THE ULTIMATE TEEN BOOK GUIDE

THE ULTIMATE TEEN BOOK GUIDE

Editors **Daniel Hahn & Leonie Flynn**
Associate Editor **Susan Reuben**

Walker & Company ✺ New York

As always, to L. M. H. Also to my father, mother, and uncle, who shared with me their love of books —L. F.

For Isaac Harry —S. R.

To Iannis, Ilan, James, Leon, Paul, and Sara— my fellow teens —D. H.

First published in Great Britain in 2006 by A & C Black Publishers Ltd.
Published in the U.S.A. in 2008 by Walker Publishing Company, Inc.
Distributed to the trade by Holtzbrinck Publishers

For information about permission to reproduce selections from this book, write to
Permissions, Walker & Company, 175 Fifth Avenue, New York, New York 10010

Library of Congress Cataloging-in-Publication Data
The ultimate teen book guide / editors, Daniel Hahn & Leonie Flynn ;
associate editor, Susan Reuben.
p.   cm.
Originally published: London : A & C Black Publishers Ltd., 2006.
Includes index.
ISBN-13: 978-0-8027-9730-8 • ISBN-10: 0-8027-9730-X (hardcover)
ISBN-13: 978-0-8027-9731-5 • ISBN-10: 0-8027-9731-8 (paperback)
1. Young adult literature—Book reviews. 2. Teenagers—Books and reading.
I. Hahn, Daniel. II. Flynn, Leonie. III. Reuben, Susan.
Z1037.A1U44 2008   028.1'62—dc22   2007024238

Visit Walker & Company's Web site at www.walkeryoungreaders.com

Printed in the U.S.A. by Quebecor World Fairfield
2 4 6 8 10 9 7 5 3 1 (hardcover)
2 4 6 8 10 9 7 5 3 1 (paperback)

All papers used by Walker & Company are natural, recyclable products made from wood grown in well-managed forests. The manufacturing processes conform to the environmental regulations of the country of origin.

Contents

Check These Out!
Exciting Extras for Exploring the Guide

Introduction
by David Almond

Books. There they are lined up on shelves or stacked on a table. There they are wrapped in their jackets, lines of neat print on nicely bound pages. They look like such orderly, static things. Then you, the reader, come along. You open the book jacket, and it can be like opening the gates into an unknown city, or opening the lid on a treasure chest. You read the first word and you're off on a journey of exploration and discovery. When you find your own best books, which might be nothing like the best books for other readers, a kind of magic occurs. The language and the story and your own imagination blend and react and fizz with life and possibility. Sometimes it's like the book was written just for you, as if it's been waiting just for you, its perfect reader. It doesn't always happen, of course. Sometimes a book will fall flat for you. What's all the fuss about? you'll ask. But then you'll find another one that excites you, that speaks clearly to you, that sets up weird resonances in you. It goes on happening all through your life. It's happening to me now, this week, as I read Yukio Mishima's *The Sailor Who Fell from Grace with the Sea*. Why have I waited till now to read this wonderful book? Because I've been reading other books, of course.

Reading is a lifelong adventure. Mishima's is just the latest in a long line of books that have gripped me. Other recent highlights include Sarah Waters's hypnotic narratives and the novels of Ha Jin. In my teenage years? Two out-of-print books: *The Grey Pilot* by Angus MacVicar that took me from my Tyneside home to flee through the Western Isles with Bonny Prince Charlie; and *The Adventures of Turkey* by Ray Harris that allowed me to share the adventures of a Huckleberry Finn-ish Australian boy. Then John Wyndham's marvelous *The Day of the Triffids* (UTBG 90), followed quickly by his *The Chrysalids*, *The Midwich Cuckoos*, and *The Kraken Wakes*, as I discovered the excitement of exploring an author's whole oeuvre for the first time. Next an astonishing book called *The Third Eye* by the ex-Tibetan monk T. Lobsang Rampa. For a time I felt that I was Lobsang in some weird way. Then he turned out to be some guy from southeast England. Did I care? Not a bit. His book had worked its magic on me. The "hoax" was just another part of that magic. Then Hemingway came along. I remember pulling out a collection of his short stories from the library shelf, opening the book, reading the first line of a story called "A Clean, Well-Lighted Place," a story in which hardly anything seems to happen, but that set up resonances inside me that have never stopped. Then Stevie Smith's poems, and Sylvia Plath's, and Kafka, and so it went on and so it goes on.

The wonderful book that you're holding in your hands now is a kind of traveler's guide. It points you to many sidetracks and highlights and landmarks that other travelers have found worth visiting. Many of them will be as exciting to you as they were to the folks who recommend them. Others might not be. The world of books is almost limitless. As you travel, you'll hit upon your own best books, the books that have a particular fascination and excitement for you. You'll keep moving on, free to roam and explore and discover at will . . .

David Almond

How to Read the Recommendations

You'll find that the majority of this book is self-explanatory, and we hope you'll find it easy to use. But here's a bit of help just in case.

Most of *The Ultimate Teen Book Guide* is made up of book recommendations. Our team of contributors has recommended more than 700 books for you, so there's bound to be stuff you'll like, whatever your tastes. The book recommendations are listed alphabetically by title, and they work like this:

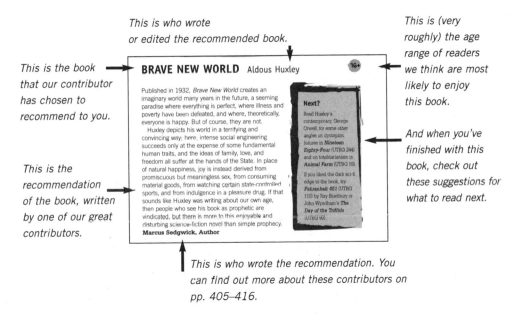

This is who wrote or edited the recommended book.

This is (very roughly) the age range of readers we think are most likely to enjoy this book.

This is the book that our contributor has chosen to recommend to you.

BRAVE NEW WORLD Aldous Huxley 16+

Published in 1932, *Brave New World* creates an imaginary world many years in the future, a seeming paradise where everything is perfect, where illness and poverty have been defeated, and where, theoretically, everyone is happy. But of course, they are not.

Huxley depicts his world in a terrifying and convincing way; here, intense social engineering succeeds only at the expense of some fundamental human traits, and the ideas of family, love, and freedom all suffer at the hands of the State. In place of natural happiness, joy is instead derived from promiscuous but meaningless sex, from consuming material goods, from watching certain state-controlled sports, and from indulgence in a pleasure drug. If that sounds like Huxley was writing about our own age, then people who see his book as prophetic are vindicated, but there is more to this enjoyable and disturbing science-fiction novel than simple prophecy.
Marcus Sedgwick, Author

Next?

Read Huxley's contemporary, George Orwell, for some other angles on dystopian futures in *Nineteen Eighty-Four* (UTBG 244) and on totalitarianism in *Animal Farm* (UTBG 19).

If you liked the dark sci-fi edge to the book, try *Fahrenheit 451* (UTBG 110) by Ray Bradbury or John Wyndham's *The Day of the Triffids* (UTBG 80).

This is the recommendation of the book, written by one of our great contributors.

And when you've finished with this book, check out these suggestions for what to read next.

This is who wrote the recommendation. You can find out more about these contributors on pp. 405–416.

The Next? box gives you ideas of what you might like to read once you've finished the recommended book. It might include other books by the same author, or books that are funny / exciting / inspiring / terrifying in the same way as the book you've just finished, or that deal with a similar subject in a different way. The letters UTBG mean the book to read next has a recommendation in *The Ultimate Teen Book Guide* too, which you can find on the page(s) indicated. For example, if you see . . .

For another powerful story of racism, read the classic *To Kill a Mockingbird* (UTBG 360) by Harper Lee.

. . . then you can turn to p. 360 to read about *To Kill a Mockingbird* and decide whether it might be just the book for you.

About the Editors

Daniel Hahn is a writer, editor, and translator. His writing includes a history book about a zoo, called *The Tower Menagerie*, which is a slightly odd kind of book. As an editor he has worked with Leonie and Susan on this award-winning series of Ultimate Book Guides (a set of three that began in the UK) about reading for young people, and with several other people on lots of other reference books about many other things. His recent translations include two Angolan novels and the autobiography of Brazilian soccer player Pelé. He also works regularly with Shakespeare's Globe and Human Rights Watch. Daniel lives in Brighton, on the south coast of England.

Leonie Flynn is editor of the popular Ultimate Book Guide series—the next volume is available in the UK and is all about books for ages zero to seven. With a day job that keeps her occupied as a librarian at a small private elementary/middle school in North London, Leonie spends most of her time reading, persuading kids to read, writing (about reading), and writing (about other things). Sometimes, when she is very lucky, she even gets to read for pleasure.

Susan Reuben has been editing children's books for 10 years and now co-owns a freelance editorial and design business. She has recently edited books about astronomy and how to be a wizard, as well as the Bible and Thomas the Tank Engine. She is married with a two-year-old son.

THE ULTIMATE TEEN BOOK GUIDE
GENRE TOP TENS

HORROR

- *Salem's Lot* by Stephen King
- *Frankenstein* by Mary Shelley
- *The Historian* by Elizabeth Kostova
- *I Know What You Did Last Summer* by Lois Duncan
- *Interview with the Vampire* by Anne Rice
- *Blood and Chocolate* by Annette Curtis Klause
- *Tales of Mystery and Imagination* by Edgar Allan Poe
- *Thirsty* by M. T. Anderson
- *The Wereling* by Stephen Cole
- *Cirque du Freak* by Darren Shan

NONFICTION

- *Into Thin Air* by Jon Krakauer
- *Fast Food Nation* by Eric Schlosser
- *Friday Night Lights* by H. G. Bissinger
- *Hitler Youth* by Susan Campbell Bartoletti
- *John Lennon* by Elizabeth Partridge
- *In Cold Blood* by Truman Capote
- *Longitude* by Dava Sobel
- *Midnight in the Garden of Good and Evil* by John Berendt
- *The Perfect Storm* by Sebastian Junger
- *Black Hawk Down* by Mark Bowden

BIOGRAPHY/MEMOIR

- *Angela's Ashes* by Frank McCourt
- *The Diary of a Young Girl* by Anne Frank
- *A Heartbreaking Work of Staggering Genius* by Dave Eggers
- *Hole in My Life* by Jack Gantos
- *Night* by Elie Wiesel
- *Persepolis* by Marjane Satrapi
- *Chinese Cinderella* by Adeline Yen Mah
- *The Burn Journals* by Brent Runyon
- *A Child Called "It"* by Dave Pelzer
- *John Lennon* by Elizabeth Partridge

GRAPHIC NOVELS

- *American Born Chinese* by Gene Luen Yang
- *Batman: The Dark Night Returns* by Frank Miller, et al
- *Bone* by Jeff Smith
- *Blankets* by Craig Thompson
- *Jimmy Corrigan, the Smartest Kid on Earth* by Chris Ware
- *Maus* by Art Spiegelman
- *Persepolis* by Marjane Satrapi
- The Sandman series by Neil Gaiman
- *Watchmen* by Alan Moore and Dave Gibbons
- *The Plain Janes* by Cecil Castellucci and Jim Rugg

ADVENTURE

- *Airborn* by Kenneth Oppel
- *Maximum Ride: The Angel Experiment* by James Patterson
- *The Call of the Wild* by Jack London
- *Hatchet* by Gary Paulsen
- *Jurassic Park* by Michael Crichton
- *Master and Commander* by Patrick O'Brian
- *The Princess Bride* by William Goldman
- *SilverFin* by Charlie Higson
- *Stormbreaker* by Anthony Horowitz
- *Treasure Island* by Robert Louis Stevenson

FANTASY

- *A Great and Terrible Beauty* by Libba Bray
- *The Amulet of Samarkand* by Jonathan Stroud
- The Harry Potter series by J. K. Rowling
- *The City of Ember* by Jeanne DuPrau
- *East* by Edith Pattou
- *Eragon* by Christopher Paolini
- *Faerie Wars* by Herbie Brennan
- The His Dark Materials trilogy by Philip Pullman
- The Lord of the Rings trilogy by J. R. R. Tolkien
- *Ella Enchanted* by Gail Carson Levine

ISSUES

- *Annie on My Mind* by Nancy Garden
- *Things Change* by Patrick Jones
- *Trigger* by Susan Vaught
- *Cut* by Patricia McCormick
- *The First Part Last* by Angela Johnson
- *Give a Boy a Gun* by Todd Strasser
- *Inexcusable* by Chris Lynch
- *Speak* by Laurie Halse Anderson
- *Go Ask Alice* by Anonymous
- *Massive* by Julia Bell

DYSTOPIAN WORLDS

- *The Giver* by Lois Lowry
- *Exodus* by Julie Bertagna
- *The City of Ember* by Jeanne DuPrau
- *Nineteen Eighty-Four* by George Orwell
- The Uglies trilogy by Scott Westerfeld
- *Brave New World* by Aldous Huxley
- *A Clockwork Orange* by Anthony Burgess
- *Fahrenheit 451* by Ray Bradbury
- *Do Androids Dream of Electric Sheep?* by Philip K. Dick
- The Foundation trilogy by Isaac Asimov

SERIES BOOKS

- A Series of Unfortunate Events by Lemony Snicket
- Harry Potter by J. K. Rowling
- Gossip Girl by Cecily von Ziegesar
- Alex Rider by Anthony Horowitz
- The A-List by Zoey Dean
- The Dark Is Rising by Susan Cooper
- Sweep by Cate Tiernan
- The Princess Diaries by Meg Cabot
- The Sisterhood of the Traveling Pants by Ann Brashares
- James Bond by Ian Fleming

MYSTERY

- *The Da Vinci Code* by Dan Brown
- *The Big Sleep* by Raymond Chandler
- *Kiki Strike* by Kirsten Miller
- *Montmorency* by Eleanor Updale
- *The No. 1 Ladies' Detective Agency* by Alexander McCall Smith
- *One for the Money* by Janet Evanovich
- *The Talented Mr. Ripley* by Patricia Highsmith
- *The Body in the Library* by Agatha Christie
- *The Lovely Bones* by Alice Sebold
- *A Northern Light* by Jennifer Donnelly

ROMANCE

- *Twilight* by Stephenie Meyer
- *What My Mother Doesn't Know* by Sonya Sones
- *Bridget Jones's Diary* by Helen Fielding
- *Nick & Norah's Infinite Playlist* by Rachel Cohn and David Levithan
- *Pride and Prejudice* by Jane Austen
- *Beauty* by Robin McKinley
- *Ella Enchanted* by Gail Carson Levine
- *Forever* by Judy Blume
- *The Princess Diaries* by Meg Cabot
- *Scrambled Eggs at Midnight* by Brad Barkley and Heather Hepler

COMING OF AGE

- *Looking for Alaska* by John Green
- *Rats Saw God* by Rob Thomas
- *Prep* by Curtis Sittenfeld
- *The Secret Life of Bees* by Sue Monk Kidd
- *What My Mother Doesn't Know* by Sonya Sones
- *The True Meaning of Cleavage* by Mariah Fredericks
- *The Catcher in the Rye* by J. D. Salinger
- *Dairy Queen* by Catherine Gilbert Murdock
- *Gingerbread* by Rachel Cohn
- *The Adventures of Huckleberry Finn* by Mark Twain

HISTORICAL FICTION

- *Al Capone Does My Shirts* by Gennifer Choldenko
- *Catherine, Called Birdy* by Karen Cushman
- *Code Talker* by Joseph Bruchac
- *Girl with a Pearl Earring* by Tracy Chevalier
- *Blood Red Horse* by K. M. Grant
- *Gone with the Wind* by Margaret Mitchell
- *Hattie Big Sky* by Kirby Larson
- *At the Sign of the Sugared Plum* by Mary Hooper
- *The Other Boleyn Girl* by Philippa Gregory
- *Out of the Dust* by Karen Hesse

HUMOR

- *The Hitchhiker's Guide to the Galaxy* by Douglas Adams
- *Angus, Thongs and Full-Frontal Snogging* by Louise Rennison
- *Can You Sue Your Parents for Malpractice?* by Paula Danziger
- *Son of the Mob* by Gordon Korman
- *Confessions of a Teenage Drama Queen* by Dyan Sheldon
- *King Dork* by Frank Portman
- *Another Roadside Attraction* by Tom Robbins
- *ttyl* by Lauren Myracle
- *All's Fair in Love, War, and High School* by Janette Rallison
- *Bucking the Sarge* by Christopher Paul Curtis

AWARD WINNERS

- *American Born Chinese* by Gene Luen Yang
- *Parrot in the Oven* by Victor Martinez
- *Godless* by Pete Hautman
- *Holes* by Louis Sachar
- *Sold* by Patricia McCormick
- *How I Live Now* by Meg Rosoff
- *Looking for Alaska* by John Green
- *Monster* by Walter Dean Myers
- *Postcards from No Man's Land* by Aidan Chambers
- *A Step from Heaven* by An Na

WAR

- *Black Hawk Down* by Mark Bowden
- *All Quiet on the Western Front* by Erich Maria Remarque
- *Flags of Our Fathers* by James Bradley
- *Empire of the Sun* by J. G. Ballard
- *War and Peace* by Leo Tolstoy
- *A Tale of Two Cities* by Charles Dickens
- *Doctor Zhivago* by Boris Pasternak
- *Troy* by Adéle Geras
- *Catch-22* by Joseph Heller
- *Tamar* by Mal Peet

HOW TO GET THE MOST OUT OF
THE ULTIMATE TEEN BOOK GUIDE

Within these pages, you'll find a lifetime's worth of stories—adventures, mysteries, romances, tragedies. Open this Guide and you'll be opening the door to tons of lovable heroines, deplorable villains, or fantastical worlds. With more than 700 books recommended—from single books to sequels, trilogies, or series—and thousands more described in the "Next" suggestions, you'll never be at a loss for what to read again!

Ever wonder what your favorite author's favorite book is? Many of today's most popular authors have weighed in on the books *they* love the most. There are also recommendations by other teens, as well as by librarians, illustrators, editors, and other people who work with and love books.

In surveys from around the country, teens across the board have said that not knowing what to read next or where to start are some of the main factors that keep them from reading. The Guide is here to solve that problem—in addition to the recommendations, there are top ten lists by genre that suggest where to begin. Like to peek into the future? Check out the list of dystopian worlds and read all ten. A fan of horror movies? Pick up one of the horror books and see if it's your thing. Currently falling in love? Be swept away by the romance picks. And once you've found the genre for you, there are tons of books throughout the Guide to keep you reading.

There are also 13 features that go into each genre in a bit more depth.If you'd like to try something in a genre you don't know much about, the features will give you a good idea of where to start. They are all written by experts in the field—authors who write that kind of book themselves (for instance, Catherine Fisher on fantasy, Cathy Hopkins on pink lit, E. Lockhart on love and relationships, K. K. Beck on detective stories). Or if you're looking for something not too challenging that will grip you from the first line, Patrick Jones has some great suggestions for you in his Short and Gripping Books feature. And next to each feature you'll find lists of relevant titles, most of which you can read about elsewhere in the Guide.

Throughout the Guide you'll also find mini-features with lists of other fun types of books—such as books written in diary format, books about siblings, books with a Latin beat—so no matter what your mood, you're bound to find the right book for you. You'll also come across the results of our teen readers' poll, which was originally conducted in the UK and then updated for the US market, to give you an even better idea of some of the most popular books out there today. And finally, you'll find reviews by winners of our schools' competition. In 2005 the *Ultimate Teen Book Guide* editors invited students from every high school in England to submit book recommendations—of the hundreds of competing entries, you'll find the ones that won a place in the book on pages 11, 105, 114, and 230.

So have fun, and get reading!

33 SNOWFISH Adam Rapp

 14+

Next?

Rapp has a handful of other books including *Missing the Piano* and *The Buffalo Tree*, but if you enjoyed *33 Snowfish*, try *Under the Wolf, Under the Dog* next.

Rapp's writing skill is hard to match, but Chris Lynch (*Freewill* [UTBG 128]), Iain Lawrence (*The Lightkeeper's Daughter*), David Almond (*Kit's Wilderness* [UTBG 197]), and M. T. Anderson (*The Astonishing Life of Octavian Nothing, Traitor to the Nation* [UTBG 25]) are authors to look for if you're craving incredibly well-crafted teen books.

Custis, Curl, and Boobie are all running from their own personal demons. Custis has escaped the man who "kept" him, Curl has only recently left her life of prostitution and drugs, and Boobie, with his baby brother in tow, is so tormented by his immediate past that he cannot speak. Each teen tells a piece of the story from his/her individual point of view—Custis and Curl through text, Boobie through haunting drawings.

While the three are certainly damaged goods, and not all of their stories end well, there is a real growth and an amazing amount of strength among them, and a ray of hope for one at the end.

Adam Rapp's dark, brooding tales—some with heavy doses of black humor—are incredibly memorable. His stories stick with you long after the last page is turned.

Kimberly Paone, Librarian

52 PICKUP Elmore Leonard

14+

The difficulty with an author like Elmore Leonard is he's written so many books—all never less than very good—that it's almost too hard to choose which one to point to and say "*that*'s the one you should read!" In the end I went with *52 Pickup* because I read it ages ago and still clearly remember it. Like every Leonard book, this one is tightly plotted, has razor-sharp dialogue, and comes with a real sting; it's a thriller, it's about blackmail and revenge, and it's very cool.

People often look down on crime fiction as being somehow less than literature, but this book has style, class, and a great story. What more could you want?

Graham Marks, Author

Next?

The films *Get Shorty* and *Jackie Brown* were both based on books by Elmore Leonard—why not read the originals?

Lots of films have been made of Raymond Chandler's books too; try *The Big Sleep* (UTBG 34) or *Farewell, My Lovely*.

Carl Hiaasen's books are also set in Florida; try *Hoot* (UTBG 159) or *Tourist Season* (UTBG 361).

And check out our feature on detective stories on pp. 96–97.

84, CHARING CROSS ROAD Helene Hanff

84, Charing Cross Road is a collection of letters exchanged between down-to-earth New York writer Helene Hanff and London bookseller Frank Doel between 1949 and 1969. Miss Hanff, who had a passion for obscure and out-of-print books, initially wrote to Marks & Co., a bookshop at 84 Charing Cross Road, with a list of secondhand books she would like, if they could supply them, so long as they didn't cost more than $5 each. Mr. Doel replied, saying that they had managed to find some of the items on her list and were sending them on, with an invoice.

Thus a wonderful correspondence and a 20-year association began. Rereading a few of the letters today, I was captivated all over again—this is one of the most delightful books ever published.
Michael Lawrence, Author

Next?

Helene Hanff's *The Duchess of Bloomsbury Street* is a sequel to *84, Charing Cross Road*. *Apple of My Eye* is about her native New York and *Q's Legacy* is about her education in English literature.

Anne Fadiman's *Ex Libris* charts a lifelong love affair with books.

A Particular Friendship by Dirk Bogarde charts another friendship between two people who never met.

The 87th PRECINCT series Ed McBain

Next?

Start the series with the early ones: *Cop Hater* or *The Mugger*.

More detective stories? Try a British version with the **Inspector Morse** books (UTBG 177) by Colin Dexter, starting with *Last Bus to Woodstock*; or try *Murder on the Orient Express* by the great Agatha Christie.

One of the great classic detective writers is Dashiell Hammett; try *The Maltese Falcon* or *The Glass Key*, both of which are tautly plotted.

I wish I'd known Ed McBain's 87th Precinct series of police procedural mysteries when I was a teenager. They're short and beautifully written with tight plots, sharp social detail, and vivid characters. There are more than 50 of them, written over as many years. The quality dipped a little halfway through, but the late ones show him back in top form, which is unusual for a long-running series.

Each title is set in a fictionalized version of New York with multiple story lines and recurring characters like detectives Steve Carella, Meyer Meyer, and Fat Ollie Weeks. They're carefully researched and shot through with world-weary attitude. Many crime writers have borrowed from McBain (as have loads of TV cop shows), but nobody did it better.
David Belbin, Author

THE A-LIST series Zoey Dean

Anna is living what seems to be the perfect Manhattan life. But there is one major thing missing: fun! She is tired of being predictable and wants to be able to let loose. So she flies out to California to live with her so-called "father" and to start a new and exciting life. Within the first 24 hours of her trip she attends a celebrity's wedding with a hot date. Everything seems to be going great, until she meets the three girls who make her want to take the next flight back to New York. But Anna is determined not to let them ruin her fun.

Zoey Dean has created a book so amazing you won't be able to put it down. I really enjoyed this book and I look forward to reading the rest of the series. Even though living Anna's life may sound perfect, sometimes it is not at all close to that.
Madalyn Gibson, age 16

Next?

If you liked the first book in the A-List series, try *Girls on Film*, book #2, or *Blonde Ambition*, book #3.

Love the look inside the good life? Try Cecily von Ziegesar's **Gossip Girl** series (UTBG 140), Lisi Harrison's **Clique** series, or J. Minter's **Insiders** books.

ABARAT Clive Barker

Next?

If you liked this, read the sequel: *Abarat: Days of Magic, Nights of War*.

If you're fond of tales about children escaping the boring, everyday world, try C. S. Lewis's **The Chronicles of Narnia**.

Or for a creepier take on the same theme, check out Neil Gaiman's *Coraline* (UTBG 76). Brrr.

Candy Quackenbush lives in Chickentown, Minnesota, the most boring place in the world. But Candy has a destiny. Fate is leading her to an extraordinary land: the Abarat, a great archipelago where each island sits at a different hour of the day. There she must fight the evil that is overtaking the islands, helped and hindered by a cast of bizarre allies and enemies.

Barker's imagination is astonishing, and he leaves most other writers in the dust. *Abarat* is a dizzying ride for children and adults alike. It is sometimes scary, sometimes funny, but always enthralling. If you thought fantasy was all about wizards and elves and fairies, read *Abarat* and find out what real fantasy feels like.
Chris Wooding, Author

ABOUT A BOY Nick Hornby

Next?

All Nick Hornby's books are worth reading. Try *High Fidelity* (UTBG 152) or *Fever Pitch* (UTBG 116).

Man and Boy by Tony Parsons also deals with a grown man facing up to his emotional responsibilities—sounds heavy, but it's very readable!

This should really be called *About Two Boys*: it tells of 36-year-old big-kid Will, whose independent income means he doesn't have to work. He owns all the latest state-of-the-art gadgets and his main ambition is to sleep with as many women as possible, with no ties. Into this emotionally barren existence stumbles Marcus, age 12, a vegetarian hippie with the dress sense of a middle-aged geography teacher. Bullied at school, he craves a father figure and imagines Will ideal for the role. Unfortunately, Will disagrees and resents this geeky kid impinging on his life and (God forbid!) feelings.

Somehow, though, their lives become intertwined, and each learns something important from the other. Witty, cynical, and touching—seriously cool stuff!

Catherine Robinson, Author

AN ABUNDANCE OF KATHERINES

John Green

Although I generally prefer books with female narrators, I quickly found myself hooked by the story of Colin Singleton: a child prodigy and recent high school graduate who has just been dumped by his 19th girlfriend named Katherine. To distract himself, Colin and his eccentric best friend, Hassan, embark on a road trip. They end up in Gutshot, Tennessee, lodging with a bizarre woman and her daughter, while Colin tries to compose a math formula that will predict the outcome of any romantic relationship. He also finds love in the process . . . and with a girl not named Katherine!

Despite his obvious nerdiness, I found Colin's story charming. The anagrams, footnotes, and Katherine anecdotes are clever, and Green's cast of characters is unique, hilarious, and totally believable. I found myself laughing out loud and wishing I had friends like Colin and Hassan. A quirky coming-of-age novel, and highly entertaining.

Claire Easton, age 16

Next?

For another novel with a math wiz, try Anna Fienberg's *Number 8*, about a numbers genius on the run from the mob.

Or you could try *The Gospel According to Larry* by Janet Tashjian, also about a young prodigy trying to find his place in the world.

John Green's other award-winning novel, *Looking for Alaska* (UTBG 207) should not be missed.

ACROSS THE NIGHTINGALE FLOOR

Lian Hearn

From its opening, in which a young boy wanders back from a carefree afternoon to find a massacre going on in his village, this story grips the reader and refuses to let go. It's an extraordinarily powerful and highly original fantasy packed with scenes of haunting beauty and horrifying violence. In a world where warring clans vie for supremacy, while hidden strings are pulled by the mysterious Tribe, the boy Takeo must make a painful choice between power, love, and revenge.

This is fantasy at its most sophisticated—but it's not for the squeamish.

Brian Keaney, Author

Next?

There are two sequels: *Grass for His Pillow* and *Brilliance of the Moon*, which continue the story of Takeo and Kaede.

If this makes you wonder about Japanese society, try Katherine Paterson's *The Master Puppeteer*.

Catherine Jinks's **The Pagan Chronicles** series (UTBG 266), set in the 12th century at the time of the Crusades, is just as exciting—and gory!

Or try a classic adventure such as Alexandre Dumas's *The Count of Monte Cristo*.

THE ADVENTURES OF HUCKLEBERRY FINN Mark Twain

Next?

Try *The Further Adventures of Huckleberry Finn* by Greg Matthews. Written in 1983, this sequel takes Twain's characters and uses them in a much darker Western that nevertheless manages the near-impossible task of capturing the spirit of Twain's original. One warning: it's much more adult.

For modern stories of the American West, read Annie Proulx's *Close Range*.

For another classic tale of the ills of slavery, try Harriet Beecher Stowe's *Uncle Tom's Cabin*.

Scared that his drunken father might pursue him for the money he discovered with Tom Sawyer, Huckleberry Finn signs his fortune over to Judge Thatcher; but this doesn't stop his dad from dragging him off to an old cabin and beating him every day. Huck escapes to Jackson's Island, where he meets his friend Jim, a runaway slave. Leading the townspeople to believe Jim has murdered Huck for his money, the two of them set sail on the Mississippi River, beginning a series of adventures that are far more elaborate, amusing, and exciting than those in *The Adventures of Tom Sawyer*. Considered one of the best sequels ever, and a great novel in every respect, this is a must-read.

Matt Thorne, Author

AFTER THE FIRST DEATH Robert Cormier

14+

Terrorists have hijacked a school bus and are threatening to blow it up. Among them is Milo, a teenager who has known nothing but war and believes only in violence. Kate is the bus driver. Seventeen years old, she fears that she doesn't have the strength to look after the children suddenly in her charge. Unknown to both, the general in charge of the effort to resolve the crisis is sending his 15-year-old son to the terrorists as a show of good faith. All are, in their own ways, morally and politically innocent, and Cormier shows how innocence can have terrifying and deadly consequences.

Fifteen years after I first read it, *After the First Death* still has the power to make me gasp. Complex and multilayered, it yields new meanings and fresh insights on every rereading.

Graham Gardner, Author

Next?

All of Cormier's books are dark adventures in reading. Try **Heroes** (UTBG 152).

Or try **The Chocolate War** (UTBG 67), also by Robert Cormier.

The Song of an Innocent Bystander (UTBG 333) by Ian Bone is about a girl taken hostage.

AIRBORN Kenneth Oppel

12+

Next?

Read the sequel, **Skybreaker**, in which Matt encounters a ghost ship and lost treasure.

Or try the exciting **Mortal Engines** (UTBG 232) by Philip Reeve, which has cities on wheels and more airships!

For another action-adventure on the high seas, check out Rick Riordan's **The Lightning Thief**.

Matt Cruse is a cabin boy aboard the luxury airship *Aurora*. Matt has called this airship home for three years. He has a good chance of being promoted to a junior sailmaker. That is, until a girl named Kate de Vries arrives onboard. She has been sent on a mysterious quest and they soon become good friends.

However, one night in the middle of the ocean, they are attacked by deadly Sky Pirates. The ship crash-lands on a strange island, Matt and Kate are thrown into adventures beyond imagining, and the mystery unfurls.

I loved this book. It was like a jigsaw puzzle, every page like a piece fitting together to make a superb adventure full of humor.

Edward Fry, age 12

AL CAPONE DOES MY SHIRTS

12+

Gennifer Choldenko

Moose Flanagan's family moves to Alcatraz, where his dad is to be a guard of the infamous inmates at the famous prison there. Life is tough at first and his parents are both so tied up looking after every need of his autistic sister that they have no time or energy left to consider how Moose is settling in. Angry, he goes out to find new friends and adventures of his own. This enjoyable and exciting insight into the imagined life and times of gangster Al Capone packs a huge emotional punch.

Eileen Armstrong, Librarian

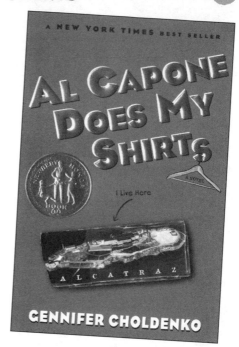

Next?

Choldenko's *Notes from a Liar and Her Dog* tells of a girl trying to come to terms with her adoption with the help of her tiny Chihuahua and her chicken-drawing best friend, Harrison.

Theresa Breslin's *Prisoner in Alcatraz* offers another compelling insight into conditions in the infamous prison.

For a different look at the history of kids on the island, try *Children of Alcatraz: Growing Up on the Rock*, a photo essay by Claire Rudolf Murphy.

THE BEST BANNED BOOKS OF THE LAST CENTURY

To Kill a Mockingbird by Harper Lee

I Know Why the Caged Bird Sings by Maya Angelou

The Chocolate War by Robert Cormier

The Adventures of Huckleberry Finn by Mark Twain

The Harry Potter series by J. K. Rowling

Forever by Judy Blume

Bridge to Terabithia by Katherine Paterson

The Giver by Lois Lowry

ALANNA: THE FIRST ADVENTURE
Tamora Pierce

Alanna wants to be a knight but is supposed to become a magician. Her twin brother, Thom, wants to be a magician but is supposed to become a knight. So they decide to swap places. The only catch is that to become a knight, Alanna has to pretend to be a boy. But keeping her true identity secret and dealing with the harsh routine of knightly training turn out to be the least of Alanna's problems—there's a conspiracy in the royal castle, and Alanna's friendship with Prince Jonathan is going to drag her into the middle of it! Alanna is one of the most likable heroines you'll ever find in a story—good-hearted, adventurous, and brave.
Benedict Jacka, Author

Next?

This is the first part of the **Song of the Lioness** quartet. Alanna's quest to become a knight continues in *In the Hand of the Goddess*.

If you want a story in which the heroine chooses to be a wizard, try *So You Want to Be a Wizard* by Diane Duane.

And if you want a longer story with castles, knights, and magic, try *Magician* by Raymond E. Feist.

THE ALCHEMIST Paulo Coelho

Next?

Paulo Coelho has written many other books about searching for meaning; try *The Pilgrimage*.

Other stories to make you think? Try *Jonathan Livingston Seagull* (UTBG 184) by Richard Bach, or *Zen and the Art of Motorcycle Maintenance* by Robert M. Pirsig, which really does have something to do with both things in its title.

Try Kahlil Gibran's *The Prophet*, a book that packs an incredible amount of philosophical meaning into a very short text.

This is, on the face of it, a simple fable about Santiago, an Andalusian shepherd boy, and his search for treasure. But the more you read this wonderful story, the more you begin to truly see within its pages. The book describes Santiago's journey from Spain to Tangiers and on into the deserts of Egypt, where he meets the mysterious alchemist. With his mentor's help, Santiago begins to listen to the Soul of the World and learns that the treasure he seeks is right under his nose.

This is a brilliant story that asks us to believe in our dreams and listen to our hearts. Coelho is a master storyteller and this is a masterful tale. Remember all that glitters is not gold and prepare to be enchanted. This novel really does live up to the hype.
Bali Rai, Author

THE ALCHEMIST'S APPRENTICE

Kate Thompson

12+

Next?

Go on to read more Kate Thompson—try her **Missing Link** series next, or her latest novel, *The New Policeman*.

For another alchemy book, this time set in modern-day San Francisco, try *The Alchemyst* by Michael Scott.

For more atmospheric chills, check out *Skellig* (UTBG 325) by David Almond.

Since his mother died, Jack has been apprenticed to a blacksmith. But—frankly—he's not very good at it. So one day, having crashed his master's cart, Jack decides to run away. He leaves London, heading south, and soon finds himself at the house of Jonathan Barnstable. Barnstable, it seems, is an alchemist, secretly working away at the mysteries of how to create gold . . .

And this Mr. Barnstable—tall and extraordinary, with white hair and piercing blue eyes—invites Jack to be his apprentice. Under his guidance, Jack learns the secrets of the alchemist's art, and a lot more besides. But this is just the beginning of his adventure!

Full of 18th-century atmosphere, with a likable hero in Jack and a fascinating character in the mysterious Barnstable, this is an enthralling read.

Daniel Hahn, Editor

ALCHEMY Margaret Mahy

14+

Roland has it all—he's going out with the sexiest girl in school, he's effortlessly clever, he's a natural leader. But then things start to go bizarrely awry—his teacher catches him shoplifting and uses this knowledge to blackmail him into making friends with a girl in his class he normally wouldn't be seen dead talking to.

Then when Roland goes to the girl's house, he enters a disturbing world where nothing in the rooms ever changes, and there's a peculiar presence at the top of the stairs that is definitely not human.

Alchemy combines a seriously sinister story of the supernatural with all the normal concerns of a boy on the verge of adulthood—and the result is gripping, scary, and life-affirming, too.

Susan Reuben, Editor

Next?

For another Margaret Mahy ghost story, try the award-winning *The Changeover*. Or for a Mahy book set entirely in this world, try *Memory*.

For another novel that involves magic in the real world, try Meg Cabot's **Mediator** series, starting with *Shadowland,* about a girl who is a medium between the dead and the living.

Orson Scott Card's *Magic Street* tells the story of a neighborhood caught in the middle of a war between the king and queen of the fairy world.

The Blue Girl by Charles de Lint blends the contemporary and fantastical worlds, and involves the emergence of a ghost.

The ALEX RIDER series   Anthony Horowitz

Alex Rider is certainly no ordinary teen. While most kids worry about acne and homework, Alex has a far bigger priority—saving the world! At the mere age of 14 and after the mysterious death of his uncle, he is thrown into the dangerous world of espionage. He quickly learns the tricks of the trade and, armed with an array of amazing (and well-disguised) gadgets, he is sent to the lavish mansion of millionaire Herod Sayle for his first mission.

If that whets your appetite, Alex's adventures don't stop there. They span over six incredible books (to date), each more exciting and gripping than the last. The characters are unique and believable, the plots are inventive, and the scrapes Alex gets himself into are absolutely amazing. It's definitely recommendable to anyone with a thirst for espionage and mystery.

Gareth Smith, age 14

SCHOOLS' COMPETITION WINNER

STORMBREAKER

Anthony Horowitz

Tied for 3rd

Have you ever been bored at school and wished you were running from a dozen armed guards instead? Alex Rider has. And when his uncle dies in a "car accident," Alex investigates and is thrown into the world of spies and espionage. When he does find out the truth about his uncle's death, he is sent to an SAS training camp where he learns that survival is everything. Then he is whisked away on his first mission armed only with state-of-the-art technology and a fake identity.

Stormbreaker really played with my emotions, which jumped from grief to curiosity, concern to suspense and excitement, and finally to relief. This book is just so hard to put down—I would recommend it to everyone I know.

Liam Hallatt, age 15

Next?

The **Alex Rider** books in sequence are: *Stormbreaker*, *Point Blank*, *Skeleton Key*, *Eagle Strike*, *Scorpia*, *Ark Angel*.

Rick Yancey's Alfred Kropp novels—*The Extraordinary Adventures of Alfred Kropp* and *Alfred Kropp: The Seal of Solomon*—provide plenty of action and adventure.

Horowitz also writes about the paranormal. His new series, **The Power of Five**, begins with *Raven's Gate* (UTBG 286).

The ALICE series Susan Juby

14+

Next?

Try the second book of the series, *I'm Alice (Beauty Queen?)*.

Another girl who dresses kind of different? Try Dyan Sheldon's *Confessions of a Teenage Drama Queen* (UTBG 75).

Or, of course, try the very funny *The Secret Diary of Adrian Mole, Aged 13 3/4* (UTBG 306) by Sue Townsend.

As a big fan of novels featuring funny teen "diarists," I was delighted to discover Susan Juby's Alice series. Sixteen-year-old Alice MacLeod lives in tiny Smithers, British Columbia, where she has been homeschooled since the age of six, after having made the grave mistake of arriving at first grade dressed in a hobbit costume. When the first book in the series opens, Alice is going back to school hoping that this time she'll fit in. Alas, her hobbit days are still vividly remembered by her fellow Smithers teens, and Alice is not exactly welcomed with open arms. Between her thrift-shop wardrobe and her aspirations of becoming a novelist, Alice has no hope of ever going "mainstream"!

Alice MacLeod is the Canadian answer to Sue Townsend's hilarious Adrian Mole, and, like Adrian, I hope she'll be around for a very long time.

Meg Cabot, Author

ALL QUIET ON THE WESTERN FRONT

14+

Erich Maria Remarque

First published in Germany in 1929, later banned by the Nazis, this is the classic anti-war novel. All the horrors of the trenches are here: the sheer terror of shellfire, rats, lice, hand-to-hand combat with sharpened spades, and how it feels to be trapped in a shell hole with a man you've just killed.

But it's as much about youth as it is about war. There's a lyrical quality to the quieter scenes, such as a visit to see a wounded comrade in the hospital or a brief romantic interlude with a local girl. The final chapter is as moving as it is cathartic: a fitting epitaph for a lost generation.

Thomas Bloor, Author

Next?

For another powerful and unforgettable novel about war and its atrocities, try Dalton Trumbo's classic *Johnny Got His Gun*.

For a different perspective on war—one that can be humorous as well as heart-breaking—try Kurt Vonnegut's *Slaughterhouse-Five* (UTBG 327) or Joseph Heller's *Catch-22* (UTBG 59).

Jane Yolen's *The Devil's Arithmetic* takes a first-person view of the atrocities of World War II and the Holocaust.

ALL THE PRETTY HORSES Cormac McCarthy

This is the first of a trilogy about the border country between America and Mexico, a land where cowboys ride hard, love deep, and hurt so much it almost kills them. I had never read a Western when I picked up this book and for me it is Hemingway on horseback, with the most poetic and heartbreaking descriptions of landscape and people inhabiting it that I know. Even if you are the most couch-potato person on earth, you will find your mind riding with Cormac McCarthy, and it is a journey no one should miss.

Raffaella Barker, Author

Next?

The Crossing and *Cities of the Plain* complete **The Border** trilogy.

It is claimed that McCarthy's prose style is similar to William Faulkner's. Try *As I Lay Dying* and see for yourself.

Brokeback Mountain by Annie Proulx is a slim but powerful book about the West and growing up; it's also in the collection *Close Range*.

Or try Ernest Hemingway's *The Snows of Kilimanjaro*.

ALL-AMERICAN GIRL Meg Cabot

Next?

There is a sequel! *All–American Girl: Ready or Not*. Cabot's books all make ordinary characters take on extraordinary roles—as a chaperone to a drop-dead-gorgeous star in *Teen Idol*, the heir to the throne in *The Princess Diaries* (UTBG 281), a ghosthunter in the **Mediator** series, and a specially gifted crime solver in the **Missing** series.

Ella Enchanted (UTBG 103) by Gail Carson Levine takes a new twist on the most famous princess story of all: *Cinderella*.

Sam is an ordinary teenager who dresses in black and tries hard to be different. She has an extraordinary talent for drawing celebs, and she loves music. She's also fallen for her perfect–cheerleader older sister's boyfriend, Jack. Skipping her art class one day, Sam ends up saving the president's life outside a record shop, in a completely believable and inventive plot twist. Suddenly she is catapulted into fame and life in the spotlight as teen ambassador to the UN—which isn't as easy as it sounds. Luckily, the president's son, David, is on hand to help her out.

This is an exciting, action-packed teen rom-com with realistic and riveting Top 10 Lists of Everything separating the chapters.

David Gardner, age 16

ALL'S FAIR IN LOVE, WAR, AND HIGH SCHOOL Janette Rallison

12+

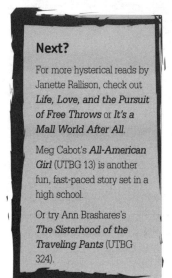

Next?

For more hysterical reads by Janette Rallison, check out *Life, Love, and the Pursuit of Free Throws* or *It's a Mall World After All.*

Meg Cabot's *All-American Girl* (UTBG 13) is another fun, fast-paced story set in a high school.

Or try Ann Brashares's *The Sisterhood of the Traveling Pants* (UTBG 324).

A cheerleader running for class president, a bet with her ex, and a boy competing for her attention—sounds like high school to me!

When Sam finds out that she scored only an 810 on her SATs, she realizes she has to do something drastic to get into college—so she decides to run for class president. It isn't an easy task. At the same time, Sam's ex-boyfriend Logan makes a bet with her that she can't go a week without saying something critical. Though both of these challenges are difficult, Sam takes them on. Sam's story truly depicts how high school life works. Sam's character is easy to relate to and makes the book a very fun read.

If you laughed hysterically at the movie *Mean Girls*, if you like romance, or if you just want a peek at what Pullman High is like, this book is for you!

Elizabeth Rice, age 18

THE AMAZING ADVENTURES OF KAVALIER & CLAY Michael Chabon

14+

Sammy Clay wakes one night to find that his cousin Joe Kavalier has escaped from Nazi-occupied Prague and has come to live in New York with him and his family. As the two cousins sit on the fire escape, Sammy realizes that Joe can help him achieve his dreams of fame and money. Joe is intrigued by Sammy's plan, hoping to make enough money to bring his immediate family over to America, and the two create a partnership that will change their lives. The Escapist, a new superhero based on Joe, is born, and the cousins are propelled into the world of comic-book making.

This Pulitzer Prize-winning novel is an enthralling read. The exciting plot, marvelous characters, and fast-paced writing make it impossible to put down. I often found myself becoming so absorbed in the book that I missed my subway stop. I can highly recommend it without any reservation.

Clio Contogenis, age 14

Next?

You shouldn't miss any of Michael Chabon's other novels—move on to *Wonder Boys* or *The Yiddish Policemen's Union.*

Richard Russo has a similar writing style—try his *Empire Falls*, which also won the Pulitzer Prize.

THE AMAZING MAURICE AND HIS EDUCATED RODENTS Terry Pratchett

Smart, sharp, wickedly funny, and very fast-moving sums up this, Terry Pratchett's first book for younger readers set in the fabulous Discworld universe. The story itself is loosely based on the traditional tale of "The Pied Piper of Hamelin." The Amazing Maurice of the title is a streetwise tomcat, always on the lookout for the perfect scam. He even has his own "plague" of educated rats, who travel ahead to "infest" a given town. Maurice then arrives with a "stupid-looking kid" who plays a pipe, and the townspeople pay him to persuade the boy to charm the rats away. A nice little earner all round. It usually works like magic, but oh dear, not this time . . . Evil awaits . . .

Chris d'Lacey, Author

Next?

Terry Pratchett is one of the most prolific authors around. So, good news: there are LOTS of other Discworld books to read; try *The Color of Magic*. Need I say more?

Okay, I will. For a fun-packed trip around our universe, why not try *The Hitchhiker's Guide to the Galaxy* (UTBG 154) by Douglas Adams?

For a different kind of humor, try Philip Ridley's *Mighty Fizz Chilla*.

AMERICA E. R. Frank

E. R. Frank's *America* is a trip into the most hellish childhood imaginable. The child of a crack-addicted mother and an unknown father, America has been taken from his foster mother, abused, and abandoned. When we first meet him, he has tried to kill himself. From page one, the suspense is fierce: is this kid going to make it?

It is tempting to read *America* as a story of how others live. (And yes, I'm in awe of Frank's ability to capture a voice and experience presumably not her own.) But America's tortured pursuit of the truth raises questions we all must ask at some point: What has my life been? Who has it made me and where do I go now? The subject matter is raw and the language is graphic at times. To tell this story any other way would have been absurd. Still, it has been challenged by people who are apparently more disturbed that some kids speak this way than they are that some kids live this way.

Mariah Fredericks, Author

Next?

If you enjoyed E. R. Frank's gritty writing, try *Life Is Funny* or *Wrecked* next.

Han Nolan's *Born Blue* also follows a young girl who is raised in the foster home system.

The Facts Speak for Themselves by Brock Cole is a similarly written tale about a girl trying to break free of an incredibly difficult situation

AMERICAN BORN CHINESE Gene Luen Yang

Every once in a while a book comes along and takes our understanding of fiction and story to a new level. This graphic novel by Gene Yang not only explores issues of identity and teen angst from the rarely seen perspective of an Asian American male young adult, but he perfectly captures the spirit of the story in his vibrant artwork.

The novel, broken into three segments, weaves together the legend of the Monkey King, the story of Chin-Kee as the embodiment of Asian stereotypes, and the heartbreaking quest of the central character, Jin Wang, as he longs for acceptance and love. While distinct and separate from the outset, by the conclusion of the novel each strand of the three stories perfectly fits and augments the others, until we are left to marvel at the richness and complexity of emotions and thoughts presented in that single braid.

An Na, Author

Next?

Amy Tan's *The Joy Luck Club* (UTBG 186) gives two different generations' perspectives on being Chinese in America.

Balzac and the Little Chinese Seamstress (UTBG 27) by Dai Sijie tells a compelling story set against the backdrop of 1970s China.

If you enjoy the graphic novel format, you shouldn't miss Craig Thompson's *Blankets* (UTBG 40), about a boy's coming-of-age in middle America.

THE AMULET OF SAMARKAND

Jonathan Stroud

Next?

The Golem's Eye and *Ptolemy's Gate* complete **The Bartimaeus Trilogy**.

Or take a sideways step into high fantasy with Garth Nix's *Sabriel* (UTBG 298) and its sequels.

For different settings with a strangely realistic touch try Mary Hoffman's *Stravaganza: City of Masks*.

In a modern-day London controlled by magicians, Simon Lovelace is a master magician who possesses the fabled Amulet of Samarkand. Nathaniel is a young magician's apprentice with a rather precocious talent, who summons the querulous 5,000-year-old djinni Bartimaeus to relieve him of it.

What starts out as a smallish act of revenge eventually leads to a largish web of intrigue, murder, and rebellion. The plot is thrilling enough, but much of the story (including hilarious footnotes) is told by Bartimaeus himself in such a quirky and cranky fashion that it makes it very hard to put down. In fact, I challenge you not to want to read straight through all three books (this is the first of a trilogy) without stopping.

Chris d'Lacey, Author

ANGELA'S ASHES Frank McCourt

When Frank McCourt was four years old, his parents took him back from America to live in Ireland. You might think that the story of his childhood, from poverty in New York to absolute poverty in the back roads of rain-sodden Limerick, would make for depressing reading. In fact, due to the beauty of the writing and the wry humor that worms its way through even the bleakest of scenarios, it's a wonderful, life-enhancing read. Although many of the characters in the book are not so lucky, Frank's is a story of survival of body and spirit against all the odds. A deeply moving, powerful, and unforgettable book.

Malachy Doyle, Author

Next?

Frank McCourt wrote two other compelling memoirs about his life: *'Tis* and *Teacher Man*.

For another intriguing (if sometimes bizarre) story, try Augusten Burroughs's *Running with Scissors* (UTBG 298).

Or try *Reading Lolita in Tehran* by Azar Nafisi, another important memoir that gives a glimpse into a little-known culture.

ANGUS, THONGS AND FULL-FRONTAL SNOGGING Louise Rennison

I read this book when I was tired and fed up. I bought it at a station kiosk to read on the train. Three minutes later, the train was clattering out of London, and I was already smiling. Two hours later, when I arrived back home in tree-lined Gloucestershire, I was grinning from ear to ear. It's about the daily life of Georgia Nicolson (a lovable teen rogue); her beloved cat, Angus; and the human males in her universe who offer much in the way of aggravation.

One of Georgia's many issues is, if she ever gets up close and personal with the boy of her dreams, how will she cope with the challenging business of "snogging," aka kissing boys? Luckily for Georgia, there's a boy in the neighborhood who's ready to give girls private lessons in the sacred art. Although he doesn't charge, it still beats a paper route. Sheer entertainment from cover to cover. Laughs guaranteed.

Sue Limb, Author

Next?

Next in the series is *It's OK, I'm Wearing Really Big Knickers* . . .

For more hilarious "Brit chick lit," try Sue Limb's *Girl, 15, Charming but Insane* (UTBG 133) or Tyne O'Connell's *Pulling Princes*.

Jaclyn Moriarty's *The Year of Secret Assignments* (UTBG 402) is another funny comedy of errors involving a group of girls and their male pen pals.

ADULT BOOKS FOR TEENS

Prep by Curtis Sittenfeld

The Secret Life of Bees by Sue Monk Kidd

Bee Season by Myla Goldberg

The Lovely Bones by Alice Sebold

The Kite Runner by Khaled Hosseini

A Prayer for Owen Meany by John Irving

Running with Scissors by Augusten Burroughs

ANIMAL FARM George Orwell

14+

Next?

Orwell will make you think about the world. Check out the equally alarming *Nineteen Eighty-Four* (UTBG 244).

For a dystopian world that's real, not fantasy, try *One Day in the Life of Ivan Denisovich* (UTBG 256) by Alexander Solzhenitsyn.

Sometimes it's easier to see something clearly by stepping away from it. Pigs on a farm, for instance—or mice in a concentration camp. To some, the Holocaust may not seem a suitable subject for comics, but the allegory *Maus* (UTBG 223) by Art Spiegelman proves them wrong.

The animals at Manor Farm are unhappy—their drunken master is letting the farm go to ruin and they're all starving, so they stage a revolution to take over. To begin with everything seems rosy—the animals all work overtime, and everyone's belly is full of food. But it doesn't take long for the pigs to decide that because of their intelligence, they are superior to the stupid chickens and the workhorse Boxer.

A simple animal story? Yes, but this is also an allegory of the Russian Revolution and the society it created. As the pigs famously say, "All animals are equal, but some animals are more equal than others." This is a rare kind of book that works as both a political satire and as a great read.
Julia Bell, Author

ANITA AND ME Meera Syal

14+

Meena is nine and growing up fast. She lives with her Punjabi family in a small, otherwise all-white, mining village on the edge of Wolverhampton in England. She longs to be someone, to run with the pack and be accepted—not because of her color, but because she wants to be seen as an equal among her peer group. She lies and steals—and idolizes the feisty, brassy, blonde Anita, who, Meena's parents worry, is leading her astray.

At first, despite their Indian dress, food, and Diwali celebrations, Meena and her family seem to fit into the village. But in one searing moment the scales fall from her eyes when Sam Lowbridge, the Bad Boy of the village whom she has always secretly admired, sneers about "darkies" and "wogs." Nothing will feel the same again.
Jamila Gavin, Author

Next?

Another Meera Syal? Try *Life Isn't All Ha Ha Hee Hee*: three friends, three weddings, three stories.

A book that will also make you look differently at racism: Malorie Blackman's *Noughts & Crosses* (UTBG 252) and its sequels.

Serving Crazy with Curry by Amulya Malladi is another great novel that explores the traditional Indian family.

ANNA KARENINA Leo Tolstoy

I first read *Anna Karenina* when I was 13, and although it is a very long book with a complicated plot, I was transfixed by it. I think it is the best story about the different kinds of love between men and women that has ever been written—and when I was 13, this was a subject that fascinated me. Anna herself is a real, living woman, with a real woman's virtues and failings, and her life forms the main thread of the narrative. But through the other characters, the book also gives us a living picture of a society different from ours that miraculously becomes as real to us as our own.

Nina Bawden, Author

Next?

If this has given you a taste for huge, heartrending novels, try Tolstoy's epic, *War and Peace* (UTBG 379), or *Doctor Zhivago* (UTBG 94) by Boris Pasternak.

There's lots of doomed love from French novelists too—try Gustave Flaubert's unbeatable *Madame Bovary*.

Or for something epic and English, try George Eliot's *Middlemarch*, a magnificent, all-encompassing novel of both society and individuals.

ANNIE ON MY MIND Nancy Garden

14+

Next?

Good Moon Rising by Nancy Garden is just as moving and true to her subject as her debut.

Another novel about the turbulent first love between two girls is Paula Boock's *Dare Truth or Promise*.

Lauren Myracle's *Kissing Kate* is a contemporary novel dealing with the fallout from an unplanned kiss between two best friends.

Annie on My Mind is the now-classic story of two high school girls who tentatively, fearfully, hopefully discover their love for each other during one magical winter in New York City. Liza has gone to a protective private school her whole life, but when she meets Annie, her world cracks open. Annie attends a rowdy, raucous public high school; she's a fresh breeze blowing through Liza's stuffy life.

Nancy Garden's book is as romantic and filled with longing as any novel of heterosexual teen love. The girls become awkward and argumentative with each other when their unresolved sexual tension grows stronger. Their emotions are clearly those of first, innocent love, no matter the sexual orientation of the lovers.

Published in 1982, the book doesn't gloss over the difficulties of the girls' relationship—shocked parents, a possible expulsion from school, and the problems the girls cause for two lesbian teachers who get caught up in the subterfuge. But through it all, readers will root for the tender love of these two heartbreakingly real characters.

Ellen Wittlinger, Author

ANOTHER ROADSIDE ATTRACTION

Tom Robbins

For some writers, language is just this great big box of tricks to have fun and play with. True, reading a book that plays with language can be amusing for a while, but it can often be like going to a party and not being allowed to join in. And then there's Tom Robbins, who has the most fun with language of any writer I know; as he says, "if little else, the brain is an educational toy."

Another Roadside Attraction, written in 1971, was his first novel, and 30 years later he's only published a total of eight books. It has an astonishing cast of memorable characters and is about all kinds of things, including flea circuses, religion, and the possible end of Western civilization.

Graham Marks, Author

Next?

What else should you read after this? Another Tom Robbins! Try *Villa Incognito*.

There are no other authors quite the same, but try John Irving and his *A Prayer for Owen Meany* (UTBG 274).

Many graphic novels have a surreal quality to them; try Chris Ware's *Jimmy Corrigan, the Smartest Kid on Earth* (UTBG 183) or Neil Gaiman's **The Sandman** series (UTBG 302).

AN ANTHROPOLOGIST ON MARS

Oliver Sacks

Next?

Others by Oliver Sacks: *The Man Who Mistook His Wife for a Hat* or *Awakenings*.

Berton Roueche's *The Medical Detectives* also takes an in-depth look at bizarre medical cases and the doctors who try to solve them— it's like reading the TV show *House*!

Nicola Morgan's **Mondays Are Red** (UTBG 227) is about a boy whose senses are muddled by synesthesia.

Sometimes truth is stranger than fiction. Who'd believe a story about an artist who wakes up in the hospital after an auto accident and discovers to his horror that he can see only in black and white? Or the account of a woman who keeps hearing strange songs on a radio, only to find the music is inside her own head? Or a man with violent tics and mannerisms who becomes a surgeon? Or a 14-year-old boy who can't speak but can take a quick look at a palace and draw it perfectly from memory? Oliver Sacks introduces us to these people. And because he didn't just study them, but lived with them, you get a real glimpse into their minds.

Caroline Lawrence, Author

APOCALYPSE

Tim Bowler

When Kit and his family survive a dramatic boating accident, they are lucky to get washed up on a small island. Unfortunately it doesn't provide the sanctuary they need. The inhabitants are openly hostile, and the family soon realizes their lives are in great danger. What is more disturbing is that Kit starts to notice the presence of a strange, naked man with a birthmark on his face, just like his own. In his ensuing struggle to stay alive and make sense of what is happening around him, Kit finds himself dealing with far more than he'd bargained for.

If you enjoy books that are rich in atmosphere, with nail-biting plots, you will love *Apocalypse*. Tim Bowler has written a wonderful, haunting book that kept me on the edge of my seat as events careened toward their thrilling conclusion.

Susila Baybars, Editor

Next?

Tim Bowler's books are all edgy; try *Stormchasers*, about a boy trying to save his kidnapped sister, or *River Boy* (UTBG 291).

Darkhenge (UTBG 88) by Catherine Fisher is another dark adventure about the blurring of the real and the imagined.

Or for a very different shipwreck—try Daniel Defoe's *Robinson Crusoe*! Okay, it's a classic, but it's a rip-roaring read nonetheless!

The Ultimate Teen Readers' Poll

YOUR FAVORITE AUTHOR

1 J. K. Rowling

2 Anthony Horowitz

3 Roald Dahl

4 Lemony Snicket

5 J. R. R. Tolkien

6 Malorie Blackman

7 Darren Shan

8 Philip Pullman

9 Meg Cabot

10 Christopher Paolini

ARABELLA Georgette Heyer

Next?

Heyer's *The Unknown Ajax* is a warm and refreshingly realistic romance; *The Grand Sophy* is sheer sparkling fun.

You might also try one of her witty detective stories, like *Duplicate Death* or *No Wind of Blame*.

And of course, anyone who likes Heyer's romances should be reading the real thing—Jane Austen's *Pride and Prejudice* (UTBG 276).

Arabella was the first Georgette Heyer book I ever read—the first of very many. I fell in love with the humor, the elegant prose, and the amazingly accurate period detail that set Heyer's above other historical romances.

Arabella is the Cinderella story of an impoverished Yorkshire girl who comes to London and meets the wealthy Mr. Beaumaris—but his pride and her prejudice threaten to get in the way of their romance. Today, several decades later, I might prefer one of Heyer's more sophisticated stories, like *The Nonesuch* or *The Foundling*. But *Arabella* is still one of the great Regency romances; sweet as an ice-cream sundae, but never, ever sickly.

Sarah Gristwood, Author

ARCHER'S GOON Diana Wynne Jones

Archer sends his goon to collect the two thousand that Quentin Sykes owes him. Only the "two thousand" are words, not money, and Sykes is an English lecturer and writer. His children, Howard and Anthea (known universally as Awful), become fascinated by the goon and by what on earth their father is doing for Archer.

Gradually we discover that the town in which the Sykes family live is governed by seven megalomaniac wizard siblings, two of whom are women. Archer is one of this family, but who is his goon and what has happened to the youngest brother, Venturus?

The complex plot gets weirder and weirder toward the end—only Diana Wynne Jones could pull this off!

Mary Hoffman, Author

Next?

Other titles by Wynne Jones include *Howl's Moving Castle* (UTBG 167), *Fire and Hemlock* (UTBG 117), and *Eight Days of Luke*.

Debi Gliori's *Pure Dead Magic* has some of the same exuberance, especially with names.

For a more serious magic book, read Michael Lawrence's *A Crack in the Line* (UTBG 79).

ARTEMIS FOWL   Eoin Colfer

12+

Next?

The other books starring Artemis are *The Arctic Incident*, *The Eternity Code*, and *The Opal Deception*. There's also a World Book Day special, *The Seventh Dwarf*, which has a story that fits in between books one and two.

Faerie Wars (UTBG 109) and its follow-up novels by Herbie Brennan are a slightly more serious take on fairies.

Or, for something else action-packed, try Robert Muchamore's *The Recruit* (UTBG 288).

Artemis Fowl is one of those books that is able to combine magic, adventure, and humor into one roller-coaster read. Artemis Fowl—a 12-year-old boy with a girl's name!—is on a quest to find fairy gold. He plans to kidnap Captain Holly Short of the LEPrecon unit and get the gold as ransom. But he doesn't realize what he's getting into . . . From Bio-bombs to tri-barreled blasters, Artemis is in great danger.

You'll meet many interesting and hilarious characters: Mulch Diggums, a smelly dwarf on the run from the authorities; 20-foot trolls who can kill anything they think is edible; and one of my favorites, Artemis's bodyguard, Butler.

Eoin Colfer keeps you spellbound and even manages to involve the reader in a bit of code breaking. Intrigued? Well, there is only one way to find out more . . . Read the book!

Benjamin Cuffin-Munday, age 11

ARTHUR: THE SEEING STONE

Kevin Crossley-Holland

Set in the Welsh Marches in 1199, this is the tale of Arthur de Caldicot, who discovers his namesake, the legendary boy-king Arthur, in his "seeing stone." In a time of transition between one century and another, one king and another, between childhood and manhood, the "between places . . . tremble like far horizons" and all certainties and loyalties are brought into question.

Bullied by his older brother Serle and supported by his friend Gatty, Arthur increasingly identifies with the boy-king as he unravels the true nature of his quest, while the enigmatic figure of Merlin moves effortlessly between one dimension and another. A dense, absorbing tale told in a beautiful, spare style.

Livi Michael, Author

Next?

For a completely different take on Arthurian legend, try *The Once and Future King* (UTBG 255) by T. H. White, or Susan Cooper's **The Dark Is Rising** series (UTBG 87).

Or, for a marvelous interpretation of who Merlin might have been, try Mary Stewart's *The Crystal Cave* (UTBG 81).

THE ASTONISHING ADVENTURES OF FANBOY AND GOTH GIRL Barry Lyga

12+

The days that everyone ignores Donnie are the good days. On bad days he's tormented by bullies. When Mitchell Frampton hits him repeatedly with a dodgeball, the teachers and the other kids don't see (or don't want to see) what's going on. But when Donnie gets an IM the next day asking, "Why do you let him hit you?" he realizes that he might have an ally. When Donnie finally meets Kyra she calls him "Fanboy," and their unusual friendship begins.

Everyone understands bullying. But what do you do about it? Donnie doesn't deserve to be a target, but he is, and he needs a friend who will support him. This story is told with compassion and humor, and will leave readers thinking about it long after they've finished.

Andrea Lipinski, Librarian

> **Next?**
>
> For another story about an unlikely pair who find solace in reading and writing, try Ellen Wittlinger's *Hard Love* (UTBG 146).
>
> K. L. Going's *Fat Kid Rules the World* (UTBG 114) also deals with the difficulty of being bullied and the redemption found through a friend.
>
> A book that features comics at its center is Michael Chabon's *The Amazing Adventures of Kavalier & Clay* (UTBG 14).

THE ASTONISHING LIFE OF OCTAVIAN NOTHING, TRAITOR TO THE NATION VOLUME ONE: THE POX PARTY M. T. Anderson

14+

> **Next?**
>
> If you like disturbing twists and provocative style, read more M. T. Anderson, especially *Feed* (UTBG 116) and *Thirsty* (UTBG 356).
>
> For alternative histories, Gary Blackwood is a good choice. *The Year of the Hangman* is set just after the Revolutionary War.

This distinctive, disturbing book set during the first days of the American Revolution sticks in your mind long after the last page. Octavian and his mother are African slaves owned by a group of free-thinking scholars. They are treated like exotic royalty, but in truth, they're just another scientific experiment. When a harsh new benefactor takes control, the experiment takes a dark turn. Some truly horrible things happen, and Octavian's polite, well-reasoned voice goes silent. The story picks up in other sources instead, such as newspaper clippings and a soldier's letters. Besides fascinating characters and a plot that doesn't let go, the story is chock-full of ideas about human rights, freedom, friendship, and the fuzziness of right and wrong. You should know, this is not an easy read. Give it a chance, though, and you'll never forget it.

Alicia Anderson, Librarian

AT THE SIGN OF THE SUGARED PLUM

Mary Hooper

Summer 1665, and Hannah journeys to London to work in her sister's candy shop, The Sugared Plum. She never receives the letter forbidding her visit, as plague threatens the city; once there, she cannot return. "At home in Chertsey, life had been peaceful . . . Here though, now, there was a bitter, heart-stopping danger in each day." As more people die, the bustling city that first intoxicated Hannah becomes increasingly gruesome, and the sisters are forced into action to save just one life from the carnage.

It is the details—of clothes, smells, foods, plague-symptoms (nasty!), mass burials—that bring this novel to life. Hannah's curious and determined viewpoint really draws you into this absorbing historical story, and parts of her plague-ridden London are recognizable today.

Helen Simmons, Bookseller

Next?

Mary Hooper has written more about Hannah in *Petals in the Ashes*, which chronicles the Great Fire in London.

Laurie Halse Anderson's historical fiction novel *Fever 1793* is about a fever epidemic in Philadelphia that killed 10% of the city's population.

Out of the Dust (UTBG 263) by Karen Hesse takes on the Depression and the migration out of the Oklahoma Dust Bowl, and is written in a lyrical stanza form.

ATONEMENT Ian McEwan

Next?

None of Ian McEwan's books are easy reads, but you might want to try two others he's written: *Enduring Love* and *The Cement Garden* (UTBG 63).

You might also like *The Wasp Factory* (UTBG 380) by Iain Banks.

I guess I started reading "grown-up" fiction when I had gone through my own stack of books and the library was closed. I picked up something my mother had left on the coffee table and discovered a new world, complete with the adult stuff. I was hooked.

Atonement is a novel I would have gobbled up back then. The story starts in 1935 when 13-year-old Briony witnesses a moment that she's not quite old enough to understand, between her older sister and a young man. Her interpretation of this moment leads us into a world of secrets, lies, and unbearable damage.

The book spans a lifetime and the ending is one you'll probably read at least twice.

Sara Nickerson, Author

BALZAC AND THE LITTLE CHINESE SEAMSTRESS Dai Sijie

14+

This book should be full of anguish, but it's uplifting rather than tragic. It's about two Chinese students who, during China's Cultural Revolution, are forced to work as manual laborers in a remote and extremely primitive area. Their misery is relieved in the most unlikely way—by the discovery of a chest full of novels by Balzac. Such books were banned at the time so the students have to keep their treasure secret, but they can't help sharing the stories with the gorgeous little local seamstress, with whom they both fall in love. This novel is funny, sad, but never solemn, and it gave me an unforgettable picture of China during one of the greatest upheavals in its history.
Elizabeth Laird, Author

Next?

If you want to read more about the appalling realities of life in 20th-century China, read *Wild Swans* (UTBG 391) by Jung Chang.

For another interesting look at Chinese culture, try Gene Luen Yang's award-winning graphic novel *American Born Chinese* (UTBG 16).

Fahrenheit 451 (UTBG 110) is a very different and horrifying story: Ray Bradbury's look at a future where books are banned.

BATMAN: THE DARK KNIGHT RETURNS

Frank Miller, Lynn Varley, and Klaus Janson

Next?

After seeing Batman's future, check out his past in *Batman: Year One*, also by Frank Miller, illustrated by David Mazzucchelli and Richmond Lewis.

For more gorgeous artwork and dark futures, try *Kingdom Come* by Mark Waid and Alex Ross.

Candy-colored movies and silly TV series might have caused you to forget the dark origins of the Batman—a man driven to vengeance and forever haunted by the murder of his parents. In *The Dark Knight Returns*, Frank Miller returns Bruce Wayne to his shadowy roots. In the bleak future of Gotham City, an aging Bruce Wayne hung up his cowl years ago, but now a group of thrill-killing teens convinces him to take to the rooftops once again. However, Bruce is not the man he was, and an aging body and tortured spirit hamper the Dark Knight's quest for justice.

Frank Miller takes the world's most recognizable comic book character and reintroduces and reinvents him. He is assisted in this by the moody, meticulous artwork of Lynn Varley and Klaus Janson. Together, the three not only created a great book, they also ushered in a new age of gritty, grown-up superheroes. Not for young readers or the faint of heart, *The Dark Knight Returns* is required reading for anyone who loves a great superhero story.
Merideth Jenson-Benjamin, Librarian

BE MORE CHILL Ned Vizzini

Definitely not a book to be left lying around for your grandma to pick up, *Be More Chill* is both very funny and surprisingly realistic.

Jeremy is the biggest geek in high school. Desperately in love with the beautiful Christine, he can't even bring himself to talk to her—but then a friend tells him about "squips."

Squips are nano-technology quantum computers, small enough to swallow. Once you have one lodged in your brain it takes over, tells you who to talk to (and how), what clothes to wear—in short, how to be the coolest dude around. Unfortunately, there's always user error to mess things up!

If you enjoy this book, Ned Vizzini suggests Googling "squip"—it's a strange world out there on the Net!

Laura Hutchings, Teacher

Next?

M. T. Anderson's *Feed* (UTBG 116) looks at what might happen if computer and television technologies were connected to people's brains at birth.

A much more serious book about peer pressure and victimization is Robert Cormier's *The Chocolate War* (UTBG 67).

If you want more Ned Vizzini, try his *Teen Angst? Naaah . . .*, which is exactly what it says it is about!

THE BEACH Alex Garland

Next?

Alex Garland's *The Tesseract* is more sophisticated than *The Beach*—a better book, though a harder one.

Lord of the Flies (UTBG 209) is William Golding's classic story of a paradise that quickly becomes a living hell.

Want more stories about backpacking? Try William Sutcliffe's *Are You Experienced?* or John Harris's disturbing *The Backpacker*.

Imagine you're on vacation, backpacking somewhere exotic. You check into a cheap and crummy hotel. There you meet a man who calls himself Daffy (as in Duck), who tells you about a secret place he knows—a secluded beach, almost inaccessible, beautiful and unspoiled, where a young community lives in paradise. Sounds tempting, doesn't it?

So Richard decides to find this heavenly spot, and when he does find it, well, it's just too good to be true. Too good, perhaps, to last.

Alex Garland's first novel was an instant bestseller—for a while, every time you sat down on a bus or train, the person sitting next to you was reading it. And it was a worthy success—it's an enthralling tale, sometimes enchanting, and sometimes very dark and savage. And the ending, well . . . Many people didn't think it worked, but I thought it was amazing—read it and judge for yourself!

Daniel Hahn, Editor

BEAU GESTE P. C. Wren

14+

At 13, I wanted desperately to join the French Foreign Legion. The newspapers said that legionnaires were the scum of the earth—but I knew differently. *Beau Geste* was the book responsible for my inside information and I read it over and over again.

When the fabulous Blue Water sapphire is stolen, suspicion immediately falls upon Michael Geste, who mysteriously disappears only hours after it vanishes. Protesting their brother's innocence, John and Digby Geste follow Michael into the French Foreign Legion in an attempt to solve the puzzle of the missing jewel.

What follows next is a marvelous, heartbreaking adventure. They really don't write books like this anymore, and the world is poorer for that.

Laura Hutchings, Teacher

Next?

A lot of people don't know that there are two sequels—*Beau Sabreur* and *Beau Ideal*.

If you enjoy this kind of historical novel, try D. K. Broster's *The Flight of the Heron* or A. E. Mason's *The Four Feathers*.

Or for another story involving a missing jewel: *The Moonstone* (UTBG 231) by Wilkie Collins.

BEAUTY Robin McKinley

12+

We all know the story of *Beauty and the Beast*: in order to save her father, Beauty, the unselfish heroine, goes to live in the house of the Beast, only to find her self-sacrifice eventually rewarded. So far, so fairy tale.

Robin McKinley's poetic retelling sticks close to the established story (though in this book Beauty's older sisters are much more sympathetic than in the original tale) and the growth of Beauty's true love for the Beast is satisfying, as are her trials and suffering en route. (The luxury that surrounds her in the Beast's castle may help.) The story is focused on the heroine's crises and responses, and will be particularly enjoyed by readers like me with a taste for tales in which real life blends into fantasy.

Margaret Mahy, Author

Next?

More Robin McKinley? Try *Spindle's End* (UTBG 335).

Kate Petty and Caroline Castle's collection *Tales of Beauty and Cruelty* are based on old tales by Hans Christian Andersen.

Patricia McKillip also delves into fairy tales to create magical worlds. Read *Winter Rose*, a dark story of love, murder, and obsession.

Or try *The Tower Room* (UTBG 362), part of the **Egerton Hall Novels** by Adèle Geras, which retells the tales of *Rapunzel*, *Sleeping Beauty*, and *Snow White*.

BEE SEASON Myla Goldberg

16+

Next?

For another book that explores the highs and lows of being Jewish, try Chaim Potok's *The Chosen* (UTBG 68) or Dana Reinhardt's *A Brief Chapter in My Impossible Life*.

Myla Goldberg's second novel, *Wickett's Remedy*, is a historical novel about a family riddled by disease in Boston during World War I.

For another adult book with teen appeal, try Sue Monk Kidd's *The Secret Life of Bees* (UTBG 308).

Bee Season is a story about a family—father Saul, a scholar and cantor at the local Reform temple; mother Miriam, a hardworking and single-minded lawyer; son Aaron, a soft-spoken future rabbi; and daughter Eliza, an average student and lover of television reruns. On the surface, they look just like everyone else. But beneath the surface, they are breaking apart . . .

When Eliza surprises everyone by winning the school spelling bee, she sets in motion a series of events that brings out new traits in everyone. Saul starts expending all of his energy training her for the national bee and introducing her to the Jewish Kabbalah, while neglected Aaron seeks out new spiritual meaning in an Eastern religious group, and Miriam falls prey to the harmfully compulsive behavior buried deep inside her. Myla Goldberg weaves effortlessly in and out of each family member's perspective, her complex narrative giving us a complete and utterly compelling look into the search for spirituality, the defining of self, the need for companionship and acceptance, and the ultimate love of family that drives us all.

Stacy Cantor, Editor

THE BEET FIELDS Gary Paulsen

14+

The boy—we never learn his name—runs away from an abusive home, leaving everything behind. It's time to grow up, fast. He takes the first job he finds, hoeing beets on the prairie farms of North Dakota, working in fields so vast they stretch from horizon to horizon. He moves on to driving a tractor, is robbed of his hard-earned wages by a corrupt cop, and finally joins a carnival—a traveling fair. In one summer he becomes a man—first work, first wages, first woman—and learns a lot about people, from the illegal immigrant Mexican workers in the beet fields to the geeks and shills of the carnival. Short, punchy, easy to read, hard to forget.

Jan Mark, Author

Next?

Hatchet (UTBG 147), also by Gary Paulsen, is about another boy learning to survive, this time alone in the wilderness; there are sequels, too.

For more about the kind of life Paulsen is describing, try *Of Mice and Men* (UTBG 253) and *The Grapes of Wrath* by John Steinbeck, set about 20 years earlier.

Want a stranger tale of laboring outside? Try *Holes* (UTBG 157) by Louis Sachar.

BEIGE Cecil Castellucci

12+

Katy's mom, a university student, is off to Peru on an archaeological dig and unfortunately, Katy isn't invited. Instead, she must leave all her friends in Montreal and go spend two weeks with her father, the Rat from the late great—but never financially successful—punk band Suck, in LA. Katy hasn't seen her dad since she was seven, when he was banned from Canada forever for smuggling heroin. Now he's off drugs and Suck is getting ready to go back on tour. One of the really horrible things the Rat does is hire Lake Suck, the daughter of Suck's lead singer, to act as Katy's friend for her visit. Lake dubs Katy "Beige."

What is interesting about this book is that you see a conservative outsider thrust into the punk community. Every punk song you ever heard will start running through your head. It helps that the chapter titles work as a playlist using titles and artists. This is a funny, sweet, and painful tale of a 14-year-old beginning to see what life is all about.

Diana Tixier Herald, Librarian

Next?

Many of Cecil Castellucci's books focus on an "alternative" narrator—if you liked reading about the punk scene, try *Boy Proof* (UTBG 47) for another wonderfully different voice.

Laurie Halse Anderson's *Twisted* is a look into the issues of self-identity and sticking out from the crowd, but from a boy's point of view.

The Return of Death Eric by Sam Llewellyn is a hilarious look at siblings who must deal with an aging rock-star dad.

THE BELGARIAD series David Eddings

14+

Next?

Try the **Mallorean** series, another epic by David Eddings.

The Sword of Shannara by Terry Brooks and *The Magician* by Raymond E. Feist are epic fantasy stories that will keep you absorbed for hours.

For something set in a fantasy world but somehow much more real, try Robin Hobb's **The Farseer** trilogy (UTBG 112).

I read the five books of The Belgariad more times than I can recall when I was a teenager. I was a big fantasy fan, and these were some of the best fantasy books I'd ever read. It's the story of a young, seemingly ordinary boy, who gets swept away from his village and involved in the world of wizards and kings. It lacks the imaginative scope of Tolkien, but it's fun, exciting, intriguing fantasy in which the characters are as important as the quest and magical elements. Easy to read and great to share, this was one of the most popular series at my school, appealing even to those who didn't read fantasy. Immerse yourself and enjoy!

Darren Shan, Author

THE BELL Iris Murdoch

16+

Next?

Another Iris Murdoch? Try *Henry and Cato* or *The Unicorn.*

Murdoch's husband, John Bayley, wrote a tender portrait of their life together and her final years with Alzheimer's—*Iris.*

Another story set against summer heat and a turmoil of emotions is Ian McEwan's *Atonement* (UTBG 26).

George Eliot's *Middlemarch* is another novel that brings the reader into the world of 19th-century manners and customs through a wide cast of characters.

I can't overemphasize the impact of reading *The Bell* at age 16. It kick-started a chain reaction and I did not stop reading Iris Murdoch until around 10 books and a year later, when I came up for air. Iris Murdoch is a must for anybody seriously interested in human relationships, beliefs, beauty, darkness, and extraordinarily powerful writing.

Be prepared to enter a world that is immediately riveting, disturbing, and totally adult. Dora is the wife of handsome, powerful, but brutal older man Paul; she tries to leave him but finds she cannot. Instead, she joins him at a strange "spiritual" community deep in the English countryside. Against a seething backdrop of summer heat, there is far more that goes on than meets the eye. Who is in love with whom? Who believes in what? And will they find the old bell that legend says has lain buried for years in the great lake?

Rebecca Swift, Editor

THE BELL JAR Sylvia Plath

16+

Sylvia Plath is perhaps better known for her poetry and for being the wife of Ted Hughes, but her only novel, *The Bell Jar*, is undoubtedly one of the greatest of modern novels. It's about Esther Greenwood, a 19-year-old girl who suffers a mental breakdown. We watch her gradually becoming disconnected from the world around her while she's working in New York on a magazine, then witness her descent as she returns home to the Boston suburbs, and see her behavior becoming increasingly erratic until she is finally admitted to a mental hospital. As dark as *The Bell Jar* is, it's shot through with an unforgettable lyrical beauty. It's a demanding and harrowing read—a real classic.

Sherry Ashworth, Author

Next?

The Catcher in the Rye (UTBG 60) by J. D. Salinger is about a boy in the grip of a breakdown.

Susanna Kaysen's *Girl, Interrupted* is a collection of autobiographical essays about being hospitalized for mental illness.

Or there's *Cut* (UTBG 83) by Patricia McCormick, about the treatment of a self-harmer.

BELOVED Toni Morrison

Beloved is the story of Sethe, a woman haunted by a terrible decision she made back in her past—to slit the throat of her baby girl rather than give her up to slavery.

This deeply powerful novel taps veins of history, folkloric tradition, and memory. In often beautiful prose, Morrison conjures up pain and suffering, guilt and torment, love and sacrifice. This author is at her best when writing about feelings, about yearnings, and about the human spirit. And *Beloved* is full of these ingredients. It's a huge-hearted, tragic story that tugs constantly at your emotions.

Neil Arksey, Author

Next?

There are some great African American women writers: try Alice Walker's *The Color Purple* (UTBG 75) or Maya Angelou's *I Know Why the Caged Bird Sings* (UTBG 170).

Toni Morrison's other books are all outstanding too. Try *The Bluest Eye* or *Jazz*.

Another writer who makes you understand the most powerful of emotions is Gabriel García Márquez; try *Love in the Time of Cholera* (UTBG 212) or *One Hundred Years of Solitude* (UTBG 257).

BEYOND THE DEEPWOODS
Paul Stewart and Chris Riddell

12+

I found this book almost impossible to put down. It features a teenage boy named Twig. Twig is the son of a sky pirate—though he doesn't realize it. As a baby he was left on the outskirts of a woodtroll village and is brought up by them. Being weak, he is bullied and comes home with bumps and scars. Then one day, he's finally told by his "mother" of his origins.

The book is about how Twig spends a year wandering the Deepwoods. Along the way he finds friendship, danger, and fear. He also stumbles upon his father, Cloud Wolf, who then abandons him again, and Twig finds the most feared creature in all the Deepwoods. I loved this intriguing and exciting book—and the detailed illustrations are amazing!

Andrew Barakat, age 12

Next?

This is the first of **The Edge Chronicles,** and you're in luck as there are lots more—try *Stormchaser* next.

Brian Jacques's *Redwall* (UTBG 288) is just as fast and exciting.

Or try Bernard Cornwell's *Sharpe's Company* (UTBG 317) for an adventure in a real historical context.

THE BIG SLEEP Raymond Chandler

14+

The Big Sleep tells the story of the quick-thinking, fast-talking California private eye Philip Marlowe. He becomes involved in the affairs of the Sternwood family after he's asked by the old, dying General Sternwood to deal with the blackmail of his younger daughter, Carmen.

Philip Marlowe is cool, smooth, and everything a private eye should be. The girls seem to like him too, seeing as both the Sternwood daughters fall for his charms early on in the book.

This is a fantastic story filled with overwhelming description and laden with twists and great one-liners: "She looked as if she'd been poured into the dress and someone forgot to say whoa." "It was a blonde. A blonde to make a bishop kick a hole in a stained glass window." "He looked as inconspicuous as a tarantula on a slice of angel cake."

Raffaella Barker, Author

Next?

How about some spies? Try the **James Bond** books (UTBG 181) by Ian Fleming, starting with *Casino Royale*.

All the other Raymond Chandlers are must-reads. Try *The Long Goodbye* next.

More hard-boiled detective novels? Read Dashiell Hammett, starting with *The Maltese Falcon* or *The Glass Key*. Both Chandler and Hammett had most of their books made into great films!

BINDI BABES Narinder Dhami

12+

Next?

Read the sequels: next is *Bollywood Babes*, in which a faded actress plays havoc with the sisters' lives.

The **Mates, Dates . . .** series (UTBG 222) by Cathy Hopkins is about three friends, boys, parents, and everything girly.

Does My Head Look Big in This? by Randa Abdel-Fattah is about the trials and tribulations of a Muslim teen.

Amber (Ambajit), Jazz (Jasvinder), and Geena are sisters. They live with their dad as their mom is dead. They have a pretty cool life: they're popular, even the teachers like them, and the only things they hate are people pitying them or trying to control their lives. Everything's fine, isn't it? They have great clothes, fun friends, lots of freedom, and, best of all, each other. But then their bossy, interfering, unmarried aunt comes over from India and the fun can't last. She makes them go to bed early and won't let them eat junk food. What's to be done? Hmm, how about an arranged marriage? Matchmaking begins and, well, things get complicated—and very funny.

Fast-paced, full of Bollywood sparkle, serious fun, and girls you'll really sympathize with!

Leonie Flynn, Editor

BIRD BY BIRD: SOME INSTRUCTIONS ON WRITING AND LIFE Anne Lamott

One of my favorite stories about getting things done, that I tell myself whenever I feel hopelessly behind and overwhelmed, is the story of the title of *Bird by Bird*. Anne Lamott's brother had a huge report about birds to write that he had put off for months. As he sat in anguish in front of a blank piece of paper on the night before it was due, he asked his father how in the world he would ever get it done, and the father replied, "Bird by bird, buddy. Just take it bird by bird."

This funny and inspiring book about writing breaks down the process bird by bird, but not in a preachy or overly instructional way. Reading it is like sitting at the kitchen table with Lamott as she treats you to anecdotes and advice that make you want to immediately pull out your pad of paper and start putting down your stories. This is a must-read for anyone with a poem in their heart.

Laura Lehner-Ennis, Librarian

Next?

Stephen King's *On Writing* is a great tool for inspiring new and old writers.

The Freedom Writers Diary by the Freedom Writers and Zlata Filipovic—originally inspired by the diary of Filipovic, a group of California urban teens are challenged by an innovative teacher to keep a diary of their difficult lives.

For a fun and practical guide to the publishing process, try *A Teen's Guide to Getting Published* by Jessica and Danielle Dunn.

BIRDSONG Sebastian Faulks

Next?

After this big, demanding read, how about a first-hand perspective on the Great War? *Memoirs of an Infantry Officer* by Siegfried Sassoon is incomparable.

For a good historian's overview, try any of Lyn Macdonald's books. *1915* and *To the Last Man* are particularly good.

Two more of Sebastian Faulks's books you should try are *Charlotte Gray*, set in World War II, and *The Fatal Englishman*, about some real-life casualties of war.

Birdsong is one of the most powerful novels I've ever read. It is a love story, and a deeply moving one at that. It's also a story about discovering the past, but first and foremost it's a story of war. Stephen Wraysford falls in love with a French woman, loses her, and is sent back to France as a lieutenant in the early stages of World War I. The horrors of that war—the endless mud, the unspeakable waste of life, the despair—can rarely have been as clearly conveyed. This is an unforgettable book and I urge you to read it.

Malachy Doyle, Author

FANTASY
by Catherine Fisher

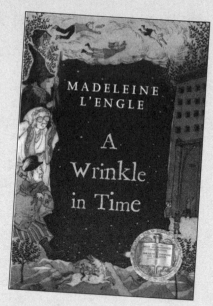

Fantasy is a wide field. Or if you like, a dark wood. Somewhere in its depths tangle ghost stories and sci-fi and legends and psychological archetypes. But all of them grew from the seeds of myth.

Like many readers, I first ventured into fantasy through fairy tale, reading Japanese and Russian and Scandinavian versions of tales where girls defeat witches and third sons kill dragons, and then found they led to myth: to the wild and crazy tales of Wales and Ireland—you can find some of these in *The Mabinogion* translated by Jones and Jones, or *Early Irish Myths and Sagas* (trans. J. Gantz). In *The Tain*, Thomas Kinsella brilliantly retells the story of the hero Cu Chulain's lone stand against the armies of Connaught, which is epic fantasy of the best kind, up there with Homer, and in the wonderful translations of *Beowulf* we can confront the terrors of the monsters that crawl from the dark swamps of the Viking imagination.

Most literary fantasy is a direct continuation of these themes. The Lord of the Rings trilogy (UTBG 210) and *The Silmarillion* by J. R. R. Tolkien are steeped in Tolkien's enormous knowledge of Norse languages and stories; they are wonderful, sweeping tales of adventure and cosmic questions. Along with C. S. Lewis (especially perhaps his sci-fi trilogy *Out of the Silent Planet, Perelandra*, and *That Hideous Strength),* it was Tolkien who founded the modern genre, though he himself was influenced by early writers like William Morris (try *The Well at the World's End*), and Lewis loved George MacDonald's books.

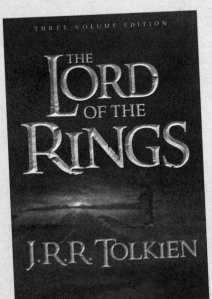

Writing a little before them was William Hope Hodgson, whose bizarre mixes of sci-fi and fantasy are now cult classics. Look out for *The House on the Borderland* and the amazing *Night Land*, which is sometimes so bad it's unreadable, and yet its nightmare landscapes are breathtaking.

A contemporary of Tolkien's was E. R. Edison, mostly known now for *The Worm Ouroboros*. If you're not afraid of flamboyant costumes, endless names, fantastic swordplay, and a very mannered style, you might love this. I do, though it's not for everyone.

A writer who built his own creations on these and other foundations was Mervyn Peake, whose superb Gormenghast trilogy has to be on anyone's list of great imaginative achievements. The endless ramifications, corridors, halls, and towers of Gormenghast castle are mirrored throughout later films and trilogies, album covers, and comics.

In children's fiction in the 1960s fantasy really took off too, especially in the books of Susan Cooper and the brilliantly gifted Alan Garner, whose style grew more clipped and taut with each novel, culminating in two of the best young adult books ever, *The Owl Service* (UTBG 265), with its terrifying loop of relived Celtic myth, and *Red Shift*, a complex triple-time story that really moves up a gear into an almost unbearable intensity. Garner's later books have been for adults, but I'd recommend his most recent, *Thursbitch*.

Fantasy these days is immensely popular. Spurred in large part by the enormous success of J. K. Rowling's Harry Potter series (UTBG 146), interest in the genre has skyrocketed in recent years. Christopher Paolini's *Eragon* (UTBG 105) and the other books in his Inheritance trilogy have developed cult followings, as have Philip Pullman's His Dark Materials trilogy (UTBG 153). Other fantasy reads worthy of their popularity are *Tithe* (UTBG 359) by Holly Black, *The Amulet of Samarkand* (UTBG 17) and the other books in The Bartimaeus Trilogy by Jonathan Stroud, *Faerie Wars* (UTBG 109) by Herbie Brennan, *Artemis Fowl* (UTBG 24) by Eoin Colfer, and *The Thief Lord* (UTBG 355) by Cornelia Funke. Start with these, and a whole world of fantasy will follow. Keep exploring.

A few favorite series:

The Earthsea Quartet by Ursula K. Le Guin

The Dragonriders of Pern by Anne McCaffrey

Harry Potter by J. K. Rowling

The Inheritance trilogy by Christopher Paolini

The Belgariad series by David Eddings

His Dark Materials by Philip Pullman

Time-travel stories:

The Time Machine by H. G. Wells

The Sterkarm Handshake by Susan Price

A Wrinkle in Time by Madeleine L'Engle

THE #1 NEW YORK TIMES BESTSELLER

ERAGON

Christopher Paolini

BLACK HAWK DOWN: A STORY OF MODERN WAR

14+

Mark Bowden

If you think nonfiction equals boring, think again. If you want to know what modern war feels like, this book will have you ducking AK-47 rounds and praying you're not blown to pieces by an RPG (Rocket-Propelled Grenade).

One day in 1993, a team of elite Delta Force operators and US Army Rangers are sent into a war-torn African city to kidnap two associates of a renegade warlord. But things go horribly wrong when their Black Hawk helicopter is shot down. For the next 18 hours they are trapped in a nonstop firefight against hundreds of enemy combatants.

Maybe you've played the video game or seen the movie. But read this book: it will make you feel like you're experiencing what really happens in modern war.

Todd Strasser, Author

Next?

Inside Delta Force by Eric Haney chronicles Haney's military career and gives an in-depth view of a secret military unit .

James Bradley's *Flags of Our Fathers* (UTBG 119) gives a gritty account of the heroic aid James's father, John, administered to a wounded Marine.

Stephen Ambrose tells the story of a regiment of soldiers from their training through D-Day and beyond the war in *Band of Brothers*.

The Ultimate Teen Readers' Poll

BOOK YOU COULDN'T PUT DOWN

1 **The Harry Potter series**

2 **The Alex Rider series**

3 **A Series of Unfortunate Events**

4 **The Lord of the Rings trilogy**

5 **The Saga of Darren Shan**

6 **His Dark Materials trilogy**

7 *Twilight*

8 *A Child Called "It"*

9 *Girl, 15, Charming but Insane*

10 *Holes*

BLACK JUICE Margo Lanagan

Next?

Gothic, edited by Deborah Noyes, is a who's who of teen authors and a great collection of creepy stories.

The folklore of the Caribbean influences Nalo Hopkinson's *Skin Folk*, another collection of strange and beautiful short stories.

And of course, *White Time* by Margo Lanagan, her second short story collection published in the U.S., is full of even more wonderful stories.

Could you watch and celebrate as a beloved sister sinks to her death? Would you seek a demonic angel to save someone who loved you? Can you imagine being an animal separated from the one human you love? Would you take part in empty and ancient rituals you don't care about to change who you are? Read *Black Juice* by Margo Lanagan and you'll do all of this and more.

Strange, strong, beautiful, challenging—all these words can be used to describe the stories that Lanagan tells. Most of the stories in *Black Juice* are less than 20 pages long, but don't let their length fool you—each one packs a major punch, and they don't fall into the category of "easy reads." But like a song that gets stuck in your head for days, these stories stay with you long after you've put them down.

Merideth Jenson-Benjamin, Librarian

THE BLACK MAGICIAN trilogy

14+

Trudi Canavan

In Imardin, magicians of the Guild gather yearly for the Purge of vagrants, miscreants, and street urchins from the city. As the gathered mob is herded, a young slum girl called Sonea throws a stone filled with her anger. To the surprise of everyone present, the stone breaks the shield of the magicians and knocks one unconscious. As the situation develops, the Guild's worst fear is realized. A desperate race starts to find Sonea before her uncontrolled power obliterates her and the whole city. Filled with magic and conspiracy, this is one trilogy that cannot be missed.

Gary Chow, age 17

Next?

Tamora Pierce's **Song of the Lioness** quartet, starting with *Alanna* (UTBG 9), is about a girl's quest to become a knight.

Dream Merchant by Isobel Hoving is a magnificent fantasy (with the most gorgeous cover!).

Terry Brooks's **The Sword of Shannara** starts another epic fantasy series.

BLANKETS Craig Thompson

12+

Growing up is never easy. Especially if you live in a fundamentalist Christian household, your younger brother wets the bed you share, and you secretly want to be an artist in a world where art is considered the work of the devil. Well, there's always winter church camp. Except that only the rich kids can afford ski passes and Craig, the hero of this stunningly drawn "illustrated novel," hasn't got enough money for even a day pass. Then he falls in love for the first time with fascinating Raina, and everything changes. But his troubles are only just beginning. Craig Thompson takes us on a moving journey of discovery about love, friendship, and the importance of a good blanket.

Ariel Kahn, Academic

Next?

Goodbye Chunky Rice by Craig Thompson deals with the close friendship between two unlikely animals.

Marjane Satrapi's *Persepolis* (UTBG 269) is another amazing graphic novel.

Oranges Are Not the Only Fruit (UTBG 259) by Jeanette Winterson is a love story set in a deeply religious community.

A Portrait of the Artist as a Young Man (UTBG 273) by James Joyce shows the way an artist develops, falls in love, and comes to terms with his past.

BLOOD AND CHOCOLATE Annette Curtis Klause

14+

Next?

Annette Curtis Klause's first novel, *The Silver Kiss*, is about a girl who, while attempting to cope with her mother's inevitable death from cancer, falls in love with a vampire set on avenging his own mother's death.

Try Anne Rice's classic *Interview with the Vampire* (UTBG 178) if you like vampire tales.

Blood and Chocolate tells the story of a modern-day werewolf named Vivian, and it puts an interesting spin on popular werewolf legends. Posing as a normal human teenager at high school, Vivian struggles to balance two complex social lives: one with her close-knit, lovable, yet sometimes vicious pack, and one with a mysterious, strangely attractive human boy at school named Aiden. As Vivian realizes the fantasy-loving Aiden may love her more for the real magic she can show him, she has to decide whether she will abandon her werewolf pack for him or vice versa—but keeping both is not an option.

Cunning and suspenseful, *Blood and Chocolate* is a mystical read, walking the fine line between fantasy and contemporary fiction. It will have you on the edge of your seat wondering if Vivian will, in the end, choose blood or chocolate.

Claire Easton, age 16

BLOOD RED HORSE K. M. Grant

I never was a fan of horse books, being more of a puppy/kitten/bunny girl myself. I read *Blood Red Horse* because it was a historical novel about medieval England and the Crusades, but I wound up falling for the horse.

Oh, I liked the people a lot: the young Crusaders Gavin and Will, their beloved Ellie who had to stay behind, and the Muslim boy, Kamil, an enemy who becomes an ally and a friend. Theirs is a story of adventure, of the futility and horror of war, of the importance of friendship, loyalty, courage, and love. They and the other characters are realistically and respectfully drawn, so I did not have to choose sides but could understand their conflicts and cheer for all of them.

And I did—but most of all for the magical horse, the blood red Hosanna, who inspired people by his example to be more than they thought they could be. And in his honor, I plan to read another horse book soon.

Karen Cushman, Author

BOOKS WITH A LATIN BEAT

How the García Girls Lost Their Accents
by Julia Alvarez

The House on Mango Street
by Sandra Cisneros

Parrot in the Oven: Mi Vida
by Victor Martinez

Heat by Mike Lupica

Next?

The next two books in the **de Granville** trilogy, *Green Jasper* and *Blaze of Silver*, should not be missed if you enjoyed the action and adventure of the first.

If you like the bloodier side of history, try Adèle Geras's *Troy* (UTBG 366), a teenaged retelling of Homer's *The Iliad* (UTBG 173).

The Minister's Daughter (UTBG 227) by Julie Hearn is another compelling historical novel; this one focuses on the witch hunts in England in 1645.

41

THE BLOOD STONE Jamila Gavin

This is the tale of Filippo Veroneo, born in Venice in the 14th century, who journeys in search of his father, missing since just before his birth. He travels from Venice to Afghanistan, carrying a ransom—the invaluable jewel, the Ocean of the Moon—sewn into his head for safekeeping. Love, loyalty, betrayal, and cruelty are fundamental to Filippo's world, and there is risk on every page. This great epic is fabulous and atmospheric and gives us tastes of worlds long since gone, including that of the great Moghul court in Agra, home of the Taj Mahal. It is a huge adventure, a compelling journey, as rich and desirable as the jewel that is its title.

Wendy Cooling, Books Consultant

Next?

Jamila Gavin's *Coram Boy* (UTBG 77) tells the story of two boys, one a rescued slave, the other the illegitimate son of the heir to a great estate.

Or try Gavin's trilogy, beginning with *The Wheel of Surya*, which tells a gripping story of war and peace.

For another journey of challenge, adventure, and survival, read Michael Morpurgo's *Kensuke's Kingdom*, a story of a shipwreck.

THE BODY IN THE LIBRARY Agatha Christie

Next?

Definitely more Miss Marple is in order—*The 4:50 from Paddington* is another favorite of mine.

Dorothy L. Sayers wrote classy murder mysteries. My favorite is *Murder Must Advertise*, but they're all worth a read.

For another series of (altogether different) books from the same time period as Agatha Christie's mysteries, with classy country houses aplenty, try the **Jeeves** stories (UTBG 182) by P .G. Wodehouse.

I think this is my favorite Miss Marple story. In it, Agatha Christie takes a conventional detective-story opening (body in library) and adds layer upon layer of intrigue, with twists and red herrings—just enough to make you feel really clever and smug for working out the whodunit all on your own and then really stupid when it turns out that you got it altogether wrong. And of course Miss Marple has got it right.

She's a lovely old woman, Miss Marple, apparently quite harmless (meaning that suspects routinely let down their guard in her presence), but at the same time harboring no happy, optimistic faith in human nature whatsoever; she is a delightful, prim old cynic. And in this story, as in them all, she shines.

Daniel Hahn, Editor

THE BODY OF CHRISTOPHER CREED

Carol Plum-Ucci

Next?

For another hard-hitting novel by Carol Plum-Ucci, try *What Happened to Lani Graver*, about a character who's more than a little bit different.

Or try Gail Giles's *What Happened to Cass McBride?* (UTBG 385), a mystery that also addresses the problem of school bullying.

Chris Creed had always been a little different—an outcast, a weirdo, a freak. But when he disappears, leaving only a cryptic e-mail message detailing his loneliness and exclusion, the entire town becomes abuzz with speculation. Was it suicide? Murder? Or did he simply leave town? After finding out he was mentioned in Chris's final note, golden boy Torey Adams becomes fixated with the need to solve the mystery and begins to search for clues. But as the town becomes more and more suspicious, gossip spreads, fingers are pointed, and no one is safe.

While *The Body of Christopher Creed* is undoubtedly a fascinating, suspenseful mystery novel, it is also a compelling coming-of-age story and an important look at the issues of teenage isolation and oppression. And it builds fantastically to a shocking, memorable ending.

Stacy Cantor, Editor

BONE
VOLUME ONE: OUT FROM BONEVILLE

Jeff Smith

Bone starts out as a simple graphic novel telling the story of three cousins who find themselves lost in the wilderness. Throw in talking animals, some dragons, and a society that deals in eggs rather than dollars, and you know you're in for a treat. *Bone* follows the epic journey of these three rogues as they get into all kinds of trouble, creating a hilarious combination of wit, adventure, and even puppy love. Much of the humor arises from the visual aspects of this graphic novel, where author and illustrator Jeff Smith never fails to impress. Additionally, the fairly simple setup of the paneled pages provides a good introduction for the inexperienced graphic novel reader, making the humor both appreciable and accessible. Always an entertaining read, *Bone* is a must.

Noah Cantor, age 19

Next?

For more in the **Bone** series, try Jeff Smith's second volume, *The Great Cow Race*, or the third volume, *Eyes of the Storm*.

Alan Moore and Dave Gibbons's *Watchmen* (UTBG 381), another critically acclaimed graphic novel, is a sophisticated, complex story with startlingly detailed illustrations.

THE BOOK THIEF Markus Zusak

14+

Next?

For a different viewpoint on the Holocaust, try *The Boy in the Striped Pajamas* (UTBG 46) by John Boyne; Lois Lowry's classic, *Number the Stars*; or Bette Greene's *Summer of My German Soldier*.

For more by Markus Zusak, pick up *I Am the Messenger* (UTBG 169) for another wonderful read with a completely different topic and tone.

When I learned the narrator of this book was Death, I knew I had to read it. How intriguing it would be to be led around Nazi Germany by the one thing I fear most. Death was fascinated by Liesel. She was so young, yet so mature, calm, and collected. He had stolen her brother from her hands at a young age, but she managed to carry on with her life. After her mom left her, she was forced to move in with the Hubermanns on Himmel Street. She liked her new dad. He taught her to read and played the accordion for her. Life was looking pretty good with her new family. Then the bombings came and everything changed. Liesel was forced into a life of stealing, fighting for every meal and living each day knowing it may be her last. The only things helping her through the hard times were the books.

How did she get the books, you ask? You will have to read this amazing story full of courage, fear, and accomplishment to find out.

Haley Fletcher, age 17

BORN CONFUSED Tanuja Desai Hidier

14+

Born Confused is a big, technicolor novel, swirling with the music, smells, and images of two continents. Dimple's 17th birthday present from best friend Gwyn is a fake ID. But for Dimple, identity is complicated: she's an ABCD—American Born Confused Desi. Should she date a "suitable *Indian* boy" or follow Gwyn, dating American college boys? And when the "suitable boy" isn't the loser she'd thought and Gwyn embraces Indian-ness to snare him—then what?

Dimple discovers "you have to get lost to get found": in getting lost, she comes to understand more about her parents' history, about India, and about friendship. I love Dimple's unsureness, her devotion to her camera, and her sound heart in this funny/sad quest for belonging.

Helen Simmons, Bookseller

Next?

You might also like *Monsoon Summer* by Mitali Perkins, a realistic look at Indian life.

For sheer exuberance, *Anita and Me* (UTBG 19) by Meera Syal is another great account of growing up in an Indian family in another country—this time, Britain.

Or for a poetic look at life in India, try Arundhati Roy's *The God of Small Things*.

BOUND   Donna Jo Napoli

Fourteen-year-old Xing Xing is the Cinderella of Ming Dynasty China. Left with her stepmother and stepsister, Wei Ping, after her father's death, Xing Xing is forced to become the family's servant, tending to household chores and her older stepsister's newly bound feet, which Xing Xing's stepmother believes will make Wei Ping a more attractive bride to possible suitors.

Xing Xing, despite her maltreatment, continues in secret to practice the arts of painting, poetry, and calligraphy as her father had taught her. Donna Jo Napoli weaves a story rich with the history of China and poetic detail. Xing Xing's journey, which includes a prince, a lost slipper, and small animals (that are more significant than the Disney films of old), is one that will feel as if you're following it for the first time— and hoping for the heroine's happily ever after every step of the way.

Norma Perez-Hernandez, age 17

Next?

Donna Jo Napoli's other novels should not be missed. Some greats include *Beast*, *Song of the Magdalene*, and *Sirena*.

And if you still want clever twists on fairy tales, try Vivian Vande Velde's more comedic take on the genre, *The Rumpelstiltskin Problem* or Shannon Hale's *The Goose Girl* (UTBG 140).

THE BOY IN THE BURNING HOUSE
Tim Wynne-Jones

Next?

Dangerous Skies (UTBG 86) by Suzanne Fisher Staples brings together an unsolved crime and a powerful and unusual friendship.

For another exciting and engaging adventure, read Mark Twain's fantastic *The Adventures of Huckleberry Finn* (UTBG 6).

Or try the classic *Treasure Island* (UTBG 363) by Robert Louis Stevenson for a great adventure starring another Jim Hawkins!

Jim Hawkins is just beginning to get over the disappearance of his dad, now presumed dead. So when wild Ruth Rose appears with her crazy theories about what happened to him, accusing Father Fisher, the beyond-reproach local priest, Jim doesn't want to know. But he can't ignore a niggling doubt— what if Ruth Rose is right? Their urgent investigation takes them back to the events of a generation earlier, when a wayward local boy died in a fire no one has yet been able to explain . . .

Consistently engaging and beautifully crafted, this is a real read-in-one-sitting book.

Daniel Hahn, Editor

THE BOY IN THE STRIPED PAJAMAS
John Boyne

12+

I've got a real problem here. You see, I can't give anything away about this book, as finding out the "secret" is part of its excitement, but this is a book you finish and then want to talk about to everyone, and I want to share it, too! So, all right, here goes . . .

The Boy in the Striped Pajamas is different, exciting, and one of the saddest and most terrifying stories I've read. It's also told in such a simple way that you start off thinking, "Hey! This is a book for kids!" But it isn't. It's powerfully strong stuff, and reading it is a bit like discovering Grimm's fairy tales when you're old enough to see through all the prettiness to the horror underneath—it's unsettling, thought-provoking, and utterly amazing.
Leonie Flynn, Editor

> ### Next?
>
> Most recommendations would give the secret away, so you'll have to look out for a certain sort of book. Otherwise, try the stories of the Brothers Grimm or Perrault and be amazed at how different they are from how you remember.
>
> Something else just as shocking? Try *Private Peaceful* (UTBG 282) by Michael Morpurgo.

BOY KILLS MAN Matt Whyman

14+

> ### Next?
>
> *The Power of One* by Bryce Courtenay, about a lonely boy growing up in South Africa, is sure to inspire .
>
> *Keeper* (UTBG 190) by Mal Peet is also partially set in South America.
>
> For another sort of child killer—just as distressing—read Anne Cassidy's gripping *Looking for JJ* (UTBG 207).

Based not on a true story exactly but on the genuine existence of child assassins in modern-day Colombia, *Boy Kills Man* is a short, powerful book that thrills but also emotionally engages the reader.

The book follows the life of Shorty, a young teenage boy who gets sucked into the underworld of life in the city: a world where the drug lords use children to kill their rivals, since a loophole in Colombian law means they are exempt from prosecution for murder. Desperate for money, but more desperate to prove himself to his peers and his family, Shorty quickly finds himself in way over his head.

This is a book with a troubling ending and no easy answers, but that is its power—it is unashamedly honest and brutal, and at the same time it does not sensationalize its material.
Marcus Sedgwick, Author

BOY MEETS BOY David Levithan

14+

Paul doesn't have a problem being gay—he's lived with the knowledge since his kindergarten teacher declared it. Loads of his friends are gay, too. But that doesn't make forming new relationships easy. Especially when the ex who dumps him wants him back and Noah, his new beau, finds out. Keeping old friendships alive is just as hard—everyone around Paul is freaking, it seems, and pretty soon he's freaking himself. It's time to get a grip and get the guy he wants. But there's so much more to this wonderfully funny book than that. Sometimes the characters seem over the top, but everything about this book is true to life.

Jon Appleton, Editor

Next?

For more by David Levithan, try *Wide Awake, Are We There Yet?* or *The Realm of Possibility*.

Annie on My Mind (UTBG 20) by Nancy Garden is a powerful love story between two teen girls.

Freak the Mighty (UTBG 127) by Rodman Philbrick isn't a "gay" novel, but it features another unique and memorable main character.

For another warm and funny love story, try Meg Cabot's *All-American Girl* (UTBG 13).

BOY PROOF Cecil Castellucci

 12+

Next?

For more by Cecil Castellucci, don't miss *Beige* (UTBG 31) or her graphic novel with Jim Rugg, *The Plain Janes* (UTBG 272).

If you like narrators with an alternative side, try Rachel Cohn's *Gingerbread* (UTBG 132).

Or try *The Astonishing Adventures of Fanboy and Goth Girl* (UTBG 25) by Barry Lyga for a look at two outcasts who find each other.

Tough, intelligent teenager Victoria, aka Egg, is too busy watching sci-fi films, helping out her dad with special effects for big Hollywood movies, and basking in her self-induced outcast-hood, to get involved with members of the opposite sex. She considers herself boy proof—boys are not attracted to her shaved head and long cloak—and she's perfectly content with that notion. But then gorgeous, unique Max comes to her school, and Egg can't help wishing she wasn't so boy proof. He shares her love for science fiction and helps her realize she can be herself without blocking everyone out. I found myself laughing with Egg and feeling a bit anti-mainstream myself afterward. Cecil Castellucci's novel is really funny, insightful, and reluctantly romantic—an enjoyable quick read.

Claire Easton, age 16

BOY2GIRL Terence Blacker

 12+

Next?

For a boy and girl switching bodies, try Michael Lawrence's *A Crack in the Line* (UTBG 79).

More Terence Blacker? Try *The Angel Factory*, about a seemingly perfect world that is actually dark and treacherous.

Pete Johnson's *Faking It* is about a boy pretending a gorgeous girl in a photo is his girlfriend—what happens when the real girl turns up?

In most stories involving the theme "distant orphan cousin arrives," the cousin is often a wimp or a nerd. But Sam Lopez, who comes to live with his English cousin Matthew, is smelly, rude, and full of brassy confidence. And he also has a certain glamour: he is from California, after all.

Matthew and his friends impose an amazing initiation test on Sam. He has to attend school dressed as a girl. Astonishingly, he is very convincing . . . But I'll leave you to discover the delicious sequence of events.

"This book will make you laugh—or your money back," it says on the cover. But this is not an easy way to make a fast buck, unfortunately. To avoid laughing at Terence Blacker's book you'd have to be clinically dead.

Sue Limb, Author

THE BOYFRIEND LIST E. Lockhart

14+

After her fifth panic attack, Ruby "Roo" is sent to a poncho-wearing shrink named Dr. Z, who has her write up the boyfriend list—a list including, but definitely not limited to, the boy she was teased about in second grade, the boy who wasn't real, and the guy who never called. And, of course, Jackson—her only actual boyfriend, the guy she used to have lollipop taste-tests with and who put zany notes in her locker; he then dumped her for Kim, the girl who used to be her best friend.

It's a hard year for Ruby. Not only does she have to deal with the downward-spiraling, or simply nonexistent, relationships with those who used to be closest to her, but she also has to learn that life *isn't* a movie and her feelings are *never* logical. This book is a humorous and sweet read.

Jordyn Turney, age 17

Next?

For more accounts of Ruby's travails through high school, try E. Lockhart's sequel, *The Boy Book: A Study of Habits and Behaviors, Plus Techniques for Taming Them*.

For more hilariously funny books, try Catherine Clark's *Truth or Dairy* or Louise Rennison's *Angus, Thongs and Full-Frontal Snogging* (UTBG 18).

BRAT FARRAR   Josephine Tey

14+

Next?

More Josephine Tey? Try
The Franchise Affair, about
a girl accusing two old ladies
of kidnapping, and *The
Daughter of Time*, in which
a convalescing detective
tries to solve the mystery of
the Princes in the Tower.

For modern mysteries set in
the world of horses, Dick
Francis's thrillers cannot be
beaten. Try *Whip Hand*
(UTBG 387) to start with.

You get two books for the price of one with *Brat Farrar*, and it's this unique combination that makes it the best mystery story that I've ever read.

The premise is simple: Patrick Ashby, heir to a considerable fortune, disappears when he is 13. For eight years his family believes that he committed suicide, but then, just weeks before his twin's coming-of-age, Pat turns up again. Everyone is happy to see him and accepts that he is who he says he is—everyone except his supplanted twin, Simon.

What really happened to Patrick is, of course, the mystery, but this book also serves as a time machine. When you read it, you are transported back to the 1940s and a way of life that has vanished forever.

Laura Hutchings, Teacher

BRAVE NEW WORLD   Aldous Huxley

16+

Published in 1932, *Brave New World* creates an imaginary world many years in the future, a seeming paradise where everything is perfect, where illness and poverty have been defeated, and where, theoretically, everyone is happy. But of course, they are not.

Huxley depicts his world in a terrifying and convincing way; here, intense social engineering succeeds only at the expense of some fundamental human traits, and the ideas of family, love, and freedom all suffer at the hands of the State. In place of natural happiness, joy is instead derived from promiscuous but meaningless sex, from consuming material goods, from watching certain state-controlled sports, and from indulgence in a pleasure drug. If that sounds like Huxley was writing about our own age, then people who see his book as prophetic are vindicated, but there is more to this enjoyable and disturbing science-fiction novel than simple prophecy.

Marcus Sedgwick, Author

Next?

Read Huxley's
contemporary, George
Orwell, for some other
angles on dystopian
futures in *Nineteen
Eighty-Four* (UTBG 244)
and on totalitarianism in
Animal Farm (UTBG 19).

If you liked the dark sci-fi
edge to the book, try
Fahrenheit 451 (UTBG
110) by Ray Bradbury or
John Wyndham's *The
Day of the Triffids*
(UTBG 90).

THE BREADWINNER Deborah Ellis

Four days after her father's arrest, food runs out for Parvana's family. Though Taliban rule absolutely forbids women to leave the house alone, Parvana has no option but to take the risk, disguising herself as a boy and dodging the deadly landmines in an attempt to save her family from starvation.

Using the imagined life story of a young Afghan teenager, Ellis clearly conveys the brutality and fear of Taliban rule, and brings the human stories behind the headlines to life in a way that is far more hard-hitting and emotionally striking than any TV news report. A brave, timely, and topical book—continued in the equally eye-opening *Parvana's Journey,* in which Parvana flees across war-torn Afghanistan in search of her father.

Eileen Armstrong, Librarian

Next?

The third book, *Mud City*, takes up the story of one of Parvana's friends.

Ellis's *The Heaven Shop* (UTBG 151) tells the story of AIDS-stricken families in Malawi through the eyes of one young girl.

Persepolis (UTBG 269) by Marjane Satrapi tells of one girl's experience of life in Iran.

BREAKFAST AT TIFFANY'S Truman Capote

Next?

For more short stories by Truman Capote, try *The Complete Stories of Truman Capote*.

Edith Wharton's *The House of Mirth* also stars a spirited heroine who is attempting to climb up the social ladder.

One of the greatest of barbed wits belonged to an author named Dorothy Parker. Read her in *The Collected Dorothy Parker*.

Holly Golightly is a Carrie Bradshaw in waiting. Today she would write a column about her adventures in the captivating city of New York, meeting her equally successful friends for brunch and buying herself presents at Tiffany's. Half a century ago, young women who wanted to reinvent themselves needed to do it through men. Capote's short novel is less frothy than the Audrey Hepburn film. Holly's barbed wit barely masks her insecurity; her casual racism and shallowness is jarring to a modern reader. Nevertheless, it's hard not to become smitten with her as the narrator does, and even when you fall out of love with her, you still wish her well.

Geraldine Brennan, Editor

BREATHING UNDERWATER Alex Flinn

14+

Next?

Two more excellent novels that deal with abuse in teenage relationships are Sarah Dessen's *Dreamland* and Patrick Jones's *Things Change* (UTBG 355).

For another compelling read that gets inside the head of a perpetrator of violence, try Chris Lynch's *Inexcusable* (UTBG 175).

Another novel with a similar stylistic narrative, Rob Thomas's *Rats Saw God* (UTBG 285) follows the same dual time-frame structure .

Breathing Underwater is a riveting story that starts out with Nick, a troubled, 16-year-old high school student, going to court in an attempt to escape a restraining order that his former girlfriend Caitlin is trying to pin on him for abusing her. Throughout the book, Nick struggles to control his raging anger as well as to deal with his problems at home. Author Alex Flinn intricately weaves Nick's past and present experiences, creating a heartrending story that keeps the reader guessing from beginning to end.

Breathing Underwater is one of my favorite books. Flinn's wonderful writing brings forth many powerful emotions in the reader. It's one of those books that you read again and again, and every time you read it you love it more.

Cecile Svensgaard, age 18

BRIDESHEAD REVISITED Evelyn Waugh

16+

Oh, man! Describing why I like *Brideshead* in 120 words is like trying to sum up the Bible in one sentence. Saying it's about a doomed aristocratic Catholic family isn't going to make you want to rush out and buy it. But it's about so much more—it's a great love story; it's a heartrending tale of loss and rejection; it's a great sweeping narrative that takes place in prewar Oxford, Venice, Paris, and Morocco, with a large cast of brilliantly drawn characters. It deals with religion and morality, guilt, repression, and pain; it's dark, complex, powerful, evocative, poetic, compelling, sumptuous, passionate, moving, at times extremely funny, and ultimately tragic. In short, it's a masterpiece and I totally love it!

Catherine Robinson, Author

Next?

The Great Gatsby (UTBG 143) by F. Scott Fitzgerald is also a classic tale of glittering wealth, love, unhappiness, and loneliness.

Another novel with a prewar setting that deals with changing attitudes toward class is E. M. Forster's *Howard's End*.

For those on a Waugh path (!), try *Decline and Fall* or *Vile Bodies*—both very different, dark satires.

BRIDGE TO TERABITHIA

Katherine Paterson

Next?

Anne of Green Gables (and sequels) by L. M. Montgomery; set on Prince Edward Island, Canada, the stories show how intimate rural life can be, as does Karen Wallace's *Raspberries on the Yangtze* (UTBG 285).

Or try *The Secret Garden* (UTBG 307) by Frances Hodgson Burnett—in which a lonely boy and girl find redemption in a magical place.

Walk Two Moons (UTBG 377) by Sharon Creech is another stunning story about coming to terms with tragedy.

Jess doesn't really have any friends until new girl Leslie comes to his rural school. Leslie is rich and lives in a big house but her parents don't even own a television. Like Jess, Leslie is an outsider. Together they create a magical kingdom—Terabithia—down by the creek, and as king and queen of Terabithia they can make a world just as they want it to be. Life is perfect . . . until tragedy strikes. This is a moving and insightful book about friendship, death, and creativity.

Ann Jungman, Author

BRIDGET JONES'S DIARY

Helen Fielding

Bridget is in her 30s and worried. Although she has a good job, a home of her own, and many good friends, she is single, and more than anything, she wants a boyfriend. But the men in her life seem to be too standoffish or too untrustworthy to fit the bill. Her family teases her for being alone, and she worries endlessly about how much she weighs, drinks, and smokes. Only her closest friends can make her see that life is not so bad after all. Written as a diary, this sweet and very funny book takes us through a year of Bridget's life, as she searches for love, happiness, and the perfect diet while dodging unsuitable men, annoying parents, and the horrible "smug marrieds."

Marianne Taylor, Editor

Next?

Bridget Jones: The Edge of Reason, the next installment of Bridget's chaotic life.

Louise Rennison's *Angus, Thongs and Full-Frontal Snogging* (UTBG 18) also chronicles the hilarious travails of a well-meaning British girl searching for love.

Want the male perspective? Try Nick Hornby's *High Fidelity* (UTBG 152).

BRIGHTON ROCK Graham Greene

14+

Next?

Graham Greene's short stories are wonderfully varied, as are his novels. Check out *Our Man in Havana* (UTBG 262) or *The End of the Affair*.

The **Maigret** books (UTBG 215) by Georges Simenon, featuring the bumbling inspector, have a cast of crooks and seedy thugs and a similar feel to *Brighton Rock*.

For another story of murder with a powerful setting, this time prewar London, try *Hangover Square* by Patrick Hamilton.

More than 40 years ago, the first page of *Brighton Rock* made me want to be a writer. It's an opening to die for . . . and somebody does. Graham Greene's story walks out of Brighton Station and straight off the page; it intrigues and appalls you, and then goes on haunting the streets of your imagination for the rest of your life. Its characters, their desperate lives, the busy seafront and dark alleys of the dangerous town where Good and Evil are in relentless pursuit of one another stay with you forever. Because, like all the very best books, *Brighton Rock* lives on long after you've turned the last page. Join the crowd on the promenade and you'll see what I mean.

Michael Cronin, Author

THE BROMELIAD trilogy Terry Pratchett

12+

For the Nomes in the Store there is no day and night, no sun and rain. All these things are just old myths—just like "the Outside." However, all that changes when a group of Nomes from the Outside arrive.

In *Truckers*, the Nomes capture a truck, and escape in it before their home, the Store, is demolished. In *Diggers*, the Nomes try to survive in the Quarry—but this becomes a nightmare, especially when the humans intervene. In *Wings*, three Nomes try to get to America to find a spacecraft to take them home, using the Thing (a micro-computer) as a guide.

This gripping fantasy adventure is full of humor, misunderstanding, and deeper meaning too—strongly recommended!

Samuel Mortimer, age 11

Next?

Follow up with more Pratchett, of course. Try the **Johnny Maxwell** series, beginning with *Only You Can Save Mankind*; or one of his **Discworld** books— *Discworld: Monstrous Regiment* (UTBG 92) is a good place to start.

For another fantasy that'll make you laugh, read Paul Stewart and Chris Riddell's **Muddle Earth**; or **The Edge Chronicles**, beginning with *Beyond the Deepwoods* (UTBG 33).

For a more serious fantasy that deals with the divide between aboveground dwellers and belowground dwellers, try N. M. Browne's *Basilisk*.

BUCKING THE SARGE Christopher Paul Curtis

There are a lot of books out there about teens who have issues with their parents. Very few of these books have heroes as justified in their hatred as Luther T. Farrell, aspiring philosopher and son of the Sarge—Flint, Michigan's slumlord (well, lady) extraordinaire.

At 15, Luther works an 80-hour week out of his mom's Happy Neighbor Group Home for Men as caretaker to a group of eccentric old guys, while aspiring to be "America's best-known, best-loved, best-paid philosopher." Oh, and his best friend, Sparky, has a get-rich-quick scheme: he plans to sue Taco Bell for being hit in the head by a roof tile (well, actually whacked in the head by a very reluctant Luther) in their parking lot. Somewhere in his busy life he's got to find the time to get away from the Sarge for good.

Kristin Anderson, Librarian

Next?

You shouldn't miss Christopher Paul Curtis's Newbery award-winning novel *Bud, Not Buddy*.

Chasing Tail Lights by Patrick Jones also features a character desperate to escape from the confines of Flint, Michigan.

Melina Marchetta's novel *Saving Francesca* takes a female viewpoint of the obstacles of living with a difficult mother.

THE BURN JOURNALS Brent Runyon

Next?

For another inside-the-head look at a suicide attempt and recovery, try Susan Vaught's *Trigger* (UTBG 365).

Zibby Oneal's *The Language of Goldfish* and E. L. Konigsburg's *Silent to the Bone* also look at a teen's emotional breakdown.

Patricia McCormick's *Cut* (UTBG 83) expertly deals with self-destructive behavior and a teen's eventual recovery.

The Burn Journals is a great book for every teenager to read, because as teenagers we always feel our lives are so much worse than anyone else's. This book showed me that life can always be worse and if you try to punish yourself, it won't make it any better. This book is a story (the author's true-life story) about how a boy named Brent recovers from his attempt at suicide. It starts with a regular day in his life at school and proceeds to when he finally goes back to school after his recovery. Brent's recovery from trying to kill himself is an emotional roller coaster, and you tag along for every second of it and feel his pain. I would recommend that every teenager reads this book.

MacKenzee Nicely, age 15

THE BURNING CITY Ariel and Joaquin Dorfman

In the summer before the tragic events of September 11, 2001, Heller Highland has just turned 16 and is the star employee of Soft Tidings, a courier service delivering personal messages all over the city. Heller specializes in bad news, cycling at breakneck speed through Manhattan's crowded streets to deliver sad tidings with a detached sensitivity born of a supreme confidence in his own invulnerability. But suddenly in the course of three or four days, Heller experiences his own loss and suffering and learns the hard way what is important in life. This is a cinematic and fast-moving contemporary fable about the coming-of-age of a boy, a city, and a nation.
Kathryn Ross, Literary Agent

Next?

Refugees by Catherine Stein is an imaginative response to the events of 9/11. Art Spiegelman's *In the Shadow of No Towers* boldly tries to make sense of that terrible day in comic-strip form.

The classic coming-of-age story is, of course, *The Catcher in the Rye* (UTBG 60) by J. D. Salinger.

Carl Hiaasen is another adult author who has started writing for younger readers too—try *Hoot* (UTBG 159).

BURNING UP Caroline B. Cooney

Next?

For more by Caroline B. Cooney, you should try *The Face on the Milk Carton* (UTBG 109) next—it's a classic, suspenseful mystery.

Han Nolan's *Send Me Down a Miracle* (UTBG 310) also follows a girl whose connection to her town's church is brought into question.

Macey, who has always thought her family, her town, and her state were close to perfect, unveils some ugly truths when she decides to research a barn fire that happened long before she was born on a property near her grandparents' beachside home. Fire has earned a critical place in her consciousness because, when working on a community service project at an inner-city church, her hair catches fire in an arson incident. The few hours spent working at the church open her eyes to the disparity between her idyllic life and that of a girl from the church with whom she feels an instant kinship.

This book is powerful and involving, looking at an issue that is of great importance. The realizations that Macey comes to are hauntingly memorable, and the blend of suspense and romance make it unputdownable!
Diana Tixier Herald, Librarian

THE CALL OF THE WILD Jack London

Next?

Jack London wrote amazingly about animals; try another of his classics, *White Fang*. Or *The Sea-Wolf*—it's different but just as good.

Roll of Thunder, Hear My Cry (UTBG 292) by Mildred D. Taylor is about humans being cruel to humans.

Another book that's set in a wild landscape is J. Fenimore Cooper's *The Last of the Mohicans*.

This is a book about appalling animal cruelty. Buck is kidnapped from his home and taken to the wild north of Canada. Beaten, clubbed, and whipped until he obeys, he is harnessed to a sled with eight other dogs and forced to pull his new owners and their belongings across rock and snow in their search for gold. He learns to fight for his place in the pack, to survive the cruelty of man, dog, and nature, and eventually finds a new pride in himself. But things get worse and worse for Buck, until it seems that a happy ending is impossible—or is it?

Leonie Flynn, Editor

CALLING A DEAD MAN Gillian Cross

A sick man with no memory awakes in a snowy Siberian wood. All he knows is that something has happened that is too terrible to recall. Meanwhile, far away, a family obliterates every trace of an adored son; a gangster organization senses a threat to its security; and a bereft lover sets out into the unknown with only the thinnest of hopes to support her.

Calling a Dead Man takes place after the fall of Communism. We see a frozen world of small, valiant people, some acting with extraordinary generosity and heroism in the face of death, cruelty, and relentless poverty.

This is an amazing book, not just for being a taut thriller in an exotic setting but for describing huge emotions in a barren landscape and portraying the Siberian people with insight and compassion.

Sally Prue, Author

Next?

Gillian Cross has written another thriller about a criminal organization in *Tightrope*.

A brilliant thriller set around the Cold War is John le Carré's *The Spy Who Came in from the Cold* (UTBG 336).

A true story of Russia, Communism, and Siberia is *One Day in the Life of Ivan Denisovich* (UTBG 256) by Alexander Solzhenitsyn.

CAN YOU SUE YOUR PARENTS FOR MALPRACTICE? Paula Danziger

After being dumped by her boyfriend, Lauren Allen has decided she's devoting her life to a career in law. It's a good thing they just added a new class at her high school: "Law for Children and Young People." She thinks that knowing her rights will come in handy with her overprotective parents. She's going to start making her own decisions, and if her parents have a problem with that, too bad! Her plan seems foolproof, until her parents find out about her newly pierced ears. Then she meets Zach, who makes her think twice about swearing off men forever.

Lauren's family is one that anyone can relate to, and between the romance, high school drama, and just growing up in general, there's enough teen angst to go around. With snappy wit and a fun, fast-moving plot, this is a light read that will make readers feel like they aren't alone in thinking that their parents are crazy.

Mary Kate Castellani, Editor

Next?

More Paula Danziger? Try *The Cat Ate My Gymsuit*, about a teenage girl who campaigns to have her recently fired teacher rehired.

For another story about family and growing up, try *Just Listen* (UTBG 187) by Sarah Dessen.

Also try *The Sisterhood of the Traveling Pants* (UTBG 324) by Ann Brashares for more fun reading.

CANDY Kevin Brooks

Next?

Read Kevin Brooks's other titles; *Martyn Pig* (UTBG 220), *Lucas* (UTBG 213), or *Kissing the Rain* (UTBG 195).

Boy Kills Man (UTBG 46) by Matt Whyman also depicts a boy in an extreme and dangerous situation.

London Zoo, one of the settings for *Candy*, also features in another, quite different book— Russell Hoban's *Turtle Diary*.

Kevin Brooks pushes his characters into situations you hope will never happen to you: extreme situations but ones you will believe in absolutely. Candy is a beautiful girl, trapped in heroin addiction and prostitution—and Joe Beck, bass guitarist and genuine good guy, falls madly in love with her. Iggy, Candy's utterly terrifying pimp/drug dealer, is not happy, and when Iggy is not happy, violence is inevitable.

This is a story about lack of control, whether because of drugs, or love, or pure chance, or the adults who run the world that teenagers have to live in. Lock your door when you read this dark, dangerous, and utterly gripping book—you will not want to be interrupted.

Nicola Morgan, Author

CANNERY ROW / SWEET THURSDAY

John Steinbeck

These two short books make up a beautifully written portrait of a group of people living on the margins of society. Set in a rundown California fishing town in the 1940s, both are based around a community of characters who exist on the edges of life—idlers, tramps, lowlifes, wasters.

There isn't much of a plot in these novels—the stories are more like a jigsaw of relationships and events—but the characters are so fascinating and the writing so hypnotically good that they don't need a plot.

Although both books can be read independently, the characters are first introduced in *Cannery Row*, so it's probably a good idea to start there.

Kevin Brooks, Author

> **Next?**
>
> John Steinbeck's most famous books are *The Grapes of Wrath* and *East of Eden*, but you might like to try some more of his lesser-known stuff. My favorites are *The Wayward Bus* and *Travels with Charley*.
>
> Another writer who deals in misfits is Flannery O'Connor. Try *A Good Man Is Hard to Find*.

CAT AMONG THE PIGEONS Agatha Christie

> **Next?**
>
> Other great detective stories? Try Dorothy L. Sayers's *Gaudy Night* (set in a women's college), or Margery Allingham's *Sweet Danger*.
>
> Ngaio Marsh and Patricia Wentworth are other brilliant female writers from the same period; look out for any of their books—they're all worth a read.
>
> Like Poirot? Try *Murder on the Orient Express*, in which he's the lead of the show.

There are two distinct pleasures in reading an Agatha Christie novel—and the whodunit is only one of them. The other is the particular period flavor of the worlds she creates. *Cat Among the Pigeons* is set in a famous girls' boarding school (much more convincing than the ones in school stories), where the gym teacher gets shot, the gardener comes from the British military, and one of the students carries a whiff of Middle Eastern mystery. Enter Christie's great Belgian detective Hercule Poirot . . . though in this particular book, he plays more of a walk-on part than in other novels, like *Murder on the Orient Express*.

Sarah Gristwood, Author

CATALYST Laurie Halse Anderson

Next?

More by the same author? Try *Speak* (UTBG 334).

For another emotional and intelligent ride through adolescence, try *The Moth Diaries* (UTBG 232) by Rachel Klein.

What the Birds See (UTBG 306) by Sonya Hartnett is a painfully wonderful book with a similar feel, though it's less direct and raw.

You Don't Know Me (UTBG 403) by David Klass is about a boy pushed to the edge by his stepfather.

Kate is brilliant and seems in control of everything; everyone expects her to succeed. The fact that she seems to have taken her dead mother's place so seamlessly makes everyone believe that she is fine. But inside, she is losing control and carries unbearable burdens. When a truly shocking event occurs, will this tip her over the edge or save her?

If this is one of the most painful books I have ever read, why am I recommending it? Perhaps because it captures so perfectly some of the pain of growing up. Parents should read it too—then they'll think twice before putting their sons and daughters under the intense pressure that Kate Malone faces.

Nicola Morgan, Author

CATCH-22 Joseph Heller

When I was a teenager, reading *Catch-22* changed the way I thought about life, and it changed the way I thought about books. It made me see, for the first time, that war is a kind of insanity. And it made me realize that a book could be funny and intensely serious at the same time. The book's antihero, Yossarian, is an American fighter pilot stationed in Italy during World War II, desperate to be excused from flying more missions and to escape the madness of a situation where every kind of military double-think and capitalist excess seems to thrive. The book has fantastic comic energy and builds toward a triumphant surprise ending.

Jonathan Coe, Author

Next?

Yossarian and friends reappear in *Closing Time*, where this time the enemy is death itself.

A scathing look at the contemporary world, particularly America, is *Dude, Where's My Country?* by Michael Moore.

Kurt Vonnegut's *Slaughterhouse-Five* (UTBG 327) is another novel that looks at war from a dual perspective of humor and horror.

Read our feature on cult books on pp. 250–251 for more inspiration.

THE CATCHER IN THE RYE J. D. Salinger

I was 19 and not enjoying my first year at college when I first met Holden Caulfield, the 16-year-old protagonist of *The Catcher in the Rye*. Holden is having a bad time too—we soon discover he is about to flunk out of yet another school and doesn't know what to do with his life. So he sets out for a weekend in New York before going home to his parents.

Holden is trapped between childhood and maturity, desperate to grow up but afraid of it too, and disgusted by the "phony" way adults behave. He is also the original teen and one of the great characters of literature. His story is both funny and very moving. Most of us have had a Holden Caulfield moment at some time—and I know he helped me with mine.

Tony Bradman, Author

Next?

Another 16-year-old who deals with a crisis a little differently is the hero of Gary Paulsen's *The Beet Fields* (UTBG 30).

For an interesting take on *The Catcher in the Rye*, try the contemporary novel **King Dork** (UTBG 194) by Frank Portman.

For more Salinger read **Nine Stories** (UTBG 244), his collection of short stories about youth and childhood.

CATHERINE, CALLED BIRDY Karen Cushman

Next?

Try Karen Cushman's other award-winning historical fiction, **The Midwife's Apprentice**.

The Ramsay Scallop by Frances Temple tells the story of a young betrothed couple in the Middle Ages who take a pilgrimage together in order to allow them time to become familiar with one another.

In **The Edge on the Sword** by Rebecca Tingle, 15-year-old Aethelflaed becomes betrothed in order to strengthen an alliance against the Danes in ninth-century Britain. The sequel, **Far Traveler**, picks up the story with Aethelflaed's daughter.

The daughter of a knight in medieval England didn't have many choices as to what her life would be like. But 13-year-old Catherine is determined that her father shouldn't marry her off to the highest bidder in this hilarious historical tale of a strong-willed girl. Her adventures in marriage avoidance and research into the best curse words of the time are laugh-out-loud funny.

Karen Cushman infuses Catherine's diary accounts with all the sights, sounds, and smells of the Middle Ages, without sparing anyone the flea bites.

Charli Osborne, Librarian

CAT'S CRADLE   Kurt Vonnegut

This story is told by a man who is planning a book about the day the first atomic bomb was dropped on Japan. In the course of his research he meets Newt Hoenikker, son of Dr. Felix Hoenikker, "father of the bomb." This leads him to a small Caribbean island where he comes into contact with a brand-new religion based on lies, falls in love, and becomes president. He also learns about Ice-9, a substance created by Dr. Hoenikker that, when brought into contact with water, instantly freezes it and spreads—endlessly.

Kurt Vonnegut is one of the easiest writers to read, and often one of the funniest, but he also puts a very individual spin on the most serious subjects. Everyone should give Vonnegut a try. Even if you don't like the way he writes, you'll have to admit he's an original.

Michael Lawrence, Author

Next?

Ken Kesey's *One Flew Over the Cuckoo's Nest* (UTBG 256), while about a decidedly different topic, has a similar sense of irreverence as Vonnegut's writing.

More Vonnegut? He lived through the bombing of Dresden and wrote about it in *Slaughterhouse-Five* (UTBG 327). There's also *The Sirens of Titan* (UTBG 323), *Breakfast of Champions*, and many more. All are weird and wonderfully brain expanding.

For a look at what the world might be like before and after The Bomb, read Raymond Briggs's graphic novel, *When the Wind Blows*.

CAT'S EYE   Margaret Atwood

Next?

If you enjoy the theme of art and what it says about life, read *To the Lighthouse* by Virginia Woolf.

Another novel that deals with the precarious relationships between girls and their ability to hurt each other is Simmone Howell's *Notes from the Teenage Underground*.

For more by Margaret Atwood, try *The Handmaid's Tale* (UTBG 145) or *The Edible Woman*.

As a successful artist, Elaine Risley returns to Toronto, where she grew up, for an exhibition. Elaine's paintings have been inspired by her own experiences, and the truths she splashes on her canvases aren't ones that her former friends are ready for. In order to move on with her adult life, Elaine is forced to confront her past and to relive the bullying she endured at the hands of her fascinating and manipulative friend Cordelia.

Cat's Eye is a brilliant and absorbing novel about art, about the nature of time, about friendship, and about how the child you were will always be a part of the adult you become.

Antonia Honeywell, Teacher

CAUSE CELEB Helen Fielding

14+

Next?

Try *Bridget Jones's Diary* (UTBG 52) and its sequel, both by Helen Fielding.

Gordon Korman's *Born to Rock* is also an irreverent novel about celebrity and the path to love.

Then move on to anything by Nick Hornby: *About a Boy* (UTBG 5) is a great place to start.

Helen Fielding's massively successful Bridget Jones books can't have passed you by—even if you only know them through the films. This book came out a good three years before Bridget, and is even funnier. It's about a disillusioned TV journalist who tries to escape the shallowness of media life and a broken heart by dropping everything to work in a refugee camp in Africa. When famine strikes, she uses her old skills to set up a celebrity TV fund-raiser.

Fielding lampoons the vanity of it all, and some of her most savage portraits of stars with their hearts on their sleeves have been proved true in the years since the book was written. It's a laugh—but it makes a very serious point.

Eleanor Updale, Author

CELL Stephen King

14+

Stephen King is one of the only authors who can kick-start my imagination into creating something truly frightening. In his novel *Cell*, a phenomenon known as "The Pulse" turns civilized, regular people into flesh-hungry "phone crazies." Their only purpose is to rip people limb from limb—at least for a time. After the phone crazies create mass chaos, they begin to evolve into much more than mindless zombies—they begin to gather and create what seems to be a leaderless army. Readers will follow Clayton Riddell in his search to find his son amid the blood and carnage that has taken the place of order and individual thought in this world of cellular dependency.

King has created something truly thought-provoking, something morbidly graphic and terrifying that relates to the present day with painful clarity. Anyone who enjoys the bloody and all-too-humiliating scenarios King puts his unfortunate characters through will quickly devour this novel.

Kelli Konicek, age 15

Next?

You should definitely read some of Stephen King's classics—try *The Stand*, *It*, or *Salem's Lot* (UTBG 300) for starters.

Stephen King has also written some less gory but equally interesting novels such as *The Green Mile* and *The Body* (the inspiration for the movie *Stand by Me*).

THE CEMENT GARDEN   Ian McEwan

Next?

A *"Lord of the Flies* of the family"? So read **Lord of the Flies** (UTBG 209) by William Golding and see what you think.

Or try Joy Nicholson's **The Tribes of Palos Verdes**, a Californian take on a family meltdown as viewed by teenagers.

For more by Ian McEwan, try **Enduring Love** or **The Comfort of Strangers**.

For another disturbing tale of twisted adolescence, read **The Wasp Factory** (UTBG 380) by Iain Banks.

As a teenager, I was not a reader. I had always been a TV and video games kid. Then, at 16, I was given Ian McEwan's *The Cement Garden*. I was gripped, and I still remember the feeling of staying up late into the night, in my own private pool of bedside light, reading and reading, unable to contemplate sleep until I had reached the end of the book. From that moment on, I was transformed from a TV watcher into a reader, and possibly even into a writer.

The story is dark, gory, weird, twisted, funny, and contains sex, bad language, masturbation, gender-bending, and the improvised burial of parents. It's a sort of *Lord of the Flies* of the family, with a suburban house standing in for the desert island. Your English teacher could get into serious trouble for giving you this kind of book!

William Sutcliffe, Author

CHANDA'S SECRETS   Allan Stratton

Chanda first captivated me as she waits to see Mr. Bateman to make funeral plans for her little sister. Staring at the angelfish in his aquarium, she wonders if it knows it is trapped in the tank for the rest of its life. This story is about how Chanda is both trapped and has free will to move in and out of her world.

Allan Stratton has written a moving story about a fictional character, Chanda, who struggles with the realities of AIDS in Africa. It is a story about friendship, honesty, shame, and family that feels very close to our lives, wherever we live.

Susan Ettenheim, Teacher

Next?

Many Stones (UTBG 217) by Carolyn Coman also takes place in Africa and deals with the poverty and hatred that followed the end of apartheid.

Or read Deborah Ellis's **The Heaven Shop** (UTBG 151) for another searing portrait of the horrors of AIDS in Africa.

Beverley Naidoo writes expertly about the struggles of African children. Try **Out of Bounds** (UTBG 262) to learn more about apartheid, or **The Other Side of Truth** (UTBG 261) for a fictional story about two exiles who find themselves in London.

THE CHICKEN DANCE — Jacques Couvillon

12+

Set in a Louisiana town populated by chicken farmers, this is the story of Don—a smart, sensitive boy who has a knack for going unnoticed, even by his own parents. But he can't seem to shake the curiosity he feels when he finds his birth certificate and realizes it actually says "Stanley." Suddenly things in his life don't add up, and he's determined to get to the bottom of it all.

This book is a slice of life that most people could only imagine. Full of kooky characters and even crazier situations, it is both hysterical and touching. Best of all is Don, whose quirks and anxieties are entirely endearing. The scenes in which he dances to KC and the Sunshine Band or he reads out loud to chickens are priceless, and when the big mystery surrounding his family's past allows Don to show his true colors, you will love him even more.

Mary Kate Castellani, Editor

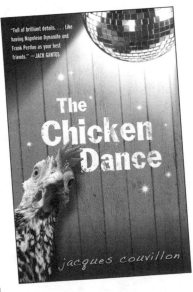

"Full of brilliant details. . . . Like having Napoleon Dynamite and Frank Perdue as your best friends." —JACK GANTOS

The Chicken Dance

jacques couvillon

Next?

For another heartfelt story with a boy protagonist, try *The Wednesday Wars* by Gary D. Schmidt.

A similarly written tale, *The Curious Incident of the Dog in the Night-Time* (UTBG 82) by Mark Haddon, should not be missed.

Or try Ann M. Martin's *A Corner of the Universe*, which is also set in a small town in the South and deals with family secrets.

There isn't much to do on a farm in Horse Island, Louisiana, so Don Schmidt passes the time by confiding in his chickens and listening to KC and the Sunshine Band. But after Don wins the prestigious chicken judging contest, he becomes a local celebrity and everything changes.

The best parts of this book are easily the characters. So many of them are just hilarious: Don's mother, Janice, who keeps chickens "for ambience" and who will drive you crazy and crack you up at the same time; the bully, Leon Leonard, who calls Don "new kid" years after he has transferred to the school; or Bobby Bufford, the general-store owner who buys Don's eggs after stealing a chicken for him. And then there are the characters who will break your heart: Don's father, Dick, who quietly watches Don's family spiraling out of control but can't speak up to stop it; and even the bully, Leon, whose own ridiculous parents aren't shy about voicing their disappointment in him. And at the center of it all is Don— genuine, naive, charming, and completely unforgettable.

Claire Easton, age 16

A CHILD CALLED "IT" Dave Pelzer

14+

This is a true story. As a child, Dave Pelzer was brutally beaten, emotionally tortured, and starved by his unpredictable, unstable, alcoholic mother, while his fireman father, who had "broad shoulders and forearms that would make any muscle man proud," did nothing but watch. No longer considered a son but a slave, no longer a boy but an "it," he slept on an old army cot in the basement, dressed in smelly rags, and when he was allowed the luxury of food it was scraps from the dogs' bowls.

What singled out Dave from his two brothers? Perhaps it was that his voice just carried farther than others. He had to learn to play his mother's games—every humiliation a victory, as it meant he had survived yet another day.

Told from the child's point of view, this is a heartbreaking yet heartwarming tale of courageous endurance, of one child's dream of finding a family to love and care for him, to call him their son.

Elena Gregoriou, Teacher

Next?

Read the sequels: *The Lost Boy* and *A Man Named Dave*.

Dave's brother Richard B. Pelzer has written his own account of their childhood in *A Brother's Journey*.

Other writers have been brave enough to tell of their own terrible childhoods. Read Alice Sebold's memoir, *Lucky*, about her attempts to readjust to life after being raped.

Or read Augusten Burroughs's take on surviving life with an alcoholic father; read his book *Running with Scissors* (UTBG 298).

BEING DIFFERENT

Tangerine by Edward Bloor

Face by Benjamin Zephaniah

Mondays Are Red by Nicola Morgan

The Curious Incident of the Dog in the Night-Time by Mark Haddon

Freak the Mighty by Rodman Philbrick

Stargirl by Jerry Spinelli

One child's courage to survive

A Child Called 'It'

THE NUMBER ONE BESTSELLER

DAVE PELZER

CHILD X Lee Weatherly

When Jules's dad leaves home, things are bad enough. He takes all his possessions, but leaves behind his favorite photo of Jules. Why? What has she done? And why are the newspapers suddenly hounding Jules and her mother? Why are they all trying to get pictures?

As she uncovers the long-buried secret that has torn her world apart, Jules is forced to question everything she has taken for granted about herself and the people closest to her. Lee Weatherly really helps us feel what Jules is going through—one of the worst nightmares of any child's life.

Yvonne Coppard, Author

Next?

More Lee Weatherly? Try *Missing Abby*, about a girl whose friend goes missing.

Jules performs in a stage version of *The Golden Compass*—so read the first part of Pullman's **His Dark Materials** trilogy (UTBG 153).

For another book in which a girl must uncover hidden secrets from her family's past, try *So B. It* (UTBG 331) by Sarah Weeks.

CHINESE CINDERELLA: THE TRUE STORY OF AN UNWANTED DAUGHTER Adeline Yen Mah

Next?

There is a sequel: *Chinese Cinderella and the Secret Dragon Society*. These books tell of her childhood; if you want to know what happened next, read *Falling Leaves*, written for adults.

If you find yourself interested in Chinese traditions and spirituality, read Mah's *Watching the Tree*.

Amy Tan's *The Joy Luck Club* (UTBG 186) follows the lives of four Chinese women who have immigrated to America.

This isn't a fairy tale; it's a true story, an autobiography. When Adeline was born in China, she was named Jun-ling. Shortly afterward her mother died, and baby Adeline was blamed. Her family thought she was unlucky and wished she had been the one who had died. All of them, especially her stepmother, treated her with contempt. Her "fairy godmother," an aunt who loved her, protected her as much as she could, but that wasn't much. Despite all the ill treatment, Adeline's story is inspiring. She doesn't fight back—sometimes you wish she would—but she doesn't give up either, and now she's a doctor and businesswoman and writer, free of her cruel family. If you like learning about different lives and different cultures, you'll love this.

Julia Jarman, Author

CHOCOLAT Joanne Harris

14+

Life in the tiny French village of Lansquenet-sous-Tannes is turned upside down when two strangers arrive and almost overnight open a shop selling the most delicious chocolates imaginable. At first, many of the villagers are suspicious of the glamorous Vianne and her little girl, Anouk, but they soon realize that the newcomers have a knack for finding out people's problems, working out solutions to them, and generally making life better. Only the village priest remains unfriendly—he doesn't trust Vianne or her seductive chocolates, and he thinks she may be a witch.

Chocolat is a lovely, richly detailed story, full of enchanting characters, magical moments, and, above all, mouthwatering chocolate!

Marianne Taylor, Editor

Next?

Blackberry Wine gives you magical realism and sumptuous settings from the same author.

For another story in which food plays an important role, try *Like Water for Chocolate* by Laura Esquivel.

For another story of a stranger, try *Lucas* (UTBG 213) by Kevin Brooks.

Elizabeth Gilbert's memoir *Eat, Pray, Love* takes a similarly seductive and healing approach to the act of eating food.

THE CHOCOLATE WAR Robert Cormier

12+

Next?

If you like dangerous, uncompromising novels, you'll enjoy Robert Cormier's other books, such as *I Am the Cheese* (UTBG 168).

Or try Kevin Brooks's (in my opinion most brilliant) book *Candy* (UTBG 57).

Paul Zindel's *The Pigman* (UTBG 270) also takes a look at teens' ability (or inability) to break free of the mold of conformity.

S. E. Hinton's *The Outsiders* (UTBG 264) is another no-holds-barred story of the strengths and weaknesses of gangs and groups.

For me, *The Chocolate War* is the perfect example of teenage fiction. Actually, it's a perfect example of fiction. It was published in 1974, after being rejected by seven publishers as too dark, too complicated, too downbeat, too violent. It's set in a Catholic boys' high school, which Cormier called a "metaphor for the world," a school riddled with corruption, bullying, and rigid systems that depend on frightened obedience. On another level, the book is about what happens when a boy refuses to sell chocolate for the annual chocolate sale. And continues to refuse. The book is shot through with scenes that leave you reeling with questions—questions like, "Is this what humans can do to each other?" Read a newspaper and you'll have to say "yes."

Nicola Morgan, Author

THE CHOSEN Chaim Potok

The Chosen is the story of the unlikely friendship between two Jewish boys growing up in Brooklyn during World War II. Danny is a Hasidic Jew, son of a powerful Orthodox rabbi, while Reuven's father teaches at a liberal school. Although the book is told from Reuven's perspective, it is really Danny's story. Hasidic customs and his father's wishes dictate that Danny will become a rabbi and lead the congregation after his father's death. But Danny yearns to be a psychologist. He secretly goes to the library and reads a multitude of books, including those that contradict his religious beliefs.

This is not really a book about losing faith, though. It's a book about friendship, education, belief, and finding meaning in life. After the characters learn about the slaughter of six million Jews in Europe, Reuven's father tells him, "A man must fill his life with meaning, meaning is not automatically given to life."

Janette Rallison, Author

Next?

Any of Chaim Potok's novels are great reads, but you should read *The Promise* next—it's the sequel to *The Chosen*.

The Amazing Adventures of Kavalier & Clay (UTBG 14) by Michael Chabon is an older, more challenging novel that also follows two Jewish friends through their childhoods and into their adult lives.

John Knowles's classic *A Separate Peace* (UTBG 310) is about boys at a preparatory school during World War II.

CHRISTINE Stephen King

Next?

Carrie, King's first novel, follows the torment of teenager Carrie White.

The Shining, King's most literary novel, is a tale of madness, isolation, and writer's block.

James Herbert and Clive Barker are both British writers of the most chilling horror stories, but they have different approaches—if you like being scared witless, try them both!

Stephen King writes the best horror stories, and *Christine* is the most enjoyable of his early books. Arnie Cunningham is a bit of a nerd, but his friend Dennis finds him more interesting than their cooler classmates. Christine is a classic car, a '58 Plymouth Fury that 17-year-old Arnie buys for $250 from a weird old man named Roland D. LeBay. From the moment Arnie buys Christine, Dennis senses something malevolent about her—a suspicion only confirmed when LeBay's brother tells Dennis that LeBay's daughter died, and his wife committed suicide, in the car. As Arnie becomes increasingly obsessed with Christine, Dennis realizes his friend's love for the car is going to lead to death and destruction, but he's powerless to stop it.

Matt Thorne, Author

A CHRISTMAS CAROL Charles Dickens

Next?

Read the Bible, if only for Luke 2 and Matthew 2—the origins of that Christmas story.

Oliver Twist, the story of another great Dickensian creation: Fagin, and his gang of boys.

Or what about the story of a ragged young pickpocket in the backstreets of 18th-century London? Try *Smith* by Leon Garfield.

For more of a challenge, read about another great literary miser in *Silas Marner* (UTBG 322) by George Eliot.

It is Christmas Eve. Bitterly cold. Snow underfoot. Ebenezer Scrooge, a hard-hearted old miser, makes his way home through the narrow, gaslit streets of London. What does he think of the season of goodwill? "Christmas! Bah! Humbug!"

But Scrooge was not always such a bitter skinflint. As a boy he was good-hearted. What happened to change him? That night four ghosts visit his cold, bare house and he is taken on a journey to Christmases past, present, and future. Scrooge is terrified . . .

This is a wonderful story, nearly perfect, and worthy of its place (after the Bible) as the best-known Christmas story in the world.

Alan Temperley, Author

CIRQUE DU FREAK Darren Shan

The muddy piece of paper promised a freak show, and Steven and Darren couldn't be happier. All the acts are amazing; none more than Madam Octa, a trained spider, who is controlled telepathically by Mr. Crepsley. Darren is fascinated by the spider. After the show, Darren returns to the theater to steal Madam Octa. He can control the spider, but only through intense acts of concentration. When the two boys attempt a trick that ends with Steve in a coma, Darren must make a horrible choice.

Fast moving and full of creepy details, this book is a sure thing for horror fans. While you might feel sorry for Darren, you know he has an amazing adventure ahead of him. That adventure is told in the books that follow *Cirque du Freak*, all part of the Saga of Darren Shan series.

Merideth Jenson-Benjamin, Librarian

Next?

Got a strong stomach? Then try Shan's series for older readers, the **Demonata**, starting with Book 1: *Lord Loss* (UTBG 208).

A small town in Alaska is the scene of unimaginable horror in the graphic novel *30 Days of Night* by Steve Niles and Ben Templesmith.

PINK LIT by Cathy Hopkins

In the current marketing trend (or obsession) to brand and pigeonhole, pink lit has emerged as the 10- to 16-year-old equivalent of adult chick lit. The books are recognizable by their brightly colored "girlie" covers. Pink lit is frothy and funny, with a twist of escapism, while also managing to deal with serious(-ish) contemporary teenage girl preoccupations: mainly, relationships (especially with the opposite sex), annoying or embarrassing parents, school life, friends, and questions such as, "How do boys tick?," "Where do I fit in?," or "Where is my life heading?"

These books have become incredibly popular because the characters and situations are instantly recognizable and easy to identify with. They are realistic but not threateningly over-gritty or grim. There is romance without sexually transmitted diseases; embarrassing parents without extreme poverty or distressing abuse. Pink lit books are light and easy reading. They have a wide appeal, being read voraciously by literate teen bookworms, by boys (in secret) who want to get a handle on what goes on in girls' minds, and by many who claim normally not to read anything more than the side of a cornflake box.

Pink lit is often dismissed by critics as trivial or shallow, probably because of its lighthearted approach. But I think the reviewers miss the point. As well as providing a bit of welcome leisurely escapism, pink lit also provides a chance to explore some of the problems that beset teenagers at an often miserable and difficult time in their lives.

I've written two series that fit into the pink-lit genre: Mates, Dates . . . (UTBG 222), which is set in North London, and

"Sure to leave readers in stitches." — *Publishers Weekly*

Sue Limb

GIRL 15 Charming BUt Insane

Other pink lit books you can read about in the *UTBG*:

The Sisterhood of the Traveling Pants by Ann Brashares

The Princess Diaries by Meg Cabot

All-American Girl by Meg Cabot

Girl, 15, Charming but Insane by Sue Limb

The **Confessions of Georgia Nicolson** series (*Angus, Thongs and Full-Frontal Snogging*, etc.) by Louise Rennison

Girls in Love series by Jacqueline Wilson

Confessions of a Teenage Drama Queen by Dyan Sheldon

Sloppy Firsts by Megan McCafferty

The Earth, My Butt, and Other Big Round Things by Carolyn Mackler

The Boyfriend List and *Dramarama* by E. Lockhart

Rhymes with Witches by Lauren Myracle

Truth, Dare . . . , set in Cornwall, England. There is the usual mix of romance, family, school life, and questions such as, "Is there a God?" or "What am I going to do with my life?" But the main thread that runs through these books is the importance and affirmation of friendship. My publisher has coined a subgenre, calling them friend lit.

I find my writing very rewarding for two reasons in particular. It is great to know that my stories are popular all over the world: the series have been sold in 21 countries. And I love to get e-mails from my readers. The most gratifying thing for me is to hear how I have turned someone onto reading. This sort of message is fairly typical: "I hated reading, but then I picked up your books and it was like reading about my own life." Score.

"A creepy, can't-put-it-down thriller."

rhymes with witches

FROM THE AUTHOR OF THE *NEW YORK TIMES* BEST-SELLER *ttyl*

LAUREN MYRACLE

THE CITY OF EMBER Jeanne DuPrau

12+

Next?

Of course, the remaining books of Ember must be read— *The People of Sparks* and *The Prophet of Yonwood*.

Other terrific otherworldly titles include *Kiki Strike* (UTBG 192) by Kirsten Miller, where a group of 12-year-old girls—each with a special (criminal) talent— uncovers a mystery in New York City; and *Gregor the Overlander* by Suzanne Collins, about Gregor, who nearly sacrifices everything to save his little sister Boots, who has accidentally discovered a whole new world right under their noses.

Imagine a world of complete darkness—a city where the only light source is run by an aging generator that more and more often just shuts down. Picture a whole bustling city going through its day as always, when suddenly the lights go off and people are frozen in the blackness of a day with no sun, no moon, no stars. This is the City of Ember.

Lina and Doon have only ever known Ember—in fact, no one ever leaves there, and no one new ever arrives. But the two friends figure there must be a way out to a world beyond their dying city, and they set out to find it before the supplies and the light run out. Do they learn the secret of Ember? And if so, what will they do with the knowledge? These questions will leave the reader in suspense from the first page on—this is a fabulous start to a great series, the Books of Ember.

Laura Lehner-Ennis, Librarian

CLAUDINE AT SCHOOL Colette

12+

Claudine is an attractive, headstrong, and precocious adolescent who lives with her unworldly father in the French village of Montigny. This, the first novel in Colette's Claudine series, is about her mischievous and disruptive behavior at school. Claudine is bright enough to cruise by on little work, so she devotes most of her energy to battling her formidable headmistress for the amorous attention of the pretty, golden-eyed classroom assistant Aimée. This witty novel is packed with flirting, bullying, and the petty horrors of taking exams.

Francesca Lewis, Publicist

Next?

Claudine Married is the next book in the series. And look out for Colette's story of *Gigi*, a girl destined to be a courtesan.

In *The Prime of Miss Jean Brodie* (UTBG 277) Muriel Spark breathes life into a band of schoolgirls and their teacher.

If you enjoy Colette's descriptions of beautiful clothes and objects, try *The Picture of Dorian Gray* (UTBG 270) by Oscar Wilde.

CLAY David Almond

Stephen Rose, the odd boy with a tragic past, has just arrived at Felling. Stephen Rose, who forms stunning, lifelike figures in clay. Local boy Davie soon learns just how remarkable Stephen Rose is; but is his gift a force of good or of evil?

As always, David Almond paints a world we seem to recognize; but as we read on we realize that we recognize it only in part, we see only its surface. For around us there are always things that we don't see or understand—things hidden in shadows, spirits of the past, powers we can't explain. Throughout his books, these inexplicable things emerge in ways that are sometimes beautiful, sometimes terrifying, but always haunting.

This is a book of secret magic, of faith and doubt, of death and life (no less). And it's one of Almond's best, I think. And if you knew how highly I rate all his work, you'd know just what praise that is.

Daniel Hahn, Editor

Next?

For a classic tale of learning to animate lifeless matter, read Mary Shelley's *Frankenstein* (UTBG 126). Or for a rather less alarming tale of a boy's relationship with a great inexplicable giant, Ted Hughes's *The Iron Man*.

If you want another David Almond, try *Secret Heart* or *Kit's Wilderness* (UTBG 197).

Pete Hautman's *Godless* (UTBG 137) is a similarly chilling tale of two boys who create something that gets out of control—in this book, it's a religion.

A CLOCKWORK ORANGE Anthony Burgess

 16+

I was coerced into reading this story of ultraviolence and rape by my 16-year-old son. I thought my feminist soul would hate it. Wrong. It's Burgess's extraordinary achievement to make you empathize with his appalling hero, Alex. Using Nadsat, a brilliant invented language that borrows from Slavic, Burgess contrives to make you into one of Alex's "droogs." It's a big book, dangerous, one that grapples with choice and morality. All the more extraordinary for the fact that Burgess wrote it after an attack on his wife, which resulted in her miscarrying their child. He might have written it from the perspective of the victim, but instead he writes as the aggressor. I only wish I'd read it as a teenager.

Nicky Singer, Author

Next?

Chris Lynch's *Inexcusable* (UTBG 175) and Alex Flinn's *Breathing Underwater* (UTBG 51) also tell stories about violence from the viewpoint of the aggressor.

Requiem for a Dream by Hubert Selby, Jr., is another heavy read, replete with addiction and illness.

Another group of antisocial friends appear in *Trainspotting* (UTBG 363) by Irvine Welsh.

Want to know more about cult books? Read the feature on pp. 250–251.

CODE TALKER: A NOVEL ABOUT THE NAVAJO MARINES OF WORLD WAR TWO

Joseph Bruchac

Next?

For another book about the Navajo code talkers, try Kenji Kawano's photo essay *Warriors: Navajo Code Talkers*.

If you are fascinated by the culture of Navajo people, read David and Aimee Thurlo's *The Spirit Line*.

Read *Flags of Our Fathers* (UTBG 119) by James Bradley for a different perspective on the horrors of World War II.

When Ned Begay was a child, he was taught that his own Navajo language was inferior to English and that he would be punished if he was ever caught speaking it. He followed the rules but was careful to retain his knowledge of his language, speaking it in secret with his friends and family. Imagine his surprise when, at the beginning of World War II, the US government began looking to recruit Navajos into the Marines. The Navajo language was considered almost impossible to learn by non-native speakers, so it was the perfect code for the United States to use during World War II. Ned and men like him were critical to the United States' victory over Japan. What they did was considered so top secret that they were not allowed to talk about the role they played until 1969, more than 20 years after the war ended. Joseph Bruchac's *Code Talker* tells the story of a "useless" language that became incredibly useful.

Kristin Anderson, Librarian

COLD COMFORT FARM Stella Gibbons

Stella Gibbons's first novel, *Cold Comfort Farm*, published in 1932, remains fresh, relevant, and witty today.

Flora Poste, 20, newly orphaned, with no property and only £100 a year, has to decide which relatives to live with. She goes for the Starkadders on their farm in Howling, Sussex. There she finds an extraordinary collection of individuals, locked into age-old family feuds, stirring lumpy porridge, and washing dishes with a thorn stick. At their center sits Aunt Ada Doom, malevolent, brooding, and implacable, haunted by the "something nasty in the woodshed" she saw as a child.

Flora is determined to create order out of chaos, to inject sanity into the madness, in a novel that is sheer delight from beginning to end.

Valerie Mendes, Author

Next?

Dodie Smith's *I Capture the Castle* (UTBG 169) is a similarly witty read, set in the same time and place as *Cold Comfort Farm*.

Or try another comic novel, such as *Miss Pettigrew Lives for a Day* by Winifred Watson.

Sophie Kinsella's frothy *The Undomestic Goddess* takes another sophisticated urbanite and drops her in the country.

THE COLOR PURPLE Alice Walker

This unforgettable tale about Celie, a black woman growing up and living in the American South, must have touched more lives than just about any other book I know.

Raped by the man she believes to be her father, Celie twice falls pregnant and each time has to give up her child for adoption. This awfulness is just the beginning of a long journey through suffering so heartbreaking that on more than one occasion the reader is left wondering how Celie can possibly carry on. But carry on she does. Inspired and loved by the stunning *femme fatale* blues singer Shug Avery, Celie realizes for the first time that she doesn't have to put up with the appalling treatment meted out to her by men. And so her life begins to change.

Walker's story is deeply intimate, and her characters are so complex, well-rounded, and deftly drawn, you feel they could walk right off the page.

Neil Arksey, Author

Next?

Tashi (from *The Color Purple*) gets her own story told in *Possessing the Secret of Joy*—another dark and heart-wrenching story.

John Irving's *The Cider House Rules* is a complex tale of love and redemption that addresses similar issues of paternity and racism.

Another classic African American novel is *Beloved* (UTBG 33) by Tony Morrison.

CONFESSIONS OF A TEENAGE DRAMA QUEEN Dyan Sheldon

For Lola, the whole world is a stage and she's the star of the show. Funny, goofy, infuriating, kind, and totally over the top, Lola (whose real name is Mary) tells the story of her new life after her parents separate and she and her twin sisters move to New Jersey and a new school.

Wearing clothes to match her mood (velvet capes are the least of it), Lola makes friends with Ella and seriously annoys the most popular girl in the school by winning the coveted lead role in the school play. Then her favorite band, Sidartha, breaks up and the story spins back to New York as Lola and Ella meet rock gods and more police than is ever really necessary. Fun? You bet.

Leonie Flynn, Editor

Next?

There is a sequel, *My Perfect Life*, which tells more about Ella and Lola, this time from Ella's point of view.

Meg Cabot's *The Princess Diaries* (UTBG 281) also stars a goofy and lovable heroine.

And don't forget to read our Pink Lit feature on pp. 70–71 for lots more good reads.

THE CONTENDER Robert Lipsyte

Robert Lipsyte wrote this book 40 years ago, but like all classic novels it is a sharp, compelling, and wise story that will always be relevant. Master of the tough/tender style of writing, Lipsyte shows us the struggle of a 17-year-old Harlem teen to become a champion boxer, a true friend, and ultimately a man. He does this skillfully and dramatically, never resorting to street language although he could have claimed the milieu called for it, respecting his young audience by presenting them with a solid, exciting story and a sound philosophy: "It's the climbing that makes the man. Getting to the top is an extra reward."

Lipsyte is a writer who's reached the top, and here he is at the start of the climb.

M. E. Kerr, Author

Next?

The sequel to *The Contender*, *The Brave*, follows Alfred Brooks back to the gym where he trained in boxing, except this time he is training a troubled youth.

For a dramatic sports story about basketball and an unlikely friendship, try Bruce Brooks's *The Moves Make the Man* (UTBG 234).

If you love wrestling stories, try Rich Wallace's *Wrestling Sturbridge* (UTBG 400), in which two friends are both trying for the state wrestling championship.

CORALINE Neil Gaiman

Next?

Neil Gaiman writes adult horror, graphic novels, and kids' books! Try *The Wolves in the Walls* (UTBG 395), a picture book illustrated by long-time collaborator Dave McKean.

Stephen King's *The Shining* is another haunting and completely terrifying read about a family that goes mad while taking care of an empty hotel for the winter.

And you should also read Lewis Carroll's *Alice's Adventures in Wonderland*!

Coraline lives in just part of a big old house with her mom and dad and a bunch of eccentric neighbors. One day when she's bored, she opens a door she's never opened before and discovers a parallel universe. It's much more exciting in there! The food is delicious, her bedroom captivating, the toys magical—and there are a new mom and dad who love her very much and want her to stay. At first it all seems very cozy, but then stranger and stranger things start to happen.

Neil Gaiman writes in a matter-of-fact, nonsensational way, and this only serves to enhance the strange and haunting quality of his tale. I can still see the deeply creepy "other mother" with her shiny, black button eyes . . .

Mary Hooper, Author

CORAM BOY Jamila Gavin

12+

Next?

There are many great stories set around this period in history—try Leon Garfield's *Smith* or *Black Jack*.

For something about slavery, try Rosemary Sutcliff's *The Outcast*, set in the ancient world, or Gary Paulsen's *Nightjohn*, set in the South. Both are very different, but both pack a strong emotional punch.

Captain Thomas Coram was a philanthropist who opened a hospital for abandoned children in the mid-18th century. This book tells the tale of Otis Gardiner, who purported to collect children for Coram's hospital, but actually murdered them, neglected them, or sold them as slaves. The sordid story of Gardiner and his simpleton son is set alongside the tale of a young woman who falls in love with an aristocrat and then, sadly, comes to need Gardiner's services. It's a densely embroidered story contrasting rich and poor, and city and countryside, and is crammed with detail. This is real edge-of-the-seat stuff, the plot carefully woven and the characters fascinating, and I defy you to finish it without a tear in your eye.

Mary Hooper, Author

CORBENIC Catherine Fisher

12+

Since he was six, Cal has spent a miserable childhood in Bangor, England, with his mother, who is schizophrenic and an alcoholic. He is offered a new life with his uncle Trevor in Chepstow, and tries to leave the past behind. On the way he falls asleep on the train and gets off at the wrong station, Corbenic, where he is directed to the Castle Hotel. He finds himself at the castle of the Fisher King, and from then the novel intertwines the Arthurian myth of the Grail and Cal's own journey to find self-knowledge and peace of mind. It's an exciting and moving story with a contemporary theme, a sense of place, the mystery of legend, and strong characterization.

Brenda Marshall, Librarian

Next?

Another wonderful Catherine Fisher book is *Darkhenge* (UTBG 88), about a boy trying to save his sister.

For more Arthurian legends try *Arthur: The Seeing Stone* (UTBG 24) by Kevin Crossley-Holland or Rick Yancey's *The Extraordinary Adventures of Alfred Kropp*.

Or read C. S. Lewis's **The Chronicles of Narnia** books, for classic adventure stories.

CORELLI'S MANDOLIN Louis de Bernières

Next?

More de Bernières? Try *The War of Don Emmanuel's Nether Parts*.

For another novel that deals graphically with war (and love), try *Birdsong* (UTBG 35) by Sebastian Faulks.

Or what about *For Whom the Bell Tolls* by Ernest Hemingway?

As much a harrowing tale of wartime occupation as it is a profound love story, *Corelli's Mandolin* tells the story of Dr. Iannis and his beautiful daughter, Pelagia, who live a simple life practicing medicine on the Greek island of Cephallonia. Pelagia believes she is in love with Mandras, a local fisherman, and when World War II breaks out, she becomes engaged to him before he leaves the island to serve in the army. But her life becomes complicated with the arrival of the Italian army and a gentle, cultured captain named Corelli. Over the sweet tings of his mandolin, they fall in love. But love during wartime is never simple—especially when the lovers are on opposite sides of the fray.

Corelli's Mandolin seamlessly blends historical fact with a tender love story and an element of fiction; de Bernières tells his tale from many different perspectives and challenges readers' perceptions of wartime and loyalty. An intriguing and touching look at how everyone, soldier or not, is affected by war.

Stacy Cantor, Editor

COUNTING STARS David Almond

This is an autobiographical collection of short stories about the childhood of my favorite author. Many of the stories in here were written before any of Almond's novels were published, so reading *Counting Stars* feels like peering into the author's heart and soul to learn what makes him tick.

I love the way Almond writes. He never wastes a word, only tells you about things that matter, and from the first page of this book you know the center of his universe is family, living and dead. Sisters. Brother. Mom. Dad. It's hard to write about how much you love and cherish and miss people without being schmaltzy and sentimental, but Almond does this amazingly throughout *Counting Stars*. It's a wonderful book about the important things in life: love, loss, childhood . . . But so is everything Almond writes.

Catherine Forde, Author

Next?

Now go and read all of David Almond's other books. *All* of them.

For a more snarky look at a childhood, read David Sedaris's *Me Talk Pretty One Day*.

Or read another author's autobiography, such as Walter Dean Myers's *Bad Boy*.

A CRACK IN THE LINE Michael Lawrence

I've come close to death at least three times—which means that in alternate realities I've died at least three times. Running flat out in the woods at home and coming to a teetering halt on the edge of a sheer drop that I didn't know was there, is a moment that still haunts me! So what are those alternate worlds—the ones without me—like?

This is a concept that Michael Lawrence sets out to explore in his trilogy The Withern Rise. Alaric Underwood's mother has a 50/50 chance of survival after a train crash. In this world she dies—in an alternate reality she lives. When Alaric finds a way to cross between these two worlds he finds himself having to rethink everything he ever knew about space and time.

Laura Hutchings, Teacher

Next?

In *The Homeward Bounders* by Diana Wynne Jones, a boy from the 19th century is forced to wander from world to world, trying to get home again.

The House on the Strand by Daphne du Maurier and "The Time Machine" in H. G. Wells's *Short Stories* (UTBG 320) are both about going back in time.

A Wrinkle in Time (UTBG 401) by Madeleine L'Engle is a classic story of two siblings on a fantastic journey through time.

CRAZY Benjamin Lebert

Next?

Try *The Old Man and the Sea* (UTBG 254) by Ernest Hemingway—if you've read *Crazy* you'll know why.

The Catcher in the Rye (UTBG 60) by J. D. Salinger—another troubled teenager goes AWOL in the city.

Troy reads Stephen King's terrifying *Misery*; but I think you should try King's *The Body* instead. Like *Crazy*, it's about the bonds of friendship, and a tale of discovery.

Benjamin is 16 and starting at a new school—his fifth. He keeps failing math, and he's not very good at German; he's "different," too, partially paralyzed down his left side, and finds it hard to fit in.

But this time Benjamin settles quickly into a group of friends. There are five of them: Janosch (the ringleader), Fat Felix and Skinny Felix, Florian aka Girl, and silent Troy. Benjamin fits right in. After all, none of his friends are really "normal" either—and anyway, who is?

Crazy is an engagingly told story of a few months in the lives of a group of friends—they get drunk, get laid, get into trouble, and get on each other's nerves. They talk for hours about profound things like life and death, and they complain about school food, teachers, rules—just school in general, but you know they'll miss it when the time comes to leave. And when the book ends you'll be sorry to leave them, too.

Daniel Hahn, Editor

CRIME AND PUNISHMENT Fyodor Dostoyevsky

Don't be scared off by the weighty title and this novel's reputation as a Great Work of Russian Literature; this is a gripping read right from the start—a psychological/crime thriller as unputdownable as any bestseller.

Rashkolnikov is an intelligent, proud, and embittered young man, living in poverty in St. Petersburg. To escape his desperate situation, he plans a robbery and murder. His intended victim is a vile old pawnbroker, whom he feels society will be better off without. He rationalizes the murder to himself and is confident that he will be able to get away with it. The reality of the deed is very different.

The inner world of Rashkolnikov is at the heart of the story. Dostoyevsky takes us deep into the nightmare of Rashkolnikov's conscience as he confronts the horror of what he's done.

Katie Jennings, Editor

> **Next?**
>
> For a gripping tale of murder and guilt, there's nothing better than Shakespeare's *Macbeth*.
>
> For something shorter by Dostoyevsky, but still full of atmosphere and energy, try his *Notes from Underground*.
>
> For high drama, this time in France, try Émile Zola's *Thérèse Raquin* (UTBG 354).
>
> Or Patrick Süskind's extraordinary tale of an extraordinary man, *Perfume* (UTBG 268).

THE CRY OF THE ICEMARK Stuart Hill

> **Next?**
>
> For other battle-filled books try Adèle Geras's *Troy* (UTBG 366), her magnificent account of the fall of the legendary city; or *Warrior Girl* (UTBG 380) by Pauline Chandler, a reworking of the true story of Jeanne, the teenage girl who led France against the English in medieval times.
>
> For another Norse-based epic full of battles and really good names, try *The Sea of Trolls* (UTBG 305) by Nancy Farmer.

If you like fantasies on an epic scale, with desperate battles against invincible armies, you can't go wrong with *The Cry of the Icemark*. Thirrin Freer Strong-in-the-Arm Lindenshield, Wildcat of the North, Monarch of the Icemark, earns every one of her titles before she has been queen for a year. At the start of the book she's eager for battle with the mighty Polypontian army bent on conquering the world; by its end, she's a seasoned warrior, bloodied and battle-scarred, understanding loss and pain as well as the euphoria of victory. She's also become an astute politician, holding together an unlikely alliance of Greek-style archers and lancers, vampires and werewolves, gigantic white leopards, and her own army of the Icemark.

Gill Vickery, Author

THE CRYSTAL CAVE Mary Stewart

Next?

The series continues with *The Hollow Hills* and *The Last Enchantment*.

The Mists of Avalon by Marion Zimmer Bradley is the Arthurian legend told by the women involved. There are sequels, too.

Or you could read the original—Thomas Malory's *Le Morte d'Arthur*.

Catherine Jinks's own **The Pagan Chronicles** (UTBG 266) recreates the past with just as much realism.

Meet the historical Merlin—or be the closest you'll ever get to him! He's not so much a magician as a seer, and his gift is more of a burden than a blessing. A thinker surrounded by fighters, and an illegitimate outcast to boot, he's condemned to a life of rejection and isolation. Yet he battles on single-handedly to ensure that his nephew, Arthur, is born and raised to fulfill the prophecies that plague poor Merlin like a recurring headache.

These fabulous novels are not only drenched in utterly convincing detail about post-Roman Britain and the Gaelic culture, but also introduce one of the wisest, loneliest, most convincing heroes you'll ever encounter. Even readers who aren't fantasy fans will enjoy them.

Catherine Jinks, Author

THE CRYSTAL SINGER Anne McCaffrey

Killashandra is a music student with her heart set on becoming a high-ranking opera singer—until the day she learns her voice contains a fatal flaw, which means she can never be a top performer. Not content to be second best, she walks away from her old life and is recruited by the "Crystal Singers," who use their voices to mine crystal from the beautiful but dangerous planet of Ballybran. Killashandra seizes the chance to realize her ambitions but discovers she must change in more ways than one before she can finally sing crystal.

This is one of the few books on my shelf I reread regularly, getting as much enjoyment out of Killashandra's determined character now as I did the first time.

Katherine Roberts, Author

Next?

Don't miss the sequels, *Killashandra* and *Crystal Line*.

Or Anne McCaffrey's **The Dragonriders of Pern** series (UTBG 98), set on Pern, where people ride—and fight—on the backs of telepathic dragons. The first of these is *Dragonflight*.

Or Katherine Roberts's **Echorium** series, beginning with *Song Quest*.

THE CUP OF THE WORLD /
THE WIDOW AND THE KING John Dickinson

Next?

For a recreation of the real Middle Ages, try Kevin Crossley-Holland's **Arthur** trilogy; set in the 13th century; it begins with **Arthur: The Seeing Stone** (UTBG 24).

The Sterkarm Handshake (UTBG 340) and *A Sterkarm Kiss* by Susan Price combine sci-fi with the violent history of the Scottish border country.

The Princess Bride (UTBG 280) by William Goldman is a crazy, exhilarating fairy tale for adults (and anyone else), set in a time that never was or could have been.

Phaedra runs away from a dynastic marriage to join the man who has wooed her by means of "undercraft." Other people mistakenly call this witchcraft, and there is a fearful price to pay for practicing it. Everything else in these two wonderful novels is entirely human as the players in a power game struggle for control over whole kingdoms, over other people, or simply over their own lives, never knowing that someone else is manipulating their every move. Phaedra, discovering how she has been used, learns to play the game herself; and her son, as he grows up, finally brings it all to a conclusion. Set in an imaginary but intensely real medieval country, the story is just as relevant to the times we live in now.
Jan Mark, Author

THE CURIOUS INCIDENT OF
THE DOG IN THE NIGHT-TIME Mark Haddon

It's always great to read exciting books about magic and faraway lands filled with mystical creatures, but every now and then a great book comes along that, despite the absence of all things fantastical, still has the power to amaze you. This is one of them. It follows teenager Christopher Boone as he grows up with a condition called Asperger's. Christopher is brilliant at math but can't understand simple human emotions. One night Christopher finds his neighbor's dog, Wellington, brutally murdered in the garden, and so begins his quest to find the killer.

Despite dealing with some serious issues, this story is told in a light and witty style, and as it progresses the characters really feel alive.
Gareth Smith, age 14

Next?

Try reading other stories of people who see the world in a different way, like those collected by Oliver Sacks in *The Man Who Mistook His Wife for a Hat*.

Al Capone Does My Shirts (UTBG 8) by Gennifer Choldenko charts life growing up with an autistic sister on Alcatraz at the time of Al Capone.

CUT Patricia McCormick

14+

Next?

Famous novels about teenagers suffering breakdowns? Try *Girl, Interrupted* by Susanna Kaysen or *The Bell Jar* (UTBG 32) by Sylvia Plath, both complex and challenging—but worth it!

Impulse by Ellen Hopkins is a free-verse novel that tells the stories of three teens who are now in a psychiatric hospital after having survived suicide attempts.

Massive (UTBG 220) by Julia Bell treats the subject of eating disorders with care and compassion.

Cut is a sensitive treatment of the subject of self-harm. The heroine, Callie, who tells the story, has been cutting herself and is admitted to Sea Pines—or Sick Minds as she calls it. Callie used to be a great runner until her obsession led her to withdraw from the world completely, to the point where she chooses not to talk anymore—not even to the people who are trying to help her. But as she gets to know the other girls at Sick Minds—anorexics, drug addicts, other self-harmers—she begins to come out of her self-imposed isolation. Reading about Callie's struggle to want to get better is moving, absorbing—and realistic, too.

Sherry Ashworth, Author

THE DA VINCI CODE Dan Brown

14+

This book has topped the bestseller lists for ages. Why? Well, the story revolves around a truly astonishing secret that challenges the very basis of the world's most deeply held Christian beliefs. This secret has been protected for centuries by a hidden society that is still active today. It's wildly controversial and stirs up ferocious, even murderous, passions.

This is a real page-turner, with an endless series of cliff-hangers that catapult you through chapter after chapter.

The book begins with a murder, and the body is weirdly arranged to resemble a famous drawing by the old master Leonardo da Vinci. Perhaps da Vinci actually belonged to one of those secret societies. Maybe more of his paintings contain hidden signs and symbols, messages we must try to decode . . .

You get the picture. I don't normally read thrillers, but this one's like a movie in your head: dark, mysterious, and compelling.

Sue Limb, Author

Next?

Holy Blood, Holy Grail by Michel Baigent, Richard Leigh, and Henry Lincoln is a real-life investigation into the same mysteries.

More religious controversy? Nikos Kazantzakis's novel *Last Temptation* explores the "did Jesus really die on the cross?" question.

Blue Balliett's *Chasing Vermeer* has been called a *Da Vinci Code* for kids if you like it, try the sequel, *The Wright 3*, as well.

DAIRY QUEEN Catherine Gilbert Murdock

D. J. Schwenk has a lot of responsibility. Her father has hurt himself, so it's up to her to run their dairy farm while her mother works two jobs. She and her younger brother do a lot of work, but they're just barely keeping up. And D. J. is having serious difficulty with her schoolwork. After all, when is she supposed to find the time to do it?

Meanwhile, a family friend sends over the rival football team's quarterback to give them a hand. Spoiled, rich Brian Nelson endures D. J.'s constant taunts, and soon she begins to train him for football. Who better to be a trainer than the younger sister of a past school football star? But the real question is, can D. J. and Brian be friends at all, or even more than friends? This is a great look at life on a dairy farm, and what it's like to want to just be yourself sometimes, even when the rest of the world won't let you figure out who that is.

Kelly Jo Lasher, Librarian

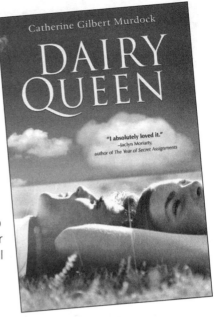

Catherine Gilbert Murdock

DAIRY QUEEN

"I absolutely loved it."
–Jaclyn Moriarty,
author of *The Year of Secret Assignments*

BOOKS ABOUT THE BOMB

Cat's Cradle by Kurt Vonnegut

Slaughterhouse-Five by Kurt Vonnegut

When the Wind Blows by Raymond Briggs

How I Live Now by Meg Rosoff

Z for Zachariah by Robert C. O'Brien

Next?

Of course, if you enjoyed this book, you'll want to check out the sequel, *The Off Season*.

For another farm girl sort of story, check out *Peaches* by Jodi Lynn Anderson. It's more focused on friendship, but it does take place on a peach farm.

D. J. does a great job of describing her life. Many of Sarah Dessen's books have the same feel to them: try *The Truth About Forever* and *Just Listen* (UTBG 187).

Another author great at capturing the voice of her characters is Joan Bauer. *Rules of the Road* and its sequel, *Best Foot Forward*, follow a girl in a unique working situation.

DAISY MILLER Henry James

Winterbourne is a good-natured but idle young American man, with not much to do with his life but drift from one European town to another, visiting friends and enjoying "Society." But at Vevey he meets Daisy Miller, and he is quite changed.

He's never met anyone like Daisy. She's both so smart and so naive, totally innocent and yet an incorrigible flirt. And she's extremely pretty. Winterbourne can't stop thinking about her.

I think Henry James is one of the greatest of all novelists, and *Daisy Miller* is just the way to meet him first. This is only the slimmest of novels—a novella, really—but in the hundred or so pages, James creates a portrait of a character (and a society she can't help being at odds with) that is perfectly poised and thoroughly enchanting.

Daniel Hahn, Editor

Next?

For another Henry James, this time with more substance, move on to his *Portrait of a Lady*.

For more turn-of-the-century innocent young ladies traveling around Europe, try E. M. Forster—*A Room with a View* (UTBG 293) or *Where Angels Fear to Tread*. After James's prose you'll find him an easy read!

Or for another dark sort of love story, read *Ethan Frome* (UTBG 106), by James's close friend Edith Wharton.

DANDELION WINE Ray Bradbury

14+

Ray Bradbury is a master of short stories. Whether they're about ghosts, Martians, his childhood, Mexico, Ireland, or a thousand other subjects, he can tell a great story using a minimum of words. For this book, he wove several tales together to create what is arguably his best novel. It's the tale of a young boy and his adventures one magical, mysterious summer. Funny, scary, but above all *warm*. This is a book that leaves you with a smile on your face—a book that you're truly sorry to put down. Bradbury has been one of my biggest influences, and if you read this book then one of mine, you'll find shades of the master in just about everything I write.

Darren Shan, Author

Next?

Try some of Bradbury's sci-fi: *The Martian Chronicles* or *Fahrenheit 451* (UTBG 110).

Or the short-story collections of Clive Barker, *The Books of Blood*, which are just as scary and gory as they sound.

Or something by Darren Shan—the horrifically gruesome *Lord Loss* (UTBG 208) or *Cirque du Freak* (UTBG 69), in which the hero's name is Darren Shan!

DANGEROUS SKIES Suzanne Fisher Staples

This is a beautifully written and deeply moving account of two teenagers—a black girl, Tunes, and a white boy, Buck. Tunes's father works for Buck's family and they have grown up together. But friendship and loyalty are tested when Tunes becomes the suspect in a local murder.

You never doubt for one minute that Tunes has been falsely accused and that the threatened injustice is a result of racism. And any momentary doubts that Buck has are quickly brushed aside. But as the story progresses, with Tunes's young life in the balance, the teenagers' desperate struggle against the blinkered attitudes of local white adults is painful to follow—all the way to its sad and courageously truthful end.

Neil Arksey, Author

> **Next?**
>
> Something else by the same author? Try *Shiva's Fire*, about a girl in India born with strange abilities and a gift for dance.
>
> Rosa Guy's *The Friends* is about prejudice of all sorts.
>
> For another powerful story of racism, read the classic *To Kill a Mockingbird* (UTBG 360) by Harper Lee.
>
> Or try Mary Ann Rodman's *Yankee Girl*, about a white girl moving to the Deep South in 1964.

THE DARK GROUND Gillian Cross

> **Next?**
>
> Some questions are left unanswered in this book—so read the sequel, *The Black Room*.
>
> *Calling a Dead Man* (UTBG 56) is another gripping thriller by Gillian Cross.
>
> William Golding's classic, *Lord of the Flies* (UTBG 209), also shows human behavior under extreme conditions, as does Tim Bowler's chilling *Apocalypse* (UTBG 22).

Gillian Cross's novels always grip you in a stranglehold from the very first page. Her writing is compelling, direct, and thought-provoking. This, the extraordinary first book of a trilogy, is no exception. Part thriller, part fable, it made me look at the world in a totally different way.

Robert regains consciousness, after what he supposes is a plane crash, to find himself alone in a thick jungle. There is no sign of his family or any other survivors. For a few days he struggles to stay alive. And then he becomes aware that someone—or something—is watching him.

I can't write more for fear of giving away the original and ambitious idea behind this novel. All I can say is *read it*!

Patricia Elliott, Author

THE DARK IS RISING series Susan Cooper

Next?

The full order is *Over Sea, Under Stone*; *The Dark Is Rising*; *Greenwitch*; *The Grey King*; and *Silver on the Tree*.

Try Alan Garner's fantastic *The Owl Service* (UTBG 265), or Mary Stewart's **Merlin** books, beginning with *The Crystal Cave* (UTBG 81).

The Various by Steve Augarde is a sprawling magical fantasy. Or try Catherine Fisher's **The Book of the Crow** series or *The Glass Tower*, a collection of some of her short, intense, and unsettling novels.

Moving from the fairly unsophisticated treasure hunt of *Over Sea, Under Stone* to the wonderful final battle under the midsummer tree in *Silver on the Tree*, this quintet of novels is a classic fantasy series. Cooper's books grow in depth and allusion as the reader journeys through them; they move from Cornwall to Wales, and the quest to possess the Grail becomes a cosmic war between the powers of light and darkness, fought through Celtic myth and the archetypes of the Arthurian legend. Cooper is good at atmosphere and brooding landscapes, and these books are a gripping read.

Catherine Fisher, Author

THE DARK LORD OF DERKHOLM

Diana Wynne Jones

Where teenager Blade lives, they reenact "Dark Lord"-type fantasies for tourists from another world. This year, the Oracle puts Blade's father in charge, and suddenly everything turns dangerous. Why? For one thing, the wizards, magic, dragons, demons, griffins, and flying pigs are all real; and Blade's father is the last wizard anyone would have chosen to run things. When Blade and his siblings get drafted to help, they have to grow up quickly.

   This is a very exciting book full of elegant magic, but also touching as the pressures and tensions act on Blade's family. Oh, and I should add: while Blade and his parents are human, his siblings have feathers and wings—they're griffins, and they're delightful!

Rosemary Cass-Beggs, Author

Next?

There's a sequel, *The Year of the Griffin*, in which a griffin daughter and her classmates (accidentally) transform their shoddy university into a center of excellence.

You should also look for Diana Wynne Jones's *Hexwood* (puzzling at first, but deeply satisfying).

And try Mercedes Lackey's **Valdemar** series, in which the horses have strange powers! Start with *Take a Thief*, about a pickpocket chosen to become a Herald.

DARK SONS Nikki Grimes

Dark Sons is the story of two boys, Sam and Ishmael. Though these two boys have never met, their lives are similar in more ways than they could ever know. Both of their fathers love them very much at the beginning of the book. But then each of their fathers has another child, born to another mother. When this happens both Sam and Ishmael are a thing of the past; their fathers pay no attention to either of them anymore. This book, written in a free-verse narrative, is a very fast read. It's a sad and captivating book that doesn't let you' stop. I read the entire book in one sitting and it only took me an hour! You should read this book because it's lifelike and is based on the life of a biblical character, Ishmael.

Maggie Whitacre, age 16

Next?

For another award-winning book by Nikki Grimes told in free verse, try *Bronx Masquerade*, which centers on an open-mic night at a multicultural high school.

For another perspective on the difficulty of being a parent, check out Angela Johnson's *The First Part Last* (UTBG 119), about a 16-year-old father.

If you enjoy biblical allusions, try Walter Dean Myers and Christopher Myers's *A Time to Love*, biblical stories told in first-person narratives.

DARKHENGE Catherine Fisher

Next?

Corbenic (UTBG 77) by Catherine Fisher also weaves legend into the fabric of today, and it is equally exciting and mysterious.

Or try *The Mabinogion* itself—a series of Welsh legends that you'll find surprisingly familiar. Read the version lyrically translated by Lady Charlotte Guest.

Alan Garner also writes books full of mystery and magic; try one of his stories based on Welsh legend, *The Owl Service* (UTBG 265).

Catherine Fisher is a magician of a writer. Imagine a world where a woman can turn into a bird, and the bird's skin can be made into a magic bag that is full when the tide is high and empty when the tide is low. Where a man can live many lives, each of them hunted because he stole wisdom from a goddess's well.

When Rob sees a bird turn into a hare, the hare into a fish and the fish into a man, he has to believe what he sees. Doesn't he? The man is a druid, and together he and Rob walk through a world of pain and loss, in an adventure that is a skein of legend, a taste of *The Mabinogion,* and a terrifying look at the power of jealousy and dreams.

Leonie Flynn, Editor

THE DAY OF THE JACKAL

Frederick Forsyth

In 1963, a young English assassin is hired by a secretive group to kill the French president at a public parade. This assassin's code name is The Jackal, and the account of his bid to stay ahead of the detective on his trail makes for gripping thriller writing. The book is hailed as a classic of the genre, and rightly so. The suspense never lets up, but the detail makes it so convincing. Often research can weigh down a novel, but here it fuels the story. Famously, Forsyth begins with a criminal master class on how to acquire a foolproof false identity. As long as you harbor no plans to follow in the footsteps of the story's antihero, you won't fail to be rewarded by this compelling read.

Matt Whyman, Author

Next?

More Forsyth? Try *The Dogs of War*, about a group of mercenaries.

Jarhead by Anthony Swofford, the true story of a Gulf War sniper, is packed with military knowledge.

Or for another nail-biting thriller, try Robert Ludlum's *The Bourne Identity*

The Ultimate Teen Readers' Poll

BOOK YOU'VE READ OVER AND OVER

1   **The Harry Potter series**

2   **The Lord of the Rings trilogy**

3   **The Saga of Darren Shan**

4   **His Dark Materials trilogy**

5   *Holes*

6   **The Alex Rider series**

7   **A Series of Unfortunate Events**

8   **The Princess Diaries series**

9   *Of Mice and Men*

10   **The Sisterhood of the Traveling Pants series**

THE DAY OF THE TRIFFIDS John Wyndham

A mysterious comet fills the sky with green shooting stars, and the next day everyone who has seen them is struck blind. William Masen is one of the few who can still see. Now he has to survive, but it won't be easy. There are triffids—walking poisonous plants—to deal with, and other humans, who want to rebuild the world their own way.

Nowadays there are a lot of "post-apocalypse" books and movies, in which some disaster strikes the entire planet, leaving only a handful of people alive; but *The Day of the Triffids*, written more than 50 years ago, is the original and still the best. You'll worry about staring at shooting stars for years to come!

Benedict Jacka, Author

Next?

More Wyndham? Try *The Kraken Wakes* first.

The War of the Worlds (UTBG 379) by H. G. Wells is another classic science-fiction story that's still just as effective now as when it was first written.

Hatchet (UTBG 147) by Gary Paulsen is the story of a boy on his own, without any resources at all.

Or what about people fighting off other dangerous creatures? Try *Jurassic Park* (UTBG 187) by Michael Crichton.

DEFINE "NORMAL" Julie Anne Peters

Next?

Two more great novels by Julie Anne Peters are *Far from Xanadu* and *Luna*.

For another look into the "alternative" world, try Cecil Castellucci's *Beige* (UTBG 31) or Barry Lyga's *The Astonishing Adventures of Fanboy and Goth Girl* (UTBG 25).

Antonia does everything right—from getting excellent grades to taking care of her two brothers and keeping her mother's clinical depression a secret. In her attempt at perfection she signs up to be a peer counselor at school and to her great dismay is assigned to work with Jazz, of the black lipstick, colorfully dyed hair, tattoos, and artfully ripped clothes. When Antonia lets slip that she really wants to learn how to swim, Jazz invites her to learn how. Returning home after the swimming lesson, Antonia discovers that her mother took her brothers to a motel and then totally lost it, and Antonia has no one to call but Jazz.

Going into foster care, Antonia finds Jazz to be a lifeline, and she tries to help Jazz connect with her own mother and realize that sometimes her rebellion hurts herself more than anyone else. A sweet tale of two girls who despise each other until they discover that outward appearances are meaningless.

Diana Tixier Herald, Librarian

DESIRE LINES Jack Gantos

14+

Next?

Another novel that challenges our—and society's—idea about what makes a hero: Robert Cormier's *Heroes* (UTBG 152).

Jack Gantos has also written a memoir about his time in prison, *Hole in My Life* (UTBG 156), though it is a harsh, uncompromising read.

Aidan Chambers's *Postcards from No Man's Land* (UTBG 273) is also about making choices.

This is that rare thing, a novel without heroes, or indeed anyone you can really like, but it is not without the power to involve and keep you reading. Walker is gutless, easily preyed upon, and in the end, corrupted and treacherous. When a fundamentalist preacher comes to Walker's small Florida town, the preacher's boy, a bigoted zealot like his father, starts a rumor that Walker is gay in order to make him "out" any "ho-mo-sexuals" in his school. A bullying and vicious gang of boys also get hold of Walker and involve him in their delinquencies. Walker, caught between the devil and the deep, finally betrays two girls upon whom he's spied in the woods making love.

Gantos is a powerful writer who is challenging his readers' loyalty and integrity here as much as the preacher's boy challenges Walker's.

Lynne Reid Banks, Author

THE DIARY OF A YOUNG GIRL Anne Frank

12+

Anne Frank, a Jewish girl living in Amsterdam, was 13 when she began her diary in June 1942. The city was under German occupation. With her family and friends, she hid in a secret annex of a house. She was 15 when she made her last entry in the diary on August 1, 1944. On August 4, the eight people in hiding were caught and sent to Auschwitz concentration camp; from there she and her sister Margot were sent to the Bergen-Belsen camp, where they both died—a month before the camp was liberated. Telling us everything about her life, from her boredom and fear to her feelings about herself, boys, and the future, Anne's remarkable diaries were found scattered all over the floor after the police left. Luckily for us, as this is probably the most moving war diary ever written. Unmissable.

James Riordan, Author

Next?

The Boy in the Striped Pajamas (UTBG 46) by John Boyne or *When Hitler Stole Pink Rabbit* by Judith Kerr are both stories of an innocent in wartime.

Surviving Hitler by Andrea Warren is a book about life in a concentration camp.

Lois Lowry's *Number the Stars* is the classic tale of a girl caught up in the evacuation of Jews from Denmark during World War II.

Susan Campbell Bartoletti's *Hitler Youth* (UTBG 155) shows another perspective of youths put in the middle of war.

DINKY HOCKER SHOOTS SMACK! M. E. Kerr

Next?

For more by M. E. Kerr, try *Deliver Us from Evie*, *Slap Your Sides* (World War II historical fiction), or the three books in the **Fell** series (a group of mysteries).

Alice Childress's *A Hero Ain't Nothin' but a Sandwich* explores the world of a young teen addicted to drugs.

Susan "Dinky" Hocker and Tucker Woolf meet when Tucker needs to find a new home for his cat. When Tucker worries that the cat is inheriting Dinky's compulsive eating problem, he goes to her house to confront her. There, he meets Dinky's troubled cousin, Natalia, and the three of them develop an unusual friendship. Meanwhile, Dinky's mother can't see that her own daughter is desperate for help. Dinky tries a million ways to get her attention, but nothing works. Well, almost nothing.

The story is told through Tucker's perspective as he tries to figure out how to be a friend to Dinky, a boyfriend to Natalia, and a good son to his parents. I love Tucker's observations about his friends and family and himself, and the way he sees the humor and tragedy in all of it. I also love Dinky Hocker, who says that "the meek shall inherit the shaft" and is angry enough to do something to make sure she finally gets what she needs.

Sara Zarr, Author

DISCWORLD: MONSTROUS REGIMENT
Terry Pratchett

The old ballad "Sweet Polly Oliver" is a wonderfully sentimental tale, but by the time Pratchett is done with it, the result is blackly witty and scathing. It's also a thrilling read.

We meet Polly in the act of cutting off her long golden hair—she is signing up with the Borogravia army disguised as a boy. But as Polly soon learns, things in the army are not all as they seem. Not being a patriot, the fact that her country is losing the war does not much bother her. Finding herself on the front line does, since no one expects her regiment to survive.

Pratchett delights in building then releasing tension in tour-de-force action sequences. The motley regiment is full of startling characters, and the real revelations are saved for the end.

Geraldine McCaughrean, Author

Next?

Terry Pratchett has fortunately written loads, including more **Discworld** books; read *The Color of Magic* next.

Or try Robert Rankin for offbeat, crazy humor—and wacky titles such as *The Hollow Chocolate Bunnies of the Apocalypse*.

DIZZY Cathy Cassidy

Next?

Rachel Cohn's *The Steps*, set in the United States and Australia, looks at life in a dysfunctional but very happy family.

Heaven Eyes by David Almond and *You Can't Kiss It Better* by Diane Hendry are both excellent glimpses into the lives of looked-after children—while Hendry's is very realistic, Almond's has a more magical edge.

Birthdays for Dizzy are extra-special because each brings a gift from the ditzy mom who abandoned her as a baby to travel the world—a rainbow stripy hat, a rag doll, a pink jeweled necklace, an exotic dream catcher. The best present of all comes on her 12th birthday, when her mom turns up in person to whisk her off for the summer into a very different life—on the road, under canvas, and at festivals—meeting up with some colorful characters along the way, in places Dizzy has never even dreamed of. Suddenly she is forced to rethink her life with her dad and the values she's always accepted, and do some growing up of her own.

Not just another pink girly book, this one is essential teen reading. Sparkling with warmth, humanity, and hope, it will make you laugh and cry.

Eileen Armstrong, Librarian

DO ANDROIDS DREAM OF ELECTRIC SHEEP? Philip K. Dick

When I was about 10 or 11 I outgrew Nancy Drew and fell in love with science fiction. I discovered the sci-fi ABC: Asimov, Bradbury, and Clarke, but it wasn't till I was over 30 that I discovered D—Philip K. Dick. This book was made into a brilliant film called *Blade Runner*. The book is quite different, though it is still about bounty hunter Rick Deckard, and it's set in a dystopian future. The thing I love most about Philip K. Dick is something I don't get excited about with any other author: his *ideas*. But be warned. He was a strange Californian who used to play with his daughters' Barbie dolls.

Caroline Lawrence, Author

Next?

Read more by Philip K. Dick: *Second Variety*, a collection of short stories.

And Caroline's ABC? Try one of each: Isaac Asimov's **Foundation** trilogy (UTBG 126), Ray Bradbury's *Fahrenheit 451* (UTBG 110), and Arthur C. Clarke's *2001: A Space Odyssey*.

And don't forget to read our sci-fi feature on pp. 218–219.

DOCTOR ZHIVAGO Boris Pasternak

Boris Pasternak was a poet and novelist who fell out with the Soviet dictator Stalin, so he was unable to publish any works in Russia after 1933. He had to have his greatest work smuggled abroad: *Doctor Zhivago* was published in 1957 in Italy. This is a thrilling if challenging read, encompassing half a century of Russian history: the excitement of revolution and civil war, the labor camps to which Zhivago's love is confined. Whose side would you have been on? That was the question that the gentle, aristocratic doctor, Yuri Zhivago, has to answer to himself.

James Riordan, Author

Next?

Another great Russian classic is Leo Tolstoy's *War and Peace* (UTBG 379).

If you want to read more about the Russian Revolution, try Mikhail Sholokhov's *And Quiet Flows the Don*.

For an epic account of another country's revolution, this time China, try *Wild Swans* (UTBG 391) by Jung Chan.

DOING IT Melvin Burgess

Next?

If you liked reading about navigating the strange waters of relationships, Nick Hornby's *High Fidelity* (UTBG 152) has the same mixture of humor and honesty.

Forever (UTBG 125) by Judy Blume gives the girl's perspective on sexuality.

Smack (UTBG 329), also by Melvin Burgess, is about the treacherously easy slide into heroin addiction.

This is a story about sex. The main characters (three 17-year-old boys and their girlfriends) spend 330 pages talking, fantasizing, worrying, planning, and thinking about sex. Oh, yes, and doing it. There's a lot of doing it. There are things in this book you wouldn't want your mother to read, and I wasn't sure I should be reading it myself.

But this is Melvin Burgess writing, so you know he's going to be ruthlessly honest as well as laugh-out-loud funny, and that in the end he's going to burrow his way down to the truth. And when he does, the truth is wonderfully liberating.

It's an excellent book. Why not ask your parents to give it you for Christmas? No, seriously. Go on, I dare you.

Andrew Norriss, Author

DON'T LET'S GO TO THE DOGS TONIGHT

Alexandra Fuller

I bought this for my son when he was just back from two incredible weeks in Zambia staying with a school friend. He read it in one hungry gulp and wanted to know if the author had written any more. This is a painful memoir of growing up in Zimbabwe and Zambia and every page screams with the sufferings of change and the grief of not changing. The raw ferocity of Africa takes you by the throat and the complexity of trying to exist and bring up a family in such an environment is brilliantly evoked and humbling to read. But it is also a story about being a child, and the honesty dazzles.

Raffaella Barker, Author

Next?

Mukiwa by Peter Godwin is another intriguing memoir about living in Africa.

Chanda's Secrets (UTBG 63) by Allan Stratton is also about growing up in an Africa torn apart by disease, and the importance of allowing the processes of change to take place.

A Long Walk to Freedom is the memoir of Nelson Mandela, one of the people who made change happen in South Africa.

DR. JEKYLL AND MR. HYDE

Robert Louis Stevenson

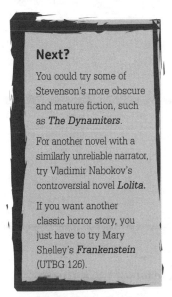

Next?

You could try some of Stevenson's more obscure and mature fiction, such as *The Dynamiters*.

For another novel with a similarly unreliable narrator, try Vladimir Nabokov's controversial novel *Lolita*.

If you want another classic horror story, you just have to try Mary Shelley's *Frankenstein* (UTBG 126).

This short novel is a very sophisticated story, but it drips with the darkness to be found in the best of Stevenson's writing.

Piece by piece unfolds the story of Dr. Jekyll, a respectable London medical man, and Mr. Hyde, an unsettling and plainly evil man who seems to have become an acquaintance of the doctor's, much to the horror of his friends. You may already know the secret of the connection between the two men because this story became so famous, but if you do not, then you are lucky enough to get to read this story as its Victorian audience would have done. To contemporary reviewers the book was weird and shocking, and I think it still is, as it speaks of the potentially horrific nature of humankind, as well as its more noble aspects.

Marcus Sedgwick, Author

DETECTIVE STORIES

by K. K. Beck

There are many reasons to read detective novels. First of all, you are pretty much guaranteed that things will happen and the plot will move along. That's because, with very few exceptions, a crime has already been, or is about to be, committed and must be solved. So the characters cannot just sit around. They are forced into action, which makes for a plot-driven, engaging read. And, because the criminals are still at large, and presumably don't want to be caught, the detectives are often in jeopardy as they go about their work. This means that the reader can enjoy the suspense of knowing the characters are in danger.

There's also something very satisfying about seeing a crime solved, getting everything properly resolved, and making sure the guilty are exposed and presumably punished. If only justice always prevailed in real life! Plus, the reader can detect along with the characters. In classic, old-school detective fiction, the clues are usually arranged hiding in plain sight. The author's goal in these kinds of books is to get the reader to say, "Of course! Why didn't I see that?!" Agatha Christie is famous for these sorts of stories. In *The Secret Adversary*, two friends who've recently returned to London from World War I start their own detective agency, trace a girl named Jane Finn who has disappeared with a packet of important government papers, and foil a plot to take over the world. Agatha Christie was also, of course, the creator of the great sleuths Miss Marple and Hercule Poirot. You can read more about them on p. 42 and p. 58.

There are all kinds of detectives, from amateurs who accidentally stumble onto a

Some teen spies:

The **Alex Rider** series by Anthony Horowitz

SilverFin by Charlie Higson

Artemis Fowl by Eoin Colfer

The Extraordinary Adventures of Alfred Kropp by Rick Yancey

Kiki Strike by Kirsten Miller

The Recruit by Robert Muchamore

The **Spy High** series by A. J. Butcher

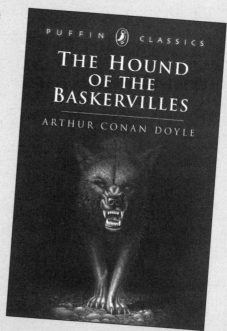

PUFFIN CLASSICS

THE HOUND OF THE BASKERVILLES

ARTHUR CONAN DOYLE

RAYMOND CHANDLER
The Big Sleep

"RAYMOND CHANDLER IS A MASTER." —THE NEW YORK TIMES

crime to hardened private eyes and police detectives. Because detective stories often feature the same detective in multiple books, after a little dabbling in the field it's easy to find the ones you know you'll enjoy. One of the first and best amateur detectives is Sir Arthur Conan Doyle's Sherlock Holmes. *A Study in Scarlet* is the first Holmes mystery, but you don't have to start there. Try *The Hound of the Baskervilles* (UTBG 319) or any of the 56 short stories. There's a reason Holmes and his sidekick, Dr. Watson, have lasted so long.

Detective novels can be hard-boiled—violent and action-packed tales of guns and gangsters. Think of Raymond Chandler's *The Big Sleep* (UTBG 34). They can be soft-boiled—gentle stories of pale corpses found neatly on the fireplace rug in the vicarage in a quiet village—like Dorothy L. Sayers's Lord Peter Wimsey books (UTBG 211). Or anything in between.

Detective novels can also take the reader on interesting journeys to exotic settings and different time periods. Some were written long in the past (traditionally, experts date the beginning of the form back to 1841 and Edgar Allan Poe's short story "Murders in the Rue Morgue," featuring an eccentric Paris detective named Auguste Dupin). Many of those written more recently are set in historic periods; some of the best are Lindsey Davis's Falco stories (set in the year AD 79), which start with *The Silver Pigs*.

Many different sorts of books can fall under the banner of detective fiction. You could try *I'm Not Scared* (UTBG 174) by Niccolò Ammaniti, scary, gripping, and beautifully written; Mark Haddon's funny, moving, fascinating *The Curious Incident of the Dog in the Night-Time* (UTBG 82); the deliciously creepy *Strangers on a Train* (UTBG 341) by Patricia Highsmith; *The No. 1 Ladies' Detective Agency* (UTBG 245), the first book in Alexander McCall Smith's popular Precious Ramotswe series; or Lee Child's page-turner *Killing Floor*, which begins with drifter Jack Reacher suddenly being arrested for murder . . .

Some older, more hard-boiled (or lightly simmered) detectives:

52 Pickup by Elmore Leonard

Tourist Season by Carl Hiaasen

The Big Sleep by Raymond Chandler

The **87th Precinct** series by Ed McBain

One for the Money by Janet Evanovich

DRACULA Bram Stoker

Next?

More Gothic fiction? Try *Carmilla* by Sheridan Le Fanu or Stevenson's *Dr. Jekyll and Mr. Hyde* (UTBG 95).

The world of young adult literature abounds with great vampire stories: try Stephenie Meyer's *Twilight* (UTBG 369), Scott Westerfeld's *Peeps* (UTBG 267), or Elizabeth Kostova's *The Historian* (UTBG 154).

Or what about a Gothic parody in Jane Austen's *Northanger Abbey* (UTBG 247)?

Bram Stoker wrote many novels and short stories, but he is best known for one extraordinary book, which, if not actually originating a genre, has become the undisputed foundation of not just vampire fiction but the gothic genre in general.

I won't waste time expounding the intricacies of the plot here, but simply implore you to forget almost any film version you may have seen (with the possible exception of 1922's *Nosferatu*) and delight in discovering the slow beauty of the original book. Quite adventurous stylistically for its time, it uses several different narratives which weave together to create a momentum that by the end of the book is simply unstoppable. A true masterpiece.

Marcus Sedgwick, Author

THE DRAGONRIDERS OF PERN series
Anne McCaffrey

The first three books about the planet Pern tell the story of the huge, fire-breathing dragons who defend their world against the periodic fall of deadly spores from a neighboring planet. But dragons cannot do this alone—riders have to guide them in battle. As soon as they hatch, the green, blue, brown, and bronze dragonets bond with boys, and the golden queens with girls, to become their lifelong soulmates. Lessa, one of the Dragonriders, impresses Ramoth, the last surviving queen, and together they risk everything to save their planet. By the third book, Jaxom, the boy lord of Ruatha, accidentally impresses a small, unique white dragon with extraordinary abilities who is destined to help Pern in a way no one dreams possible.

Gill Vickery, Author

Next?

Anne McCaffrey has worked out the science of Pern (an acronym of Planet Earthlike Resources Negligible) so if you like hard-science sci-fi, you will enjoy reading about the colonizing of the planet and the creation of dragons from the native fire lizards in *Dragonsdawn*.

Try **The Black Magician** trilogy (UTBG 39) by Trudi Canavan, or, for a new take on the dragon book, Jessica Day George's *Dragon Slippers*.

DRAMARAMA E. Lockhart

You don't have to adore gold lamé or even musicals to fall in love with E. Lockhart's novel *Dramarama*. All you have to do to fall in love with the story of big-boned, straight, theater girl Sarah/Sadye and her best friend—super-fine, gay, theater guy Demi—is to pick up the book and read. Within minutes you're hooked for good.

In the beginning of the book Sarah decides she needs to jazz herself up a bit. She cuts her hair. She goes more razzle-dazzle. She becomes Sadye. She ends up at theater camp, hoping to finally fit in, hoping to finally fight the loneliness. She does. Sort of.

Demi begins to shine, shine, shine and Sadye becomes chorus material. So what does this do to their new friendship? That's where the good stuff really comes in. E. Lockhart delivers the truths of friendships and relationships with humor, poignancy, and some funky Sadye riffs that will have you standing up, stomping your feet, and screaming ENCORE before you even finish the last page. Trust me. It's just that good.

Emily Ciciotte, age 13

Next?

If you loved E. Lockhart's writing, try her popular *The Boyfriend List* (UTBG 48), about a girl who must relive all of her painful crushes when she lands in a shrink's office.

For more dramatic books about high school plays, try *Fame, Glory, and Other Things on My To Do List* by Janette Rallison and *No More Dead Dogs* (UTBG 246) by Gordon Korman.

Laurie Halse Anderson's *Prom* is similarly funny and heartfelt, but it centers around the drama of a high school prom gone wrong.

Don't miss E. Lockhart's feature on love and relationships on pp. 162–163.

OUT IN THE COUNTRY

Dairy Queen by Catherine Gilbert Murdock

Walk Two Moons by Sharon Creech

Hattie Big Sky by Kirby Larson

Out of the Dust by Karen Hesse

A Long Way from Chicago by Richard Peck

When Zachary Beaver Came to Town by Kimberly Willis Holt

The Chicken Dance by Jacques Couvillon

DRUMS, GIRLS & DANGEROUS PIE

Jordan Sonnenblick

In Steven's eyes, everything about his life is just plain normal. He lives with his parents and his slightly annoying younger brother, Jeffrey. He attends school every day where the hottest girl in the eighth grade continues to ignore him. He plays drums in the All-City jazz band and feels best when he's holding his special set of sticks. Then Jeffrey is diagnosed with leukemia, and things are suddenly not normal.

Steven's hysterically funny commentary takes us through the ups and downs of Jeffrey's diagnosis and treatment, as his family struggles to hold on. This is not a typical book about cancer—you will laugh out loud repeatedly, probably while the tears are still drying on your cheeks (if you're the type who cries). In the end, Steven shows that no matter how difficult the situation, a bit of humor and a lot of kindness can go further than anyone ever imagined.

Mary Kate Castellani, Editor

Next?

Jordan Sonnenblick's second novel, *Notes from the Midnight Driver*, is another perfect blend of humor and real life.

Try Daniel Ehrenhaft's *Drawing a Blank* for a similar story about a teen whose sense of humor gets him by in life.

King Dork (UTBG 194) by Frank Portman is an edgier read about a teen boy who wants to learn more about his dead father.

DUNE Frank Herbert

Next?

Any of the *Dune* sequels—there are six books in total.

Robert Heinlein's *Stranger in a Strange Land* is a classic science-fiction epic that calls into question both religious and political beliefs.

Ursula K. Le Guin's *The Dispossessed* contrasts the stories of two planets, each with political and ecological problems to solve.

Dune is a desert planet inhabited by enormous sandworms that produce a mind-altering substance called "melange." This and water are the most precious commodities. The story describes the battle for supremacy between the Atreides family and their enemies, most notably the fantastically spooky Bene Gesserit sisterhood, which is dedicated to harnessing the pure power of thought and thus dispensing with science and technology. But it becomes clear that in the course of learning to control their environment and their own fateful vulnerability, the inhabitants cannot do without either technology or mysticism.

If you love traveling in alien worlds, then this book is a must—a science-fiction epic of grandeur and complexity, realized in intricate detail.

Livi Michael, Author

DUSK Susan Gates

Curtis is a lab assistant at a secret military research base. There's one door he isn't allowed to enter—behind this door is a creature who shrieks and cries, who eats microwave-defrosted mice, and who can demand dinner in a little girl's voice. Behind this door is Dusk. Only once does Curtis dare to break the rules—but once is enough, because when the door is opened, things spiral beyond anyone's control. Dusk's terrifying existence is powerfully described as this fast-paced sci-fi novel explores the boundaries between human and animal and the ethics of genetic engineering.

Noga Applebaum, Academic

Next?

Eva by Peter Dickinson also examines the relationship between humans and animals, through the eyes of a girl whose brain has been transplanted into a chimp's body.

The ethics of cloning are explored in *The House of the Scorpion* (UTBG 164) by Nancy Farmer and *Sharp North* (UTBG 316) by Patrick Cave.

Two more books that explore the issues of genetic engineering are H. G. Wells's *The Island of Dr. Moreau* or Kate Thompson's **The Missing Link** trilogy.

THE EARTH, MY BUTT, AND OTHER BIG ROUND THINGS Carolyn Mackler

I confess: Carolyn Mackler is a close friend of mine. But our friendship does not preclude me from writing an unbiased rave of *The Earth, My Butt, and Other Big Round Things*. See, I wasn't her friend when I first read it. But after meeting Virginia Shreves—follower of the Fat Girl Code of Conduct and self-proclaimed –3 on the Popular (+10) to Dorky (–10) scale—I was determined to become friends with her creator. Anyone who backs up that hilarious title with an opening sentence like, "Froggy Welsh the Fourth is trying to get up my shirt" is a person I want to hang with.

But this novel isn't just for laughs—though there are many. Virginia copes with the insecurities and identity crises *all* teens suffer through—no matter where they fall on the Popular to Dorky scale. But when her family life gets messy in a very unexpected way, Virginia's resilience makes her a heroine worth looking up to. You may not be as lucky as I am to have befriended Carolyn, but getting to know Virginia Shreves is the next best thing.

Megan McCafferty, Author

Next?

If you like Carolyn Mackler's writing, you shouldn't miss her other novels: *Love and Other Four-Letter Words* and *Vegan Virgin Valentine*.

Other books that explore the plight of overweight narrators are Julia Bell's *Massive* (UTBG 220) and *Big Fat Manifesto* by Susan Vaught.

EAST Edith Pattou

12+

Remember when you were a child and your parents read you fairy tales? Fairy tales come from all over the world, and many stories are basically the same though they are told in different countries. *East* is a retelling of the Scandinavian folktale *East of the Sun and West of the Moon*. To save her family from further hardship, Rose agrees to go with the white bear when he comes to ask for her. He takes her to a beautiful castle, where she has everything she could want but she cannot leave. The story is related from five different points of view: Rose (the main character), Neddy (her brother), the white bear (the enchanted character), the Troll Queen (the enchantress), and Father (Rose and Neddy's father). Each point of view gives the reader a different look at the tale and completes the enchanted picture Pattou paints.

Deborah Nicholl, Librarian

Next?

If you enjoy reading retold fairy tales, you should try the books of Shannon Hale or Donna Jo Napoli. Start with Hale's *The Goose Girl* (UTBG 140) or Napoli's *Bound* (UTBG 45).

For another take on the same Scandinavian folktale, try *Sun and Moon, Ice and Snow* by Jessica Day George.

THE ECLIPSE OF THE CENTURY Jan Mark

 14+

Next?

Another Jan Mark? Try *Useful Idiots* (UTBG 372), about a world where the seas have risen and what's left of civilization is a dystopian nightmare.

Douglas Coupland's *Girlfriend in a Coma* is another novel dealing with the (possible) end of the world.

Or try *The Blue Hawk* by Peter Dickinson, about a world controlled by priests and a boy who commits sacrilege.

Keith's near-death experience brings him not to the gates of heaven but to Qantoum, a city in "the armpit of Asia," which has been all but forgotten by the rest of the world. After his recovery, he finds himself taking part in an extraordinary drama that is destined to conclude "beneath a black sun, at the end of a thousand years."

A must-read for anyone 14 and up who is interested in imaginative fiction. This book reaches the parts of the mind that other books don't. Reading it is like participating in a vivid dream and, as though the dream were your own, the characters and events will remain with you for a long, long time.

Kate Thompson, Author

ELLA ENCHANTED Gail Carson Levine

Next?

Gail Carson Levine has written many other fairy tale-themed novels; try *Fairest* (UTBG 111) or *The Two Princesses of Bamarre* next.

If you want to write fiction just like Gail Carson Levine's, her writing manual for teens, *Writing Magic*, is a must-read.

Try *The Goose Girl* (UTBG 140) by Shannon Hale for another rich novel based on a fairy tale.

Ella Enchanted is about a girl named Ella who is cursed by her aunt. Ella's curse is the gift of "obedience"—she has to do everything she is told to do. Then, she falls in love with a prince named Char. Char's uncle is trying to kill him in order to keep the throne. For the first time, Ella finds that she has to try to do something different from what she is being told to do, because of her love for Char. Can Ella fight against the spell and get rid of it for good?

I felt so bad for Ella because she would try so hard to be herself, but she couldn't because every time someone told her to do something, she would have to do it. I really liked *Ella Enchanted* because Ella's enchantment was kind of like peer pressure. A lot of people give in to peer pressure. So in a way, Ella is kind of like us.

Caitlin Mohwinkel, age 16

ELSEWHERE Gabrielle Zevin

While crossing the road (and not looking both ways), Liz is hit by a car. She is now dead. *Elsewhere* is the story—in her words—of what happens next.

I can't count the number of stories I've read that have been narrated from beyond the grave. Dozens, probably. But this one is special. This is not like any book I've ever read. The world beyond death is so well imagined and so consistent it feels totally realistic—which is a strange thing to say about a book about the afterlife, I know. But that's how it is—the dreamlike elements of the tale are blended with what feels like absolute reality and clarity; and throughout, Zevin's writing is impeccable.

Elsewhere is full of character and warmth; it's a book about death, but more than that it's about life. It's an uplifting story about how Liz lives hers, and about how to live yours, too.

Daniel Hahn, Editor

Next?

Of the various other beyond-the-grave stories, I'm a fan of Alex Shearer's *The Great Blue Yonder*, too.

Toward the end of *Elsewhere*, Owen reads to Liz from *Tuck Everlasting* by Natalie Babbitt, another beautiful tale of endless life. Try it.

The best companion to *Elsewhere* would probably be Alice Sebold's *The Lovely Bones* (UTBG 213), which also follows a little girl into the afterlife.

EMPIRE OF THE SUN J. G. Ballard

14+

Next?

Some of the most powerful books about war are memoirs, such as *The Diary of a Young Girl* (UTBG 91) by Anne Frank and Livia Bitton-Jackson's *I Have Lived for a Thousand Years*.

Try James Bradley's *Flags of Our Fathers* (UTBG 119) for a gritty account of the atrocities of the Battle of Iwo Jima in Japan.

Wild Swans (UTBG 391) by Jung Chang tells of one family's struggle to live through China's recent history.

In 1942, at the age of 12, J. G. Ballard was interned in a Japanese prisoner-of-war camp in Shanghai. This powerful, moving novel is based on his own experiences and gives us a real insight into the horrors of war. Jim, the 11-year-old narrator, is separated from his parents when the Japanese invade Shanghai, and he spends weeks living alone until he is captured. Over the next four years, malnutrition, violence, and death become everyday facts of life to Jim, whose survival instinct draws him into a kind of rapport with his Japanese guards whom, despite their cruelty, he admires for keeping the inmates secure from the chaos outside. Jim's incomprehension of war, plus his utter determination to survive and be reunited with his parents, makes for an unforgettable piece of writing.

Malachy Doyle, Author

ENDER'S GAME Orson Scott Card

12+

Set in the not-so-distant future, a group of children and teenagers are being trained in Battle School to fight an extraterrestrial race of insectlike beings. Each child is specially chosen: they are the brightest in the world, they are the most adaptable; together, working in teams, the army commanders believe that they will come up with new ways of fighting that no adult could ever conceive.

And they do—or rather, Ender does. Ender Wiggin. This is the story of his personal struggle, put under constant, relentless pressure, to become the next military commander. It is a striking book, believable, full of thrilling battles, unusual aliens, and well-crafted characters—but in the end what you remember is Ender. You'll grow to love Ender Wiggin.

Cliff McNish, Author

Next?

You can go straight on to the sequel, *Speaker for the Dead*. Or, if you can't bear to leave the Battle School (like me), read about them all over again, but from the perspective of the character Bean, in *Ender's Shadow*.

Or what about being a cadet on an airship? Try Kenneth Oppel's *Airborn* (UTBG 7).

ERAGON Christopher Paolini

12+

A hunter, quietly creeping through the undergrowth. A boy, orphaned when only a baby. Eragon, the dragon rider, legacy of a legend.

Christopher Paolini has successfully woven a beautiful tale of such magic and wonder it makes readers hurry frantically to the last pages. The touching story of Eragon, a young farm boy whose life is drastically changed the day he finds a dragon's egg, has enticed many people to pick it up so that they too can be part of the intimate bond between boy and dragon. Paolini takes readers far away to his mysterious world of Alagaësia, where the land's future lies heavily on the shoulders of a young boy, and follows his quest as he makes new friends and encounters new dangers.

I would recommend this book to anyone who enjoys a good read that they can curl up with and be transported to a whole different universe.

Shazia Mirza, age 15

Next?

If you enjoyed *Eragon*, the next book in the **Inheritance** trilogy is *Eldest*.

Also try *The Cry of the Icemark* (UTBG 80) by Stuart Hill.

Another great series of (very different!) dragon books starts with Chris d'Lacey's *The Fire Within*.

THE #1 NEW YORK TIMES BESTSELLER

ERAGON
Christopher Paolini

Eragon is the first part of the Inheritance trilogy. It follows the tale of a boy, Eragon, who discovers a dragon's egg near his home. When strange figures come to look for the newly hatched dragon, his home is destroyed and he embarks on a quest to seek revenge and discover his heritage as a mythical dragon rider. Along the way he befriends Brom the storyteller, magical elves, and the mysterious Murtagh.

Eragon is very fast-paced, without a single boring moment. It is well written, and emotions are wonderfully conveyed. *Eragon*'s world of Alagaësia is described so well that it seems almost real.

Eleanor Milnes-Smith, age 13

ETHAN FROME Edith Wharton

16+

Next?

Read Wharton's *Summer*—she nicknamed it "Hot Ethan." Her very different, but equally powerful, novel of repressed sexuality is *The Age of Innocence*.

Another excellent short novel set in 19th-century America is Henry James's *Washington Square*.

There are many wonderful tragic love stories out there; try Gustave Flaubert's *Madame Bovary*.

This little book is one of the saddest love stories you'll ever read. Ethan, a lonely farmer in 19th-century Massachusetts, has married his older cousin Zena for company. But she has quickly turned into a miserable, complaining hypochondriac.

When a young woman, Mattie Silver, comes to live with them, Ethan finds himself fascinated by her energy and joyfulness. A kind, inarticulate man, he hardly admits to himself his real feelings for Mattie, as he walks her home from a dance through starlit snows. Chance allows them one night together in the isolated farmhouse.

It's a passionate love story. We know from the outset it will end tragically, but the cruel twist will still take you by surprise.

Jane Darcy, Teacher

ETHEL & ERNEST Raymond Briggs

12+

This is Raymond Briggs's beautiful, candid, and moving illustrated account of his parents' married life. Ernest, a milkman, brazenly courts Ethel, a lady's maid. They marry in 1930 and stay together in the same house until they die within months of each other in 1971.

As well as a loving biography, the book is an illustrated social history of what used to be called The Respectable Working Class in Great Britain. During this middle span of the 20th century, the clothesline in the backyard gives way to the laundromat, the bike gives way to the car, Hitler and Stalin come and go, ordinary people acquire telephones and television, the Welfare State is born. And so (with difficulty) is Raymond, who later horrifies his parents by going off to art school. ("That lot's all long hair, drink and nude women," Ernest tells Ethel, wistfully.) There's nothing rose-tinted here. Briggs doesn't flinch from relating and drawing his parents' deaths, either, and it makes you gasp.

Mal Peet, Author

Next?

Search out all of Raymond Briggs's books, from the altogether gross *Fungus the Bogeyman* to the pathos of *The Snowman*. Read them and weep—from sadness or laughter.

If you learn anything from *Ethel & Ernest*, it's that even the most ordinary people are extraordinary. Read Craig Thompson's illustrated memoir *Blankets* (UTBG 40) for another "ordinary" story of growing up that will leave you feeling anything but.

EXILE AND THE KINGDOM Albert Camus

16+

I read four of Camus's novels in my late teens, plus the six stories in this slim volume. I found the novels a little hard going, but I really liked these stories. As a fairly unworldly guy struggling to write my first serious fiction, I was impressed by the directness of the language (albeit in translation from the French). I found the writing crisp and clean, never fussy. Every word seemed to count, and there was a feeling of detachment that appealed to me. You got the impression (well, I did) that if one of the characters died, the author would not be among the mourners. But if you want a taste of genuinely good writing, give *Exile and the Kingdom* a try.

Michael Lawrence, Author

> ## Next?
>
> The most accessible of Camus's novels is *The Outsider* (UTBG 263).
>
> For unfussy writing in short stories, Raymond Carver is best of all. Check out *Where I'm Calling From*.
>
> Franz Kafka also has a fondness for writing rather bleak stories; try *Metamorphosis and Other Stories*.

EXODUS Julie Bertagna

14+

> ## Next?
>
> *Useful Idiots* (UTBG 372) by Jan Mark also takes place in a futuristic drowned world.
>
> *Watership Down* (UTBG 382) by Richard Adams describes another kind of community looking for a safe haven, only this time they are wild rabbits!
>
> *Life as We Knew It* (UTBG 203) by Susan Beth Pfeffer is another chilling story about the consequences of environmental change.

2099—the ice caps have melted due to environmental damage and Britain is covered in water. Mara watches as the waters slowly rise around Wing, her island home, threatening to swallow everything she has ever known. Cooped up due to violent storms, Mara escapes into the Weave, a virtual-reality cyberspace, now in ruins as civilization has disintegrated and communities have lost touch. A chance virtual encounter sends Mara's community on a treacherous journey to find shelter in New Mungo, a sky-city erected on the site of today's Glasgow; they are unaware of the cruel fate that awaits them there.

This fascinating futuristic sci-fi quest-adventure raises crucial questions about the consequences of the way we live our lives today.

Noga Applebaum, Academic

THE EYRE AFFAIR Jasper Fforde

16+

When the publishers came to publicizing this, Jasper Fforde's first book, they didn't spend their money on advertising. They just sent out free copies saying "READ IT." So how can I hope to describe it if they couldn't?

Well, if you're into literature you'll get the joke. Picture "grammarcites" that eat the punctuation out of sentences. Picture Heathcliff from *Wuthering Heights* meeting Miss Havisham from *Great Expectations* at an anger-management session. Picture Jane Eyre kidnapped out of *Jane Eyre*. Picture knitting narrative loopholes. Picture critical analysis of *The Flopsy Bunnies*, quotes from nonexistent books, and Prose Portals that let fugitives hide out inside *Hamlet*. It's Douglas-Adams-meets-*Pagemaster*. It defies the laws of time, place, probability, boredom, and sanity. Oh, and it's sort of an ongoing crime novel with a great heroine. Beyond all that, all I can say is "READ IT."
Geraldine McCaughrean, Author

Next?

The **Thursday Next** series continues with *Lost in a Good Book*.

Is Heathcliff a Murderer? by John Sutherland is literary detection—this time for real.

More irreverent humor can be found in *Good Omens* (UTBG 139) by Terry Pratchett and Neil Gaiman, where the target is religion.

For another irreverent look at classical literature, try Shannon Hale's *Austenland,* in which a woman goes to a retreat for Jane Austen lovers.

FACE Benjamin Zephaniah

14+

Next?

Benjamin Zephaniah has written several hard-hitting books that deal with real-life situations. Check out *Gangsta Rap* and *Refugee Boy* (UTBG 289).

For a book that explores racism in an imaginative and surprising way, try Malorie Blackman's *Noughts & Crosses* (UTBG 252).

Finally, for the best book I know about being different, you have to read Rodman Philbrick's *Freak the Mighty* (UTBG 127).

This is the story of a teenage boy named Martin Turner. After a night out, Martin and his friends are walking home when two older boys offer them a ride. The fateful journey ends in disaster. The police chase them and the car overturns and catches fire. Martin is taken to the hospital with serious facial burns.

The book goes on to tell how people deal with Martin's disfigurement. Life moves on and Martin forges new friendships and goals.

This book is very realistic, and I think we can all relate to the characters. I have certainly gained sympathy for people who suffer any injuries, and I think I am a better human being for having read it. I couldn't put this book down.
Jamie Caplan, age 11

THE FACE ON THE MILK CARTON

Caroline B. Cooney

The moment 15-year-old Janie Johnson sees the face of a missing child on a milk carton, her idyllic life comes to a screeching halt. She knows the face of that little girl. It is her own. Janie struggles to accept the shocking truth, that she was kidnapped twelve years earlier. Fragmented, shadowy memories of her early childhood begin to emerge. Could her loving parents have abducted her from someone else? Is she Janie Johnson or Jennie Spring, the name given on the milk carton? Determined to find out about her hidden past, Janie decides to search for answers.

What follows is a suspenseful tale full of complex issues of identity, trust, and family. Janie's emotions are believable and well written. The relationship between her and her boyfriend, Reeve, is both touching and awkward, an honest portrait of teen romance. This fast-paced and thought-provoking book is the perfect choice for any reader.

Debbie Reed Fischer, Author

Next?

If you enjoyed *The Face on the Milk Carton*, check out the companion books, **Whatever Happened to Janie?**, **The Voice on the Radio**, and **What Janie Found**.

If you like mysteries, try Carol Plum-Ucci's **The Body of Christopher Creed** (UTBG 43).

Another novel that explores a girl's unknown biological past is Dana Reinhardt's **A Brief Chapter in My Impossible Life**.

FAERIE WARS Herbie Brennan

Next?

For more adventures with Henry and the world of the Faerie Realm, try the next three books in the **Faerie Wars Chronicles**: *The Purple Emperor*, *Ruler of the Realm*, and *Faerie Lord*.

Holly Black's *Tithe* (UTBG 359) is another fast-paced fantasy that takes place in the world of faeries.

Artemis Fowl (UTBG 24) by Eoin Colfer blends the same kind of high fantasy but weaves in a good amount of humor, too.

Believing is what gets Henry Atherton into a huge mess with his boss, Mr. Fogarty. A very simple thing—the emergence of a butterfly—is what happens, but a closer look reveals a secret that some believe in and others just think is an old faerie tale. At first, Henry's world starts to fall apart, then slowly, as the tale goes on, he finds a stable landing to stand on and learns to deal with his life. He also finds true friends in the process.

Ever believed in the unbelievable—something that no one but you thought was true? That, and trying to save what you have just started to love with all of your heart, is what the high fantasy *Faerie Wars*, the first in a series by Herbie Brennan, is all about.

Amber Lyon, age 16

FAHRENHEIT 451 Ray Bradbury

This is the story of a world where books are forbidden, a world where free thought is firmly discouraged, where people feel closer to television characters than to their spouses or children or friends. It's a world where firemen like Guy Montag aren't employed to put out fires but to start them—to track down people who have secretly been hoarding books and then to burn down their houses. All for the public good, of course.

This is no fantasy world, though, but our own, some years in the future. *Fahrenheit 451* takes a chilling look at where we might be going, and it does so with imagination and momentum and often-brilliant writing. Bradbury has said that he writes "at the top of my lungs"—and in this book you can't help but listen to his warning.

Daniel Hahn, Editor

Next?

Classic dystopian novels include *Brave New World* (UTBG 49) by Aldous Huxley and *Nineteen Eighty-Four* (UTBG 244) by George Orwell , another tale of a man standing up against the system.

If you like Bradbury, try his magical *Dandelion Wine* (UTBG 85).

Or try reading about the formative years of a real revolutionary hero in Ernesto "Che" Guevara's *The Motorcycle Diaries* (UTBG 233).

The Ultimate Teen Readers' Poll

CHARACTER MOST LIKE YOU

1 Harry Potter (The Harry Potter series)

2 Hermione Granger (The Harry Potter series)

3 Ellie (Girls in Love series)

4 Alex Rider (The Alex Rider Series)

5 Ron Weasley (The Harry Potter series)

6 Darren Shan (The Saga of Darren Shan)

7 Lena (The Sisterhood of the Traveling Pants series)

8 Klaus Baudelaire (A Series of Unfortunate Events)

9 Tibby (The Sisterhood of the Traveling Pants series)

10 Jessica Darling (*Sloppy Firsts*)

FAIREST Gail Carson Levine

Aza knows two things about herself: she has a beautiful singing voice, and she is the ugliest person she knows. In the kingdom of Ayortha, a good voice is highly respected. Aza has another, secret talent: she can make anyone or anything sound like it's singing beautifully, a unique skill she names "illusing."

At first, Aza can't believe her luck when she becomes lady-in-waiting to Ivi, the king's new wife—but then the queen discovers her talent. To impress (and deceive) her new husband and his people, Ivi demands that Aza illuse for her. The one bright spot is her friendship with the king's nephew, Prince Ijori. When Ivi brings the kingdom to the brink of revolt, Aza is forced to flee. During her exile she learns some very surprising truths about herself.

This enthralling, charming Snow White retelling is set a few kingdoms over from *Ella Enchanted*. Aza's self-loathing and her struggle with concepts of beauty ring true, and the ending is very satisfying without falling into the syrupy. Highly recommended for fans of fairy-tale retellings.

Alicia Anderson, Librarian

> **Next?**
>
> If you haven't read *Ella Enchanted* (UTBG 103) by Levine, that's a must.
>
> *Bella at Midnight* by Diane Stanley is not based on one particular fairy tale, but it feels just like one.
>
> Or if you like the intrigue, politics, and romance of the royal court, try *Crown Duel* by Sherwood Smith.

FALLEN ANGELS Walter Dean Myers

> **Next?**
>
> *Sammy and Juliana in Hollywood* (UTBG 301) by Benjamin Alire Sáenz is about a young man living in Hollywood, New Mexico, during the Vietnam War era.
>
> *Full Service* by Will Weaver gives us a look into life in the Midwest, and into all kinds of beliefs regarding our involvement in Vietnam.
>
> *Habibi* (UTBG 144) by Naomi Shihab Nye reveals the violence and peaceful hope of teens living in Jerusalem.

Perry questions whether enlisting and getting flown off to Vietnam was actually a good idea. He left behind his broken dreams of becoming a basketball star, along with his troubled mother and younger brother in New York, to find a situation that is much, much worse than he imagined.

Myers creates a story of brotherhood and the harsh realities of war. His cast of characters fights and jokes with one another and dreams of returning home. You will laugh at Peewee's wisecracking and be brought back to the core of the story when soldiers are in danger and sometimes die.

Will Perry make it through Vietnam? Will he get back home to his family in New York? Read this book and find out!

Kathy Fredrickson, Librarian

FAR FROM THE MADDING CROWD

Thomas Hardy

Bathsheba Everdene was one of the first romantic heroines of my teenage years. Beautiful, self-possessed, clever, independent—and somehow both grown-up and still growing up. The story follows Bathsheba as she makes choices (plenty of which she gets wrong) about how to live her life. While her story is not short of suffering, compared to many other Hardy novels it is a load of laughs, and it has all the advantages of a fantastic costume drama combined with the perennial dilemma of how to find Mr. Right—or whether such a thing as "Mr. Right" really exists.

Philippa Milnes-Smith, Literary Agent

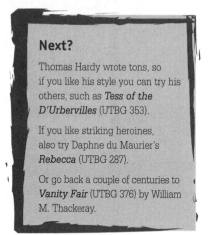

Next?

Thomas Hardy wrote tons, so if you like his style you can try his others, such as *Tess of the D'Urbervilles* (UTBG 353).

If you like striking heroines, also try Daphne du Maurier's *Rebecca* (UTBG 287).

Or go back a couple of centuries to *Vanity Fair* (UTBG 376) by William M. Thackeray.

THE FARSEER trilogy Robin Hobb

Do you want books you can immerse yourself in? Where the created world is so perfect, so real, that you feel you are there, breathing the strange scents, walking in distant alleyways? Then look no further than these amazing books.

Fitz is the bastard son of a prince. He grows up with nothing. Apprenticed to the king's master spy and assassin, Fitz can kill in hundreds of ways and is an adept spy. He also learns (sometimes painfully) about his own magic: the Skill that comes from his father, and the Wit, a forbidden and reviled beast-magic.

With only two friends—a Wolf, Night-eyes, who he is Wit-bonded to, and the strange boy who is the king's fool—Fitz has to survive. He must, for fate has plans for him—plans that will lead him into desperate danger.

Leonie Flynn, Editor

Next?

This trilogy consists of *Assassin's Apprentice*, *Royal Assassin*, and *Assassin's Quest*. There is a further sequence, the **Tawny Man** trilogy.

If you find Robin Hobb addictive, there is another series set in the same world, with some of the same characters: the **Liveship Traders** trilogy.

Another epic that feels real is Frank Herbert's *Dune* (UTBG 100) and its sequels.

FAST FOOD NATION Eric Schlosser

When I was in college, a friend and I watched the documentary *Super Size Me*, in which the filmmaker ate nothing but McDonald's for a month. At the end of the movie, my friend said, "I could really go for a Big Mac right now."

She might have felt differently had she read award-winning journalist Eric Schlosser's exposé, *Fast Food Nation*, which could make even the most ardent fast-food fanatic think twice. From the slaughterhouses run by giant corporations to the counters with inhumanely treated employees to the chemistry labs where flavors are engineered, each detail is more shocking than the last.

Cholesterol or calories may not be on your radar yet, but when junk food isn't just fattening but a detriment to your mood, your values, and ultimately your life, it's time to think twice. *Fast Food Nation* is an important read for anyone who's ever been affected by the fast-food industry—and according to Eric Schlosser, that's everyone.

Stacy Cantor, Editor

> ### Next?
>
> Another shocking exposé, Barbara Ehrenreich's *Nickel and Dimed* is a compelling example of how hard it can be to break out of poverty in America.
>
> The original meatpacking industry exposé, Upton Sinclair's *The Jungle*, should not be missed.
>
> Eric Schlosser's next book, *Reefer Madness*, is about America's underground drug trade.

FAT BOY SWIM Catherine Forde

> ### Next?
>
> *Dark Waters* by Catherine MacPhail is another read set in Scotland, and it's a gritty thriller.
>
> *Girls Under Pressure* by Jacqueline Wilson tackles weight issues seen from a female perspective, as does *Big Fat Manifesto* by Susan Vaught.
>
> The hero of Kevin Brooks's *Kissing the Rain* (UTBG 195) is another boy bullied for being heavy.

"Fatso" Jimmy Kelly is endlessly bullied because of his size, he's useless at gym, and school is a nightmare. But at home, in the kitchen, he can really shine, with his enviable talent for creating truly fantastic food.

Over the summer, however, things change for Jimmy in all sorts of ways. Being forced into serious swimming leads to self-discovery, plus the unearthing of family secrets. There's the challenge of the Swimathon. And he gets together with Ellie. It's an absorbing tale with totally believable characters, and the turmoil of Jimmy's life is beautifully depicted. For anyone whose heart sinks at the thought of gym class, the first chapter captures to perfection the horror of school soccer while the descriptions of Jimmy's cooking will have you drooling and desperate to try some tablet, the Scottish version of fudge.

Nick Sharratt, Illustrator

FAT KID RULES THE WORLD

14+

K. L. Going

Have you ever felt alone in the world? That you are the one person who doesn't quite fit in? If the answer is yes, read this book. If the answer is no, read it anyway.

Troy knows he could never fit in. He is hugely, morbidly obese and thinks he has no real future. Just as he's about to throw himself in front of a train and save himself further pain, his life is saved by a homeless punk by the name of Curt McCrae. At first, Troy is in awe of the guitar genius, a legend at his school. Then, slowly, a strange and unstable friendship develops between the pair. Troy's life is about to change dramatically: Curt wants him to be the drummer in his new band! Great, except Troy can't play the drums.

This is a book for anyone who escapes reality through music. Read it, and be alone no more. Misfits unite!

Zoe Holder, age 16

Next?

For more by K. L. Going, try *Saint Iggy* (UTBG 300) or *The Liberation of Gabriel King*.

Freak the Mighty (UTBG 127) by Rodman Philbrick and *When Zachary Beaver Came to Town* (UTBG 387) by Kimberly Willis Holt also look at the unlikely friendship between two very different teens.

Or try *Staying Fat for Sarah Byrnes* (UTBG 338) by Chris Crutcher, about a teen and his disabled best friend.

Sure, K. L. Going's first novel features one of the darkest and funniest narrators in contemporary young-adult fiction—the extravagantly fat, copiously perspiring 16-year-old Troy Billings. But it is his friendship with gutter punk Curt that makes this novel one of my all-time favorites. Troy is a marine's son; Curt is seemingly no one's son. Troy is hugely fat; Curt "looks like a blond ferret." But really, they're perfect for each other: Curt needs a drummer, and Troy needs something to hit. Going writes about troubled guys in a way that isn't boring or didactic or false—and in the end, *Fat Kid* brilliantly evokes the salvific power of friendship and punk rock music.

John Green, Author

FATHERLAND   Robert Harris

14+

This is a rare thing, a thriller that makes you think. Set in 1964, in a world in which Germany won World War II and Hitler is still alive and celebrating his 75th birthday, it concerns Xavier March, a Berlin policeman who starts off investigating a murder and ends up uncovering a deep, dark secret that puts his life at risk.

Aside from the great plot, there's also all the detail of how life would be different: like if Prince Edward and Mrs. Simpson had become king and queen of England. Written in a taut, spare style, this is a true thriller. You need to keep reading to find out what's happening—and if March will survive.

Leonie Flynn, Editor

> ### Next?
>
> Robert Harris has a talent for taking the past and making it real. Try *Pompeii*, about the eruption of Vesuvius; or *Enigma*, about the code-breakers of Bletchley Park in the UK, who deciphered many difficult codes during World War II.
>
> Someone else who writes terrific thrillers is Dan Brown; try *The Da Vinci Code* (UTBG 83).
>
> Or try a thriller set in 1930s Berlin: Philip Kerr's *Berlin Noir* is bleak, dark, and very exciting.

FEATHER BOY   Nicky Singer

 12+

> ### Next?
>
> Another Nicky Singer? Try *The Innocent's Story* (UTBG 177).
>
> Other books about a journey of self-discovery are *The Shell House* (UTBG 318) by Linda Newbery and *Postcards from No Man's Land* (UTBG 273) by Aidan Chambers.
>
> For other stories about bullying, try *Kissing the Rain* (UTBG 195) by Kevin Brooks or *Fat Boy Swim* (UTBG 113) by Catherine Forde.

Robert Noble has a hard time at school; nicknamed Norbert Nobottle by his classmates, his chief tormentor is a boy named Niker who is full of the casual self-confidence that Robert lacks.

But Robert's life changes when he meets an old lady with a tragic past. She lost her son years back, when he fell out of the top window of their apartment. The old lady is dying, and on her request, Robert finds himself going back to the abandoned building where the disaster took place. This is the beginning of a journey that gives him a whole new sense of purpose—although ultimately he discovers that life does not always have simple answers.

Susan Reuben, Editor

FEED M. T. Anderson

Imagine a world in which everyone has a live Internet feed hard-wired into his or her brain, and is online all the time. The teenage hero of *Feed*, Titus, has grown up barraged with advertising, information, and e-mail chat that all come into his head with the speed of mental telepathy. He's completely content until the day he meets Violet, an eccentric girl who wonders what it might be like to live without the Feed. Her questions awaken in Titus a curiosity and intellect he never knew he had. But they both discover, with tragic consequences, that it's not so easy to free themselves. The novel is both science fiction and contemporary satire; it's a technological and environmental cautionary tale; it's a moving love story. It's told with astonishing energy and inventiveness, and it's nothing short of a masterpiece.

Kenneth Oppel, Author

Next?

Another M. T. Anderson? Try *Thirsty* (UTBG 356), about a boy who gets very thirsty—for blood.

For more futuristic worlds where technology rules, try Philip K. Dick's *The Minority Report*, Isaac Asimov's *I, Robot* (UTBG 171), or Ray Bradbury's *Fahrenheit 451* (UTBG 110).

Ned Vizzini's *Be More Chill* (UTBG 28) is a more lighthearted, humorous take on the technology-as-brain story.

FEVER PITCH Nick Hornby

Next?

More Nick Hornby? Try *Long Way Down* or *High Fidelity* (UTBG 152).

For great British soccer novels, try the superbly atmospheric, rainforest-based *Keeper* (UTBG 190) by Mal Peet.

Soccer players' memoirs include the autobiographical *David Beckham: My Side*, and *Off the Record* by Michael Owen. Both are very reader-friendly and each offers fascinating looks behind the scenes of today's world of soccer megastars.

When this book came out, I thought it had been specifically written for me! It tracks one man's life passage as seen through the prism of Arsenal, the British soccer club. Everything in his world is inexorably linked with the fortunes of his favorite team. For the soccer fan, it strikes a tremendously deep chord. For the non-soccer fan, it is a brilliant invitation inside the mind of an obsessive fan's allegiance to his club. It's funny, clever, thoughtful, and fresh.

Fever Pitch started a stampede of books that plot people's lives in tandem with their most cherished cultural icons, in sports, music, art, et al. But in my view, this one remains the original and best.

Jonny Zucker, Author

FIRE AND HEMLOCK Diana Wynne Jones

A photograph that 19-year-old student Polly has had since childhood now looks different from how she remembered: where are the horse and the figures that once ran among burning cornfields? Fragments of long-suppressed memories begin to force themselves into Polly's consciousness and she realizes that her recollection of the events of the past five years is false. The truth has something to do with an evil, ageless woman and a gifted musician, Tom Lynn, who was once the most important person in her life. How—and why—has she forgotten him? Polly searches for the truth in one of Diana Wynne Jones's most fiendishly complex plots.

Gill Vickery, Author

Next?

Another of Diana Wynne Jones's wonderful novels where memory plays tricks and time is turned upside-down is *Hexwood*.

If you like books based on myths and legends, try Catherine Fisher's novels: *The Lammas Field*, also based on the ballad of "Thomas the Rhymer," or *Corbenic* (UTBG 77), based on the legend of the Holy Grail.

Jennifer Donnelly's *A Northern Light* (UTBG 247) is another romantic mystery that involves a series of peculiar letters.

FIRE FROM HEAVEN Mary Renault

You think you have a dysfunctional family? Try Alexander's . . . His mom hates his dad (but has a thing for snakes), his dad hates his mom and has tons of girlfriends (no, Mom does not approve). Oh, and Alexander? He has ambitions. BIG ambitions (they didn't call him The Great for nothing!).

This is a true story. It tells of Alexander in all his godlike, insane glory, and of his lovers—both male and female. If you've ever thought that history is boring, read this. Here a legend steps off the page and becomes human: flawed, imperfect, yet utterly wonderful. In fact, be careful, because you might fall in love. I did.

Leonie Flynn, Editor

Next?

There are two sequels; next is *The Persian Boy*, Alexander's story told by Bagoas, a Persian eunuch who becomes his lover.

If you want to read a nonfiction account of Alexander the Great, try Robin Lane Fox's biography. Or Mary Renault's own book about him, *The Nature of Alexander*.

Or how about another great portrayal of history that makes it real? Try Robert Graves's *I, Claudius*.

THE FIRE-EATERS   David Almond

This memorable story starts with Bobby's first encounter with the fire-eater McNulty, on a particular Sunday in late summer 1962: "It was like my heart stopped beating and the world stopped turning." Bobby and his friends Ailsa (from a sea-coaling family), Daniel (newly moved to the area), and Joseph are living under the shadow of the Cuban missile crisis: World War III might start at any moment. The world is at the edge of the abyss. There are other scary things happening too: Bobby's dad, a shipyard worker, is sick, and Bobby is starting at a new preparatory school.

Darkness, inhumanity, and war threaten life and love and family throughout the story, and for me make this book seem particularly relevant now. As with Almond's other novels, the writing is beautifully honed and polished, and at the novel's heart, holding back the darkness, are strong, tender friendships and family bonds, and a sense that the world is truly an amazing place. Wonderful.
Julia Green, Author

Next?

Try David Almond's *Clay* (UTBG 73), about belief, friendship, and evil.

You might also like *Thursday's Child* (UTBG 358) by Sonya Hartnett, another extraordinary and original writer.

What about another book that shows how hope can triumph over the darkest of circumstances? Try Markus Zusak's *The Book Thief* (UTBG 44).

THE FIRM   John Grisham

Next?

For another fast-paced thriller by John Grisham, don't miss *The Runaway Jury* (UTBG 297) or *A Time to Kill*.

If you like quick, engrossing reads, try *The Da Vinci Code* (UTBG 83) by Dan Brown.

But if you're looking for another story with the law at its center, you should try Jodi Picoult's *Plain Truth*, about a woman defending a teenager who killed her newborn child.

The Firm is a book that exceeds all others of its kind. It's fast and relentless, and it puts you within the action until the very end. Mitch McDeere is in for the ride of his life when he joins the appealing Bendini, Lambert & Locke law firm. Straight out of Harvard Law, he is looking for the best job—and this seems like the one. Upon joining, Mitch thinks he's stumbled upon a great opportunity—the firm has presented him with a car and a house and paid off all of his loans. There has to be a catch, though. It turns out that the firm is run by the mob, and the FBI knows all about it. Mitch has become a puppet. Now it's up to Mitch—does he run? Does he take the money? No matter what, he must use his own wits if he wants to survive.
Sahil Goswami, age 15

THE FIRST PART LAST Angela Johnson

The last two things Bobby expects to hear in the same conversation are "Happy 16th Birthday!" and "I'm pregnant." But Nia, Bobby's girlfriend, has said those things and now everything's changed. Then, Nia is out of the picture and Bobby finds himself trying to juggle school and homework and his friends while caring for baby Feather on his own—it's just not what he ever imagined his life would be.

In "THEN" and "NOW" alternating chapters, Bobby's story unfolds—before and after Feather. A teenage pregnancy story with a twist, it puts a face on the teenage dad and his difficulties and triumphs. Johnson also breaks a stereotype or two along the way, portraying a young African American male who is a dedicated father and a hardworking student.

Kimberly Paone, Librarian

Next?

You'll want to read all of Angela Johnson's books, but make sure to check out *Heaven*—the sequel to *The First Part Last* (even though it was written first).

Another great teenage dad story is *Hanging on to Max* by Margaret Bechard. It has different choices and very different outcomes.

You might also want to try Connie Porter's *Imani All Mine*. This is a more traditional teenage pregnancy novel (it's about a teenage mom).

FLAGS OF OUR FATHERS James Bradley

Next?

In *Flyboys*, James Bradley investigates the experiences of eight pilots who were taken captive in Japan.

Check out *The Things They Carried* by Tim O'Brien for a harrowing look at the horrors of Vietnam.

For a fictional experience of an American family during World War II, try William Saroyan's *The Human Comedy*.

You've seen the photo in your history books and maybe even visited the memorial on a class trip. *Flags of Our Fathers* is the story behind the story of the iconic image of US Marines raising the American flag at the Battle of Iwo Jima during World War II. Focusing on the lives of the six men who planted the flag after storming the beach of that tiny Japanese island, this book is a blend of history and memoir that emphasizes the cold hard truth that "the real heros of Iwo Jima were the guys who didn't come back."

From the first page, the raw emotion of this book will suck you in as the author explains why he decided to research this one moment in history. His own father was one of the six marines, and it was only after his death that Bradley started to learn about his father's experience at Iwo Jima. Although it might be easier to watch one of the many World War II movies, the fascinating details in this powerful book make it worth every minute you spend with it.

Mary Kate Castellani, Editor

FLESHMARKET Nicola Morgan

14+

Next?

Robert Louis Stevenson's classic *Dr. Jekyll and Mr. Hyde* (UTBG 95) is a more difficult read but equally rewarding.

Then try Julie Hearn's *Follow Me Down*, an extraordinary time-travel novel.

For more historical fiction where siblings must struggle to survive, try Mary Hooper's *At the Sign of the Sugared Plum* (UTBG 26).

This novel transports you immediately—and shockingly—to the raw, rough Edinburgh of the 19th century, where the teenage protagonist, Robbie, is on a seemingly futile mission of revenge. As a small boy, he witnessed a brutal operation on his mother at the hands of a renowned surgeon, Dr. Knox. Days afterward, she died. Now Dr. Knox has come into Robbie's life once more.

Dr. Knox is a real historical character, as are the corpse-stealers Burke and Hare, with whose murderous work Robbie becomes involved. The writing is so vivid, you can almost taste the reeking fog, while you suffer with Robbie and his younger sister in their struggle to survive deprivation and danger.

Patricia Elliott, Author

FLIPPED Wendelin Van Draanen

12+

A sycamore tree, some chicken eggs, and a pair of eighth graders are at the heart of this tale of neighbors Julianna Baker and Bryce Loski. The two take turns telling the story of their very up and down relationship. Julianna confesses to having "flipped" for Bryce the very first time she saw him at the tender age of five. But Bryce has no interest in the bossy girl with the muddy shoes, and he sees her as an annoyance to be avoided.

As the years pass, Julianna begins to wake from the trance of Bryce's blue eyes and to take her father's advice and "look beyond the landscape." Meanwhile Bryce, coached by his grandfather, finally realizes there is more to Julianna than just the "pest" he thought her to be.

Van Draanen tells a unique not-quite-love story through the authentic voices of two teens. Filled with heartache and humor, the pages will quickly turn as readers wonder: will they or won't they?

Shari Fesko, Librarian

Next?

Van Draanen's **Sammy Keyes** mysteries capture the middle school experience while adding a dash of mystery.

Another light and frothy teen romance is *Flavor of the Week* by Tucker Shaw— a modern-day interpretation of the Cyrano story.

Bradley and the Billboard by Mame Farrell is about 13-year-old Bradley—a boy in a family of women, who finds himself thrust into the world of modeling.

FLOODLAND Marcus Sedgwick

"Zoe ran. Harder than she had ever run in her life . . ."

For such a slim book, *Floodland* packs quite a punch. It's a story set in the not-too-distant future, when global warming has caused the waters to rise and cover large parts of England. Zoe has been stranded on Norwich—now an island, cold and inhospitable. Her attempts to get away and find her parents land her on Eels Island, which is even worse—inhabited by wild children, all under the leadership of the sinister and violent Dooby. Her only friend on Eels Island is old William, and he's crazy. Isn't he?

This is a story of bravery and resilience, a story about unusual friendships; it's sometimes very dark, but always beautiful, and it grips you from the first line.

Daniel Hahn, Editor

Next?

Read more Marcus Sedgwick. Maybe *The Book of Dead Days* next or the stunning *Dark Horse*.

Another odd tale of being stranded at sea is Yann Martel's wonderful and peculiar *Life of Pi* (UTBG 203).

You shouldn't miss Julie Bertagna's *Exodus* (UTBG 107) for another tale of global warming's consequences on a future society.

FLOWERS FOR ALGERNON Daniel Keyes

Next?

For another heartrending tale full of doctors and loners, try Ken Kesey's *One Flew Over the Cuckoo's Nest* (UTBG 256).

Two more classics that showcase a mentally handicapped character are John Steinbeck's *Of Mice and Men* (UTBG 253) and *The Sound and the Fury* by William Faulkner.

Flowers for Algernon is quite an engrossing tale. It tells the story of Charlie Gordon, a 37-year-old man who is mentally handicapped. Charlie gets selected to participate in a scientific experiment that will attempt to enhance his intelligence. The novel, which is told in Charlie's journal entries, tracks his progression from diminished to superhuman intelligence. His early, pre-experiment entries are primitive in style. But as the experiment continues and Charlie gets smarter, his writing drastically improves.

Eventually, Charlie's intelligence progresses to extraordinary levels. He can now speak 20 languages, whereas before the experiment he couldn't even master one. Things start to go downhill, however, when Algernon, a mouse who has undergone the same experiment as Charlie, begins to rapidly lose his enhanced intelligence. And then, Algernon dies. Will Charlie lose his intelligence as well? Will he suffer the same horrible fate as Algernon? The only way to find out is to read this powerful page-turner.

Jeremy Tramer, age 17

GRAPHIC NOVELS
by Mal Peet

I was in a bookstore recently and asked where the graphic novels were. "We don't keep them anymore," I was told, "they just get stolen." It's a small triumph for the form, I suppose, that it encourages reading among the thieving classes; but it's a shame that it gets harder to buy graphics just when it seems that they are beginning to win the struggle for serious critical recognition. Of course, there are still diehards who dismiss graphic novels *en masse* as immature or flippant reading matter best suited to young readers reluctant to read "real" books.

It's true that there's a pretty iffy border between "comic books" and graphic novels, and that movie and TV spin-offs and fantasy books (often daringly and beautifully drawn) are predominant. Yet the term "graphic novel" was coined in 1978 to describe Will Eisner's immensely serious *A Contract with God*, and some of the greatest graphics of the last 20 years have dealt with extremely somber matters: the Holocaust in Art Spiegelman's two-volume *Maus* (UTBG 223) and Joe Klubert's *Yossel*; the Hiroshima bombing in Keji Nakazawa's two Barefoot Gen books; nuclear war in Raymond Briggs's *When the Wind Blows*; war and ethnic cleansing in Joe Sacco's *Palestine* and *The Fixer: A Story from Sarajevo*. Indeed, if there is a criticism to be made of the form generally, it would be that graphics tend not toward the lightweight and the comical but toward the shadowy and the bleak. Even the good old escapist superhero genre has turned darkly ironic; see, for examples, *Batman: The Dark Knight Returns* (UTBG 27) by Frank Miller, et al, and *Watchmen* (UTBG 381) by Alan Moore and Dave Gibbons.

The fact is, though, that there are now as many genres of graphic novels as there are of mainstream prose fiction; and in one important respect the graphic novel is far more challenging and experimental than the prose novel. By combining text, art, and the "grammar" of movies and animation, graphic novelists have devised new, startling, and complex narrative techniques that make interesting demands on the reader's verbal and visual literacy. Actually, strip cartoonists have always taken a subversive approach to logical narration; look at collections of Winsor McCay's weird and beautiful *Dreams of the Rarebit Fiend* and *Little Nemo*, and George Herriman's brilliant *Krazy Kat*, which date from the early years of the 20th century and were a major influence on the "underground" comics of the 1960s and '70s.

Contemporary graphic sci-fi/fantasy novelists, such as Bryan Talbot (*The Adventures of Luther Arkwright*) and Neil Gaiman (the extraordinary *Black Orchid*, illustrated by Dave McKean, as well as the ongoing Sandman series [UTBG 302]) make it a point of honor to offer few concessions to the reader, weaving together different time frames and points of view to create a "parallel universes" style of narration, which, in a prose novel, would deter all but the most sophisticated readers.

Some graphic novels you can read about in the *UTBG*:

Blankets by Craig Thompson

Ethel & Ernest by Raymond Briggs

Jimmy Corrigan, the Smartest Kid on Earth by Chris Ware

Maus by Art Spiegelman

Persepolis by Marjane Satrapi

The Sandman series by Neil Gaiman

V for Vendetta by Alan Moore and David Lloyd

Watchmen by Alan Moore and Dave Gibbons

Bone by Jeff Smith

FLOWERS IN THE ATTIC V. C. Andrews

14+

Four children in 1970s America have a perfect and happy family life, until their father dies tragically, their mother is left destitute, and they go to live with their evil grandparents. There they are locked out of sight "just for one night" for reasons they don't understand. And the one night turns into weeks, the weeks into months. Food becomes scarce, their treatment increasingly harsh . . .

This book is genuinely harrowing with some violent and some sexually explicit scenes. It's a story full of high melodrama, and literary it isn't; but if you want a really gripping and engrossing read that won't let you stop thinking about it until you've reached the last page (and probably not even then), it's definitely worth the ride.

Susan Reuben, Editor

Next?

Try the other books about the Dollanganger family, *Petals on the Wind*, *If There Be Thorns*, and *Seeds of Yesterday*.

Another story of a girl locked in an attic (or is she?) is Josephine Tey's *The Franchise Affair*.

Or for more Gothic and overheated prose, try Anne Rice's *Interview with the Vampire* (UTBG 178).

FORBIDDEN Judy Waite

16+

Elinor has grown up with The Chosen, following the True Cause. She is especially privileged, as she is destined to be the "bride" of the cult leader when she reaches her 16th birthday. Elinor is happy to be a part of all that—until she happens to meet an "outsider" boy. She begins to question what the cult is all about and what she really wants to do with her life. But when she thinks about making a break, Elinor discovers how little freedom she truly has. Can she, will she, break free? This tense and gripping story takes the reader through many twists and turns to find out.

Yvonne Coppard, Author

Next?

The Book of Fred by Abby Bardi takes a slightly more humorous approach, when a teen who grew up on a commune must learn to adapt to life with an undisciplined American family.

Pete Hautman's *Godless* (UTBG 137) looks at what happens when two teens invent a religion and the worship gets out of hand.

Try something else by Judy Waite; *The Next Big Thing* is about a boy discovered singing in his garage who becomes a reluctant superstar.

FOREVER Judy Blume

Forever follows the developing relationships of teenage couples and their interaction with the adult world. How do liberal parents deal with the reality of their teenage daughter's long-term and developing sexual relationship?

Until I read this book, I thought nothing could shock me. First published in the 1970s, *Forever* talks more graphically about teenage sex than anything I've read that was written since. Of course, being shocked is not necessarily a bad thing. The book gives a very realistic insight into the workings of teenage relationships and answers questions young people cannot always ask their parents. Well worth reading.

Anna Posner, age 16

Next?

More Judy Blume, of course: *Tiger Eyes* or *Are You There God? It's Me, Margaret*.

For a more recent take on teenage sex, try Melvin Burgess's *Doing It* (UTBG 94).

For two more books that deal with the "first time" experience (as either positive or negative), try Sara Zarr's *Story of a Girl* (UTBG 340) or Kristen Tracy's *Lost It* (UTBG 211).

Or for more books on love and life, read E. Lockhart's Love, Sex, and Relationships feature on pp. 162–163.

#1 *NEW YORK TIMES* BESTSELLING AUTHOR

judy blume

forever...

is there a difference between first love and true love?

Erica has insight. She knew Katherine liked Michael the moment they met at a New Year's Eve party. Katherine admits the fact to herself, which allows the attraction to develop. Eventually she is sure it is love and not childish infatuation. Michael feels it too, and after a few failed attempts, they make love.

Their relationship becomes intense and exclusive. But with their future plans all figured out, the couple have to face up to the fact that their senior year at high school is coming to an end and they will be going to different universities. To make matters worse they both have summer jobs. They put their love to the test with a long separation. For Katherine it's a time to reflect and wonder if their love really is forever.

Elena Gregoriou, Teacher

The FOUNDATION trilogy Isaac Asimov

The human race has spread across the galaxy to occupy millions of worlds, all ruled from the metal-covered planet Trantor. Only one man, Hari Seldon, realizes that the Galactic Empire is in decline. Charting the fall of civilization by means of the predictive science of Psychohistory, Seldon sets up two secret Foundations "at opposite ends of the galaxy" to hold it together over the next thousand years. In the course of the trilogy we meet buccaneering mayors, deep-space traders, merchant princes, thieves, mutants, emperors, scheming generals, and a host of other colorful characters. Generations and crises come and go, centuries pass, with considerable excitement and a great many surprises and twists. The greatest of all sci-fi epics.
Michael Lawrence, Author

Next?

After completing the trilogy—*Foundation*, *Foundation and Empire*, and *Second Foundation*—Asimov wrote more **Foundation** books. *Foundation's Edge* is next.

Asimov also wrote some of the most brilliant sci-fi ever. Try *I, Robot* (UTBG 171), which starts the excellent **Robot** series.

Philip K. Dick's *Do Androids Dream of Electric Sheep?* (UTBG 93) is also full of amazing and original ideas.

Another series that spans time and space starts with *Dune* (UTBG 100) by Frank Herbert.

FRANKENSTEIN Mary Shelley

Next?

Angelmonster by Veronica Bennett is based on this book and Mary Shelley's life.

For another experiment that goes wrong, read H. G. Wells's *The Invisible Man*.

Another classic horror story that's still appallingly scary is *Dr. Jekyll and Mr. Hyde* (UTBG 95) by Robert Louis Stevenson.

And read our horror feature on pp. 346–347.

If you think that Mary Shelley just played the dutiful wife to her famous poet husband, Percy Bysshe Shelley, think again!

Frankenstein started out as a challenge by the great Lord Byron to each of his guests at the Villa Diodati on Lake Geneva: "Write a horror story." So Mary sat down to write a book that would have more readers than those of all her poetic contemporaries; it turned out to be one of the most chilling stories ever written. Dr. Frankenstein puts pieces of dead bodies together to assemble a creature that he brings to life. The monster escapes and roams the hills and villages nearby, wreaking havoc. But the monster also gains our sympathy, for within a misshapen body there is a lost soul that craves affection.
James Riordan, Author

FRANNY and ZOOEY J. D. Salinger

16+

For some people, *The Catcher in the Rye* is the only important Salinger book. But his true masterpiece remains incomplete. Since the early 1950s, Salinger has been writing an epic narrative series about a New York family called the Glasses. "Franny" and "Zooey" are two of the stories from this sequence, with a sweet simplicity that makes them incredibly enjoyable to read. "Franny" is a short story about a young female student who meets her boyfriend for dinner and can't help disagreeing with everything he says. "Zooey" is a longer novella, narrated by Buddy Glass, who claims his family hate him writing about them but don't protest because they know he'd burst into tears. All the children in the Glass family are prodigies, appearing on a radio quiz show called "It's a Wild Child," but when they grow up their problems drive them to depression and suicide.

Matt Thorne, Author

Next?

The Cheese Monkeys by Chip Kidd, a novel about a year in art school, has some of Salinger's sarcastic humor.

Studs Lonigan by James T. Farrell tells of teenage dissatisfaction, but Studs is a harder character than Salinger's whimsical Glass siblings.

For another book about a complex family, plus the trials of growing up, try Colette's *Gigi*.

FREAK THE MIGHTY Rodman Philbrick

12+

Even though he's six feet tall, Max Kane is scared of a lot of things: being noticed, being hugged, and most of all becoming like his father, who's been in prison since Max was four. Kevin, aka Freak, is half Max's height and not scared of anything, not even the disease that might kill him. The summer before eighth grade they become Freak the Mighty—Freak is the brain, Max is the brawn. It may sound whimsical, but this is realistic fiction. In the course of the book, both Freak and Max have to stare down their most terrifying enemies.

What really makes this story a favorite is Max's voice. It's self-effacing and heartbreaking, while also funny and real. Max claims (without exactly saying so) that he isn't lovable, isn't worth the space he takes up, and doesn't have a future. Everything about his friendship with Freak tells you otherwise.

Sara Zarr, Author

Next?

If you loved *Freak the Mighty*, you shouldn't miss the sequel, *Max the Mighty*.

Other books that feature unlikely friendships are Pete Hautman's *Invisible* or Ron Koertge's *Stoner & Spaz*.

Jordan Sonnenblick's *Notes from the Midnight Driver* is a heartwarming tale about a rebel teen who finds solace with a senior citizen.

FREEWILL Chris Lynch

Next?

Chris Lynch has an amazing body of work full of complex characters—*Inexcusable* (UTBG 175) is one of his very best.

Pete Hautman's *Invisible* will keep you guessing about guilt and innocence, sanity and insanity.

And if you were mesmerized by Lynch's writing, read Adam Rapp's similarly powerful books, especially *33 Snowfish* (UTBG 2) and *Under the Wolf, Under the Dog*.

Will has endured the death of his father and step-mother and is now living with his paternal grandparents, struggling to adjust to his new life. Sickly and sullen, Will displays his emotions only in the odd objects he carves in his shop class and, occasionally, when outcast athlete Angela is in his proximity.

When questionable deaths begin to occur in his small town, and mysteriously, Will's sculptures become integral parts of the memorials that sprout up at each location of the victims' deaths, the voices inside his head and those outside have to compete for Will's attention.

This disturbing yet completely engrossing tale is not for the faint of heart. But readers who share in Will's isolation and desperation even in the smallest way will feel forever changed by Lynch's slim masterpiece.

Kimberly Paone, Librarian

FRENCHMAN'S CREEK Daphne du Maurier

Romance was never quite as passionate or daring as in *Frenchman's Creek*. Prepare to fall in love right along with our heroine, Dona; for never was there quite as elusive, romantic, or swashbuckling a lover as the pirate known as "the Frenchman"!

Dona is married, the mother of two, and about to turn 30. She had been the toast of London (of the men at least), but one day, she decides to leave it all and move to her husband's country estate in Cornwall, and her life changes forever. All of Cornwall is desperately trying to capture a French pirate—but who would have thought that his hideout was right in the middle of Dona's estate? And what exactly happens after he offers her a place on his ship? Will Dona choose adventure and love or stay faithful to her husband and children? You will find yourself holding your breath as the story unfolds . . .

Candida Gray, Teacher

Next?

There's more breathless West Country romance in R. D. Blackmore's classic, *Lorna Doone*, or for corsets and passion try *Wuthering Heights* (UTBG 402) by Emily Brontë.

Richard Hughes's *A High Wind in Jamaica* is a story of pirates, unsuitable obsession, and adventure.

Daphne du Maurier has written many books, but *Jamaica Inn* (UTBG 181) is the closest you'll find to *Frenchman's Creek*.

FRIDAY NIGHT LIGHTS: A TOWN, A TEAM, AND A DREAM H. G. Bissinger

14+

Next?

Bissinger's *3 Nights in August* does for baseball what *Friday Night Lights* did for football.

Raiders Night by Robert Lipsyte explores the pressures of being a high school football star.

Michael Lewis's *The Blind Side* is a compelling, in-depth look at the game of football.

Even if you *don't* daydream of being your school's top athlete, would you turn down the opportunity to be him? Read this book before you decide.

This story isn't only about being the best football player in town. It's about a town where high school football is the only thing that matters. Where the ultimate goal is winning the state championship. If you can help your team do that, you'll be treated like a king. But if you let these people down, your life will never be the same.

And the book doesn't stop there. It's about race, prejudice, and small-town attitudes about education. It's about fathers and mothers living through their sons, and about the institutionalized inferiority of daughters in a world that values football above all else.

So, do you want to be a hero?

Todd Strasser, Author

FROST ON MY MOUSTACHE Tim Moore

14+

Once it gets started, this is one of the funniest books ever. About 150 years ago, fearless, swashbuckling Lord Dufferin went off on his daring travels, battling with icebergs and polar bears through Iceland and Norway. Modern-day author Tim Moore is a self-confessed "girl's blouse," and, oozing with lack of daring, he sets off in his footsteps. As Tim watches himself fall so far short of the fearless Victorian in pluck and stamina on the demanding Arctic journey, he gets funnier and funnier. Skip chapter one the first time if you must and start, as does Tim, at 4:30 A.M. in Grimsby, England, boarding a boat in a Force-8 gale. ("Eat, like, twelve Mars bars," suggests the taxi driver. "So you'll have something to chuck up.")

Anne Fine, Author

Next?

For more crazy men doing heroic (or crazy) things, read *The Worst Journey in the World* (UTBG 399) by Apsley Cherry-Garrard, or *Terra Incognita* (UTBG 353) by Sara Wheeler for a woman's view of ice adventure.

Or less heroic, but as funny as Tim Moore: *Round Ireland with a Fridge* (UTBG 294) by Tony Hawks.

Or more Tim Moore? Try his hilarious *Do Not Pass Go*.

129

FULL TILT Neal Shusterman

12+

Do you like to ride roller coasters? Sixteen-year-old Blake does not. His younger brother, Quinn, is the adrenaline junkie in the family. So when Blake gets a mysterious invitation to a secret amusement park, he chooses to ignore it. Quinn has different plans, and Blake ends up at the sinister amusement park, where he must go on seven rides before dawn if he wants to save his brother's life. The trouble is, getting on seven rides before dawn is easy; getting off them is a slightly harder task. Blake has to face all his fears in order to save his brother—and himself. This fast-paced horror thriller is definitely worth checking out!
Kristin Anderson, Librarian

Next?

For more eerie chills by Neal Shusterman, try any of the books in his **Dark Fusion** series, or, for a more seriously scary book, try *The Shadow Club*.

The books of Chris Wooding are great scary reads. Try *Poison* (UTBG 272) or *The Haunting of Alaizabel Cray* (UTBG 148).

If you like horror books, be sure to check out our Horror and Ghost Stories feature on page 346–347.

GENERATION X Douglas Coupland

16+

Next?

More Douglas Coupland? Try his *Shampoo Planet*.

The Catcher in the Rye (UTBG 60) by J. D. Salinger was the defining book for a generation—obviously a different one than Douglas Coupland's!

The Beach (UTBG 28) by Alex Garland is another book that started as a cult novel—then they made a film of it.

And read our feature on cult books on pp. 250–251.

Dag, Claire, and Andy are good friends in their 20s who live in neighboring bungalows in quiet Palm Springs, California. Their jobs are dull, they have little money, and they see the future as frightening, full of the threat of nuclear bombs and environmental catastrophe. So they escape from all of this by telling one another bizarre, beautiful stories about other worlds where things make more, or sometimes less, sense to them. This is a thoughtful book about friendship, human nature, and trying to understand an uncertain world. It is a true "cult novel," its popularity spread by word of mouth. It is full of new and clever words and terms, like "McJob" for a low-paid and unimportant job, which are explained in amusing side notes to the main text.
Marianne Taylor, Editor

GEORGIE Malachy Doyle

Georgie lives in a home for disturbed children. He has a terrible secret he won't talk about to anyone. He destroys anything given to him. He rejects anyone who attempts to win his trust.

Then he moves to a new home, where he meets Shannon and Tommo. Shannon is a girl with her own secrets. Tommo is a care worker who won't let Georgie push him away. Together, they help Georgie overcome the nightmares in his past and develop the courage to love again.

Georgie is no easy read. At times, it's so honest it's painful. It's also one of the most positive and uplifting books I've ever read.

I'm still not sure about the last chapter, which doesn't quite ring true, but other than that, *Georgie* is utterly believable and totally compelling.

Graham Gardner, Author

Next?

Disconnected by Sherry Ashworth is about a girl escaping life through the solace of alcohol.

Who Is Jesse Flood? is another great Malachy Doyle, about a boy coming to terms with life and himself.

For another tale of problematic children finding their place in life, read Sharon Creech's gentler *Ruby Holler* (UTBG 295).

GIFTS Ursula K. Le Guin

Next?

For more Ursula K. Le Guin, try *The Dispossessed*.

How about Virginia Euwer Wolff's *The Mozart Season* or Mark Haddon's *The Curious Incident of the Dog in the Night-Time* (UTBG 82)?

For another fantasy about teens with unrealized powers, try N. M. Browne's *The Story of Stone*.

Lene Kaaberbol's *The Shamer's Daughter* (UTBG 316) is about a gift that can also be a curse.

This is a story of strange countries and magic powers. But nobody in Caspromont can work general, all-purpose magic; instead, each family has a traditional "gift." Orrec's friend Gry can call creatures to her, but Orrec's family has the gift of "Undoing," the gift of completely destroying things—a gift so terrible that Orrec must be blindfolded until he can control it. Can Orrec and Gry reach a true understanding of how best to use their gifts? You won't be able to stop reading this book, with its strange sense of foreboding. And maybe it'll make you wonder about any gift you yourself may have . . .

Jill Paton Walsh, Author

GINGERBREAD Rachel Cohn

"Recovering hellion" Cyd Charisse, recently kicked out of boarding school and stuck at home with her overbearing mother and doting stepdad, just wants to be herself—working as a barista on the beach and spending time with her surfer boyfriend, Shrimp. But when Shrimp decides he needs a break and things reach a boiling point at home, Cyd and her rag doll, Gingerbread, are sent off to New York to live with "Frank real-dad" and the half-siblings Cyd has wanted to meet her entire life. Against the sparkling backdrop of New York City, Cyd will learn a thing or two about life, love, and the meaning of family.

There are elements to *Gingerbread* that may remind readers of other YA fare: a rebellious "wild child" narrator, a touch of romance, a girl out trying to find her place in the world. But *Gingerbread* goes way beyond the light, fluffy teen novel to something much more. Cyd's slang-heavy first-person narrative flows almost like stream-of-consciousness thought, her revelations about life spot-on and moving. *Gingerbread* is an all-too-quick read; funny and touching—you'll fall in love with its narrator and, by the end, feel just a little bit cooler by association.

Stacy Cantor, Editor

Next?

If you fell in love with Cyd Charisse, don't miss the next two novels starring her—*Shrimp* and *Cupcake*.

Rachel Cohn has also written two books in conjunction with YA novelist David Levithan: start with *Nick & Norah's Infinite Playlist* (UTBG 242) and then try *Naomi and Ely's No Kiss List*.

If you like a narrator with a bit of an edge, you'll enjoy Cecil Castellucci's writing. Try *Boy Proof* (UTBG 47) or *Beige* (UTBG 31) for starters.

GIRL Blake Nelson

14+

The early 90s is the time. Portland is the place. Andrea Marr is the girl. Somehow Blake Nelson has opened up the head of a teenage girl and put what he found directly on paper without filter, censor, or brakes. Andrea's story hurtles at us in a compelling, nonstop monologue across three years of high school. Bored by the suburban status quo of homecomings, proms, and résumé-building "activities," Andrea plunges headlong instead into the burgeoning Seattle/Portland grunge rock scene. Andrea's new life revolves around amped-up concerts, edgy fashion, and sexual trysts interspersed with mundane lunch period visits to Taco Time and writing articles for the school newspaper. Navigating this tricky territory results in incredible highs as well as painful losses, but as Andrea succinctly puts it, "At least I was pushing myself." *Girl* is a YA classic that captures a time, a place, and maybe even a generation.

Bob Krech, Author

Next?

Girl's tone and themes are not unlike *Absolute Beginners*, Colin MacInnes's 1950s gem.

For more by Blake Nelson, try *The New Rules of High School*, which shows Nelson's mastery of teen dialogue.

For another book about a girl's coming-of-age, try Sonya Sones's *What My Mother Doesn't Know* (UTBG 386).

GIRL, 15, CHARMING BUT INSANE
Sue Limb

14+

Next?

Jess continues her adventures in *Girl, Nearly 16: Absolute Torture; Girl, Going on 17: Pants on Fire;* and *Girl, Barely 15: Flirting for England.*

To fully appreciate the story, go back and read Jane Austen's *Emma,* the original matchmaker tale.

For another hilarious view of British girl life, try the first in the **Calypso Chronicles,** *Pulling Princes* by Tyne O'Connell.

Limb's novel is a riotous take on Jane Austen's *Emma* and—like *Clueless* before it—is modern, charming, and very up-to-date. Jess Jordan feels that in comparison to the blonde, beautiful, rich Flora, she is hideous, poor, and doomed. She spends her time being mesmerized by the fabulously handsome Ben Jones—who is so totally wrong for her.

Jess has been invited to do a stand-up routine at the school show, the one thing she knows she's good at. But the glamorous Flora and her vile band, Poisonous Trash, threaten to steal the show. It's classic stuff and laugh-out-loud funny.

John McLay, Literary Scout

GIRL WITH A PEARL EARRING

Tracy Chevalier

Girl with a Pearl Earring is narrated by servant-girl Griet, and it simmers with her passion. Griet is a tile maker's daughter, taken to be a maidservant to the great artist Vermeer. With her we are drawn into the Vermeer family house, a small world full of almost unbearable tensions. It is fraught with struggles of class and religion, servants vying for superiority over each other, and rivalries for the affection of a genius who cares only for his painting.

Griet reveals the process of painting as magically as she evokes the mood of the house and its people, and we sense that she herself might have been an artist, had she not been a girl and of the servant class. I am not sure I like Griet, and I can never predict what she will do next. Yet her narrative is as spellbinding as Vermeer's portraits themselves.

This is a dazzling book with erotic undercurrents. Look out for the ear-piercing scene.

Caroline Pitcher, Author

> ### Next?
>
> Lynn Cullen's *I Am Rembrandt's Daughter* does for the paintings of Rembrandt what Tracy Chevalier did for Vermeer.
>
> *Lady Chatterley's Lover* (UTBG 197) by D. H. Lawrence tells the story of a lady and a game-keeper.

GIRLS IN LOVE Jacqueline Wilson

> ### Next?
>
> *Girls Under Pressure*, *Girls Out Late*, and *Girls in Tears* continue the series.
>
> Louise Rennison's books are funny and familiar: try *Angus, Thongs and Full-Frontal Snogging* (UTBG 18) for starters.
>
> For more friends, families, and the tribulations of life in general, read Cathy Hopkins's hilarious **Mates, Dates . . .** series (UTBG 222).
>
> Or for a more serious look at girls' friendships, read Simmone Howell's *Notes from the Teenage Underground*.

This series of books is about three teenage girls who are going through the usual teenage problems. It's full of jealousy, tears, boys, and family difficulties. The main character, Ellie, thinks she's fat and boring and is very insecure. Her two best friends are Magda (who is gorgeous and totally boy-crazy) and Nadine (who is very cool and striking, though sometimes blunt and rude).

Jacqueline Wilson's books are light but gripping, and I felt I had a real connection with the characters. I would recommend this book to anyone who wants an easy, enjoyable read.

Rachel Shaw, age 13

GIVE A BOY A GUN Todd Strasser

12+

Next?

Nineteen Minutes
(UTBG 245) by Jodi
Picoult also looks at the
issue of school violence
from multiple points of
view.

For more by Todd
Strasser, try *Can't
Get There from Here*,
about a group of teens
living on the streets,
or *Boot Camp*, a look
at the ills of teen
incarceration.

Using fictitious transcripts, facts about school violence, and excerpts from actual books, newspapers, and magazines, Todd Strasser tells a powerful story. Written not long after the Columbine shooting, *Give a Boy a Gun* imagines a similar situation in which two teens stage an attack at a school dance.

The story is told through the eyes of classmates, teachers, and school administrators, some of whom were friends, others tormentors. Although high school caste systems and the glorification of athletes are seen as sources of the violence, what comes through loud and clear is the role that guns played. Footnotes relating comparisons such as the 35,957 Americans killed by gun violence in 1995 compared to the 33,651 deaths during the entire three years of the Korean War will not only surprise readers but also give them a great deal to think about long after they've finished the book.

Dorian Cirrone, Author

THE GIVER Lois Lowry

12+

Picture a civilization where no one can see in color. Picture a civilization where children are assigned to parents, names are preset, and jobs are selected for people. In *The Giver*, everything is perfect. There is no hunger, scarcity, or conflict.

When Jonas turns 12, he gets his Assignment, or occupation. During the Ceremony of Twelve, Jonas is shocked to find that he has become the new Receiver. Jonas will receive private training from the Giver, who holds the memories of what ordinary life was like in an ordinary civilization. But after a year of being the Receiver, Jonas can no longer handle this responsibility. An outrageous discovery creates a need to bring the community back to reality.

The Giver is a fascinating book about a fictional civilization. It makes you realize how exciting our lives are in contrast to the boring, redundant, and inexpressive lives of the members of Jonas's community. I recommend *The Giver* to anyone with a creative interest in strange new worlds!

Justin Mahes, age 12

Next?

Ray Bradbury's *Fahrenheit
451* (UTBG 110) also details
a frightening society of the
future.

For another book by Lois
Lowry, try *Number the
Stars*, about a little girl
during the Holocaust.

If you loved the futuristic
society detailed in *The
Giver*, be sure to go back
and look at the Dystopian
Worlds Top Ten List at the
beginning of this book.

GO AND COME BACK Joan Abelove

Next?

Shabanu by Suzanne Fisher Staples is also about a girl on the brink of marriage, this time in the Pakistan desert.

The Moorchild by Eloise McGraw is fantasy, but it's also another look at our world with fresh eyes—the eyes of a half-fairy inserted into a human family.

For more outsiders trying to understand an alien culture, read An Na's *A Step from Heaven* (UTBG 339) or Elizabeth Laird's *Kiss the Dust* (UTBG 195).

I know this book inside out—that's how many times I've read it. *Go and Come Back* changed me forever.

Alicia is on the brink of marriage when two white women, anthropologists, arrive in her Peruvian village for a year's stay. To Alicia and the others in Poincushmana, the tall blonde woman is ugly and the short fat one, beautiful. They're not even related to each other. They're friends, a word that doesn't exist in Isabo. The anthropologists ask a million questions, and they're incredibly stingy.

Months pass. Alicia adopts a *nawa* (outsider) baby. The rains come and go. Army recruiters come and young men flee. The two white women learn the values of the village. You will, too. You'll see yourself and your life in a new way—and dental floss will never seem the same again!

Gail Carson Levine, Author

GO ASK ALICE Anonymous

What happens when you're so desperate for acceptance that you'll do just about anything to get it?

This is the real diary of a 15-year-old girl whose name is never revealed. She feels like the odd one out in her well-off, over-achieving family; she's snubbed by the boy she adores; she has problems with her looks and with the new school that she attends when she moves. Then a spiked drink at a party changes her life. She plunges into the local drug scene, eventually running away from home and ending up in a psychiatric ward.

Though sad and scary, her story is so painfully honest, vivid, and touching that it's hard to put down.

Catherine Jinks, Author

Next?

Jim Carroll's *The Basketball Diaries* is another searing look at an addicted teen's life on the streets.

Smack (UTBG 329) by Melvin Burgess also looks at heroin addiction.

Or try Ellen Hopkins's semi-autobiographical *Crank*, about a troubled teen addicted to crystal meth.

Read our Off the Rails feature on pp. 188–189 for more ideas.

GODLESS   Pete Hautman

What if? In this National Book Award winner, Hautman applies this question to one of the most taboo subjects in YA literature: religion. What if a teenager, disgusted with "formal and normal" religion, decided to start his own faith brand? The results run deep, like the water in the tower that 15-year-old Jason starts worshipping. What was originally a joke turns serious when Jason's best friend, Shin, grows obsessed with the water-tower worship. And just as important to the story is the love triangle between Jason, the unrealized crush Magda, and the bully Henry.

But there's another core question: what happens when a teenager gets his first taste of power? Hautman catches, in the skeptical and sarcastic voice of Jason, an innocent yet brave teenager taking his first big dive into adult experience. Jason is questioning what he's been taught as a child so he can reject or embrace those lessons as an adult. Hautman is exploring questions not so much about a deity, as about teenagers making decisions, thus about the twin towers of power and responsibility.

Patrick Jones, Author

> ### Next?
>
> Try Pete Hautman's *Rash*, which takes place in 2076, in the "United Safer States of America."
>
> Morton Rhue's classic story *The Wave* deals with similar issues of group pressures and power.
>
> Try Avi's *Nothing but the Truth* (UTBG 249) for a satire on high school politics.

GOLDKEEPER   Sally Prue

> ### Next?
>
> There are not enough really funny books around, but another to try is Alan Temperley's *Harry and the Wrinklies* and *Harry and the Treasure of Eddie Carver*.
>
> If you like this book you'll almost certainly enjoy Jonathan Stroud's *The Amulet of Samarkand* (UTBG 17).
>
> For fast-paced adventure try Eoin Colfer's *Artemis Fowl* (UTBG 24) and its sequels.
>
> For a magical story with an interesting twist on demons, try Sally Prue's first book, *Cold Tom*.

I don't love the title of this book, but don't let that put you off, as the story itself is excellent: very funny and packed with bizarre twists and turns. It spins the yarn of Sebastian, a surprise candidate for the job of high priest's apprentice in the temple of Ora, and his pet rat, Gerald. Not everyone is pleased by Sebastian's apparent good fortune, particularly a certain Mr. Meeno (a gangster) and his nephew Horace (who was expecting to be chosen himself). The tale darkens as Sebastian and Gerald survive several nasty—and unusual—accidents. Is there a plot to get rid of them? Well, of course there is, but that's only the start of their problems . . .

Chris d'Lacey, Author

GONE WITH THE WIND

14+

Margaret Mitchell

At the beginning of this book, the heroine, Scarlett O'Hara, is 16. She is a willful, flirtatious Southern belle from a wealthy Irish American family. But it is 1861 and Scarlett and her family are soon plunged into the violence and chaos of the American Civil War.

In five years Scarlett loses everything: her home, her family, and two husbands. She eventually marries the dashing captain Rhett Butler, a man as passionate and determined as she is. Her troubles have barely begun.

Scarlett does much to invite the reader's disapproval, but her indomitable spirit and her refusal to accept defeat in hopeless situations win our admiration, and we crave her survival. The book is 1,000 pages long, but the protagonists are so lively and the story so rich in events, it is hard to put down.

Jenny Nimmo, Author

Next?

If you are interested in books set in the American Civil War, *Cold Mountain* by Charles Frazier is a beautifully written novel about a soldier's desperate and dangerous journey home to the woman he loves.

Stephen Crane's *The Red Badge of Courage* vividly depicts the emotions and experiences of a young soldier during the Civil War.

For another romance on an epic scale, try *Katherine* (UTBG 190) by Anya Seton.

The Ultimate Teen Readers' Poll

CHARACTER YOU'D MOST LIKE TO BE

1. Alex Rider (The Alex Rider series)

2. Bella (*Twilight*)

3. Hermione Granger (The Harry Potter series)

4. Harry Potter (The Harry Potter series)

5. Mia Thermopolis (The Princess Diaries series)

6. Darren Shan (The Saga of Darren Shan)

7. Artemis Fowl (The Artemis Fowl books)

8. Violet Baudelaire (A Series of Unfortunate Events)

9. Legolas (The Lord of the Rings trilogy)

10. Ron Weasley (The Harry Potter series)

GOOD OMENS Terry Pratchett and Neil Gaiman

Next?

If you haven't read Terry Pratchett's **Discworld** series, then do so at once. Start with *Discworld: Monstrous Regiment* (UTBG 92).

Try Neil Gaiman's *Neverwhere*, or the eerie *The Wolves in the Walls* (UTBG 395), a picture book that will make you shiver.

For another end-of-the-world tale, try *Apocalypse* (UTBG 22) by Tim Bowler.

Terry Pratchett's Discworld novels are fabulous. I didn't think he could get any better. Then he got together with Neil Gaiman, the incredibly dark writer of the Sandman comics, and the result was *Good Omens*. This book starts out simply, with a small boy playing with his dog in a rural setting. Then it turns out that the little boy is the Antichrist, his dog is the hound of hell, and Armageddon is approaching. The story also features a reliable prophet, an angel, a demon, the four horsemen of the apocalypse, and the explanation of the satanic origins of the M25 motorway in London. It's undoubtedly the best book ever written!

Anthony Reuben, Journalist

GOODBYE TO ALL THAT Robert Graves

This autobiography covers the first 33 years of poet and author Robert Graves's extraordinary life. He joins the army when he leaves school in 1914 and, for me, this is the best account we have of the trenches. The book, with its matter-of-fact and darkly humorous tone (it is often very funny), reminds me of the old men's stories I heard as a child of something that sounded just like hell. Robert Graves is the most independent-minded of soldiers, and his is an honest, though very personal, story that gives us a glimpse of Siegfried Sassoon, T. E. Lawrence (of Arabia), and Wilfred Owen.

There are lots of World War I novels about the unfairness and butchery of the trenches. Read this wonderful real-life book about a young man determined to be a good soldier, while refusing to accept anyone's principles but his own.

Sally Prue, Author

Next?

Another autobiography that looks at the war from a young nurse's point of view, Vera Brittain's *Testament of Youth* is a fascinating story.

Under Fire by Henri Barbusse tells the true story of the author's experiences as a French soldier in the trenches.

Regeneration (UTBG 289) by Pat Barker is a novel, but it has many real people as characters.

Ernst Jünger's *Storm of Steel* is another autobiographical account of a soldier's experiences.

THE GOOSE GIRL Shannon Hale

Anidori-Kiladra Talianna Isilee, Crown Princess of Kildenree, spent the first years of her life listening to her aunt's incredible stories and learning the language of the birds. She feels a failure as a princess: only her father and her horse, Falada, accept her as she is. Her only friend is her maid—or so she thinks.

When her father dies, Ani inherits the throne, and she has to marry the prince of the neighboring country in order to avoid a war. The plot twists and Ani becomes a goose girl. Falada plays a memorable role as Ani learns to understand herself before she can overcome her enemies. The book is a beautifully written tale of magic, excitement, and courage.

Brenda Marshall, Librarian

Next?

Grimm's Fairy Tales by the Brothers Grimm has an earlier version of "The Goose Girl."

Beauty (UTBG 29) by Robin McKinley is a retelling of the story of *Beauty and the Beast*.

The Picture of Dorian Gray (UTBG 270) by Oscar Wilde will intrigue you and get you thinking about both appearances and consequences.

The GOSSIP GIRL series Cecily von Ziegesar

Next?

If you're completely pulled into the world of the Gossip Girl, don't miss the next two books in the series: *You Know You Love Me* and *All I Want Is Everything*.

For a similar series, try J. Minter's **Insiders** books, which look at privilege from the point-of-view of the guys, or the spin-off, *Inside Girl*, narrated by one of their sisters.

The A-List series (UTBG 4) by Zoey Dean, while undoubtedly a "wannabe title," deviates in that it takes the catty Manhattanites to Los Angeles.

Welcome to the world of the Gossip Girl—privileged, catty, and irresistibly impossible to put down. With her long-running series (12 books will have been published at the time of this printing), Cecily von Ziegesar has coined a new phrase in teen literature: the "guilty pleasure read." She's also spurred a whole host of wannabe titles, but if you're really looking for a juicy read as delicious as gossip itself, look no further than the original.

In Book #1, you meet all the major players: popular Blair; her ex-best friend, Serena; Nate, the boy they're both fighting over; Dan, the sensitive, artistic type; and many others. In the Manhattan-elite world of the Gossip Girl, anything can happen—sex is consequence-free, alcohol flows no matter the age, and money is absolutely no object. It is a fun, fast-paced, and utterly fantastical look at teenage life that, while it may not bear even a slight resemblance to your own life, will certainly entertain you from the series' beginning to end.

Stacy Cantor, Editor

A GREAT AND TERRIBLE BEAUTY
Libba Bray

Okay, first can I tell you that I don't like fantasy books? I have great appreciation for them, but fairies and vampires and supernatural worlds—these books usually leave me going, "That's nice, but . . . huh?" *A Great and Terrible Beauty* is the book that changed this perception for me.

Gemma Doyle has been raised in Victorian times to be a proper English girl. When tragedy strikes, Gemma is sent away from her home in India to a posh British boarding school called Spence, where Gemma discovers she might not so much be the "proper" English girl after all. At Spence, Gemma starts having disturbing visions that have a strange habit of coming true. These visions lead Gemma to discover unsettling truths about her mother, and about Gemma's own royal place in a lush and scary otherworld where she discovers she can transport herself and her powerful circle of boarding-school friends. Gemma's newfound powers lead her on a journey of excitement, betrayal, splendor, and danger that will keep you up all night furiously flipping the pages to see what happens next. And to find out more about that very hot guy named Kartik who may or may not know more about Gemma and her role in this otherworld.

A Great and Terrible Beauty is the fantasy book that left me going, "That's nice, and . . . GREAT and not at all terrible!" It also left me very grateful that Libba Bray made a trilogy of these books, so once you get addicted to the first book, there are two more about Gemma to feed the hunger.
Rachel Cohn, Author

Next?

If you want to read more about Gemma, the sequel, *Rebel Angels*, and the third book, *The Sweet Far Thing*, pack just as much intrigue and excitement as the first.

For another historical fiction story with a bit more realism, try Jennifer Donnelly's *A Northern Light* (UTBG 247), which interweaves the fictional heroine's story with the true tale of a drowned woman through a series of letters.

For another atmospheric tale with a supernatural leaning, *A Certain Slant of Light* by Laura Whitcomb does the trick.

THE GREAT DIVORCE C. S. Lewis

This book is about a group of people on an outing from Hell, visiting Heaven. Most of them, once they've arrived, can't wait to get back.

If you've read C. S. Lewis's Narnia books, you've probably realized that the stories were his way of talking about Christianity. This book is a more grown-up version of some of the beliefs he explored there. I read it first when I was 14, have read it a dozen times since, and find something new in it every time. It is seriously clever stuff—and a good story as well—though the language he uses is from the middle of the last century and not always easy to understand.

Andrew Norriss, Author

Next?

You might enjoy *The Screwtape Letters* (UTBG 304), also by C. S. Lewis—advice on temptation from a senior devil to a junior.

And if you're in the mood to ponder the meaning of life, then *Sophie's World* (UTBG 333) by Jostein Gaarder is a neat guide to the theories the Big Brains have come up with.

Philip Pullman is an outspoken critic of C. S. Lewis, but you'll find Pullman's rich and allegorical **His Dark Materials** trilogy (UTBG 153) an interesting and satisfying counterpoint to Lewis's work.

GREAT EXPECTATIONS Charles Dickens

Next?

A prolonged diet of Dickens can be a little rich, so have a break before you start your next meal, and then you might try the wonderful *Nicholas Nickleby*.

The Moonstone (UTBG 231), by Dickens's contemporary Wilkie Collins, is a mystery involving a missing jewel and a cast of thousands.

If you like Dickens's style, why not try something by Jane Austen—perhaps *Pride and Prejudice* (UTBG 276) or *Emma*—for a new take on the "novel of manners."

Pip starts off in life as a humble country boy. As we follow him through the years, we encounter escaped convicts, spooky graveyards, unrequited love, and of course the unforgettable Miss Havisham, languishing in her eerie, dust-filled house, still in her bridal gown from years before.

Reading Dickens is like watching the performance of a play given just for you. This was one of the first "grown-up" books that ever made me cry and laugh out loud too. It frightened and delighted me. It made me realize that those were the things that good books did. It did all the things that Dickens, the consummate actor, the writer with boundless energy and more feelings sometimes than even his enormous heart could contain, loved to do and does better than anyone else.

P.S. Make sure you read the "Canceled Conclusion," the alternative ending Dickens discarded, and make up your own mind whether he was right.

Michael Cronin, Author

THE GREAT GATSBY F. Scott Fitzgerald

A compact but engrossing read, *The Great Gatsby* propels you into a world of fast cars, fancy cocktails, and the cool of 1920s New York and Long Island. Through the narrator, Nick Carraway, we meet an array of characters who epitomize the glamour, opulence, and wealth of the Jazz Age. Everything revolves around Jay Gatsby and his legendary parties in rich and trendy West Egg. However, Gatsby soon discovers that he can't have it all when he falls in love with Nick's cousin Daisy—who, despite her feelings, remains with her adulterous husband, Tom.

Fitzgerald immerses us in life in the fast lane, but the pace inevitably burns out and the decadence descends into a gripping and tragic climax.

Melanie Palmer, Editor

Next?

Try Salinger's *Nine Stories* (UTBG 244) or Hemingway's *A Moveable Feast* (UTBG 233).

Also try Truman Capote's *Breakfast at Tiffany's* (UTBG 50). Not the same period, but something about the yearning strikes the same chords.

THE GREAT RAILWAY BAZAAR

Paul Theroux

Paul Theroux is the doyen of modern travel writing, and to my mind, this is his best book. Theroux chronicles a railway odyssey from London's Victoria station to the Trans-Siberian Express, with a cornucopia of journeys in between, including the Mandalay Express from Rangoon, a local Burmese train to Naung-Peng, and, in Vietnam during the war, a rattling ride from Saigon to Bien Hoa. It's purposeless travel for fun and adventure by a writer with a gift for luminous prose, as well as an eye for telling detail and a robust sense of humor (not to mention irony). There is acerbic social commentary and plenty of serious stuff there, too.

Sara Wheeler, Author

Next?

Move on to Theroux's *The Old Patagonian Express*.

For a fictional look at an around-the-world trip, try Maureen Johnson's *13 Little Blue Envelopes*.

Bill Bryson writes very, very funny books about his travels; the best is definitely the fabulous one about Britain—*Notes from a Small Island* (UTBG 248).

Or try Stephen Clarke's *A Year in the Merde*, a hilarious look at an Englishman in France.

HABIBI Naomi Shihab Nye

12+

Next?

Like Sisters on the Homefront by Rita Williams-Garcia is about Gayle, sent from her home in New York to live with Southern relatives.

The Loud Silence of Francine Green by Karen Cushman is the story of a girl who befriends an outcast at her school in the 1950s.

Teenager Liyana Abboud has grown up in the United States but her family has decided to move back to her father's homeland, Jerusalem. Liyana doesn't know the language, religion, or restrictive customs of her new home. And she isn't allowed to be friends with Omer, a Jewish teenager. Because he is Jewish and Liyana is Palestinian, their budding relationship is forbidden by both of their cultures. Think Romeo and Juliet, but with two cultures prohibiting the match instead of just two families.

Though the forbidden love story is important, the novel shouldn't be dismissed as a simple romance. Liyana's transplant causes her to question her own beliefs, and instead of quietly disagreeing, she makes decisions and takes action to change what she believes is wrong. Her story will strike a chord with any teenager trying to do the same, whether they are in a foreign land (high school, a new city) or their hometown.

Heather Miller, Librarian

HAMLET William Shakespeare

14+

I hated Shakespeare in school. I couldn't understand the plays and was convinced that no one really liked them. People just pretended they did, to seem intelligent. But I wasn't used to reading poetry, and one day I realized that I was mentally putting a period at the end of each line, chopping the words up into nonsense. So I read "To be or not to be—" while paying strict attention to the punctuation. A revelation! I was a depressed teenager, and it was as if Shakespeare had put my mood into words—"How weary, flat, stale, and unprofitable seem to me all the uses of this world."

I read the rest of the play and loved it. The drama, humor, and magnificent poetry had been there all along—I'd just been blind to them. Give Bill a chance. He really did write the most amazing stuff.

Susan Price, Author

Next?

More Shakespeare, of course. *Romeo and Juliet* and *A Midsummer Night's Dream* are old favorites. And if you get the chance you really ought to try and see these plays too.

For a look at the *Hamlet* story from a different character's point of view, try Lisa Klein's reimaging, *Ophelia,* or Tom Stoppard's classic play, *Rosencrantz & Guildenstern Are Dead.*

Dating Hamlet by Lisa Fiedler also tells the story from Ophelia's point of view.

THE HANDMAID'S TALE
Margaret Atwood

In some ways this book is really science fiction, but you'll find no spaceships or laser guns here. The story opens in a high-school gymnasium, converted into a dormitory and patrolled by "aunts" armed with electric cattle prods. It is a frightening near-future scenario, where men have taken away women's independence by the simple method of cutting off their access to money.

The handmaid of the title is a young woman named Offred ("Of Fred"), whose job it is to have babies for Fred's infertile wife. She has no choice in this, because much of the population is infertile following a nuclear disaster. Right from the start we know this is going to be a sinister tale, and it becomes more chilling with every page.

Katherine Roberts, Author

Next?

If you like Margaret Atwood's style, look for her science-fiction tale *Oryx and Crake*, or *Cat's Eye* (UTBG 61), her classic of childhood and memory.

Another good mix of science fiction and feminism? Read Ursula K. Le Guin's *The Dispossessed* and *The Left Hand of Darkness* (UTBG 202).

HARD CASH Kate Cann

Next?

Kate Cann has written many highly popular teen novels—try *Footloose*, about three girls going on vacation together, or *Shacked Up,* the second in the Hard Cash trilogy.

Many of Sarah Dessen's novels involve teens with unique summer jobs—try *The Truth About Forever* or *Keeping the Moon* (UTBG 191).

A series about being very rich? Try the **Gossip Girl** series (UTBG 140) by Cecily von Ziegesar, about a group of New York friends.

Richard Steele is a hard-up art student—and his life suffers from his lack of cash. In this very funny, highly readable contemporary novel, the author takes a look at what happens when Rich makes some serious money from getting an ad agency interested in his drawings. Suddenly the girl he's been lusting after for ages actually seems interested in him, and he enters a world of trendy parties, posh restaurants, and designer gear. But is selling his talent the same as selling out? And is Portia, the girl of his dreams, worth the trouble it takes to get her? With her customary light touch, Kate Cann answers these questions and creates a very believable hero in Rich.

Sherry Ashworth, Author

HARD LOVE Ellen Wittlinger

John and Marisol are unlikely friends. Marisol, who has spiky hair and always dresses in black, is a lesbian, and John has his emotions so thoroughly tamped down that he doesn't know what he is—besides lonely, and angry at his divorced parents. John and Marisol meet because of 'zines, the homemade magazines they both write, and *Hard Love* is the story of the deep and difficult relationship that ignites between them. It's always an interesting story and often funny—there's a lovelorn best friend, a terrible prom date, a dash toward freedom. But it's the feelings, true and alive on every page, that make *Hard Love* a book that strikes the heart.
Jeanne DuPrau, Author

Next?

For more by Ellen Wittlinger, be sure to try *Heart on My Sleeve*, a modern-day epistolary novel told in IMs, e-mails, letters, and more.

Another book that deals with the sensitive relationship between two teens, one straight and one gay, is Barbara Wersba's *Whistle Me Home*.

For a more humorous, lighthearted approach to the gay–straight friendship, try E. Lockhart's *Dramarama* (UTBG 99).

The HARRY POTTER series J. K. Rowling

Next?

In order they are: *Harry Potter and the Sorcerer's Stone*; *Harry Potter and the Chamber of Secrets*; *Harry Potter and the Prisoner of Azkaban*; *Harry Potter and the Goblet of Fire*; *Harry Potter and the Order of the Phoenix*; *Harry Potter and the Half-Blood Prince*; *Harry Potter and the Deathly Hallows*.

More wizards and a wizarding school? Try Ursula K. Le Guin's *A Wizard of Earthsea* (UTBG 394).

The only fantasy in recent years that's come close to the popularity of Harry Potter is Christopher Paolini's *Eragon* (UTBG 105) and the rest of his **Inheritance** trilogy.

We first meet Harry as a small baby; his parents are dead and the only family he's got left are his muggle (non-wizard) aunt and uncle, Petunia and Vernon Dursley. Harry has a painful upbringing; he is bullied by his cousin, Dudley, and forced to live in a dingy cupboard under the stairs.

During his time at Hogwarts School for Witchcraft and Wizardry, Harry develops from a young boy into an adolescent who seems to get moodier by the chapter! But he still has time to save the day, with the help of his loyal friends Ron Weasley and Hermione Granger.

J. K. Rowling has written a colorful masterpiece full of suspense, action, and magic. Millions of people have read and loved these books, and I'm sure they'll continue to do so for decades!
Olivia Armes, age 14

HATCHET   Gary Paulsen

12+

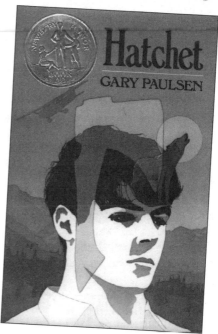

In seventh grade, I read two different books that would shape my future as a writer: *It*, by Stephen King, showed me how completely warped you could get if you wrote for adults, and *Hatchet*, by Gary Paulsen, showed me how rich you could get if you wrote for children.

I closed *Hatchet* disbelieving that it had been written for kids. It was just too good. Looking at it vs. *It*, there wasn't much difference and there were startling similarities: the horror of the unknown; the strange magic of survival that seems to come with being a child.

The part in *Hatchet* where Brian realizes that animals never cry, never feel sorry for themselves, is a profound moment that I still take strength from. And when he goes into ecstasy over "first meat," we see the same eye for the grotesque that Stephen King mines so well in childhood. This book remains fierce, disturbing, weird, hopeful, and as good as adult literature of any kind.

Ned Vizzini, Author

Next?

There are sequels—*The River; Brian's Winter; Brian's Return; Brian's Hunt*.

Another great Paulsen book is *The Beet Fields* (UTBG 30), about a boy learning to survive on his own.

True survival-in-the-wilderness stories can be amazing; try *The Worst Journey in the World* (UTBG 399) by Apsley Cherry-Garrard.

Fourteen-year-old Brian is the sole survivor of a plane crash in the Canadian wilderness. Stranded hundreds of miles from civilization, he must survive a harsh, unforgiving environment. All he has to help him are his wits and a small hatchet.

At first Brian makes mistake after mistake—one of them almost fatal—as he attempts to build a shelter, find food, protect himself from wild animals, and make fire. Then, slowly, he learns to look after himself. As his body and mind adapt to his new life, he undergoes a profound change in outlook and attitude.

Hatchet is a gripping story of survival against all odds—of a teenager from the city up against nature in the raw. It is also the story of a boy coming to a new understanding of himself, his abilities, and the natural world.

Graham Gardner, Author

HATTIE BIG SKY Kirby Larson

It's early in the 1900s, and World War I is beginning. Hattie's parents have died, and she lives with distant cousins in Iowa, earning her keep by doing chores, until word comes that her long-lost uncle has died and left her a claim in Vida, Montana. If she wants the land (320 acres!), she needs to live on it for a year, fencing part of it in and growing crops. In her time on the land, she meets all sorts of people, finds out about prejudice, and learns how to cook, clean, and rely on the barest of essentials to survive.

I can't imagine living as Hattie did, and even more amazing is realizing that many more people lived just like this. Luckily for us, those early settlers survived to tell their stories. This book is based on the author's great-grandmother and her experiences, and it's a great story about having courage. It's also an interesting look at World War I and the prejudices some people held at that time.

Kelly Jo Lasher, Librarian

> ### Next?
>
> For more fiction set in the past, try *A Northern Light* (UTBG 247) by Jennifer Donnelly—like *Hattie*, this one is based on a true story.
>
> Also, *Fever 1793* by Laurie Halse Anderson is an interesting look at how a teenager reacts as yellow fever spreads through Philadelphia.
>
> And, if you're interested in prejudice set in modern times, try *Fade to Black* by Alex Flinn.

THE HAUNTING OF ALAIZABEL CRAY

Chris Wooding

> ### Next?
>
> Chris Wooding writes dark and atmospheric novels. Try *The Storm Thief* and *Poison* (UTBG 272).
>
> Or try *The Last Apprentice* by Joseph Delaney—Thomas Ward is the seventh son of a seventh son so he can do battle with demons and spirits.
>
> Marcus Sedgwick writes wonderfully shady, moody books. Try *The Book of Dead Days*.

If you like a macabre, eerie story set in a vividly portrayed cityscape, full of action, with foul enemies and ghoulish creatures, then this is the book for you. Hideous things lurk within the labyrinth of the city's Old Quarter, and those who venture out at night are easy prey for the wolves and murderers that stalk the crooked streets, and for creatures far more deadly—the wych-kin. But evil disguised is the deadliest kind of all. Behind the facade of wealth and charity that surrounds the uppermost levels of society lies a terrifying pact with the wych-kin that threatens humankind's very existence. And the key to the conspiracy? The enigmatic Alaizabel Cray.

Brenda Marshall, Librarian

THE HEART IS A LONELY HUNTER

Carson McCullers

The Depression still grips McCullers's small town in the Deep South on the eve of World War II, with rumors of fascist activity drifting from Europe. A deaf-mute jeweler's-engraver named Singer takes the pulse of the segregated community throughout a year, as black and white townsfolk alike tell him their troubles. They are all lonely and desperate, but Singer is lonelier still since his one friend was incarcerated in an asylum—unsatisfactory though that friendship was, as his role of confidant only worked one way. This book is intensely sad, but it's rewarding for the depiction of human relationships and of people who fail to see that they already have what they need.

Geraldine Brennan, Journalist

> **Next?**
>
> More by the same author? Try the *Collected Stories of Carson McCullers*.
>
> *Of Mice and Men* (UTBG 253) by John Steinbeck is a story of pain and friendship also set in the Deep South.
>
> For a different sort of cold-and-lonely, in a different America, try *The Great Gatsby* (UTBG 143) by F. Scott Fitzgerald.

HEART OF DARKNESS   Joseph Conrad

> **Next?**
>
> *Lord Jim* has always been my favorite Conrad novel—not only is Marlowe again the narrator but it also shares the theme of a man discovering essential truths about himself.
>
> If you want to know how this turn-of-the-19th-century novel could be adapted for Hollywood, read Michael Herr's book, *Dispatches*, and then watch *Apocalypse Now* to see how the two books were melded into a cinematic masterpiece.

Say Joseph Conrad to most people and this is the book that they will think of; between the covers of this slim novel lurks an unforgettable indictment of man.

The premise is simple: Marlowe (the narrator) is employed by a trading company to locate its most effective operative, who is living in the heart of the Congo. The journey that Marlowe undertakes, the man he finds at the end of his travels, and his dawning insight into himself form the bulk of the narrative.

It's not an easy read, but when Francis Ford Coppola wanted to make a film about the horrors of the Vietnam War and the way in which it had corrupted good men, this was the book that he turned to.

Laura Hutchings, Teacher

HEART TO HEART: NEW POEMS INSPIRED BY TWENTIETH-CENTURY AMERICAN ART

Edited by Jan Greenberg

Next?

If you love reading poetry, try Tracie Vaughn Zimmer's *Sketches from a Spy Tree*, a series of poems about a family, or Naomi Shihab Nye's *The Words Under the Words*.

If you like reading stories influenced by famous paintings, try Tracy Chevalier's *Girl with a Pearl Earring* (UTBG 134), Blue Balliett's *Chasing Vermeer*, or Lynn Cullen's *I Am Rembrandt's Daughter*.

Poetry can uncover your true self. There are so many ways to express your feelings through poetry. In the book *Heart to Heart*, multiple authors contribute their insights about many different situations through their responses to famous paintings. You will very easily be able to relate your own life to one of the poems in this book, which deals with the various choices you must make during life. From reading this book, I've learned that the outcomes to these choices will never necessarily be the same. Reading poetry can let your mind interpret outcomes in multiple ways instead of having only one, as you would with a novel. Poetry helps your mind travel beyond the words into a new level of thinking.
Becca Hiekel, age 16

A HEARTBREAKING WORK OF STAGGERING GENIUS   Dave Eggers

Written on pure joy and adrenaline, this autobiographical book more than lives up to its title, which pokes fun at the things reviewers write. This is all the more amazing considering its subject. The deaths of both parents leave Dave in charge of his younger brother, Toph. To help them deal with their grief, he gives Toph the most anarchic education possible, struggling with the demands of suddenly becoming a single teenage parent while also trying to run a magazine and have a love life. A rip-roaring journey into the heart of modern America, dealing with heartbreak with a swagger, this may be the funniest book you ever read. With such a humble author, how could you miss it?
Ariel Kahn, Academic

Next?

Dave Eggers's subsequent book, *You Shall Know Our Velocity*, is about a crazy road trip.

The original crazy road trip with a friend is Jack Kerouac's *On the Road* (UTBG 255).

Augusten Burroughs's *Running with Scissors* (UTBG 298) takes a look at a boy's nontraditional childhood.

HEAT Mike Lupica

Cuban-born Michael Arroyo has baseball running through his veins and Yankee Stadium practically in his backyard. Yet his only hope of seeing the inside of this magical place is by pitching his Bronx All-Star team to the district finals and a shot at the Little League World Series.

Michael is good enough to make it happen, but envious coaches and players from rival teams are convinced he is too seasoned a player to be only 12 years old. How can he prove them wrong with his birth certificate miles away in his Cuban homeland? Throw in a mysterious and beautiful girl who keeps turning up to watch Michael pitch and you have one rousing baseball tale.

Lupica's talent for sports writing translates perfectly into fiction as he blends the action of baseball with one boy's search for his identity. This book will make even non-sports fans sit up and cheer!

Shari Fesko, Librarian

Next?

Travel Team by Mike Lupica tells the story of Danny, who may be small but he can play ball, and he may take a ragtag team of misfits all the way to victory!

Sportswriter John Feinstein has written two teen mysteries that capture the excitement of sports while stirring in romance and suspense: *Last Shot* and *Vanishing Act*.

Night Hoops by Carl Deuker tells the story of Nick, a team player who dreams of varsity basketball.

THE HEAVEN SHOP Deborah Ellis

Next?

More Ellis? Try *The Breadwinner* (UTBG 50).

Chanda's Secrets (UTBG 63) by Allan Stratton also paints a picture of a family trying to survive AIDS-ridden Africa.

Reporter Stephanie Nolen's *28 Stories of AIDS in Africa* is a searing collection of nonfiction portraits of the AIDS epidemic in Africa.

No Turning Back by Beverley Naidoo also lets the reader into the reality of life as part of a gang of street children struggling to survive, this time in South Africa.

Binti is a rising star of the most popular radio soap in Malawi and loves nothing more than helping her father in the Heaven Shop, where they make coffins to "take you more quickly to heaven." When her father falls victim to the AIDS virus, as her mother did, Binti is split up from her brother and the sister who finds that "men will give you money if you are nice to them." Refusing to give up, Binti sets out to look for her grandmother and finds a new way to fight back.

Powerful and poignant, this is an original and ultimately hopeful story that highlights the individuals caught up in a global tragedy on a massive scale. Overflowing with strength and courage and raw humanity, it reveals appalling ignorance and prejudice, and it packs a powerful punch.

Eileen Armstrong, Librarian

HEROES   Robert Cormier

14+

Next?

More Cormier? Try *After the First Death* (UTBG 7) and *The Chocolate War* (UTBG 67).

More books about war—although World War I in this case—are *Private Peaceful* (UTBG 282) by Michael Morpurgo and *Lord of the Nutcracker Men* by Iain Lawrence.

Slightly more challenging war novels are *Johnny Got His Gun* by Dalton Trumbo and *All Quiet on the Western Front* (UTBG 12) by Erich Maria Remarque.

Two men, both with medals for bravery, both survivors of World War II—but one comes home to Frenchtown to kill the other. Why?

Prompted by the 50th anniversary celebrations of D-Day, Cormier wrote this book to express his ideas about heroism. Larry and Francis are inextricably linked by their involvement with Nicole Renard, but guilt and the desire for revenge, rather than love, are the forces that really drive this narrative.

I've never read a Cormier novel that didn't make me think long and hard about the subject matter—and this book is no exception. Personally, I find it hard not to feel sorry for Francis, but you'll have to make up your own mind about him!

Laura Hutchings, Teacher

HIGH FIDELITY   Nick Hornby

14+

A great read, this book. It's about a guy who's trying to come to terms with having just been dumped by his girlfriend. When he's not thinking about sex, which he is almost constantly, he's thinking about music (he works in a secondhand record shop). It's about male obsessions, and it's one of the funniest (and saddest and truest) books I've ever read. If you're female and you want to find out why men are like they are, read it. If you're male, read it and find yourself laughing and cringing at the same time. It clues into the mind of just about every teenage boy I've ever known, except that our hero—and this is what makes it even funnier and even sadder—is actually 35 years old.

Malachy Doyle, Author

Next?

More Nick Hornby? Try *About a Boy* (UTBG 5) or *Fever Pitch* (UTBG 116); or the wonderful history of his own musical passions, *31 Songs*.

Simmone Howell's novel *Notes from the Teenage Underground* does for movies what Nick Hornby does for music here.

Doing It (UTBG 94) by Melvin Burgess is another hard-hitting novel about male obsession—this time the sexual obsessions of teenage boys.

Nick & Norah's Infinite Playlist (UTBG 242) by Rachel Cohn and David Levithan uses punk rock music as the background for an unforgettable night in the teens' lives.

152

The HIS DARK MATERIALS trilogy

Philip Pullman

Philip Pullman manages to make you believe a fantasy novel is real with his clever wit and suspenseful endings. This is a series of three stunning books (*The Golden Compass*, *The Subtle Knife,* and *The Amber Spyglass*), each one better than the last.

A young girl, Lyra, is drawn into a fantastic adventure when her friend Roger disappears under mysterious circumstances. She soon finds out that Mrs. Coulter and her evil friends are after her, for some purpose she must discover for herself. An expedition to the North turns into a flight for her life. And now that she's started there's no turning back . . .

Be warned. Once you've started, you won't want to be interrupted.

Hattie Grylls, age 12

> ### Next?
>
> More Philip Pullman? Some of his best are the historical **Sally Lockhart** books (UTBG 301), starting with *The Ruby in the Smoke*.
>
> Jonathan Stroud's **The Bartimaeus Trilogy** is also a sophisticated fantasy—start with *The Amulet of Samarkand* (UTBG 17).
>
> If you're interested in the debate on religion, try C. S. Lewis's *The Screwtape Letters* (UTBG 304).
>
> Or try **The Lord of the Rings** trilogy (UTBG 210) by J. R. R. Tolkien or **The Chronicles of Narnia** by C. S. Lewis for more classic fantasy.

If like me you're not a huge fan of fantasy, don't be put off reading this trilogy. Philip Pullman is one of the finest storytellers and once you've been sucked into this intriguing world you won't want to stop till you've read all three volumes.

Grounding his fictional world in the hauntingly familiar, Pullman weaves reality and imagination with a masterful touch. There are witches, angels, talking polar bears, and other much stranger creatures. There is also Oxford and London, canal boats and cowboys, Milton, and cutting-edge science.

Since the publication of His Dark Materials, Pullman has famously attacked C. S. Lewis for the religious subtext of his Narnia stories. I, for one, read Lewis as a child and remained totally oblivious to any religious message. I have grown up to be a lying, cheating gambler addicted to Turkish Delight, a cannibal, and a devout nonbeliever to boot. If Lewis was out to Christianize young minds, he failed.

Pullman, on the other hand, in his crusade against organized religion, stuffs his trilogy full of imaginary beings and figures from Christian mythology. Despite his intentions, I'd wager that Lyra's adventures will lead far more young readers to religion than Narnia ever did. Oh, the irony.

Pullman's His Dark Materials trilogy cannot be praised enough. Read it and marvel!

Neil Arksey, Author

THE HISTORIAN Elizabeth Kostova

14+

Next?

Go back and read Bram Stoker's *Dracula* (UTBG 98)—the classic vampire story has just as much suspense and horror as any of its successors.

For other books on teen "creatures of the night," try Annette Curtis Klause's *Blood and Chocolate* (UTBG 40) (werewolves), M. T. Anderson's *Thirsty* (UTBG 356) (vampires), or Jean Thesman's *The Other Ones* (witches).

Hold onto your vampire-loving hat (and cloak, and most especially your library of rare and mysterious books), and get ready to embark on a journey through time and space in search of the truth about Dracula (who yet lives! and is yet dangerous!) with our bookish 16-year-old heroine, who (although she did not know it) comes from a family already seriously involved in the deadly quest. There are lots of old letters, stories within stories, dark nights, parental disappearances and reappearances, reasons to scream, and reasons to run. Romance! Danger! Death! And of course, you'll get to travel all over Europe while you read (including Transylvania, naturally). Be prepared to enjoy yourself for several days at least with this long, juicy, well-written book.

Nancy Werlin, Author

THE HITCHHIKER'S GUIDE TO THE GALAXY Douglas Adams

12+

Arthur Dent is an ordinary Earth guy having a very bad day when his old friend Ford Prefect reveals he's not really an Earthling. Ford, it turns out, is a roving reporter from a distant planet, on Earth to compile an entry for a travel guide to the galaxy. But unfortunately that entry will now be unnecessary as the planet Earth is about to be demolished.

The Hitchhiker's Guide to the Galaxy is a subversive and zany jaunt through space, poking fun along the way at all manner of familiar earthly institutions—science and science fiction, bureaucrats, alcohol, gadgets, geeks, jargon, philosophy, and pomposity, to name but a few. The surreal universe Adams creates for his travelers is filled with the ridiculous and the absurd. The adventures of our two heroes are comic to the end. Do not leave the planet without it.

Neil Arksey, Author

Next?

The "trilogy" continues with *The Restaurant at the End of the Universe*.

There's nothing really like *Hitchhiker*, but try *Good Omens* (UTBG 139) by Terry Pratchett and Neil Gaiman, in which a devil and an angel conspire to prevent the apocalypse.

Or anything by Philip K. Dick. Try *Do Androids Dream of Electric Sheep?* (UTBG 93).

HITLER YOUTH: GROWING UP IN HITLER'S SHADOW Susan Campbell Bartoletti

12+

Next?

For more on the Hitler Youth, try *Parallel Journeys* by Eleanor Ayer, which weaves together two disparate stories about a German girl and boy—one Jewish and the other not.

Susan Campbell Bartoletti has written many fascinating nonfiction titles—if you enjoyed *Hitler Youth*, try *Kids on Strike!* next.

For excellent fiction about growing up German during World War II, try John Boyne's *The Boy in the Striped Pajamas* (UTBG 46) or Markus Zusak's *The Book Thief* (UTBG 44).

Hitler used his youth movement to subvert schools, churches, and families and replace them with a series of paramilitary groups run by the Nazis and loyal only to him. Bartoletti's ambitious book depicts this movement by focusing on the stories of young Germans who went through it or even resisted it, while putting the youth groups in the context of Nazi society in general, and of World War II specifically.

While this is undoubtedly a lot to pack into 159 pages of text, the dozens of individual stories attached to the well-chosen pictures are as well-rounded a look at the Hitler Youth experience as I have ever read. The book reads like a photo album, or a yearbook from a sinister high school. Read this book and you will ask yourself, "What would I have done? What would I do now?" The book also includes an index, notes, a time line, a bibliography, an essay on the photographs, and an interesting author's note.

Douglas Rees, Author

THE HOBBIT J. R. R. Tolkien

12+

The Hobbit is a prelude to The Lord of the Rings trilogy. Since it was written in 1937, this classic tale has delighted generations of readers throughout the world. Bilbo Baggins is a friendly hobbit who is content with his quiet life. One day he receives some strange visitors: a wizard named Gandalf and a band of dwarves. He joins them on a dangerous and exciting quest to raid the treasure hoard of Smaug the dragon. At first Bilbo is nervous and uncertain. He worries about getting back home. As the journey progresses he encounters elves, goblins, and trolls and finds himself surprised by his own enthusiasm. Life will never be the same again.

Brenda Marshall, Librarian

Next?

The Lord of the Rings trilogy (UTBG 210) is Tolkien at his greatest.

Eragon (UTBG 105) by Christopher Paolini is another quest-with-a-dragon book.

Or try Lloyd Alexander's **Chronicles of Prydain**, starting with *The Book of Three*, and find out about Taran, the heroic pig-keeper!

HOLE IN MY LIFE Jack Gantos

Jack Gantos is a normal kid; he's lazy, bored, constantly stoned, and not really sure what he wants to do, though he kind of thinks he wants to write. Which means college. Which means money—something he doesn't have. Then one day a guy offers him a way to make ten grand. All he has to do is help sail a boat to New York— and not care that there are more than 900 kg of hash hidden in the bows. Great? No way!

Caught and sent to prison, he does time surrounded by violence, rape, and misery. Somehow though, he still wants to write—and that need alone is what saves him. This is a true story that reads like a thriller—one full of brutality and steeped in drug culture. Read and be shocked—I promise it'll put you off smuggling for life.

Leonie Flynn, Editor

Jack Gantos

Think *you* can *get away* with it? So did Jack.

Next?

Jack interprets his life through the books he reads. Try Jack Kerouac's *On the Road* (UTBG 255) for the road trip of a lifetime. Or *The House of the Dead* by Dostoyevsky, which tells of the author's own imprisonment.

Or try another novel that spins around drugs—*Trainspotting* (UTBG 363) by Irvine Welsh, though it's a much harder read.

Jack Gantos has also written the disturbing *Desire Lines* (UTBG 91).

PHILOSOPHY 101

The Alchemist by Paulo Coelho

Jonathan Livingston Seagull by Richard Bach

Siddhartha by Hermann Hesse

The Screwtape Letters by C. S. Lewis

Sophie's World by Jostein Gaarder

HOLES Louis Sachar

12+

Stanley Yelnats IV is an 11-year-old boy wrongly accused of stealing a pair of sneakers. Stanley serves his punishment at Camp Green Lake (where there is no lake). In the unbearable heat he is made to dig holes: a five-by-five-foot hole each day, starting at 4:30 every morning!

During breaks in the digging the reader is introduced to such characters as Kissin' Kate Barlow, an avenging outlaw; Madame Zeroni, a gypsy fortune-teller, and of course Stanley Yelnats, a palindrome in himself! It is Stanley's destiny to be the fourth generation to fall foul of Madame Zeroni's curse.

Will Stanley and his newfound friends unravel the mystery of Camp Green Lake and lift the terrible curse that has been laid upon his family?

Benjamin Cuffin-Munday, age 11

This story starts with poor and luckless Stanley Yelnats being sent to Camp Green Lake, a correction facility for wayward boys. Upon arrival he is told his punishment will be to dig a hole five feet wide and five feet deep, every day in the scorching heat, for the next 18 months. Anything he finds must be handed over to the warden, no questions asked. It all sounds straightforward, but it's anything but.

Louis Sachar has woven the cleverest of plots around characters with fabulous names such as Armpit, Mr. Sir, and Kissin' Kate Barlow. In a nutshell, *Holes* is one of the best children's books I have ever read—and I've read a lot of them!

Helena Pielichaty, Author

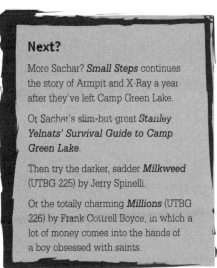

Next?

More Sachar? *Small Steps* continues the story of Armpit and X-Ray a year after they've left Camp Green Lake.

Or Sachar's slim-but-great *Stanley Yelnats' Survival Guide to Camp Green Lake*.

Then try the darker, sadder *Milkweed* (UTBG 225) by Jerry Spinelli.

Or the totally charming *Millions* (UTBG 226) by Frank Cottrell Boyce, in which a lot of money comes into the hands of a boy obsessed with saints.

HOMBRE Elmore Leonard

14+

Next?

Valdez Is Coming is another great Western by Elmore Leonard.

Some more fantastic Westerns (if you've never read them, give them a try; they're better than you think!): *Shane* by Jack Schaefer; *Lonesome Dove* (UTBG 204) by Larry McMurtry; and anything by J. T. Edson (check out your library!).

Or what about Elmore Leonard writing crime? Try *52 Pickup* (UTBG 2) or any of his other books!

I've always loved reading Westerns, and this is my all-time favorite. John Russell has lived with the Apaches since he was six years old, but now he's back in the white man's world. It's an ugly world—full of prejudice, greed, and exploitation—but John Russell walks through it all with pride and silence. And when things begin to go wrong, he does what has to be done.

That's what this book is all about: doing what has to be done, regardless of the consequences. It's a thrilling read—tough and uncompromising—and when you get to the end, you'll wish that you could live your life like the man they called Hombre.

Kevin Brooks, Author

HOMECOMING Cynthia Voigt

12+

What would you do if your mother left you in charge of three younger siblings and just disappeared? Dicey does a great job. Having decided that the family should stay together, she avoids the police and sets off across America. When they discover that they have a grandmother in Maryland, they wonder whether she will give them a home. Full of hope, they set off to find her. Will their gran take them in?

A wonderful picture of a family and the rich, complex web of American society, full of interesting and sympathetic characters and a really exciting plot. Dicey, James, Maybeth, and Will make terrific traveling companions.

Ann Jungman, Author

Next?

The story continues with *Dicey's Song*, *A Solitary Blue*, *The Runner*, *Sons from Afar*, and *Seventeen Against the Dealer*.

For a different kind of orphaned siblings story, try Lemony Snicket's *A Series of Unfortunate Events* (UTBG 311).

Journey to Jo'burg by Beverley Naidoo is about two children traveling across South Africa to find their mother.

Another group of children coping without adults are those in *How I Live Now* (UTBG 165) by Meg Rosoff.

HOMELESS BIRD Gloria Whelan

Next?

Suzanne Fisher Staples's *Shabanu* and *Haveli* are both remarkably similar stories set in modern-day Pakistan.

Deborah Ellis's *The Breadwinner* (UTBG 50) is about Parvana, who has to disguise herself as a boy in Taliban-ruled Afghanistan to help her family survive.

Patricia McCormick's *Sold* (UTBG 332) is a verse novel about Lakshmi, a 13-year-old girl sold into prostitution in India.

What if at 13 you were married to a boy you had never seen, and had to live with his family, whom you had never met? This is Koly's story. It's a tale of her survival after everything she knows and trusts is stripped away. Set in India, *Homeless Bird* provides a window on a world very different from what many of us know, but with people who will seem instantly familiar. With a recognizable plot that parallels many classic fairy tales and quickly moving chapters, this book will pull you into Koly's life of heartbreak, love, hard work, and triumph. You will cry with her in her dark moments and root for her as she struggles to win out in the end. Gloria Whelan spins an excellent tale of a girl forced to rely on her own resourcefulness and her talent with a needle and thread to make her way out of a bad situation.

Megan Webb, Librarian

HOOT Carl Hiaasen

This is a conservation story with a difference. It carries a powerful eco-message, but it's hilariously funny too and packed with quirky characters and crazy situations. Roy Eberhardt has recently moved to Florida; he's bright, resourceful, and used to being the new kid in town. Roy soon makes friends with Mullet Fingers—a boy who lives on the fringes of society—and his stepsister Beatrice, and he finds himself caught up in their campaign to save a colony of rare owls. The tiny birds live in burrows on land that's earmarked to be the site of yet another Mother Paula's All-American Pancake House. The three unlikely allies take up their cause against a corrupt adult establishment, in a lively story with plenty of suspense, wit, and great good humor.

Kathryn Ross, Literary Agent

Next?

More Carl Hiaasen? Try *Flush*.

If you like Hiaasen's humorous, off-beat characters, try Jonathan Kebbe's *The Bottle-Top King*.

If you want to know the real story behind the fast-food industry, read *Fast Food Nation* (UTBG 113) by Eric Schlosser—it could put you off burgers for life!

Move on to an adult Hiaasen book—*Tourist Season* (UTBG 361) is a good place to start.

HOPE WAS HERE

Joan Bauer

This is a book to touch all the emotions as the narrator, Hope, tells the story of her life—and her hopes. There's a gentle thread of humor throughout the book, centered in a sleepy Wisconsin town. Sixteen-year-old Hope works in the local diner with her wonderful cooking aunt Addie and other great characters. She's soon caught up in the intricacies of small-town politics as she helps her sick boss campaign against the corrupt mayor standing for reelection. *Hope* is a joy to read as it swings between cooking, serving, eating, and politics—there's a good deal of love interest too, and moments of anxiety over Hope's unreliable mom.

Wendy Cooling, Books Consultant

Next?

More Bauer? Try *Squashed*, an extraordinary story of first love—and of a girl who is determined to grow the biggest pumpkin in the world. Or *Rules of the Road*, about a drive from Chicago to Texas—though it's about the rules of life, really.

Look for Joan O'Neill's books, always full of truth and always telling strong family stories. Start with *Daisy Chain War*, the first of a quartet of books that follow the life of an Irish family.

Meg Rosoff's *How I Live Now* (UTBG 165) is another special story of love and war, one told in a strong, distinctive voice that demands to be heard—or read.

The Ultimate Teen Readers' Poll

CHARACTER WHO'D BE THE BEST BOYFRIEND

1. **Harry Potter (The Harry Potter series)**

2. **Ron Weasley (The Harry Potter series)**

3. **Russell (The Girls in Love series)**

4. **Alex Rider (The Alex Rider series)**

5. **Michael Moscovitz (The Princess Diaries series)**

6. **Legolas (The Lord of the Rings trilogy)**

7. **Draco Malfoy (The Harry Potter series)**

8. **Edward (*Twilight*)**

9. **Klaus Baudelaire (A Series of Unfortunate Events)**

10. **Shrimp (*Gingerbread*)**

THE HOURS Michael Cunningham

16+

The Hours is an uplifting novel about death. Because it's about death, it's also about life— three lives. Virginia Woolf, in the 1920s, struggles against suicidal depression and writes her novel, *Mrs. Dalloway*. In the 1940s, Mrs. Brown, suffocated by domestic bliss, longs only for the time to read. And in the 1990s, Clarissa organizes a party for Richard, who is dying of AIDS.

It's intriguing to discover the connections between the characters, and the story is fascinating. For me, though, the novel's beauty lies in the way the various protagonists discover the difference between the choices they would like to make for the sake of the people they love and the choices they must make for themselves.

Antonia Honeywell, Teacher

Next?

If you liked the lyrical, poetic writing, try Michael Cunningham's *Home at the End of the World*.

If you felt sympathy for Mrs. Brown, try *The Lovely Bones* (UTBG 213) by Alice Sebold or *Mrs. Dalloway* itself.

Another novel with a large cast of characters from every different walk of life, Richard Russo's *Empire Falls* is a funny tale about small-town life.

THE HOUSE OF SLEEP Jonathan Coe

Next?

Try some more Jonathan Coe: *The Closed Circle* and *The Rotters' Club* are particularly good, though if you like this one, try them all!

Time for Bed by David Baddiel is about one man's battle with insomnia.

Life of Pi (UTBG 203) by Yann Martel is a completely different but equally quirky and entertaining read.

For a younger read that is a humorous, behind-the-scenes look at the sleep process, check out *The Seems: The Glitch in Sleep* by John Hulme and Michael Wexler.

Sarah has an alarming tendency to fall asleep suddenly, with no warning, at any time of day. Terry swears that he hasn't slept at all for years and spends his nights watching movies. And Gregory Dudden studies sleep as a science, gradually coming to see it as a disease that must be eradicated at all costs.

A group of students are all linked by their obsession with sleep, and though they drift apart when they leave college, this same obsession brings them together again a decade later.

This very odd subject for a novel results in a read that is touching, gripping, sometimes shocking, and occasionally laugh-out-loud funny. I became a Jonathan Coe fan practically from the first page.

Susan Reuben, Editor

LOVE, SEX, AND RELATIONSHIPS
by E. Lockhart

People often ask me why I write about high school. One of the reasons is that when you go to high school you are stuck there.

Human beings can be cruel, and no matter if someone hit you yesterday, stomped on your heart, stole your best friend, talked trash about you, threatened you—in high school, you have to show up and probably sit next to that person in math class. You are legally obligated to attend.

This is not true of a college class or even of most jobs; it's true of relatively few adult situations. High school is a pressure cooker, and it's also filled with people who are extremely likely to behave badly. They're just figuring out sex, adult responsibilities, their independence from their families, their identities. They're having love relationships for the first time. This pressure cooker packed

Friendship. Not love. Well, maybe a little love, but mostly friendship:

ttyl by Lauren Myracle

Peaches by Jodi Lynn Anderson

The Sisterhood of the Traveling Pants by Ann Brashares

Saving Francesca by Melina Marchetta

An Abundance of Katherines by John Green

Love stories, but not exactly romances:

Boy Proof by Cecil Castellucci

Sloppy Firsts by Megan McCafferty

I Capture the Castle by Dodie Smith

The Earth, My Butt, and Other Big Round Things by Carolyn Mackler

What My Mother Doesn't Know by Sonya Sones

Nick & Norah's Infinite Playlist by Rachel Cohn and David Levithan

with badly behaving and inexperienced humanity is an ideal setting for high drama.

Love and relationships—that's the stuff of life, the stuff of our most intense emotions. We need to know we're not alone, people! And friendships break up just like romances do.

Some of the books I love in this genre take the emotions seriously, while others play it all for laughs more than tears (as my own books do)—but leave you thinking at the end.

And now for sex—which is tied up with love (and even with friendship), but which is also its own complicated thing. Naturally, it's fun to read about. But reading about it also lets you experiment with different attitudes toward sex without taking any action until you're ready. It lets you figure out your own path, outside of pressure or desire to actually do anything.

So read, laugh, cry, let your eyes bug out of your head, hide the books in the list below from your parents—and remember, you won't be in high school forever.

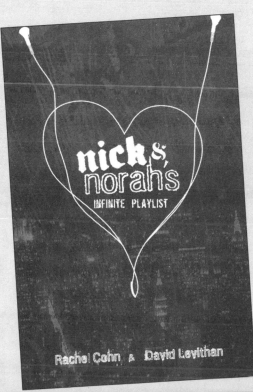

Not racy, but still good for thinking about and exploring sexuality:

Angus, Thongs and Full-Frontal Snogging by Louise Rennison

Ready or Not by Meg Cabot

The Bermudez Triangle by Maureen Johnson

Gingerbread by Rachel Cohn

Storky by D. L. Garfinkle

Oh, these are totally racy. But also thought-provoking:

Doing It by Melvin Burgess

Fly on the Wall by E. Lockhart

Wide Awake by David Levithan

A Bad Boy Can Be Good for a Girl by Tanya Lee Stone

Good Girls by Laura Ruby

How I Paid for College by Marc Acito

nick & norah's
INFINITE PLAYLIST

Rachel Cohn & David Levithan

THE HOUSE OF THE SCORPION

Nancy Farmer

Next?

Nancy Farmer is amazing—
read the very different *The
Sea of Trolls* (UTBG 305) next.

Another fast, gripping story
set in the future, where the
hero battles for survival, is
Ender's Game (UTBG 104)
by Orson Scott Card.

The camaraderie of the
imprisoned boys will remind
readers of Louis Sachar's
magnificent *Holes* (UTBG
157).

Opium is a country that was once Mexico—and its
only crop is field upon field of white opium poppies.
Matteo grows up hidden away, but some secrets
cannot be kept forever, and one day the outside
world comes crashing in. Whether caged as an
animal or pampered as a pet, Matt finally realizes
that in order to survive he has to escape. But if he
leaves Opium, could worse await him outside?

Thought-provoking, brilliantly told, with characters
you feel for and situations that leave you chewing
your fingers in anxiety, this book is amazing. With
issues of drug culture gone crazy, cloning, and
slavery, this book is full of gory detail and packed
with suspense. Will Matt survive? And when he finds
out what is planned for him, will he even want to?
Leonie Flynn, Editor

THE HOUSE OF THE SPIRITS Isabel Allende

Clara is a sparky and spirited girl, gifted
with telepathic abilities, who delights in
making objects move and predicting the
future. Falling mute upon the mysterious
death of her beautiful sister, Clara speaks
again only to tell of her foreseen wedding
to the dark and brooding Esteban, once
her sister's fiancé. He builds her a
magnificent house that becomes home to
their children, grandchildren, and an
assortment of colorful characters from the
neighborhood. Allende's magical realism
and poetic prose are widely acclaimed, but
her real achievement here is in making
readers feel as much a part of the Trueba
family as they do of their own.
Eileen Armstrong, Librarian

Next?

Other equally compelling stories by
Allende include *City of the Beasts*, an
exciting adventure about 15-year-old
Alexander, who joins his grandmother
on a dangerous expedition. Or
Allende's *Daughter of Fortune* has a
more historic feel, charting the life of
the courageous and unconventional
Chilean Eliza, caught up in the gold
rush to California.

Eva Ibbotson's *Journey to the River
Sea* (UTBG 186) is an easier, but
equally riveting, adventure read with
a similar Amazonian flavor.

THE HOUSE ON MANGO STREET

Sandra Cisneros

Life in Esperanza's neighborhood in the Latino section of Chicago is not easy, but it's all she knows. Her family has just moved to a new house, and although it isn't the one she's been dreaming of, it is a step up from that crowded old apartment where they used to live. Each day on Mango Street brings a new experience, expertly told through Esperanza's eyes. Her innocent observations of life on the street are refreshing and heartbreakingly honest. They reflect not just this young girl's situation but society as a whole, complete with the injustices that she might not yet fully understand.

I've reread this book several times now—the short chapters make it easy to pick up and put down—and every time, I walk away with a new understanding of Esperanza's life. Her thoughts and feelings will take on new meaning as your own perspectives shift, and you won't be able to get enough of this beautifully written novel.

Mary Kate Castellani, Editor

Next?

Julia Alvarez is another author who has captured similar Latin American experiences. Try *How the García Girls Lost Their Accents* (UTBG 166).

American Born Chinese (UTBG 16) by Gene Luen Yang offers a different look at how a person of another culture found his place.

More Sandra Cisneros? Try *My Wicked Wicked Ways*, a collection of short stories.

HOW I LIVE NOW Meg Rosoff

Next?

The Fire-Eaters (UTBG 118) by David Almond, set during the Cuban missile crisis, similarly shows both the wonder and fear that life holds.

For a story of a real girl caught up in a real war, read Anne Frank's *The Diary of a Young Girl* (UTBG 91).

Something with the same feel (though utterly different) is *I Capture the Castle* (UTBG 169) by Dodie Smith.

Not far in the future, teenage Daisy is sent to England to stay with her aunt, two male cousins, and their little sister. The aunt goes abroad, leaving them "home alone" on the farm. For a short while, Daisy lives in blissful limbo without adult rules, without anyone telling her she's too young for sex with cousin Edmond—a psychic bond even the war can't break. Then a bomb goes off in London. Britain is under attack. And, as the unnamed enemy closes in, Daisy and her cousins are forced to survive in a terrifying world they no longer recognize.

How I Live Now has an ingenious plot, it's beautifully written, and is all the more scary since 9/11. (Damn, I wish I'd written it!)

Jeanne Willis, Author

HOW THE GARCÍA GIRLS
LOST THEIR ACCENTS Julia Alvarez

Carla, Yolanda, Sandra, and Sofía García de la Torres are grown women living in the United States. Their lives are full, but each feels that she is missing something. Some part was left behind in the Dominican Republic when they fled for their lives so many years ago. But exactly what they are missing is unknown. Is it the family still living in the Caribbean? The tropical climate? Their heritage?

As the book progresses, the story regresses, taking the reader back through the turning points in the lives of each of "the four girls." Their marriages, their arrival in New York as young children, the day their father had to hide from the "bad men," and before, when everything was peaceful and the García de la Torres family was respected. This time shift develops the characters in a unique way, letting us see just how the girls' personal experiences have led them to their current lives and showing us the pieces they could be missing.

Heather Miller, Librarian

A FEW CHILDHOODS YOU WOULDN'T WANT FOR YOURSELF

Angela's Ashes by Frank McCourt

Chinese Cinderella by Adeline Yen Mah

Wild Swans by Jung Chang

You Don't Know Me by David Klass

Running with Scissors by Augusten Burroughs

A Child Called "It" by Dave Pelzer

This Boy's Life by Tobias Wolff

Next?

Before We Were Free, also by Julia Alvarez, is a more in-depth story of a young girl whose family is involved in the plot to overthrow dictator Rafael Trujillo.

Esperanza Rising by Pam Muñoz Ryan is another story of a Latino girl who is forced to flee Mexico for the United States just before the Great Depression.

Marilyn Sachs's *Lost in America* is another story of adjusting to American life—this time for teenage Nicole, a French Jew, during the 1940s.

HOWL'S MOVING CASTLE Diana Wynne Jones

Next?

There is a sequel, *Castle in the Air*.

Other books with a similar flavor are *A Wrinkle in Time* (UTBG 401) by Madeleine L'Engle and Geraldine McCaughrean's *A Pack of Lies*.

Moving cities appear in Philip Reeve's dazzlingly imaginative *Mortal Engines* (UTBG 232).

Sophie is the oldest of three sisters in a world where fairy-tale conventions hold sway, and she never expects to be the one who finds fortune. So she is not really surprised when the Witch of the Waste puts her under an age spell. For most of the book Sophie becomes the aged crone of traditional stories, but it doesn't stop her from being the heroine and the only person who has any control over Wizard Howl.

It was during a school visit that a boy suggested Wynne Jones could write a book about a moving castle, and Wynne Jones has interpreted the idea with characteristic quirkiness. The four doors of the castle each open onto a different place, one of which is in Wales, where Howl becomes known as "Howell," a local rugby player.

Mary Hoffman, Author

HUNTER'S HEART Julia Green

Fourteen-year-old Simon Piper lives on the Cornish coast with his mother and little sister. They're new to the area. Across the road from Simon lives 16-year-old Leah, who decides to manipulate him for her amusement. He is to be her "summer project." Told from alternate points of view, Leah and Simon reveal their frustrations with life in their own unique ways. Authentic teenage angst and wild emotions rage on every page, and both Leah and Simon are powerfully portrayed. This book is about many things—love, jealousy, obsession, and growing up—and is in the immensely likable "one of those summers where everything changed" formats that make it a delight to read.

John McLay, Literary Scout

Next?

Blue Moon is Julia Green's earlier novel about growing up—this time from a girl's point of view.

If you like the dual-perspective love-story format, try *Flipped* (UTBG 120) by Wendelin Van Draanen or *Scrambled Eggs at Midnight* (UTBG 304) by Brad Barkley and Heather Hepler.

John Green's *Looking for Alaska* (UTBG 207) is a tough but absorbing look at how a college girl dominates the lives of some of her fellow students.

For lighter relief, but similar poignancy, try *Stargirl* (UTBG 337) by Jerry Spinelli.

I AM DAVID Anne Holm

 12+

Next?

Another boy trying to find a way home is the hero of Ian Serraillier's *The Silver Sword*.

Donna Jo Napoli's *Stones in Water* is about a group of Italian boys taken captive during the war and forced into being slave laborers far away from home.

For a Holocaust story that'll make you weep, read Jerry Spinelli's *Milkweed* (UTBG 225).

Or try the simply told *The Boy in the Striped Pajamas* (UTBG 46) by John Boyne.

David is a young prisoner. He is undernourished, has very little experience with "people," and knows nothing of the big and dangerous world outside the concentration camp.

Late one night, a helpful guard helps him escape. With few resources and only a little money, David goes in search of his family. He encounters many people, some friendly and some less friendly; all the while knowing that the enemy might catch up with him.

This story touched me in a way that is hard to describe. It brought me to tears at some points, both happy and sad. It's a book about one small boy's outlook on life, how he makes the most of having very little, and it's incredibly moving. Don't be surprised if you're reduced to tears while reading it too.

David Bard, age 12

I AM THE CHEESE Robert Cormier

14+

Robert Cormier was a brilliant writer—I deliberately haven't read all his books, because I would hate to feel there were no more left to read. I'm not really a risk taker but reading his books is the sort of risk taking I can cope with: you don't know what Cormier is going to do and his books take you to the edge of fear and emotion. This is definitely the most powerful one I've read. It's a simple story—Adam Farmer is on a journey, on his bike, delivering a package for his father. But all is not as it seems and the truth is clever, surprising, and deeply moving. And as for the ending . . .

Nicola Morgan, Author

Next?

Obviously, read any Robert Cormier books. Try *The Chocolate War* (UTBG 67), *The Rag and Bone Shop* (UTBG 284), and *Heroes* (UTBG 152).

For another psychological thriller involving a mysterious past, try Graham Marks's *Zoo* (UTBG 404).

Kit's Wilderness (UTBG 197) is eerier, and like all of David Almond's books, dark and amazing. Like Cormier, he takes risks—and thank goodness for us he does!

I AM THE MESSENGER   Markus Zusak

I Am the Messenger is a mesmerizing and intriguing story about a 19-year-old cab driver named Ed. Ed leads a pretty meaningless existence until the day he happens to be at a bank during a robbery and he ends up helping to thwart the thief. His resulting 15 minutes of fame seem to be the cause of a sudden and mysterious change in his life: he begins receiving anonymous and cryptic messages written on the backs of playing cards.

As Ed begins to decipher these bizarre messages, he discovers that they are instructions for tasks. Who is sending Ed these weird playing card messages? And why are they telling him to do all these strange things? Is Ed helping or harming the people with whom these playing cards bring him into contact? Questions like these will keep you devouring the pages of this book, unable to stop reading until you find out the answers. This intricately woven and fascinating story makes you laugh and makes you think, and it's got one of the most powerful endings ever.

Sonya Sones, Author

> **Next?**
>
> For more by Markus Zusak, his award-winning *The Book Thief* (UTBG 44) is another weighty read that will not disappoint.
>
> *Millions* (UTBG 226) by Frank Cottrell Boyce also deals with the desire to help others, while Meg Cabot's *1-800-Where-R-You* series takes on a similar issue of helping versus harming the people around you.

I CAPTURE THE CASTLE   Dodie Smith

> **Next?**
>
> *Cold Comfort Farm* (UTBG 74) by Stella Gibbons takes place in a similar time and is just as interesting.
>
> Dodie Smith's novel is often likened to the books of Jane Austen—try *Pride and Prejudice* (UTBG 276), *Northanger Abbey* (UTBG 247), or *Sense and Sensibility*.
>
> Elizabeth Goudge's *The Little White Horse* also involves a girl moving to an ancient, mysterious manor.

This book sparkles and bubbles like vintage champagne. Generations of readers have loved it as teenagers and gone on loving it throughout the years. It captivates from its very first line: "I write this sitting in the kitchen sink." Who could resist?

Seventeen-year-old Cassandra is practicing her writing skills by keeping a diary. Through her eyes we follow the lives of her eccentric family members as they struggle to survive in genteel poverty, amidst the ruins of an ancient castle. With the arrival of two brothers from America, love with all its complications enters Cassandra's life and nothing will ever be quite the same again. We share her awakening to the joys and pains of unrequited passion, right through to the unexpected ending.

Funny, romantic, witty, charming, *I Capture the Castle* is a total delight from beginning to end.

Jean Ure, Author

I KNOW WHAT YOU DID LAST SUMMER
Lois Duncan

For anyone who sat through 1997's *I Know What You Did Last Summer* movie, please note that the book of the same title, while similar in premise, does not include a character with a hook for a hand. The novel, written in 1973, concerns a group of friends who accidentally kill a young boy and then make a pact to keep their involvement in his death a secret. One year later, one of the members of the group, Julie, receives a letter in the mail that spells out that someone outside of the group is aware of the friends' guilt.

In my opinion, Duncan still reigns supreme and the enduring appeal of *I Know What You Did Last Summer* is one of the reasons why. A horrifying secret from the past, an anonymous note-leaver, escalating suspense, and violence: hook or no, what more could you ask for?

Amy Pattee, Librarian

Next?

Lois Duncan's earlier suspense novels—*Daughters of Eve*, *The Third Eye*, *Down a Dark Hall*, and *Killing Mr. Griffin*—are must-reads.

Christopher Pike's **Chain Letter** series has often been compared to Lois Duncan's work.

Joan Lowery Nixon's "older" young adult novels—such as *The Specter*, *The Kidnapping of Christina Lattimore*, and *A Deadly Game of Magic*—are just as eerie as Lois Duncan's novels.

I KNOW WHY THE CAGED BIRD SINGS
Maya Angelou

Next?

Next in the series is *Gather Together in My Name*.

If you enjoyed reading about the experience of being African American, try *The Color Purple* (UTBG 75) by Alice Walker.

For an actual account of being a slave, read Frederick Douglass's *The Narrative of the Life of Frederick Douglass*.

I Know Why the Caged Bird Sings is the autobiography of a young black girl struggling against the brutal racial discrimination of America in the 1930s and 1940s. But it's also the story of a woman finding herself in the experiences of her childhood and celebrating the people she loves, especially her beloved older brother and her fierce-but-brilliant grandmother. Even though she's caged by segregation and injustice, Maya still sings of hope and self-respect. Cruel things happen (and at times, this isn't the easiest book to read), but she never presents herself or her family as victims. This fascinating life story is blisteringly honest but never bitter, and that's what makes it so difficult to put down.

Antonia Honeywell, Teacher

I, ROBOT   Isaac Asimov

This is a collection of short stories by one of the masters of sci-fi—the man who invented the idea of robots as we know them today. Originally published in "pulp" magazines in the 1940s, most of them take the form of an "interview" with Susan Calvin, founder of U.S. Robotics, who is looking back over the development of robots in her lifetime and discussing the problems the manufacturers faced along the way.

Asimov had a fantastic imagination, and although the language is a little dated, these are truly great stories. One of them was recently used as the basis for a movie of the same name. They're immensely readable and filled with the sense of what it would be like to live in a world served by intelligent machines.

Andrew Norriss, Author

Next?

You'll probably enjoy some of the other "robot" books by Asimov. "The Rest of the Robots" and "Caves of Steel" are more short stories; *Bicentennial Man* was turned into a movie with Robin Williams.

And if you just like science fiction, well, frankly, you've got choices galore. Read our feature on pp. 218–219.

THE ICE ROAD   Jaap ter Haar

If you read Nicola Morgan's feature on pp. 312–313, you'll see that she defines good historical fiction as writing that "can make you feel the cold." This book does just that. Boris is living in Leningrad in 1942, during that city's appalling siege in which 700,000 people died. For 150 pages you'll be there, too. You will feel cold and hungry, just as Boris does; you will despair at the death and desolation that surrounds him; and you will be entranced, utterly elated at every little sign of hope. You will fear for the health of Boris's ailing mother; delight in the company of his best friend, Nadia; and when a death comes, it will hit you hard. But don't be put off if it sounds grim—you'll come away from this book sober, certainly, but Boris's generosity and courage will make you stronger too, and full of admiration and hope.

Daniel Hahn, Editor

Next?

Mary Renault's *The Last of the Wine* (UTBG 199) is set around the siege of Athens during the Peloponnesian War, and it's just as harrowing.

Or try something else cold and Russian—*One Day in the Life of Ivan Denisovich* (UTBG 256) by Alexander Solzhenitsyn, or Slavomir Rawicz's *The Long Walk* (UTBG 205).

Another novel that shows the despair of war is Helen Dunmore's *The Siege*.

IF ONLY THEY COULD TALK
James Herriot

James Herriot is a vet in a UK national park, and this is the first collection of stories about the strange creatures (animal and human) he meets. Look out for the psychotic pig, the sliding seat, the flying chickens, the wailing Labrador, the story of the lightning strike, the great pig disaster, James's wonderfully inconsistent partner, Siegfried, and his younger brother, Tristan. Some of the stories are of triumph, some are of failure, and others are just really, really embarrassing, but all are incredibly funny. If you like animals, you'll love this book. I guarantee it.

Benedict Jacka, Author

Next?

James Herriot wrote six more books in the same series, of which the next is *It Shouldn't Happen to a Vet*.

Another very funny story about animals and people is *My Family and Other Animals* (UTBG 236) by Gerald Durrell.

And if you just want a pure animal story, without any humans around, you can't do better than *Watership Down* (UTBG 382) by Richard Adams.

IF YOU COME SOFTLY Jacqueline Woodson

This love story has a touch of *Romeo and Juliet* about it, and it is gentle, heartrending, and unforgettable. The growing love between two 15-year-olds—a black boy and a white girl—is threatened by prejudice but never defeated by it. Ellie and Miah have a very special relationship, something apart from the rest of the world, so why can't the rest of the world see it like that? It takes an act of fate to change the story, and you will be aching for a happy ending. This is a universal tale that should appeal to young people everywhere.

Wendy Cooling, Books Consultant

Next?

Malorie Blackman looks at black/white relationships (with a twist) in *Noughts & Crosses* (UTBG 252).

For more by Jacqueline Woodson, try *Hush* or *The Dear One*.

My all-time favorite story of first love is *I Capture the Castle* (UTBG 169) by Dodie Smith, a very different but equally compelling story—it was the first book that gave me some idea of what adult love was about.

THE ILIAD and THE ODYSSEY Homer

The Iliad is the story of a great war between the Greeks and the Trojans that broke out after Paris, son of King Priam of Troy, ran off with Helen, beautiful young wife of Menelaus, King of Sparta in Greece. The Greeks gathered a massive army and set sail in "a thousand black ships" to lay siege to the city of Troy—a siege that lasted for 10 full years. It's a story full of rivalry, jealousy, heroism, and love, plus a fair share of meddling from the dear old gods.

The Odyssey is the story of Odysseus, one of the Greek warriors of *The Iliad*, sailing home at the conclusion of the siege of Troy. The journey takes him another decade to complete because so much happens on the way. Among other diversions, Odysseus and his crew are held captive by the Cyclops, visit the land of the dead, and battle a man-eating sea monster. What happens when he eventually makes it back is worth waiting for.

These two books are not always an easy read, but once you have read them, these heroes, adversaries, and adventures will stay with you for life.

Michael Lawrence, Author

Next?

Homer's books are available in many translations, some in verse, some in prose. There is a really accessible modern version by Robert Fagles.

Christopher Logue's *War Music* is a segment of the story retold in modern language and verse.

In Adèle Geras's *Troy* (UTBG 366), the story of the siege is told from the point of view of the women involved.

THE ILLUSTRATED MUM Jacqueline Wilson

Next?

More Jacqueline Wilson? Try *The Diamond Girls*, about sisters fending for themselves while Mom has a baby—and what happens when Mom and baby come home.

Anne Fine also writes about families and friends in crisis; try *The Tulip Touch* (UTBG 368).

Or for a lighthearted look at life, try Meg Cabot's *The Princess Diaries* (UTBG 281).

Two sisters, Star and Dolphin, have a mother who is romantic, tattooed, and clinically crazy. From the first page, this story exudes apprehension. It subsequently moves through a series of nightmarish domestic crises to a hopeful end, though that initial apprehension is not totally dismissed. Love will continue to strengthen the two young heroines as they sustain their deeply confused "illustrated" mother, but we know their hard times are not yet over. The story is not only concerned with eccentric events but also with the way in which vulnerable Star and Dol move toward maturity and strength.

This story somehow manages to deal with a frightening family situation without becoming too depressing; and like anything by Jacqueline Wilson, it is compulsive reading.

Margaret Mahy, Author

I'M NOT SCARED Niccolò Ammaniti

It is the scorching summer of 1978. A hideous discovery in a ruined farmhouse deep in the Italian countryside tears nine-year-old Michele Amitrano's childhood apart in this dark, claustrophobic novel. The sense that something terrible is about to happen grips you from its opening sentence and keeps you turning the pages. (And in my case flicking them back to find the clues I'd missed the first time around.)

This story will haunt you. Guaranteed. It's a chiller, a thriller, a horror, and a heartbreaking study of the evil and cruelty that can lurk in the hearts of those you love and trust more than anyone. And like all the best stories, it's beautifully written and there is final redemption. But at what a price!

Catherine Forde, Author

Next?

Robert Cormier writes about the dark side of human nature; try *The Chocolate War* (UTBG 67) or *I Am the Cheese* (UTBG 168).

Thursday's Child (UTBG 358) by Sonya Hartnett is another claustrophobic novel.

Another exquisite book about death: Alice Sebold's *The Lovely Bones* (UTBG 213).

And read our Detective Stories feature on pp. 96–97.

IN COLD BLOOD Truman Capote

Next?

Gerald Clarke's *Capote* gives a comprehensive view of the man from his childhood through the writing of *In Cold Blood*, and the obsessions and addictions that led to his untimely death.

Breakfast at Tiffany's (UTBG 50) will give you a taste of Capote's writing before he took on the Clutter family murders.

Some critics today may tell you that to find a great work of young adult literature one should look to the contemporary: carefully planned, packaged, and processed, only complete with the most modern of issues filed behind the most symbolic of covers. And although in some cases this may be true, it is also safe to say that a classic can at times be just as, if not more, challenging and teasing as the newest published work.

Truman Capote's *In Cold Blood* is just this kind of a classic. The constant plays between empathy and anger are sure to challenge anyone with a heart, and what could be more teasing, more taunting, then the ever-present question of why? This remarkable account of two men's horrific act and its effects on a small Kansas town are nothing short of simple storytelling at its best. Truly a book for everyone—with its ability to connect to raw emotion and yet also to be able to portray such violence so vividly that even the most reluctant of readers can't help but read at least a few chapters. Bottom line: *In Cold Blood* may be construed as a classic, yet its story is nothing short of modern!

Katie Heaton, age 18

IN THE SHADOW OF THE ARK

Anne Provoost

According to the Old Testament, God sent a flood to wipe out mankind but spared one righteous man, Noah, and his family. Re Jana, a shipwright's daughter, forms a relationship with Ham, Noah's youngest son, and when the flood comes she is hidden aboard the Ark, where she sees the terrible story unfold as Noah tries to carry out God's instructions to the letter. What kind of a man builds a great ship, packs it with animals, and leaves his fellow humans to drown? What kind of man employs a huge workforce to build it, allowing the workers to believe that they are earning a place on it before abandoning them? What kind of a god would tell them to do it?

Jan Mark, Author

Next?

Because of global warming, writers are beginning to think hard about floods. *Not the End of the World* (UTBG 248) by Geraldine McCaughrean is also about what might have happened aboard Noah's Ark, as is David Maine's *The Flood*.

Another look at the possible truths behind myths and legend are Mary Renault's novels about the Greek hero Theseus: *The King Must Die* (UTBG 194) and *The Bull from the Sea*.

INEXCUSABLE Chris Lynch

Next?

Pete Hautman's *Invisible* also revolves around a mysterious "happening," one that keeps you guessing the whole way through.

Speak (UTBG 334) by Laurie Halse Anderson should not be missed—it is another gritty read about a similar subject.

For more by Chris Lynch, try *Sins of the Fathers*—a story about three best friends and the secrets of the Catholic Church's priests.

Keir Sarafian considers himself to be a good guy . . . sort of. He likes it when people like him, and after a football accident, he gets the popular nickname of "Killer." Popularity clouds his views, and as his love for Gigi Boudakian is intensified by every second, Keir's view of himself gets even more clouded. Keir loves her so much, he isn't careful with his actions and doesn't want to take responsibility for his choices. Keir is surrounded by friends and parties but doesn't know what to do.

This story is told with a mix of suspense and reality. Chapters are switched between the past and the future to keep the reader interested and intrigued—it works. Did Keir really do it? What really happened between him and Gigi? The book comes with its own set of twists and turns, and there's no guidance as to where it's going to take you next. "The way things look are definitely not the way they really are."

Rosa Mateo, age 17

THE INHERITORS William Golding

16+

This book was written 100 years after the first Neanderthal skull was discovered. Even so, little was known about these early humans and they were generally thought to be more ape than man; this was the first attempt to think of them as people. They use fire but cannot make it; they scavenge but do not hunt; they have a little speech but find it difficult to share ideas; and when the new people come with their canoes and weapons, they have no way of defending themselves. From what we've learned since, the end of the Neanderthals was probably not like this, and it is still not certain if they actually did die out as Golding hints, but it is still a moving, very human story.

Jan Mark, Author

Next?

Golding wrote many books, the best of them set in the past. *The Scorpion God* comprises three novellas that give an unusual interpretation of historic and prehistoric events. Or leap forward in time and read *The Spire*, about the building of a medieval cathedral.

The Kin by Peter Dickinson is another novel about early humans.

INNOCENT BLOOD P. D. James

14+

With all the confidence of her new freedom as an adult and aided by a new law passed by the government, 18-year-old Philippa Palfrey sets out to find the birth mother who gave her up for adoption as a small child. She discovers that her parents were the infamous Ductons, guilty of murdering a child. Philippa confidently thinks she can rebuild a life with her mother, who is due for release from jail—she even eschews older, established relationships in preparation. But is Philippa truly equipped to operate in a murky new world—and is she truly naive enough to think she can "own" her mother exclusively? A brilliant thriller about innocence and guilt, from a master storyteller.

Jon Appleton, Editor

Next?

P. D. James has been called the Queen of Crime—but so has Ruth Rendell! Try Rendell's *A Sight for Sore Eyes* (UTBG 321) and decide for yourself.

Another mystery in which no one is quite as they seem is Patricia Highsmith's chilling *The Talented Mr. Ripley* (UTBG 348).

For a younger take on the spy thriller, try Kirsten Miller's *Kiki Strike* (UTBG 192).

For more crime and mystery, turn to our Detective Stories feature on pp. 96–97.

THE INNOCENT'S STORY Nicky Singer

14+

The first thing that has to be said about this book is it's a brave book to have written. Our narrator, Cassina, has recently been killed in a suicide bombing, and her disembodied spirit hangs around in the brains of her parents and her killer, listening to their thoughts. But the book's bravery isn't just because of the subject matter—suicide bombs, religious extremism, death—but also in the narrative techniques Nicky Singer uses to tell the story. The idea of having a dead spirit floating around visiting other people's brains is hard to pull off—but in *The Innocent's Story* it's done with imagination and confidence. As a reader you'll quickly forget the device and start relishing the details of the story. And (without saying too much) the ending is extraordinary. My friends and I have had long discussions about whether it works or not—see what you think!

Daniel Hahn, Editor

Next?

For more Nicky Singer, read her award-winning *Feather Boy* (UTBG 115) next.

Malorie Blackman's **Checkmate**, the third book in her **Noughts & Crosses** series (UTBG 252), is also about the makings of a suicide bomber.

The most imaginative and enchanting story of the afterlife that I've read is Gabrielle Zevin's debut novel, **Elsewhere** (UTBG 103).

Or try Alice Sebold's **The Lovely Bones** (UTBG 213) for another story whose narrator has died.

The INSPECTOR MORSE books Colin Dexter

14+

Next?

Read Sir Arthur Conan Doyle's **Sherlock Holmes** stories (UTBG 319), starting with **The Hound of the Baskervilles**. Sherlock Holmes is one of the all-time great literary detectives.

Agatha Christie's Miss Marple—try **The 4:50 from Paddington** or **The Body in the Library** (UTBG 42).

Try a wonderful story that involves solving a crime, this one set in the past—**A Northern Light** (UTBG 247) by Jennifer Donnelly.

John Thaw's TV portrayal of Chief Inspector Morse has helped to popularize the novels of Colin Dexter. Morse is intelligent, well-read, a lover of Wagner, a swiller of ale, and a solver of crossword puzzles. Together with his faithful partner, Sergeant Lewis, he unravels a succession of crimes based around Oxford. The books are well written with plenty of twists and red herrings. My favorite is *The Dead of Jericho*, in which the corpse discovered is Anne, one of Morse's ex-girlfriends. Apparently it is suicide, but Morse digs beneath the world of publishing and the bridge society in Oxford to get at the truth behind the tragedy. It is an intriguing page-turner.

Brenda Marshall, Librarian

INTERVIEW WITH THE VAMPIRE

Anne Rice

In a dingy room a boy listens to a despairing vampire tell his story. While a tape spools on he hears of centuries of life, of love and passion, of the enigmatic and captivating Lestat, of the beautiful vampire child Claudia, and above all of Louis, the one cursed with hating his own life and its eternal craving for blood.

Lush, compelling, horribly beautiful, this macabre, gruesome, and exquisite book is steeped in the erotic, the sensual, and the perverse. Though there had been vampire books before it, and there have been many since, this is the one that started a cult and made Anne Rice the heroine of black-clad teens across the world.

Leonie Flynn, Editor

> ### Next?
>
> The **Vampire Chronicles** continue with *The Vampire Lestat* and *The Queen of the Damned*, both of which are amazing. (The series goes on, but the later stories are not quite as good.)
>
> Or try Holly Black's *Tithe* (UTBG 359) and *Valiant* for all-out sex, drugs, and faeries.
>
> A really different take on vampires is Joss Whedon's TV series, *Buffy the Vampire Slayer*. There are some great tie-in novels; try any of them, or those about the *Buffy* spin-off, *Angel*.

INTO THIN AIR: A PERSONAL ACCOUNT OF THE MT. EVEREST DISASTER Jon Krakauer

> ### Next?
>
> *The Perfect Storm* (UTBG 268) by Sebastian Junger is a true story about the men of the *Andrea Gail* trawler who are set upon by the "perfect storm."
>
> *Alive* by Piers Paul Read is a horrific true story. When a Uruguayan rugby team's plane crashes high in the Andes, they struggle to survive.

When Jon Krakauer, a veteran journalist and accomplished climber, was offered the chance to write about Everest from Base Camp, he declined. He didn't want to just stay behind while others climbed—he wanted to climb the mountain and fulfill a lifelong dream. When the opportunity came to join a professionally guided team, Krakauer jumped at the chance. The harsh reality of the mountain and its extremes pushed his abilities to the limit and others to their deaths.

His minute-by-minute, first-person retelling of the 1996 Everest tragedy, in which five of his fellow climbers died in a sudden storm, is a thrilling, roller-coaster read that puts you right there in the clouds. The fact that the story is true makes it all the more compelling and poignant.

Charli Osborne, Librarian

INVENTING ELLIOT   Graham Gardner

Next?

Inventing Elliot was inspired by Orwell's ***Nineteen Eighty-Four***, the book from which Graham Gardner took his epigraph. So read ***Nineteen Eighty-Four*** (UTBG 244) next.

For another heroic individual standing up against the gang that rules his school, read Robert Cormier's classic ***The Chocolate War*** (UTBG 67).

Maybe at the new school everything will be different. Nobody knows Elliot there; nobody knows anything about him—so he can be whomever he wants to be, right? Well, yes, but . . .

Scratch the surface and you'll see that Holminster High is really run not by the teachers but by a powerful and sinister group of older students called the Guardians. And the Guardians want Elliot. Joining them will allow him to belong, but to what exactly? The Guardians aren't a warm and friendly social club; they're cold and clever and manipulative. And they're used to getting what they want. Is Elliot strong enough to resist?

The first page will grab you and then won't let go; Gardner keeps the momentum and tension up right to the thrilling closing sentence. It's a gripping, often terrifying book—a great piece of spare and powerful writing.

Daniel Hahn, Editor

THE INVENTION OF HUGO CABRET

Brian Selznick

Hey, you! Want to read a 525-page book in a couple hours? Want to read a book that seems a lot like watching a movie? Look no further!

Assistant timekeeper Hugo Cabret works to keep all 27 clocks in the Paris train station running smoothly. He is also obsessed with fixing up a small automaton, a mechanical man that will write something when it's fixed. Hugo is sure the writing will be a message from his dead father. Instead, it leads him to an early French silent film and its legendary creator, Georges Méliès.

Out of 525 pages, 284 are filled with original drawings by the author, plus there are photos, stills from silent movies, and reproductions of sketches by the real Georges Méliès. The illustrations don't accompany text, they replace it in large chunks. I don't think I've ever read a book quite like this.

Alicia Anderson, Librarian

Next?

If you enjoyed the black-and-white illustrations, you might also like *Foundling* (UTBG 229), the first book in the **Monster Blood Tattoo** series by D. M. Cornish.

If you want another mystery-adventure with enigmatic clues, try *The Mysterious Benedict Society* by Trenton Lee Stewart.

IT'S KIND OF A FUNNY STORY   Ned Vizzini

Fifteen-year-old Craig worked very hard to get into one of the top high schools in Manhattan, but just when he thought he had what he wanted, he begins to battle severe depression. Finding himself overwhelmed by suicidal thoughts, Craig checks himself into the psychiatric unit of a local hospital. There he meets an eccentric group of characters who are battling their own illnesses. With the help of his family, his therapist, and the friends he makes in the hospital, Craig learns how to handle his life by anchoring it in his long-forgotten artistic talents.

Craig is a near-typical teen, who is unsure about drugs, sex, and what the future holds. How Craig deals with these stressors reveals a raw and stark side of life that can so often be hidden to everyone. This intimate and humorous look at teenage depression is for you if you are also suffering, but it will also open your eyes if you have never had to deal with an illness such as this.

Rachel Wadham, Librarian

> ### Next?
>
> For more by Ned Vizzini, try *Be More Chill* (UTBG 28) or *Teen Angst? Naaah . . .*
>
> Other great books about teenagers dealing with the raw realities of life include *Saint Iggy* (UTBG 300) by K. L. Going, *Dancing on the Edge* by Han Nolan, and *Get Well Soon* by Julie Halpern.

IVANHOE   Sir Walter Scott

> ### Next?
>
> Charles Dickens's story *A Tale of Two Cities* (UTBG 345), set at the time of the French Revolution, is also about love and hatred and is just as exciting as *Ivanhoe*.
>
> Alexandre Dumas was influenced by Sir Walter Scott; try *The Three Musketeers* (though try and forget the films!) or the classic, *The Man in the Iron Mask*.
>
> Sir Walter Scott wrote many books, mostly set in his native Scotland; try *The Pirate* or the wild adventure that is *Rob Roy*.

In an England torn apart by civil war, where Saxons battle Normans, Wilfred of Ivanhoe returns from the Crusades. Disinherited by his scheming father, he battles for his name, his country, his life, and his love, Rowena. From the deadly games of jousting to witch trials, near death and rescue, and healing by the black-eyed, beautiful Jew Rebecca, *Ivanhoe*'s story is fast, furious, and compelling. And in Brian de Bois-Guilbert it also has one of the best villains ever.

This is a story of hatred and conflict, of Christians, Jews, Muslims, families, and kings. It is also about the healing power of compassion and the enduring strength of love. In weaving all the threads together, Scott spins a tale that has become a true legend.

Leonie Flynn, Editor

JAMAICA INN Daphne du Maurier

12+

Next?

For the ultimate scary hotel story, don't miss Stephen King's *The Shining*.

More Daphne du Maurier? Try *My Cousin Rachel*, about love, doubt, and murder.

A classic tale that involves characters who are not what they seem and a mysterious visitor who comes and goes in the dead of the night is Charlotte Brontë's *Jane Eyre* (UTBG 182).

Mary Yellan couldn't possibly have imagined the wild and twisted adventure she would embark on after she moved into Jamaica Inn. She quickly realizes that it's no ordinary inn, since there are no guests staying there, and before long she starts to hear mysterious visitors who come and go in the dead of the night . . . Uncle Joss, a monstrous hulk and brute of a man, is not really her uncle but rather her half-witted, terrified aunt Patience's husband. But Mary isn't scared of Uncle Joss, and she is not about to leave her aunt alone in his clutches, so she chooses to stay at the inn. In doing so, she is swept up in all its dark secrets.

Your hair may be on end before you finish *Jamaica Inn*; if you enjoy a good suspenseful romance, this one won't disappoint you.

Candida Gray, Teacher

The JAMES BOND books Ian Fleming

16+

When I was about 12, and a student at a boys' boarding school in England, we all read The Saint books avidly. The author, Leslie Charteris, was our hero, and we all wanted to be just like his hero, Simon Templar—the Saint himself.

But then one day a man named Ian Fleming wrote a book called *Casino Royale*, about a superspy with a license to kill. Almost overnight, every one of us boys dropped the Saint books and picked up James Bond. The Fleming books weren't better written than the Charteris books and Bond's adventures weren't more exciting than Templar's; but they contained a treasure trove of meticulous and grown-up details—Walther PPK pistols and supercharged Bentley cars, vodka martinis ("shaken, not stirred"), and gambling dens and shadowy Soviet organizations that were into really *horrible* torture. Last, but most important, Ian Fleming wrote about beautiful girls with wonderful names who did a whole lot more than just kiss the hero fleetingly on the lips. With that sort of competition, poor old Simon Templar didn't stand a chance.

Ian Ogilvy, Author

Next?

If you like James Bond, try the detailed and realistic books by Tom Clancy. Start with *Patriot Games*.

Curious about Bond's backstory? Try the brilliant *SilverFin* (UTBG 322) by Charlie Higson.

For more spies but a slightly tougher read, try John le Carré's *The Spy Who Came in from the Cold* (UTBG 336).

JANE EYRE Charlotte Brontë

12+

Jane Eyre caused a real storm of protest when it was first published. Politicians, the press, and churches wanted it destroyed. It was too dangerous, too depressing, and full of controversial "issues" and revolutionary ideas that had no place in a novel read by impressionable young people. In fact, it was cutting-edge stuff, a roaring success with the young readers who were supposedly threatened by it.

Having survived a grim and loveless childhood, Jane ventures into the world on her own, still a teenager, and falls in love with her rich employer. But this man has a dark secret . . .

This story of a young character's ultimate survival in a brutal world has resonated with generation after generation—and it's still gripping stuff for readers today.

Julie Bertagna, Author

> ### Next?
>
> Mr. Rochester's early life is imagined in *Wide Sargasso Sea* (UTBG 390) by Jean Rhys.
>
> Charlotte's sisters wrote of love and passion too. Try *Wuthering Heights* (UTBG 402) (Emily) or *Agnes Grey* (Anne).
>
> Mrs. Gaskell knew Charlotte Brontë; her *Life of Charlotte Brontë* is a warm, fascinating study.

The JEEVES stories P. G. Wodehouse

12+

P. G. Wodehouse wrote dozens of novels and short stories about Jeeves, and they almost all have the same basic plot. Likable upper-class goofball Bertie Wooster gets himself into some sort of jam; his efforts to put things right only make it worse, and in the end his super-capable manservant, Jeeves, exerts his mighty brain to save the day. But in P. G. Wodehouse's hands the formula never stales, and the fact that the world of gentleman's clubs and country house parties he writes about is so dated that it feels like fantasy doesn't matter either. The writing is fresh and chatty, the jokes are funny, and the plotting is fantastic. The short stories in particular are perfect little pieces of comic engineering and wonderfully entertaining.

Philip Reeve, Author

> ### Next?
>
> P. G. Wodehouse's many **Blandings** stories are every bit as good as the Jeeves ones.
>
> Or for something from the same era that is equally funny, yet also much deeper and darker, try Stella Gibbons's *Cold Comfort Farm* (UTBG 74).
>
> Margery Allingham's detective stories also have a delightful relationship between a rich man and his butler; start with *Mystery Mile*.

JEMIMA J Jane Green

14+

Reading *Jemima J* is as satisfying as a Sunday afternoon on the sofa with a box of cookies. A deliciously compulsive read, it tells the story of Jemima Jones's transformation from overweight and lonely reporter for the *Kilburn Herald* to size 10, sought-after, glamorous feature writer, and international jet-setter. This is a totally feel-good book that has you laughing, crying, and falling in love along with Jemima. There are some positive messages too: about dieting, best friends, fashion, and learning to love yourself. Plus some hints about surviving long-haul transatlantic flights that I have found invaluable!

Abigail Anderson, Theater Director

Next?

Other books by Jane Green you will enjoy: **Mr. Maybe** and *Bookends*.

Tales of the City (UTBG 349) and its sequels by Armistead Maupin are unputdownable, quick to read, and full of characters to fall in love with.

There's a whole world of must-read pink lit out there; read our feature on pp. 70–71.

JIMMY CORRIGAN, THE SMARTEST KID ON EARTH Chris Ware

14+

If you thought that comics were just about superheroes, think again. Chris Ware is probably the greatest comic artist working today, and this novel about three generations of the Corrigan family is both moving and beautiful. Two men, grandfather and grandson, both named Jimmy Corrigan and living in Chicago a hundred years apart from each other, are abandoned by their fathers. Both lead lonely, difficult childhoods and spend their lives searching for love and family in a fumbling, sometimes tragic way. The story shuttles back and forth between them; in the past, one is abandoned as a child, while in the present, his adult grandson is contacted out of the blue by his father and makes a fateful journey to meet him.

Ariel Kahn, Academic

Next?

If you like Chris Ware's style, his comics collection *The Acme Novelty Library* will not disappoint.

Jar of Fools by Jason Lutes has a magician searching for his disappeared father.

Michael Chabon's *The Amazing Adventures of Kavalier & Clay* (UTBG 14) is also a moving tale that follows two men from childhood through adulthood.

JOHN LENNON: ALL I WANT IS THE TRUTH

Elizabeth Partridge

Next?

Try *John's Secret Dreams* by Doreen Rappaport and illustrated by Bryan Collier.

Elizabeth Partridge also did a biography of Woody Guthrie called *This Land Was Made for You and Me*.

In 1964, I was five years old when I got my first Beatles album. At my neighbor Sherry's house, we listened to the album and pretended to be married to the Beatles. Sherry married Paul, leaving me with John, and that was fine with me. Paul may have been the cute Beatle, but John was the smart one.

More than 40 years have passed, but as I read Elizabeth Partridge's unflinching biography, I found myself captivated by John all over again. The more Partridge reveals about John's early life, the more I see the etchings of his early genius. She portrays the boyish John, the John on *The Ed Sullivan Show*, the John in the music I memorized.

But John's music and subsequent fame came with a cost, and Partridge reveals the conflicted genius who alchemized inner torment into brilliant songs. This is also the John who made me angry as I wondered why he did the things he did—and yet, all it took was a song to forgive him. Partridge gives us an amazing portrait of a complex artist.

Susan Campbell Bartoletti, Author

JONATHAN LIVINGSTON SEAGULL

Richard Bach

This book was a massive bestseller on publication and has retained its iconic status. It is one of those rare, utterly simple stories that achieve the enduring quality of myth.

Dedicated to "the real Jonathan Livingston Seagull who lives within us all," the book tells the tale of a bird who is expelled from his flock for trying to do so much more than fly. Outcast and alone, he learns that "boredom and fear and anger are the reasons a gull's life is so short," and discovers the compassion he needs to return to the flock.

The book is enhanced by the close and detailed observations of nature and flight. A powerful tale of freedom and transcendence that speaks to us all.

Livi Michael, Author

Next?

Try *Wind, Sand and Stars* by Antoine de St Exupéry next.

Or Paulo Coelho's road trip of self-discovery, *The Alchemist* (UTBG 9).

For a novel that explores what it is to be human, try Hermann Hesse's *Siddhartha* (UTBG 321).

JONATHAN STRANGE & MR NORRELL

Susanna Clarke

14+

Strange by name and strange by nature, at first glance this huge book looks like a historical novel, complete with old-fashioned spellings and elaborate footnotes. But start reading and you find yourself drawn into a fantasy 19th century where magic works and lost roads lead into the wild and dangerous realms of the mysterious Raven King . . . The complex story revolves around the rivalry between two magicians: the reclusive Mr. Norris and his rebellious pupil Jonathan Strange. It has been compared to Harry Potter but it is far better than that; Ms. Clarke's magic seems rooted in a deep love of British landscape and folklore, and her intensely visual writing makes this the most fully realized imaginary world since Tolkien's.

Philip Reeve, Author

Next?

Try Charles Dickens's vast and brilliant *Bleak House*.

Something more modern? Glen David Gold's *Carter Beats the Devil* relates the rivalry between two very different magicians.

Or for much more British myth and legend, introduce yourself to Merlin in *The Once and Future King* (UTBG 255) by T. H. White.

The Ultimate Teen Readers' Poll

CHARACTER WHO'D BE THE BEST GIRLFRIEND

1 **Hermione Granger (The Harry Potter series)**

2 **Lyra (His Dark Materials trilogy)**

3 **Mia Thermopolis (The Princess Diaries series)**

4 **Sabina (The Alex Rider series)**

5 **Bella (*Twilight*)**

6 **Alice (*Alice in Wonderland*)**

7 **Lucy (The Chronicles of Narnia)**

8 **Luna Lovegood (The Harry Potter series)**

9 **Éowyn (The Lord of the Rings trilogy)**

10 **Pandora (The Adrian Mole series)**

JOURNEY TO THE RIVER SEA
Eva Ibbotson

This is classic storytelling! The heroine, Maia, has been tragically orphaned. Word comes that she has an uncle and aunt who are willing to adopt her; the only snag is that they live on the Amazon in South America. But Maia is a plucky girl, always keen to see the best in everything. While her schoolmates fear she could be eaten by crocodiles or poisoned by snakes, she sets off with excitement at the prospect of seeing this magnificent river and all the wonderful plants and animals that live in the forest. Best of all, she looks forward to meeting her cousins—the twins, Beatrice and Gwendolyn. But when she arrives, the family isn't nearly as welcoming as she'd hoped.

Underneath the almost fairy-tale atmosphere of bad people and hapless children is the power of the human spirit to overcome adversity. And there is such a sense of fun in the brilliant way Ibbotson allows her plot to twist and turn right to the bitter, and wonderful, end.

Jamila Gavin, Author

Next?

Another Eva Ibbotson? Try *The Star of Kazan*, about an orphan girl in Vienna.

Karen Wallace's *Raspberries on the Yangtze* (UTBG 285) is a wonderful evocation of both a place and sibling rivalries/friendships.

Or Jamila Gravin's vivid story of growing up in India, *The Wheel of Surya*.

THE JOY LUCK CLUB Amy Tan

Next?

Try *The Kitchen God's Wife* by Amy Tan, her second novel, which will transport you to China in the 1940s.

American Born Chinese (UTBG 16) by Gene Luen Yang is a fascinating look at the revelatory experiences of an Asian American boy in graphic-novel format!

Shizuko's Daughter by Kyoko Mori introduces us to Yuki, a strong young Japanese woman who must face life after her mother commits suicide.

Ever wonder why you and your mom are not getting along? Wish that you came from a different family?

The Joy Luck Club follows the lives of four young women and the mothers who preceded them. These eight women will take you on very personal journeys through different regions of China and different neighborhoods of San Francisco. Amy Tan weaves the stories of their pasts and the trials of their present situations with fluid prose.

From Waverly Jong's days as a chess champion and Jing-Mei Woo's unique piano recital to Lindo Jong's clever escape from a doomed marriage, this novel will take you to new places and help you to experience the lives of eight extraordinary women!

Kathy Fredrickson, Librarian

JURASSIC PARK Michael Crichton

14+

When I was about 12, I read *The Lost World* by Sir Arthur Conan Doyle and was entranced by an adventure in which brave men found themselves having to cope with dinosaurs. After all, though dinosaurs have a prehistoric reality, they somehow contrive to be fabulous too. *Jurassic Park* gets off to a scary beginning and is able to call on modern genetics to give a science-fiction credibility to the dinosaurs in this story, but at heart it has a lot in common with Conan Doyle's original fantasy. A park intended to display recreated dinosaurs has been scientifically contrived, but inevitably things go wrong and once again brave men have adventures as they confront prehistoric monsters.

Margaret Mahy, Author

Next?

The Lost World by Sir Arthur Conan Doyle has the same premise— though it was written much earlier.

Other Michael Crichtons to look out for are **The Andromeda Strain**, which is about the threat of alien bacteria capable of wiping out the human race, or **Sphere**, about a 300-year-old spaceship found on the Pacific Ocean floor.

Or for a fast-paced mystery story, try **The Da Vinci Code** (UTBG 83) by Dan Brown .

JUST LISTEN Sarah Dessen

12+

Next?

For more by Sarah Dessen, try *Someone Like You* and *That Summer*: together they provided the inspiration for the movie *How to Deal*.

Another novel with a lovable heroine dealing with the ups and downs of being a teen is Megan McCafferty's *Sloppy Firsts* (UTBG 328).

Ibi Kaslik's *Skinny* deals with some of the same eating issues that *Just Listen*'s cast of characters are avoiding.

Have you ever needed someone just to sit down and listen to what you have to say? In Sarah Dessen's book *Just Listen* the main character, Annabel Greene, needs just that. Annabel is going through the hardest year of her life, dealing with harsh friends, the pressure to model, and a family that is slowly falling apart. In the midst of all the turmoil she is unexpectedly falling in love. As an ordinary teenage girl myself, I found that I am going through many of the same things that Annabel is. Sarah Dessen expresses the reality of tough, controversial topics while still touching upon love and life, like many other young teen novels. So take the time, and just listen.

Sarah Whitson, age 17

OFF THE RAILS
by Kevin Brooks

The first book I read that really grabbed hold of me and took me away to another world was *The Catcher in the Rye* (UTBG 60) by J. D. Salinger. I read it when I was about 14. My English teacher just gave it to me one day and said, "See what you think of that." He was one of those crazy English teachers who actually encourage you to read stuff you don't have to read for school. He was also fond of throwing chairs at people, but that's another story. Anyway, I read *The Catcher in the Rye* and I loved it, and I've never forgotten it. You can read more about this classic story on p. 60, but basically it's about a teenage boy named Holden Caulfield who goes a little crazy and runs away from school, and then his life starts spiraling out of control. *That* was the

"Everyone should read *Smack*."
—*The Sunday Times*

part that really grabbed me —the spiraling-out-of-control part—and ever since then I've always been drawn to reading (and writing) books about people whose lives go off the rails.

It's not a uniquely teenage experience—there are plenty of books about adults losing control of their lives—but in the teenage world the dividing line between order and chaos is so much more fragile than in the adult world, which makes it a perfect setting for journeys into chaos and confusion. When we're growing up, everything is unsettled—our lives, our emotions, our relationships—and so it doesn't take much to step over the line and become lost in the spiral.

That's how it was for me, anyway.

In fact, that's *still* how it is for me!

Which is where the fascination comes from, I suppose. I like to read about stuff that *could* happen to me, but probably—and hopefully—won't, because it allows me to experience all the fears and the thrills and the confusion of going off the rails without actually doing it myself.

All books, of course, work on lots of different levels—which is part of what makes reading so great—and this kind of story is no different. Take *Peace Like a River* (UTBG 267) by Leif Enger, for example. Yes, it tells the story of a young boy whose life suddenly changes when his older brother kills a man and goes on the run, and, yes, it's all about that spiraling journey into an unknown world—but there's so much more to it than that. There's tragedy, poetry, mystery. There's stuff to make you think. There's beautiful language, unforgettable characters, a compulsive story . . . Basically, there's everything you could ever wish for in a book.

Another example is *Hole in My Life* (UTBG 156) by Jack Gantos. This book tells the true story of what happened to the writer Jack Gantos when he was convicted of smuggling drugs as a young man. We learn about his somewhat chaotic early life, his constant struggle to find himself, and his time in prison, where he finally began to do what he'd always wanted to do—write books. It's an amazing story, and I suppose one of the most fascinating things about it is that the wonderful books that Jack Gantos now writes are often about the kind of young people whose lives are prone to tumbling out of control, just like his did.

Is that a neat ending, or what?

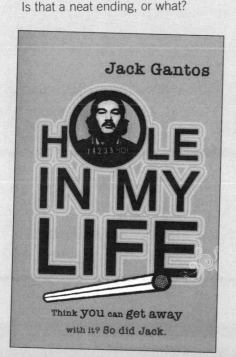

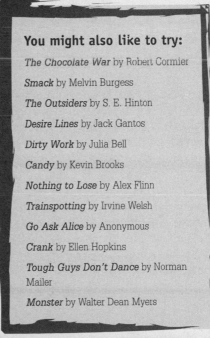

You might also like to try:

The Chocolate War by Robert Cormier

Smack by Melvin Burgess

The Outsiders by S. E. Hinton

Desire Lines by Jack Gantos

Dirty Work by Julia Bell

Candy by Kevin Brooks

Nothing to Lose by Alex Flinn

Trainspotting by Irvine Welsh

Go Ask Alice by Anonymous

Crank by Ellen Hopkins

Tough Guys Don't Dance by Norman Mailer

Monster by Walter Dean Myers

KATHERINE Anya Seton

14+

This was the first historical novel I ever read, and it won me over completely, luring me into a medieval world of lust and intrigue. When I was at school, the only way you could get away with reading anything even a little bit sexy was to have it wrapped in a historical cover, and I'm sure my teachers must have thought I was more interested in the court of Edward III than Katherine's love affair with his son, Prince John, which is at the heart of the book. Having said that, this book did get me into reading about the past, and I ended up studying history at college, so perhaps the teachers knew what they were doing after all!

Eleanor Updale, Author

Next?

Many books mix historical fact with fiction. Josephine Tey wrote a book called *The Daughter of Time* about the Princes in the Tower.

The Other Boleyn Girl (UTBG 260) by Philippa Gregory tells the story of Anne Boleyn's sister, Mary, who was another of Henry VIII's mistresses.

If you enjoy historical novels, you absolutely should not miss M. T. Anderson's *The Astonishing Life of Octavian Nothing, Traitor to the Nation, Volume 1: The Pox Party* (UTBG 25). Don't let the overbearing title fool you—this is one engrossing read.

KEEPER Mal Peet

12+

Don't be put off this book if you don't like soccer—it will still captivate you. *Keeper* tells the life story of El Gato—the Cat—the world's greatest goalkeeper. During an interview with journalist Paul Faustino, El Gato reveals how he, an impoverished boy from the South American rain forest, became the iconic figure Faustino reveres. As the interview progresses, El Gato reveals how the mysterious figure he calls "The Keeper" taught him almost everything about goalkeeping from a makeshift goalmouth in the heart of the rain forest. Peet's story is as original as it is gripping, building up tension as skilfully as any penalty shoot-out. Once you've read this book, I guarantee you will never watch a goalkeeper in the same way again.

Helena Pielichaty, Author

Next?

This was Mal Peet's first book; his second, very different novel is *Tamar* (UTBG 350).

If you're a fan of British soccer, you should check out *Fever Pitch* (UTBG 116) by Nick Hornby, about an extreme fan of the sport.

Eva Ibbotson's *Journey to the River Sea* (UTBG 186) is set in an unspoiled rain forest in South America.

KEEPING THE MOON   Sarah Dessen

14+

This is a book about fitting in, not fitting in, and being yourself. It's not a rip-roaring adventure, but the power is in the utterly wonderful characterization (every single character is beautifully drawn and fascinating) and the mood. It feels like a drifty book, a summer's dream of a book, a growing-up book; poignant, gentle, and lovely, but nevertheless with decent pacing. I love this kind of young adult fiction for its controlled intensity and bravery. This doesn't have a particularly teenage voice, because it is quiet and the characters are a little older, but I do think it speaks genuinely to teenagers. And adults will definitely enjoy eavesdropping.

Nicola Morgan, Author

> **Next?**
>
> To be honest, I haven't read anything like it, but for some reason, which I can't explain, these books come to mind as ones you might also enjoy: *A Northern Light* (UTBG 247) by Jennifer Donnelly, *The Fire-Eaters* (UTBG 118) by David Almond, *Starseeker* or *Apocalypse* (UTBG 22) by Tim Bowler, and *The Shell House* (UTBG 318) by Linda Newbery.

KEESHA'S HOUSE   Helen Frost

12+

> **Next?**
>
> In *What My Mother Doesn't Know* (UTBG 386) by Sonya Sones, a year in poems describes Sophie's hopes, dreams, and search for the perfect boyfriend.
>
> Told in verse, *Make Lemonade* (UTBG 215) by Virginia Euwer Wolff is a compelling look at young motherhood and choices. To make money for college, 14-year-old LaVaughn babysits for Jolly, a 17-year-old mom who is struggling to make her family's life a little better.
>
> Eleven interlocking teen voices make for a realistic and touching portrait of youth in urban society in the impressive debut novel *Life Is Funny* by E. R. Frank.

Frost's Printz Honor-winning novel in verse is a great story about seven teens in trouble. The house is a safe place for teens to rest and get their heads together while they deal with their problems, including pregnancy, coming out, abuse, and underage drinking. Even so, the book resonates with hope. It is also a remarkable achievement in poetry. Once you read it through for the story, go back and read it again for the structure and grace inherent in the poetical forms, which range from Shakespearean and Italian sonnets to sestinas—one of the hardest forms of poetry to write—to the triumphant ending crown of sonnets.

Charli Osborne, Librarian

KIDNAPPED Robert Louis Stevenson

It's the year 1751, and orphaned David Balfour has set out to claim his inheritance from his uncle Ebenezer. But his uncle has other plans, and David finds himself a prisoner on the high seas—until he befriends exiled Jacobite Alan Breck Stewart. Together they escape, but before David can wreak his revenge on Ebenezer, he and Alan are pursued across Scotland by the English, who regard Alan as a dangerous rebel.

You can't get better historical fiction than this. Alan is wonderfully believable, full of flaws, but brave and shrewd and cocky. David is the perfect foil, with his even temper and dogged good sense. The language and attitudes take you straight back in time; you'll find yourself speaking with a Scottish accent after reading this book.

A classic!

Catherine Jinks, Author

> ### Next?
>
> Try *The Three Musketeers* and *Twenty Years After* by Alexandre Dumas, for a flawless portrayal of 18th-century action adventure.
>
> Want another adventure set in Scotland? Try John Buchan's *The Thirty-Nine Steps* (UTBG 357).
>
> You shouldn't miss Robert Louis Stevenson's *Treasure Island* (UTBG 363), the classic pirate adventure.

KIKI STRIKE: INSIDE THE SHADOW CITY

Kirsten Miller

> ### Next?
>
> Miller's second book about Kiki, *Kiki Strike: The Empress's Tomb*, follows the Irregulars through the streets of Chinatown, this time with Oona in charge.
>
> Try the **Spy Girls** series by Elizabeth Cage, starting with *License to Thrill*, if you like to read about girls kicking butt.
>
> Or how about *I'd Tell You I Love You, but Then I'd Have to Kill You* by Ally Carter—the first in a series about boarding school girls who are secretly spies-in-training.

Who is Kiki Strike? Evil, or victim of evil? Good girl who just happens to be able to kick your butt, or adventuress on a mission? You decide. But be sure you start reading this book in the morning, or when you have lots of time. It will hook you and you will suffer withdrawal if you put it down. Never has the world been introduced to this much adventure, mystery, and thrill. I feel like I know all the Irregulars personally and can't wait until their next adventure. Now, every time I walk past a manhole in the street, I wonder if a slight blonde girl and her friends are running around under me. Watch out world, Kiki Strike is coming.

Logan Ragar, age 14

KIM Rudyard Kipling

Next?

Kipling was a great writer of short stories, many of them set in India. Try the collections *Plain Tales from the Hills* and *Soldiers Three*.

More undercover (and underground) activities, this time in prewar Europe, are to be found in Geoffrey Household's *Rogue Male*.

J. R. R. Tolkien's **The Lord of the Rings** trilogy (UTBG 210) combines friendship and adventure with a quintessential fantasy story.

Kim reads like a fantasy quest through a fabulous landscape of sweltering plains, snowy passes among towering mountains, roads, trains, and cities teeming with people—holy men, soldiers, pilgrims, thieves, spies. But this is not a fantasy, this is 19th-century India, pre-Partition, and the quest is twofold: a Buddhist lama seeking a sacred river and a youth involved in "The Great Game" of espionage between the British Raj and the expansionist Russian Empire across the North-West Frontier. This is old-style spying, with codes, passwords, disguises, and secret agents. Some aspects of Kipling can be hard to like these days, but in *Kim* he celebrates every race and religion; it's a story as much about tolerance and friendship as it is about adventure.

Jan Mark, Author

THE KIN Peter Dickinson

This epic tale was originally published as four books, each told from the viewpoint of a youngster growing up in Africa at the dawn of humanity. Suth, Noli, Ko, and Mana have to face bears, tigers, famine, and human enemies on their long and hazardous journey toward adulthood.

The individual stories fit beautifully together, and I especially liked the invented myths between the chapters—such as "How People Were Made"—which feel as though they have been transcribed from ancient cave walls, even though we have no written records from so long ago. Mixing myth and history with a moving and entertaining story, this is one of those books that lingers in the soul long after the final page has been turned.

Katherine Roberts, Author

Next?

Another brilliant Peter Dickinson is the fantasy-based *The Ropemaker* (UTBG 294).

You might like *Wolf Brother* (UTBG 395) by Michelle Paver, which is set at the time of the first humans and is totally exciting.

If you like a bit of romance and are looking for a more adult read, you should enjoy Jean M. Auel's **Earth's Children** sequence, starting with *The Clan of the Cave Bear*.

KING DORK Frank Portman

14+

Tom Henderson is one of his high school's undesirables and, for the most part, he likes it that way. Why would he want to hang out with any of the kids in his class when they, like everyone else at school, seem to be under the sway of Holden Caulfield of *Catcher in the Rye* fame? Tom would rather hang out with his best friend Sam, fantasize about the rock-and-roll band the two vow to start, and make snarky comments about everyone else. When Tom discovers his dead father's copy of that dreaded book, the aforementioned *Catcher in the Rye*, he begins to believe that the notes in the book's margins are clues to his father's death. As if one mystery isn't enough, Tom gets involved in another, more personal, puzzle: he kissed a girl at a lame school party and now it appears that she doesn't even exist. What would Holden Caulfield do?

Amy Pattee, Librarian

Next?

There's something kind of funny about Tom Henderson's story; *Youth in Revolt*, by C. D. Payne, smacks of the same desperation that tinges Tom's narrative, but plays the whole thing for laughs (and a little bit of raunch).

If you're not into funny but are into introspection, Stephen Chbosky's *The Perks of Being a Wallflower* (UTBG 269) is a good one to read.

For a feminine perspective, try *Girl* (UTBG 133) by Blake Nelson.

THE KING MUST DIE Mary Renault

14+

Next?

The good news is that there's a sequel: *The Bull from the Sea*.

Mary Renault wrote many other books about the ancient world, and they're all worth looking out for, particularly *The Last of the Wine* (UTBG 199) and *Fire from Heaven* (UTBG 117).

Or try some detective stories set in Ancient Rome with Stephen Saylor's **Gordianus the Finder** stories, starting with *The House of the Vestals*.

Or for rip-roaring adventure, try P. C. Wren's books about the Foreign Legion, starting with *Beau Geste* (UTBG 29).

Plunged headlong into the colorful world of ancient Greece, you identify so strongly with the hero that you, too, would have sacrificed yourself rather than your honor and sailed to Crete to dance the dance of death with the bulls. Theseus comes across as a real person: a womanizer and a warrior, thoughtful though not academic, ambitious but not ruthless. When he reaches Knossos and the Labyrinth, he must take part in the dangerous rite of bull leaping. No one survives for long—but Theseus really *is* made of kingly stuff. This is one of the most exciting books I have ever read; I reread it every few years and enjoy it just as much each time.

Elizabeth Kay, Author

KISS THE DUST   Elizabeth Laird

Tara's father is involved with the Kurdish rebels under the terrifying regime of Saddam Hussein. The family are forced to flee their home, and eventually they arrive in London as refugees. They have lost everything: their friends and neighbors, their possessions, and the community who spoke their language and understood their ways. Set in the time of the first Gulf War in the 1990s, this is the book to read if you want to try and understand what life must be like for refugees and asylum-seekers today.

Yvonne Coppard, Author

Next?

Elizabeth Laird also wrote *Red Sky in the Morning*, about a girl living with the prejudices surrounding her family life with a disabled brother.

Refugee Boy (UTBG 289) by Benjamin Zephaniah describes what it's like to be a refugee in Britain today.

Mud City by Deborah Ellis is about an Afghan girl's life in a Pakistan refugee camp.

KISSING THE RAIN   Kevin Brooks

Next?

If you enjoyed this, try some more Kevin Brooks—the gripping *Martyn Pig* (UTBG 220), the gentler *Lucas* (UTBG 213), or the shocking *Candy* (UTBG 57).

For another story about a boy who's bullied for being overweight, read *Fat Boy Swim* (UTBG 113) by Catherine Forde.

Grass by C. Z. Nightingale is the story of a girl who witnesses a racist attack and the subsequent decisions she is forced to make.

"I shoulda kept my big mouth shut. I DIN'T SEE *NOTHING*, ALL RIGHT?"

Moo Nelson has it really tough. Bullied at school for being fat, his greatest pleasure is standing on a bridge, staring at the traffic and letting it shut him into a world of his own . . . until the day he witnesses a murder from the bridge, and gets deeply involved in another, far more seedy and sinister world where he's forced to make some impossible choices.

Moo narrates his own story at breakneck speed, in a tone that's aggressive and defensive at the same time, so you can just feel what it's like to be inside his head. And it's not a comfortable place to be, I can tell you

Susan Reuben, Editor

THE KITE RIDER Geraldine McCaughrean

12+

Next?

All Geraldine McCaughrean's books are great. Try *Plundering Paradise* for a brilliant, fast-paced story about pirates, or *The White Darkness* for obsession and loneliness.

Try *Lost Horizon* by James Hilton, about finding paradise hidden in the Himalayas.

If you want to read the original—and still the best—"son seeking revenge for his father's death" story, don't miss Shakespeare's classic *Hamlet* (UTBG 144).

Haoyou's father flies up into the clouds and comes back without a soul, his heart having burst with fear "like a sack of grain." Now Di Chou, the man who sent his father to his death, wants to marry Haoyou's mother. While escaping from both his grasping uncle Bo and Di Chou, Haoyou is taken on by the Great Miao Je, owner of an exotic circus, and becomes a virtuoso kite rider, seeking his father's spirit in the sky. But Miao Je is on a dark quest of his own.

This is a stunning story of revenge and restoration that will keep you hooked until the final page.
Livi Michael, Author

THE KITE RUNNER Khaled Hosseini

14+

I couldn't put this book down once I'd started reading it. There are three things I like in a book: 1) a good, gripping story; 2) that it's well written and a pleasure to read; and 3) that it gives an insight into another way of life. This book does all three. It is about the value of friendship and family with 1970s Afghanistan as the background and starting point. It is written with true warmth, and I came away feeling that I knew more about what had happened over there than I could have gained from watching a hundred in-your-face documentaries. Everyone (and I mean everyone) I have recommended this to has loved it as much as I did!
Cathy Hopkins, Author

Next?

Memoirs of a Geisha (UTBG 224) by Arthur Golden also gives a glimpse into another culture and time.

My Forbidden Face by Latifa is a searing account of life under the Taliban.

The Bookseller of Kabul is Asne Seierstad's story of her time living with a family in Kabul.

KIT'S WILDERNESS David Almond

12+

Next?

Among David Almond's other books, *The Fire-Eaters* (UTBG 118) is my favorite. It has the same quality of looking at the real, everyday world and seeing something mysterious.

The Owl Service (UTBG 265) by Alan Garner does this, too.

If you like David Almond's ability to describe real places, linking past and present, you might enjoy **Sea Room** by Adam Nicolson. It's a non-fiction book about the little islands that his father gave him when he was 21, and I think it's magic.

Kit's Wilderness explores "the desire we have to be terrified, to look into the darkness." When Kit Watson makes friends with John Askew and Allie Keenan, they play the game called Death, and Kit finds himself drawn into a strange place where the darkness of the past links somehow with the darkness inside his own head and the dark tunnels of the abandoned mines.

There is danger and cruelty and, in the end, a real death, but the book is full of warmth, too. In Kit's stories and Askew's drawings, in the acting of Allie, "the good-bad ice girl," and in the character of Kit's grandfather, the darkness becomes a source of strength and beauty. It's an extraordinary book. But don't take my word for it. Read it yourself.

Gillian Cross, Author

LADY CHATTERLEY'S LOVER D. H. Lawrence

16+

Chatterley is arguably the most controversial book of the 20th century. What shocked its readers (and those who didn't read it but followed the famous obscenity trial in the newspapers) wasn't the boundary-breaking story of a married aristocratic lady having an affair with a working-class man, a gamekeeper on her estate, but the way the book was written—or more particularly the way the sex scenes were written. The rough, honest earthiness of the language was unlike anything any respectable person had ever read before. Or at least would admit to having read before. Such language! In print! Outrageous!

And it's great. The whole book—not just those few famous and controversial scenes—is energetic and rough and uncomplicated, and the characters live and breathe from the first page to the very last. Read it and see what all the fuss was about.

Daniel Hahn, Editor

Next?

Another D. H. Lawrence? *Sons and Lovers* is probably the best known; I've always liked his short stories, too.

A Clockwork Orange (UTBG 73) by Anthony Burgess is in no way like *Lady Chatterley*, except that it, too, was scandalous when it was first published. See if you're shocked.

For another exploration of the tensions in the British class system, read E. M. Forster's *Howard's End*.

THE LAND Mildred D. Taylor

12+

Next?

Roll of Thunder, Hear My Cry (UTBG 292), *Let the Circle Be Unbroken,* and *The Road to Memphis* are three more installments in the saga of the Logan family.

A book about slavery—and about what constitutes freedom—is *Nightjohn* by Gary Paulsen, about an escapee who returns to slavery in order to teach reading and writing to his fellow slaves.

Here is a compelling prequel to Mildred D. Taylor's great *Roll of Thunder, Hear My Cry*. Remember Cassie Logan? This coming-of-age story is told by her grandfather, Paul-Edward, who is born into slavery shortly before the end of the Civil War. His father is a wealthy white landowner. Paul-Edward looks almost white. That complicates relationships with both his white family and black peers. Although he is the son with the greatest feeling for his father's land and horses, he will never inherit them. Injustice, humiliation, and betrayal lead him to run away at 14. His determination to make his own way and realize his dream of acquiring his own land drives the novel and the reader.

Beverley Naidoo, Author

LARKLIGHT Philip Reeve

12+

Creatures, swashbuckling pirates, and more abound in this Victorian space adventure. Art Mumby, his older sister, Myrtle, and their scientist father live at Larklight, their home in orbit just beyond the moon. Art dreams of adventure, and Myrtle dreams of visiting proper society on Earth. They both find much more excitement than they bargained for when giant white spiders attack Larklight and capture their father. The siblings manage to escape and soon find themselves rescued by the notorious pirate Jack Havock, who turns out to be no older than Myrtle.

The action is nonstop, the world is clever and imaginative and full of great creatures like hoverhogs and the Tentacle Twins, and the characters are vivid and likable. If *20,000 Leagues Under the Sea* took place 20,000 miles into the aether instead, it might look a little like this.

Alicia Anderson, Librarian

Next?

If you liked *Larklight*, you shouldn't miss the sequel, *Starcross*.

Airborn (UTBG 7) by Kenneth Oppel also offers nonstop off-the-ground adventure with mysterious creatures.

Gregor the Overlander by Suzanne Collins is the first of five books about a boy from New York who discovers that an entire underground world has been waiting for him.

LAST CHANCE TO SEE

Douglas Adams and Mark Carwardine

14+

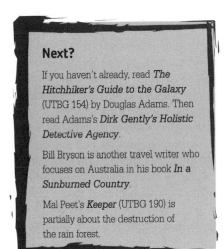

Next?

If you haven't already, read *The Hitchhiker's Guide to the Galaxy* (UTBG 154) by Douglas Adams. Then read Adams's *Dirk Gently's Holistic Detective Agency*.

Bill Bryson is another travel writer who focuses on Australia in his book *In a Sunburned Country*.

Mal Peet's *Keeper* (UTBG 190) is partially about the destruction of the rain forest.

Douglas Adams takes the writing style that we all adored in *The Hitchhiker's Guide to the Galaxy* and applies it to a series of trips to see some of Earth's most endangered species. And it works! The descriptions of the creatures themselves are beautifully interwoven with tales of the people who devote their lives to trying to save them. In one part, Adams is going to an area with lots of poisonous snakes so he goes to see an expert on venom. He asks what he should do if he gets bitten by a deadly snake and is told: "You die, of course. That's what deadly means."

Anthony Reuben, Journalist

THE LAST OF THE WINE Mary Renault

 16+

This book takes place about 2,500 years ago, when Athens was at the height of its glory. Mary Renault takes you into the homes, courtyards, baths, and temples of the ancient Greek city. The young hero Alexias is fictional, but he meets real historical figures of his time—Socrates, Plato, and Xenophon. He competes in the games, takes a dream cure, fights in wars, and falls in love. (Renault deals very sensitively with homosexuality in the ancient world.)

This is one of those rare historical novels that does what all historical novels should: it transports you to another place and time. I read this book as a teenager, and it changed my life.

Caroline Lawrence, Author

Next?

Read Mary Renault's *Fire from Heaven* (UTBG 117), the first in the **Alexander** trilogy, for a wonderful evocation of the ancient world.

For one of her stories set in the more recent past—World War II—and dealing with love between two men, read *The Charioteer*.

Another author who makes history real is Bernard Cornwell. Try his **Grail Quest** series about the Hundred Years War, beginning with *The Archer's Tale*.

THE LAST SIEGE Jonathan Stroud

12+

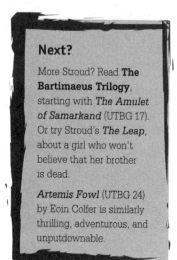

Next?

More Stroud? Read **The Bartimaeus Trilogy**, starting with *The Amulet of Samarkand* (UTBG 17). Or try Stroud's *The Leap*, about a girl who won't believe that her brother is dead.

Artemis Fowl (UTBG 24) by Eoin Colfer is similarly thrilling, adventurous, and unputdownable.

The nearby ruined castle has never interested Emily and Simon—for them it's just a place for tourists. Then one snowy winter, when the castle is locked up, they meet Marcus. His vivid imagination and fascination with the castle's murderous past bring the ruin to life. He persuades them to break in and spend the night there. But the place starts to exert a more powerful grip than any of them could have imagined. And when they feel the castle is under siege, they are prepared to defend it.

Stroud has written a powerful psychological thriller. His depiction of the castle is especially vivid, and as it goes from being a place of refuge to a nightmarish trap, you really feel as though you're there.

Katie Jennings, Editor

THE LASTLING Philip Gross

12+

Paris is in the Himalayas on a trek with her uncle and his friends. They meet Tahr, a young Tibetan monk, who reluctantly joins them as his protector has died in an accident. Paris and Tahr are thrown together and each learns something about themselves. As the journey progresses, Paris realizes the purpose of her uncle's quest—he and his friends are part of an exclusive gourmet dining club, dedicated to eating the rarest possible animals. When a young yeti-like creature is discovered, Tahr convinces Paris that they have a duty to protect her, no matter what.

This book is full of powerful descriptions of places and feelings. It stimulates the imagination and raises questions about moral and environmental issues. It is also a gripping read!

Brenda Marshall, Librarian

Next?

More Philip Gross? Try *Turn to Stone*, about a boy involved with a strange, cultlike group.

If you like stories about intrepid journeys, try Thor Heyerdahl's *Kon Tiki*, which describes his journey across the Pacific; or Captain Scott's diary of his epic journey to the South Pole.

If you like lighter travel writing, you will enjoy Bill Bryson's humorous *Notes from a Small Island* (UTBG 248).

LBD: IT'S A GIRL THING Grace Dent

Next?

The bambinos are back in *LBD: The Great Escape*. They're a little older but are still determined to go the Astlebury Festival. Somehow.

There's more girl power on display in *Guitar Girl* by Sarra Manning, which is about a teenage girl's rise to rock stardom.

Try E. Lockhart's *Dramarama* (UTBG 99), which employs all the same fun and drama, this time at a summer theater camp.

Fourteen-year-old Ronnie Ripperton and her best friends, Claude and Fleur, are the feisty trio who call themselves the LBD—*Les Bambinos Dangereuses*. They love boys and music and are all longing to go to a local music festival, which naturally offers great make-out opportunities, and where even the gorgeous Spike Saunders will be playing. When their parents forbid them from going, Claude comes up with the brilliant idea of staging their own charity concert at the school. They start organizing auditions, but things start to go awry almost immediately and there's soon drama and excitement to be had all around. Very funny, and totally believable—it's a great summer read.

John McLay, Literary Scout

LE GRAND MEAULNES Alain-Fournier

A magical novel set in the dreamy hinterland between childhood and adulthood. Augustin Meaulnes, 17 and bursting with energy, if a bit rude, explodes into life at a small rural boarding school in France. Confiding only in his friend François, Meaulnes departs on a journey involving a house in the woods in the dead of night, enchanted revelries, scarlet waistcoats, and vagabonding in Paris, all of which slip away from our hero as quickly as they present themselves.

In a blend of fantasy and reality, Alain-Fournier conjures a quest for the unobtainable, at the same time painting a memorable portrait of lost love and lost youth. Marvelous.

Sara Wheeler, Author

Next?

Sadly, Alain-Fournier died before writing any other books. But why not try *Claudine at School* (UTBG 72) by Colette, another French coming-of-age story?

As is the dark and adult *Bonjour Tristesse* by Françoise Sagan.

Read our feature about coming-of-age books on pp. 278–279.

THE LEFT HAND OF DARKNESS

Ursula K. Le Guin

Next?

If you liked this book, you'll love Le Guin's *A Wizard of Earthsea* (UTBG 394), about the wizard Ged and the responsibilities of magic; also her short stories in *The Wind's Twelve Quarters*, which are superbly imaginative.

Virginia Woolf's *Orlando* (UTBG 260) has a life that spans centuries and crosses the gender divide.

On the glacial planet of Gethen it's always deepest winter. When an ambassador from the Ekumen (a federation of planets) visits, he discovers that the inhabitants live a feudal existence and that they have only one gender, becoming male or female at different times in their lives. In a wonderful story of love and danger and journeying through landscapes of ice, Le Guin plays havoc with our preconceptions of male and female, and imagines how it would be if a person could be both a mother and a father. This isn't just an ideas book though—it's a rich, exciting story. Definitely one of the all-time classic fantasies.

Catherine Fisher, Author

LETTERS FROM THE INSIDE

John Marsden

I can do no better than to quote Robert Cormier, who described this book as "absolutely shattering as it brings to vivid life two teenage girls and then strangles your heart over what happens to their relationship."

The girls start as strangers writing letters to each other, pen pals with secrets and fears that they slowly reveal. But what they reveal will change them in ways they could not have predicted, and their lives become entangled. You have to concentrate while you are reading, because the whole story is in the letters and you don't quite know what to trust. But the effort will be rewarded, I promise, and you will not forget this book.

Nicola Morgan, Author

Next?

For a book about secrets and lies and the harm they can do, try E. R. Franks's *Friction*.

You may enjoy another book by John Marsden, such as *Tomorrow When the War Began*, in which a group of friends return from a camping trip to find their families dead and the world a changed place.

You might also like any of Robert Cormier's dark, edgy books. Start with *Heroes* (UTBG 152).

LIFE AS WE KNEW IT Susan Beth Pfeffer

14+

What would you do, if in only a few seconds your life changed completely? Everything Miranda knows changes one night when the moon is knocked out of orbit and closer to the earth, causing chaos throughout the world. Miranda and her family are suddenly struggling to survive. Due to the weather changes and food shortages, school is closed, the grocery store is closed, and gas is outrageously priced. Just when Miranda thinks things can't get worse, they do.

Life as We Knew It is a powerful story told in diary entries written by Miranda. It is nearly impossible to put down, and once you do, the way you look at life will never be the same.

Shelbi Ball, age 16

Next?

Robert C. O'Brien's *Z for Zachariah* deals with the aftermath of a nuclear holocaust, while Julie Bertagna's *Exodus* (UTBG 107) shows a near future plagued by global warming.

Meg Rosoff's *How I Live Now* (UTBG 165) is a similarly compelling novel in which a teen must put aside her daily concerns when her country is invaded and a war begins.

Susan Beth Pfeffer's classic young adult novel, *The Year Without Michael*, is a must-read, even though it deals with a completely different topic—the abduction of a family member.

LIFE OF PI Yann Martel

14+

Next?

Did you like the tale of boy and tiger? Try Rudyard Kipling's *The Jungle Book*. He also wrote another marvelous story about a boy in India, *Kim* (UTBG 193).

If you liked the magical realism, there are many more wonderful books to look out for. Try Isabel Allende's *The House of the Spirits* (UTBG 164), or García Márquez's *Love in the Time of Cholera* (UTBG 212).

After the tragic sinking of a cargo ship carrying his family and their zoo, 16-year-old Pi is left shipwrecked. Think things could not get any worse? Add the endless Pacific Ocean, a hyena, a zebra with a broken leg, a female orangutan . . . and a 450-pound Royal Bengal tiger. Well, it's not a normal story.

Life of Pi is a captivating novel written from Pi's point of view as he bobs around in the middle of a never-ending expanse of ocean. It's a story of courage, survival, and nerve, with a mixture of suspense, tension, surprise, and cleverness. It takes a while to get going, but patience is a virtue as the story culminates in an interesting twist . . .

Louise Manning, age 14

LIZZIE BRIGHT AND THE BUCKMINSTER BOY Gary D. Schmidt

12+

Even in the context of the early-20th-century setting, fans of contemporary and historical fiction alike will enjoy this coming-of-age story of friendship and self-discovery. Turner Buckminster wishes he could just "light out for the Territories" instead of facing the realities of being son of Phippsburg, Maine's new First Congregational minister. But things start to look up when he meets Lizzie Bright, who lives on the neighboring island founded by former slaves, the same island that is targeted by the town's leaders as a future tourist development. The subsequent tension within Turner's own family, and throughout the entire town, serves as the backdrop for the evolving friendship forged between these two unlikely souls. Based on factual events, this is a touching and very human look at the tragic story of Malaga Island in 1912.
Karen Santamaria, Librarian

Next?

Schmidt's *The Wednesday Wars* also endears the reader to a young male protagonist, this time during the 1960s.

Katherine Paterson's *Bread and Roses, Too* offers a look at another family in the eastern United States during the early 1900s.

For other stories on racially charged friendships try *A Summer of Kings* by Han Nolan or *Black and White* by Paul Volponie.

LONESOME DOVE Larry McMurtry

Next?

Dead Man's Walk is next in the saga.

Riders of the Purple Sage by Zane Grey is just about the oldest Western, and in it you'll find some of the ideas that became clichés of the genre (girl disguised as boy; terse, hard-eyed heroes; etc.).

Or how about another classic that was made into one of the most famous cowboy films ever—Jack Schaefer's *Shane*.

While reading this book I was thrown from my horse, trampled by stampeding cattle, bitten by rattlesnakes, struck by lightning, battered senseless by hailstorms, and washed away in flash floods. And during my quieter moments, I was regularly chased, shot at, and beaten up by the toughest and most terrifying bunch of dudes I've ever had the misfortune to get on the wrong side of. However, I enjoyed every minute of it, my worst moment coming when I dropped this brilliant adventure story in the tub, causing it to swell up to the size of a dead longhorn steer. And despite the fact that the entire masterpiece about life in the old Wild West is a mere 1,000 pages short, at the end of it I found myself yelling: "More, McMurtry! More! Reach for your pen this minute! You doggone ornery, cotton-pickin' brilliant author, you!"
Michael Cox, Author

THE LONG WALK

Stephen King writing as Richard Bachman

Next?

More Stephen King?
Start with the horror
story *Carrie*, about a
girl with psychokinetic
powers who goes on a
rampage in small-town
America.

James Herbert writes
psychologically adept
horror; try **The Rats** or
The Lair.

Stephen King is the most commercially successful author in the world. But one fine day he got suspicious and wondered if he could repeat his success as an unknown author. To find out he wrote five Bachman books, and *The Long Walk* is the best of them.

The US government has started up a race. One hundred teenage boys are selected for it. But it's no ordinary race. It's a long walk, and once you start you can't stop. If you do, the penalties are terrifying. There can be only one winner. Will it be 15-year-old Ray Garrity, or will he be "penalized" like all the others before he can reach the prize?

This is vintage King. I can honestly say that every teenage boy over the age of 14 to whom I have given *The Long Walk* has loved this dark and brilliant tale.

Cliff McNish, Author

THE LONG WALK Slavomir Rawicz

This is the most extraordinary escape story one could possibly imagine—and it's all true. The writer, Slavomir Rawicz, was a Polish cavalry officer who was taken prisoner by the Russians during World War II, tortured, and sentenced to 25 years' hard labor in one of the murderous gulags that Stalin set up in Siberia. From a guarded encampment in the middle of hundreds of miles of snowbound forest, he and six fellow captives scrambled under the wire and escaped. They set out on a journey of unimaginable hardship and endurance, crossing the icy wastes of Siberia, the Gobi desert, Inner Mongolia, and Tibet before reaching safety and freedom in India. This book had me on the edge of my seat all the way through. Trust me. Your hair will stand on end.

Elizabeth Laird, Author

Next?

Seven Years in Tibet by
Heinrich Harrer is the story of a
man's escape from a prisoner-of-
war camp and his refuge in a
monastery in Tibet.

For another harrowing true story,
try **Into Thin Air** (UTBG 178), in
which Jon Krakauer narrates his
experiences during a tragic climb
up Mt. Everest in 1996.

A climbing trip that goes
disastrously wrong is recounted in
Touching the Void (UTBG 361)
by Joe Simpson.

A LONG WAY FROM CHICAGO Richard Peck

Next?

For a similar story about small town high jinks with a lot of heart, try Jerry Spinelli's classic *Maniac Magee*.

Erik Larson's adult book *The Devil in the White City* gives a more sinister side of historical Chicago.

For another tale set in Chicago, try Blue Balliett's *Chasing Vermeer*, a detective story about a missing painting.

Looking for a historical fiction book to impress your Language Arts teacher, but worried because historical fiction always seems a little . . . um, dry? Look no further than *A Long Way from Chicago*, an action-packed, humorous, plot-intensive book from master storyteller Richard Peck.

We all love our grandparents, but spending the whole summer with them seems like it might be a tad boring. Not with Joey and Mary Alice's grandma. Granny Dowdel makes home-brewed beer at the height of Prohibition and arranges an impressive funeral for Shotgun Cheatham. This book puts you right there in the Great Depression, which doesn't seem that bad with Granny around. It seems clichéd to use words like "rollicking" and "poignant," and yet *A Long Way from Chicago* is actually both rollicking and poignant. It's also a quick read and a lot of fun.

Alex Flinn, Author

LONGITUDE: THE TRUE STORY OF A LONE GENIUS WHO SOLVED THE GREATEST SCIENTIFIC PROBLEM OF HIS TIME
Dava Sobel

Up until the late 1700s, sailors on a ship could not pinpoint their location at sea accurately and were sailing, literally, into the unknown—this problem became known as the "longitude problem." During the 18th century, England offered money to the person who could solve the problem. *Longitude* is the story of clockmaker John Harrison's 40-year struggle to receive the prize money for his invention. Mixed within Harrison's story is the tale of the British officer who became interested in Harrison's inventions and spent more than 20 years meticulously cleaning and restoring them. Solving the "longitude problem" was the greatest scientific dilemma of its day, and Sobel brings to life the personalities of those involved in the race.

Deborah Nicholl, Librarian

Next?

For other riveting true stories, try *Krakatoa* by Simon Winchester or *The Bounty* by Caroline Arnold.

More Dava Sobel? Try *The Planets* next.

LOOKING FOR ALASKA John Green

Miles Halter is sick of his safe and practically friendless life at home in Florida. So he decides to enroll in a boarding school in Alabama called Culver Creek for his last two years of high school, in the hopes of seeking a "Greater Perhaps." Upon his arrival he becomes friends with his roommate, a boy who prefers to be called Colonel. He also meets a mysterious yet drop-dead gorgeous girl named Alaska, who he wants to get to know better. Although she seems to open up to him, something tells Miles that Alaska is still hiding something important.

John Green tells a captivating tale in a serious tone, but also includes humor along the way. *Looking for Alaska* embraces day-to-day situations that almost anyone can relate to, showing the indelible impact one life can have on another.

Bailey Boron, age 16

Next?

John Green's second book, *An Abundance of Katherines* (UTBG 5), takes a more humorous tone but is similarly captivating.

Invisible by Pete Hautman is also centered on a mysterious incident in the past, and follows two friends as they attempt to come to terms with it.

For another touching and mysterious story about a school outcast, try Frank Portman's *King Dork* (UTBG 194).

LOOKING FOR JJ Anne Cassidy

Next?

Sonya Hartnett's *Surrender* (UTBG 344), about a child who has extremely violent tendencies, is an upsetting but important read.

Or for a really dark read about a boy who witnesses his father's murder and discovers a whole new life, try Graham Marks's *Zoo* (UTBG 404).

Alice Sebold's *The Lovely Bones* (UTBG 213) is a compelling read about, among other things, a little girl who is murdered, and how she tries to help prove the identity of her killer.

Children who murder other children—cases like this make BIG headlines in newspapers. But what is the real story behind the headlines, and what is it like if you are the teenage girl convicted of murder, now newly released into the world? What I liked about this brave story is that it makes you really think about the issues and see things from an unusual perspective.

"JJ" has been given a new identity upon her release—she has a job and a boyfriend and a new life to look forward to—but someone knows who she is and is looking for her. She has to go on the run yet again. At the same time as these compelling and powerful events are happening, another story is unraveling, about the murder itself: why and how it happened. I found this novel compulsive reading!

Julia Green, Author

THE LOOKING GLASS WARS Frank Beddor

Next?

Where better to start than with Beddor's inspiration, *Alice's Adventures in Wonderland* and *Through the Looking Glass* by Lewis Carroll?

Stuart Hill's *The Cry of the Icemark* (UTBG 80) involves another princess fighting for her rightful kingdom.

The Eyre Affair (UTBG 108) by Jasper Fforde takes characters from famous books and makes them do some awfully strange things . . .

Using Lewis Carroll's classic children's story *Alice's Adventures in Wonderland* as his inspiration, Beddor has created a storming, imaginative, bloody tour de force that deserves not to be overlooked.

The author imagines that Alice's Wonderland did indeed exist and that it was not a fairy tale after all. Princess Alyss Heart was heir to the throne of Wonderland but was cruelly usurped when her Aunt Redd stormed Wondertropolis and murdered her parents. Fleeing for her life, Alyss was transported to our world, the world of Charles Dodgson and literary Oxford in the late 19th century. Beddor has pulled off a wonderfully complicated twist of creativity, and his ambitious novel is a visual feast that is begging to be made into a film.

John McLay, Literary Scout

LORD LOSS Darren Shan

Everything goes wrong for Grubbs Grady from the moment he plays a joke on his sister. Though why his family gets so uptight about a few rotting rat guts is a mystery—one that gets solved pretty quickly when Lord Loss appears, along with his nightmare companions, Vein and Artery. Demons one and all, they literally tear Grubbs's family apart. Locked into a home for the mentally unstable, Grubbs is just about ready to give up, until one day his long-lost uncle comes to take him home. To peace and quiet? Not likely.

This book is not for the fainthearted! From the end of chapter one you step into a world of demons—a world that drips with gore, pain, magic, werewolves, and bloodcurdling excitement.

Leonie Flynn, Editor

Next?

If you haven't read Darren Shan's other books—and you like to be scared witless—do so! Start with *Cirque du Freak* (UTBG 69) and keep going.

Or try one of Darren's own favorites, such as Charles Dickens's thrilling story of the French Revolution, *A Tale of Two Cities* (UTBG 345).

Another bloodthirsty account of werewolves can be found in *The Wereling* (UTBG 385) by Stephen Cole.

LORD OF THE FLIES William Golding

Lord of the Flies tells the story of a group of young boys stranded without adults on a deserted island after a plane crash. After a promising beginning, the group fragments and very soon descends into savagery. It is ingenious because it gives an idea of what could happen when ordinary boys are left alone.

I could easily identify with the characters, and I used to think about my own friends and which characters from the book they would be. With such vivid descriptions of the setting, it was easy to wonder what might have happened if it had been us left alone on that island . . .

Andy McNab, Author

BEHIND BARS

Monster by Walter Dean Myers

Al Capone Does My Shirts by Gennifer Choldenko

White Oleander by Janet Fitch

Nineteen Minutes by Jodi Picoult

To Kill a Mockingbird by Harper Lee

Hole in My Life by Jack Gantos

Next?

William Golding wrote complex books—try **The Spire**, about the building of a cathedral, or **The Inheritors** (UTBG 176), about the first humans.

Brave New World (UTBG 49) by Aldous Huxley is another bleak view of how humanity has evolved.

Heart of Darkness (UTBG 149) by Joseph Conrad is about another journey into violence and madness.

lord of the flies

william golding

THE LORD OF THE RINGS trilogy

J. R. R. Tolkien

After reading *The Hobbit* and loving it, I thought I should try the trilogy that followed. So I did. For six days I spent my time reading, rereading, and losing myself in life in Middle Earth, where the story is set. The trilogy begins with *The Fellowship of the Ring*, following the journey of one hobbit, named Frodo Baggins, who must destroy the One Ring in order to save Middle Earth. Frodo starts off with a fellowship of nine, but by the end of the book the Fellowship has lost some members and the remaining ones decide to go their separate ways. Frodo's quest to destroy the Ring is continued in the next two books—*The Two Towers* and *The Return of the King*.

Florence Eastoe, age 13

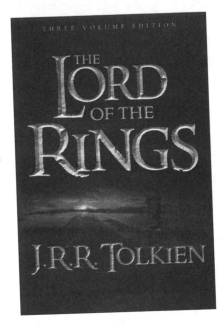

Next?

If you are one of the many who devoured the appendices at the end of The Lord of the Rings trilogy then try Tolkien's **The Silmarillion** and **Unfinished Tales**.

Gone are the days when the closest to a fantasy section that bookshops got was science fiction. Now there's almost too much to choose from. My personal favorites are: the novels of Robin Hobb—particularly **The Farseer** trilogy (UTBG 112)—and Philip Pullman's **His Dark Materials** trilogy (UTBG 153).

If you haven't read it already, try Tolkien's **The Hobbit** (UTBG 155)— the story of how the Ring was found.

Ask six different people why this book is important to them and you'll get six different answers.

For some it's the sheer scale of the story—the epic struggle between Good and Evil that will always be relevant to our own lives. For others it's the Fellowship, the friendship that binds nine disparate individuals and keeps them going through one perilous adventure after another. And then there's Tolkien's creation of an alternate world, complete with its own language and history.

For me, it's always been the realism. The characters may be hobbits and elves and walking trees, but I know what they eat, when they sleep, and how they feel. When I read this book I believe in it utterly—and that's fantasy at its best.

Laura Hutchings, Teacher

The LORD PETER WIMSEY books

Dorothy L. Sayers

Peter Wimsey is an intellectual, highly sensitive amateur detective with a taste for good wine—and a talent for solving crimes. He appears in around a dozen books, all of them full of strong, quirky characters and ingenious plots. The solutions often depend on his detailed knowledge of subjects like bell-ringing and arsenic poisoning, and the author has an exceedingly characteristic way of weaving obscure quotations into the dialogue. Only one woman can really keep up with Wimsey—and when they meet she's on trial for the murder of her lover.

Don't expect graphic details of sex and violence or serious discussion of current issues. The books are elegant puzzles, written to tantalize and entertain. But they don't trivialize life. Everything is underpinned by Wimsey's curiosity and enjoyment of the world around him, and his commitment to rigorous intellectual honesty.

Gillian Cross, Author

> **Next?**
>
> More Wimsey? My favorites are *Strong Poison*, *Gaudy Night*, and *Murder Must Advertise*.
>
> You might also enjoy the modern detective novels of Janet Evanovich, starting with *One for the Money* (UTBG 257).
>
> Or the very funny **Jeeves** stories (UTBG 182) by P. G. Wodehouse.

LOST IT Kristen Tracy

> **Next?**
>
> Reading about first love and the loss of virginity would not be complete without Judy Blume's *Forever* (UTBG 125), the first book to talk candidly about teenagers and sex.
>
> For a more serious look at a girl's first sexual experience, try Sara Zarr's *Story of a Girl* (UTBG 340).
>
> Daria Snadowsky's *Anatomy of a Boyfriend* follows two characters from their first time having sex through the changes they face when they leave for different colleges.

Lost It is a funny, lively "adventure of a story" starring Tess Whistle. Tess fears everything in her life: bears, boys, bras. She thinks of only the worst outcomes and concocts every possible tragic ending. Life challenges Tess to deal with the unusual hurdles of both parents experiencing a midlife crisis (at the same time!), her best friend having a breakdown and relocating (across the country!), and her cancer-surviving, adorable first boyfriend with whom she struggles to have a healthy, happy, and honest relationship.

Tess endears and entertains readers through her obsessive outlooks, her youthful mistakes, and her honest and heartbreaking lessons. I loved the liveliness, the laughter, the losses (and gains), and hope you will too!

Laura Gajdostik, Teacher

LOVE IN THE TIME OF CHOLERA

Gabriel García Márquez

If you long to escape from our everyday world, and would like to travel far away (to South America) and long ago (the start of the 20th century), this book will take you there. You are slowly drawn into a dazzling world of extraordinary detail, and begin to tune in to the life of two young people: Florentino and Fermina (great names, by the way). Their love affair is drawn out over decades, and years and years must pass before it will reach some kind of dreamlike resolution.

It's the kind of book you can only read very slowly, allowing one of the great writers of our age to hypnotize you with his evocation of a society that is beautiful and magical but also brutal and primitive. The book is hugely satisfying. I want to read it again NOW. Although, speaking as a hypochondriac, I felt there was maybe a *teeny* bit too much about love and not *quite* enough about cholera.

Sue Limb, Author

> ### Next?
>
> García Márquez has written some of the best-loved books of the past few decades. Try *One Hundred Years of Solitude* (UTBG 257) next.
>
> Something similar, but not similar? A Greek story by an Englishman about an Italian? *Corelli's Mandolin* (UTBG 78) by Louis de Bernières.
>
> Isabel Allende's usual subtlety is brought to the high adventure of *Zorro*.

SIBLINGS

My Sister's Keeper
by Jodi Picoult

A Wrinkle in Time
by Madeleine L'Engle

Peace Like a River by Leif Enger

The Wind on Fire trilogy
by William Nicholson

Ruby Holler
by Sharon Creech

A Series of Unfortunate Events
by Lemony Snicket

Saffy's Angel
by Hilary McKay

THE LOVELY BONES Alice Sebold

This is a startling book. Within a few lines you learn that the narrator is Susie Salmon, a murdered 14-year-old girl. She describes her own grisly murder at the hands of a neighbor. She is in a kind of heaven, a frozen place where she can only watch the life she has left behind. We see the effects of the murder on her mother and father, how it destroys their life together. We also see, with horror, that the murderer is not caught—and there is evidence of other deaths.

There is life after death for Susie, but she's in a lonely place. We often read about the loss felt by grieving relatives, but Susie's loss is greater: she has lost everything.

Anne Cassidy, Author

Next?

Lucky by Alice Sebold is the account of the author's own traumatic rape and its aftermath.

The Great Blue Yonder by Alex Shearer is told by a boy from beyond the grave.

Jacqueline Woodson's *Behind You* follows a family and those around them trying to cope with the freak accidental death of Jeremiah, their son, brother, boyfriend, and friend.

Or read one of the most enchanting life-after-death stories, Gabrielle Zevin's *Elsewhere* (UTBG 103).

LUCAS Kevin Brooks

Next?

Other books by Kevin Brooks? All of them are worth reading: *Martyn Pig* (UTBG 220), *Kissing the Rain* (UTBG 195), and *Candy* (UTBG 57).

The Fire-Eaters (UTBG 118) by David Almond is another powerful story about an outsider and the nature of fear.

What My Mother Doesn't Know (UTBG 386) by Sonya Sones captures the consequences of a relationship with an outcast.

Kevin Brooks writes powerful, original stories, and *Lucas* is my favorite so far. The main character, Caitlin, tells the story of what happened to her one extraordinary summer, when a mysterious, beautiful boy named Lucas arrived at the island where she lives with her dad and brother in a close-knit but fearful community. Caitlin's friendship with Lucas helps her to be the person she really is, rather than going along with how most of the other teenagers behave—but that's a really difficult thing to do when you're 15. Lucas, the outsider, becomes a focus for all the fear and hatred the islanders feel about someone "different" from them, with terrible and tragic consequences.

I loved the island setting, the descriptions of the sea and the mudflats and dunes, and the way we are powerfully shown the danger of the "mob mentality." You won't forget this story.

Julia Green, Author

MAGIC OR MADNESS Justine Larbalestier

Reason Cansino has spent 15 years on the run with her mother, Sarafina, traveling the Australian outback in an effort to escape her evil grandmother, Esmeralda. But when Sarafina suffers a severe mental breakdown, Reason is sent to live with the very woman she fears most. Will the horror stories that Sarafina has told turn out to be true, or is there something more complex behind the scenes? It's Reason's job to find out as she magically travels between New York and Sydney and uncovers long-hidden family secrets with her enigmatic friends Jay-Tee and Tom.

Mysteriously magical, this complex story will have you on the edge of your seat trying to figure out what is real and what is not. Reason's struggle to find out just where she fits in is something most of us have experienced, but in Reason's quest you never know just where evil may lie.

Rachel Wadham, Librarian

> ### Next?
>
> Try the rest of the Magic or Madness trilogy, which completes Reason's story: Book 2, *Magic Lessons*, and Book 3, *Magic's Child*.
>
> Or try any of the books by Larbalestier's husband, Scott Westerfeld—the **Uglies** trilogy (UTBG 370) is especially riveting.
>
> You might want to jump the pond to New Zealand and try some of Margaret Mahy's magical and romantic books, such as *The Changeover*, *Alchemy* (UTBG 10), or *The Catalogue of the Universe*.

THE MAGIC TOYSHOP Angela Carter

> ### Next?
>
> If you like the poetry of the language and the sense of magic, try *Orlando* (UTBG 260) by Virginia Woolf.
>
> If you like the way Angela Carter uses fairy-tale images, read *The Bloody Chamber*, her collection of short stories.
>
> If you like the way Angela Carter describes the decisions Melanie faces as she grows older, try *The Last September* by Elizabeth Bowen.

Fifteen-year-old Melanie secretly slips into the night wearing her mother's wedding dress. The next day she learns that her parents have been killed in an airplane crash. She is sent with her little brother and sister to live with their unknown uncle Philip, the toymaker. Burdened with guilt and responsibility, Melanie has to confront her approaching adulthood in the strange, surreal world she has entered. Surrounding her are an aunt struck dumb on her wedding day, magical mechanical birds, and puppets that are either dream or nightmare but are definitely not toys. Controlling everything is Uncle Philip. Does he see Melanie as a person, or as another puppet he can shape and control? A rich and disturbing novel with no easy answers.

Antonia Honeywell, Teacher

The MAIGRET books Georges Simenon

I love Maigret. Simenon wrote his Maigret detective books at breakneck speed, often in just a few days. Maybe that's why the stories feel so immediate and alive. I love Simenon's sparse and simple prose, his claustrophobic settings, where tensions simmer away and then explode—driving quite ordinary people to violence. I love the way Maigret bumbles about, often just as confused as we are, "feeling" his way toward a solution. And how he struggles, as we often do, to understand the darker secrets of the human heart and why people behave as they do.

Where to start? Perhaps with *Maigret Goes to School* or *Maigret Goes Home* or *Inspector Cadaver*, and if you get hooked, there are 73 more!

Susan Gates, Author

> **Next?**
>
> Simenon without Maigret? Try *The Strangers in the House* or *The Man Who Watched Trains Go By*.
>
> For something lighter, try other famous detectives like Chandler's Marlowe in *The Big Sleep* (UTBG 34), Conan Doyle's **Sherlock Holmes** stories (UTBG 319), or Christie's Poirot in *Death on the Nile*. Or Dexter's more recent **Inspector Morse** books (UTBG 177).

MAKE LEMONADE Virginia Euwer Wolff

> **Next?**
>
> There's a follow-up, which is also excellent, called *True Believer* (UTBG 366).
>
> The theme of being trapped by life as an unloved and unwanted daughter is explored in Adeline Yen Mah's autobiographical *Chinese Cinderella* (UTBG 66).
>
> For other novels told in verse, try Sonya Sones's *What My Mother Doesn't Know* (UTBG 386) or Nikki Grimes's *Bronx Masquerade*.

A beautifully written book about LaVaughn, a 14-year-old girl, who is determined to break out of the inner-city poverty of her upbringing and get to college. To raise funds she takes on a regular babysitting job for Jolly, a struggling single mother, but ends up getting drawn deeper and deeper into the seemingly hopeless situation in which Jolly has found herself.

It's a very sensitive, deeply moving but highly readable story, told in the first person without a single wasted word. It explores themes of friendship, family, and self-respect; and of young people aiming to make something of their lives against all the odds. Although it deals with the most difficult of issues, this is a book brimming with warmth, humor, and hope, and it leaves the spirit soaring.

Malachy Doyle, Author

THE MAN IN THE HIGH CASTLE

Philip K. Dick

Philip K. Dick is deservedly a legend among sci-fi writers. Several of his books formed the basis of some great movies, *Blade Runner* among them. With *The Man in the High Castle* he gave an enormous boost to the "alternative history" genre, in this case the idea that Germany and Japan actually *won* World War II and divided the defeated United States between them.

The story is set in 1962 against a background of mounting tension between Japan and a Nazi Germany bent on total world domination, and the destinies of several characters become entangled as the plot is worked out. This strange, haunting book and its Zen-like approach to history and the clash of cultures will resonate in your mind for a very long time.

Tony Bradman, Author

Next?

Other stories that tell of alternate histories are Robert Harris's *Fatherland* (UTBG 115) (Germany won the war and invaded Britain), or Ben Jeapes's *New World Order* (aliens alter the course of the English Civil War).

What about another Philip K. Dick? Try *We Can Remember It for You Wholesale* (UTBG 382).

MANCHILD IN THE PROMISED LAND

Claude Brown

Next?

Ralph Ellison's classic, *Invisible Man*, chronicles the life of a nameless black man, who searches for truth, justice, and an identity.

For another autobiographical story about growing up in Harlem, try Walter Dean Myers's *Bad Boy*.

Claude Brown's astounding narrative chronicles his tumultuous childhood in Harlem, New York. Claude, known in the book as Sonny, came to New York searching for opportunity in the "promised land." The North symbolized freedom for African Americans, but when Claude's family arrived, they were faced with the poverty, violence, and disparity that besieged their beloved yet feared neighborhood. At a young age, Claude was tempted by the dangers that stereotypically characterize an urban lifestyle—violence, drugs, and illegal activities. Claude watches as his beloved Harlem is plagued by brutality and tragedy—the very obstacles he worked so hard to overcome.

Manchild in the Promised Land makes you question your racial, social, and overall life views. It is captivating and beautiful even in its most heartbreaking moments. Claude Brown perfectly captures the voice of an era, and the story remains as relevant today as it was when the book was written.

Yardley Peresman, age 15

MANSFIELD PARK Jane Austen

Next?

Pride and Prejudice (UTBG 276) is probably Jane Austen's most famous novel. *Northanger Abbey* (UTBG 247) is wonderful too. Come to think of it, they all are!

For another comedy of manners that's every bit as sharp and telling, read William M. Thackeray's *Vanity Fair* (UTBG 376).

Or try Karen Joy Fowler's modern story of five people who meet every month in *The Jane Austen Book Club*.

This is funny, really very funny, and has great dialogue and such honesty from Fanny, the heroine, that even the most self-obsessed teenager could not help but learn something from her. At the beginning, the characters are assembled at a country house and are planning to perform a play. This device is as brilliant as any psychological workshop for showing the reader a multitude of behaviors that only intensify through the novel. Jane Austen is my favorite English novelist, and although this book is not faultless—I find the ending a little frustrating—it is clever and perceptive. Read it and recognize your friends and yourself.

Raffaella Barker, Author

MANY STONES Carolyn Coman

A heaviness hangs over Berry Morgan. Her beloved older sister, Laura, was killed while volunteering in South Africa a year earlier, and Berry's attempts to cope include submerging herself under the weight of her collection of stones, which she methodically places atop her chest. When Berry's father suggests they go to South Africa to attend Laura's memorial service, Berry feels like the stones are crashing down on her. But while on the trip, she begins to understand the many levels of reconciliation, if not forgiveness, and each stone is lifted until she can finally feel light again.

Many Stones also explores the need of a nation to lift itself up from apartheid. The most poignant moments of the novel are when Berry lets down her angry teenage front and lets in the suffering of others—the many men and women who also lost loved ones, who were wrongfully imprisoned for years, and who are still feeling the effects of the large divide between the rich and the poor. It is a moving portrayal of a girl, and a nation, learning to move forward.

Stacy Cantor, Editor

Next?

Try Sharon M. Draper's *Tears of a Tiger* (UTBG 352) for a different look at death.

Or Alice Sebold's *The Lovely Bones* (UTBG 213), which explores one family's different reactions to the loss of their daughter.

For more by Carolyn Coman, don't miss *What Jamie Saw*, about recovering from abuse.

SCIENCE FICTION by Andrew Norriss

I grew up with a comic called *The Eagle*, which had stories on the front page about a pilot in the United Planets Spaceforce named Dan Dare. He had his own spaceship, the *Anastasia*, that could take him anywhere in the galaxy, and I *so* wanted to go with him. His adventures were set far in the future—about the year 2000 as I remember—and I've been hooked on science fiction ever since. They say the genre began with people like Jules Verne and H. G. Wells, but for my money science fiction really started in the 1940s and 1950s, and the three big names that launched it were Isaac Asimov, Robert Heinlein, and Arthur C. Clarke. These were the guys, I later discovered, who had inspired the writers of Dan Dare. Heinlein wrote stories about humanity colonizing the planets and spreading out across the galaxy, much as Americans had conquered the West, but fighting off aliens instead of Indians. Asimov's Foundation trilogy (UTBG 126) went even further into the future and described the fall of the first human, stellar empire, while in *2001: A Space Odyssey* Arthur C. Clarke wondered if we hadn't already been visited by aliens in the distant past who might yet return and take humanity to the next level.

Nobody took these guys seriously as novelists, but the ideas they were coming up with were mind-blowing—and they were just the tip of the iceberg. I'll never forget the first time I came across the idea of stargates, in Murray Leinster's *The Wailing Asteroid*. Clifford D. Simak's *The Way Station* was my favorite reread for years, and I still have my dog-eared copy of Theodore Sturgeon's *More than Human*, which suggested that humanity might evolve into gestalts. The ideas went on and on, and the possibilities and the hope seemed endless.

I didn't much like it when science fiction grew up. I knew that writers like Ray Bradbury and Kurt Vonnegut were seriously clever, but they used sci-fi—in books like *Fahrenheit 451* (UTBG 110) or *Slaughterhouse-Five* (UTBG 327)—to show humanity screwing it up on a galactic scale. They were well written, but they weren't what I was looking for.

I wanted the fun stuff, and fortunately it's still around. A lot of it gets written for television these days—for *Star Trek*, *Babylon V,* or *Farscape*—but there are still some authors producing ideas that will astound, and describing worlds you wish you could live in.

Some of these writers may not be quite what you're looking for, but the good news is that bookstores these days have whole shelves stuffed with sci-fi. All you need to do is dip and pick until you find the stuff that works for you. Good luck in the hunt! And may the Force be with you as you boldly go to infinity and beyond . . .

Who am I? (cloning & more):

The House of the Scorpion by Nancy Farmer

Zoo by Graham Marks

Sharp North by Patrick Cave

Taylor Five by Ann Halam

Unique by Alison Allen-Gray

Some classic sci-fi:

Neuromancer by William Gibson

I, Robot by Isaac Asimov

Do Androids Dream of Electric Sheep? by Philip K. Dick

Starship Troopers by Robert A. Heinlein

The Left Hand of Darkness by Ursula K. Le Guin

Ender's Game by Orson Scott Card

The Hitchhiker's Guide to the Galaxy by Douglas Adams

Dune by Frank Herbert

The Day of the Triffids by John Wyndham

The War of the Worlds by H. G. Wells

NOW A MAJOR MOTION PICTURE

THE HITCHHIKER'S GUIDE TO THE GALAXY

Contains a 92-page bonus section on the making of the movie!

DOUGLAS ADAMS
New York Times bestselling author

MARTYN PIG Kevin Brooks

12+

Next?

Brooks excels at putting his characters in the kind of unusual situations you would never want to find yourself. Try *Lucas* (UTBG 213), or *Being*.

Boy Kills Man (UTBG 46) by Matt Whyman also sees young people driven to murder, this time in South America and for very different reasons.

Raymond Chandler's *The Big Sleep* (UTBG 34) contains another poignant and lonely narrative voice, hidden behind the hard-boiled front.

P. D. James's English crime novels, such as *A Taste for Death*, have an air of chilly melancholy to them, which can also be found in *Martyn Pig*.

Martyn Pig is a boy with a weird name and not much else; not particularly interesting, not really good-looking, and not very popular either. In one week, though, his life is turned upside-down and inside-out, trapping him in a web of lies and deadly events.

Martyn lives with his dad, an alcoholic, and the only thing good in his life is his best friend, Alex. She's also his only hope, the only person he can turn to when he does something wrong, very wrong. But was he in fact wrong to do what he did? Is it only wrong if he gets caught? This is a fantastic story, dark and very witty, must-pickupable and unputdownable, which thrills and shocks. Kevin Brooks amazes and provokes. He is without doubt one of the best authors for teenagers . . . ever!

David Gardner, age 16

MASSIVE Julia Bell

14+

This brilliant novel is simultaneously funny and tragic. It's about an anorexic mother driving her daughter toward the same condition.

Carmen's mother is obsessed with making her daughter thin and beautiful, but Carmen finds comfort in food . . . at first. The real horror begins when Carmen herself decides she *would* like to be thin—very thin. Then it's no longer funny.

Parents should read this book. It reveals how we often don't support or understand each other: there are teachers, girls, and parents who are ignoring pain when they should be supporting and caring for those in trouble—in the book and in real life. I laughed and cried while reading this book. It is wise and witty and wincingly poignant.

Nicola Morgan, Author

Next?

Ibi Kaslik's *Skinny* also delves into the issue of anorexia. It's written in alternate viewpoints between two sisters.

Julia Bell's second novel, *Dirty Work*, takes on the terrifying issue of human trafficking.

But for the most devastating book about the damage girls can do to each other and themselves, you must read *Speak* (UTBG 334) by Laurie Halse Anderson.

MASTER AND COMMANDER   Patrick O'Brian

This is the first in the Aubrey/Maturin series of 20 superb novels chronicling the lives and adventures of two unforgettable characters: Jack Aubrey, the dashing sea captain in Nelson's navy—gruff, courageous, magnificently flawed; and his friend, the naval surgeon Stephen Maturin—moody, taciturn, fascinatingly complex. This is historical fiction of the very highest order. Don't worry about the nautical terms. You're in the safest of hands, and, besides, these are not just stories about the sea. There are storms, shipwrecks, and battles to be sure, but there are also intrigues, affairs, scandals, duels, the murky world of secret intelligence, and much more. O'Brian's canvas is huge. These are stories of love and loyalty, humor and humanity, beautifully written and with a sense of the period so powerfully evoked you think you're there.

Tim Bowler, Author

> **Next?**
>
> If you want more about life under sail, try the **Hornblower** books by C. S. Forester.
>
> A classic story of the sea is Herman Melville's epic *Moby-Dick*.
>
> For warfare on land you can't get much better than Bernard Cornwell's **Sharpe** books, starting with *Sharpe's Company* (UTBG 317).

THE MASTER OF BALLANTRAE

Robert Louis Stevenson

> **Next?**
>
> More Stevenson? *Kidnapped* (UTBG 192) and *Dr. Jekyll and Mr. Hyde* (UTBG 95) are both fine reads.
>
> Alexandre Dumas wrote some fast, brilliant adventure stories. Try *The Count of Monte Cristo*.
>
> Or for something even more romantic, try *The Prisoner of Zenda* (UTBG 281) by Anthony Hope.

This exciting story, set in 18th-century Scotland, opens at the ancestral home of the Duries of Durisdeer and Ballantrae. Narrated by Mr. Mackellar, steward of the estate, it deals with the intense rivalry between two brothers who could not be less alike. The eldest, James, Master of Ballantrae, is a charming swashbuckler who despises his dour, unadventurous brother, Henry. When James is reported killed at the battle of Culloden, Henry assumes his place as head of the household and marries James's betrothed. The story might end there, but James returns from the dead and upsets everything. A rich and moving tale, strong in character and action. Read it by firelight in an old, creaky house for best effect.

Michael Lawrence, Author

The MATES, DATES . . . series
Cathy Hopkins

Lucy, Nesta, TJ, and Izzie seem as real as the people you meet at school, in the mall, at the market, and so on. These four girls come from very different backgrounds, but their friendship bonds them together for life—more so than with boys (although their friendship is strained on more than one occasion *because* of boys). Each book tells the story of a few weeks of change in one of the girls' lives, but we always know what the others are thinking and doing, and most importantly, how they all help each other resolve their problems. Frank and funny, moving and thought-provoking, the Mates, Dates . . . series makes for compelling reading about what it's like being a teen today.

Jon Appleton, Editor

BAD BREAKUPS

The Boyfriend List by E. Lockhart

Gingerbread by Rachel Cohn

The True Meaning of Cleavage by Mariah Fredericks

Bridget Jones's Diary by Helen Fielding

Things Change by Patrick Jones

Breathing Underwater by Alex Flinn

Next?

More Mates? Try *Mates, Dates, and Comic Kisses* next.

Girl, 15, Charming but Insane (UTBG 133) by Sue Limb also entertainingly tackles what it's like being a teenager today.

Make sure you read the **Confessions of Georgia Nicolson** series, starting with *Angus, Thongs and Full-Frontal Snogging* (UTBG 18) by Louise Rennison.

Tyne O'Connell's **Calypso Chronicles** series follows an American girl at a British boarding school, where she meets and falls in love with an English prince.

MAUS   Art Spiegelman

Maus is an extraordinary graphic, or comic-book, novel about the Holocaust. In Poland in the 1940s, Jews hide from the Nazis, who are seeking to exterminate them. It's a game of cat-and-mouse, and Spiegelman makes that metaphor the basis of his drawings. The Polish Jews are mice, the Nazis are cats; *Maus* becomes a darkly fascinating version of Beatrix Potter's quaint fantasies.

Two narratives run side by side: the story of Spiegelman's parents and their struggle to survive, and an account, set in contemporary America, of Spiegelman's thorny relationship with his aging and difficult father, Vladek.

At the heart of the book is a painful question. To paraphrase Vladek, addressing his son, the author: "I survived Hell so that you could be born; why aren't you what I wanted you to be?" It's a question that survivors of tyranny continue to ask and their children still struggle to answer. Maybe a book as good as this is the answer.

Mal Peet, Author

Next?

Persepolis (UTBG 269) by Marjane Satrapi uses pictures to illuminate a dark story—better than any amount of text.

Or for something else about the Holocaust, try either *Stones in Water* by Donna Jo Napoli (about two boys stolen from their homes to be slave workers in Eastern Europe) or *Daniel Half Human* by David Chotjewitz (about how a friendship is torn apart when one boy is found to be half-Jewish).

For another compelling look at the Holocaust from an insider's point-of-view, you shouldn't miss Elie Wiesel's heartbreaking memoir, *Night* (UTBG 243).

MAXIMUM RIDE: THE ANGEL EXPERIMENT James Patterson

14+

Max is 14; she's a wise-cracking, quick-witted girl. Oh, and she has wings. With two percent bird DNA, she and her group, or "flock," are the result of genetic engineering. Light-boned, strong, fast, they live as outcasts from the "school" that bred them. Until the day the Erasers—half-wolf killing machines—steal away Max's youngest flock member, Angel, and the race to save her from being no more than a lab rat is on.

This is a book where you dive straight into the action and keep on going. With love and friendship, great villains, and enough thought-provoking backstory to keep you thinking as well as frantically page turning, this is fast and furious fiction at its best.

Leonie Flynn, Editor

Next?

Another James Patterson? Mostly he writes for adults, but try *When the Wind Blows*, which has some of the same characters as *Maximum Ride*.

Something with more horror and just as much excitement: Darren Shan's *Lord Loss* (UTBG 208).

Or for a different sort of flying, this time on the backs of dragons, try **The Dragonriders of Pern** series (UTBG 98) by Anne McCaffrey.

MEMOIRS OF A GEISHA Arthur Golden

16+

Next?

If this starts you off on a quest to find out more about geishas, try Liza Dalby's *Geisha*.

The real-life geisha Arthur Golden interviewed tells her own story in *Geisha of Gion* by Mineko Iwasaki.

To read of the wartime experiences of a US Japanese community, try *Snow Falling on Cedars* (UTBG 330) by David Guterson.

This has everything I want in a book. Beautifully written, it gives an insight into another time and culture—in this case from 1929 to the postwar years of Japan. It is told from the point of view of Sayuri, a geisha girl.

The closed world of geishas has always fascinated me, from the rituals that dominate every aspect of their days to the intimate details of their personal lives. Part of the appeal of this book was that the author claimed to have obtained his information from a real geisha who told him her life story. But it is what he has done with this story that makes this such a great read—he has woven fact and fiction into a heartbreaking and breathlessly lovely tale.

Cathy Hopkins, Author

MIDNIGHT IN THE GARDEN OF GOOD AND EVIL John Berendt

16+

Next?

There really isn't another book quite like *Midnight in the Garden of Good and Evil* (though there is a film version, starring Kevin Spacey and John Cusack).

John Steinbeck's **Cannery Row** (UTBG 58) has some of the same flavor.

John Grisham's legal thrillers are set in the similar worlds of New Orleans and Mississippi—try **The Partner** first.

When this book first came out, readers thought it was a fictional story. But according to Berendt, he really did have the luck to meet this extraordinary cast of characters and to witness the bizarre plot.

It all takes place in the Deep South, in Savannah, Georgia, where Berendt, a New York journalist, finds himself captivated enough by the place to rent a home there for several months every year. He meets society belles and lowlife characters too, like the sleazy lawyer Joe Odom, whose life is one long traveling party. But the real stars are the transvestite African American cabaret artist, the Lady Chablis, and the ambiguous millionaire Jim Williams, who is tried four times for the same murder.

Some of the subject matter is very "adult," but not gratuitously so; the city of Savannah plays a central part in this book, and it's this subject matter that gives the city its decadent character.

Mary Hoffman, Author

MILKWEED Jerry Spinelli

12+

Milkweed is an utterly compelling and engrossing story with a main character whose life at the beginning is worse than most of us could imagine, and it deteriorates steadily throughout. It is also a book about the Holocaust.

Misha Pilsudski is a wild thief without family, home, or education. Is he Jew, gypsy, or neither? It makes little difference as he is herded into the Warsaw Ghetto with the rest of the boys in his gang and begins to live through the horrors of life there.

Jerry Spinelli has an uncanny ability to plunge right to the heart of a character. Misha whirls you along with his story, which, like him, is endlessly energetic with a spirit that is never crushed.

Susan Reuben, Editor

Next?

For the most famous true account of the Holocaust, read **The Diary of a Young Girl** (UTBG 91) by Anne Frank.

For a "based on a true story" account of the Warsaw Ghetto uprising, read *Mila 18* by Leon Uris.

My Secret Camera by Mendel Grossman and Frank Dabba Smith is full of photos taken in a Polish ghetto, showing what life was like there.

THE MILL ON THE FLOSS George Eliot

Next?

More Eliot—try *Silas Marner* (UTBG 322) next. Or the wonderful (wonderful!) *Middlemarch*.

For another book about 19th-century siblings, read *Little Women* by Louisa May Alcott.

Or Virginia Woolf's *A Room of One's Own* (UTBG 293), which is about the role of creative and exciting women in society.

One of George Eliot's most famous and best-loved books, this is the tragic story of Maggie Tulliver and her brother Tom. An intelligent and passionate teenager, Maggie is bored by the stifling and judgmental villagers of St. Ogg's. She longs for the love and approval of her brother, who is forced to study. Tom, embarrassed by his sister's passionate nature, ultimately rejects and humiliates her. This isn't an easy book to read, but the portrait of Maggie's conflicted and frustrated character is subtle and moving and gives the reader a real sense of how hard growing up must have been for girls in the 19th century who weren't allowed equal access to education.

Julia Bell, Author

MILLIONS Frank Cottrell Boyce `12+`

I like nothing better than being drawn into a story right from page one and *Millions* does just that. It's about a boy named Damian Cunningham who lives with his older brother, Anthony, and their widowed father.

Damian is obsessed by the saints and knows all there is to know about each and every one of them, much to the consternation of his teacher and classmates, who can't shut him up. Fast paced, multilayered, and humorous, the plot really takes off when the brothers find a bag of stolen money at the back of their yard, with mixed but hilarious consequences.

Read the book first, laugh, cry, and enjoy, then go see the film and buy the T-shirt. Then read the book again.

Helena Pielichaty, Author

Next?

Joey Pigza Swallowed the Key by Jack Gantos is about a boy with ADHD who has the same heart-tugging warmth as Damian.

Holes (UTBG 157) by Louis Sachar is another multilayered, real-life adventure story with an edge.

Ruby Holler (UTBG 295) by Sharon Creech is a poignant story of a brother and sister using humor and cunning to overcome life's perils.

In *Hoot* (UTBG 159) by Carl Hiaasen, the new kid in town overcomes the bullies in an ingenious way.

THE MINISTER'S DAUGHTER Julie Hearn

14+

Next?

Julie Hearn's first novel, *Follow Me Down*, is a time-travel novel set in contemporary London, among the "monsters" of old Bartholomew Fair.

Also try another wonderful historical novel about witch hunting: Celia Rees's powerful *Witch Child* (UTBG 393).

Or try Diana Wynne Jones's *Witch Week*, about a school for children of witches.

Do people see only what they believe they can see? In this rollicking, rambunctious historical novel set in the superstitious West Country during the English Civil War, boundaries are blurred between delusion, illusion, magic, and the everyday.

Nell is a Merrybegot, a child conceived on May Morning and thus sacred to nature. She is gradually learning her craft so that she can follow her grandmother as the cunning woman of the village. But if you are an unconventional, feisty girl in a period of witch hunting, you are surrounded by malice and danger. Characters both human and supernatural romp through the story, which sparkles with audacious humor, yet is touching, too.

Patricia Elliott, Author

MONDAYS ARE RED Nicola Morgan

14+

Following a near-fatal case of meningitis, Luke discovers that his senses have been strangely altered; he sees music, smells colors, and can taste through his fingertips. He has developed a condition called synesthesia, and the author's dexterity with language allows us to experience the world as richly as Luke does. "Mondays are red. Sadness has an empty blue smell. And music can taste of anything from banana puree to bat's pee." But there's a flip side to this sensation-drenched world, and it's Dreeg, a foul creature who has taken up residence in Luke's brain and who persuades him that he can do anything. Ugliness as well as beauty is heightened and in his fight to recover his full health, Luke grows ever more selfish and mean, even putting his family at risk. This is a startlingly original novel and a sensory roller coaster that will leave you breathless.

Kathryn Ross, Literary Agent

Next?

No two novels by Nicola Morgan are the same, but all are superbly written. Try *The Highwayman's Footsteps* or *The Passion Flower Massacre*.

The hero of Tim Bowler's *Starseeker* is a musical genius who also has synesthesia.

Two novels that explore the heightened senses of smell and taste to very different effect are Patrick Süskind's *Perfume* (UTBG 268), and *Chocolat* (UTBG 67) by Joanne Harris.

MONSTER Walter Dean Myers

Monster by Walter Dean Myers is one of the most interestingly written books I have ever read. What makes it so original is that it is a combination of the main character's journal entries and a regular narration of his life. Walter Dean Myers did an amazing job. As I read the book I was able to imagine the story playing out in front of me and I could hear the characters speaking as I read their lines. This book has as much style as any classic novel and the originality makes it twice as fun to read. The story is able to stay true to the seriousness of the plot it is telling. I was able to feel Steve Harmon's fear and felt as if I were sitting beside him experiencing the same anticipation.

As you learn more about what happened on that day in December, you will not want to put the book down. As Steve's court trial goes on, you are able to follow along with the jury as they try to figure out whose testimony is real and who is lying. Is this 16-year-old boy guilty of murder, or was it all a mistake—was he in the wrong place at the wrong time? How did the small role as a lookout for a robbery suddenly turn into something much bigger? The ending of this unique book will not let you down and will leave you thinking about how lost innocence can change one's life forever.

Anna Plociak, age 16

Next?

Tears of a Tiger (UTBG 352) by Sharon M. Draper looks at the inner turmoil of a teen who feels he murdered his best friend by driving drunk.

Paul Volponi's **Black and White** is about the friendship between two teens—one black, one white—and the one night that changed everything.

For more hard-hitting fiction by Walter Dean Myers, try either *Autobiography of My Dead Brother* or *Somewhere in the Darkness* next.

CLASSICS THAT NEVER FEEL OLD

The Great Gatsby by F. Scott Fitzgerald

Great Expectations by Charles Dickens

Lord of the Flies by William Golding

Fahrenheit 451 by Ray Bradbury

On the Road by Jack Kerouac

The Catcher in the Rye by J. D. Salinger

To Kill a Mockingbird by Harper Lee

MONSTER BLOOD TATTOO BOOK ONE: FOUNDLING

12+

D. M. Cornish

Monster Blood Tattoo is a story about a young boy, Rossamünd, who must take a long journey. The book is about his adventures and the people and monsters he meets along the way, including a fulgar named Europe. A fulgar is someone who has had surgery so that he can shoot lightning and control electricity. Rossamünd also gets into fights. When a big monster is killed, its blood is mixed with chemicals and made into a tattoo on the person who killed it.

I liked the book because it's very descriptive and has details of some awesome fights. In one of the best scenes, Rossamünd must jump into monster-infested waters after a fight breaks out on a ship! If you like fantasy and adventure stories, you should definitely read this book.

Casey Chartier, age 11

Next?

Don't miss *Lamplighter*, the second book in the Monster Blood Tattoo series.

Brian Selznick's *The Invention of Hugo Cabret* (UTBG 179) is similarly peppered with black-and-white drawings.

The Death Collector by Justin Richards is an atmospheric monster story.

The Ultimate Teen Readers' Poll

BOOK YOU DON'T WANT YOUR PARENTS TO KNOW YOU'VE READ

1. *Angus, Thongs and Full-Frontal Snogging*

2. *The Girls in Love series*

3. *A Child Called "It"*

4. *Bridget Jones's Diary*

5. *Smack*

6. *Good Girls*

7. *The Kama Sutra*

8. *Doing It*

9. *Forever*

10. *Ready or Not*

Tied for 3rd

MONTMORENCY: THIEF, LIAR, GENTLEMAN? Eleanor Updale

12+

Montmorency follows the story of rich gentleman Montmorency and his servant, Scarper. Problem is, they're the same person!

Montmorency is a young thief who has a terrible accident that nearly costs him his life. Instead, a doctor turns him into a scientific wonder in an age where people still died from drinking bad water. Montmorency will do anything to maintain a life of dignity. And he knows how to do it: the sewers. He learns to imitate the rich by copying the movements of a friend, and soon he has enough money to live the life he wants without stealing. But when Scarper's life calls, can Montmorency resist?

Stephen McGruer, age 14

Next?

Montmorency installments so far are: *Montmorency on the Rocks*, *Montmorency and the Assassins*, and *Montmorency's Revenge*.

James Bond might have made a good thief. Try Charlie Higson's *SilverFin* (UTBG 322), about Bond's first spy case as a teen.

Raffles was the first famous gentleman thief; try *Raffles: The Amateur Cracksman* by E. W. Hornung.

Montmorency's life in Victorian London is a challenge after his body's been put back together by a surgeon and he's spent time in prison. He has a double persona—there's Montmorency the wealthy, upper-class gentleman, who turns into the degenerate servant Scarper, a thief who uses the sewers of London to rob the city's rich. The police are baffled by the wave of mysterious and seemingly unstoppable thefts, but Montmorency must always remain on his guard—the smallest mistake could destroy both his lives.

The book is full of intrigue and ingenious plots, and it's a real page-turner.

Wendy Cooling, Books Consultant

AFRICAN AMERICAN WOMEN TELL IT LIKE IT IS

The Color Purple by Alice Walker

Beloved by Toni Morrison

I Know Why the Caged Bird Sings by Maya Angelou

Roll of Thunder, Hear My Cry by Mildred D. Taylor

Their Eyes Were Watching God by Zora Neale Hurston

THE MOON RIDERS Theresa Tomlinson

The legendary Amazon warriors were a tribe of women from what is now Turkey, who lived without men and fought their own battles on horseback. Their culture is seldom explored very deeply, but in this book they are called "Moon Riders" and dance under the moon, as well as fighting when called upon to do so.

Myrina, a young Moon Rider, rides to the aid of Troy when the city is besieged by the Greeks, which gives us a familiar tale told from a different point of view. The dramatic cover adds to the atmosphere, and by the end of the book I wanted to leap on a horse and join them!

Katherine Roberts, Author

Next?

For more by Theresa Tomlinson, try *Against the Tide* next.

If you are interested in the story of the siege of Troy, then try Adèle Geras's *Troy* (UTBG 366).

Or you could seek out a translation of Homer's *The Iliad* (UTBG 173)—the epic Greek poem about Achilles's adventures, which Alexander the Great kept under his pillow so he could read about his hero every night!

THE MOONSTONE Wilkie Collins

14+

The poet T. S. Eliot described this book as "the first modern English detective fiction." When Rachel Verinder inherits the Moonstone—a huge and cursed yellow diamond stolen generations ago from an Indian shrine—from her distant relative John Herncastle, she has no idea what havoc this gift is about to wreak. We discover that Herncastle, alienated from his family, has bequeathed the stone to Rachel as a form of revenge, and as the events of the novel unfold it becomes almost impossible to put it down. Both this novel and *The Woman in White* were Victorian equivalents of blockbuster bestsellers like *The Da Vinci Code*—hugely popular and read by almost anyone who could.

Julia Bell, Author

Next?

Other Wilkie Collins to look for are *The Woman in White* (UTBG 398) and *No Name*.

Beau Geste (UTBG 29) by P. C. Wren is a mystery and adventure that hinges on the theft of the Blue Water sapphire.

Or for a mystery involving an ancient chalice and a curse, try Margery Allingham's *Look to the Lady*, involving her aristocratic sleuth, Albert Campion.

MORTAL ENGINES Philip Reeve

12+

Mortal Engines follows the fortunes of city boy Tom and a disfigured outcast girl, Hester. It's set in a world where gigantic motorized cities roam the earth; a future in which our civilization is just a fragment of memory and technological advancement has proved flawed and fleeting. The story introduces a host of richly drawn characters as it rushes toward an apocalyptic conclusion.

This is adventure on a grand scale, but Tom and Hester never get lost in it all. Reeve is also determined to keep the moral waters murky, challenging preconceptions at every turn.

Thomas Bloor, Author

Next?

The sequel, *Predator's Gold*, is every bit as good, as is the third, *Infernal Devices*, set 16 years later, centering on Tom and Hester's daughter, Wren.

For a different kind of adventure story penned by Reeve, try *Larklight* (UTBG 198), a Victorian space odyssey with spiders, pirates, and a floating house.

Different views of how the future might be are found in *Children of the Dust* by Louise Lawrence and *Ender's Game* (UTBG 104) by Orson Scott Card.

Or what about airships, pirates, and huge adventure? Try *Airborn* (UTBG 7) by Kenneth Oppel.

THE MOTH DIARIES Rachel Klein

14+

Next?

Try Cynthia Leitich Smith's *Tantalize* (UTBG 351) for another creepy, gothic, vampiric tale.

And *Catalyst* (UTBG 59) by Laurie Halse Anderson brilliantly depicts the intensity of friendships and of life during adolescence.

Another series about intense emotion, passion, and friendship set in a boarding school is Adèle Geras's **Egerton Hall Novels**, starting with *The Tower Room* (UTBG 362).

There is simply nothing else like this book. I could read it again and again. Set in a girls' boarding school in the late 1960s, it delves deep into the intense world of female adolescence, through the extraordinary eyes of a girl with a "borderline personality disorder, complicated by depression and psychosis."

The book is gothic and dangerous, oozing passion, paranoia, and blood. Not to mention deaths—several. Is creepy Ernessa merely creepy, or is she a vampire? And is Lucy becoming weak through anorexia, or is her blood being sucked by Ernessa? The ironic tone is perfect, the voice utterly original. It is absolutely my favorite book in the world. Can you tell?

Nicola Morgan, Author

THE MOTORCYCLE DIARIES
Ernesto "Che" Guevara

14+

You've seen the T-shirts—and you probably know something of the most romantic revolutionary of all time. This is the backstory, the man before he became the myth, in his own words.

Che Guevara was born in Argentina and fought alongside Fidel Castro in the three-year guerrilla war in Cuba. He became Minister for Industry following the victory of the Cuban revolution, but he found "ordinary" life unfulfilling and went to fight for freedom in the jungles of Bolivia, where he was caught and murdered under orders from the US. Written eight years before the Cuban Revolution, these are Che's diaries as he drives a 500cc Norton motorbike across Latin America, with his friend Alberto. Their adventures, written by Che during and after the journey, make up this wonderful, beautiful, and painful book.

James Riordan, Author

Next?

Read his fellow-traveler Alberto Granado's book: *Traveling with Che Guevara*; or for the whole life story, read the excellent biography *Che Guevara* by Jon Lee Anderson.

For something more political, try Che's own book, which explains his politics: *Guerrilla Warfare*.

A MOVEABLE FEAST Ernest Hemingway

16+

Next?

Stephen Clarke's *A Year in the Merde* is a hilarious, fictionalized account of his experiences in Paris as a young man.

More Hemingway? Try *To Have and Have Not*, a love story set during the Spanish Civil War.

F. Scott Fitzgerald admired Hemingway. Read the jazz-age classic *The Great Gatsby* (UTBG 143), written while he was in France in the 1920s.

A Moveable Feast is a retrospective account of Hemingway's days in Paris as a young man trying to write fiction, mostly in cafés. Some elements of the account might be considered fiction —such as the degree of poverty supposedly experienced by Hemingway and his first wife, Hadley—but this is incidental. Although much of the dialogue sounds like a translation from a language the author doesn't speak too well, the book is an exuberant, mostly warmhearted evocation of Paris in the 1920s, when he hung out with a host of other young writers and artists trying to make their way in the world. Hemingway killed himself in 1961, shortly before his 62nd birthday. This book was published posthumously.

Michael Lawrence, Author

THE MOVES MAKE THE MAN   Bruce Brooks

12+

Thirteen-year-old Jerome Foxworthy takes everything in stride. When everybody else plays baseball, he shoots hoops solo. When he's the only black kid integrated into an all-white junior high, he excels. And when his momma is laid up in the hospital, he learns to cook for his two brothers. But Jerome doesn't know what to make of Braxton Rivers the Third—"Bix" for short. Here's a white boy who picks up the game of basketball without even knowing how to dribble first, and who just may be the best friend Jerome has ever had.

But why does Bix go nuts and hurt himself when Jerome tries to teach him head fakes and ball tricks? And what does his madness have to do with Bix's beautiful, crazy mother and his overbearing stepfather? Jerome wants to know the answers—and help his friend—but how can he convince Bix that the moves make the man when it's the last thing Bix wants to hear?

The Moves Make the Man is just about the best book ever written about basketball, and that's not even what it's really about.
Alan Gratz, Author

> **Next?**
>
> *Face Relations* is an anthology of stories about teens' views of their skin color, heritage, and more.
>
> If you like basketball stories, try *Rebound* (UTBG 287) by Bob Krech or *Taking Sides* by Gary Soto.

MR. MIDSHIPMAN EASY
Captain Frederick Marryat

14+

Don't be put off by the rather dated philosophizing in this book. It was written in the mid-19th century, after all. The author was himself a midshipman in Nelson's navy and rose to be a captain. Many of the escapades he describes are based on real events.

Reading the book, you can understand why the beginning of the 19th century was the heroic age of sailing, when boys as young as 12 fought the great sea battles alongside hardened sailors. This book is especially dear to me because my great-great-great-grandfather was serving on this very ship. He was 15 and a third-class boy. Fred Marryat was 16 and a junior officer. They can't have been friends, but they must have known each other.
Elizabeth Laird, Author

> **Next?**
>
> If you like the idea of sea warfare, try Paul Dowswell's *Powder Monkey* and its sequel, *Prison Ship*.
>
> Another series of famous sea stories: the **Hornblower** series by C. S. Forester. *Mr. Midshipman Hornblower* is first.
>
> If you enjoy stories of ships at sea, you should also try the **Aubrey/Maturin** series, starting with *Master and Commander* (UTBG 221) by Patrick O'Brian.

MURKMERE Patricia Elliott

Next?

You might also enjoy the imaginative **Gormenghast** trilogy by Mervyn Peake.

Garth Nix's *Sabriel* (UTBG 298) is another fantasy novel grounded in a reimagined historical period, where trenches and barbed wire provide little protection against the walking dead.

Jane Eyre (UTBG 182) by Charlotte Brontë is the classic tale of a troubled master with a dark secret and is well worth a read.

Aggie comes to Murkmere Hall and Leah's story begins. Two teenagers of wildly differing character and background meet in turbulent times, setting in motion a chain of dark and richly mysterious events.

Murkmere is set in an alternative 18th-century England, ruled by a corrupt elite who lord over a downtrodden people. There's an oppressive state religion that sees wild birds as objects of both veneration and terror. This divided society is mirrored in Murkmere Hall, where the reclusive Master, crippled in a mysterious accident, broods in his library while his predatory butler exerts a sinister control over the household.

Murkmere blends gothic fantasy with invented history, to create a world as convincing as it is enthralling.

Thomas Bloor, Author

MY BRILLIANT CAREER Miles Franklin

Written in 1895 when the author was 16, the language of *My Brilliant Career* is old-fashioned but vivid. "Do not fear encountering such trash as descriptions of beautiful sunsets and whisperings of wind," writes heroine Sybylla, promising the reader stronger stuff. She longs to be a writer, but her life in the Australian bush is drudgery. She loathes and loves her resigned mother, drunken father, pretty younger sister, and dirty little brothers. Escape looks unlikely, till rich, handsome Harry Beecham offers marriage. Should she accept?

This book has realism, romance, humor, big feelings, and big ideas. It captures the longings and conflicts of teenage life—and the even greater frustrations of that life a century ago—and you may find it inspiring.

Julia Jarman, Author

Next?

Jane Austen writes about another world where women escaped drudgery through the right marriage—try **Pride and Prejudice** (UTBG 276) or the matchmaking **Emma**.

The Yellow Wallpaper (UTBG 403) by Charlotte Perkins Gilman is of the period, and it tells of a marriage and one woman's breakdown.

Or try *The Awakening* by Kate Chopin, a classic feminist manifesto.

MY DARLING, MY HAMBURGER   Paul Zindel

Next?

Other books by Paul Zindel are a must: *The Pigman* (UTBG 270), *Pardon Me, You're Stepping on My Eyeball*, or *Rats*. Nobody else writes quite like him, so you really should read them all.

Are You There, God? It's Me, Margaret and *Forever* (UTBG 125) by Judy Blume are great if you want to see the world from a girl's perspective.

This isn't *Dawson's Creek*, and it's certainly not *The OC*. It's a no-glamour look at American teen life—losing your virginity and parents/teachers totally missing the point.

This book packs a real emotional punch and—I think I can say this—doesn't have a happy ending. Maggie, Liz, Sean, and Dennis are all in their final year at high school, negotiating the world of dating, first love, and sex. Just when *is* the right time to stop making out and suggest going for a hamburger?

The story is told in a mixture of letters, short stories, notes passed in the cafeteria, and the usual "Liz got out of the car"-type narrative. It's like having hidden cameras in each of the characters' homes, so you really get to know them.

Abigail Anderson, Theater Director

MY FAMILY AND OTHER ANIMALS
Gerald Durrell

First published in 1956, this is the autobiography of an English schoolboy whose family moved to the Greek island of Corfu. Gerald Durrell loved animals, and in this laugh-out-loud tale he recounts the astonished and often-horrified reaction of his mother, two brothers, and sister as he ferries home a selection of strange and wonderful insects, birds, and beasts (including the odd octopus, toad, and glowworm).

Durrell paints a beguiling portrait of the Ionian landscape and a rural way of life that has since vanished. He explores the island with his dog Roger, gets into scrapes, has adventures, and conveys wonderfully to the reader how simple it can be to drink in the exuberance of living. A natural-history classic.

Sara Wheeler, Author

Next?

The series continues with *Birds, Beasts, and Relatives.*

All Creatures Great and Small is the first of James Herriot's autobiographical tales about being a vet in Yorkshire, England.

Gerald Durrell's brother Lawrence also wrote a book about a Mediterranean island—a lyrical evocation of southern Cyprus, *Bitter Lemons*.

MY FRIEND FLICKA Mary O'Hara

Rereading Mary O'Hara's *My Friend Flicka* was a shock. I had discovered the book early and read the trilogy often. The shock was to learn, later, how much I owe *My Friend Flicka* not only as a reader but as a writer. Mary O'Hara turns what could be a dated and childish story about a dreamy boy and his sorrel filly into a deeply satisfying, timeless epic about a ranch family, in which every character, every scene, every horse (and there are a lot of horses) is memorable. At 10, I fell in love with it and at 16 was still in love, largely due to O'Hara's style. Clear and purposeful, full of sentiment but never sentimental, she tells her tale: no tricks or trickery, just a great writer telling a great story filled with characters with four legs and two that you will long to meet.

K. M. Grant, Author

Next?

Continue with Mary O'Hara's trilogy with the next two books: *Thunderhead* and *The Green Grass of Wyoming*.

Love horse stories? Then you shouldn't miss the timeless classic **Black Beauty** by Anna Sewell.

For a classic tale with a charming heroine, try **Anne of Green Gables** by L. M. Montgomery. If you like it, there are many more stories featuring Anne—**Anne of Avonlea** is next.

MY HEARTBEAT Garret Freymann-Weyr

Next?

Nancy Garden's **Annie on My Mind** (UTBG 20) is an honest and real account of two female best friends who fall in love.

Who Am I Without Him? by Sharon Flake examines the important roles boys play in the lives of girls in African American society. Uplifting, funny, sad, and thought provoking all at the same time.

Garret Freymann-Weyr's most recent novel for young adults, **Stay with Me**, chronicles a young girl trying to make sense of her much older sister's suicide.

Ellen is 14 and more than anxious for life and love to begin in what she decides is her incredibly boring and normal life. Her brother, Link, and his best friend, James, are the only really close friends Ellen has. Ellen has hung around Link and James since she was little, falling deeply in love with James, who treats her like a younger sister. Yet as suspicion among peers and parents mounts about the boys' true relationship, the two best friends begin to fall apart. Link turns to his math skills and his new love of music for support, and James, much to her delight, turns to Ellen. As Ellen embarks on her first real relationship, she discovers the meaning of "bisexual" through her new, brilliant boyfriend. Ellen must now decide what's more important: her one and only brother and best friend, or her confused, artistic new lover.

Surely Garret Freymann-Weyr's best novel, *My Heartbeat* will educate and amaze you with every page that you turn.

Allison Van Siclen, age 16

MY SIDE OF THE MOUNTAIN

12+

Jean Craighead George

Next?

If you liked the wildlife aspect of this book, try *A Kestrel for a Knave* by Barry Hines.

Other great books about animals and the wilderness are *The Call of the Wild* (UTBG 56) and *White Fang*, both by Jack London.

Woodsong by Gary Paulsen is about growing up in northern Minnesota and training sled dogs for a race.

Some books manage to capture your dreams, and for me this is one of them. It tells the story of a young boy named Sam Gribley, who runs away from his cramped New York home to live off the land in the woods of the Catskill mountains. With only himself and his tamed animals for company, Sam spends a lot of time thinking about things that he hasn't really thought about before—life, living, other people, his family—and gradually he begins to find out all about himself. This book's got it all—adventure, escapism, insights, and feelings—and it's told in such a wonderfully simple way that you feel as if Sam is talking directly to you.

If you read it, you'll never forget it.

Kevin Brooks, Author

MY SISTER'S KEEPER Jodi Picoult

14+

Since she was born, Anna Fitzgerald has had the responsibility of keeping her older sister, Kate, alive. Now, after enduring 13 years of time-consuming, painful medical procedures to stave off her sister's leukemia, Anna just wants it all to end. Anna has decided to sue her parents for the rights to her own body, and this decision will tear her family apart.

My Sister's Keeper is told from alternating perspectives, which gives readers a more complete understanding of the situation than they can get through any one character in the novel. This adds shades of gray where others see things as so clearly black and white. The ethical and moral questions in this poignant novel are moving and at times mind-boggling. As you read, and when you finally put it down, it's hard not to think—what would I have done?

Mary Kate Castellani, Editor

Next?

More Jodi Picoult? She has written many novels, most about family, relationships, and love. Try *Nineteen Minutes* (UTBG 245) or *Picture Perfect*.

For another story about sisters struggling to deal with serious issues, try *Skinny* by Ibi Kaslik.

And there's always *Little Women* by Louisa May Alcott for a wonderful story of family and sisterly love.

For a more lighthearted look at cancer, try Jordan Sonnenblick's hilarious *Drums, Girls & Dangerous Pie* (UTBG 100).

NAILED Patrick Jones

Next?

For another intense story by Patrick Jones, try *Chasing Tail Lights*, about a girl trying to escape abuse.

Gail Giles's *What Happened to Cass McBride?* (UTBG 385) is another powerful, frightening tale about the difficulties of high school relationships.

The Perks of Being a Wallflower (UTBG 269) by Stephen Chbosky also chronicles a teen trying to manage the ups and downs of high school.

This novel is about Bret Hendricks who, like many teens, is an outcast in school who does everything the hard way. But when he starts dating Kylee, a beautiful girl with the same interests, his life starts filling with upward and downward spirals. With a father who cares more about a car than his own family, Bret only has his mother and his closest friend, Alex, to turn to in times of need. Battling life in high school, from being picked on every day by a bully who knows no boundaries to dealing with school staff members who care more about the student athletes than anyone else, Bret must rise above all in order to decide his own future.

This is a magnificent story of the true struggles of teen life, and it is a must-read and must-have for every teen. Patrick Jones portrayed the characters and events so well that through the entire book I felt I was looking through the eyes of Bret, enduring the same hardships, and learning the same life lessons. The book is an amazing read that I will never forget.

Nicholas Campbell, age 17

NAKED WITHOUT A HAT Jeanne Willis

Naked Without a Hat is a story about love and acceptance. Throughout the book an underlying secret waits to be discovered. The story is highly original and the twist at the end is unpredictable. The book touches on modern subjects that have previously been taboo. It exposes people's judgments. It is interesting to see, once you have learned the secret of the book, if you can reread it without prejudice. I found it to be a highly enjoyable read and was eager to discover the secret. It was interesting to see the world through the eyes of a young man in love and this story made me, a self-confessed cynic, believe that young love could exist.

Anna Posner, age 16

Next?

Any of Chris Crutcher's books would be a good place to go from here—try *Staying Fat for Sarah Byrnes* (UTBG 338) or *The Sledding Hill* (UTBG 327).

If you like reading young love stories, Sarah Dessen's books may be right for you. Start with *That Summer* or *This Lullaby*.

The Shell House (UTBG 318) by Linda Newbery is an atmospheric novel of trying to fit in and the problems of first love.

NARCISSUS AND GOLDMUND

Hermann Hesse

A book for "seekers"! I read this when I was a teenager and loved it. I was going through my "looking for the answers to the universe" phase (and still am, I think . . .) and I found Hermann Hesse's books a joy as he seemed to be asking similar questions to my own. What is the way to happiness? The pleasure of the flesh or its denial?

In *Narcissus and Goldmund*, Hesse creates two very different characters to represent the flesh versus the spirit: Narcissus the aesthete, who lives a life of serenity in a monastery, and Goldmund the artist, restless and discontent, who seeks answers through pleasure, art, and beauty. Different roads but with the same destination in mind. Reading what they both have learned at the end is a revelation.

Cathy Hopkins, Author

> **Next?**
>
> *Siddhartha* (UTBG 321) by Hermann Hesse is about another seeker and his path to find knowledge and happiness.
>
> *The Prophet* by Kahlil Gibran is a collection of beautifully written passages about life, from love and work to death.
>
> *Illusions* by Richard Bach is another cult exploration of why we are.

NEUROMANCER William Gibson

> **Next?**
>
> William Gibson wrote two more books set in the world of Neuromancer: *Count Zero* and *Mona Lisa Overdrive*.
>
> Or, try *Ghost in the Shell* by Masamune Shirow, a manga that depicts a future society dependent on cyborgs.

Long before Neo first plugged into the Matrix, William Gibson told the story of Case. Case was the best hacker there was, physically jacking into computers and using his mind to manipulate data—for the right price. But when he crossed the wrong people, they destroyed his gift, and now he lives in the dark underbelly of a future Tokyo, waiting to die. So when a dangerous and beautiful mercenary named Molly tells him of a chance to regain his skills in return for his services, Case jumps at it. But who is her mysterious employer, Armitage, and what exactly does he want with Case and the cybernetically enhanced "razor girl" Molly?

Gibson serves up all the staples of cyberpunk here—hackers, urban decay, drugs, artificial intelligence, sex, virtual reality, violence, greedy corporations—and does it better than anybody before or since. Rich with ideas and action-packed, readers who like their sci-fi dark and thought provoking will lose themselves in this classic.

Merideth Jenson-Benjamin, Librarian

THE NEVERENDING STORY Michael Ende

Next?

The Last Unicorn by Peter S. Beagle is another book about fantasy itself.

The Princess Bride (UTBG 280) by William Goldman is the only other book I know of with the same "feel."

For another book that blurs the lines between fantasy and reality, try Alan Garner's *Elidor*.

Bastian Balthazar Bux loves stories—they're a way for him to escape from the school he hates and the other boys who bully him. So when he finds *The Neverending Story*, he just has to read it.

But *The Neverending Story* is no ordinary book—it's a gateway to Fantasia, where Atreyu the Hunter is on a quest to save the Childlike Empress. As the story unfolds, Bastian realizes that he is what Atreyu is searching for, and to save the Empress he will have to enter Fantasia. In Fantasia, Bastian can have everything he's ever wished for, but there's a hidden danger waiting to trap him: while entering Fantasia was hard, leaving it will be all but impossible . . .

Benedict Jacka, Author

NEW MOON Stephenie Meyer

New Moon, the second in the Twilight series written by Stephenie Meyer, left me thirsting for more by the end of the book. I became hypnotized by this fairy tale-esque reality like no other book I've ever read.

The very relatable, 17-year-old main character, Bella, seems to be a magnet for danger, harm, and just plain bad luck. In *New Moon*, Bella is long past the point of falling in love with Edward, the breathtaking vampire. They've been inseparable for months. But when Edward leaves, thinking it's for the best, Bella is left speechless, alone, and most of all, hurt. Yet Edward's departure only means another dangerous, fateful twist in Bella's life. Stephenie Meyer once again takes readers on an adventure that leaves everyone wanting more.

Brittny Dunlop, age 17

Next?

Stephenie Meyer's first story about Edward and Bella, *Twilight* (UTBG 369), is not to be missed if you liked *New Moon*.

Peeps (UTBG 267) by Scott Westerfeld is another masterfully penned vampire story.

Julie Hearn's historical fiction *The Minister's Daughter* (UTBG 227) or Libba Bray's *A Great and Terrible Beauty* (UTBG 141) are also complex, romantic tales.

NICK & NORAH'S INFINITE PLAYLIST

Rachel Cohn and David Levithan

Nick & Norah starts off with Nick asking a perfect stranger, Norah, for a kiss. It's just to make his newly ex-girlfriend jealous, but . . .

Well, I fell in love with Nick and got a big old girl-crush on Norah. What's the book about? It's about one long night of Nick and Norah bumping into each other here and there, sometimes on purpose and sometimes not, on the streets of New York and in and out of the punk music clubs there. But that's just the setup. What's it *really* about? It's about being vulnerable. And pretending you aren't. Then changing your mind. And losing your nerve. And missing your chance. Then finding some luck. And passing someone by—again. Then chasing them down. All in one night. To the backbeat of the New York punk-rock club scene.

It's about being dumped and wounded, then finding out that in pining for the wrong person you let the right person get away. Or maybe not. It's about wanting to pull your hair out because you can't decide. It's about two people with their force fields up to protect themselves, finding those force fields clattering into one another.

It's about the evil girlfriend that might not be evil but just wrong for you. And the horrible boyfriend that might be just horrible.

And yes, then there are the transvestite nuns. I loved the nuns. Well, I'm not sure they were real transvestites but I'm sure they were man nuns. And they were hilarious. The book is worth the money just for the nuns.

Be ready for the language. It's real. It sounds like a walk down the hallway in the school where I taught when the kids didn't see a teacher around. It fits.

I loved this book. It is so—aware. It pulled out emotions and made them fresh and new for me. It's not my world, it's Nick and Norah's, but I loved traveling in it with them for a while. I keep feeling like I need to send them a postcard.

Gail Giles, Author

Next?

The second collaboration from these two authors, *Naomi and Ely's No Kiss List*, is just as fun as the first.

E. Lockhart's *Dramarama* (UTBG 99) explores a different kind of relationship, set to Broadway musicals.

High Fidelity (UTBG 152) by Nick Hornby also uses music as the backdrop for a funny, heartfelt love story.

NIGHT Elie Wiesel

In spare language, Wiesel tells the heartrending story of his village, ravaged physically and emotionally by the Nazis. Oblivious to the atrocities occurring around them, the Jews of Sighet think they will live out World War II in peace. Then their rights start evaporating: first curfews, then yellow stars on their clothes, relocations, evacuations to concentration camps, and the final "selection" of those who will perish in the crematoria. Wiesel describes the Nazis' systematic dehumanization of Jews: herding into cattle cars, constant roll calls, lengthy marches, incessant showers, meager nourishment. He is numbed by the sight of Jews attacking other Jews over scraps of bread, weak sons abandoning weaker fathers, people collapsing in the snow, abandoned there to die. He recounts his transformation from Talmudic student to a teenager and adult who has lost his faith in God. The last lines in the book are haunting. Upon seeing himself in the mirror after liberation, he states, "From the depths of the mirror, a corpse gazed back at me. The look in his eyes, as they stared into mine, has never left me." *Night* is a unique, must-read memoir.

Ed Goldberg, Librarian

Next?

Any book by Elie Wiesel is just as compelling as *Night*, including the remaining two books of his Holocaust trilogy: *Dawn* and *Day*. For another true-life account of the war, try *The Diary of a Young Girl* (UTBG 91) by Anne Frank.

The Book Thief (UTBG 44) by Markus Zusak is a compelling story about Liesel Meminger, a foster girl living outside Munich who steals books and shares them with her neighbors, as well as with the Jewish man hidden in her basement during bombing raids.

Yellow Star by Jennifer Roy is the fictionalized story of Syvia Perlmutter and her family, who were among more than 250,000 Jews forced into Poland's Lodz Ghetto and among only 800 people alive when it was liberated.

NINE STORIES J. D. Salinger

J. D. Salinger is best known for his classic (and only) novel, *The Catcher in the Rye*, but he also wrote some other lesser-known stories which are just as good, if not better. As the name implies, this is a collection of nine short stories, many of which deal with the relationships between children and adults—a theme that Salinger approaches like no other writer. He not only sees things from children's points of view, but he takes us into their minds and their hearts and shows us the world through their eyes.

These are weirdly wonderful stories—"A Perfect Day for Bananafish," "Uncle Wiggily in Connecticut," "Just Before the War with the Eskimos." They're funny, sad, tragic, mad . . . and every one is a perfect gem.

Kevin Brooks, Author

Next?

Raise High the Roof Beam, Carpenters and *Seymour: An Introduction*, and *Franny and Zooey* (UTBG 127), also by J. D. Salinger, are worth seeking out, as is of course the classic **The Catcher in the Rye** (UTBG 60) if you haven't read it yet.

If you like short stories, also try **Black Juice** (UTBG 39) by Margo Lanagan.

NINETEEN EIGHTY-FOUR George Orwell

It is the future. Britain is ruled by a totalitarian government. The Party demands total obedience; dissent is a crime punished by imprisonment, torture, or death. There is no freedom: whoever you are, wherever you are, somebody could be watching you.

Winston Smith works for the Ministry of Truth, fabricating the present and rewriting the past. He does his best to conform—to love The Party and all that it stands for—but he dreams of rebellion, revolution, and liberation. Captured by the dreaded Thought Police, he is imprisoned and subjected to terrifying interrogation and indoctrination. Can he maintain his freedom of mind and spirit—particularly after he finds out what is inside Room 101?

First published in 1949, George Orwell's novel is as powerful and relevant today as it was more than half a century ago. Utterly convincing, utterly terrifying, it will change the way you look at the world.

Graham Gardner, Author

Next?

For another view of a totalitarian future where hope is at a premium, try *Fahrenheit 451* (UTBG 110) by Ray Bradbury.

For a world where slavery is legal and to be Jewish is a crime, try *The Man in the High Castle* (UTBG 216) by Philip K. Dick.

Something quite different by Orwell? Try *Keep the Aspidistra Flying*.

NINETEEN MINUTES Jodi Picoult

Jodi Picoult always writes stories about sensitive issues, but this book is one of her most timely. Peter Houghton, a high school student in Sterling, New Hampshire, has had enough of feeling like an outsider, and so he takes a gun to school one day and starts shooting. When the police find him, he has killed several and wounded more. Among the wounded is Josie, his childhood friend. Josie must move on with her life and try to remember what happened that day.

Josie's mother, a judge, is prepared to see this trial in her own court. As the novel continues, the stories of Josie, her mother, Peter, his mother, and Patrick DuCharme (a police detective on the case) become intertwined. The best part about reading Picoult is that you know there will be a twist at the end (there always is)—but what will it be?

Kelly Jo Lasher, Librarian

Next?

My Sister's Keeper (UTBG 238) by Jodi Picoult is another great emotional thriller about two teenage sisters facing tough decisions.

For more stories about school shootings, look at Todd Strasser's *Give a Boy a Gun* (UTBG 135), Walter Dean Myers's *Shooter*, or Nancy Garden's *Endgame*.

THE NO. 1 LADIES' DETECTIVE AGENCY

Alexander McCall Smith

This is a humorous first novel of a series of books set in Botswana, Africa. The story follows the movements of the colorfully named Precious Ramotswe as she founds a detective agency.

The book is so much fun to read and the author describes the scenes so vividly that it is easy to imagine the landscape, the people, and of course the cattle—a subject that everyone refers to regularly during conversation.

So open the cover and pack your sunscreen. Before you know it, you'll be driving along a dusty road named Zebra Drive in a rickety, old white van, passing such landmarks as Tlokweng Road Speedy Motors, The Botswana Secretarial College, and, of course, The No.1 Ladies' Detective Agency.

Alexander Carn, age 12

Next?

More quirky detective stories? *The Eyre Affair* (UTBG 108) by Jasper Fforde is a harder read, but if you know anything about books it's completely original.

Brat Farrar (UTBG 49) by Josephine Tey is a very English detective story.

West with the Night by Beryl Markham tells of her youth in Kenya and life as a pioneer aviator.

Or the rest of the No. 1 Ladies' Detective Agency books—there are lots in the series. *Tears of the Giraffe* comes next.

NO MORE DEAD DOGS Gordon Korman

12+

Wallace Wallace, a reluctant football hero, is sick of reading classic books where the dog dies. He never lies, so his review of *Old Shep, My Pal* isn't exactly flattering. Wallace ends up in drama club as detention, where he manages to completely overtake his teacher's adaptation of *Old Shep, My Pal*. The play is being systematically sabotaged, and even though most people believe Wallace is guilty, they don't care because they like what he's doing to the play. In the process, much to Wallace's dismay, he becomes even more notorious and famous.

Korman is a master of timing and witticisms that sneak up on you. This story is told in multiple voices, with many different perspectives on the same situation, which makes for interesting and amusing reading.

Charli Osborne, Librarian

Next?

For more great reads by Gordon Korman, check out *Son of the Mob* (UTBG 332) or *Born to Rock*.

David Lubar's take on freshman year, in *Sleeping Freshmen Never Lie*, is extremely funny. Scott is overwhelmed not only by beginning a new school as a geek but also with the changes in his family, which is soon to include a baby.

A Long Way from Chicago (UTBG 206) and *A Year Down Yonder* by Richard Peck are both set during the Great Depression, but they are anything but depressing. A brother and sister who are plucked from the urbanity of Chicago go to live with their grandmother downstate, and they have an interesting time coping with the differences.

JOINING THE ELITE— PREP SCHOOL

A Separate Peace by John Knowles

Prep by Curtis Sittenfeld

A Great and Terrible Beauty by Libba Bray

Looking for Alaska by John Green

The Gossip Girls series by Cecily von Ziegesar

The Harry Potter series by J. K. Rowling

NORTHANGER ABBEY Jane Austen

Next?

More Jane Austen?
Try *Sense and
Sensibility* next.

If you're interested in
gothic novels, try the
one Catherine is
hooked on: *The
Mysteries of Udolpho*
by Ann Radcliffe.

For a more modern
Gothic novel, read *The
Woman in Black* by
Susan Hill.

Catherine leaves her dull village to visit the city of Bath, with its parties and fashionable people. She is daunted at first—but she is not a complete innocent, as she has read all about such exciting places in novels. So she knows very well that, while everyday people are kind, honest, and respectable, there are also villains in the world who commit dark deeds of gore and horror. Distinguishing one from the other, however, proves strangely difficult, and this leads Catherine into all sorts of embarrassments and dangers.

Northanger Abbey, like all of Jane Austen's novels, is a comedy about a girl testing her beliefs about the world and finding love on the way. It's full of marvelous characters and jokes, but at the same time it's very subtle. It's a bit like a whodunit (it contains what is almost a murder mystery), for everyone has their own agenda, and no one is quite as they appear. Or at least not to the poor heroine!

Sally Prue, Author

A NORTHERN LIGHT Jennifer Donnelly

This wonderful book brilliantly combines fiction and reality. Set in a small New England resort town in 1906, it tells the story of Mattie and how her life intertwines with that of drowned Grace Brown.

Mattie is torn between her duty to help her father run his farm and look after her motherless siblings, and her desire to be a writer. When handsome Royal Loomis starts to show an interest, there is an extra reason for Mattie to turn her back on her dreams and stay put. She has in her possession the letters Grace wrote to her lover Chester, and these help Mattie resolve the dilemma about what to do with her own life.

Sympathetic, beautifully written, and wonderfully constructed, this is an outstanding read.

Ann Jungman, Author

Next?

Another novel that borrows
elements from the real murder of
Grace Brown is Theodore
Dreiser's *An American Tragedy*.

Anne of Green Gables by L. M.
Montgomery shows the toughness
of life on a farm and the warmth of
small communities.

Libba Bray's *A Great and Terrible
Beauty* (UTBG 141) is set in a
similar time and is similarly
atmospheric, although it has an
element of the supernatural.

NOT THE END OF THE WORLD

Geraldine McCaughrean

Next?

Try Julie Bertagna's *Exodus* (UTBG 107) for a story about escaping from a flood.

Or try a slightly more adult version of the story, *In the Shadow of the Ark* (UTBG 175) by Anne Provoost.

Meg Rosoff's *How I Live Now* (UTBG 165) is another tale told after a disaster.

This is simply a fantastic book: a retelling of the story of Noah that asks the most profound questions about faith, the relationship of man to animals, and what it might actually be like to be plunged into the "dark reeking paradise" that is Noah's Ark.

What is it like to leave behind neighbors, your best friend, the rest of your family, to certain death? What is it like when you have to butcher the last of a species that a future world will never know? As everything degenerates into madness, sickness, and squalor, it is up to the overlooked member of the family, Timna, the one whose name will not be remembered when the Old Testament version is told, to find a new way in a wholly new world.

This is a small book with many dimensions—an epic, thundering read.

Livi Michael, Author

NOTES FROM A SMALL ISLAND   Bill Bryson

This book should come with a health warning: *Do Not Read on Public Transportation or You'll Laugh Out Loud and People Will Think You're Nuts*. Bryson is journeying around Britain on a farewell tour before moving back to the United States; on the way he manages to take a wry, sideways swipe at the British and their eccentricities both endearing and baffling (he lists steam trains and making sandwiches from bread you've sliced yourself among the things he doesn't really get), without ever making you think he holds anything other than great fondness for the Brits. He's a writer who understands irony—just don't get him started on 1960s and '70s UK town planners or you'll regret it!

Catherine Robinson, Author

Next?

Bill Bryson's *Notes from a Big Country* repeats the same funny formula, this time in the US.

Round Ireland with a Fridge (UTBG 294) by Tony Hawks isn't serious travel writing but it is seriously funny!

The classic British travelogue is Paul Theroux's *The Kingdom by the Sea*.

Queenan Country by Joe Queenan: another American laughing at Britain, but—like Bryson—loving it really.

NOTES ON A SCANDAL Zoë Heller

Sheba is having an affair with a male pupil at her school. The only problem with this is that she's a teacher. Sheba confides in trusted colleague Barbara, who is flattered by being party to this secretive tryst.

Barbara starts a journal—tracking the development of Sheba's teacher-pupil relationship along with insights about her own friendship with Sheba. It is through Barbara's eyes that we see Sheba's increasingly complex entanglement with the student.

But as petty rivalry and jealousy ignite Barbara's insecurities, her loyalty and devotion to Sheba wrench into acts of spite and revenge. The tale unfolds darkly, with cruel twists that make you wince.

I literally could not put this book down—it's sharp, menacing, and totally outstanding.

Jonny Zucker, Author

Next?

The Painted Veil by W. Somerset Maugham also chronicles a woman fallen from grace and her struggles to maintain herself in a misogynistic society. (It was also made into a film.)

Friction by E. R. Franks is a tense story based in school, this time about bullying.

Doing It (UTBG 94) by Melvin Burgess is about a group of boys and their sex lives (including an affair with a teacher).

NOTHING BUT THE TRUTH Avi

Next?

Monster (UTBG 228) by Walter Dean Myers has a similar format and a serious approach to the theme of truth.

The Gospel According to Larry by Janet Tashjian has the same political bent, and *Speak* (UTBG 334) by Laurie Halse Anderson features a female protagonist as the outcast at school.

Can we ever know the whole truth? *Nothing but the Truth* presents a many-faceted story in which each character has his or her own version of the truth, complicated by personal agendas, poor communication, and bureaucracy. Philip Malloy is a potential track star and class clown freshman. Peg Narwin is a veteran teacher struggling to get her students to love literature as she does. Their clash over humming "The Star-Spangled Banner" is fraught with misunderstanding, controversy, and half-truths. And as more people become involved, the less of the "truth" there is. An early example of alternative formats, the story is told in conversations, memos, and journal entries. This is an excellent example of how people have their own versions of a story, creating a widely divergent understanding of what the reality is. A Newbery Honor book, *Nothing but the Truth* withstands the test of time, remaining funny, relevant, and poignant.

Mary Ann Harlan, Librarian

CULT BOOKS

by William Sutcliffe

What is a cult book? Is it more than just a book that your granny would hate?

To qualify as a cult book, you have to be popular, but only with the right people. You can't be too popular, and your readers must absolutely not be grandmas or golfers; they should be tattoo artists or rock stars. Jane Austen's *Pride and Prejudice* (UTBG 276) is not a cult book. Dan Brown's *The Da Vinci Code* (UTBG 83) certainly isn't a cult book.

Even though it has sold at least a million copies, *Trainspotting* (UTBG 363) by Irvine Welsh is still a cult book, but only because those million readers are mostly under 30, and because the book is exclusively populated by drug addicts, weirdos, and psychopaths. *The Beach* (UTBG 28) by Alex Garland was once a cult book, but since the Leonardo DiCaprio film, it probably doesn't qualify anymore. It's hard to define a cult book, but you know one when you see one.

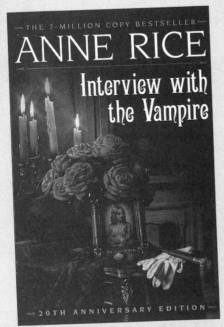

I had always wanted to write one, and first began to think I might have done it when I saw a heap of pirated, xeroxed editions of my book *Are You Experienced?* for sale near an Indian beach. Although the bookseller was, in effect, robbing me, the strange thing was, I felt more flattered than annoyed. It felt, in some way, like an induction into an exclusive gang.

One of the most important things about cult books is that they don't go away. When I was 18, you just had to read Jack Kerouac's *On the Road* (UTBG 255), Joseph Heller's *Catch-22* (UTBG 59), Hermann Hesse's *Steppenwolf,* and Anthony Burgess's *A Clockwork Orange* (UTBG 73), and that's just as true today. When my son hits that age in another 17 years, I expect he'll probably want to turn to them, too.

You could say that it's something to do with sex, drugs, traveling, or adventure, and there's an element of truth in all those things. These books are all about forbidden or dangerous ways of life. They are culty because they give you intimate contact with people you'd be a little afraid to sit next to on the bus. The characters in these books are bigger, louder, crazier, and more reckless than anyone your parents will ever introduce you to.

And that's exactly why these books are so important to read as you enter adulthood. As you begin to chafe at the restrictions of your life in the parental home, these are the books that take you out of your safe little nest and show you all the best, worst, riskiest, brightest, and stupidest things that you could possibly do with your life.

At 18, anything is possible, and you have to read these books to find out what "anything" really means. You'd be dumb to think about emulating the characters in these novels, but if you're intelligent and curious about the world, this is where you turn to find out what the limits are, and what happens if you reach them.

More cult books:

The Lord of the Rings trilogy by J. R. R. Tolkien

Discworld: Monstrous Regiment by Terry Pratchett

The Buddha of Suburbia by Hanif Kureishi

Jonathan Livingston Seagull by Richard Bach

Narcissus and Goldmund by Hermann Hesse

Generation X by Douglas Coupland

Interview with the Vampire by Anne Rice

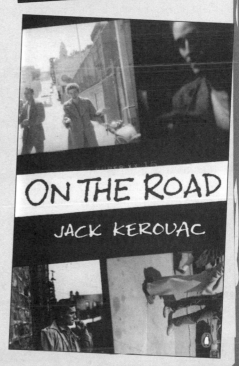

NOUGHTS & CROSSES Malorie Blackman

Book One: Noughts & Crosses

Once in a while you discover a mind-blowing, thought-provoking, gut-wrenchingly emotional book that changes your life. Not often, but it does happen, and *Noughts & Crosses* is one such book. If you don't read another book all year, read this and you will never look at issues such as bullying or racism in the same way again.

Malorie Blackman is such a master at creating believable characters, you feel you've known them all for years. This means, of course, that when they face pain, danger, or tragedy, you share it with them; so grab a box of tissues before you start reading.

The two main characters are Sephy, a Cross (and you'll understand what that means within the first few pages), and Callum, a Nought, who has been Sephy's best friend since childhood. The problem is that in their world Noughts and Crosses don't mix, never mind profess eternal friendship to one another. Their parents, locked in their own worlds of prejudice, tunnel vision, and fear, battle to make their children understand the rules they live by.

The wonderful thing about this book is that it shows us all that, in the end, you can and must live by your own conscience and follow your own star. There is no other way.

Rosie Rushton, Author

Book Two: Knife Edge

Eighteen-year-old Sephy is alone and terrified—as she gazes down at her newborn daughter. Sephy lives in a world where the ruling Crosses treat the Noughts as second-class citizens. But while Sephy is a Cross, the baby's dad was a Nought.

Jude, a Nought terrorist, blames Sephy for what happened to his brother, the father of Sephy's baby. Full of bitterness and hatred, his actions take him to the brink of disaster . . .

Louise Manning, age 14

Next?

When you've read these two, you'll be desperate to read the story's thrilling conclusion in book three: *Checkmate*.

Or for slavery and prejudice in the recent past, read Mildred D. Taylor's *Roll of Thunder, Hear My Cry* (UTBG 292) and the rest of the Logan family saga.

For a story about slavery in Britain, try Philippa Gregory's *A Respectable Trade*.

OF MICE AND MEN

John Steinbeck

14+

Two migrant workers, Lennie and George, travel from farm to farm. Lennie thinks that they look after each other, but really all the looking-after is done by George: Lennie has the mind of a four-year-old. Trusting, affectionate, he understands nothing of what goes on around him, the hopes and disappointments of adulthood, sexuality, racial prejudice. He does not know that he is a man, dangerously strong, unaware of how he seems to women and to other men. George's whole life is dedicated to caring for his childhood friend who is still a child, until the day comes when something happens that George has always dreaded.

Although not a love story, this is one of the greatest stories ever written about love.

Jan Mark, Author

Next?

Cannery Row and *Sweet Thursday* (UTBG 58), also by Steinbeck, are tragicomic stories about the people who live in a poor area of Monterey on the California coast.

Another strange friendship is movingly explored in Ursula K. Le Guin's *The Left Hand of Darkness* (UTBG 202), a science-fiction novel.

THE OLD MAN AND THE SEA

Ernest Hemingway

Next?

If you liked this Hemingway, you could try his novel based around his experiences in the Spanish Civil War, *For Whom the Bell Tolls*, or his account of life as a poor writer in Paris in the 1920s in *A Moveable Feast* (UTBG 233).

Another epic battle between a man and a fish? *Moby-Dick* by Herman Melville (okay, not technically a fish, but you know what we mean).

The Old Man and the Sea is really just a long short story, but part of Hemingway's attraction is his ability to convey an emotional world with spare and simple prose.

Santiago is an old fisherman down on his luck. He hasn't caught a fish for 84 days and the other fishermen think he's all washed up. But far out to sea he finally hooks a huge marlin—the largest he has ever hooked—and so ensues a battle between the old man and the fish that lasts not hours but days.

It may not sound like much to build a story on, but this is a powerful book about the hopes and fears that life is founded on, played out through the tired but noble figure of the old man.

Marcus Sedgwick, Author

OLIVIA JOULES AND THE OVERACTIVE IMAGINATION   Helen Fielding

Olivia Joules, a bold, independent, and beautiful journalist, is desperate for excitement. She's convinced that there's something suspect about the suave and sexy Pierre Ferramo, whom she meets at a face-cream launch. But is he really as sinister as he appears, or is it just Olivia's overactive imagination at play?

Either way, Olivia is determined to find out what lies behind Pierre's immaculate exterior—in more ways than one! And her trail leads her on an adventure to some of the most glamorous spots in the world.

This is an extremely silly but entertaining and fast read for all fans of Bridget Jones, and anyone who enjoys a light, girly thriller.

Susan Reuben, Editor

Next?

If you haven't already read *Bridget Jones's Diary* (UTBG 52), it's an absolute must. Or try Helen Fielding's earlier *Cause Celeb* (UTBG 62).

For another chick-lit-meets-detective story, try *One for the Money* (UTBG 257) by Janet Evanovich.

Or the massively successful *The No. 1 Ladies' Detective Agency* (UTBG 245) by Alexander McCall Smith.

ON THE ROAD Jack Kerouac

Next?

Heart of Darkness (UTBG 149) by Joseph Conrad is a quest into the heart of the African jungle as well as the human heart.

One Flew Over the Cuckoo's Nest (UTBG 256) by Ken Kesey is about an outsider who takes on the authorities in a mental institution.

The Adventures of Huckleberry Finn (UTBG 6) by Mark Twain is the original road trip, following Huck's adventures with escaped slave Jim.

Join Sal Paradise for the journey of a lifetime across the United States in search of love, music, and inspiration. In *On the Road*, Kerouac recasts his own experiences in the company of madman, prophet, and con man Neal Cassady (Dean Moriarty in the novel). They don't know where they're going, only that they have to go, and the faster, the better, in search of the ultimate high, until they cross the border into magical Mexico. Kerouac captures the intense joys and sorrows along the way, in a book that opens the wide spaces of America on the page until you can almost smell them. Once you've read this book, no journey you make will ever be the same.

Ariel Kahn, Academic

THE ONCE AND FUTURE KING T. H. White

From the magic-infused good humor of the opening chapters, this vivid retelling of the Arthurian legends gradually moves into darker territory. The plot sweeps from the Welsh borders to the Scottish islands and to England, covering the length of the land.

But the drama is painfully human in scale. Witness the Orkney brothers, desperately seeking their mother's attention through a horrifying unicorn hunt, or Lancelot running wild in the forest, or Arthur, alone in his pavilion before the final battle, contemplating the collapse of all his hopes.

This is less a story of good versus evil and more a depiction of idealism set against mankind's innate destructiveness. Though grounded in an alternative medieval Britain, this is still very much a parable for our times.

Thomas Bloor, Author

Next?

More King Arthur? Try the historically accurate *Sword at Sunset* by Rosemary Sutcliff, or her younger trilogy: *The Sword and the Circle*, *The Light Beyond the Forest,* and *The Road to Camlann*. Like most of her books, they are powerful and engrossing.

Marion Zimmer Bradley's *Mists of Avalon* tells the Arthur story through the eyes of the women involved.

Rick Yancey's *The Extraordinary Adventures of Alfred Kropp* is about a plot to steal Excalibur.

ONE DAY IN THE LIFE OF IVAN DENISOVICH Alexander Solzhenitsyn

In Stalin's USSR, five million people were locked up in prison camps (called gulags). Most were innocent. You could find yourself imprisoned for a "wrong" opinion or for being a Baptist. At a whim, sentences were increased by ten years. Countless numbers of people died.

This novel is an account of a single day in the life of Ivan Denisovich, imprisoned for escaping from the Germans in World War II. Life in the gulag is harsh: thick ice inside the dormitory windows, filthy soup, inadequate clothes, cruelty. Stupidity too: attempting to build a power station when the earth is as hard as granite and concrete freezes in the bucket before it can be used.

Solzhenitsyn, a Nobel Prize winner, was such a prisoner. This short, readable, and explosive novel brought the gulag system to the attention of the world.

Alan Temperley, Author

Next?

Papillon by Henri Charrière is an account of life and escape from the "hellhole of disease and brutality" that was Devil's Island.

The Wooden Horse by Eric Williams is the story of one of the most famous escapes from a German prisoner-of-war camp in World War II.

The Shawshank Redemption by Stephen King also tells an engrossing tale of a prison escape.

ONE FLEW OVER THE CUCKOO'S NEST
Ken Kesey

Next?

Tom Wolfe's *The Electric Kool-Aid Acid Test* is the account of Ken Kesey and his friends The Merry-Pranksters' road trip across the US.

On the Road (UTBG 255) by Jack Kerouac is another essential read from this time period and the soul of the Beat movement.

Set in a mental ward run by the iron-fisted, tyrannical Nurse Ratched, this book is a classic of 1960s counterculture. When Randle McMurphy, a free-spirited, fun-loving inmate joins the ward, the rest of the patients are amazed by his antagonistic behavior toward the hospital staff. As his antics inspire other patients to act out, Nurse Ratched's hold over the ward is threatened. A battle of wills ensues, capturing the spirit of individuality and rebellion against the conformity of the time.

The dated approach to mental health—electroshock therapy and frontal lobotomies—will surprise readers, but once the many characters and Kesey's language become familiar, the plot quickly moves toward an unforgettable ending.

Mary Kate Castellani, Editor

ONE FOR THE MONEY Janet Evanovich

When Stephanie Plum loses her job in a lingerie store, she decides to become a bounty hunter. I guess that's what you do if you're born in Trenton, New Jersey. The hunt for sadistic prizefighter Benito Ramirez takes her into some dark and gruesome territory. But things aren't all doom and gloom—the love of Stephanie's life so far has been Rex the hamster, but soon she's torn between cool cop Joe Morelli and Ranger, the macho mercenary.

The Stephanie Plum series has run to 10 books already, and every one of Evanovich's fans wait for another with bated breath.

Sarah Gristwood, Author

Next?

If you liked *One for the Money,* try some of the other Stephanie Plum novels—*Two for the Dough, Three to Get Deadly,* and *Four to Score* come next.

For a historical slant, try Elizabeth Peters's *Tomb of the Golden Bird* about Egyptologist Amelia Peabody.

Olivia Joules and the Overactive Imagination (UTBG 254) by Helen Fielding is a take on the female detective heroine.

The classic murder-mystery writer Agatha Christie wrote a series of detective stories starring Miss Marple that may appeal to readers of the Stephanie Plum novels, but Agatha Christie's best will always be *And Then There Were None.*

ONE HUNDRED YEARS OF SOLITUDE
Gabriel García Márquez

Next?

García Márquez has written many wonderful books. Try *Love in the Time of Cholera* (UTBG 212) or the haunting *Of Love and Other Demons.*

If you found the South American setting interesting, try anything by Isabel Allende—start with *The House of the Spirits* (UTBG 164); or try the strange and fairy-tale-like *The Alchemist* (UTBG 9) by Paulo Coelho.

Often prize-winning books aren't the classics we are led to believe they are. This novel is. Winner of the 1982 Nobel Prize for Literature, this is a journey into South America, following the fortunes of generations of the Buendía family as they found and then strive to retain the town of Macondo. With its wonderful writing, often-insane characters, and a charm that many so-called classics lack, you fall into this story and start to question what is real and what isn't, as flying carpets, women who birth iguanas, and clouds of yellow flowers escape from the pages. A magical, fantastical book—a real triumph of the imagination. Novels do not come much better than this.

Bali Rai, Author

ONLY FORWARD   Michael Marshall Smith

16+

Stark is our gun-toting, cat-loving hero—a detective with a special talent that no one else alive possesses. He travels within the strange, future city of a thousand neighborhoods on a seemingly impossible rescue mission, beset at every twist and turn by ever-more bizarre and life-threatening challenges.

This wholly original adventure will linger in the minds of readers not simply because of the whirlwind blur of genres, jokes, and violent thrills, but because of its powerful emotional core. You not only want Stark to win, you actually care for him, too.

More poignant than Terry Pratchett, more bloodthirsty than Douglas Adams: get ready for a bumpy ride. I guarantee you will not have read anything like this before.

Keith Gray, Author

> ### Next?
>
> *Spares* by Michael Marshall Smith is a sci-fi/comedy/thriller all wrapped up in one, with just as many weird thrills as his first.
>
> Read anything by Douglas Adams, who must have been a huge inspiration for M. M. S.
>
> And don't forget the original (and perhaps still the best) wise-cracking detective, Philip Marlowe. *The Big Sleep* (UTBG 34) by Raymond Chandler is the first time we meet him.

OPERATION RED JERICHO   Joshua Mowll

12+

> ### Next?
>
> For a pirate story that is more than it seems, try Tanith Lee's *Piratica*.
>
> For secret societies, of course there is Dan Brown's very popular *The Da Vinci Code* (UTBG 83).
>
> And definitely try Philip Pullman's *The Ruby in the Smoke* and the rest of his **Sally Lockhart** books (UTBG 301).

Mowll takes that cheesy old device, the hidden archive of a secret society, and fills it with zing. The plot is preposterous, the narrative action so incessant that it makes an Indiana Jones adventure look half-asleep, and the book itself is a thing of beauty.

The setting is Shanghai and the South China Seas in 1920. Becca and Douglas McKenzie get involved with the activities of the Honorable Guild of Specialists (founded 1533) in their search for a lost gravitational device of awesome power. They get more than they bargained for: tons of violence and an awful lot of pseudo-science. Beautifully designed, the book features maps, period photos, cut-away diagrams, pencil sketches, and ephemera of all sorts. A must-read for nerdy swashbucklers and swashbuckling nerds.

Mal Peet, Author

THE ORACLE PROPHECIES trilogy

Catherine Fisher

Next?

For more absorbing, believable other-worlds, *A Wizard of Earthsea* (UTBG 394) by Ursula K. Le Guin and its sequels are modern classics.

All of Catherine Fisher's novels are exceptional. Try the atmospheric *Darkhenge* (UTBG 88).

In *The Sterkarm Handshake* (UTBG 340) by Susan Price, the future clashes with the past in an original time-travel novel.

This compelling trilogy, set in an invented yet highly believable Greco-Egyptian world, drew me in immediately.

In the first book, *The Oracle*, Mirany has become the new Bearer of the terrifying scorpion bowl in the service of the Oracle. The old Archon has died and Mirany must search for the new god in secrecy. For a girl who has always questioned the existence of the god, her quest is especially fraught. This is powerful writing, as vivid as a painting, yet with concise, intense sentences conveying an almost unbearable sense of danger.

The second book, *The Archon*, is just as gripping, but there are deeper truths to be found—about faith, choice, and loyalty—in these extraordinary, breathtaking novels that culminate in *Day of the Scarab*.

Patricia Elliott, Author

ORANGES ARE NOT THE ONLY FRUIT

Jeanette Winterson

Jeanette doesn't have an easy time of things. Adopted, growing up in a fiercely religious Pentecostal family, she has to endure endless church meetings, and her mother's conviction that she is actually God's Chosen One. Jeanette is not even sure she believes in God.

As if that weren't enough, she falls in love with a fiery-haired girl from the fishmonger's, and she starts having visions of her very own personal orange demon. She has to decide if she is to live up to the expectations of her community or follow her heart and her visions.

Threaded through this funny, moving, semi-autobiographical story of first love and big ideas are cool retellings of fairy tales that comment on the unique, entrancing story.

Ariel Kahn, Academic

Next?

Blankets (UTBG 40) by Craig Thompson also describes a boy's struggle to break away from his religious community.

Sugar Rush (UTBG 343) by Julie Burchill explores what happens when Kim falls for her best friend, Maria.

In *Candy* (UTBG 57) by Kevin Brooks, Joe falls for a mysterious girl who isn't what she seems.

ORLANDO Virginia Woolf

14+

Virginia Woolf jokingly called *Orlando* "a biography"—and also "a writer's holiday." The title character was based on her own lover, Vita Sackville-West, and the book is set in Vita's family home of Knole. The novel follows him/her through a magically long, ever-youthful life, with a sex change from man to woman along the way.

It may sound bizarre, but Woolf's sheer exuberance and pleasure sweeps you along, from the Elizabethans through the Victorians to Woolf's own day. Racy, lush prose, and a loving, intimate knowledge of 400 years of English history.

Sarah Gristwood, Author

Next?

More Virginia Woolf? Try the slim, satisfying, and thought-provoking *A Room of One's Own* (UTBG 293).

Other historical novels that are also great classics include *Ivanhoe* (UTBG 180) by Sir Walter Scott and *A Tale of Two Cities* (UTBG 345) by Charles Dickens.

For more recent takes on past times, try a Philippa Gregory novel such as *A Respectable Trade*, or historical detective stories like Lindsay Davis's *The Silver Pigs*.

THE OTHER BOLEYN GIRL
Philippa Gregory

16+

Next?

Gregory's *The Virgin's Lover* focuses on the impossible love triangle involving Elizabeth and her married lover, Robert Dudley. High drama, intrigue, passion, and court politics combine in an unforgettable read. Gregory's *The Constant Princess* tells the story of Catherine of Aragon.

In *Mary, Bloody Mary* by Caroline Meyer, Mary Tudor, daughter of Henry VIII, tells the story of her childhood.

This is the riveting story of Anne Boleyn's sister, Mary, who at the age of 13 was first introduced to Henry VIII by her family to further their ambitions at court, and was gradually replaced in Henry's affections by Anne.

Gregory creates cold and calculating characters so completely nasty and manipulating that we cannot help but empathize with Mary and enjoy the comeuppance Anne receives after her rise to greatness. The equally fascinating historical detail of daily life at court creates a stunning backdrop to the drama of the characters' relationships, really bringing the history books to life.

Eileen Armstrong, Librarian

OTHER ECHOES Adèle Geras

Next?

Another book about growing up abroad is *Oleander, Jacaranda* by Penelope Lively.

You can learn about the events that provide the background to Flora's story in J. G. Ballard's *Empire of the Sun* (UTBG 104).

For books about going to boarding school, as the older Flora does, read Adèle Geras's wonderful **Egerton Hall Novels**, beginning with *The Tower Room* (UTBG 362).

Flora is a thoughtful sixth-grader convalescing after fainting dramatically at her boarding school. Unsettled by a dream of her childhood in Borneo, Flora makes a record of that long-ago time, painstakingly sorting and arranging vivid, sometimes half-remembered memories into a coherent story. *Other Echoes* is a jewel of a book about a teenager looking back at a pivotal time in her life. What could have happened then that makes her feel so compelled to write it down now? The answer is partly young Flora's discovery of who lives in the haunted house on the hill, but mostly it concerns ghostly memories, loss, and the realization of how cruel life can be even in the midst of beauty.

Gill Vickery, Author

THE OTHER SIDE OF TRUTH Beverley Naidoo

When Sade and Femi's mother is shot in front of them as punishment for their journalist father's controversial newspaper articles, they see no choice but to trust a female contact to take them to safety in Britain, where their uncle lives. The woman, however, takes their money and abandons the children in London. The rest of the book follows Sade and Femi in their increasingly desperate attempts to find their uncle and stay in Britain. Help comes in the unlikely form of a well-known news broadcaster.

If you have ever heard other people make negative comments about refugees and secretly agreed with them, then this is a book that you really need to read. I guarantee that it will make you think differently.

Laura Hutchings, Teacher

Next?

You can see what happens to Sade and Femi in the sequel, *Web of Lies*.

Another very powerful book by Beverley Naidoo is *Journey to Jo'burg*, which deals with what life was like under apartheid rule in South Africa.

If you like books that make you think about real-life issues, then try *Noughts & Crosses* (UTBG 252) by Malorie Blackman, *Stone Cold* by Robert Swindells, or *Private Peaceful* (UTBG 282) by Michael Morpurgo.

OUR MAN IN HAVANA Graham Greene

Next?

In Graham Greene's *The Comedians*, a hotelier, a confidence trickster, and an innocent American, pass time in Papa Doc's Haiti.

Another exciting novel set in Cuba? Read Elmore Leonard's *Cuba Libre*.

Or why not try a novel by a Cuban writer? The dense, eccentric, playful *Three Trapped Tigers* by G. Cabrera Infante is written in a style unlike Greene's.

Graham Greene specialized in creating and perfecting his own vivid world, inhabited by lonely men, spies, and assassins. His heroes are ordinary men who find themselves out of their depth in James Bond-style adventures.

In *Our Man . . .* Jim Wormold has a humdrum job selling vacuum cleaners in 1950s Cuba. But he needs more money. So he accepts an offer to become an agent of the British Secret Service, which asks him to recruit his own network of agents in Cuba, something Wormold has no idea how to do. So he decides, simply, to make it all up. But his lies soon develop a life of their own. The more Wormold invents, the more dangerous his life becomes.

James Reynolds, Journalist

OUT OF BOUNDS: SEVEN STORIES OF CONFLICT AND HOPE Beverley Naidoo

For 50 years South Africa was ruled by the system of apartheid, the white minority making sure they remained in control by color-coding the rest of the population and making it progressively harder for them to live, work, and get an education. These stories show how the lives of ordinary people were destroyed: families were forced to leave their homes; people were beaten and jailed for having friends of a different color; a father was separated from his children for being a different shade of brown. First they endured, then they began to fight back, and finally Nelson Mandela was set free to lead them to a new future. It's likely to leave you seething in furious disbelief, but it's all true.

Jan Mark, Author

Next?

Other books by Beverley Naidoo about South Africa under apartheid include *Journey to Jo'burg, Chain of Fire,* and *No Turning Back*.

Cry the Beloved Country by Alan Paton gives another view of the same times.

To Kill a Mockingbird (UTBG 360) by Harper Lee is a story of growing up in the racially segregated southern United States.

OUT OF THE DUST Karen Hesse

Deservedly, Hesse won the 1998 Newbery Medal with this tight, spare novel. It is written as a series of free-verse poems that depict a year in the Oklahoma Dust Bowl in the 1930s.

The narrator is 14-year-old Billy-Jo, and through her eyes we watch the land giving itself up to the dust storms; dust invades her family's fields, their home, their food, their minds. It is like another character, mercilessly wearing down all hope as the weeks and months progress.

Then a terrible disaster strikes the family: Billy-Jo's mother dies. She and her father blame themselves and each other and can't find a way of talking about it and healing the grief. But there's another character too—music. Like her mother, Billy-Jo is a brilliant pianist. The accident that killed her mother scarred Billy-Jo's hands, and she despairs that she will ever play again. And if she can't, what's left for her?

This is a story about tremendous courage and strength, and the personality of the narrator sings through every line.
Berlie Doherty, Author

Next?

If you're interested in reading about the Oklahoma Dust Bowl and the will to survive, try John Steinbeck's *The Grapes of Wrath* next.

Try *The Simple Gift* (UTBG 323) by Steven Herrick, about running away from an alcoholic father, or *Locomotion* by Jacqueline Woodson. Both are told in verse form.

THE OUTSIDER Albert Camus

Written in the first person, *The Outsider* opens with the death of the narrator Meursault's mother. Meursault is a young bachelor in Algiers. Shortly after his mother's funeral, he gets involved in some violence with Arabs in the town, which results in him shooting one of them on the beach later that day. He goes to court, but the court seems to be more interested in his apparent lack of grief for his mother than his killing of the Arab.

Camus was an interesting man—a French Algerian, a philosopher, and a pretty good goalkeeper too. *The Outsider* is a product of the existentialist philosophy that Camus explored—the nature of what it is "to be," whether life has meaning or not, and by implication, questions of how we should exist within the rules of society.
Marcus Sedgwick, Author

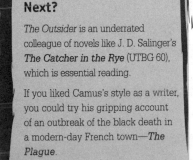

Next?

The Outsider is an underrated colleague of novels like J. D. Salinger's *The Catcher in the Rye* (UTBG 60), which is essential reading.

If you liked Camus's style as a writer, you could try his gripping account of an outbreak of the black death in a modern-day French town—*The Plague*.

For something equally bleak try Franz Kafka's *The Castle* or *Metamorphosis*. Both are surreal yet deeply real.

THE OUTSIDERS S. E. Hinton

14+

Hinton was 17 when she wrote this great novel and it is her most popular book to this day. Set in the Southwest in the late 1960s, it's a story about social divisions and gangs.

According to Ponyboy Curtis there are only two types of people in this world— Greasers and Socs (short for "socials"). The Socs have it all and they flaunt it to Ponyboy and his friends, who come from the wrong side of town. Life is tough if you're a Greaser, but the long nights are often livened up when the Socs and the Greasers have a rumble. The problems start when Ponyboy's friend Johnny kills a Soc during yet another fight. Ponyboy feels the death more than he thought he would and begins to question all the things he's ever taken for granted.
Bali Rai, Author

Next?

S. E. Hilton's follow-up to *The Outsiders* was **That Was Then, This Is Now**, about two friends, Mark and Bryon, whose friendship endures many struggles. You might also want to try **Rumble Fish** (UTBG 297) by Hinton, which has a similar theme to *The Outsiders*.

The Battle of Jericho by Sharon M. Draper is about an exclusive high school club and the ramifications and terrors of peer pressure, hazing, and fitting in.

Robert Cormier's **The Chocolate War** (UTBG 67) also deals with peer pressure and bullies, and is just as heartrending of a tale.

BOOKS TO MAKE YOU LAUGH OUT LOUD

No More Dead Dogs by Gordon Korman

Angus, Thongs and Full-Frontal Snogging by Louise Rennison

Son of the Mob by Gordon Korman

Lost It by Kristen Tracy

All's Fair in Love, War, and High School by Janette Rallison

Be More Chill by Ned Vizzini

264

THE OWL SERVICE Alan Garner

A teenage girl becomes obsessed by the owl patterns on an old dinner service found in an unused attic. At the same time, her stepbrother and the son of their housekeeper become rivals for her affections. What none of them realize is that they are replaying a tragedy that occurred centuries before. As ancient jealousies are translated into fresh hatred, it seems they will destroy each other unless they can overcome terrifying forces they barely comprehend.

The Owl Service is a rare and special book that combines mythology and fantasy with social realism. Its real strength comes from the way it shows how good and evil stem from the passions of individual human beings, and how the battle between them takes place in all of us.

Graham Gardner, Author

Next?

Alan Garner has written some of the most amazing books ever! Try the strange and haunting *Red Shift* or the vivid excitement of *Elidor*.

Margaret Mahy writes complex, dark, and scary books too; try *Alchemy* (UTBG 10).

Someone else who mixes the very real and the altogether unworldly is David Almond; try *Skellig* (UTBG 325) first.

Catherine Fisher often weaves Welsh legends into her stories. *Corbenic* (UTBG 77) is a good mystery.

PADDY CLARKE HA HA HA Roddy Doyle

Next?

Roddy Doyle's **Barrytown** trilogy, about the life of the Rabbitte family in Dublin, starts with *The Commitments* and continues with *The Snapper* and *The Van*.

For an earlier look at life in Ireland, read *Angela's Ashes* (UTBG 17) by Frank McCourt.

Maeve Binchy's *Circle of Friends* is the story of three girls growing up in a small Irish village and leaving to attend university in Dublin.

Paddy Clarke is a 10-year-old boy growing up on a council estate in Dublin in the late 1960s. His world revolves around his gang, his school, and thinking of ways to torture his younger brother Sinbad. In Paddy's world parents argue, teachers whack you, and everything is a sin. It's cutting edge—these kids are one step ahead of the law.

The book is narrated as a diary, and we really feel sympathy for Paddy. He's worried his parents are about to split up. His world is cruel and yet loving—he's confused. The book is funny, but also sad. And beware—it's full of Irish slang that you may have to work at to understand at first!

Anne Flaherty, Journalist

THE PAGAN CHRONICLES series

Catherine Jinks

12+

Next?

For another orphan who is befriended by a knight, try *Across the Nightingale Floor* (UTBG 6) by Lian Hearn, though the Japanese setting makes it very different.

Or for something else set during the Crusades, try K. M. Grant's **de Granville** trilogy, starting with the stunning first book, *Blood Red Horse* (UTBG 41).

These books are set in the 12th century, but don't expect to find any antiquated language—the hero thinks and speaks as if he's around today. Sixteen-year-old Pagan Kidrouk is a streetwise, foul-mouthed monastery brat who sees life as a series of opportunities—usually opportunities that aren't totally legal. Employed as squire to a Templar knight, Lord Roland, he thinks he'll be escorting pilgrims to the Holy Land, but instead of the easy life, he ends up in Jerusalem fighting Saladin.

Pagan is a great character, with a sharp wit and sharper tongue. The books chart his relationship with Lord Roland and his own journey into adulthood. Full of huge battles, brutal violence, and fascinating historical detail, these books are incredible and should be read by everyone!

Leonie Flynn, Editor

PARROT IN THE OVEN: MI VIDA

Victor Martinez

12+

Manny Hernandez is trying to grow up in his impoverished Southern California neighborhood, and he's having a tough time. His unemployed dad drinks away the family's money at the local pool hall, and his loafing older brother isn't any better as a role model. Manny doesn't ask for a lot, but what he wants seems out of reach: a baseball glove, a girlfriend, and acceptance in a community where brown-skinned Mexican Americans are viewed with mistrust by the lighter-skinned, wealthier folks.

Parrot in the Oven is a beautifully written, vivid portrait of a teenage boy, his troubled family, and the daunting obstacles they face. It's a novel of failure and success, bitter hatred and deep loyalties, and just enough tough love to hold everything together. It—and sensitive, courageous Manny—will stay with you for a long time.

Deborah Davis, Author

Next?

Try the autobiographical stories of Francisco Jiménez, beginning with *The Circuit* and continuing with the sequel, *Breaking Through*. Both books recount his trials moving from Mexico to the United States.

For a lighter look at the Latin coming-of-age story, try *Estrella's Quinceañera* by Malin Alegria.

PEACE LIKE A RIVER Leif Enger

Eleven-year-old Reuben Hand begins life by not
breathing for 12 minutes. But by a miracle he
survives "in order to be a witness" to other miracles.
Reuben has a poetic younger sister, a brave older
brother, and a wise father. He suffers from terrible
asthma but survives to become the narrator of this
funny, tragic, and ultimately uplifting story. *Peace
Like a River* has elements of *To Kill a Mockingbird*,
Cold Mountain, and Cormac McCarthy's modern
Westerns, but it is also a masterpiece in its own right.
Every sentence is a joy, every thought is fresh, every
character believable. Without being preachy or
moralizing, it does what stories are meant to do: it
inspires you to live a better life.
Caroline Lawrence, Author

> ## Next?
>
> Read some of Cormac
> McCarthy's stories—
> start with *All the Pretty
> Horses* (UTBG 13).
>
> Charles Frazier's *Cold
> Mountain* is set during
> the American Civil War.
>
> Other classic Western
> novels include *Hombre*
> (UTBG 158) by Elmore
> Leonard and *Shane* by
> Jack Schaefer.

PEEPS Scott Westerfeld

> ## Next?
>
> If you like vampire books,
> try Annette Curtis
> Klause's *Blood and
> Chocolate* (UTBG 40), or
> Stephenie Meyer's
> *Twilight* (UTBG 369).
>
> For more by Scott
> Westerfeld, check out his
> **Uglies** trilogy (UTBG 370).
>
> Scott Westerfeld's wife,
> Justine Larbalestier, is also
> a talented writer—check
> out *Magic or Madness*
> (UTBG 214).

"Parasite Positives" (PEEPS) have been mistaken for
vampires. They have wide eyes, translucent skin, sharp
cheekbones, a thirst for blood, and an aversion to
everything that made them happy before the parasite
(sunlight, family members, Ashlee Simpson . . .).

Cal Thompson carries the parasite, and he inadvertently
infects several of his girlfriends. Once he realizes his
condition, he enters a secret organization filled with
immune PEEPS who track down those they infected for
care. It is a noble life, secretive and chaste. However, after
a few encounters in the apartment in which he was
infected, Cal begins to wonder how noble it truly is.

Written in a compelling way with defined voices and
developed characters, *Peeps* is a fast-paced narrative
that raises questions of medical and human ethics
when it comes to diseases and differences. It also has
a parasite lesson every other chapter! *Peeps* is
compulsively readable and extremely worth your while.
Angela Bryan-Brown, age 15

THE PERFECT STORM: A TRUE STORY OF MEN AGAINST THE SEA Sebastian Junger

12+

The forecasters called it the most ferocious storm of the century. Six commercial swordfishermen found themselves 500 miles from shore on the *Andrea Gail*, a 72-foot fishing trawler, being tossed around in the huge waves like a popsicle stick in a washing machine.

This is a minute-by-minute account of how the men fought to survive a storm with 100-mph winds so violent it tore doors off hinges and ripped planks off the deck. Until finally, they faced the ultimate challenge—a massive rogue wave as tall as a 10-story apartment building.

It is also a tale of the rescue efforts of some of the bravest people on earth—the Coast Guard's helicopter rescue crews and rescue swimmers, who jump into 80-mph winds and 50-foot waves to save the crews of sinking ships.

But can they reach the *Andrea Gail* in time?

Todd Strasser, Author

Next?

Sebastian Junger also compiled a collection of newspaper articles chronicling some of the most dangerous adventures survived today in a book called *Fire*.

Stolen by the Sea by Anna Myers is a narrative about a teenage girl caught up in the worst hurricane in American history.

If you'd rather read about what happens to the survivors of a shipwreck, try Daniel Defoe's *Robinson Crusoe* or Theodore Taylor's *The Cay*.

PERFUME Patrick Süskind

 16+

Next?

The Interloper by Antoine Wilson is another murder-mystery with a character steeped in obsession.

If you enjoy true crime, on the other hand, try Truman Capote's *In Cold Blood* (UTBG 174).

Another book that is both a mystery and a window into another world is Umberto Eco's *The Name of the Rose*, set in a monastery during the Middle Ages.

I once lent my copy of *Perfume* to my teenage daughter. I never got it back. A murder story steeped in sensuality, utterly original, and often shocking, it's set in stinking 18th-century Paris and is about a man named Grenouille who has "the finest nose in Paris and no personal odor." His ambition is to make the most wonderful perfume in the world—distilled from the scent of murdered girls.

This is a richly written book that will open your eyes (and nose) wide, and you will learn and think and wonder. It's the sort of adult book that teenagers often love—it reaches deep inside and changes you.

Nicola Morgan, Author

THE PERKS OF BEING A WALLFLOWER

Stephen Chbosky

It's hard enough being a freshman in high school, but Charlie has just lost his best friend, Michael.

Last year, Michael killed himself. Since then, Charlie has drifted away from all his old friends. He soon hooks up with wild, fun seniors Patrick and Samantha. Sam and Patrick are able to teach Charlie how to navigate teenage life in ways his own siblings—former football star brother and lovelorn older sister—never could.

Charlie develops from a lonely observer into a boy who speaks his mind. He defends Patrick against gay-bashing, stands up to his prejudiced grandfather, helps his pregnant sister make a decision that will affect the rest of her life, and faces his own painful past. In this book, Charlie realizes that there are benefits to being the kind of person who notices things and says something about them. These are the perks of being a wallflower.

Melinda Howard Flores, Author

Next?

A short story collection with multiple authors and a foreword by Stephen Chbosky, *Pieces* introduces the winners of a writing competition held by MTV—and the result is edgy and real.

You Don't Know Me (UTBG 403) by David Klass also tackles issues of growing up and fitting in.

Another book about what happens when you stand out from the crowd is Jerry Spinelli's *Stargirl* (UTBG 337).

PERSEPOLIS: THE STORY OF A CHILDHOOD   Marjane Satrapi

Next?

Try *Maus* (UTBG 223), about the Holocaust, and *In the Shadow of No Towers*, about the 9/11 attacks, from the master graphic artist Art Spiegelman.

Joe Sacco's eyewitness book *Palestine* is a heart-stopper.

Or try Deborah Ellis's *The Breadwinner* (UTBG 50), about an Afghan girl trying to save her family from starving.

Marjane Satrapi draws in unique, powerful black-and-white comic-strip images in *Persepolis*, her own story about growing up in Iran as the outspoken child of wonderfully open-minded parents. When the Shah is overthrown by the Islamic revolution, a beloved Marxist uncle and friends return from the Shah's barbaric jails. But joy is short-lived. A new religious tyranny takes over. War follows with Iraq. To have a rebel spirit is dangerous, so for her own safety, 14-year-old Marjane is sent away to school in Austria.

Persepolis 2 follows the lonely story of this witty, sharply honest teenager into young adulthood as "a Westerner in Iran and an Iranian in the West." It's powerfully personal, opening our eyes to the politics and human beings behind black veils. I laughed, gasped, and cried.

Beverley Naidoo, Author

THE PICTURE OF DORIAN GRAY Oscar Wilde

Next?

Dr. Jekyll and Mr. Hyde (UTBG 95) by Robert Louis Stevenson takes on the similar theme of the purity of one's soul.

Natalie Babbitt's beautiful novel *Tuck Everlasting* will make you think about the disadvantages of immortality.

For more by Oscar Wilde, be sure to check out *The Importance of Being Earnest*, a hilarious and witty play about mistaken identity and finding true love.

You will find some of the attitudes in this book—taken for granted in Wilde's time—unacceptable today. The style is also overblown and more florid than you might be used to. But if you can accept these limitations, you will be fascinated by the story of Dorian Gray, who sacrifices his soul for eternal youth and good looks. The corrupting effects of Dorian's lifestyle, however, have to show up somewhere, and they are mirrored in his portrait; the more violent and decadent Dorian's actions, the more warped and ugly the painting becomes. Eventually it degenerates into such a hideous parody of Dorian that he destroys it, thus bringing about an unpredictable and terrifying climax to the novel.

Gill Vickery, Author

THE PIGMAN Paul Zindel

John and Lorraine are ordinary kids with ordinary names and ordinary lives. The Pigman, or Mr. Pignati, is a sad and lonely old man who is somewhere between ordinary and extraordinary. Their friendship with him becomes the catalyst for extraordinarily awful events. On page four you learn that the Pigman eventually dies, but this knowledge does not lessen the impact of the way in which John and Lorraine each tell their stories of the shockingly realistic and ultimately heartrending events leading up to his death.

This is a story of what happens when simple events spiral out of control. It's also a story of taking responsibility—even if it's too late.

Nicola Morgan, Author

Next?

The sequel to *The Pigman*, *The Pigman's Legacy*, reunites John and Lorraine as they come to terms with the Pigman's death.

Boy Kills Man (UTBG 46) by Matt Whyman and *Friction* by E. R. Frank both portray situations where someone gets in too deep and everything spirals out of control.

Freak the Mighty (UTBG 127) by Rodman Philbrick also stars a scarred but lovable hero, and an unlikely friendship that changes everyone involved.

PIRATES! Celia Rees

Boys have had juicy adventure stories forever, while girls have generally had to make do with much tamer stuff. But not always—for Celia Rees writes adventure stories for girls, every bit as juicy as those for boys.

Pirates! has scenes set on the docks of 18th-century Bristol, England, in the turquoise bays and emerald mountains of pirate-haunted Jamaica, and in the jungles of Madagascar. The heroine finds life as a merchant's daughter narrow and unsatisfying; especially when her stepmother decides to make a young lady of her. After her father's death, she's shipped off to Jamaica, and she's shocked by the ugly truth about how her family made its money—slavery. She learns that the law tolerates great injustice and cruelty; and she has to join an outlawed pirate crew to find a sort of democracy, as well as friendship, loyalty, and love.

It's all so exciting and well-told that you won't even notice the solid knowledge and research that underpins it all. You simply believe that Celia Rees could captain a fast yankee schooner from the Indies to Africa's shores. A wonderful read!

Susan Price, Author

Next?

For another girl pirate, *Piratica* by Tanith Lee is about a girl whose life is not quite what she thinks it is. *Plundering Paradise* by Geraldine McCaughrean is also a tale of pirates, adventure, and Madagascar.

And pirates in icy waters? Try *The Sea of Trolls* (UTBG 305) by Nancy Farmer.

For another, altogether different Celia Rees, try her acclaimed *Witch Child* (UTBG 393).

CALLING ALL ANIMAL LOVERS

Redwall by Brian Jacques

Watership Down by Richard Adams

Animal Farm by George Orwell

The Amazing Maurice and His Educated Rodents by Terry Pratchett

The Call of the Wild by Jack London

THE PLAIN JANES

Cecil Castellucci and Jim Rugg

I loved *The Plain Janes*. It is a fabulous graphic novel with compelling characters and a superb plot. This book is about a group of girls who share one thing in common, and one thing only—the name Jane, just spelled differently. Yet with four distinctly different girls comes a wonderful friendship. The Main Jane (the main character) comes up with the idea to create random acts of art through a secret club called P.L.A.I.N., or People Loving Art In Neighborhoods. From there the trouble, as well as the fun, escalates to new proportions . . . but a wicked good story comes from it all. I would highly recommend this book to someone who enjoys graphic novels, or even just a good short read.
Katherine Krauland, age 18

Next?

Try some of Cecil Castellucci's other novels, like *Boy Proof* (UTBG 47) or *The Queen of Cool*.

Re-Gifters by Mike Carey and Marc Hempel uses the same short, graphic-novel format to tell a story of a contemporary Korean girl in L.A.

For the antithesis of *The Plain Janes*, try the ultimate mean girl books: the **Gossip Girl** series (UTBG 140) by Cecily von Ziegesar or **The A-List** series (UTBG 4) by Zoey Dean.

POISON Chris Wooding

Next?

If you liked the atmosphere and writing of *Poison*, try Chris Wooding's *The Haunting of Alaizabel Cray* (UTBG 148), a darker, older fantasy.

Angie Sage's **Septimus Heap** series, starting with *Magyk*, are full of action and mystery, and also involve a switching of infants—these are switched at birth, however.

The Thief Lord (UTBG 355) by Cornelia Funke is a suspenseful, action-packed adventure about two orphaned brothers.

Sixteen-year-old Poison, a defiant, sullen girl with long black hair and violet eyes, has never been out of the Black Marshes. But when the Scarecrow comes in the middle of the night, stealing away her baby sister and leaving a changeling in her place, Poison sets out to rescue her. She must travel to the Realm of Phaerie to confront the Phaerie Lord, Alethar. Little does she know that her entire grasp on reality will soon be turned upside down. Poison was raised in a place where danger lurks around every corner, but nothing could have prepared her for what she is about to face.

Poison has a wonderful plot full of unexpected twists and turns that keep the pages turning. Chris Wooding has created a fantasy world that paints vivid pictures in your mind, making the book that much more intriguing.
Stacey Zuehlk, age 15

A PORTRAIT OF THE ARTIST AS A YOUNG MAN James Joyce

16+

James Joyce is considered by many to be the greatest writer of the 20th century. This, his first novel, is closely based on his own life, and is an amazingly convincing portrayal of the thoughts and actions of a highly sensitive young man.

The book takes us from the early childhood of Stephen Daedalus, our hero, through to college and a decision to leave Dublin, Ireland, faith, and family. Stephen is tormented by religious and sexual guilt, but also changed forever by the idea and experience of beauty. It's not always an easy read, but the writing is superb and you may well find it a truly inspirational book, as I did.

Malachy Doyle, Author

> **Next?**
>
> Another powerful story of a young man growing up is *Le Grand Meaulnes* (UTBG 201) by Alain-Fournier.
>
> *Counting Stars* (UTBG 78) by David Almond tells stories of his own youth.
>
> If you enjoy the sophisticated writing style of James Joyce, you might also enjoy Virginia Woolf. Start with her classic, *Mrs. Dalloway*.

POSTCARDS FROM NO MAN'S LAND
Aidan Chambers

14+

As compelling as all Chambers's novels, this deserves more than one reading. Jacob is in Amsterdam to visit relatives of the family who saved his grandfather, wounded in the Arnhem fighting. His experiences in the present alternate with the memoirs of Geertrui, who rescued and loved his grandfather. Readers will be equally entranced by both stories, and by Jacob's questioning of his identity as he meets the novel's other characters: Daan, Geertrui's angry, charismatic grandson; the fascinating Ton, mistaken for a girl during an attempted pick-up; Hille, an engaging possible girlfriend; and Geertrui herself, now dying of cancer and awaiting euthanasia.

All their stories weave together into a gripping, thought-provoking story.

Linda Newbery, Author

> **Next?**
>
> More Aidan Chambers? Try *Dance on My Grave*.
>
> At the start of *Postcards . . .*, Jacob has just visited the Anne Frank House; Anne Frank's *The Diary of a Young Girl* (UTBG 91) is essential reading for anyone interested in World War II, Jewish history, or in human courage and resourcefulness.
>
> *Tamar* (UTBG 350) by Mal Peet deals with similar issues—it's also a breathtaking read.

A PRAYER FOR OWEN MEANY

14+

John Irving

I've read all of John Irving's books and rate him among my all-time top authors, and this is definitely my favorite novel by him. It's funny, totally unpredictable (as all good writing is), and ultimately, gut-wrenchingly tragic. It's about a boy named Owen Meany who "SHOUTS ALL THE TIME!" and is physically small, even when he "grows up." Early on in the story Owen accidentally deprives the narrator of his mom during a baseball game, when he clobbers the ball that hits and kills her—this sort of thing always makes for an interesting narrator/character relationship.

After reading this book I was completely convinced I had hung out with Owen Meany during my own childhood and teenage years but couldn't quite remember where he lived or what school he'd gone to. All I did know was that we'd had some great times together and that he'd been my best pal ever. However, I suspect that most people feel this once they've read this great book.

Michael Cox, Author

Next?

More John Irving? *The World According to Garp* (UTBG 399) is another tragic, hilarious book to make you think.

Garrison Keillor is another author who writes about weird characters in rural America. Start with *Lake Wobegon Days*.

For a powerful true story about American youth, try Tobias Wolff's *This Boy's Life* (UTBG 357).

The Ultimate Teen Readers' Poll

BEST BOOK ABOUT OTHER WORLDS

1. **The Harry Potter series**

2. **The Lord of the Rings trilogy**

3. **His Dark Materials trilogy**

4. **The Chronicles of Narnia**

5. *Skellig*

6. **The Artemis Fowl books**

7. *Alice in Wonderland*

8. *The Amulet of Samarkand*

9. *The Giver*

10. *Eragon*

PREP Curtis Sittenfeld

Lee Fiora, 14, leaves small-town Indiana to go to (and board at) an Eastern prep school on scholarship. The other students have names like Gates and Aspeth and Cross, and come from families with piles of money. Unsurprisingly, Lee has trouble fitting in. As we follow Lee through all four years of prep school, she makes and loses friends, earns and squanders respect, and distances herself more and more from her family. In one extraordinary act of bad judgment, nearly everything she's built for herself at school in terms of place and reputation and community is wiped out.

Lee is a character who is not entirely likable. She's got feelings of inferiority and superiority that are always battling and leading her to behave badly. Maybe it's because Lee is so raw and honest that even when she's being stupid or mean or needy, I couldn't put this book down. Reading it is like watching an exquisite, beautifully choreographed train wreck.
Sara Zarr, Author

Next?

I Am Charlotte Simmons by Tom Wolfe also takes a negative view of school life and its many stressors.

Curtis Sittenfeld's second novel, *The Man of My Dreams*, is also about a young woman's coming-of-age.

Richard Russo's *Straight Man* and Andrew Trees's *Academy X* both look at academic life from the viewpoint of a teacher.

TIME TRAVEL

A Wrinkle in Time
by Madeleine L'Engle

The Time Machine by H. G. Wells

A Crack in the Line
by Michael Lawrence

Time and Again by Jack Finney

The Sterkarm Handshake
by Susan Price

"Funny, excruciatingly honest, improbably sexy, and studded with hard-won, eccentric wisdom about high school, heartbreak, and social privilege. One of the most impressive debut novels in recent memory."—**TOM PERROTTA**, author of *Little Children* and *Election*

prep

a novel

curtis sittenfeld

PREY Michael Crichton

16+

Next?

If you enjoy Michael Crichton, the novel of *Jurassic Park* (UTBG 187) is even scarier, gorier, and more suspenseful than the successful blockbuster movie.

The Big Picture by Douglas Kennedy is another movie for the mind, and a hugely addictive page-turner.

Try *A Simple Plan* by Scott Smith, in which two brothers find a million bucks, but at what price? So much better than the film adaptation.

People often dismiss books that "read like a movie." I have never understood why. I was raised on films, and the hours I spent in front of the silver screen inform my novels today. Michael Crichton knows how to write thrillers that truly play out in your mind's eye. That his novels tend to become major films speaks volumes. *Jurassic Park* may be his most celebrated work, but I think *Prey* is better. There are no dinosaurs in this cautionary tale of technology run wild. The bad guys here are nanobots—microscopic flying machines with an instinct to swarm—that turn on their scientist creators. Read the book now, before the film comes to a cinema near you!

Matt Whyman, Author

PRIDE AND PREJUDICE Jane Austen

14+

I love books that you can read over and over and still find something new to enjoy in them. *Pride and Prejudice* is that kind of a book. The very first time I read it, it was as a romance. I wanted the spirited Elizabeth to marry Darcy. I found his aloofness really sexy. And she turned him down! I could never understand how she could prefer the smarmy Wickham! The next time I read it, I laughed out loud at Mr. Collins, cringed at Mrs. Bennet, and enjoyed the dry wit of her husband.

It is a totally compelling story. There are no surprises. I know exactly what is going to happen, but I never tire of reading this book.

Catherine MacPhail, Author

Next?

More Jane Austen, of course. To compare, try *Persuasion*, a more somber tale overall but with another excellent hero, Captain Wentworth.

For a quirky look at an obsessed Jane Austen fan, try Shannon Hale's *Austenland*, where a girl in search of her own Mr. Darcy attends a camp for Austen fans.

A woman who sees marriage entirely as a means to her own ends (as in getting very rich) is Becky Sharp in *Vanity Fair* (UTBG 376) by William M. Thackeray.

For more Regency romance you can't beat Georgette Heyer; try *Arabella* (UTBG 23).

THE PRIME OF MISS JEAN BRODIE

Muriel Spark

This is an immensely readable and funny book about a group of girls in a select Edinburgh school and their unconventional teacher Miss Brodie. Set in the 1930s just before the outbreak of World War II, it charts the girls' development from the ages of 11 to 18, at Marcia Blaine School, where students wear lilac uniforms and hatlessness is an offense. Miss Brodie—who cultivates a small group of students as her elite "set"—is charismatic and inspirational but ultimately dangerous— not least because of her admiration of fascism and her dubious sexual motives. There is an excellent play (which I was in, at age 17!) by Jay Prissori based on the novel and also a great film starring Maggie Smith.

Sue Mayfield, Author

Next?

Picnic at Hanging Rock by Joan Lindsay is about a girls' school where things go very wrong during a walk in the country.

More by the great Muriel Spark? Try *The Girls of Slender Means* next.

Iris Murdoch was another writer who wrote exquisitely about relationships; try *The Bell* (UTBG 32) first.

For another book about girls in the 1930s, try *The Pursuit of Love* by Nancy Mitford.

PRINCESS ACADEMY Shannon Hale

Next?

Try more Shannon Hale, starting with the first Book of Bayern, *The Goose Girl* (UTBG 140).

If that isn't enough, check out any books by Gail Carson Levine, Tamora Pierce, Patricia C. Wrede, or Robin McKinley.

Other great adventures with strong female characters include *Crown Duel* and *Court Duel* by Sherwood Smith and *Dragon Slippers* by Jessica Day George.

Or try some retold fairy tales like *East* (UTBG 102) by Edith Pattou or *Enchantment* by Orson Scott Card.

Miri feels useless since she is not allowed to work in the quarry like everyone else on the mountain. Things change when a prophecy proclaims that the prince's wife will be found in her village. To prepare the eligible young ladies to meet and possibly to marry the prince, they are sent to a "princess academy" under the strict eyes of their tutor, Olana. If learning poise, the rules of diplomacy, and theories of commerce were not enough, the girls must face hard winters, severe punishments, and even bandits.

Miri's story is no traditional fairy tale but a suspenseful and humorous narrative, with the most perfect twist at the end that allows for a satisfying happily ever after. With just the right amounts of adventure and thought-provoking moments topped off with some true love, how can you pass up this book?

Rachel Wadham, Librarian

COMING OF AGE
by Matt Whyman

Becoming an adult doesn't require an entrance exam. There's no need to take a training course, or do anything that involves pass or fail. It's just something that happens to everyone at some stage, whether they like it or not.

So how do you graduate to the grown-up world? Is it something to do with your developing body, the way you see your place in the world, or how people relate to you? The truth is, everyone has a different experience. For some it can be a slow and subtle transformation, while others might encounter a single event that changes their life forever.

Ultimately, there is no right or wrong way to go through it. What matters is that you're able to make sense of things, so you can get on with making the most of your life. Which is where books can work wonders . . .

Whether you're into action, adventure, romance, gritty realism, or faraway fantasies, a book works best when it stirs up your heart and mind. A really good one won't end with a period either. If a story strikes a chord, it can leave a question mark hanging over your head. You're left to think about what you've just read and how it relates to your growing sense of identity. It doesn't have to be exclusively about characters on the cusp of adulthood, like the hormone-crazed boys in *Doing It* (UTBG 94) by Melvin Burgess, or the girls in Julie Burchill's *Sugar Rush* (UTBG 343). You might connect with big ideas, like those explored across Philip Pullman's His Dark Materials trilogy (UTBG 153) or simply admire the attitude that shines from any tale that grips you. It's all about stirring up emotions and making you feel alive.

James Herbert wrote my coming-of-age novels of choice. I was addicted to being scared witless as an endless chain of inescapable horror confronted the hero. It might've stopped me from sleeping at night, but the fact that these guys always managed to survive showed me the value of determination. The lovemaking scenes were an added bonus, and frankly I learned more about how to do it from *The Rats* and *The Fog* than I did when we covered human reproduction in biology. It may have led me to believe that "unsafe sex" meant getting under the covers together without first checking the room for zombies and bloodthirsty rodents, but then, I learned about life wherever I could get the information.

Nowadays, there are nonfiction books that cover all the subjects I so desperately wanted to know about. They can be a great source of information and advice, especially when it comes to issues we find hard to talk about with friends and family. You might be concerned by personal stuff that's just too embarrassing for words, and so it can come as a revelation when you find what you're looking for on the page. Knowledge, after all, is power.

With clear, balanced information at hand, you can reach decisions with confidence about how to make the most of your life. It beats just hoping for the best and then lying awake worrying at night. Besides, you need that time to enjoy the books that make your world turn.

Ten books about coming of age:

This Boy's Life by Tobias Wolff

Parrot in the Oven: Mi Vida by Victor Martinez

How I Live Now by Meg Rosoff

Drums, Grils & Dangerous Pie by Jordan Sonnenblick

Looking for Alaska by John Green

Empire of the Sun by J. G. Ballard

Love and Other Four-Letter Words by Carolyn Mackler

Le Grand Meaulnes by Alain-Fournier

The Catcher in the Rye by J. D. Salinger

The Secret Life of Bees by Sue Monk Kidd

THE PRINCESS BRIDE

William Goldman

You know a book is really good when you remember certain details about reading it: what the weather was like, what color socks you were wearing. When I plopped myself down on my green vinyl beanbag and opened *The Princess Bride*, it was raining and my socks were red. And I don't think I moved for the next six hours because Westley, the handsome farm boy, was risking death (and much worse) for Buttercup, his one true love.

This book is an amazingly fun ride—a cut-to-the-chase story of love, adventure, really good guys, and really bad ones. It's also smart, funny, hard to put down, and not just for fantasy lovers.

Sara Nickerson, Author

Next?

A very funny book that satirizes all the stories of wizards, elves, and poor boys who end up saving the world is Paul Stewart and Chris Riddell's *Muddle Earth*.

Good Omens (UTBG 139) by Terry Pratchett and Neil Gaiman is a loopy look at the battle between Good and Evil.

Want another funny fantasy story (that's also great for nonfantasy readers)? Try something by Robert Rankin, such as the anarchic *Waiting for Godalming*, about God's other son (Colin) and a private detective hired to investigate God's death.

Now, I know you guys are thinking, "There's no way I am going into a bookstore and asking for a novel with the words 'princess' and 'bride' in the title." I know this, because that's what I thought myself many years ago. Some of my more enlightened classmates had read the book and were urging me to get it, but for a while I couldn't get past my machismo. Finally the glowing reviews became too much to ignore, so I asked a friend if I could borrow it. And he said, "No, you have to buy this yourself. You have to walk up to the counter and say the words. It's like a badge of courage."

So I did. I walked in there and said the words. Then I went home and did not eat for eight hours. Instead, I devoured Mr. Goldman's masterpiece. This is simply the funniest book you will ever read, packed with hilarious one-liners, riotous characters, and sidesplitting situations. It is also jammed with swordfights, giants, riddles, revenge, magic, and torture chambers. The plot is clever, the style is hypnotic, and the conclusion is satisfying. William Goldman should be paying me for all the nice things I'm saying. But they're true, all true. Take my word for it, break open the piggy bank, go down to the store, and say the words. You will not be disappointed.

Oh, yes—there is a princess in the story, who is also a bride.

Eoin Colfer, Author

THE PRINCESS DIARIES Meg Cabot

Next?

There are 15 so far in this series—look out for them all. And, of course, all the other Meg Cabot books.

Gail Carson Levine writes totally modern fairy stories; try her *Ella Enchanted* (UTBG 103) about a princess gifted at birth with obedience.

The Sisterhood of the Traveling Pants (UTBG 324) by Ann Brashares is about a group of girls like Mia—though none of them are princesses!

Mia's your average American teenager until her dad arrives with a secret that's been hidden since she was born: she's really a princess! But how? Enter "Grandmère," to turn the 5'9" "freak" into a beautiful, graceful princess. Soon Mia is being plucked, styled, and tutored within an inch of her life, yet she still can't understand boys! Mia's life is changing, and not necessarily for the better!

I love this book. Any girl will sympathize with Mia's problems and understand her worries. Meg Cabot's way of telling the story through diary entries really works, and you end up knowing Mia and hoping that she gets her happy ending.

Issie Darcy, age 13

THE PRISONER OF ZENDA Anthony Hope

Rudolf Rassendyll, an idle English gentleman, decides to journey to Ruritania to see a distant cousin—whom he's never met—be crowned king. In Ruritania, Rassendyll dozes against a tree before continuing on to the castle. He wakes to voices discussing his striking likeness to the future king (also named Rudolf). That night the two cousins—Rudolf Rassendyll and Rudolf the soon-to-be king of Ruritania—dine together. Early next morning, Rassendyll is woken and told that the future king is out cold—he drank too much the night before—and that he, Rassendyll, must stand in for him at the coronation. But this is only the beginning of the adventure. When the king is abducted by his jealous brother Michael and his ruthless henchman Rupert of Hentzau, Rassendyll is forced to keep up the pretense that he is the king—in the course of which he falls for Princess Flavia, the king's betrothed.

The young reader who loves tales of intrigue, adventure, heroism, and villainy (and doesn't mind a little love thrown in) need look no further.

Michael Lawrence, Author

Next?

. . . except perhaps afterward, to the sequel, *Rupert of Hentzau*.

Then try *The Count of Monte Cristo* by Alexandre Dumas, which has more impersonated nobles, heroism, and romance.

Or try the historical **Sally Lockhart** books (UTBG 301) by Philip Pullman, starting with *The Ruby in the Smoke*.

PRIVATE PEACEFUL

14+

Michael Morpurgo

Nobody has written more classic children's books than Michael Morpurgo—but for me this is his best book yet.

Set against the background of World War I and the shocking fact that more than 290 soldiers were unjustly executed for cowardice, it tells the story of two brothers, Charlie and Thomas Peaceful, their life in the English countryside before the war, their recruitment, and subsequent fate.

It's a book with an angry heart, but the mood is often gentle, even elegiac. In one chapter, an airplane flies over the two brothers. It's a moment of wonder—A defining moment in an English summer, and yet also a harbinger of the horrors to come.

Private Peaceful is brilliantly structured, with a twist that took me completely by surprise. It should be read by anyone studying the Great War . . . in fact, by anyone wanting to read a great writer at the top of his form.

Anthony Horowitz, Author

"We hear the shell coming and know from the shriek of it that it will be close, and it is."

Life in the battlefields of World War I was ghastly and left men with the most horrific memories. Old and young men fought and spent long hours together in the squalid conditions of the trenches.

For young Private Thomas Peaceful it is no different. Patriotic and naive, he joins up to follow his older brother into war. He soon finds out that war is not what the posters back home said it would be like. Spending many an hour in the trenches, he reflects on his childhood and fond countryside memories.

Michael Morpurgo's writing style is amazing and brings the story to life. It leaves you shocked, stunned, and sad all at once. A mixture of reflection, romance, and a poignant climax make this book a definite must-read.

Louise Manning, age 14

Next?

For another simply told but very moving story of the same war, read Michael Foreman's *War Boy*.

Megiddo's Shadow by Arthur Slade is about a young boy who enlists in the war and survives with the help of an extraordinary horse.

Michael Morpurgo writing about a different war? Try *Waiting for Anya*. Or you might like a book of short stories he edited about war: *War: Stories About Conflict*.

A book that shows a terrible side of a different war is Jerry Spinelli's *Milkweed* (UTBG 225).

THE RACHEL PAPERS Martin Amis

Next?

Everything that Martin Amis writes is exceptional, though nothing is quite like this. Try *London Fields* next.

The Cement Garden (UTBG 63) is nothing like this book— except I suppose, that it's about teenagers and sex and is pretty shocking— but it was Ian McEwan's first novel, too.

Melvin Burgess's *Doing It* (UTBG 94) also stars male narrators who talk very openly about sex.

Charles Highway is turning 20 tomorrow and is making the most of the occasion to put his teenage years into order—to reflect on his romantic conquests and file away his collection of notes.

Charles is implausibly clever, well-read, and a methodical planner of every amorous encounter he has. But when he meets Rachel, well . . . Okay, maybe he will be able to get her to sleep with him— but what if that's not enough anymore? He soon discovers there are certain things you can't plan . . .

This dazzling novel was Martin Amis's first, published when he was just 25. It's funny and filthy and the writing is electric, and it boasts a captivating main character you cannot stop listening to. You may not altogether approve of him, but then, they're often the most interesting, aren't they?

Daniel Hahn, Editor

RACHEL'S HOLIDAY Marian Keyes

Keyes is one of the funniest so-called "chick-lit" authors you'll ever find, but she's so much better than that. Keyes's tongue-in-cheek humor, witty one-liners, and sparkling dialogue is so real you'll almost hear it.

Although the Rachel of the title swears her that she uses recreational drugs only for purely recreational reasons, she nevertheless finds herself at the Cloisters Rehab Clinic "just in case." She consoles herself by saying that she's not at all like any of the other crazy, loser residents (some of whom are truly hilarious), but soon finds her salvation—and soulmate—in Chris, definitely a "man with a past."

Like the wrapped toffee in a box of chocolates, Keyes's fiction always hides something important at the center. It's as addictive as Rachel's drugs and as tantalizing as those chocolates.

Eileen Armstrong, Librarian

Next?

All Keyes's books have equally sharp insights into love, marriage, perfect partners (or not!), and female friendship. *Under the Duvet* is a very different collection of short stories and journalistic scribblings.

For another fabulously unsorted heroine try *Confessions of a Shopaholic* by Sophie Kinsella.

And you'll find lots more recommendations in our Pink Lit feature on pp. 70–71.

THE RAG AND BONE SHOP Robert Cormier

Cormier, whose *The Chocolate War* virtually invented the modern teenage novel, once said that he had to be emotionally involved with the novel he was writing. It shows in everything he produced, his writing probing the dark side of human existence with a scalpel-like intelligence. In *The Rag and Bone Shop*, 12-year-old Jason is interrogated about the murder of Alicia Bartlett. The interview, conducted by a man named Trent, comes to resemble a priest's confessional. *The Rag and Bone Shop* is a compelling psychological thriller. At around 150 pages, it can be read in one sitting and is one of the most convincing young adult novels ever written. What's more, it concludes with one of the most stunning plot twists you will ever read. Don't miss it!

Alan Gibbons, Author

Next?

Every one of Cormier's novels is amazing. *I Am the Cheese* (UTBG 168) is about an interrogation of a quite different sort.

Another book that starts with an interrogation is Benjamin Zephaniah's *Refugee Boy* (UTBG 289).

For another fast-paced thriller, try James Patterson's *Maximum Ride: The Angel Experiment* (UTBG 224).

RAINBOW BOYS Alex Sanchez

Next?

Alex Sanchez has written two more **Rainbow** novels with the same characters— *Rainbow High* and *Rainbow Road*.

Many of David Levithan's books also broach the gay topic—try *Boy Meets Boy* (UTBG 47) or *Wide Awake*.

Kyle Meeks is a math whiz and a swim team champion, but he doesn't feel worthwhile to his sports-loving father. Then there's the problem of his years-long crush on Jason, and the fact that Kyle is still in the closet . . .

Nelson Glassman is gay and proud of it. He loves dyeing his hair across the color spectrum, cracking loud jokes, and staying true to his sexuality. But he just may be in love with his best friend, Kyle, too.

Jason Carrillo is a star of the basketball team with a steady girlfriend and tries not to see himself as anything but straight. Only he has spent months carrying around a newspaper clipping for a gay teen group called Rainbow Youth, and one Saturday, he attends the meeting . . . and Nelson and Kyle see him there.

Sanchez's writing is straightforward and true, and each character's drama is meaningful as he struggles through homophobia, adolescence, and relationships.

Norma Perez-Hernandez, age 17

RASPBERRIES ON THE YANGTZE

Karen Wallace

The brilliant first sentence of this book cannot fail to draw you in. The story seems simple and slow to start, but builds quickly as secrets unfold one by one. Nancy, the narrator, is a nosy young girl growing up in a small town in Quebec, Canada, some decades ago. She spends most of her time playing with her brother and friends. A piece of gossip she overhears leads Nancy to investigate the goings-on at the home of the prim and proper Wilkins family, where things are clearly amiss. The story is told in a very funny but also honest and touching manner. This short gem of a book is bound to charm you.

Noga Applebaum, Academic

Next?

Read more about Nancy and her adventures in an English boarding school in the sequel, *Climbing a Monkey Puzzle Tree*.

To Kill a Mockingbird (UTBG 360) by Harper Lee is also a novel told from the point of view of a girl growing up in a small town during the 1950s—this time in Alabama.

Another coming-of-age novel that takes place in a small town is Sue Monk Kidd's *The Secret Life of Bees* (UTBG 308).

RATS SAW GOD Rob Thomas

Next?

Rob Thomas has written two other fantastic books for teens: *Doing Time* and *Slave Day*.

Don't miss *The Catcher in the Rye* (UTBG 60) by J. D. Salinger, the quintessential outsider boy coming-of-age story.

Parrot in the Oven (UTBG 266) by Victor Martinez is a great boy coming-of-age story with a Mexican American narrator.

Steve York learns the hard lesson that "everything doesn't have to make sense" in his adolescent odyssey from scholar to stoner. From *Rats*'s opening phrase to its heartbreaking ending, the voice of Steve York turns a very good book about first love found, betrayed, and lost into a classic. *Rats* takes some basic YA conventions (such as part of the book being York's 100-page paper) to tell a basic YA story about innocence lost, yet it all seems fresh and new, mostly because Steve is like no other book-based teen. Stoner, scholar, iconoclast, dreamer, and sometimes a pirate, York defines himself best in the context of the girl he loves (Dub) and the father he can't stand (the astronaut), yet still wants to please.

Rats is a typical male coming-of-age story, yet told in a voice so strong, so sure, so heartbreakingly honest, it's a must-read for all teen boys, as well as anyone writing for them.

Patrick Jones, Author

RAVEN'S GATE Anthony Horowitz

Next?

The second book in the new series, *Evil Star*, is just as exciting and mysterious as the first.

Or, if you enjoy the idea of a group of people coming together to fight the powers of darkness, then **The Dark Is Rising** series (UTBG 87) by Susan Cooper can't be recommended too highly.

Darren Shan writes scary novels about fighting the powers of evil; try the first in **The Saga of Darren Shan**, *Cirque du Freak* (UTBG 69).

What I want to know is how Anthony Horowitz does it! Does he ever sleep?

Not only do we have the excellent Alex Rider books, but now there's his new series: The Power of Five.

Raven's Gate is the first book, and it introduces Matt Freeman, a 14-year-old boy with powers that even he doesn't fully understand. There's a little incident involving robbing a warehouse, and Matt finds himself an unwilling part of a new government scheme for young offenders, forced to go and live with a sinister stranger, Mrs. Deverill, in a remote village in Yorkshire, England.

Obviously, nothing is as it seems and soon Matt finds himself up against the powers of darkness, fighting for his life.

Laura Hutchings, Teacher

THE READER Bernhard Schlink

This extraordinarily original novel bears the stamp of lived experience on every page. A young German man studying in his native city shortly after World War II gets deeply involved with an older woman neighbor. She's a simple bus conductor without social graces, and he's embarrassed to introduce her to his friends and family. This, and not their love affair, makes him deeply guilty, and when she disappears he feels sure it's because of him.

Years later he learns the shattering truth about her wartime past, and a secret even deeper than that which has blighted and deformed her whole life. A profoundly moving story about love, shame, and atonement, strongly recommended for serious readers.

Lynne Reid Banks, Author

Next?

Sophie's Choice by William Styron is a heartbreaking story of decisions about love, loss, and the Holocaust.

Or try *Schindler's Ark*, Thomas Keneally's story (based on a real person and real events) about how many Jews were saved from the Nazis by the heroism of ordinary people.

Another book about how secrets change our worlds is Alan Gibbons's *Blood Pressure*, in which a boy discovers his father's dirty secret.

REBECCA Daphne du Maurier

Some people find the narrator of this classic romantic mystery, set in 1930s England, to be wimpy and insipid. And maybe, compared to today's out-there, kick-butt-style heroines she might seem a little passive. But I think anyone who's ever felt socially ill at ease, or that they don't really deserve a particular chunk of happiness, or even but-why-does-he/she-love-*me*?—and let's face it, that's pretty much all of us—will readily identify with her.

This haunting, magical Gothic tale starts as an account of how the narrator met the handsome, brooding, and irresistible Maxim de Winter. And it soon becomes apparent that his past holds a dark mystery. Du Maurier's wonderfully descriptive writing makes this page-turner one of my fave books ever—and if the ending doesn't leave you openmouthed with disbelief, turning the pages to see if some are missing, I'll eat my PC!

Catherine Robinson, Author

Next?

Read du Maurier's classic spine-tingling mystery, *Jamaica Inn* (UTBG 181).

Sally Beauman's *Rebecca's Tale* fills in some of the gaps.

The original tale of inexperienced-young-girl-meets-and-falls-in-love-with-older-man-with-a-secret is *Jane Eyre* (UTBG 182) by Charlotte Brontë.

REBOUND Bob Krech

Next?

For more books about basketball, try Bruce Brooks's *The Moves Make the Man* (UTBG 234) or Walter Dean Myers's *The Outside Shot*.

Black and White by Paul Volponi examines the friendship between a black boy and a white boy, on and off the basketball court.

The Hoopster by Alan Lawrence Sitomer also focuses on racism and a young teen.

Raymond Wisniewski's high school is divided along racial lines, but Ray—a Polish kid who loves basketball—never really thinks about his African American classmates until he tries out for the basketball team. On the first day of tryouts, he's surprised when he finds himself relieved to see a couple of other white guys in the gym. Ray never remotely considered himself to be racist, but over the course of this honest and insightful novel, he'll be forced to take a hard look at his own beliefs, and those of his family and friends.

Bob Krech has written an engrossing story about a complex topic, touching on the many shades of racism and treating his characters with compassion and understanding. The book is also jam-packed with real-time basketball action, fun characters, new friendships, and even a sweet love story.

Kieran Scott, Author

THE RECRUIT Robert Muchamore

Next?

The Recruit is first in the **Cherub** series. Sequels are *Class A*, *Maximum Security*, *The Killing*, etc.

Andy McNab's adventure stories are full of intrigue and action. Start with *Traitor*.

For more action-packed spy novels try the **Spy High** series (UTBG 335) by A. J. Butcher.

To find out about the teen years of the world's most famous spy, James Bond, read *SilverFin* (UTBG 322) by Charlie Higson.

This thriller is a cross between Anthony Horowitz's Alex Rider books and the violent Luc Besson film *Nikita*. A 12-year-old hood on the verge of becoming a delinquent is "recruited" by a special branch of the British Secret Service. He undergoes brutal training and at the end of it is sent on his first mission.

The story is never predictable, there are no clear-cut good guys or bad guys, and it's sometimes violent and crude. But all this just adds to the "real feel." If you can't bear to read a story about elves or princesses or spoiled rich kids who never go to the bathroom, try this. You won't regret it.

Caroline Lawrence, Author

REDWALL Brian Jacques

Okay, so you pick up this book and think—animals? How stupid, I'll put it back. But, I promise that if you do, you'll be missing a really good read. *Redwall* is a book full of exciting adventure and heroic battles. It's well written and full of excitement.

Redwall itself is a castle, founded by Martin the Warrior—a powerful and great fighter who appears in the first books of the series. *Redwall* features a descendant of Martin (though he doesn't realize it at first), Mathias, who, through a lot of puzzling and with the help of friends, takes up the mighty sword of Martin to defeat his enemy Cluny the Scourge. This is an excellent read and I give the whole series a 10!

Andrew Barakat, age 12

Next?

Try Brian Jacques's *Castaways of the Flying Dutchman*, about a wrecked ship, a cursed crew, and a mute boy who travel the world helping people.

The Sight by David Clement-Davies is the story of good and evil in a world of wolves.

There are tons of other Redwall books to explore if you enjoyed the first one. *Mossflower* was published second, but if you really want to start at the beginning of the story, read *Lord Brocktree*.

REFUGEE BOY Benjamin Zephaniah

14+

Next?

Zephaniah is also a poet and musician whose original work engages with many social issues. Try his poetry collections, *Too Black Too Strong* or *School's Out*.

The Frozen Waterfall by Gaye Hicyilmaz is another story about immigrants, this time a Turkish family in Sweden.

For a look at a young boy's life in a different country in Africa, try *A Long Way Gone* by Ishmael Beah. It is a shocking but worthwhile read.

Where can you go when nobody wants you? This is the dilemma that Alem Kelo faces. His father is Ethiopian, his mother Eritrean, and when these neighboring countries plunge into a bloody war, Alem and his family are persecuted wherever they go. When Alem's father suggests a short vacation in England, Alem is happy to leave the strife behind. However, he soon discovers his father's true intention. Fearing for their son's life, Alem's parents have decided to leave him behind in England to seek asylum. Through Alem's personal story, Zephaniah uncovers the trials and tribulations that refugees go through in England. The heartlessness of the law is powerfully contrasted with the kindness of the local community that reaches out to Alem to offer him a new home.

Noga Applebaum, Academic

REGENERATION Pat Barker

16+

Anyone interested in World War I will love this book. It's set in a mental hospital—at Craiglockhart near Edinburgh, Scotland—where the poet Siegfried Sassoon is sent for treatment after criticizing the war. There, Sassoon meets Wilfred Owen (another young poet) and William Rivers, a psychiatrist charged with "curing" the mentally disturbed so that they can be sent back to fight again.

It's a great story, and you'll want to keep reading just for that, but along the way it deals with poetry, bravery, friendship, and the central question of whether it is sane to fight. If you're struggling with books about the war that you read for school, reading this book will help make everything fall into place.

Eleanor Updale, Author

Next?

Regeneration is part of a trilogy. It continues with *The Eye in the Door* and *The Ghost Road*.

Read the poems themselves: *The Collected Poems of Wilfred Owen* and *War Poems of Siegfried Sassoon*.

Testament of Youth by Vera Brittain is based on her own diaries written while working as a nurse at the battlefront in World War I.

The brilliant *Birdsong* (UTBG 35) by Sebastian Faulks brings trench warfare to terrifying life.

RHYMES WITH WITCHES Lauren Myracle

A believable blending of magic, desire for popularity, and school cliques, *Rhymes with Witches* introduces readers to Jane, a nearly invisible girl and Bitch wannabe. To be a Bitch is to be accepted into the most elite and powerful group of girls in school. But you cannot just become one—you have to be invited to join and go through a series of secret tasks. With mysterious cats roaming the schools, rumors of witchcraft, and spells cast upon unsuspecting students, Jane finds herself among the elite only to discover that it is not all that she thought it would be.

With humor, convincing characters, and a touch of suspense, Lauren Myracle creates a mood that keeps the pages turning. Readers will identify with Jane and her desire to be popular and well-liked. Her magical quest for status makes her realistically face some of her not-so-likable traits, and readers will root for her as she tries to find her way back. A fun read with an ultimately deeper message of self-acceptance.

Stephanie Squicciarini, Librarian

Next?

For other blended genres read Libba Bray's **Gemma Doyle** trilogy: *A Great and Terrible Beauty* (UTBG 141), *Rebel Angels*, and *The Sweet Far Thing*.

For additional stories featuring magic and quests for popularity try *Bras & Broomsticks* and its sequel, *Frogs & French Kisses*, by Sarah Mlynowski.

Searching for other schools with magic thriving? Try the **Bard Academy** series *(Wuthering High, Scarlet Letterman)* by Cara Lockwood.

Also try *In the Cards: Love* (the first of a planned trilogy) by Mariah Fredericks for cliques and the use of tarot cards.

FIGHTING TO SURVIVE

Hatchet by Gary Paulsen

Night by Elie Wiesel

My Side of the Mountain by Jean Craighead George

The Perfect Storm by Sebastian Junger

Life as We Knew It by Susan Beth Pfeffer

Exodus by Julie Bertagna

How I Live Now by Meg Rosoff

THE RIDDLE OF THE SANDS Erskine Childers

Next?

A natural follow-up would be *The Thirty-Nine Steps* (UTBG 357) by John Buchan, an adventure novel that in 1935 was made into a classic Hitchcock film.

Brat Farrar (UTBG 49) by Josephine Tey involves a mystery about identity.

For another gripping story of drama on the high seas, try *The Perfect Storm* (UTBG 268) by Sebastian Junger.

I'm not one for sea stories, but I can't resist this one. Carruthers, a young affected Edwardian, is cooped up in London all August by work. Then he's invited by his friend Davies to join him yachting and duck shooting in the Baltic. Carruthers goes, but nothing is as expected. The *Dulcibella* is a "scrubby little craft," not for pleasure; and there are no ducks. Instead, Davies reveals his suspicions that Germany is secretly preparing for an invasion of England (this is some 10 years before the outbreak of World War I in 1914). The springboard would be the Frisian islands that fringe the North Sea coastline. The two friends sail the *Dulcibella* through treacherous tides, shifting sandbanks, and blinding fogs to outwit a prospective enemy. There are maps and charts. A breathless read.

Philippa Pearce, Author

RIVER BOY Tim Bowler

This book—which made me cry—is the story of Jess and her relationship with her unusual and cantankerous grandfather, a painter in the last stage of his life. Jess, her mother and father, and gravely ill Grandpa go on vacation to a remote cottage beside a river in the place where Grandpa lived until he was 15. Here, Grandpa struggles to complete a strange painting while Jess, a long-distance swimmer, has a series of mysterious encounters while swimming in the river.

This is a beautiful, moving, mystical novel that uses the metaphor of rivers and swimming to explore themes of death and fulfillment. Tim Bowler manages to capture deep truths without being sentimental or didactic.

Sue Mayfield, Author

Next?

More Tim Bowler? Try *Apocalypse* (UTBG 22).

Another book about grandfathers is Sharon Creech's *Walk Two Moons* (UTBG 377). Or try David Almond's haunting *Kit's Wilderness* (UTBG 197).

Another book that uses a river journey in a symbolic way is Mark Twain's *The Adventures of Huckleberry Finn* (UTBG 6). The writing is nothing like *River Boy*, though!

ROLL OF THUNDER, HEAR MY CRY
Mildred D. Taylor

Set in the violent and racist Deep South of the 1930s, *Roll of Thunder . . .* became an instant classic. The Logans, a black family, are struggling not just to survive but to make a better life for themselves in a world that is hell-bent on keeping them down.

Told from the point of view of Cassie, the Logans' fiercely defiant daughter, this vivid fictional account records the relentless everyday injustices and vicious brutalities that real people suffered at the time.

Cassie's stubborn refusal to be cowed by the racists, and the inventiveness and cunning with which she outwits them time and again, are testimony to the brave struggles that helped bring about the Civil Rights movement and transformed the South. *Roll of Thunder . . .* is unforgettable, deeply moving, and, above all, uplifting.

Neil Arksey, Author

Next?

More Mildred D. Taylor? Try other books about the Logan family: **Let the Circle Be Unbroken** and **The Land** (UTBG 198).

I Know Why the Caged Bird Sings (UTBG 170) is an inspiring real-life account of Maya Angelou's experience as a young black girl growing up in the same time period.

Ralph Ellison's **Invisible Man** is a challenging but powerful story of a young black man's search for identity.

THE ROMANCE OF TRISTAN AND ISEULT
Retold by Joseph Bédier

Next?

If you want another great epic romance, try a version of Thomas Malory's **Morte d'Arthur**, or Shakespeare's **Romeo and Juliet**.

For a more modern (but still pretty old) doomed love story, you can do no better than **Wuthering Heights** (UTBG 402) by Emily Brontë.

For more fate and passion, read Audrey Niffenegger's **The Time Traveler's Wife**.

"My lords, if you would hear a high tale of love and death . . ." is how this short, great masterpiece begins. It's one of the most famous stories in the world, and what's striking about the way it's retold by Joseph Bédier is the sense of fatality that hangs over the lovers. The language is simple, forceful, and beautiful. (Chapter headings include, for example, The Philtre, Ogrin the Hermit, The Quest for the Lady with the Hair of Gold, Iseult of the White Hands, The Ordeal by Iron.) Only a brick wall could read it without a sickening sense of rising doom, and toward the end, make sure you keep the tissue box handy.

Anne Fine, Author

A ROOM OF ONE'S OWN Virginia Woolf

Next?

Fay Weldon's *Letters to Alice on First Reading Jane Austen* is another skilled and funny take on women and writing.

Or, for first-hand experience of the problems to be faced, try the journals of some women writers—Sylvia Plath's, or Katherine Mansfield's.

Virginia Woolf features in Michael Cunningham's wonderful *The Hours* (UTBG 161).

Okay, so it's one of the building blocks of feminism. But the real point about Virginia Woolf's essay is the delicately lush writing, the angry imagination, that make reading it a pleasure every inch of the way.

Why—she asked, back in the 1920s—had women been able to tell so little of their own story? Was it because of the stumbling blocks in their way? Imagine that William Shakespeare had had a sister, just as talented as him . . . what might her fate have been? Some of the conditions Woolf describes may be different now. (In order to write, she said, a woman needs a room of her own "and five hundred pounds a year.") But some may feel that the fundamentals have not changed much.

Sarah Gristwood, Author

A ROOM WITH A VIEW E. M. Forster

With its bright social comedy and its cast of distinctive characters, *A Room with a View* (first published in 1908) is the most accessible of E. M. Forster's novels—and is also an excellent film starring Helena Bonham Carter as the young, impressionable Lucy Honeychurch.

On the Grand Tour in Italy, Lucy meets passionate George, who claims to love her for her very essence—but back at home in England, she becomes engaged to the pompous, buttoned-up Cecil. Lucy must defy convention if she's to follow her instincts rather than class expectations. Stuffy Aunt Charlotte, liberated novelist Eleanor Lavish, and the kindly Reverend Beebe attempt to guide her—although several of the characters are not what they seem.

Linda Newbery, Author

Next?

For more comedies of manners, try *Pride and Prejudice* (UTBG 276) or *Sense and Sensibility* by Jane Austen.

E. M. Forster's *Collected Short Stories* will introduce you to more of his preoccupations; several, including "The Machine Stops," have a fantasy element.

Another wonderful, colorful book set in Italy is *Miss Garnet's Angel* by Sally Vickers.

THE ROPEMAKER   Peter Dickinson

12+

Next?

For more by Peter Dickinson, try *A Bone from a Dry Sea* or *Shadow of a Hero* next.

Skellig (UTBG 325) by David Almond is another compelling, intricate fantasy that you won't be able to put down.

Try Philip Pullman's **His Dark Materials** trilogy (UTBG 153), starting with *The Golden Compass*.

Recent years have shown a great increase in the demand for children's fantasy, especially since J. K. Rowling's Harry Potter series took the world by storm. It seems as though the entire world is clamoring for high-quality fantasy written by authors who have a way with words. It is up to talents like Peter Dickinson to satisfy this hunger, and thankfully, they don't fail to deliver. *The Ropemaker* more than satisfies a reader's desire for magic and delivers a huge world with a lore and history all its own.

Dickinson's linguistic skills are to be admired, on a par with Sarah Ash and Philip Pullman. His is a voice that can be understood by children and appreciated by adults. Furthermore, readers of both *The Tears of Artamon* and the His Dark Materials series will love *The Ropemaker*. It is filled with interesting characters and has an engaging and memorable story line. It's a book not easily put down; once started, you'll find it as difficult as I did to set aside. The only thing I can ask of Dickinson is that he write faster!

Daniel Pease, age 16

ROUND IRELAND WITH A FRIDGE

Tony Hawks

This was the first of a crop of books in which somebody makes a drunken bet, does something ridiculous, and then writes a book about it. In this case, Tony Hawks is bet that he cannot hitchhike around the circumference of Ireland with a fridge within one calendar month. The premise is clearly very silly. Fortunately, Hawks is an excellent writer and a very funny man, so the fridge just becomes an icebreaker (if that's possible) in conversations with the many entertaining people he meets on his quest. Highlights include his entry into the Ballyduff bachelor festival and his bizarre decision to take the fridge surfing in Sligo.

Anthony Reuben, Journalist

Next?

The sequel, *Playing the Moldovans at Tennis*, is based on an even sillier bet and is just as entertaining.

McCarthy's Bar by Pete McCarthy is an Irish travelogue based on a less silly premise.

Bill Bryson has written several interesting and humorous books about his travels through America. Start with *The Lost Continent*.

RUBY HOLLER Sharon Creech

12+

The Boxton Creek Home for Children is run by the unpleasant Trepids. Twins Florida and Dallas won't toe the Trepids's line and are consequently on the receiving end of multiple punishments. So they spend their days dreaming of escaping.

The Trepids would love to rid themselves of Florida and Dallas, but every family they've been placed with has returned them to Boxton Creek like an unwanted package.

So when they're sent to spend time with the elderly Tiller and Sairy Morey in Ruby Holler, the twins await their inevitable return to the home. But Tiller and Sairy aren't your average couple and Ruby Holler is a truly wondrous place.

As Florida and Dallas finally enjoy the sweet taste of freedom, their hopes and dreams change radically. It's a very moving, well paced, and clever tale.

Jonny Zucker, Author

Next?

More Sharon Creech? Try *Love That Dog*, a brilliant book told in verse, or *The Wanderer* (UTBG 378), a seabound adventure.

Set in 1917, *Hattie Big Sky* (UTBG 148) by Kirby Larson is a story about a young orphan girl who goes to Montana to claim her uncle's land.

The Beet Fields (UTBG 30) by Gary Paulsen has a rural setting—a 16-year-old boy leaves home to forge a new life.

Try E. L. Koningsburg's *The Outcasts of 19 Schuyler Place*, about a girl who is sent to live with her eccentric great-uncles.

RULE OF THE BONE Russell Banks

14+

Bone, formerly Chapman Dorset, or "Chappie," is not only a petty thief, stoner, punk, runaway, and all-around drifter/criminal, but he also has a tremendous heart and capacity to love. He gets a pirate tattoo in honor of Peter Pan, because he really is one of the Lost Boys until he becomes "Bone." From the icy world of upstate New York to the warm sands of Jamaica and the Rastafarian culture, Bone's brutal story is an adventure in self-discovery and self-preservation as he learns to become a man.

Russell Banks hasn't forgotten what it's like to be 14, lost, and at the mercy of adults who don't care. He said in an interview once, "I think writing saved my life. I was so self-destructive, so angry and turbulent, that I don't think I could have become a useful citizen in any other way."

Kerry Madden, Author

Next?

Russell Banks has written many other books for adults—try *Continental Drift* or *Affliction* next.

Anthony Burgess's *A Clockwork Orange* (UTBG 73) and Adam Rapp's *The Buffalo Tree* involve slightly off-kilter narrators.

Third and Indiana by Steve Lopez depicts the world of drugs and living on the street with searing precision.

THE RULES OF SURVIVAL   Nancy Werlin

Some books are just riveting. You know the type. You pick up the book intending to read a chapter or two and instead you get sucked in for one long, nonstop, read-way-past-your-bedtime, marathon session.

Nancy Werlin's books are generally like this, but I found *The Rules of Survival* to be particularly compelling. Maybe it's the way the main character, Matt, is telling the story in a long, heartfelt letter to his little sister Emmy . . . the same little sister Matt tries to protect from their abusive mother, but whose safety is in constant jeopardy. Maybe it's the way their mother's abuse is so savagely unpredictable. Or maybe it's the hope offered by Murdoch, a stranger Matt brings into their lives after he witnesses Murdoch standing up to an abusive father at a convenience store.

All of these elements, along with Nancy Werlin's trademark suspense writing, will keep you glued to your seat as you wait to find out the fate of this family. *The Rules of Survival* never patronizes or simplifies. It just keeps you turning the pages.

K. L. Going, Author

Next?

If you want more suspenseful stories from Nancy Werlin, try *The Killer's Cousin* or *Double Helix*, both compelling mysteries.

Nothing to Lose by Alex Flinn portrays a boy on the run from his past, whose mother is on trial for the murder of her abusive husband.

Not Like You by Deborah Davis also chronicles the difficulties of living with an extremely flawed mother.

JUST AS GOOD AS THE FIRST! GREAT SEQUELS

A Great and Terrible Beauty & Rebel Angels by Libba Bray

Sloppy Firsts & Second Helpings by Megan McCafferty

Twilight & New Moon by Stephenie Meyer

Inkheart & Inkspell by Cornelia Funke

Eragon & Eldest by Christopher Paolini

RUMBLE FISH S. E. Hinton

Next?

More S. E. Hinton? Try *That Was Then, This Is Now*; *The Outsiders* (UTBG 264); or her adult novel, *Hawkes Harbor*.

Autobiography of my Dead Brother by Walter Dean Myers is a haunting look at the effect of gangs in contemporary Harlem.

For a girl gang in the 1950s, try Joyce Carol Oates's *Foxfire*.

A rare example of a classic novel becoming a cult film, *Rumble Fish* is, in my opinion, Hinton's greatest work. It centers on Rusty-James, a disillusioned tough guy who longs to emulate his absent brother Motorcycle Boy and become a gang-fight legend. But when Motorcycle Boy returns, he's changed and Rusty-James doesn't understand him anymore. Then Rusty's world begins to fall apart and things take a tragic turn.

This is a hard-hitting, no-nonsense read that takes you right into the heart of Rusty's world. Read the book then try to see the film, directed by Francis Ford Coppola and starring Mickey Rourke and Matt Dillon. Neither will disappoint you.

Bali Rai, Author

THE RUNAWAY JURY John Grisham

You know what you're going to get when you open a John Grisham book: a clear plot, plenty of suspense, a sympathetic hero, and lots of courtroom drama. If you want poetry, go somewhere else; for irresistible, page-turning, must-find-out-what-happens-next narrative, Grisham's your guy. And as an ex-lawyer himself, he knows his legal stuff, but he never lets the details get in the way of a thrilling story.

The Runaway Jury is vintage Grisham and, I think, my favorite. This time the court case in question is a suit against a massive tobacco corporation. It seems that someone is tampering with the jury selection to try and guarantee a verdict Big Tobacco will like. But one of the jurors, Nicholas Easter, has an agenda of his own too. Complications ensue. Great stuff.

Daniel Hahn, Editor

Next?

I always find I want a break between Grishams—two in a row and the similarities might be just a little too much. So I'd read something else next ... But when you do want to come back to him, go for *The Partner* or *A Time to Kill*.

For another legal thriller, a little denser, try Scott Turow's *Presumed Innocent*.

Or José Latour's gripping Miami-based thriller, *Outcast*.

RUNNING WITH SCISSORS

Augusten Burroughs

It isn't until about the third chapter of *Running with Scissors* that you realize the recklessness with which 12-year-old Augusten Burroughs has been treated by the world—by his deluded mother who abandons him to live with her psychiatrist, by the shrink who feeds him Valium like it's candy, and by the pedophile in the backyard who gives Augusten his only taste of tenderness. Soon, the author's pain is ours as we read on, compulsively, the way rubberneckers stop to watch a car wreck.

But thanks to the book's black humor, cool irony, and deadpan send-ups of the fashions of the time, its profound sadness sneaks up on you. Meanwhile, the perceptive reader will begin to see the gallows humor for what it is—a way to survive something too awful to cry over.

Patricia McCormick, Author

> **Next?**
>
> Find out what happens to Augusten in his follow-up, *Dry*.
>
> David Sedaris has a similarly dry humor and details his often-painful life experiences in *Me Talk Pretty One Day* and *Holidays on Ice*.
>
> Dave Pelzer's *A Child Called "It"* (UTBG 65) is another difficult read about an even more heartbreaking childhood.

SABRIEL Garth Nix

> **Next?**
>
> Of course you'll want to read the sequels: *Lirael* and *Abhorsen*.
>
> Another jaw-dropping fantasy series of great power and imagination: Robin Hobb's **Assassins** trilogy, beginning with *Assassin's Apprentice*.
>
> Garth Nix has also written the **Keys to the Kingdom** series, which starts with *Mister Monday*, about a boy who is supposed to die but instead becomes involved in a battle against evil.

The sun is shining in Ancelstierre. A few yards away, across the border in the Old Kingdom, it's snowing. But that's not surprising, because everything is different there. Machinery doesn't work, the dead won't stay in their graves, and the magic of the Great Charter, intended to keep the kingdom safe forever, is faltering as blood is shed on ancient stones. Grisly creatures from beyond the Seventh Gate of Death have been waiting for this moment for centuries. Now their chance has come, and only one person stands against them: Sabriel, a 16-year-old schoolgirl with a terrible destiny.

This is an utterly compelling book, and one that will make you remember why you first enjoyed reading.

Brian Keaney, Author

SAFFY'S ANGEL

Hilary McKay

Cadmium, Saffron, Indigo, and Rose Casson were named by their eccentric artist parents after paint colors. But Saffy discovers that the color saffron isn't on the paint chart and, shockingly, that Eve Casson is her aunt—not her mother. Suddenly, she no longer belongs. Only a haunting dream of a heat-filled garden and a mysterious angel link her to her past, and thus begins her quest—for the angel and for some deep part of herself.

I love the way McKay balances the sheer ordinariness of family life with its moments of emotional intensity: she perfectly captures why certain things just matter. *Saffy's Angel* is wonderfully funny—this slightly crazed but wholly believable family really stays with you.

Helen Simmons, Bookseller

Next?

The doings of the Casson family are continued in *Indigo's Star*.

You might also enjoy E. Nesbit's books about the Bastable family— *The Treasure Seekers* is the first one. They have a similar, truthful kind of humor.

And don't miss *I Capture the Castle* (UTBG 169) by Dodie Smith, another funny/sad novel about an eccentric family falling in and out of love.

The Ultimate Teen Readers' Poll

BOOK THAT SCARED YOU THE MOST

1. **The Harry Potter series**

2. *Interview with the Vampire*

3. **The Lord of the Rings trilogy**

4. *A Child Called "It"*

5. **The Alex Rider series**

6. *Salem's Lot*

7. *Cirque du Freak*

8. *Skellig*

9. *Jurassic Park*

10. *Lord Loss*

SAINT IGGY K. L. Going

Iggy Corso doesn't have a lot. He lives in the projects; his dad's always stoned; his mom's been gone "visiting" for weeks; Freddie, a drug dealer, is always messing things up; and his only friend, Mo, is becoming an addict. When Iggy gets kicked out of school, he loses what looks like his last chance.

The writing style really reminded me of a cross between *The Catcher in the Rye* and *Go Ask Alice*. Whereas I had a hard time liking Holden, I couldn't help but love Iggy. The almost-poetic writing gives a harshly honest snapshot of Iggy's Christmas. The ending left me stunned. I think I sat for a full five minutes trying to absorb what I had just read.

Kara Leonardi, age 17

> **Next?**
>
> For more by K. L. Going, try *Fat Kid Rules the World* (UTBG 114) or *The Liberation of Gabriel King*.
>
> *The Catcher in the Rye* (UTBG 60) by J. D. Salinger and *Go Ask Alice* (UTBG 136) by Anonymous are both more than worthwhile reads if you like the dark coming-of-age tale.
>
> Ellen Hopkins's *Crank* is a disturbing look at a teen's addiction to a dangerous drug.

SALEM'S LOT Stephen King

> **Next?**
>
> Try *The Hand of the Devil* by Dean Vincent Carter, about a young journalist thrown into a nightmare.
>
> Read *Dracula* (UTBG 98) by Bram Stoker—the classic.
>
> *Weaveworld* (UTBG 383) by Clive Barker is another complex and involving horror story.
>
> How would it feel to be the last human on a planet inhabited by ravenous vampires? Try *I Am Legend* by Richard Matheson to find out.
>
> Edgar Allan Poe's stories have frightened readers for over 100 years. Try *Tales of Mystery and Imagination* (UTBG 348).

This book changed my life. A modern-day riff on *Dracula*, it follows the downfall of a town besieged by vampires. The beauty of this book is in watching King build up a totally convincing cast and town then subject them to the horrors of a vampire attack. In the book, vampirism is like a plague, and King details the fallout of such a disaster. I LOVED this. It opened up a whole new world of nightmares to me, and as all horror fans know, nightmares are cool! Like most of King's books, there's stuff in here that isn't suitable for younger readers—so if your parents catch you reading this, don't tell them *I* recommended it to you!

Darren Shan, Author

The SALLY LOCKHART books Philip Pullman

Next?

Anthony Hope's *The Prisoner of Zenda* (UTBG 281) has strange happenings in a Central European country.

For something funnier, try Lindsey Davis's **Falco** books, set in Ancient Rome—start with *The Silver Pigs*, which is in fact set in Roman Britain.

The original detective of old London is, of course, Sherlock Holmes. Read the **Sherlock Holmes** stories (UTBG 319) by Sir Arthur Conan Doyle.

The first three novels are exciting mystery-adventures set in Victorian London, starring Sally Lockhart and her friends. Sally is 16 when *The Ruby in the Smoke* begins, desperate to widen the limited horizon before her as an orphaned middle-class Victorian girl of modest means, and to find out who killed her father in the South China Sea.

Her final confrontation with her enemy takes three books to arrive, and on the way through *The Shadow in the North* and *The Tiger in the Well* Philip Pullman leads us everywhere shunned by polite Victorian society: opium dens, séances, music halls, East End missions, and socialist gatherings.

In *The Tin Princess*, the focus shifts to Central Europe and the perils of a small kingdom hemmed in by rival powers. Sally makes only brief appearances, but there are two strong new heroines and a sense of the political forces pulling the strings of the story.

Geraldine Brennan, Journalist

SAMMY AND JULIANA IN HOLLYWOOD
Benjamin Alire Sáenz

Sammy and Juliana in Hollywood tells the bleak and beautiful story of Sammy Santos, a Mexican American teenager growing up not in California's city of dreams but in a bleak neighborhood in Las Cruces, New Mexico, in the late 1960s. A loner, Sammy finds all-too-brief happiness with the damaged Juliana, as he struggles to come of age in a time and place fractured by racism, poverty, and the violence of the Vietnam War.

In language that's sometimes stark, sometimes poetic, and always strikingly authentic, Alire Sáenz shows us a young man's journey from innocence to experience, and how for Sammy, as for so many others in the summer of '69, love walked hand-in-hand with loss.

Jennifer Donnelly, Author

Next?

CrashBoomLove by Juan Felipe Herrera is about a boy growing up as a migrant worker.

Fallen Angels (UTBG 111) by Walter Dean Myers is about a Harlem teenager who enlists to fight in Vietnam, and his struggle to survive.

SAMURAI SHORTSTOP Alan Gratz

Baseball is said to be America's pastime sport, but you'd be surprised how much Japan loves it as well. Alan Gratz digs all the way back into history and paints a perfect picture of Toyo, a boy who loves baseball but, like us, must find the balance between doing what he loves (playing baseball) and doing what he feels he must in life (becoming a samurai).

Together with his friends at school, Toyo discovers the correct balance and becomes a samurai shortstop. Even though most of us aren't expected to become a samurai, each of us has tension in our lives, and the way that Toyo decided to resolve his tension can help us decide how to solve ours.

Felix van der Vaart, age 14

Next?

For more contemporary baseball stories, try Mike Lupica's *Heat* (UTBG 151) or *Summer Ball*, or *The Boy Who Saved Baseball* by John H. Ritter.

The Revenge of the Forty-Seven Samurai by Erik Christian Haugaard is also a historical novel about ancient Japan, which follows a serving boy to one of the great samurai.

For another novel by Alan Gratz, try *Something Rotten*, a modern take on the story of Hamlet.

THE SANDMAN series Neil Gaiman

Next?

Death, one of the best characters in The Sandman series, gets two of her own books: *The High Cost of Living* and *The Time of Your Life*.

Alan Moore's **Swamp Thing** series is a modern retelling of *Beauty and the Beast* with added villains.

Philip Pullman's **His Dark Materials** trilogy (UTBG 153) explores similar themes of myth and religion.

Or try Neil Gaiman, writing in collaboration with Terry Pratchett, in *Good Omens* (UTBG 139).

Imagine if death were a Goth punk and she had three strange sisters: Delirium, Despair, and Desire; and three brothers: Destiny, Destruction, and the mysterious Dream. Blending myth, fantasy, and horror with powerful stories of the real world, this 12-volume series changed the face of comics.

Morpheus, the Lord of the Dreaming, is the key to the whole series. At its opening he is the prisoner of a crazy sect who wants the secret of immortality. When he frees himself, he must relearn his powers and reshape his kingdom, discovering new allies—and new enemies. His magical journey will keep you riveted, with narrow escapes, retellings of famous legends that blaze with life, and a shocking ending.

Ariel Kahn, Academic

THE SCARLET PIMPERNEL Baroness Orczy

Next?

For a more realistic and brutal but equally exciting account of the French Revolution, read Leon Garfield's *Revolution*.

A classic novel set in this period is *A Tale of Two Cities* (UTBG 345) by Charles Dickens.

And there's always the sequel—try *The Elusive Pimpernel* for more of the same.

The Master of Ballantrae (UTBG 221) by Robert Louis Stevenson is a classic story of brothers, feuds, and treachery.

Forget any film versions you've seen of this book and read the real thing. You'll find that the hero, Sir Percy Blakeney, is younger than he's shown on screen and built like Arnold Schwarzenegger. Some of the attitudes and beliefs of the time in which it was written are surprising and even distasteful to us today, yet the story of dandified young Englishmen forming a secret league dedicated to spiriting away French aristocrats from the shadow of the guillotine during the Reign of Terror is an exciting one. If you can disregard the unpleasant attitudes, you'll enjoy the novel for its plot and historical background, showing a time when fear and brutality stalked the streets of Paris.

Gill Vickery, Author

SCOOP Evelyn Waugh

John Boot, a fashionable novelist, is desperate to be a war reporter. His distant cousin William Boot is blissfully happy writing about badgers on his impoverished country estate. John's famous—William's not. John can write—William can't. John's streetwise—William's scared of London. And because, in Evelyn Waugh's comic novel, everyone knows they're right and no one listens to anyone else, it's William who ends up in a war no one knows is happening, to invent news stories he doesn't understand, to satisfy a media that is only interested in profit. *Scoop* is a bit dated, but the central cynicism about the way the media manipulates world events is, if anything, more relevant now than it was in 1938, when the novel was published.

Antonia Honeywell, Teacher

Next?

If you like Evelyn Waugh, try *Vile Bodies*, a satire that comments on social classes.

If you liked the political commentary, try reading George Orwell's *Nineteen Eighty-Four* (UTBG 244).

If you liked Mrs. Stitch, the ridiculous society hostess, try Anita Loos's *Gentlemen Prefer Blondes*.

SCRAMBLED EGGS AT MIDNIGHT

Brad Barkley and Heather Hepler

Next?

If you enjoy love stories with alternating viewpoints, don't miss *Flipped* (UTBG 120) by Wendelin Van Draanen.

Or check out *Dairy Queen* (UTBG 84) by Catherine Gilbert Murdock, a quirky story about a girl living on a dairy farm.

In and around a small town in North Carolina, two 15-year-olds follow different lives. Cal (short for Calliope) works the town's Renaissance Faire until her wench mother decides to pack and move them to another place. She takes solace in wishing for a better future and eating eggs and pancakes at night. Eliot has lived in the same mountains with his parents for seven years, but he cannot connect with his father's evangelical weight loss business. Eliot illegally creates fireworks to find beauty and creates rules of his own that are not sanctioned by his father.

Told in alternating points of view, *Scrambled Eggs at Midnight* details the summer in which Cal and Eliot discover each other, fall in love, and try to hold on to their relationship before it dies with the coming of fall. Barkley and Hepler's vivid characters bring you to a place where adolescence isn't just about hormones and rebellion, but about discovering your identity and values and fighting for them every step of the way.

Norma Perez-Hernandez, age 17

THE SCREWTAPE LETTERS C. S. Lewis

Wormwood, a raw recruit in the Infernal Civil Service, is assigned to win a young man's soul by tempting him to stray from the straight and narrow and damn himself. Since the young man is in love, the task shouldn't prove too hard.

The pressures on both are intensified by the setting: wartime London. (I'm guessing the book was some kind of spiritual bomb shelter C.S. Lewis built for himself as World War II raged around him.) Wormwood is answerable to his high-ranking uncle, Screwtape—an affectionate and patient teacher. The book takes the form of correspondence, and it is their relationship that sticks in the mind, even more than the will-he-won't-he? progress of the poor sinner. The end is a real gut-wrencher.

Think you know C. S. Lewis? Narnia this ain't.

Geraldine McCaughrean, Author

Next?

For more C. S. Lewis, try *The Great Divorce* (UTBG 142), in which the inhabitants of Hell visit Heaven and find there's no place like home.

The Alchemist (UTBG 9) by Paulo Coelho is another tale of finding a spiritual path.

Or what about a classic? Try Jonathan Swift's *Gulliver's Travels*.

THE SEA OF TROLLS Nancy Farmer

Jack is an apprentice bard. He has a hard life, but things go from bad to worse when his village is raided by Vikings and he and his spoiled baby sister are taken as slaves by Olaf One-Brow. He is taken far into the North to the court of Ivar the Boneless and his half-troll queen. After accidentally causing the queen's hair to fall out, Jack finds himself sent on a quest to find Mimir's Well, and on his journey he finds trolls, dragons, sea monsters, berserkers, battles, a troll-boar named Golden Bristles, and a shield maiden who wants to die.

Weaving Norse myth into spellbinding adventure, this is storytelling on a grand scale. I really couldn't put it down, devouring it in one (very long!) sitting, totally unable to do anything but read and read until I knew exactly what was going to happen to Jack.

Leonie Flynn, Editor

> **Next?**
>
> Norse mythology is amazing. Read any version you can find; the stories are dark, cruel, and wonderful.
>
> *Beowulf* (try the version translated by Seamus Heaney) is the story of another quest.
>
> Or for more stories based on the same legends, try Catherine Fisher's **The Snow-Walker's Son** trilogy.

SECOND HELPINGS Megan McCafferty

> **Next?**
>
> If you liked *Second Helpings*, go back and read the first book in the series, *Sloppy Firsts* (UTBG 328), and then try the third, *Charmed Thirds*, and the fourth, *Fourth Comings*.
>
> For another author who has mastered humor, Sarah Mlynowski's **Bras and Broomsticks** should not be missed.

Second Helpings is the journal of high-school senior Jessica Darling, a witty and intelligent girl stuck in the "ohmigod!"-esque world of New Jersey's Pineville High. This book is the sequel to McCafferty's previous novel, *Sloppy Firsts*, but it is easy to understand without reading the first book. Jessica hilariously and poignantly details trying to get into Columbia, her correspondence with her best friend (who has moved away), and most important, her conflicted feelings for reformed bad boy Marcus Flutie.

Second Helpings is a triumph. Jessica is a breath of fresh air in a teen-book scene cluttered with bubble-brained heiresses. The character of Marcus Flutie has a combination of a poetic sensibility, rebelliousness, and sweetness that will melt your heart. Megan McCafferty's writing will make you both laugh until your stomach hurts and cry. If you are looking for a book that stands apart from the teen pack, pick up *Second Helpings* immediately!

Zoey Peresman, age 15

SECOND STAR TO THE RIGHT

Deborah Hautzig

Next?

For more about eating disorders, try the fictional *Diary of an Anorexic Girl* by Morgan Menzie, based on the author's own experiences.

Massive (UTBG 220) by Julia Bell is about three generations of one family, all with eating disorders.

Or read *Skinny* by Ibi Kaslik, about a girl struggling to deal with her sister's eating disorder.

Leslie has the kind of life anyone would like. She has an awesome best friend, does well at school, and gets on great with her mom. But Leslie is not happy. If only she were thin, then life would be perfect, wouldn't it?

She loses her first few pounds by accident, during a spell of the flu. It's the break she needs and Leslie starts to diet seriously, egged on by the "dictator" inside her. The pounds start dropping off, but getting thinner doesn't make things perfect. What Leslie eats, or doesn't eat, becomes an obsession; it takes over her life, and in the end she risks losing everything she cares for most.

This harrowing insight into the mind of a girl with anorexia nervosa is well observed and utterly compelling.

Susila Baybars, Editor

THE SECRET DIARY OF ADRIAN MOLE, AGED 13¾ Sue Townsend

Adrian is an average teenager. He has typical problems: acne, bullies, and a troublesome love life. His parents don't care what he does (while his grandmother cares too much), and his dog's always getting sick. He looks after a beetroot-sandwich-obsessed senior citizen named Bert Baxter, who doesn't appreciate him at all.

Adrian Mole is hilarious. It's well written and I found it very true to life. And this is only the first book in a whole series, during which we watch him grow up—he's in his mid-30s in the latest installment, and he's still hopeless!

Max Arevuo, age 13

Next?

If you also grow fond of Adrian, then read the other diaries; next is *The Growing Pains of Adrian Mole*.

If you like Sue Townsend's humor, you will love her *The Queen and I*, in which the queen (and, more troublesomely, the duke of Edinburgh) move to a council estate.

Want to read a more serious book about boys growing up? Robert Westall's *Falling into Glory* is about having an affair with a teacher.

THE SECRET GARDEN Frances Hodgson Burnett

Next?

Try *A Little Princess*, also by Frances Hodgson Burnett. Instead of rags to riches, this one is from riches to rags, and like *The Secret Garden* it is ultimately a triumph-against-the-odds book.

For another classic British tale of children overcoming adversity, try E. Nesbit's *The Railway Children*.

Ruby Holler (UTBG 295) by Sharon Creech is about orphan twins finding their place in the world.

This is a timeless story of survival against the odds. It is about a completely cranky and opinionated tween who is a real pain in the butt, but who is transformed into a decent human being through finding a secret garden that is overgrown and needs a makeover (how modern is that?).

I'm a sucker for Pygmalion-type transformations with a "before" and "after" and *The Secret Garden* has a very satisfying transformation; the people's changes are mirrored by a dying garden brought back to life. Yes! It is ultimately a feel-good book, the story of a survivor that inspires and warms the heart. Aaaah . . .

Cathy Hopkins, Author

THE SECRET HISTORY Donna Tartt

Richard sees Hampden College as the chance to leave behind his unglamorous past and create a new identity. Drawn to an elite group of students, centered around their charismatic classics professor, Richard is captivated by their sophistication, eccentricity, casual affluence, and the way they seem to live in a world set apart from the everyday. But as he sets about working his way into their confidence he discovers they have a secret history far darker than his own: one involving blackmail and murder.

This psychological thriller is far more than a whodunit (we find out the facts on almost the first page). The book's skill lies in the way it makes murder appear rational and justifiable before the event, and then hits you with the true horror of its consequences. It may sound like a grim read, but Tartt injects black humor into even the bleakest situations.

Katie Jennings, Editor

Next?

Another Donna Tartt? Her most recent book is *The Little Friend*.

For another tale of a crime and its consequences, try *Crime and Punishment* (UTBG 80) by Fyodor Dostoyevsky.

F. Scott Fitzgerald's *Tender Is the Night* (UTBG 352) is about secrets among the rich. Evelyn Waugh wrote tellingly about the decadent lives of the rich, too, in *Brideshead Revisited* (UTBG 51).

THE SECRET LIFE OF BEES Sue Monk Kidd

14+

I devoured every single page of this book, each with a certain thrill. The story takes place in 1960s South Carolina, where 14-year-old Lily Owen lives with her abusive father, T. Ray, and the fear that she accidentally killed her mother when she was four years old. When she finds a picture of a black Madonna inscribed with the words "Tiburon, S.C." mixed in with her mom's old possessions, Lily and her nanny escape from T. Ray in search of the truth about her mother. The two reach Tiburon and encounter a sisterhood of bizarre yet courageous black women and their honey-making business. Here, Lily finds a connection between the bee ladies and her mother, a slew of racial tensions, and strength in herself.

Claire Easton, age 16

CROWNED PRINTZ: GOLD MEDALISTS

American Born Chinese by Gene Luen Yang

Looking for Alaska by John Green

How I Live Now by Meg Rosoff

The First Part Last by Angela Johnson

Postcards from No Man's Land by Aidan Chambers

A Step from Heaven by An Na

Monster by Walter Dean Myers

Next?

Sue Monk Kidd's second novel, *The Mermaid Chair*, is about a middle-aged woman trying to care for her aging mother. It has the same sense of mysticism and legend as her debut.

Sarah Weeks's *So B. It* (UTBG 331) also stars a main character who is trying to piece together the mystery of her mother's past.

THE SECRET OF SABRINA FLUDDE

Pauline Fisk

The Secret of Sabrina Fludde is a strange and lyrical story that transforms the everyday into the mythological. A girl is washed up on the banks of a river, with no memory of how she got there or who she is. She discovers she is in the ancient market town of Pengwern, but as she wanders its streets nothing is familiar. As she searches for clues to her identity, she finds that her past is entwined with a local legend. But with this knowledge comes danger.

What has stayed with me is the vivid and magical atmosphere of the setting, which is both contemporary—with its shopping malls and graffiti—and steeped in history and legend. The eccentric, misfit characters the free-spirited heroine encounters on her quest are equally memorable—from Phaze II, a homeless boy who lives high in the eaves of a railroad bridge, to a boatsman descended from Barbary pirates.

Katie Jennings, Editor

> **Next?**
>
> Try David Almond's *Skellig* (UTBG 325) for more lyrical magical realism.
>
> Alan Garner's *The Owl Service* (UTBG 265) has Welsh legends and magic combined with darkly atmospheric writing.
>
> *Fire and Hemlock* (UTBG 117) by Diana Wynne Jones is also wonderfully inventive, with a brilliant opening chapter in which a girl crashes a funeral . . .

SEEKER William Nicholson

> **Next?**
>
> More William Nicholson? Read **The Wind on Fire** trilogy (UTBG 392).
>
> For power struggles and mysterious tribes, try Marcus Sedgwick's *Dark Horse*.
>
> Or try one of my favorites, Susan Cooper's **The Dark Is Rising** series (UTBG 87).

For as long as he can remember, Seeker has wanted to join the Nomana, the mysterious group of powerful "warriors." Morning Star and the Wildman want to as well. They all think they understand the Nomana and ought to be allowed to join. But it's not quite that simple. The Nomana won't accept just anyone . . .

Will the three of them ever be let in? What's the terrible "secret weapon" the Nomana are saying is set to destroy them? What happened to Seeker's brother, the heroic Blaze? Where's Morning Star's mother? And what is the source of the Nomana's power?

Many of your questions will be answered in this wonderful book, and for the rest, well, there are sequels on the way. If they're as good as this book, William Nicholson has another classic series on his hands.

Daniel Hahn, Editor

SEND ME DOWN A MIRACLE   Han Nolan

14+

Next?

The year after Han Nolan was nominated for the National Book Award for this book, he was nominated again—and won—for *Dancing on the Edge*.

Bee Season (UTBG 30) by Myla Goldberg shows how Jewish mysticism takes hold of a family of intellectuals.

Maybe a Miracle by Brian Strause also looks at what happens when a town believes a miracle has occurred.

Charity Pittman, a 14-year-old in a small and very religious Southern town, doesn't know for sure what she believes when it comes to God, love, family, and what she wants to be when she grows up. That is, until Adrienne Dabney, a New York artist, comes to town. Charity is fascinated by this new woman. Then, Adrienne bursts forth claiming that she saw Jesus sitting in her living room chair. The town begins to believe Adrienne's claims, worshipping the chair and holding prayer sessions. Charity watches, awestruck, as her father, an evangelical pastor, begins a hurried plot to destroy the chair, Adrienne, and the Devil himself.

An almost comedic way of looking at small-town Christian life, *Send Me Down a Miracle* is a fast read, with vivid characters and a plot like no other.

Allison Van Siclen, age 16

A SEPARATE PEACE   John Knowles

14+

It's hard to imagine now what it's like growing up in a world truly at war, where you and/or many of your peers may well be dead within a year. That's the situation in which Gene, Phineas, and their friends—the class of 1943 at an expensive boys' boarding school in New England—find themselves. But while World War II looms large, the key battle recounted in *A Separate Peace* is fought closer to home. Gene, the narrator, is an introverted intellectual. His roommate, Finny, is a popular athlete and a natural leader who is crippled by an accident that may be Gene's fault. Knowles beautifully captures Gene's tortured brooding and the destructive jealousy that can turn even the closest friends into enemies.

Terri Paddock, Author

Next?

Peace Breaks Out—although not a sequel, John Knowles's later book is set at the same school, where war hero Pete has returned to teach.

The Catcher in the Rye (UTBG 60)— J. D. Salinger's classic portrays another memorable protagonist, Holden Caulfield, whose story begins when he's expelled from an American prep school.

Lord of the Flies (UTBG 209) by William Golding has a more exotic setting, but the shipwrecked schoolboys also explore their baser instincts.

A SERIES OF UNFORTUNATE EVENTS

Lemony Snicket

Become part of the Baudelaire orphans' grim epic as they are pursued by the dastardly and stunningly inept Count Olaf, who wants to get his hands on the Baudelaire family fortune. But these are orphans with many talents: Violet is an inventor who can fashion a solution to almost any problem; Klaus is a bookworm who has read innumerable books on every subject imaginable; and Sunny . . . well, Sunny likes biting things.

The 13 books in A Series of Unfortunate Events are written for younger children, and they go out of their way to educate the reader as to the meanings of more complicated words. But older readers will still find plenty to enjoy here, whether it is the wonderfully Gothic and dreary atmosphere of the books, the novelty of reading a children's story that flatly refuses to give you a happy ending, or simply the ghoulish glee of watching the Baudelaire orphans suffer.

Chris Wooding, Author

> ### Next?
>
> You want Gothic? Try one of the best ones: *Frankenstein* (UTBG 126) by Mary Shelley.
>
> If you like seeing children treated awfully, pick up anything by Charles Dickens. *Oliver Twist* will start you off.
>
> Or try Philip Ardagh's **Unlikely Exploits** series.

THE SERIOUS KISS Mary Hogan

> ### Next?
>
> Want to read some more about that kiss? Try *Angus, Thongs and Full-Frontal Snogging* (UTBG 18) by Louise Rennison. Pure fun!
>
> Or what about a very different sort of moving away? Try *Wendy* (UTBG 384) by Karen Wallace, which imagines the story of *Peter Pan*'s Wendy Darling.
>
> Another Mary Hogan? Try *Perfect Girl*, about a girl who decides it's time to take a chance.

Whether drunk or sober, Libby's dad is a pig. He's also a spendthrift who loses all the family money, meaning they have to move away from everything she knows, out of the city and into a trailer park on the edge of a shabby desert town. White trash lifestyle? Thank you, Dad.

Libby hates it all. Even her old best friend drops her, and the only person prepared to befriend her now is the fat school misfit. In fact, life looks like it might be just about over. But then she meets a boy and makes friends with some of the weirdest (but coolest) people. So, will her dad stop being a loser? Will her mom stop feeding them take-out and actually start cooking? And what about that kiss?

Leonie Flynn, Editor

HISTORICAL FICTION
by Nicola Morgan

So you think history is boring? Just useless facts about dead people? Not relevant to our lives? I admit I probably thought that too. My memories of history classes at school are not exactly inspirational. Mainly, I remember one teacher making us do push-ups if we got a date wrong, and another teacher punctuating her terrifying lessons with cries of "Henry VIII *never* fiddled with his pencil!" The only thing this taught us was how to clench our stomach muscles so hard that the laughter did not explode. And I can still do push-ups.

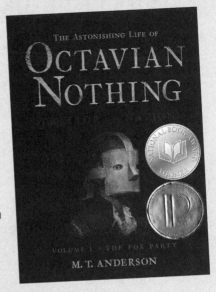

That all changed when I found myself writing a historical novel, *Fleshmarket* (UTBG 120). It happened by accident, after I heard a story—a true story—so powerful that the woman in it began to haunt me. The trouble was, I didn't know the history of the time. Okay, I knew some dates and facts—that's the easy part (and the boring part, to be honest) but I didn't really *know* the past. When I began the research, reading history books, I found I still didn't *know*, not really. Then I found primary sources, original newspapers, the actual paper touched by actual people from the time, and I began to have the inklings of connection. My heart began to beat faster. But I was still outside, looking through a doorway. Only when I began to know my own fictional characters, the characters I pushed through that door, did I properly understand. Only then did I *feel* the past.

That is why historical fiction is very different from a history lesson and why it should never feel like one (especially not like the ones I remember). Nonfiction tells you a type of truth—it can tell you the freezing point of water and even how the molecules behave as they freeze, but only fiction can make you feel the cold. The task for a novelist is to make you feel the cold without lecturing you about the behavior of molecules, without appearing to teach anything.

Historical fiction *is* relevant to us today:

Costume romances:

Pride and Prejudice by Jane Austen

Nicola and the Viscount by Meg Cabot

Frenchman's Creek by Daphne du Maurier

Jamaica Inn by Daphne du Maurier

Katherine by Anya Seton

War and Peace by Leo Tolstoy

Gone with the Wind by Margaret Mitchell

I Capture the Castle by Dodie Smith

it gives us a reflection of our own times, something we can compare our lives with, sometimes showing how much the world has changed, often showing how little anything changes. The one thing that remains the same, in past, present, and future, is human nature, in all its richness and its potential for good and for evil. And really, a historical novel is exactly like any other, just with a different setting. It shows humans behaving like humans, behaving as we always have done and always will.

Books where the past is real:

The Astonishing Life of Octavian Nothing, Traitor to the Nation, Volume One: The Pox Party by M. T. Anderson

Coram Boy by Jamila Gavin

No Shame, No Fear by Ann Turnbull

Witch Child by Celia Rees

Al Capone Does My Shirts by Gennifer Choldenko

The Ruby in the Smoke by Philip Pullman

At the Sign of the Sugared Plum by Mary Hooper

Blood Red Horse by K. M. Grant

'A powerful, absorbing and unusual novel' *The Bookseller*

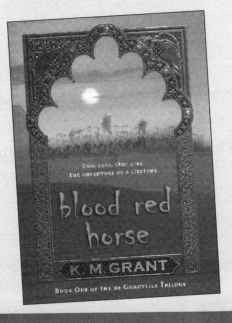

(Great) War stories:

All Quiet on the Western Front by Erich Maria Remarque

Cold Mountain by Charles Frazier

Goodbye to All That by Robert Graves

Birdsong by Sebastian Faulks

Regeneration by Pat Barker

Remembrance by Theresa Breslin

Private Peaceful by Michael Morpurgo

Black Hawk Down by Mark Bowden

SET IN STONE Linda Newbery

14+

Next?

Now try Newbery's other books, particularly *The Shell House* (UTBG 318) and *Sisterland* (UTBG 324).

For more secrets and mysteries, try *The Woman in White* (UTBG 398) by Wilkie Collins or *The Woman in Black* by Susan Hill.

Another book set among a strange family is *Titus Groan*, the first of the **Gormenghast** trilogy by Mervyn Peake.

Set in Stone begins in 1920, with successful artist Samuel Godwin looking back to his youth and his employment as tutor to the daughters of recent widower Ernest Farrow. Samuel is intrigued by the ménage he finds at Fourwinds, which includes the enigmatic Charlotte Agnew, companion to the girls. He senses a mystery involving Gideon Waring, sculptor of the magnificent carvings that give the house its name.

Linda Newbery characteristically refuses to compromise, either in narrative complexity or in subject matter. A shocking secret lies at the heart of the family; no one is quite as Samuel sees them, and nothing is quite as it seems. His shifting perspectives make *Set in Stone* a powerful page-turner, gripping to the end.

Celia Rees, Author

SEVENTH HEAVEN Alice Hoffman

16+

It is 1959. The oldest member of a small community on Long Island suddenly dies. His wife leaves town, and their empty house on Hemlock Street gradually falls apart. A terrible smell invades the street and a flock of vicious birds arrives to terrorize the neighborhood. The people wonder if they are being punished. But for what? It has always been a happy and peaceful community.

This sounds like the opening to a horror story, but *Seventh Heaven* is nothing like that. It is the story of ordinary people whose lives, gently explored, become strange and remarkable.

So when 17-year-old Ace begins to fall in love with a ghost, we are not at all surprised, just incredibly moved.

Jenny Nimmo, Author

Next?

If you like this book, you might like some of Alice Hoffman's other books that have a similar blend of ordinary lives touched by enchantment. Start with *Green Angel*.

Or you could try Anne Tyler's novels; *The Accidental Tourist* and *Dinner at the Homesick Restaurant* are not only touching but also enthralling and, sometimes, very funny.

Or how about Carol Shields's *The Stone Diaries*, the story of one woman's life from birth to death.

THE SHADOW OF THE WIND

Carlos Ruiz Zafón

This is a beguiling tale full of intrigue and heartbreak. Daniel, the son of a widowed bookseller, who lives with his father above their shop in postwar Barcelona, sets out on a quest to discover the truth about Julian Carax, a mysterious writer whose novel (also called *The Shadow of the Wind*) is at the center of the mystery. Along the way there are stories within stories, and different narrators take up the tale. Although books and writing are central to this novel, ultimately it is infatuation, young love, and heartbreak that weave together the complex plot.

With a host of fabulous characters and a backstory that unfolds through the dark times of the Spanish Civil War, *The Shadow of the Wind* captures the old-world charm of an almost forgotten Barcelona. One minute you're on the edge of your seat, the next you're reaching for the tissues. An enormously readable book.

Neil Arksey, Author

> **Next?**
>
> For an eyewitness account of the same war, try George Orwell's *Homage to Catalonia*.
>
> Ernest Hemingway's *For Whom the Bell Tolls* is a classic about the Spanish Civil War.
>
> Another complex and wonderful book: Umberto Eco's *The Name of the Rose*.

SHADOWMANCER G. P. Taylor

> **Next?**
>
> Another G. P. Taylor? Try *Wormwood*, about an astronomer, a prophecy, and an angel whose feathers are plucked one by one.
>
> For the most different slant on God and religion imaginable, you have to try Philip Pullman's **His Dark Materials** trilogy (UTBG 153).
>
> Or for more mystery and magic try Trudi Canavan's **The Black Magician** trilogy (UTBG 39).

"It is the song of the deep. They are calling the dead to feast. The Seloth will not stop until the ship is broken on the rocks. They want sacrifice not mercy."

It is the 1700s. Thomas, Kate, and Raphah are brought together in mysterious ways, and are sent on a mission from God to retake a golden statue (the Keruvim) from the cruel, power-hungry priest Demurral, before he can use it to kill God and control the universe. But there are many complications . . .

This is a fast-moving tale of magic, evil, superstition, and witchcraft that never fails to keep you in suspense. If you want to be transported into a time when not even life can be taken for granted, you will enjoy this book.

Samuel Mortimer, age 11

THE SHAMER'S DAUGHTER Lene Kaaberbol

 12+

Dina's mother, the Shamer, is haughtily summoned by Lord Drakan to prove a murderer's guilt. But the man is innocent. So she refuses to testify against him and finds herself, Dina, and the "murderer" caught up in a deadly power game. Dina struggles desperately to save her mother and the accused man from death, and in doing so she begins to come to terms with inheriting her mother's Shamer power.

I'm not a regular fantasy reader, but I loved this: filled with tension, the story whips along at a quick pace and—scary dragons notwithstanding—it's set in a very real and tangible world. Dina certainly has guts, and she will make you see that the role of the Shamer—teller of truth—isn't for fantasy worlds alone. Exciting and thought-provoking.
Helen Simmons, Bookseller

Next?

Lene Kaaberbol has written three more books about Dina and her journey to understanding the role of the Shamer: *The Shamer's Signet*, *The Serpent Gift*, and *The Shamer's War*.

You might also like *The Giver* (UTBG 135) and *Gathering Blue* by Lois Lowry, set in a world where everyone is engineered to be the same.

For another exhilarating fantasy, try Clive Barker's *Abarat* (UTBG 4).

SHARP NORTH Patrick Cave

 12+

Next?

The sequel is *Blown Away*, about Adeline. Or try *The House of the Scorpion* (UTBG 164) by Nancy Farmer, another fantastic sci-fi thriller whose protagonist has much in common with Mira.

Exodus (UTBG 107) by Julie Bertagna also takes place in a futuristic flooded Britain.

Or how about the different but equally thrilling **The Oracle Prophecies** (UTBG 259) by Catherine Fisher.

An isolated spot in the Highlands, an unknown woman pursued by gray-clad men, red blood spills on white snow as a young girl accidentally witnesses a murder. This is the atmospheric opening of Cave's intense sci-fi thriller. Mira's simple existence is shattered by the violent scene, sending her on a long journey to find her true identity. The book is set in a futuristic Britain, a half-drowned country governed by powerful families who would do just about anything to retain their control, including some very unethical experiments. A web of lies and political corruption is slowly closing in on Mira, who must use every resource she has in order to survive.
Noga Applebaum, Academic

SHARPE'S COMPANY Bernard Cornwell

Next?

You will certainly want to read other **Sharpe** books—I've got 18 on my shelf and Cornwell is still writing them. Chronologically, they start with *Sharpe's Tiger* but the first one he wrote—and one of the best—was *Sharpe's Rifles*.

C. S. Forester's **Hornblower** series is set at sea druing the Napoleonic wars, as is Elizabeth Laird's fast and action-packed *Secrets of the Fearless*.

Sharpe is a soldier in the Peninsular wars—the wars Britain fought in Spain and Portugal against Napoleon in the early 1800s. These were times of great cruelty and great heroism, and Bernard Cornwell describes them better than anyone. His hero is a rough, tough lieutenant of the 95th Rifles, and the events in which he is involved actually happened. When you read in the book about the "forlorn hope" and the attack on the great fortress of Badajoz you will be blown away—as were most of the men in the first advance.

Sharpe's Company is the third of a wonderful series and possibly my favorite. Cornwell makes you wonder how anyone could think history is boring.

Andrew Norriss, Author

SHE H. Rider Haggard

In my mid-teens I was mightily stirred by H. Rider Haggard's adventure novels, by this one most of all perhaps, partly because of the detailed drawings in my hardcover edition of the proud, deliciously bare-breasted queen Ayesha.

In *She*, Ludwig Horace Holly and his young ward Leo Vincey set sail for Africa to seek the truth behind the death, over 2,000 years earlier, of Kallikrates, an ancestor of Leo's. After hair-raising escapades on the high seas and among cannibals, Holly and Leo are taken to the concealed realm of the great white queen Ayesha (She-Who-Must-Be-Obeyed), who admits to having murdered Kallikrates herself for rejecting her several lifetimes ago. Ayesha has ruled this hidden land for all those centuries, never losing her youth and beauty. Recognizing Leo as a true descendant of her lost love, the queen leads him and his guardian on thrilling and dangerous adventures during which not all will survive . . .

Michael Lawrence, Author

Next?

Another Rider Haggard? There's a sequel, *Ayesha*. Or try the yarn *King Solomon's Mines*.

For a more modern story set in Africa, try *What Is the What* by Dave Eggers, based on the real lives of Sudanese boys who tried to escape war.

Or try some of Rudyard Kipling's short stories in *The Man Who Would Be King*.

THE SHELL HOUSE Linda Newbery

14+

This is a big and complex novel that explores in some depth, and with great honesty and tenderness, the emotional awakening of two young men from different periods of history. One is Greg, a modern teenager, drawn into the past by his involvement in the restoration of a stately home. The other is Edmund, a young soldier, who fought and loved—and subsequently disappeared—in World War I.

Sexual identity, as revealed through Edmund's sufferings, is one strand of this many-layered novel. Another is the nature of religious belief, as Greg's girlfriend, the aptly named Faith, struggles with the concept of her Christianity. Still another is the need for Greg to discover what he really feels and thinks, and to remain true to his ideals.

An astonishingly wide canvas is covered, ranging across both time and the conflicting emotional landscapes of the two main characters. All in all, a deeply satisfying read.

Jean Ure, Author

Next?

Another book that sets the troubles of sexuality against the backdrop of World War I is Susan Hill's *Strange Meeting* (UTBG 341).

Or for more Linda Newbery, read *Sisterland* (UTBG 324), which weaves a compelling story around Alzheimer's, sexuality, and racism.

Aidan Chambers's *Dance on My Grave* also deals with complex issues of sexuality.

ICE IN BEARDS— VERY COLD PLACES

The Worst Journey in the World by Apsley Cherry-Garrard

Terra Incognita by Sara Wheeler

Into Thin Air by Jon Krakauer

Touching the Void by Joe Simpson

The SHERLOCK HOLMES stories

Sir Arthur Conan Doyle

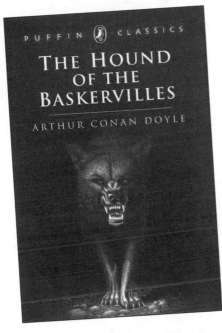

It's impossible to imagine a world without Sherlock Holmes. Sir Arthur Conan Doyle's creation is more famous than many historical figures. The actor/director Orson Welles once described Holmes as "the greatest man who never lived and who will never die."

I'd start with the very first story, *A Study in Scarlet*, and then read the first half-dozen or so short stories in order. That way you'll get to know Holmes, his faithful companion Doctor John Watson, and the Victorian world they inhabit. After that, you can pick and choose. There are 56 short stories and four short novels, offering an extraordinary mix of pure deduction, adventure, and intrigue. Like them, and they will stay with you forever.

Philip Ardagh, Author

I can remember how my heart sank when I opened a big present and found this heavy volume inside. I must have been about 14, and I couldn't imagine anything less enticing. Sometimes that's the best way to approach a book. The thrill of being sur-prised is wonderful. These four stories: *A Study in Scarlet*, *The Sign of Four*, *The Hound of the Baskervilles,* and *The Valley of Fear*, are all you need to get hooked on Holmes and Watson, and their world of crime and mystery. The stories were first published in the late 19th century, and these days there may even be an extra thrill: Holmes is wonderfully politically incorrect. A modern publisher would insist on cleaning up his habits and attitudes before allowing you anywhere near these compelling stories.

Eleanor Updale, Author

Next?

There are tons more Holmes stories found in: *The Adventures of Sherlock Holmes*; *The Memoirs of Sherlock Holmes*; *The Return of Sherlock Holmes*; *His Last Bow*; *The Casebook of Sherlock Holmes*;

If you want something more modern, go to P. D. James, Colin Dexter, or Ruth Rendell. They all write books in which the same detective returns to solve new mysteries.

Or try Dorothy L. Sayers's **Lord Peter Wimsey** books (UTBG 211), starting with *Clouds of Witness*.

SHORT STORIES H. G. Wells

Next?

Try Wells's novels. *The War of the Worlds* (UTBG 379) is a classic of alien invasion, and *The Invisible Man* takes the idea of invisibility to its logical limits.

Wells's work inspired William Hope Hodgson's bizarre and brilliant *The Night Land*.

Or try some more recent science fiction, such as Arthur C. Clarke's *Childhood's End*, or Isaac Asimov's *I, Robot* (UTBG 171).

Or see our feature and list of great sci-fi reads on pp. 218–219.

H. G. Wells is the founding father of British science fiction—a brilliant storyteller whose books are full of speculations about the future. Of the short stories, the most famous is "The Time Machine," in which the hero travels through untold millennia to the very end of the world. Then there's "The Country of the Blind," where the sighted man is at no advantage, and "The Man Who Could Work Miracles," who ends up dearly wishing he couldn't. Wells imagines what would happen if the earth stopped revolving, if diamonds could be grown, if a man could see two periods of time at once, if tentacled invaders were to crawl from the sea. Through stories, he explores his theories and beliefs, mixing terrifying fantasy firmly within the world of Edwardian Britain.

Catherine Fisher, Author

THE SHORT STORIES OF SAKI H. H. Munro

Tobermory the cat is taught human speech and starts repeating in public everything he has overheard in private. A stray child turns out to be a werewolf. Conradin makes a god of his pet ferret and prays for vengeance on his hateful guardian—successfully. Through these very short stories rampage fiendishly inventive children, dictatorial aunts, liars, bored young men who make life hell for other people just to pass the time, and every species of animal from chickens to wolves, usually wreaking havoc of some kind. Often savage, sometimes sad, always witty, these portraits of Edwardian society are like snapshots taken with a camera that has a crack in the lens.

Jan Mark, Author

Next?

O. Henry, another famous short story writer, is known as a master of irony. Try *41 Stories*.

You might also want to try Annie Proulx's stories of the west. Start with *Close Range*.

Or try G. K. Chesterton's slightly strange *The Man Who Was Thursday*, about an anarchist and a policeman.

SIDDHARTHA Hermann Hesse

14+

Young Siddhartha is loved and admired by everyone, not least the girls of the town, who sigh when he passes. But Siddhartha is not content. He feels that something is missing from his life, and with his faithful friend Govinda, he joins a band of wandering holy men. The friends travel and live with the holy men for three years until the day they hear of old Gotama, the wise man known as the Buddha, and go to hear him preach. Govinda is impressed by the Buddha and decides to follow him, but Siddhartha does not want to learn how another man acquired his wisdom: he wants to find his own, by way of his own experiences. And so his real quest begins—a difficult and complicated journey that is fulfilled only in old age.

I loved this book when I first read it, and I loved it all over again when I read it some years later—though I confess without experiencing the slightest urge to go on a quest like Siddhartha's.

Michael Lawrence, Author

Next?

More Hermann Hesse? Try *Narcissus and Goldmund* (UTBG 240) or *Steppenwolf*.

Richard Bach also writes about the getting of wisdom— try *Jonathan Livingston Seagull* (UTBG 184).

Or try the Dalai Lama's *The Art of Happiness*.

A SIGHT FOR SORE EYES Ruth Rendell

14+

Next?

Although in her 70s, Rendell knows exactly what it's like to be young. One of her best evocations of youth can be found in *The Crocodile Bird*.

P. D. James is another master of suspense. Try her mysteries about Inspector Dalgliesh, starting with *Cover Her Face*.

And of course you can turn to our feature on detective stories on pp. 96–97 for more recommendations.

Rendell is my all-time favorite author, and this thriller is one of her best. Teddy Brex is born a beautiful, lovable child into a family lacking in love. After her mother's violent murder, Francine Hill is trapped in a strict family setting that permits no room for any emotion but a desperate desire for escape. When the two young adults meet there's an instant attraction. But can a man who's never been loved learn to love? And is ugliness so corrosive that it sours even the most beautiful subject? These are two questions asked in Ruth Rendell's compulsively readable thriller, which as always spins several threads at once and culminates in a devastating, ingenious end.

Jon Appleton, Editor

SILAS MARNER George Eliot

16+

This was the first classic book I read outside school. I had heard of George Eliot, and how she was a woman hiding behind a man's name, but I was put off by the size of her books on the library shelves. So I chose the thinnest: *Silas Marner*. It's a great story, set in the early 19th century.

Silas Marner, a weaver, is turned into a reclusive, miserly outsider when falsely accused of theft. Then he is transformed again when he finds and adopts a young girl. This book has everything: tragedy, mystery, and a dissolute, sexy, aristocratic villain. At school, we read Eliot's *The Mill on the Floss* out loud in class. It took weeks. I thought I was going to die of boredom. But *Silas Marner* is fabulous.

Eleanor Updale, Author

Next?

I went on from this to *Tess of the D'Urbervilles* (UTBG 353) by Thomas Hardy (more rural England and dastardly men), and *Jane Eyre* (UTBG 182) by Charlotte Brontë, the ultimate book of unjust suffering and longing.

One of the themes of *Silas Marner* (though I don't think I realized it at the time) is the dignity of labor. You can get more of that from *Sons and Lovers* by D. H. Lawrence.

Some people do like *The Mill on the Floss* (UTBG 226), also by George Eliot. Try it and see if you are one of them.

SILVERFIN Charlie Higson

12+

James Bond is 13 and a new boy at Eton in England. School is bad enough, but then he makes enemies and his vacation in Scotland becomes something less than relaxing. With the help of a beautiful girl and a tough, streetwise kid, Bond survives the attentions of an obsessed millionaire, imprisonment, experimental drugs, torture, perilous escape, and coming to terms with the death of seemingly everyone he loves.

This is brilliantly researched and perfectly in keeping with the other Bond stories. From the gruesome opening chapter to the final scenes, this is a rip-roaring adventure, and one that Ian Fleming would surely have approved of. And best of all? This is just the first in a series—I can't wait!

Leonie Flynn, Editor

Next?

Try the sequel, *BloodFever*, of course.

Or one of the original **James Bond** books (UTBG 181) by Ian Fleming; try *Dr. No* for starters.

Robert Muchamore writes great adventures for his teen heroes. Try *The Recruit* (UTBG 288), first in the **Cherub** series.

Or for another story set in the wilds of Scotland that'll have you biting your nails, try John Buchan's *The Thirty-Nine Steps* (UTBG 357).

THE SIMPLE GIFT   Steven Herrick

Next?

The Simple Gift reminds me—weirdly, I know—of Bunyan's *Pilgrim's Progress*.

And the father-son relationship has echoes of Kevin Brooks's *Martyn Pig* (UTBG 220), although with a happier outcome.

More Steven Herrick? Try *Love, Ghosts & Facial Hair*, also told in verse, about a young, aspiring poet who falls in love.

You might also want to read *Just Listen* (UTBG 187) by Sarah Dessen, about a teen who is also struggling to deal with how tough real life can get.

Written in free verse, this story is told through short, stand-alone poems, each a little masterpiece in its own right. A most unusual novel, it opens with 16-year-old Billy abandoning his loveless home and cruel father to hit the road and live rough. But if you think you're in for a grim, downbeat read, you'll be surprised.

Basically *The Simple Gift* explores goodness and kindness. Despite his background, Billy is a character of fundamental dignity and integrity. He might be down and out, living in an old subway car, but his decency enriches the lives of others.

And ultimately in this gritty, uplifting fairy tale for our times, Billy himself trades his past for true friendship and love.

Catherine Forde, Author

THE SIRENS OF TITAN   Kurt Vonnegut

Everyone knows Vonnegut wrote *Slaughterhouse-Five*. And yes, it's a brilliant book that must be read. But he wrote a lot of other classics too. This, one of his earliest, is also one of his best. A wickedly funny satire about the meaning (and meaninglessness) of life, it features many of his trademarks—science fiction, time travel, knowledge of the future, man's role in the universe, our ultimate end.

Vonnegut's books can be bleak as well as hilarious—but they'll always make you think. He's not just a brilliant sci-fi writer—he's a great writer altogether. Don't let phrases like "chrono-synclastic infundibulum" put you off. Vonnegut's books come dressed as sci-fi, but they're always about humans and our struggles to make sense of the world and of life. But be warned: if you read this book, you might never look at the Bible in the same light again!

Darren Shan, Author

Next?

Try *Slaughterhouse-Five* (UTBG 327) and *Mother Night*, both by Kurt Vonnegut.

Childhood's End by Arthur C. Clarke is about what humanity might become, with encouragement from outside.

The Hitchhiker's Guide to the Galaxy (UTBG 154) by Douglas Adams must be the funniest sci-fi novel ever.

THE SISTERHOOD OF THE TRAVELING PANTS   Ann Brashares

12+

This is the story of one pair of pants, four very different girls, and one very special friendship. Carmen, Lena, Bridget, and Tibby are destined to go their own separate ways in the summer, but they resolve to share their lives by passing the pants (a stylish pair of jeans that somehow fits each of them perfectly) from one to the other in turn. The four girls' summer experiences, with all their highs and lows, are woven skillfully together into a satisfying story of friendship and self-discovery.

**Philippa Milnes-Smith,
Literary Agent**

> ### Next?
>
> Try *Feeling Sorry for Celia* by Jaclyn Moriarty; wry, hilarious, and written in the form of letters. Or Carolyn Mackler's *Love and Other Four-Letter Words*, about parents separating, moving to New York, and love.
>
> And *Sisterhood* . . . has sequels, too: *Second Summer of the Traveling Pants* is next.
>
> You also might like to try Meg Cabot's *Teen Idol*.

SISTERLAND   Linda Newbery

14+

> ### Next?
>
> Another wonderful Linda Newbery? Try her latest, *Set in Stone* (UTBG 314), or *Lost Boy*.
>
> David Almond's *The Fire-Eaters* (UTBG 118) is another book that manages to make international politics a part of an engaging personal story.
>
> Or for more about the contemporary Middle East, try Naomi Shihab Nye's *19 Varieties of Gazelle*.

This novel covers an enormous amount of ground very well. It's at once a story about the relationship of a British girl and a Palestinian boy, a story about memories of World War II, a tale of two sisters and the rivalry between them, and a discussion of racism and contemporary Middle East politics. This makes the book sound "high level," which it emphatically isn't. We are always engaged with the characters and their lives, and the pace ensures that readers will want to keep turning the pages.

The relationship between the British girl, Hilly, and her grandmother, and the role of memory and history in the novel, make it one that's worth rereading. There are no easy answers at the end, but the author strikes a hopeful note in the final pages.

Adèle Geras, Author

SKELLIG   David Almond

This is one of my favorite books! It's about a boy named Michael, who has just moved to a rather derelict house and whose baby sister is so seriously ill we don't know whether she's going to survive. It's about fear and sadness and loss, but also about healing and recovery and love and tenderness. At the heart of the story is the extraordinary figure of Skellig, whom Michael discovers in the dilapidated garage. At first he seems like a disgusting old man, covered in cobwebs, but bit by bit Michael's (and the reader's) view is transformed.

Michael, his friends Leaky and Coot, Mina (a homeschooled girl with a special way of seeing things), and Michael's family are all real and totally believable, but this story is also magical and extraordinary. Reading it felt to me like going on an intense, moving journey. I couldn't put it down!

Julia Green, Author

With a new house and a new school, Michael has a lot to cope with, even without his baby sister falling dangerously ill. With his parents preoccupied with the baby and the doctor always in the house, Michael is left to his own devices, and one day he finds a mysterious man—or is it a bird?—or maybe an angel?—in the ramshackle garage at the bottom of the garden. Together with his new friend Mina, they take the strange being, with wings and a peculiar liking for flies and Chinese take-out, to her grandfather's house, and Michael's life changes forever.

Words aren't enough to describe the magic of this book. It's a story about faith and hope, life, love, and death—big, serious issues—but there's humor too, and it's so well-written you feel you're there with them. Imaginative, inspired, original, full of poetry and emotion, you won't be able to put it down when you're reading it or get it out of your head when you've finished.

David Gardner, age 16

Next?

A Kestrel for a Knave by Barry Hines is a powerful story about the relationship between a boy and a wild bird.

Coraline (UTBG 76) by Neil Gaiman is a magic/reality mix with a far darker and more sinister edge, based on a backward reality, not unlike a creepier version of Lewis Carroll's *Alice's Adventures in Wonderland*.

Other David Almond books to look for include his disturbing look at good and evil, *Clay* (UTBG 73).

Or try *Big Fish* by Daniel Wallace, about a man who comes to know his father by separating myth from reality.

THE SKIN I'M IN Sharon G. Flake

Next?

Try *Begging for Change* and *Money Hungry* by Sharon G. Flake, which star a memorable young woman named Raspberry.

Or try John Howard Griffin's *Black Like Me*, in which the author, a white man, took on the appearance of a black man in the Deep South and recorded his experiences.

Firegirl by Tony Abbott is another title that deals with a young woman with scars, physical and otherwise, and the reactions of her classmates.

We all wonder how other people see us, but are the importance and the power we give others really all that relevant? Join Maleeka Madison as she discovers the strength within her beautiful skin. Will she be able to overcome the need to feel popular? Will she continue to do other girls' homework just for the privilege of hanging out in the bathroom where they smoke, gossip, and make fun of her?

This title delves into some hard-hitting issues, including grief; choices, actions, and consequences; self-esteem; friendship; adolescent and parental relationships; and love. Plus, Maleeka is an incredibly likable character who you will root for, question, and ultimately understand, given her situation and her own perception of self. *The Skin I'm In* is a quick read that is also incredibly thought-provoking.

Kathy Fredrickson, Librarian

SLAKE'S LIMBO Felice Holman

Artemis Slake is "born an orphan at the age of thirteen, small, near-sighted, dreaming, bruised, an outlander in the city of his birth." Fleeing from constant bullying, he goes underground, literally. He finds a cave in New York's subway system and doesn't go home again. From his hideout, cautiously, he builds a new, almost-independent life, forming delicate relationships with subterranean people who, to his surprise, do not want to hurt him.

The story is free of sentimentality, even of pity, and Holman's writing is wonderful. Somehow it manages to be dense and rich but laid-back at the same time; sometimes it jolts and sparks like the subway. And it's miraculously compact—a mere 90 pages in my edition. An unmissable masterpiece.

Mal Peet, Author

Next?

Want more books about running away and the problems it brings? Try Wendelin Van Draanen's *Runaway*, Christine Fletcher's *Tallulah Falls*, or Steven Herrick's *The Simple Gift* (UTBG 323).

Underworld (UTBG 371) by Catherine MacPhail is about a group of kids trapped underground and how they survive.

SLAUGHTERHOUSE-FIVE Kurt Vonnegut

Kurt Vonnegut lived through the fire-bombing of Dresden in World War II and then spent 20 years trying to find a way to write about it. He finally came up with this—one of the most famous antiwar novels of all time. Billy Pilgrim, with his blue and ivory feet, stumbles through time and space. Billy becomes an optometrist, a private in the US army, a specimen on show in an alien zoo, an innocent, a father, a son, a husband—quite often all at once. People die. A lot of people die. So it goes.

Absurd, tragic, and very funny, this is Vonnegut's masterpiece. As a plea for less butchery and less blind obedience to authority, it sears.

Leonie Flynn, Editor

Next?

For another war book—that makes you see just how horrible war is—try *Catch-22* (UTBG 59) by Joseph Heller, one of the funniest books written about this subject—and the scariest.

Or for a vision of the future that'll chill you, where knowledge and ideas are forbidden and books are burned, try Ray Bradbury's *Fahrenheit 451* (UTBG 110).

Or maybe you want something else by Mr. Vonnegut? Try *Breakfast of Champions*, a hilarious, cynical roller coaster of a novel (in which Kilgore Trout himself appears!).

THE SLEDDING HILL Chris Crutcher

Next?

For another intriguing novel by Chris Crutcher, don't miss *Ironman* or *Whale Talk*.

For another novel about censorship, try *Memoirs of a Bookbat* by Kathryn Lasky, about a girl who secretly loves the books her Christian Fundamentalist parents are fighting to ban.

For a different look at death by a narrator who has experienced it, try Alice Sebold's *The Lovely Bones* (UTBG 213) or Gabrielle Zevin's *Elsewhere* (UTBG 103).

Eddie Profit is trying to get a grip on reality. It's a tough thing to do when you've just lost your father and your best friend. Losing his father is devastating. Losing his best friend, Billy, is not as tragic because Billy has found a way to talk to Eddie from beyond the grave. Billy helps Eddie stand up for himself and make sense out of senseless tragedy. This is a great story for anyone who has experienced the loss of a loved one.

Brace yourself for a powerful look at racism and censorship.It will feel like Billy Bartholomew is talking directly to you. Chris Crutcher creates that personal touch time and time again in his novels. If you read one Crutcher novel, you will want to read them all.

Roz Monette, Author

THE SLIGHTLY TRUE STORY OF CEDAR B. HARTLEY Martine Murray

What can I say about this book, other than that it's extraordinary? It reads like an Australian Margaret Atwood with an added layer of quirkiness. For starters, Cedar B. Hartley's real name isn't Cedar B. Hartley at all, but Lana Monroe, who as well as telling the story, draws weird little pictures with captions such as "terrapin inside a sock" and "Oscar in cone shape." This is a story about being an outsider, growing up and growing friendships, with a big dose of acrobatics thrown in for good measure. And then there's Oscar with his brain injury, Kite (who's a bird person), and Stinky the dog. If there's only one book you read from this guide, make it this one!
Philip Ardagh, Author

> **Next?**
>
> Hilary McKay's *Dog Friday* is another story of friendship brought about by a lost dog.
>
> Martine Murray is also an illustrator, so why not check out her drawings in *Henrietta* or *A Moose Called Mouse*?
>
> More quirky characters? try *Stargirl* (UTBG 337) by Jerry Spinelli.

SLOPPY FIRSTS Megan McCafferty

> **Next?**
>
> This is the first book in a continuing series. If you like it, you'll definitely want to follow Jess through *Second Helpings* (UTBG 305), *Charmed Thirds*, and *Fourth Comings*.
>
> Stephen Chbosky's *The Perks of Being a Wallflower* (UTBG 269) is another book that looks at the difficulties of being a teenage outcast, but from a boy's point of view.
>
> For another hilarious novel written in multiple formats, try Jaclyn Moriarty's *The Murder of Bindy Mackenzie*.

While high school sophomore Jess Darling may have a cynical outer shell that tends to alienate her from many of the social cliques at her school, inside she is constantly worrying and wondering about how she fits in and about the person she really wants to be. The diary format, combined with an occasional letter to her best friend, Hope, allows the reader into Jess's most private musings. Among other things, she writes about the pressures of being the school brainiac, the friendships she has with so many different boys, concerns about her body, and what really matters in a friendship. Intelligent and witty, honest and confident, Jess's voice is a refreshing change from that of so many other chick-lit protagonists. She says what she thinks, and it is her ability to articulate what so many others have silently believed that endears her to the people who really matter. Or does it?
Karen Santamaria, Librarian

SMACK Melvin Burgess

This is the story of two young people, Gemma and Tar, who fall in love with each other, and with drugs. If you've ever wondered why anyone would be dumb enough to stick a needle in their arm and inject heroin, this book will tell you. It charts the downward spiral of Gemma and Tar with a clinical, terrifying precision that lets you see that the slide is easier than you'd think. This doesn't make for comfortable reading. The events are real. Many of them are highly unpleasant, and they become more so as the book goes on . . . but by then it's too late: you like and care about the main characters so much you have to keep reading.

Andrew Norriss, Author

"Everyone should read *Smack*."
—*The Sunday Times*

Next?

If you enjoy reading about tough situations, you could try *I Am the Cheese* (UTBG 168) by Robert Cormier, about a boy caught up in violence and a struggle for power in his school.

Crank by Ellen Hopkins is a similarly tough read about a group of teens caught up in drug addiction.

You'll probably enjoy *Doing It* (UTBG 94), also by Melvin Burgess, which looks at sex with the same ruthless honesty.

Candy by Luke Davies also looks at heroin addiction and the lengths people will go to in order to get it.

Todd Strasser's *Can't Get There from Here* is an intriguing read that follows a group of homeless teens and their myriad problems.

Gemma and Tar run away together, escaping their unhappy, quarrelsome families. They fall in with people who live differently, dress differently, and look at the world in a different way. Their new life is exhilarating, like flying—and part of the exhilaration comes from taking drugs.

But *Smack* isn't "a book about drugs." It's about *people*. People so real that you're right inside their heads, sharing their excitement and fears, the lies they tell themselves, and the hard lessons they learn. The questions all the characters face are: What's real? What's solid enough to last a lifetime?

Finding out takes them through painful and difficult experiences, and they don't all come up with the same answers. Not a book for the squeamish, but it's a terrific read.

Gillian Cross, Author

SMILLA'S SENSE OF SNOW Peter Høeg

Peter Høeg's novel took the world by storm when it appeared 10 years ago. It was a totally unexpected bestseller. It's the story of a Danish woman—by birth a Greenlander, an ice dweller—who stumbles on a major conspiracy.

The delight is in the detail, and Høeg's minute description of a wintry world is as magical (to those of us from less extreme climates) as anything you'd find on top of the Christmas tree.

The book falls into two distinct halves and some may find the second—when Smilla leaves Copenhagen for the Arctic seas and the heart of the mystery—to be harder to follow. But the dazzling prose will propel you all the way.

Sarah Gristwood, Author

Next?

More Peter Høeg? Try *Borderliners*, about a group of kids suffering at an experimental school.

Other surprise hits in a similar vein were David Guterson's *Snow Falling on Cedars* (UTBG 330), and Nicholas Evans's *The Horse Whisperer*.

Or Rebecca Wells's wonderful *The Divine Secrets of the Ya-Ya Sisterhood*—though this one is more contemporary.

SNOW FALLING ON CEDARS David Guterson

Next?

More Guterson? Try *Our Lady of the Forest*, about a girl who has visions, or his collection of stories, *The Country Ahead of Us, the Country Behind*.

For another portrait of a small fishing town, try Annie Proulx's *The Shipping News*.

A book that tells of Japan just after the war is *Memoirs of a Geisha* (UTBG 224) by Arthur Golden.

This book is set in the years directly following World War II, when a sleepy fishing town on San Piedro Island off the coast of Washington state is rocked by the suspicious circumstances surrounding a fisherman's death. A Japanese American man, Kabuo Miyomoto, is charged with the murder, but because of the latent sentiments toward the Japanese after the war, his arrest is also suspicious. Told through the eyes of a local newspaperman, who was once in love with Kabuo's wife, we see the events of the trial and years leading up to it unfold.

This book is brimming with elements like unrequited love, the horrid effects of war on individuals, courtroom drama, and a beautifully described Pacific Northwest setting—all the makings of a great book. Guterson's ability to weave the details from the past into the events of the trial through flashbacks that switch seamlessly from past to present makes this an unmissable read.

Mary Kate Castellani, Editor

THE SNOW GOOSE Paul Gallico

Next?

The stories in Michael Morpurgo's collection *The White Horse of Zennor* also have a haunting quality and a strong sense of place.

For another story that examines the bond between the young and old, read *The Distance from Normandy* by Jonathan Hull.

Or if you'd prefer a funnier take, try Jordan Sonnenblick's *Notes from the Midnight Driver*.

This moving and haunting little story was first published in 1940. It's about the relationship that develops between a lonely older man, Philip Rhayader, and a young girl, Frith, who brings him a wounded snow goose to be healed. Philip, an artist, feels a special connection with the wild birds on the marshes near his home on the east coast of Essex, in England. It's this same feeling that drives him to take his boat to help rescue the soldiers stranded at Dunkirk, joining many other "little ships."

The story is simply and beautifully told. It captures perfectly the remote setting, the birds, and the feelings of the girl who comes to love the lonely and isolated man.

Julia Green, Author

SO B. IT Sarah Weeks

For 12 years, Heidi and her mother, who can only speak 23 words and has the mind of a child, have depended on a benevolent neighbor. Their rent and utilities have always been mysteriously paid, and the neighbor, Bernadette, feeds and takes care of them. But when Heidi decides it's time to find out the truth about where they came from, she sets out on her own with two clues: an old photograph of her mother that shows a sign with the name of an institution in New York, and the word Soof, which her mother repeats constantly.

Sarah Weeks has created a cast of characters that belong mostly to this world, and yet have an almost magical aura around them. A wonderful read for a younger teen with a big heart.

Laura Lehner-Ennis, Librarian

Next?

In *Jumping the Scratch*, also by Sarah Weeks, Jimmy must deal with the memory of a traumatic event in his life.

Rules by Cynthia Lord, a Newbery Honor Book, explores the challenges of having an autistic sibling.

Chris Crutcher's *Staying Fat for Sarah Byrnes* (UTBG 338) delves into the difficulties of maintaining a relationship with someone who is emotionally scarred.

SOLD Patricia McCormick

14+

Lakshmi is a 13-year-old Nepalese girl traded into sexual slavery by her own stepfather. Told through a series of raw, unforgettable vignettes from Lakshmi's point of view, the reader follows her harrowing journey from her impoverished yet happy days in her rural mountain village to her hellish imprisonment in an Indian brothel called "Happiness House." There, Lakshmi and the other girls are subjected to the most inhumane and squalid conditions. And yet Lakshmi never gives up hope, inspired by the words of her beloved and long-suffering mother: simply to endure is to triumph.

I'm grateful to Patricia McCormick for this brutal yet beautiful book, and for allowing Lakshmi to speak up for those who suffer in anonymity and silence.

Megan McCafferty, Author

Next?

For more gritty reads by Patricia McCormick, try *Cut* (UTBG 83), about a girl who self-mutilates, or *My Brother's Keeper*, about a boy who tries to save his brother from drug addiction.

Elisa Carbone's *Last Dance on Holladay Street* gives a picture of prostitution in America in the late 1800s.

For more about the issue of human trafficking, try Julia Bell's *Dirty Work*.

SON OF THE MOB Gordon Korman

12+

Next?

Fans of *Son of the Mob* will undoubtedly also enjoy the book's sequel, *Son of the Mob: Hollywood Hustle*.

If you like Gordon Korman's writing, *No More Dead Dogs* (UTBG 246) or *Born to Rock* are also hilarious.

Or try Todd Strasser's **Mob Princess** series (starting with *For Money and Love*) about a girl whose dad is the head of the Mob—but she's the one running it.

Amid bodies in trunks and uncles with names like Fingers, Nose, and No Nose, Vince's life is no laughing matter. Korman's novel, on the other hand, is a hilarious story of one boy's attempt to deal with the perks and pitfalls of being the son of a Mob boss.

Up until senior year, Vince has managed to stay away from the family "vending machine business." But a noble gesture to one of his father's "clients" gets Vince more involved in the business than he planned. Soon he finds himself uncharacteristically wheeling and dealing to save the kneecaps and other body parts of those in debt to his father.

Korman manages to mix in humor with the horror of what the Luca family business is really all about. Each clever plot string is dished out and wound together in a conclusion as delicious as a bowl of Vince's mother's spaghetti.

Dorian Cirrone, Author

THE SONG OF AN INNOCENT BYSTANDER

Ian Bone

Next?

Looking for JJ (UTBG 207) by Anne Cassidy is another great book that examines how a terrible event in childhood can have resonances in later life.

Noughts & Crosses (UTBG 252) (and sequels) by Malorie Blackman also vividly portrays young people dealing with guilt and remorse within a traumatic setting.

For a fresh perspective try *The Lovely Bones* (UTBG 213) by Alice Sebold, narrated by the young victim of a brutal crime.

Imagine that when you are nine years old you are one of the hostages in a siege—a man with a gun holds you and a bunch of adults who don't know you in a fast-food restaurant because he *HATES* the company that owns it. Imagine that you survive, and 10 years later a journalist wants to interview you. But imagine too that you have worse memories—and guilt—from that horrible event than anyone knows or imagines. Except the strangers who were with you.

This book examines terrible memories, and the reader experiences them with the young girl. Has she been damaged? Can she be healed? It's gripping, sometimes horribly so, but exceptionally real and moving.

Nicola Morgan, Author

SOPHIE'S WORLD   Jostein Gaarder

This amazing book starts with two simple questions: Who are you? and Where does the world come from? When 14-year-old Sophie finds these questions written on pieces of paper in her mailbox one day, her extraordinary journey into the history and mystery of philosophy is only just beginning.

If you thought philosophy was dull and boring, or only for big-brained geniuses—think again! It really is fascinating stuff, and it's so fundamental that it relates to everything we do. The story itself is full of suspense and excitement, with plenty of twists and turns, and it'll keep you thinking and guessing right to the end.

Kevin Brooks, Author

Next?

If you want to read more about philosophy, watch out! Many books tend to be a little stiff. But anything with the word "beginner" in the title is usually a safe bet.

The Bluffer's Guide to Philosophy is glib, very funny, and very useful!

Jostein Gaarder has written many books. Try *The Solitaire Mystery*, a philosophical novel with a dwarf.

SPEAK Laurie Halse Anderson

Speak is a very accurate tale of the psychological horrors that happen to one girl. The narrative starts once the event is in the past, where readers can feel the aftermath of what happened to Melinda Sordino. She has lost her friends and a lot of her will, her fear of what happened during a summer party haunting her continually. She believes there can be no escape. But step-by-step, she slowly regains her life, starting with the help of her eccentric art teacher.

The book is chillingly accurate, especially considering that it presents the worst-case scenario—Melinda is shunned by the richest, most popular people in school, and no one believes Melinda's side of the story. Uniquely written, this novel will pull in readers of all genres, as it did with me.

Alan Thierfelder, age 18

Next?

E. L. Konigsburg's *Silent to the Bone* also chronicles a teen whose traumatic experience has led him to abandon speech altogether.

Chris Lynch's *Inexcusable* (UTBG 175) is another novel about violence, except this one is told from the aggressor's perspective.

It Happened to Nancy is a true, anonymously written account of a young girl's similarly traumatic experience, edited by the same doctor who worked on *Go Ask Alice* (UTBG 136).

DEAR DIARY . . . BOOKS IN JOURNAL FORMAT

Angus, Thongs and Full-Frontal Snogging
by Louise Rennison

Bridget Jones's Diary
by Helen Fielding

Sloppy Firsts by Megan McCafferty

Witch Child by Celia Rees

I Capture the Castle by Dodie Smith

Flowers for Algernon
by Daniel Keyes

SPINDLE'S END   Robin McKinley

Next?

Robin McKinley has also retold the story of *Beauty and the Beast* in her book *Beauty* (UTBG 29).

And if you like complex retellings of traditional tales, try Adèle Geras's *The Tower Room* (UTBG 362). Or Angela Carter's *The Bloody Chamber*, a collection of short stories based on fairy tales.

For more magic with a twist, read *Wicked* (UTBG 390) by Gregory Maguire, which challenges our notions of good and evil.

You might think you know the story of *Sleeping Beauty* but you don't, not as Robin McKinley tells it. The country in which it takes place so drips with magic that every ordinary household tries to have a fairy on hand to control it.

Katriona's aunt is a fairy, but it is Kat herself who has the adventure, which involves rescuing a certain bewitched baby princess and keeping her in hiding till she comes of age. The last part of the book involves a cunning plan to outwit the wicked witch and becomes very surreal.

Don't be put off by the slow, intense pace at which the story unfolds: you'll find complex magic, romance, and loads of atmosphere.

Mary Hoffman, Author

The SPY HIGH series   A. J. Butcher

Deveraux College is an exclusive boarding school for teenagers with great potential. But not just academic potential—these teens are training to be secret agents. To those enrolled at Deveraux, it's known as Spy High.

Book one of the series introduces six new recruits—Bond Team—and we watch them face the demands of Spy High training, including battles against Stromfeld, a virtual reality megalomaniac villain. And Stromfeld, evil as he is, isn't the toughest challenge that Bond Team will face; there's a real villain out there too, a villain who creates horrific mutant monsters—a villain named Dr. Averill Frankenstein.

This isn't a book to read if you're looking for beautifully turned passages of descriptive prose, nor for detailed and sophisticated characterization; but if you want an exciting story, an easy read with breathless pace, they don't come any better.

Daniel Hahn, Editor

Next?

If you liked this you might want to move straight on to the next in the series: *The Chaos Connection*.

For another very special training school, how about Benedict Jacka's *To Be a Ninja*?

Or for a girlish twist on the spy adventure, try the **Spy Goddess** series by Michael P. Spradlin, starting with *Book One: Live and Let Shop*.

THE SPY WHO CAME IN FROM THE COLD

John le Carré

A classic spy story. It's a story of secrets and schemes, betrayals, double agents and triple agents, barbed-wire checkpoints, interrogations. The story twists and turns back on itself, as we try to work out whose side everyone is really on.

British secret agent Leamas is on one final mission to eliminate East German head of counterespionage Mundt; but it seems that Mundt may really be a double agent for the British. Except he isn't really. Except he is. Is he?

This is a world in which you can't trust anyone, can't believe anything they say. Leamas can trust only himself; his girl, Liz; and his boss, Control. But can he really? As he gets closer and closer to the nail-biting finale, the question of who his real friends are will take on the greatest importance imaginable. Seriously engaging stuff.

Daniel Hahn, Editor

Next?

For more spies and complicated plots, check out *Patriot Games*, one of Tom Clancy's Jack Ryan novels, or for another classic le Carré: *Tinker, Tailor, Soldier, Spy*.

For the opposite take on spies—this time heroic and glamorous rather than slightly dark and seedy—try the **James Bond** books (UTBG 181) by Ian Fleming.

A wartime story about boys who take their spying a little too seriously is Michael Frayn's *Spies*.

STAR OF THE SEA   Joseph O'Connor

Next?

For more stories about the Irish try Roddy Doyle's *Paddy Clarke Ha Ha Ha* (UTBG 265) or Seamus Deane's *Reading in the Dark*.

Herman Melville also wrote about life at sea in *Billy Budd* and his classic tale of the white whale, *Moby-Dick*.

This book tells the stories of the captain and passengers of the *Star of the Sea*, a ship sailing to New York in 1847. Through them, the author examines the misery caused by the Irish potato famine, one of the greatest disasters of the 19th century, which killed as many as one million people and forced another two million to emigrate. We see the issues through the eyes of all levels of society, from the fallen aristocrat eating fine food in first class to the peasants eating gruel below deck, who have had to sell everything they own to pay for their passage. In the background is a deeply political story of social upheaval, but the narrative is strong enough to make it feel like more of a murder-mystery than a historical document.

Anthony Reuben, Journalist

STARGIRL Jerry Spinelli

12+

I recommend *Stargirl*, unreservedly, wherever I go. It's a fabulous, lyrical, magical book about individuality and being different; about being yourself and having the maturity to allow everyone else to be themselves, too. It's also about being one of the herd, peer pressure, and the cautionary tale of what happens when you give in to that force and don't follow your own heart and your own star. Furthermore, it's a joyous story of first love, bittersweet and poignant, full of tension and emotion, beauty and tragedy, thrilling, inspiring, and a homage to nonconformity.

If ever there was a book that should be compulsory "rite-of-passage" reading for everyone, male and female, from age 12 to age 112, this is the one. Unforgettable.

Chris d'Lacey, Author

Next?

Love, Stargirl is the equally fabulous follow-up to *Stargirl*.

Milkweed is another, completely different type of novel from Jerry Spinelli.

Quirky reads are my favorites. I thoroughly recommend *Holes* (UTBG 157) by Louis Sachar, *Joey Pigza Swallowed the Key* by Jack Gantos, and *Saffy's Angel* (UTBG 299) by Hilary McKay.

STARSHIP TROOPERS Robert Heinlein

Next?

You'll certainly enjoy other books by Heinlein. Probably best to start with the early stuff—*Stranger in a Strange Land* and *The Moon Is a Harsh Mistress* are both pretty amazing, and he wrote some wonderful short stories, too.

For other great battles in space, read *Ender's Game* (UTBG 104) by Orson Scott Card, in which the hero goes through training before being thrown into the realities of war.

Try *The War of the Worlds* (UTBG 379) by H. G. Wells if you'd rather read about aliens invading your own turf.

Robert Heinlein is one of the founding giants of science fiction and if you want to know why, read *Starship Troopers*. Set 5,000 years in the future, on one level this is the story of how John Rico joins the military and learns to defend human civilization against the alien Bugs. But it is so much more than that. Heinlein spits out more ideas in a page than many writers put in an entire novel. You may not agree with them—Heinlein was very right-wing on some issues—but they are always well-woven into the story, which has rightly become one of the classics of science fiction.

Andrew Norriss, Author

STAYING FAT FOR SARAH BYRNES

Chris Crutcher

How far would you go for a friend? What secrets would you keep? In *Staying Fat for Sarah Byrnes*, Eric "Moby" Calhoune must make these decisions when faced with his friend's chosen muteness and psychiatric stay. Moby and Sarah Byrnes are both outcasts—Moby because of his weight and Sarah Byrnes for the scarring on her face. Now in their senior year, Sarah Byrnes has stopped talking, and that scares Moby.

   Like many of Crutcher's novels, *Staying Fat for Sarah Byrnes* tackles a host of issues that many teens deal with every day—abuse, religion, abortion, and suicide. While Sarah Byrnes (it is always her full name) is the main focus, no character escapes lightly. Crutcher's distinct blend of humor and seriousness keeps a book about so much sorrow readable, enjoyable, and ultimately hopeful.

Mary Ann Harlan, Librarian

Next?

Any Chris Crutcher is going to be a great read, but *Ironman* is especially poignant.

A Room on Lorelei Street by Mary Pearson and *Dreamland* by Sarah Dessen both deal with struggling teens and issues of abuse.

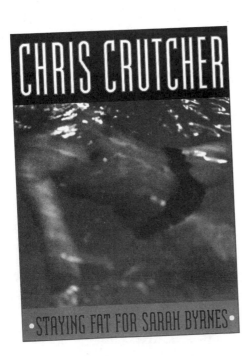

BOOKS THAT ROCK

Nick & Norah's Infinite Playlist by Rachel Cohn and David Levithan

High Fidelity by Nick Hornby

Just Listen by Sarah Dessen

Beige by Cecil Castellucci

Confessions of a Teenage Drama Queen by Dyan Sheldon

John Lennon: All I Want Is the Truth by Elizabeth Partridge

Fat Kid Rules the World by K. L. Going

King Dork by Frank Portman

A STEP FROM HEAVEN An Na

We have all had an experience where everything is new and intimidating, and we're afraid of taking that first step. Imagine, then, four-year-old Ju coming from her native Korea to the new country of Mi Gook, America, where everything, even the language, is new and surprising and a little frightening. An Na's Printz winner, *A Step from Heaven*, follows Ju and her family in their struggles to find their way in their adopted country.

Nothing is easy for Ju. She must protect her mother, younger brother, and herself from an abusive, alcoholic father who resists leaving the traditions of his old world behind.

Wonderfully woven through An Na's story are Korean words and customs so that just as Ju "learns" America, we learn something of Korea. We learn, too, that though culture and language may separate us for a time, if we open our hearts we find in one another the mirror image of our own selves.

Gloria Whelan, Author

Next?

Another Printz award winner, Gene Luen Yang's *American Born Chinese* (UTBG 16) also chronicles the difficulties of an Asian teen attempting to fit in.

Linda Sue Park's *A Single Shard* takes place in 12th-century Korea, but the ideals and beliefs of traditional Korean culture are much the same as in An Na's novel.

The Ultimate Teen Readers' Poll

BEST BOOK ABOUT RELATIONSHIPS

1 **The Sisterhood of the Traveling Pants series**

2 **The Girls in Love series**

3 *Noughts & Crosses*

4 *Romeo and Juliet*

5 **The His Dark Materials trilogy**

6 **The Princess Diaries series**

7 *Angus, Thongs and Full-Frontal Snogging*

8 *Sloppy Firsts*

9 *Twilight*

10 *What My Mother Doesn't Know*

THE STERKARM HANDSHAKE Susan Price

Like all great fantasies, *The Sterkarm Handshake* is simple. Every part clicks into place, making exact sense.

A multinational corporation develops the technology to travel into the past to exploit untapped resources, but fails to take into account the people they will encounter. The time tunnel is situated in the Borders. Twenty-first century scientists meet 16th-century Sterkarms: a fierce, amoral clan of border raiders who live by stealing and fighting. The Sterkarms think the scientists are elves, so that's all right with them.

Susan Price makes use of history, language, and myth, setting past and present at angles to act as mirrors, each world illuminating the other. The cultural differences can be very funny, but the implications are ominous and the consequences potentially tragic, not least for lovers Per and Andrea, caught between worlds.

Celia Rees, Author

Next?

Find out what happens next in *The Sterkarm Kiss*. It won't disappoint.

Or try the fascinating **Uglies** trilogy (UTBG 370) by Scott Westerfeld set in a futuristic conformist society.

For those who love classic fantasy based on myth and folk belief, try *A Wizard of Earthsea* (UTBG 394) and its sequels by Ursula K. Le Guin.

STORY OF A GIRL Sara Zarr

Next?

Harmless by Dana Reinhardt is another novel that deals with the fallout from a mistake, this time involving three friends and a lie.

Laura Ruby's *Good Girls* has a similarly frank message that having sex doesn't necessarily make a girl a "slut."

For the "first time" experience from a boy's point of view, try Gary Paulsen's *The Beet Fields* (UTBG 30), an autobiographical coming-of-age novel.

Three years ago, Deanna Lambert's father caught her in the back of a car with 17-year-old Tommy. Now 16 years old, Deanna is still the talk of her high school and is labeled "school slut," even though she wishes her past would disappear. Ever since that embarrassing encounter, Deanna's father hasn't looked at or treated her the same. Her older brother, the only one in her family she can talk to, is living in her parent's basement with his girlfriend and their daughter. Plus, Deanna's friends Jason and Lee are dating, which leaves her feeling like she is alone.

Sara Zarr writes about our need for redemption from all of our past mistakes and the importance of the people who stick with you through the rough patches in your life. This is the best book I have ever read. Anyone who has ever been in high school and made a mistake can relate to this book.

Laura Fox, age 16

STRANGE MEETING   Susan Hill

It's 1916, in the midst of World War I (which will be over by Christmas, so they're told). After three months' active service, John Hilliard returns to his family, wounded. Back at the front line he finds that his battalion has altered drastically—fatally. More changes occur, of which the most significant is meeting David Barton. Barton seems able to articulate a wealth of feeling that Hilliard never knew possible. He writes endless letters back home, describes heartfelt emotions about the brutality of war, and becomes close to Hilliard. Yet Hilliard still feels he does not understand him. Their bond intensifies as death looms ever closer. Compelling and devastating.

Jon Appleton, Editor

Next?

One of the most famous books about World War I is the brilliant *All Quiet on the Western Front* (UTBG 12) by Erich Maria Remarque.

Susan Hill wrote a bunch of short, brilliant novels and then stopped, in favor of other kinds of books. Seek out her early books, especially *I'm the King of the Castle* and the terrifying *The Woman in Black*.

Losing Julia by Jonathan Hull is another bleak book about World War I.

STRANGERS ON A TRAIN   Patricia Highsmith

Next?

Almost everything Highsmith has written is worth reading, particularly *The Tremor of Forgery* and *The Talented Mr. Ripley* (UTBG 348).

How about another book that Hitchcock filmed? Try Robert Bloch's *Psycho*.

Another great crime novel is Dashiel Hammett's *The Glass Key*, with its TB-ridden, gambling, drinking hero.

Two men get talking on a train. Both want somebody murdered. Each needs a perfect alibi. So they agree to swap murders. Or at least one of them—an alcoholic named Bruno who turns out to be a psychopath—thinks they've agreed. So he carries out the murder. Complications arise . . .

Highsmith's a great suspense novelist rather than a crime writer, and this novel was ideally suited to become a fine Hitchcock film with a script by Raymond Chandler. I can't easily explain why I'm so drawn to her work, which shows remarkable sympathy for sociopaths, yet little for her own sex. Her work is dark, laconic, unsettling, and almost always gripping.

David Belbin, Author

STRIPES OF THE SIDESTEP WOLF

Sonya Hartnett

This is a novel to read slowly, taking in the detail of the Australian landscape and wildlife, lingering over Hartnett's striking and original imagery, and letting the story work its way quietly into your mind. The story moves between three main characters: 23-year-old Satchel O'Rye; Chelsea Piper, sister of his best friend, Leroy; and the wolf of the title. All three are outsiders, all are struggling to survive in a place under threat: a little town that has been bypassed by the new highway, causing businesses to fail and families to move away. Satchel's difficult, complex relationship with his family (and his dog, Moke) is very well described. Satchel and Chelsea's developing connection with the "wolf" becomes the clue to their own survival, and ultimately a symbol of hope.

Julia Green, Author

Next?

Try *Thursday's Child* (UTBG 358) by the same author and see what an original and challenging writer she is.

She also wrote *Surrender* (UTBG 344), a book about friendship, the truth of memory, and a dog.

Or try *The Lastling* (UTBG 200) by Philip Gross, about a social club that eats rare species.

STUCK IN NEUTRAL Terry Trueman

Next?

For another character who has cerebral palsy, try Tracie Vaughn Zimmer's *Reaching for Sun* or *Small Steps* by Louis Sachar.

Love Terry Trueman? Try two more: *Cruise Control* or *Inside Out*.

Kissing Doorknobs by Terry Spencer Hesser looks at a teen with obsessive-compulsive disorder.

Shawn McDaniel has had to deal with a difficult medical condition, cerebral palsy, all of his life. He can think like a normal human being—he wants to tell his mother he is not in pain from his condition—but he can't walk or talk.

What kept me reading this story was the fact that Shawn believes his father wants to kill him. When Shawn was born, his father loved him but hated the condition. When he would go into his seizures, Shawn's dad would hold him and make sure everything would be all right. But now Shawn's seizures are getting more frequent.

This book helped me see how kids with CP can still have thoughts and feelings like we do, but they can't share them like we do. I'll never forget that Shawn was unable to hug his own father and unable to communicate his love for him. I feel as though I have gained an understanding toward people who cannot communicate. In my opinion, this book will definitely give you a new outlook on life and about how you see other people.

Cress Hanson, age 17

SUGAR RUSH Julie Burchill

14+

Next?

You'll find a more intense look at falling for another girl in *Oranges Are Not the Only Fruit* (UTBG 259) by Jeanette Winterson or *Annie on My Mind* (UTBG 20) by Nancy Garden.

Weetzie Bat (UTBG 384), part of the **Dangerous Angels** series by Francesca Lia Block, is about a group of friends/lovers living in LA.

Or for more streetwise girls trying to deal with life, read Catherine Johnson's *Face Value*, set in the cutthroat world of modeling.

Sugar Rush does exactly what it says on the cover. It's a high-speed, toxic slice of teen life, an emotional melting pot, a story that's so evocative you can smell the perfume, taste the vodka, hear the soundtrack. This is Julie Burchill's first teen novel, although she's been writing (mostly journalism) since punk rock upset the music-biz applecart back in the 1970s. Her debut follows Kim, who, having had to move schools, meets, falls for, and has a full-on relationship with Maria, aka Sugar. The book, which has no pretensions to be anything but as entertaining as possible, is set in England and holds a very honest mirror up to what it's like to be young and in lust.

Graham Marks, Author

THE SUPERNATURALIST Eoin Colfer

12+

The Supernaturalist is an exciting and intriguing book about Cosmo Hill, who lives in Satellite City, the city of the future. Cosmo is an orphan, stuck in an orphanage where the inhabitants are used to test new products. Statistics say he has only about a year to live—unless he escapes. He succeeds but nearly dies in the process, and he is found by the Supernaturalists, a group of youngsters who save people by shooting at the invisible parasites that come to the scene of accidents and suck life from the injured. When the Supernaturalists realize that Cosmo can see the parasites too, they allow him to join their group. I loved this book and its unusual characters and was entranced while reading it.

Adam Cohen, age 13

Next?

If you enjoyed this book you will love *The Wish List* or *Artemis Fowl* (UTBG 24) by the same author.

For something a little darker, try Garth Nix's *Sabriel* (UTBG 298) and its sequels.

If you liked the James-Bond-style adventure, try *SilverFin* (UTBG 322) by Charlie Higson, about young James and his first journey into the world of the spy.

SURRENDER Sonya Hartnett

surrender

SONYA HARTNETT

Surrender isn't a pretty book. But it is beautiful and powerful, dark, and elegantly written. And yet, I read so many posts online from readers that are disgusted by it. I am not saying anyone is wrong or discounting those emotions—in fact, the readers that react this way tend to be the norm. I am struck, however, that it's not only in fiction, but in how adults react to children in the justice system in real life, that mirrors this reaction.

In *Surrender* we meet Anwell, who renames himself Gabriel when he meets the forest wild child Finnigan, who vows to do bad deeds to the people who would harm them. Gabriel's parents are unloving, remorselessly punishing adults, and there's a dirty secret about their younger, deceased son.

We read books like *America*, *The Rules of Survival*, or *Little Chicago*, and we heap praise on them. Is there anything in these books that is by nature less awful than *Surrender*? There are burnings, rapes, beatings, neglect—but they happen to children. And we have some redemption in the end. But, if a book deals with a child or teen who turns on an adult—suddenly the book disgusts, angers, upsets the readers. And in the courts, a 14-year-old is suddenly an adult if this happens in real life.

What I think Hartnett wrote about was the story of parents that killed a child. In every way but physical, they killed Anwell. He has no moral compass, he has no joy, no love, nothing to stop him.

I find *Surrender* a beautifully written book about the damage done when someone withholds love from a child. But books like this frighten us. They don't soothe. In my mind, that doesn't reduce their power.

Gail Giles, Author

Next?

For more excellent fiction by Sonya Hartnett, try **What the Birds See** (UTBG 386) or **The Silver Donkey**.

33 Snowfish (UTBG 2) by Adam Rapp is another novel in which a child takes action against his parents—a difficult and shocking novel.

Han Nolan's **Born Blue** follows an emotionally devastated girl through her search for stardom and love.

SWEEP: BOOK OF SHADOWS Cate Tiernan

This is the first in a long teen series that is both addictive and very spooky. Sixteen-year-old Morgan is smitten when Cal Blaire, a real hottie, transfers to her school and throws a party in a huge field to which everybody goes. Around the campfire, he asks them to join him in a Wiccan thanksgiving ritual. Reactions range from curiosity to fear. Most leave but others, including Morgan and best friend Bree, stay. Some are curious about Wicca. Some are attracted to others present and want to stay near them. And some, like Morgan, have more complex motivations. She's an orphan and curious about her origins, and it turns out Wicca might hold all the answers.

John McLay, Literary Scout

Next?

Read on about Morgan in the rest of the Sweep series. Next is *The Coven*.

Holly Black's *Tithe* (UTBG 359) is a powerful drama with more magic and supernatural excitement.

Witch Child (UTBG 393) by Celia Rees is a historical story featuring a teenager accused of being a witch.

The Minister's Daughter (UTBG 227) by Julie Hearn delves into a period of history when it was unsafe to be different.

A TALE OF TWO CITIES Charles Dickens

I'd read a few Dickens books, and enjoyed them, but hadn't been blown away. Then I read this and my opinion of him changed completely. This is a masterful, suspenseful novel with more twists than any modern thriller. Set at the time of the French Revolution, the two cities are Paris and London, and the story centers on a few unfortunate individuals who get caught up in the madness of the time. Both epic and personal, this is a book that will take your breath away. Plus, it has maybe the strongest opening and closing lines in all literature! Brooding and incisive, it also boasts some sly scenes—the revelation of why one character always has dirt under his nails had me howling out loud with laughter! Even if you think you don't like Dickens, read this book!

Darren Shan, Author

Next?

More Dickens? Try the very different *Nicholas Nickleby*.

Fleshmarket (UTBG 120) by Nicola Morgan brings a cruel, gory, and brutal 19th-century Edinburgh to life.

Or for another classic about the French Revolution, try Baroness Orczy's *The Scarlet Pimpernel* (UTBG 303).

HORROR AND GHOST STORIES—
Spooks, Crooks, and Mystery Books
by Hugh Scott

Listen. Weird things happen. I was sitting alone and a pen rose up off the arm of an armchair, then it dropped to the floor. When I was in elementary school my best friend passed me on the stairs, and when I got to the playground, he was walking along the sidewalk.

Other strange events have stirred my imagination; but the main fascination for me is this: if such things can happen, then there is more to life than being born, doing things, and then dying. So I write spooky stories. I love to be involved in puzzles that gradually reveal solutions.

When I wrote *The Place Between*, I was creating a ghost story in which somebody walked through walls, and somebody else disappeared before the eyes of startled witnesses. These things happen; but when you write them as a story you

must explain how it all works; and I was astonished to discover, when the book was finished, that I had come up with an explanation for ghosts.

And this is what writing (and reading) are about: *discovery*! Finding out what is possible, and occasionally revealing an answer to a great mystery. Aren't we all fascinated by mystery? Isn't every child and adult at least slightly curious about the Loch Ness monster? And UFOs?

We are always asking questions, and sometimes we find answers. Then we dig into the next mystery, swiftly and keenly, because we love the unknown. If there is no mystery in our lives, we make one by writing or reading the next book, and send the hairs on the back of our necks rising in terror.

Let me tell you this: if you love weird stories, go to your local Goodwill and look for volumes of ghost stories. Most of these

stories will be old-fashioned, like *The Upper Berth* by F. Marion Crawford, in which the storyteller books his passage to sail to America and finds that his companion in the upper berth is a drowned man, and he himself will be next to go overboard—unless he can find a way of escaping!

Or find perhaps "The Whistling Room," which is a scream-making tale of a room with a past—and also a horrifying present. My heart almost stopped beating when I was reading this amazing story. It was written by William Hope Hodgson. Some of the scariest stories of ghosts and the macabre were written a while ago—try E. F. Benson's *The Tale of an Empty House*; Edgar Allan Poe's *The Fall of the House of Usher*, or his *Tales of Mystery and Imagination* (UTBG 348); or Algernon Blackwood's *Ancient Sorceries and Other Weird Tales*. H. P. Lovecraft wrote short stories and novellas that take you into other dimensions, leaving you gasping with relief when you remember you are merely reading.

Books to stop you sleeping at night:

Interview with the Vampire by Anne Rice

Lord Loss by Darren Shan

The Wereling by Stephen Cole

Blood and Chocolate by Annette Curtis Klause

What Happened to Cass McBride? by Gail Giles

I Know What You Did Last Summer by Lois Duncan

Cell by Stephen King

Frankenstein by Mary Shelley

THE TALENTED MR. RIPLEY Patricia Highsmith

Next?

Patricia Highsmith wrote four follow-ups to *The Talented Mr. Ripley*; they are all good, but the first two, *Ripley Under Ground* and *Ripley's Game*, are the best.

A different Highsmith? Try *Strangers on a Train* (UTBG 341), about planning a perfect murder.

For another story with an antihero, try the difficult but amazing *Crime and Punishment* (UTBG 80) by Fyodor Dostoyevsky.

In 1950s Italy, a penniless young American named Tom Ripley charms his way into a group of rich, artsy expatriates. Tom's envy of his host's carefree life and beautiful possessions propels him into murder, several changes of identity, and a tense game of cat-and-mouse as he tries to evade the Italian police and his victim's family. Tom Ripley is a fascinating character: nervy, audacious, imaginative, and almost completely amoral. But despite his tendency to bludgeon people to death with blunt instruments, he never becomes a mere monster; this brilliant and unsettling book is written in such a way that you sympathize with Tom entirely in both his crimes and his panicky, improvised attempts to cover them up, and the short chapters and constant twists will keep you turning the pages right to the end.

Philip Reeve, Author

TALES OF MYSTERY AND IMAGINATION
Edgar Allan Poe

My aunt Nancy had a spooky bookcase in a dark corner of the hall, and among the books there was this one.

Now, I loved language when I was a boy; I loved the way words fitted themselves together in my mouth, and I loved finding words I didn't recognize; and in that volume Poe fitted words together with such precision that I was delighted; and as for words I didn't know—well, the stories were stacked with them and made reading his tales not only a journey into mystery, terror, and imagination but into a revelation of new language. Edgar Allan Poe's stories are still published, even though he lived in the early 19th century, and they are still as terrifying! Stories like "The Black Cat," "The Gold Bug," "Hop-Frog" and, oh, so many more. Treat yourself to a good scare. I dare you.

Hugh Scott, Author

Next?

For more tales of horror, try a short story or novella by H. P. Lovecraft. Start with the **Dream Cycle** stories.

How about scary stories in pictures? Start with the first volume of **The Sandman** series (UTBG 302) by Neil Gaiman and see how far you dare to go.

Or for a classic, try *Frankenstein* (UTBG 126) by Mary Shelley.

TALES OF THE CITY Armistead Maupin

Next?

The series is best read in order. *Tales of the City, More Tales of the City, Further Tales of the City, Babycakes, Significant Others, Sure of You.*

Maupin's *Maybe the Moon* and *The Night Listener* are good, too.

Edmund White's trilogy of fictionalized memoirs about growing up gay will be too explicit for some and loved by others; it starts with *A Boy's Own Story*.

I devoured Armistead Maupin's *Tales of the City* on a three-hour bus journey across Crete, then had to wait until I got home before I could read the next in the series. These novels, originally written as a newspaper serial, are compulsive reading: a soap opera about a San Francisco full of promise (and secrets) for gay and straight characters alike. They're insightful and enormous fun, with lots of mysterious twists and aspects that will challenge some readers' prejudices.

But overall the mood gets darker and the writing even better as the series progresses. Maupin's one misstep is when he sets one novel in the UK—*Babycakes*.

David Belbin, Author

TALES OF THE UNEXPECTED Roald Dahl

As well as his famous children's books, Roald Dahl wrote a series of fantastic short stories for adults, many grotesque and with a twist in the tale.

Billy Weaver, 17 years old, stays in a B&B run by a sweet old lady. Her hobby, it turns out, is taxidermy. Who knows Billy is there? His tea tastes a bit funny. . .

After the death of a crabby old professor, his brain is kept alive in a laboratory basin. It has one floating eye. His wife, whose life he has made a misery, wishes to take him home . . .

Mary Maloney, six months pregnant, kills her husband with a frozen leg of lamb then pops it in the oven. Detectives searching for the murder weapon eat it with relish . . .

Would you risk a bet with a smart, old gentleman? If you win you get his gorgeous Cadillac; if you lose he gets to chop off one of your fingers . . .

Great fun.

Alan Temperley, Author

Next?

Roald Dahl's children's stories can be enjoyed by anyone. Read *The BFG, The Witches,* and *Danny, the Champion of the World.*

H H Munro and O. Henry are two other fine writers of short stories. I am also a fan of the **Rumpole** stories by John Mortimer.

Or if you fancy something more macabre, try Edgar Allan Poe's *Tales of Mystery and Imagination* (UTBG 348).

TAMAR Mal Peet

14+

Next?

Between Silk and Cyanide by Leo Marks is the true story of World War II secret agents and their wireless codes.

Intrigued by special operatives in World War II? Try *Code Talker* (UTBG 74) by Joseph Bruchac, about the Navajo Native Americans who served as Marines.

Keeper (UTBG 190) by Mal Peet is completely different but no less absorbing.

1944: Two young Dutchmen code-named Tamar and Dart, trained in England by the Special Operations Executive, are parachuted into the occupied Netherlands to organize local resistance groups that are by no means united in their struggle against the invaders. The liberation of Europe is imminent but conditions are desperate.

Fifty years later, the suicide of Tamar sends his granddaughter in pursuit of a secret of identity enclosed in the events of that last terrible winter of the war. This is not a testosterone-fueled novel but a quiet, remorseless account of civilian heroism, of men and women living in continuous fear, driven to unthinkable acts.

Jan Mark, Author

TANGERINE Edward Bloor

12+

Paul Fisher is legally blind and wears thick glasses that only begin to help correct his vision. Oddly enough, he's also a really good soccer goalie. When his family moves to Tangerine, Florida, to position his football star brother for a shot at the NFL, Paul begins to question everything he took for granted. Why don't his parents see how genuinely evil his brother is? And how did Paul really lose his sight?

Tangerine is a novel of suspense, but this tension is not typically evoked. The descriptions of the Florida landscape and the town of Tangerine— where severe storms descend every day and sinkholes open up out of nowhere—make the town a character in itself. There's a sense of foreboding throughout the novel that I found absolutely delicious, like when it's hot and muggy and you can't wait for a good storm to clear the air.

Amy Pattee, Librarian

Next?

Since writing *Tangerine*, Bloor has published many novels; the one that comes closest to *Tangerine* is *Crusader*.

Stephen Fair by Tim Wynne-Jones mines similar territory and is concerned with the repressed memories of its main character.

Kirsten Miller's *Kiki Strike* (UTBG 192) also features deeply buried secrets and young narrators whose ages are belied by their intellects.

TANTALIZE Cynthia Leitich Smith

Darkly delicious, *Tantalize* offers a winning blend of werewolves, vampires, romance, betrayal, and Italian food.

The story is told from the point of view of high school senior Quincie Morris, whose parents died years ago and left her with a restaurant, Fat Lorenzo's. Unfortunately, Fat Lorenzo's is not doing so well, so Quincie's uncle devises a plan to "revamp" the restaurant into "Sanguini's: A Very Rare Restaurant."

The plot is crafted very carefully and develops slowly. The characters are devilishly original and they all have motivations hidden from view. *Tantalize* is written at a higher level than most YA books these days, and as such is a moderately challenging read. However, this only adds to the book's appeal, making it accessible for adult readers and more desirable for older teens who feel the need for "juicier" reads.

Robert Johnston, age 18

Next?

There are tons of other great horror-thrillers—try Stephenie Meyer's *Twilight* (UTBG 369), Scott Westerfeld's *Peeps* (UTBG 267), or Annette Curtis Klause's *Blood and Chocolate* (UTBG 40).

Elizabeth Kostova's *The Historian* (UTBG 154), in addition to being about vampires, is also a challenging read for an older YA reader.

TAYLOR FIVE Ann Halam

Is a clone a whole human being or just a photocopy of one? Taylor asks herself this question as she grows up at a remote jungle refuge for orangutans. From an early age she is aware that she was cloned so that her body tissues could be used to develop a cure for a terrible disease. Taylor finds this hard to take and refuses to meet her gene mother, an extraordinary scientist. However, Taylor's world is about to collapse as terrorists invade the refuge and she escapes into the jungle with Uncle, an intelligent orangutan. This is the start of a treacherous journey, and Taylor experiences fear and loss on the way to discovering her true self. Pain and violence are powerfully described in this action-packed sci-fi novel.

Noga Applebaum, Academic

Next?

Many books discuss the ethical dilemma presented by human cloning. Try *The House of the Scorpion* (UTBG 164) by Nancy Farmer or *Sharp North* (UTBG 316) by Patrick Cave.

My Sister's Keeper (UTBG 238) by Jodi Picoult is a contemporary novel about a young girl who is consistently asked to be a donor for her ailing sister.

TEARS OF A TIGER Sharon M. Draper

It's almost too horrific to imagine what life would be like after accidentally killing your best friend in a drunk-driving accident. But such are the circumstances of Andy Jackson's painful reality. Guilt consumes him. Loneliness pervades every waking moment. Anger, deception, and wild mood swings distance him from his friends, his teachers, and even his girlfriend. Told exclusively in dialogue, poems, essays, letters, and diary entries, this deeply affecting book is impossible to put down.

The most interesting aspect of the book, however, is the honest and direct manner with which the urban African American experience is depicted. Characters speak frankly about what it feels like to be followed in department stores, and question why there's no such thing as a black department-store Santa, and why evil fictional characters are represented by the color black.

Judy Goldschmidt, Author

Next?

The other two books in the **Hazelwood High** trilogy, *Forged by Fire* and *Darkness Before Dawn*, should not be missed.

Sharon G. Flake's *The Skin I'm In* (UTBG 326) is also a profound book about race and self-perception.

Another boy loses his best friend in Chris Crutcher's *The Sledding Hill* (UTBG 327).

TENDER IS THE NIGHT F. Scott Fitzgerald

Next?

Another Fitzgerald? Try *The Beautiful and the Damned* about a wild, rich couple whose lives fall apart when they run out of money.

Another great novel about mental instability is Sylvia Plath's *The Bell Jar* (UTBG 32).

The landmark work on psychoanalysis is Freud's *The Interpretation of Dreams*; but there's also a condensed, more manageable version, the 25-page "On Dreams," which is fascinating. (You can find it in Peter Gay's *The Freud Reader*.)

This had a huge impact on me as a teenager because it is about the fine line we all walk between sanity and madness. I spent months marveling that the only thing that stopped me driving my car into a brick wall or a knife into the heart of my boyfriend was the fact that I am sane. Dr. Dick Diver's affair with Nicole Warren echoes Zelda Fitzgerald's relationship with her psychiatrist and is a compelling examination of moral breakdown, and of how society shuns those it considers weak, whether mentally or morally. And of course it's so beautifully written that it leaves a glimmer in your heart like a diamond necklace.

Raffaella Barker, Author

TERRA INCOGNITA Sara Wheeler

Next?

More classic travel writing? Try Robyn Davidson's *Tracks* (about crossing Australia on a camel), Bruce Chatwin's *Songlines*, and Patrick Leigh Fermor's *A Time of Gifts*, (about walking across Europe in the 1930s).

The best account of the Scott expedition, by a man who was on it, is *The Worst Journey in the World* (UTBG 399) by Apsley Cherry-Garrard.

This travel book has everything: eye-opening descriptions (Antarctica—the Terra Incognita of the title—is "intact, complete and larger than my imagination could grasp"); very funny characters, including José, who married his Harley Davidson, and the penguin experts who can tell individual penguins apart; and there's even a recipe for Antarctic bread-and-butter pudding. The author spent months with polar scientists, who are as much a part of her story as are the famous explorers whose lives she recounts. Incidents range from the funny—the seal that unexpectedly pops up through the ice-hole latrine—to the sublime—playing Beethoven's *Fifth* in the virgin landscape.

A warning: you might not think you're interested in Antarctica now, but after this book you will be.

Jane Darcy, Teacher

TESS OF THE D'URBERVILLES Thomas Hardy

Maybe the best known of Hardy's novels set in his semi-fictional county of Wessex, *Tess of the D'Urbervilles* is both beautiful and sad. The story draws the reader quickly into the life of Tess Durbeyfield, an unassuming servant girl who comes to discover that her true heritage lies with the powerful D'Urberville family. But this is no joyous rags-to-riches story. Tess is a tragic figure, manipulated and misled, and makes a striking heroine for this classic novel of suffering.

The greatest strength of the book is the poetry of Hardy's writing, with which he creates wonderfully dark and mysterious atmospheres. Tess was Hardy's favorite heroine and this is a good place to start reading his work. But be warned! There are no happy endings.

Marcus Sedgwick, Author

Next?

If you liked this novel by Hardy, then there are many more to choose from—*Under the Greenwood Tree* and *Far from the Madding Crowd* (UTBG 112) are many people's favorites.

Another dark love story set against the backdrop of a wild landscape: Emily Brontë's *Wuthering Heights* (UTBG 402).

A Northern Light (UTBG 247) by Jennifer Donnelly is also about a girl (in the past) who gets involved in a murder.

THERE'S A BOY IN THE GIRLS' BATHROOM   Louis Sachar

No one likes Bradley Chalkers, so when new fifth-grader Jeff offers to sit next to him, you hope this will be the start of a friendship. But life isn't that simple with Bradley. His opening words to Jeff are, "Give me a dollar or I'll spit on you."

Bradley is so out of control he's sent to the school guidance counselor, Carla. To his surprise she doesn't criticize him, even when he's discovered in the girls' bathroom. Bradley's big moment comes when one of the girls invites him to her birthday party—his first invitation since that time he sat on someone's birthday cake.

This is a very funny book that might help you to understand why some people behave the way they do.

Jane Darcy, Teacher

Next?

Other funny and thoughtful books about troublesome boys include Louis Sachar's *Holes* (UTBG 157) and Jerry Spinelli's *Crash*.

A sadder (and harder) book is Cynthia Voigt's *A Solitary Blue*, about a boy torn between his parents. It's one of the **Tillerman** series.

THÉRÈSE RAQUIN   Émile Zola

16+

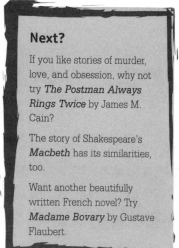

Next?

If you like stories of murder, love, and obsession, why not try *The Postman Always Rings Twice* by James M. Cain?

The story of Shakespeare's *Macbeth* has its similarities, too.

Want another beautifully written French novel? Try *Madame Bovary* by Gustave Flaubert.

Passion, murder, ghosts, and guilt—what more can a teenager ask for in a novel?

Thérèse lives with her sickly husband, Camille, and his adoring mother. Then Laurent comes into her life, and Thérèse throws herself into adultery, and ultimately the murder of her husband, with complete abandon.

But even Camille's death can't bring them happiness. His drowned ghost haunts them, standing in the shadows of their room night after night, turning their life into a constant nightmare, until in the end their passion turns to hatred.

This is a claustrophobic story steeped in atmosphere. I loved it when I was 15, and I love it now.

Catherine MacPhail, Author

THE THIEF LORD Cornelia Funke

12+

I was in desperate need of a good book to stop the line of mediocre ones I had been reading when a friend suggested *The Thief Lord* by Cornelia Funke. I was immediately enthralled. This story wraps you up and doesn't let you go until you finish the last page.

In the book you follow the characters of Prosper and his brother, Bo. They run away together when they find out that their nasty aunt wants to adopt Bo but not Prosper. The brothers escape to Venice, where they are taken under the wing of the Thief Lord, Scipio, and his gang of street children. Race along with these intense action scenes, and fall in love with all of the endearing characters. This book's twists will keep you guessing!

Allison Hawthorne, age 16

Next?

For more by Cornelia Funke, try *Inkheart* and its sequel, *Inkspell*.

Another fantasy set in Italy, Mary Hoffman's **Stravaganza** series takes readers on a similarly fast-paced journey.

Charles Dickens's *Oliver Twist* is also about street urchins trying to survive under the guidance of a gang leader.

Jonathan Stroud's **The Bartimaeus Trilogy**, starting with *The Amulet of Samarkand* (UTBG 17), does not disappoint for fantasy lovers.

THINGS CHANGE Patrick Jones

14+

Next?

For more novels that deal with the issue of teen violence, try Sarah Dessen's *Dreamland* or David Klass's *You Don't Know Me* (UTBG 403), which features a protagonist who is both the receiver and the giver of abuse.

Patrick Jones has written three more novels for young adults: *Nailed* (UTBG 239), *Chasing Tail Lights*, and *Cheated*.

Fault Line by Janet Tashjian also looks at an abusive relationship, and it's equally compelling.

Things Change is about a girl, Johanna, whose boyfriend, Paul, abuses her. Although she is really smart, Johanna is shy and she doesn't have a lot of experience with guys. Paul is two-faced, alternating between being angry and charming.

Johanna is so innocent that it made me feel enraged that Paul could seduce her into believing he could change. This book taught me that things do change sometimes, but usually not, and that the person you love must love you in return to make that love true. I believe that if you hurt someone you love, you truly do not love them. People cannot be blinded by a false sense of "love." *Things Change* is probably one of the most compelling novels I have ever read.

Bjorn Carlson, age 16

THINGS FALL APART Chinua Achebe

16+

Next?

The Song of Solomon by Toni Morrison begins with an African folk tale and transforms it into a quest for identity.

For an anticolonial view, read the masterpiece *Heart of Darkness* (UTBG 149) by Joseph Conrad.

More Achebe? Try *The Arrow of God*, about an Ibo village priest in conflict with the British in 1920s Nigeria.

"Okonkwo was well-known throughout the nine villages and even beyond." Thus begins *Things Fall Apart*. Okonkwo is a member of the Ibo tribe in an area of Africa now known as Biafra. The story of Okonkwo is in many ways the story of black Africa and its confrontation with white colonialism and Christianity.

When the story opens, Okonkwo has been a champion wrestler for more than 20 years. He is famous. He is feared. He is respected by all. His is the world of the rain forest: spirits and drums and unflinching tradition. Into this world comes the white man with his religion and guns and civilized ways. Okonkwo has met the match of his life.

Jerry Spinelli, Author

THIRSTY M. T. Anderson

14+

Bodies piling up around your town? Garlic hanging from your front door? Can't see your reflection in water? Has a celestial being been sent to give you a hand? Maybe you are like Chris, a teen whose Massachusetts town is getting ready for the annual Festival of Sad Vampires.

Would you believe that an entity from the "Forces of Light" could help you save the world? Could you trust an object called the "Arm of Moriator" to destroy a very powerful creature? Would you attend "a gruesome kegger of death" to accomplish this feat?

If you are brave enough, pick up *Thirsty* and see if you can escape the bloodlust! I dare you!

Kathy Fredrickson, Librarian

Next?

If you like your creatures of the night with a little spice, try Annette Curtis Klause's *Blood and Chocolate* (UTBG 40).

Can't get enough of that vampire stuff? Read *Peeps* (UTBG 267) by Scott Westerfeld and its sequel, *The Last Days*.

Maybe zombies give you chills. Check out William Sleator's *The Boy Who Couldn't Die*. Creepy.

THE THIRTY-NINE STEPS John Buchan

This is a classic thriller—a story of pursuit and escape. The hero, Richard Hannay, bored with his return to life in Britain, finds himself unexpectedly involved in an adventure in which he is hunted not only by the police for a murder he did not commit but also by a rather more sinister group bent on destroying Britain, and anxious (since he has clues to their identity) to eliminate him. He evades his pursuers with a variety of innovative disguises and hair's-breadth escapes, enriching his story with an account of his moods and responses, and with descriptions of the varying landscapes (especially that of Scotland), which themselves become part of the adventure. Despite certain racist elements (it was written a long time ago), this is a great story told at breakneck pace.

Margaret Mahy, Author

Next?

Another classic story that still grips is *The Riddle of the Sands* (UTBG 291) by Erskine Childers, one of the first spy novels to kick off this genre.

For more action-packed espionage novels, try Tom Clancy, starting with *The Hunt for Red October*.

Another adventure that starts with a mistaken identity is *The Prisoner of Zenda* (UTBG 281) by Anthony Hope.

Tamar (UTBG 350) by Mal Peet is about spies and espionage in World War II, and it's a thrilling read.

THIS BOY'S LIFE Tobias Wolff

14+

This story begins with ten-year-old Toby and his mother driving from Florida to Utah "to get away from a man my mother was afraid of and to get rich on uranium." In Utah it'll all be different—and to prove it Toby changes his name. From now on, we are to call him Jack. He's borrowing the name from Jack London.

Of course, Utah isn't what Jack expected. There's no fortune to be made, and his mother just ends up with another man Jack can't stand, the violent car mechanic Dwight. We watch Jack face those same challenges that we all have to deal with—how to find out who we are, to understand other people, to find our way in the world. In short, we watch him grow up.

Wolff's writing is simple and effective—and it's a true story, too. Ten-year-old Toby grew up to be a very fine writer.

Daniel Hahn, Editor

Next?

There's a sequel to this—*In Pharaoh's Army*—but I think you should go on to read Wolff's fiction instead. His short stories are very good; his novel *The Old School* is stunning.

Toby's brother Geoffrey has also written a memoir—*The Duke of Deception*; read it to find out about the other half of the family . . .

The Sea-Wolf by Jack London is about a literate, civilized man up against a brutal ship's captain.

THREE MEN IN A BOAT Jerome K. Jerome

14+

Next?

Other hilarious travel books include Pete McCarthy's *McCarthy's Bar* and Bill Bryson's *Neither Here Nor There*.

And don't miss another 19th-century classic, *Diary of a Nobody* by George and Weedon Grossmith.

Or one of the great American humorists—James Thurber. Anything he wrote, anything at all.

This is a comic classic. Three Victorian young men: the unnamed narrator, George, and Harris, together with Montmorency the dog, set off on a leisurely boat trip up the Thames. They've dreamed of picnics on riverbanks, evenings beneath the stars, and some comfortable nights at country inns. The reality is somewhat different, as the narrator finds when he accidentally takes an early-morning plunge in the river, or when Harris claims he's been attacked by 32 swans.

Along the way are memories of other mishaps, including the time when Harris said he knew how to get around the maze at Hampton Court (he didn't) and when he tried to sing a funny song without knowing the words. Priceless.

Jane Darcy, Teacher

THURSDAY'S CHILD Sonya Hartnett

14+

From the very first sentence, this remarkable book grabs you by the throat. The narrator is Harper Flute, telling of her childhood in rural Australia between the two World Wars when her father, a scarred survivor of World War I, brings his family to live on an almost unsustainable parcel of land during the Great Depression. Tin, Harper's young brother, becomes obsessed with tunnelling beneath the earth, and he is the pivot on which the story turns . . . "Born on a Thursday and so fated to his wanderings . . ."

This book has an immensely powerful realization of place, compelling characters, soul-tearing moments, and atmosphere that seeps into your life.

Theresa Breslin, Author

Next?

Read about a boy who uses fire as a way of dealing with the pressures in his life in Chris Wooding's *Kerosene*.

Of Mice and Men (UTBG 253) by John Steinbeck is a novel of the American Depression.

For a tale of staying alive in the Australian outback, try James Vance Marshall's *Walkabout* (UTBG 377).

TIME BOMB Nigel Hinton

Four friends experience one final summer of freedom before beginning junior high. But this is postwar Britain and the bomb site where they play hides a terrible danger.

The book is narrated by the grown-up Andy, but the story mainly concerns his friend, Eddie. When Eddie is betrayed by one adult after another, he swears his friends to secrecy and takes his revenge.

You'll find yourself thinking about this story long after you've put the book down. Not only does Nigel Hinton manage to conjure up the ghost of the long, hot summer of August 1949, but he lets you into the lives of Andy and his friends to such an extent that the epilogue comes almost as a body blow.

Unforgettable!

Laura Hutchings, Teacher

Next?

Richard Peck's *On the Wings of Heroes* provides an American perspective on World War II, as a boy from Illinois finds his place in a world at war.

Postcards from No Man's Land (UTBG 273) by Aidan Chambers offers a modern perspective on the same war, when a teen goes back to visit the battlefield where his grandfather died.

Another Nigel Hinton? Try the excellent *Collision Course*, about a boy who accidentally kills an old lady when he's out joyriding.

TITHE Holly Black

Next?

For the next two books from the world of Faerie, try *Valiant* and *Ironside*.

Faerie Wars (UTBG 109) by Herbie Brennan also takes readers into a differently imagined world of faeries.

For a different kind of eerie tale, try Laura Whitcomb's *A Certain Slant of Light*.

Tithe is a fresh approach to the traditional world of fairies. Holly Black captures not only the cunning and cheekiness of the fairy folk but also captures the magic and mystery of them. It is also refreshing to the reader to find out that our heroine is not an angelic, two-dimensional character, but a spunky and delightfully frayed creature from another world. I really enjoyed reading this book. The world of fantasy is only enjoyable if the characters and the fantastical world are able to rise out from the confines of the book and play out like reality. The fantasy world of *Tithe* manages to do this elegantly and convincingly.

May Aung, age 17

TO KILL A MOCKINGBIRD

Harper Lee

Scout was in grammar school when it happened—the thing that rocked her family and divided her sleepy Southern town. She is a patient storyteller, telling of the odd neighbors down the block with their dark history; her life in a single-parent household; the angst of a southern girl who doesn't have it in her to be a lady. And then there's her father, Atticus. If you're looking for father figures, like I was as a teenager, he's your man. This book changed my life and continues to challenge me as a writer and a reader. It introduced me to characters of honor who stood for their ideals despite raging injustice. This is a stunning story about childhood colliding with ignorance and prejudice, and the grace people need to build a better world.

Joan Bauer, Author

This is one of those astonishing books that stay with you forever. Set in the Deep South during the Great Depression of the 1930s, it tells the story of Scout and Jem Finch and their father, Atticus, a lawyer who defends a black man wrongly accused of raping a white girl.

On one level, it's a seemingly simple tale about the fears and prejudices of a small-town community, and how one man stands up for what he thinks is right; but within that simplicity there's so much more. It's a story about innocence and growing up, about conscience and courage, about seeing the world for what it is.

Wonderfully told by nine-year-old Scout, *To Kill a Mockingbird* has everything you could ever want in a book: a gripping story, strong emotions, engaging characters, and—best of all—that very special feeling of being alive.

Kevin Brooks, Author

Next?

A Separate Peace (UTBG 310) by John Knowles brilliantly brings to life the world of a wartime boarding school.

John Steinbeck's *Of Mice and Men* (UTBG 253) is also set in the South and is about difference and acceptance.

If you liked the style and subject matter of *To Kill a Mockingbird*, you should enjoy *Peace Like a River* (UTBG 267) by Leif Enger.

For another stunning book set in 1930s America, try *The Grapes of Wrath* by John Steinbeck.

Harper Lee published only one book, but try *In Cold Blood* (UTBG 174) by Truman Capote. Lee and Capote were good friends, and she helped him research his book.

The Timeless Classic of Growing Up and the Human Dignity That Unites Us All

TO KILL A MOCKINGBIRD
Harper Lee

TOUCHING THE VOID Joe Simpson

An astounding adventure story, with the extra-special ingredient of being true. Author Joe Simpson and fellow mountaineer Simon Yates tackle one of the highest unclimbed peaks in the Peruvian Andes. They get to the top, but on the way down Joe falls and breaks his leg. Simon, in an astonishing feat of bravery, somehow manages to lower him down, until Joe topples over an edge and is left hanging in space. Simon, tied to him, is being slowly pulled off the mountain and is eventually forced to break the last rule of mountaineering—he cuts the rope. Convinced Joe's dead, Simon descends, but meanwhile Joe, showing quite incredible courage and determination, tries to crawl to safety.

This is a riveting and inspiring read, even if you've never climbed higher than to the top of a stepladder.
Malachy Doyle, Author

Next?

More mountaineering? Try *The Kid Who Climbed Everest* by Bear Grylls, the youngest Briton at the time to have climbed Everest.

Or more by Joe Simpson— try *Dark Shadows Falling*, which reflects on recent mountaineering tragedies.

Or for more snow (but with fewer peaks), Sara Wheeler's *Terra Incognita* (UTBG 353)—about Antarctica and the men and women who have tried to understand its wilderness.

TOURIST SEASON Carl Hiaasen

Next?

Native Tongue by Carl Hiaasen—more low-life high jinks from the Sunshine State. He also writes for younger readers; try *Flush*.

Me Talk Pretty One Day by David Sedaris—everyday confessions of an ordinary guy who happens to be hugely funny.

Or try an Elmore Leonard book—more Florida, more guns. Start with *Rum Punch*.

A critic once wrote that Carl Hiaasen's comedy thrillers are "better than literature" and I agree wholeheartedly. I read *Tourist Season* after a weighty Russian classic about long winters and thin gruel. To find myself in the sweltering heat of Florida was refreshing, and the anarchy and savage exuberance packed into the story came as a revelation. A native son of the state itself, Hiaasen's novels rage against the destruction and corruption of his beloved environment. In this, his first novel, it's Florida's tourist industry that he picks apart with glee.

Just don't read it in company. You'll laugh and snort and hoot so much that everyone will want you to explain what's so funny.
Matt Whyman, Author

THE TOWER ROOM Adèle Geras

Next?

Second in the series is *Watching the Roses*.

Fairy tales make fabulous dark novels: try *Beauty* (UTBG 29) by Robin McKinley for suppressed passion and exquisite prose.

Or slightly darker than these novels, try *The Magic Toyshop* (UTBG 214) by Angela Carter.

Think you are too old for fairy tales? Not the kind Adèle Geras writes. In her magical Egerton Hall Novels, she brings well-loved stories such as *Rapunzel*, *Sleeping Beauty*, and *Snow White* right up to date. Well, not quite—her stories are set in the early 1960s in a boarding-school world of common rooms and tea with the headmistress. But don't let that put you off—the emotions experienced by her three main characters, Megan, Alice, and Bella, are totally current as they fall in and out of love, fear for their lives, or grapple with the process of growing up in a world that's becoming far too sheltered for their liking. *The Tower Room* is my favorite of the trilogy; the title refers to the bedroom shared by the three girls at school, a room that feels very safe and secluded until one day when Megan looks out of the window and her life changes forever. And the unexpected ending will leave you desperate to know what happens next . . .

Rosie Rushton, Author

A TOWN LIKE ALICE Nevil Shute

This story begins with a lawyer trying to trace a woman who is due to inherit a fortune. When he finds her, Jean Paget turns out to be a simple typist—but like all Shute's "ordinary" people, Jean is not really ordinary at all. As a prisoner of the Japanese during the war, she saw and did some extraordinary things, and how she decides to spend her money is even more extraordinary.

This is a war story and a love story combined. It moves at a slow and gentle pace, but be patient. It is a brilliant yarn about a woman determined to use all her resources to heal and create, after a period in history that had seen so much hatred and destruction.

Andrew Norriss, Author

Next?

You'll probably enjoy another Nevil Shute book, *On the Beach*, about life after a nuclear war.

If you are interested in World War II in the Far East, read *Quartered Safe Out Here* by George Macdonald Fraser. Or for a true story of life in a Japanese POW camp, try *The Railway Man* by Eric Lomax.

TRAINSPOTTING Irvine Welsh

16+

Next?

More dark Scottish writing? Alan Warner's *Morvern Callar* begins with a girl waking up next to her dead boyfriend (and a great deal of money).

Moving south to England, Jonathan Coe's *The Rotters' Club* is a bittersweet story of the adolescence of four schoolboys.

Other Irvine Welsh? Try *The Acid House*, a collection of dark short stories.

Trainspotting is about a group of drug addicts, the levels to which they'll stoop to get drugs, and how drugs dominate their lives. It doesn't glamorize drug taking; in fact, quite the reverse, it tells the story of life under the influence—exciting, dangerous, ruinously destructive, all-consuming, and ultimately soul-destroying. But it's told in such a fascinating way that you're ripped along without stopping to make judgments as you go.

This is a roller-coaster, hair-raising read—its energy, vitality, and rawness make it so fresh and new. The language, once you've got a handle on it, is evocative of the lifestyle. It gives you such an immediate sensation of the world the characters inhabit you really feel as if you're right in there with them—which, thankfully, you're not. It's daring, thrilling, frightening, and very funny.

Arabella Weir, Author

TREASURE ISLAND Robert Louis Stevenson

12+

Treasure Island is a perfect story of exotic adventure. It starts on homely dry land—but coastal—at the Admiral Benbow pub. The innkeeper's young son, Jim Hawkins, tells the tale and is its daring hero. Mystery, dread, and tension build up with the arrival of Blind Pew, *tap-tapping* his way to deliver "the black spot," a doom of execution, to a double-crossing old shipmate. We realize that these are pirates on the track of treasure. But it's Jim who lays hands on the essential treasure map and, with the local squire and doctor, sets sail. Chief among their rascally crew is one-legged, parrot-on-the-shoulder Long John Silver: he conceals black treachery under geniality and seeming honesty and helpfulness. No wonder there is bloodcurdling action on Treasure Island!

Philippa Pearce, Author

Next?

If the character of Long John Silver fascinates you, try Stevenson's *Dr. Jekyll and Mr. Hyde* (UTBG 95), a chilling story of good and evil.

More pirates? What about *girl* pirates? Try *Piratica* by Tanith Lee, about a girl who almost by accident becomes a pirate, or *Pirates!* (UTBG 271) by Celia Rees.

Okay, more *boy* pirates? Try Brian Jacques's *Castaways of the Flying Dutchman* or H. Rider Haggard's *King Solomon's Mines*.

A TREE GROWS IN BROOKLYN

Betty Smith

I don't remember how I came across *A Tree Grows in Brooklyn* but I do remember how the story stayed with me a long time afterward. The book is set in Brooklyn, New York, at the turn of the 20th century. It focuses on Francie Nolan and her younger brother, Neeley, through their poverty-stricken childhood. Guided by their hardworking, determined mother, Katie; their handsome but drunk father, Johnny; and their wonderful but wanton aunt Sissy, the children, like the hardy Trees of Heaven growing through the Brooklyn gutters, struggle to reach the sky. Problems are overcome with tough love, tenderness, humor, and in one powerful incident, carbolic acid and a bullet.

Helena Pielichaty, Author

Next?

Try *My Childhood* by Maxim Gorky—a Russian account of childhood poverty, beautifully and movingly told.

Angela's Ashes (UTBG 17) by Frank McCourt is the story of a poor Irish family.

For a modern Irish story set in Ireland, try *A Swift Pure Cry* by Siobhan Dowd.

TRICKSTER'S CHOICE Tamora Pierce

Next?

For the next novel in the series, try Tamora Pierce's *Trickster's Queen*, or try her **Song of the Lioness** series.

For two more fantastic fantasies, try Jeanne DuPrau's *The City of Ember* (UTBG 72) or Cornelia Funke's *The Thief Lord* (UTBG 355).

Sixteen-year-old Alianne hates being the daughter of national legend Alanna the Lioness. Aly dreams of being a spymaster like her father, but her parents definitely do not understand or approve. After a major family fight, Aly gets kidnapped by pirates and sold into slavery. There, she discovers a land of mystery and conspiracy, where even the gods are at war. Aly must make a bargain with the treacherous trickster god Kyprioth—a bargain that thrusts her directly into a dangerous civil war. She must use all of her wits and skills to save her own life and help free a captive nation.

Tamora Pierce always delivers magical stories with powerful, intelligent female characters who fight like nobody's business. *Trickster's Choice* reads like a fast-paced spy novel, full of twists and turns. Imagine trying to save a world when the very god who "hired" you can't be trusted! Aly rocks. If my world's ever in danger, I'm calling her first.

Susan Vaught, Author

TRIGGER Susan Vaught

Jersey Hatch did the unthinkable: he shot himself in the head. He survived the pull of the trigger—but not without consequences. Now Jersey struggles with the mental and physical effects of his impulsive decision. Mentally, Jersey has the mind of a fifth grader, and physically, he has a paralyzed arm and leg, along with other problems. Jersey's greatest problem is that he can't remember anything that happened two years before he pulled the trigger.

    Trigger is told from Jersey's perspective. Read what he is thinking as he tries to recall the past two years of his life and attempts to uncover the reason why he shot himself. *Trigger* is a compelling story told from an original viewpoint. Jersey will keep your interest and steal your heart.

Shelbi Ball, age 16

Next?

For another inside-the-head read by an author who, like Susan Vaught, doubles as a therapist, try Chris Crutcher's *Whale Talk* or *Staying Fat for Sarah Byrnes* (UTBG 338).

Alex Flinn's *Breathing Underwater* (UTBG 51) is another psychological narrative with a troubled teen boy protagonist.

Susan Vaught's previous novel, *Stormwitch*, a blend of historical fiction and fantasy, takes place in 1960s Mississippi.

TROLL FELL Katherine Langrish

Next?

Look out for *Troll Mill*, Katherine Langrish's sequel to her first Scandinavian troll-fest. It has more chilly drama and fantasy.

The Sea of Trolls (UTBG 305) by Nancy Farmer is a blockbuster of a troll novel, with more dragons and Vikings (and, yes, trolls) than you can shake a stick at. (And have you ever tried shaking a stick at a troll?)

Twilight (UTBG 369) by Stephenie Meyer is an absolute must for any fan of novels that blend fantasy with believable human experiences. Follow up with *New Moon* (UTBG 241) and *Eclipse*.

In an unspecified Nordic landscape of fjords and extreme weather, Peer's life has suddenly been turned upside down. Before the ashes of his father's funeral pyre have even cooled, up turns one of his mean uncles who then drags him off to be kept as a virtual slave in a dilapidated mill. Peer's only solace is in the company of Hilde, a neighbor from a nearby farm—together they uncover Peer's uncles' devilish plot to steal troll treasure from the dark and magical Troll Fell—a course not recommended if one values one's life.

    This is a novel that is atmospheric, dramatic, stylish, and intensely engaging. It is at times gritty and bleak, but it is also magical and uplifting.

John McLay, Literary Scout

TROY   Adèle Geras

You probably know the famous story of Helen of Troy, whose face launched a thousand ships and inspired a bloody battle that lasted for 10 long years. If you don't, it doesn't matter. Geras tells you what you need to know and more: the inside story, the woman's-eye view, the best parts. Seen for the most part by two sisters, Xanthe and Marpessa, it shows the war affecting the lives of ordinary folk as well as famous ones. Fittingly it begins in the Blood Room, where Xanthe awaits the wounded from the latest battle—for blood runs through the story. But so does humor, friendship, and love. Stories within the great story, all vividly told, will keep you enthralled to the end.
Julia Jarman, Author

Next?

Something else by Adèle Geras? Try the sequel, *Ithaka*, or the **Egerton Hall Novels**, starting with *The Tower Room* (UTBG 362).

For a marvelous retelling of Homer's *The Iliad* (UTBG 173), read Rosemary Sutcliff's *Black Ships Before Troy*.

For more vividly told and fairly bloody historical fiction, try Nicola Morgan's *Fleshmarket* (UTBG 120), set in 19th-century Edinburgh.

TRUE BELIEVER   Virginia Euwer Wolff

Next?

If you enjoyed *True Believer*, you should go back and read the first book about LaVaughn, *Make Lemonade* (UTBG 215).

Joan Bauer also writes novels with strong female protagonists—try *Rules of the Road* or *Hope Was Here* (UTBG 160).

If you like novels told in verse, try anything by Nikki Grimes (*Dark Sons* [UTBG 88]) or Sonya Sones (*What My Mother Doesn't Know* [UTBG 386])—two talented writers with two very different styles.

LaVaughn is a typical teenage girl who is trying to figure out who she is and what her purpose is in life. She has her best friends, even though they barely agree on anything anymore, and her mother, who used to support her in everything she did before her boyfriend came along. LaVaughn comes to find out that life is not as easy as it once was. In a world where everything is changing fast, LaVaughn tries desperately to catch up. This book shows what it really feels like to be a teenage girl, all about the insecurities and awkwardness of growing up and becoming who you want to be for the rest of your life. It's about growing into your own skin and not just becoming who everybody else wants you to be, but becoming who you actually believe you should be.
Lauren Villarroel, age 17

THE TRUE MEANING OF CLEAVAGE

Mariah Fredericks

The True Meaning of Cleavage reminded me of Laura, my best friend since kindergarten. We ate lunch together every day and spent Friday nights sleeping over each other's houses, singing along with the stereo and dreaming of being stars. But the summer before high school, we stopped being friends. She had grown up, and I was the same girl I'd always been, which suddenly wasn't cool enough.

Reading the story of Sari and Jess brought those memories back to me. *The True Meaning of Cleavage* is a story of cleavage, the kind that occurs when something is split apart (in this case, two friends whose friendship is cleaved when Sari becomes hot and falls "madly, psychotically in love" with a senior guy), and also the kind that occurs when one wears a very low-cut blouse (in this case, Sari's). Jess's experience of losing her best friend to sudden popularity and "hotness" is a universal one. I related to the character of Jess, as I am sure many readers will too.

Alex Flinn, Author

Next?

For more by Mariah Fredericks, try *Head Games*, in which an emotionally scarred teenage girl finds new hope in an online role-playing game.

Ann Brashares's *The Sisterhood of the Traveling Pants* (UTBG 324) also explores the complexity of teenage girls' friendships.

Feeling Sorry for Celia by Jaclyn Moriarty also involves an overly confident, eclipsing best friend.

THE MONSTER OF MY DREAMS

Twilight & *New Moon* by Stephenie Meyer

Blood and Chocolate by Annette Curtis Klause

Tantalize by Cynthia Leitich Smith

Peeps by Scott Westerfeld

Interview with the Vampire by Anne Rice

Thirsty by M. T. Anderson

ttyl Lauren Myracle

Spend hours on end chatting with your bffs? Like 2 leave crazy away messages when u r gone (or don't feel like im-ing that certain someone)? This may be the book 4 u!

Meet Angela, Maddie, and Zoe, three high school sophomores faced with the daily stresses of school, boys, mean girls, peer pressure, and teacher crushes! By reading their instant messages, you'll learn how they survive all of these. Once you get hooked, no worries, there are two more books about these teen girls and where their high school experiences take them!

I would tell you more but I have g2g!

Kathy Fredrickson, Librarian

> ### Next?
>
> *ttfn* and *l8r, g8r* by Lauren Myracle continue the (mis)adventures of Angela, Maddie, and Zoe.
>
> *The Year of Secret Assignments* (UTBG 402) by Jaclyn Moriarty includes a plethora of ways teens communicate with each other.
>
> *The Sisterhood of the Traveling Pants* (UTBG 324) by Ann Brashares follows four young women, a pair of jeans, and emotional experiences!

THE TULIP TOUCH Anne Fine

12+

> ### Next?
>
> More Anne Fine? Try *Flour Babies*, a hilarious but poignant novel about a boy who learns about his own life through his class assignment.
>
> *Big Mouth* and *Ugly Girl* by Joyce Carol Oates and *Noughts & Crosses* (UTBG 252) by Malorie Blackman look, in very different ways, at the role prejudice can play in people's judgments about other people.
>
> *Fat Kid Rules the World* (UTBG 114) by K. L. Going is another take on the impact one person can make on another.

Natalie is a good girl. Tulip is not. But when their paths cross, the relationship is almost magnetic—Natalie simply can't resist her mesmerizing friend. As their story gradually unfolds, we watch, horrified, as Tulip pushes Natalie further toward the point of no return.

Anne Fine doesn't resort to histrionics or drama to tell her stories. The language of each sentence is as clear as a bell. Yet this story, like so many of her others, keeps us wondering long after we've closed the book. That's largely because we become so engrossed in the characters that their realness extends beyond the last page. But it's also because we wonder what we might have done, and how we would have reacted in the same situation.

Lindsey Fraser, Literary Agent

TWILIGHT Stephenie Meyer

You don't have to be a regular vampire novel fan to love *Twilight*. I know I'm certainly not, but this extraordinary book makes my top five favorites, hands down. Spanning somewhere around 500 pages, it was one of the quickest reads I've ever had. My eyes tore through the book; Edward and Bella's intense romance is just that captivating.

Stephenie Meyer has breathed life into her characters—even the undead ones—like no other author has before. Shy and awkward teenager Bella, the beautiful vampire Edward, and the rest of the Cullen family are all so easy to relate to, Meyer has half her readers desperately hoping—and often convinced—that there are actual vampires wandering around the country somewhere. Bella, a reluctant newcomer to rainy Forks, Washington, (literally) stumbles upon the secret world of a gorgeous family of "vegetarian" vampires, and is instantly charmed by the magnetic Edward Cullen, who puts most teenage boys to shame. As the two face emotional and physical challenges, and toy with the seductive lure of dangerous love, readers will find themselves equally seduced by the world Meyer has created. Basically, *Twilight* is just amazing—the best teen vampire/romance book out there. It will not disappoint.

Claire Easton, age 16

Next?

Definitely don't miss the next two books about Edward and Bella: *New Moon* (UTBG 241) and *Eclipse*.

Cynthia Leitich Smith's *Tantalize* (UTBG 351) is also a sensual love story that involves undead characters.

Or try *Wicked Lovely* by Melissa Marr—about the king of the faery world who falls in love with a mortal girl.

The UGLIES trilogy   Scott Westerfeld

12+

Science fiction and fantasy are littered with great premises that never go anywhere. In the Uglies trilogy, however, the writing is just as good as the ingenious conceit. Now that the Rusties (i.e., us) have fought and famined their way to extinction, the world population is much, much smaller—and cities are way, way cooler. (For instance, hover boards. Also, buildings floating in the sky.) In this futuristic society, everyone gets an operation when they turn 16 to become a Pretty—a blemish-free body with perfect facial symmetry and endlessly gorgeous eyes. The New Pretties get to party while the younger Uglies look on, desperately craving their own Pretty surgeries. But as Tally Youngblood soon discovers, there's more to the Pretty operation than just a new face, and some people choose not to live in New Pretty Town. Westerfeld's dystopian trilogy is a wonderful parable about beauty, of course, but these books also have a lot to say about religion, consumerism, and our present historical peril.

John Green, Author

Next?

If you enjoy dystopian societies, try Lois Lowry's classic *The Giver* (UTBG 135) or Jeanne DuPrau's *The City of Ember* (UTBG 72).

Try Scott Westerfeld's **Midnighters** series, starting with the first book, *The Secret Hour*. It's a blend of horror and science fiction that follows a girl, Jessica, who is born at the exact stroke of midnight, which gives her special powers to enter a mysterious 25th hour.

For more books about dystopian futures, check out our Top Ten list at the beginning of the book.

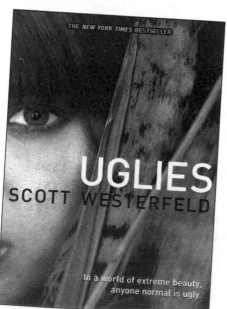

MY FRIEND, MY ENEMY

The True Meaning of Cleavage by Mariah Fredericks

The Boyfriend List by E. Lockhart

The Gossip Girl series by Cecily von Ziegesar

A Separate Peace by John Knowles

Define "Normal" by Julie Anne Peters

UNDERWORLD
Catherine MacPhail

God, what a scary book this is. You'll get sucked in by the first few harmless pages—school stuff, outsiders, little rivalries—and suddenly find you're in the middle of an appalling nightmare. But by then it's too late. You're hooked.

Underworld isn't blood 'n' guts scary—there are no vicious monsters, sharp-fanged Draculas, or anything like that—but what it has is much, much worse. It vividly portrays the terror brought by things you can't see, by things hidden in the shadows, when you find that you and your friends are trapped deep underground, in the darkness, and there are noises . . .

Daniel Hahn, Editor

Next?

To see the range of different books MacPhail writes, move on from this to *Dark Waters*.

Another spooky read is Susan Hill's chiller *The Woman in Black*.

Check out Darren Shan's **Demonata** series for another set of fast-moving, supernatural thrillers. Start with book one: *Lord Loss* (UTBG 208).

The Ultimate Teen Readers' Poll

BOOK WITH THE MOST EXCITING PLOT

1 **The Harry Potter series**

2 **The Alex Rider series**

3 **The Lord of the Rings trilogy**

4 **A Series of Unfortunate Events**

5 **The His Dark Materials trilogy**

6 *Skellig*

7 *Holes*

8 **The Artemis Fowl books**

9 **The Girls in Love series**

10 *Cirque du Freak*

AN UNSUITABLE JOB FOR A WOMAN

P. D. James

Next?

There are plenty more P. D. James books to choose from. Try *Cover Her Face* and *The Skull Beneath the Skin*.

James can be a little gory. If you want something gentler, go for Dorothy L. Sayers. *The Nine Tailors* is a good place to start.

If you want something bloodier than P. D. James, try Ian Rankin, whose **Rebus** books can be violent. Start with *Knots and Crosses*.

I read this book in one sitting on the night before my daughter Catherine was born. She has turned out to be a great fan of detective fiction, and I often wonder whether that last experience in the womb is to blame!

This is the story of Cordelia Gray, tackling the mystery of two apparent suicides: of her partner in a detective agency, and of a 21-year-old Cambridge student. It's a good introduction to the work of P. D. James, one of my favorite murder-mystery writers. Her books always have more to them than just the solution of a puzzle. Stick with them and her main character, the sleuth and poet Adam Dalgliesh, will become one of your best friends.

Eleanor Updale, Author

USEFUL IDIOTS Jan Mark

The year is 2255. Climate change has altered the shape of the world; whole countries and great cities are under water. What's left of Britain is now the Rhine Delta Islands, part of the United States of Europe. Jan Mark's wonderfully imagined new world order depends upon homogeneity; genetically engineered humans lead long and blandly pleasant lives. Anything that encourages nonconformity and individualism is deeply distrusted. Digging up the past to discover one's "primitive" roots is therefore a dangerous activity, and when a group of archaeologists unearth a rare intact skeleton on "Aboriginal" land they find themselves in deep trouble.

Part sci-fi, part crime thriller, *Useful Idiots* asks thorny and absorbing questions about what it takes to be an individual in a world submerged in historical and political amnesia.

Mal Peet, Author

Next?

For another book that looks into the future to make us consider the present, try *Exodus* (UTBG 107) by Julie Bertagna, about a girl who must save her family from floods caused by global warming.

Or try Arthur C. Clarke's *2001: A Space Odyssey*, which makes us question everything we know about our origins.

The House of the Scorpion (UTBG 164) by Nancy Farmer is a futuristic thriller on the subject of cloning. Or for another dystopia, try Aldous Huxley's classic *Brave New World* (UTBG 49).

V FOR VENDETTA

Alan Moore and David Lloyd

What if Guy Fawkes, the notorious British revolutionary who attempted to assassinate King George by blowing up Parliament, had succeeded? This dark, gripping graphic novel blends George Orwell's *Nineteen Eighty-Four* with Robin Hood. The mysterious "V" is a mask-wearing, Shakespeare-spouting terrorist, committed to bringing down the government in a 21st-century fascist Britain. On the very first page, he succeeds in blowing up the Houses of Parliament; but this is just the beginning of his plans. Evie, a young woman he rescues from a vicious police attack, gradually uncovers more about his extraordinary past. For he is a man betrayed, and he will stop at nothing to bring down those responsible. Evie herself is to play a key role in his schemes, one that no one could have predicted.

Ariel Kahn, Academic

Next?

Alan Moore and Dave Gibbons's *Watchmen* (UTBG 381) is about the end of superheroes and the beginning of the nuclear age.

Brave New World (UTBG 49) by Aldous Huxley explores a genetically engineered future.

Someone to Run With by David Grossman has two parallel stories: one about a boy who enters the criminal underworld in Jerusalem to try and return a lost dog; and the moving story of the girl to whom the dog belongs.

BREAKING BOUNDARIES

Doing It by Melvin Burgess

Smack by Melvin Burgess

Sugar Rush by Julie Burchill

Forever by Judy Blume

The Cement Garden by Ian McEwan

RACE IN YOUNG-ADULT FICTION by Bali Rai

When I was at school, finding books about ethnic minority characters was like a treasure hunt. I'd start at one end of the school library and search every shelf, scanning the titles for any hint of ethnicity. I'd take the promising novels off the shelf and read the blurb on the back, looking for tell-tale signs, such as Asian names or Caribbean settings. I'd study the covers too, hoping to see an ethnic face. Like most treasure hunts, most of the time I was doomed to failure. All the books seemed to me to be about middle-class white kids from posh families who never swore or worried about money. And mostly they never had nonwhite friends.

Someone gave me *A Little Princess* by Frances Hodgson Burnett, which did have an Indian character in it, but I didn't like it. And I'm not Indian. I am British and Asian. Where were all the characters that reflected my life, at home and at school? Finally I found books by Farrukh Dhondy and Bernard Ashley, and I was satisfied for a while. But I read those quickly and when they were gone, there were no more.

Today there are more books about all sorts of ethnic minorities but not as many as there should be. Reading rates among young men of Afro-Caribbean and Pakistani/Bengali descent in particular are very low. One of the reasons is that they don't find books that relate to them and their lives. Too often the characters that they do find are like those cell phone snap-on covers. The colors are different but the underlying component is universal. That's one of the reasons that I write about characters from different backgrounds to the literary norm—to try and represent the "real" voice of multiethnic teens—as do authors such as Benjamin Zephaniah, Malorie Blackman, Narinder Dhami, and Preethi Nair.

That is not to say that Asian youth, for example, should only read about Asian lives. That would be wrong. But they must feel as though their lives are a part of the literary tradition. And many of them do not. That is why race and writing about race is so important. To get nonreaders from ethnic minority backgrounds to start reading, you need to pull them in. One of the best ways is to give them novels about characters that they can relate to—real characters whose lives reflect the world at large today.

Not the middle-class utopia of boating lakes, boarding schools, and wizards but the streets of the inner city, which is where the vast majority of ethnic minority kids live.

Once books about such young people become a norm and not a speciality, only then can we start to say that race is truly represented in fiction. Things are changing from when I did my treasure hunts, but I still get young ethnic minority people asking me if I know of other books, like mine, which deal with their lives, their hopes, and their dreams. I'll only be happy when they stop asking me that question. And that is still a long way off.

A few suggestions:

Refugee Boy by Benjamin Zephaniah

Noughts & Crosses by Malorie Blackman

A Step from Heaven by An Na

American Born Chinese by Gene Luen Yang

Keesha's House by Helen Frost

Code Talker by Joseph Bruchac

Anita and Me by Meera Syal

How the Garcia Girls Lost Their Accents by Julia Alvarez

VANITY FAIR William M. Thackeray

14+

Next?

To find another book with the breadth and variety of *Vanity Fair*, you should move on to another Victorian novel—something like **Bleak House** by Charles Dickens.

If it's Thackeray's humor you like, you'll probably also enjoy Jane Austen's **Pride and Prejudice** (UTBG 276).

A modern American novel clearly influenced by *Vanity Fair* is Tom Wolfe's **The Bonfire of the Vanities**, set in 1980s New York.

Okay, so *Vanity Fair* is long. And it was written more than 150 years ago. But no other novel will repay you so richly for reading it. Why? Because it has everything—humor, drama (it covers the battle of Waterloo), and a fascinating cast of characters, including one of the most memorable ever invented—the classic antihero, Becky Sharp.

From the moment she leaves school and throws her copy of Dr. Johnson's *Dictionary* out of the carriage window, there are no rules for Becky. She uses her wits, her skillful reading of character, and her sly beauty to climb her way to the top of the rotting social pile that is London in the 1830s. But when she gets there, is it worth it? Read the novel and find out!

Sherry Ashworth, Author

VERNON GOD LITTLE D. B. C. Pierre

16+

Just when I start complaining that books don't surprise me anymore, along comes one like *Vernon God Little*. And *Vernon God Little* didn't just surprise me—it pretty much knocked me over. I don't know when I've last read a book with the freshness and fearlessness, the relish, the sheer hurtling momentum of this one.

It's the story of a teenager in a small Texan town, in the wake of a terrible school shooting. The town is Martirio, the barbecue-sauce capital of Texas.

The narrator's voice belongs to Vernon Little—and what a voice it is. Angry and sharp and smart and witty and profane, and with the power to blow away a stolid, cynical seen-it-all-before reader like me. It's a great feeling.

Daniel Hahn, Editor

Next?

For another distinctive and off-center American hero, try John Irving's brilliant **A Prayer for Owen Meany** (UTBG 274).

For a narrative voice that's energetic, captivating (and a little odd), try Patrick McCabe's dark and dazzling **Butcher Boy**, though for some of it you'll need a strong stomach.

And if you haven't read **The Catcher in the Rye** (UTBG 60) by J. D. Salinger, now's your chance. I think Vernon and Holden would have gotten along.

WALK TWO MOONS Sharon Creech

Sal (short for Salamanca) and her father moved a year ago, after her mother left "in order to clear her heart of all the bad things" and never returned. In this wonderful novel, Sal travels back with her gram and gramps to find her mother, and over the long journey across America to Idaho she tells them the story of her friend Phoebe; at the same time she is revealing another story, about herself. The ending of this story moves me to tears each time I read it.

There are great characters, funny bits, wise sayings: "Don't judge a man until you've walked two moons in his moccasins." Most important is Sal's utterly convincing voice telling the story. I loved this book!

Julia Green, Author

Next?

Other books by Sharon Creech—try *The Wanderer* (UTBG 378), about a yacht journey across the Atlantic, or *Chasing Redbird*.

To Kill a Mockingbird (UTBG 360) by Harper Lee is a wise, wonderful, moving story, which is also about seeing from someone else's point of view and has a strong female narrator.

Joan Bauer is another great writer; try *Hope Was Here* (UTBG 160) about a girl constantly moving from place to place.

WALKABOUT James Vance Marshall

Next?

Try *Hatchet* (UTBG 147) by Gary Paulsen—another exciting story about survival in the wilderness (Canada, this time); or Gillian Cross's *The Dark Ground* (UTBG 86), about a boy alone in a strange jungle.

Sonya Hartnett is a great Australian writer; try *Stripes of the Sidestep Wolf* (UTBG 342).

I read this as a teenager, and I loved it then for the descriptions of the Australian landscape—wild and remote, beautiful but also dangerous—as well as for the powerful story of what happens when two children crash-land in the middle of the Australian desert. They have no chance of survival: it's thousands of miles to Adelaide, where they were supposed to be going, in intense heat with no food and hardly any water.

And then they meet an Aboriginal boy, who knows everything about survival in this place. Yet the girl is full of fear. Their meeting is also the meeting of two very different cultures, and (without giving too much away) what happens is a tragic mirror of what has happened so often when people misunderstand and fear each other.

Walkabout was written back in 1959, and you'll notice some uses of language about race that we consider totally inappropriate today, but don't let that put you off this perceptive and moving story.

Julia Green, Author

WALKING NAKED Alyssa Brugman

Suicide isn't an easy subject, but *Walking Naked* tackles it head-on with starkly elegant, wry humor. Megan is one of the beautiful people; Perdita is the school outcast. Thrown together in detention, Megan is drawn to Perdita, who is unexpectedly funny, intelligent, uncompromising—and desperate. But when her friends force Megan to take sides, she shuns Perdita—and then must live with the consequences.

Megan's honesty about her own behavior—of which she's not proud—is painful, but this isn't a grim book. Perdita introduces Megan to poetry, a dialogue that underpins their unorthodox friendship, revealing Perdita's personality and Megan's growing understanding of herself—and of someone utterly different.

Helen Simmons, Bookseller

Next?

Track down *Lucas* (UTBG 213) by Kevin Brooks. It's about a mysterious, beautiful outsider who arrives on an island, but for some reason everyone hates him.

Girl, Interrupted by Susanna Kaysen deals with the feeling that you don't want to go on with your life.

Nick Hornby's funny and sad *A Long Way Down* is about four very different people who become each other's support group.

THE WANDERER Sharon Creech

Next?

For a slightly less realistic but truly captivating novel set on the open sea, try *Life of Pi* (UTBG 203) by Yann Martel.

Creech's *Ruby Holler* (UTBG 295) is also about family and loyalty, but it's more quirky and magical.

If you like swashbuckling adventure on the high seas, with some futuristic vampire pirates thrown in, look no further than Justin Somper's **Vampirates** series.

Sophie has persuaded her three uncles and two cousins to let her join them on a trip of a lifetime aboard *The Wanderer*—a 45-foot sailboat that they plan to sail north up the coast from Connecticut, then east across the ocean toward England, where Sophie's grandfather is looking forward to a visit from his three sons. Thirteen-year-old Sophie is an orphan, daydreamer, and headstrong tomboy, and an absorbing and intriguing main character. During several windswept weeks at sea, Sophie manages to inspire everyone around her, despite being on the very brink of coming to terms with her own fractured and half-remembered family history. The author's descriptions of the sea and of Sophie's emotional and physical journeys are first class.

John McLay, Literary Scout

WAR AND PEACE Leo Tolstoy

Count Tolstoy served as a military officer in the Crimea, but he turned against war and began the pacifist movement of which Gandhi was his most eminent disciple. He is also Russia's greatest novelist. He spent 10 years creating his masterpiece, *War and Peace*, an epic novel about Napoleon's invasion of Russia, seen through the lives of three aristocratic families. Tolstoy himself appears in the novel as the gentle, peaceable, bumbling Pierre Bezukhov.

Don't be put off by the length of the book, or by Uncle Reg's comment that he "started reading it once, but never finished it." This is one of the greatest books ever written, so it merits perseverance.

James Riordan, Author

Next?

After this massive book you may find yourself hooked on Russian classics. Move on to Tolstoy's *Anna Karenina* (UTBG 20) (tragic love story), Dostoyevsky's *Crime and Punishment* (UTBG 80) (tragic, thought-provoking thriller), or Mikhail Lermontov's *A Hero of Our Time* (psychological tragedy).

Or for something epic and not tragic at all, Vikram Seth's *A Suitable Boy*, set in India—many families and many classes and many generations (and many pages)—a great and glorious read.

THE WAR OF THE WORLDS H. G. Wells

Imagine invaders from Mars arriving at the end of your street! H. G. Wells's science-fiction adventure will have you on the edge of your seat as sinister cylinders rain down from space on South London and slowly unscrew to reveal Martians brandishing heat-rays . . .

The narrator of this story is one of the first to witness the Martians' war machines—huge tripods—stalking across the scorched heathland near his former home. Meeting up with a fellow survivor, he hides in a house that is hit by a second wave of cylinders. What are the Martians making in their crater? Will our hero be reunited with his wife? Will the Martians and their tripods take over the world? Can humanity—and Earth—hope to survive? H. G. Wells studied biology, and his answer may take you by surprise!

Lesley Howarth, Author

Next?

Another sci-fi classic (this time very funny) is *The Hitchhiker's Guide to the Galaxy* (UTBG 154) by Douglas Adams. It too begins with a threat to the future of Earth . . .

Or for something a bit more guns 'n' battles, try *Starship Troopers* (UTBG 337) by Robert Heinlein.

Or more H.G. Wells? Try *The Invisible Man*.

WARRIOR GIRL Pauline Chandler

A sweeping and dramatic historical epic that tells the story of Mariane, Joan of Arc's brave and trustworthy friend, whose parents have been brutally murdered by the occupying English army. Persuaded to rally to Joan's cause, Mariane hadn't planned on those wanting to have an English ruler on the throne, including her scheming and corrupt uncle, Sir Gaston. Mariane is forced to choose between saving herself and saving her country fighting at Joan's side.

Meticulous research, larger-than-life characters from every social class, a fiery heroine, fast pace, and a grand ending make this an unforgettable evocation of 15th-century France that really pulls readers back into the heart of the action.

Eileen Armstrong, Librarian

Next?

Want another compelling historical epic? Try the **de Granville** trilogy by K. M. Grant. Start with *Blood Red Horse* (UTBG 41), first in the series about young crusader Will de Granville and his beautiful horse, Hosanna.

For insight into a young girl's life in a different culture across the world, try *Memoirs of a Geisha* (UTBG 224) by Arthur Golden, set in Japan in the 1920s.

THE WASP FACTORY Iain Banks

Next?

More Iain Banks? Try *Complicity*, a cat-and-mouse thriller about a journalist accused of the murder he's trying to solve. Iain's science fiction novels have a cult following, too.

What Happened to Cass McBride? (UTBG 385) by Gail Giles is another intense story about a teen who seeks revenge, with some horrifying but truly thrilling moments.

And if you've got the taste for a graphic crime drama, try *Mystic River* by Dennis Lehance.

The Wasp Factory is not for the squeamish. Banks piles on the horror in graphic detail, BUT it is also extremely well written, compulsively readable, and studded with the author's trademark dark humor. The narrator is Frank Cauldhame, a disturbed and disturbing 16-year-old who lives on a small island with his reclusive father. He lives his life according to a series of bizarre and unpleasant rituals, which usually involve killing something and bring some kind of twisted order to his troubled world. Frank is obsessed with death; indeed he tells us that he has killed three children. But can we believe anything Frank says when he himself is so clearly deranged? Banks's skill as a writer lies in making the monstrous Frank human and in making us care about him.

Kathryn Ross, Literary Agent

WATCHMEN Alan Moore and Dave Gibbons

Don't ever let anyone tell you comics are just for kids. *Watchmen* puts that idea well and truly to rest. Alan Moore is a superb writer, Dave Gibbons a startlingly good artist, and together they serve up one hell of a story that first came out in 1986 as an award-winning, 12-issue mini-series, and later as a graphic novel. Okay, so it's almost 20 years old, but the paranoia, the multiple plot lines, the tension, and the unique mix of sci-fi, philosophy, and conspiracy theories still rings true. Moore writes as densely plotted a story line as you could wish for, while Gibbons packs more detail, thought, and design into a single page than you'll find in most complete comic books.

Graham Marks, Author

Next?

Check out Moore's *The League of Extraordinary Gentlemen*, which is drawn by Kevin O'Neill, and his collaboration with Eddie Campbell, *From Hell*, about Jack the Ripper; both are far better than the movies made from them.

And look out for Frank Miller, et al's great **Batman** story *The Dark Knight Returns* (UTBG 27).

In nongraphic terms, why not try the mind-boggling **Catch-22** (UTBG 59) by Joseph Heller.

DEATH BE NOT PROUD

Night by Elie Wiesel

Brothers by Ted van Lieshout

Elsewhere by Gabrielle Zevin

The Great Blue Yonder by Alex Shearer

The Lovely Bones by Alice Sebold

The Book Thief by Markus Zusak

WATERSHIP DOWN   Richard Adams

12+

Something terrible is going to happen to Hazel's home warren. His brother Fiver has foreseen disaster, and Fiver's sixth sense is never wrong. So, along with a handful of companions, Hazel and Fiver set off into the unknown. And so begins a great adventure, in which the small band of rabbits will face every danger imaginable in their search for a new home.

There's no other book like *Watership Down*. It's an animal story, an adventure, and an epic all rolled into one. I've read it more than 10 times, and each time I find something new.

Benedict Jacka, Author

Next?

The Incredible Journey by Sheila Burnford is another story about a group of animals traveling a long way. A nice easy read.

Redwall (UTBG 288) by Brian Jacques is an adventure in which all the characters are animals.

Or try **Urchin of the Riding Stars**, part of the **Mismantle Chronicles** by M. I. McAllister, about a world where animals are in charge.

If you want something as epic as *Watership Down*, though, your best bet is **The Lord of the Rings** trilogy (UTBG 210) by J. R. R. Tolkien.

WE CAN REMEMBER IT FOR YOU WHOLESALE   Philip K. Dick

16+

Next?

Books that'll bend your imagination abound from the pen of Philip K. Dick. Try *Do Androids Dream of Electric Sheep?* (UTBG 93) or *The Man in the High Castle* (UTBG 216).

Or what about **Neuromancer** (UTBG 240) by William Gibson, the book that spawned the whole cyber-punk genre?

A marvelous collection of sci-fi short stories with surreal titles like "The Electric Ant," "Your Appointment Will Be Yesterday," and "Cadbury, the Beaver Who Lacked." The title story was made into the film *Total Recall*. Apart from other films directly based on his stories (*Blade Runner*, *Minority Report*, etc.) you will see Philip K. Dick's influence in films such as *The Matrix*, *Twelve Monkeys*, and *Eternal Sunshine of the Spotless Mind*.

Dick loved to toy with concepts like time travel, memory, and identity. For example: a Gulliver-like time traveler finds people are tiny in the past and huge in the future. Why? Because the universe is expanding. Simple, but brilliant.

Caroline Lawrence, Author

WEAVEWORLD Clive Barker

When one of his father's racing pigeons escapes, Cal chases it to a strange gathering of birds over what looks to be an old carpet thrown out in a backyard. This carpet belongs to Suzanna, who has just inherited it from her grandmother. But the carpet contains another world—Weaveworld—inhabited by people with terrifying powers, who call us "Cuckoos."

Stalked by a sinister salesman named Shadwell and Weaveworld refugee Immocolata, Cal and Suzanna are sucked into terrifying adventures a million miles away. This book weaves fantasy with horror into a story that amazed me when I first read it, and it has continued to delight me ever since.

Katherine Roberts, Author

Next?

You might like Clive Barker's other stories, such as *Imajica*. Or, for an easier read, look for his beautifully illustrated *Abarat* (UTBG 4).

Or for more horror, try Stephen King's *Cell* (UTBG 62) and never look at your cell phone the same way again.

In Ray Bradbury's *The Illustrated Man*, a fairground worker's tattoos come alive and tell their stories.

THE WEE FREE MEN Terry Pratchett

Next?

For another fantastical adventure starring Tiffany Aching, try Terry Pratchett's *A Hat Full of Sky*.

Madeleine L'Engle's *A Wrinkle in Time* (UTBG 401) also stars a girl and her young brother who go on a quest.

The Neverending Story (UTBG 241) by Michael Ende is another fun-filled fantasy with imaginative creatures.

Tiffany Aching has some serious problems. Monsters from Fairyland are invading her world, and the wicked Fairy Queen has swiped her kid brother Wentworth. Poor Tiffany also has a bad case of Nac Mac Feegles—an infestation of six-inch-high "pictsies" with red hair and blue tattoos. The Nac Mac Feegles got pitched out of Fairyland for fighting and being drunk before two in the afternoon, but they're willing to help Tiffany any way they can. Tiffany is the only one who can control the thieving, brawling Feegles, bring Wentworth safely home, and set things right.

I laughed all the way through this book. It's fast and funny, and I want some Nac Mac Feegles of my own. Nine-year-old Tiffany has more than a touch of witch blood, and who could fail to love a heroine armed with an iron skillet and an army of insane, head-kicking pictsies?

Susan Vaught, Author

WEETZIE BAT Francesca Lia Block

Next?

The rest of the series is: *Witch Baby, Cherokee Bat and the Goat Guys, Missing Angel Juan,* and *Baby Be-Bop*. They're all about love, happiness, and the struggle to be true to both others and yourself.

Something else fantastical? Try Gabriel García Márquez's *Love in the Time of Cholera* (UTBG 212).

Or for something else about the weirdness that is LA, try Clive Barker's *Coldheart Canyon*.

Weetzie is freaky; she's way too cool for school and hates the kids who walk around blind to the beauty and wonder of Los Angeles. Then she meets Dirk, who's her soulmate, except . . . he's gay. But what does that matter? Dirk needs someone, so they find Duck. And then Weetzie needs someone, too. And all the while there's Slinkster Dog, and the city, and the whole wild brilliance of being alive, really alive.

There are some books you love so passionately that you never want them to end—for me *Weetzie Bat* is one of those. It's not a long book, or written in a fancy way. But it tells the story of Weetzie so beautifully that it makes you feel as if you're dreaming, not reading.

Leonie Flynn, Editor

WENDY Karen Wallace

14+

The heroine of this atmospheric novel set in Edwardian times is not just any Wendy, but *the* Wendy—Wendy Darling of J. M. Barrie's *Peter Pan*. The events in the novel happen before the story of *Peter Pan* takes place. We find out all about the Darling family, their neighbors (the awful Cunninghams), life upstairs in the nursery, and life at Rosegrove, where the Darlings spend their summers.

All is not well with Mr. and Mrs. Darling. Wendy becomes increasingly aware that there are hidden tensions and secrets, and she resolves to find out the truth. With a wonderful cast of characters, authentic historical detail, and a clever twist at the end, *Wendy* is a novel you won't forget.

Sherry Ashworth, Author

Next?

Karen Wallace has written three other excellent novels: *Raspberries on the Yangtze* (UTBG 285), *Climbing a Monkey Puzzle Tree*, and *The Unrivalled Spangles*.

If you're interested in more fantasy with a taste of the Edwardian background in *Wendy*, try the **Dreamhunter** duet by Elizabeth Knox.

Or you could always reread *Peter Pan* by J. M. Barrie; you may find the original is darker than you remember.

THE WERELING Stephen Cole

So you think werewolves are merely creatures of legend? You're sure? Well, Tom is pretty certain too. Until he goes for a walk in the woods and ends up rescued from a near-drowning by the strangest family. Amid secrets and lies, Tom tries to work out why his senses are suddenly so acute, why the family wants him, and why their daughter, Kate, seems so unhappy.

Paced like an episode of *Buffy the Vampire Slayer*, dripping in gore, and with characters you really feel for, this book is unnervingly realistic. Together Tom and Kate go on the run, and you'll be urging them on every step of the way. Thank goodness there are sequels!

Leonie Flynn, Editor

Next?

The sequels are *Wereling II: Prey* and *Wereling III: Resurrection*. Be warned, the series gets scarier and more violent as it goes on.

For something else scary (and even more bloodthirsty), try *Lord Loss* (UTBG 208) by Darren Shan.

For something else that makes the weird totally real, try *Tithe* (UTBG 359) by Holly Black.

WHAT HAPPENED TO CASS MCBRIDE?

Gail Giles

Next?

Definitely try other books by Gail Giles, such as *Dead Girls Don't Write Letters*.

If you can't get enough buried-alive suspense, *Deep* by Susanna Vance is just the book for you.

After his troubled younger brother, David, commits suicide, Kyle Kirby takes revenge on the popular, ambitious A-lister Cass McBride. He blames David's death on a note that Cass wrote to her best friend lamenting how that loser David Kirby had dared to ask her out. One night, Kyle drugs Cass, kidnaps her, and buries her in a coffin-shaped box, with only a small air tube and a walkie-talkie. Cass has always used her skills in reading people to get ahead; now the only way she will survive is if she says the right things and figures out what Kyle wants from her—before she runs out of time. Told in alternating chapters by Kyle, Cass, and the police detective Ben, a story unfolds—of the Kirby brothers and their messed-up mother; Cass's family and her driven, unloving father; what really drove David to hang himself; and what finally does happen to Cass McBride.

This is an intense, page-turning thriller. In spite of the fact that burying someone alive is never a good way to win friends and influence people, no one comes out seeming totally bad or good, not even Kyle. Read with caution if you are at all claustrophobic.

Alicia Anderson, Librarian

WHAT MY MOTHER DOESN'T KNOW

Sonya Sones

Sometimes what you really want to read is a love story—about how love can overcome the odds, how love requires courage, and how love is never where and what you expected. And there's actually no more unlikely spot for true love than ninth grade, because that's when your friends' opinions of who you ought to be with are actually more important than your own. Or are they?

Sophie is about to find out, because when she takes a close look at her heart, she finds that it's not Dylan she cares about but the class loser, Murphy.

I adored this book, which is written in a series of delicious poems that convey the essence of emotion, character, and plot without sacrificing depth.

Nancy Werlin, Author

Next?

For more satisfying stories in verse, try Sonya Sones's *Stop Pretending* or *One of Those Hideous Books Where the Mother Dies*.

Two more novels dealing with love in its many forms— between friends, between family, between first loves— are Diane Les Becquets's *Love, Cajun Style* and Carolyn Mackler's first novel, *Love and Other Four-Letter Words*.

WHAT THE BIRDS SEE Sonya Hartnett

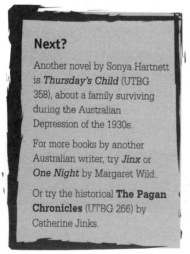

Next?

Another novel by Sonya Hartnett is *Thursday's Child* (UTBG 358), about a family surviving during the Australian Depression of the 1930s.

For more books by another Australian writer, try *Jinx* or *One Night* by Margaret Wild.

Or try the historical **The Pagan Chronicles** (UTBG 266) by Catherine Jinks.

Stories about children are not necessarily *for* children. Nine-year-old Adrian, taken from his unstable mother, abandoned by his father, is raised by his grandmother, who looks after him but never bothers to conceal the fact that she finds him a burden; her own adult children are enough of a headache. But she would be very sorry if something happened to him, especially as the neighborhood, a quiet Australian suburb, is haunted by the fate of three young children who went missing and were never found. This beautifully written, desperately sad story about a lost child and the unhappy adults who fail him, is also haunted—by a sense of unspoken horror that becomes only too real at the end.

Jan Mark, Author

WHEN ZACHARY BEAVER CAME TO TOWN Kimberly Willis Holt

12+

This story begins, "Nothing ever happens in Antler, Texas," but when Toby Wilson is 13, the "fattest boy in the world" arrives, and everything changes. Toby's been having a rough time: his mom has left town; his best friend Cal's brother is fighting in Vietnam; and Scarlett, the girl Toby adores, is in love with someone else. Toby and Cal pay two dollars each to look at Zachary Beaver, who is so fat that he can barely step out of his trailer. The last thing Toby wants is to spend time with this arrogant, unfriendly freak. But when Zachary runs into some trouble, Toby and Cal dream up a plan to help him— and in return they're helped in ways they never dreamed possible.

I've read this book more than once, and I'll read it again. Everything, from Toby's confusion and sorrow to the gap between Scarlett's teeth, seems achingly real. With its unforgettable characters, compelling story, and laugh-out-loud humor, this novel is a terrific read.

Deborah Davis, Author

> ### Next?
>
> If you like Kimberly Willis Holt, don't miss *My Louisiana Sky*, about a girl who must choose between caring for her mentally disabled parents, or moving to live with a little-known aunt.
>
> *Tangerine* (UTBG 350) by Edward Bloor takes place in an unusual town and stars an unusual narrator.

WHIP HAND Dick Francis

14+

> ### Next?
>
> The first Sid Halley story is *Odds Against*—it tells how he lost his hand.
>
> *Blood Red Horse* (UTBG 41) by K. M. Grant is the first in a trilogy of historical fiction about a young crusader and his beloved horse, Hosanna.
>
> Or try *Seabiscuit* by Laura Hillenbrand, about a runt racehorse that became a legend.

Sid Halley was a champion steeplechase jockey until a fall, and then a sadistic crook robbed him of half his left arm. Surgeons have fitted him with an electrically operated plastic hand, but it's clumsy. As a consequence he has become a private investigator, specializing in the racing world. With his friend Chico, a cheery young judo teacher, Sid is inquiring into a series of mysterious events, principally the poor performance and death of several promising young racehorses. This brings him to the attention of some very nasty criminals. Sid values his courage above all things, and it's sorely tested when a villain threatens to blow off his remaining hand with a shotgun . . .

Alan Temperley, Author

THE WHISPERING ROAD Livi Michael

12+

"There's always been Annie," says Joe; but many times he is tempted to abandon her, and for a desperate period, he does give in to that temptation. She is his little sister and they are on the run together from the cruel masters that they have been farmed out to by the workhouse. Their bid for freedom takes them to dangerous places, and they have to live by their wits to survive.

It is a roguish journey in which one extraordinary situation follows another, and characters as strange as the people of dreams or nightmares weave in and out of their lives. The incidents that the children are involved in are as wild and fascinating as the stories Joe tells and as the visions his sister has.

This is a great adventure story that works on many levels; it's both a disturbing and a heartwarming read.
Berlie Doherty, Author

Next?

No one wrote better historical adventure series than Joan Aiken. Read *Go Saddle the Sea*.

The Cup of the World (UTBG 82) by John Dickinson is an epic adventure set in a fantasy Middle Ages.

Or try Frances Hardinge's *Fly by Night*, about a girl, a goose, and a fabulously reimagined 18th-century England.

WHITE OLEANDER Janet Fitch

14+

Next?

Janet Fitch's sophomore novel, *Paint It Black,* portrays another unforgettable coming-of-age story.

She's Come Undone by Wally Lamb has a strong, determined female protagonist who has struggled to break free of the abuses of her family.

Billie Letts's *Where the Heart Is* chronicles a down-and-out teen who was abandoned by her mother at an early age.

Being the child of a beautiful yet emotionally unstable poet isn't easy. After a failed relationship with a man by the name of Barry Kolker, Astrid's mother teeters on the brink of insanity, trying desperately to make Barry love her again. Soon after, Astrid's mother is taken from her after murdering Barry with the poisonous oleander flower, thus changing the life of her daughter forever. Astrid is taken to a series of foster homes, being pushed from each for various reasons. Astrid soon sees her mother for who she truly is and vows that she'll never become what she has since grown to hate.
Jessica Harrington, age 17

WHITE TEETH Zadie Smith

16+

When Archibald Jones and Samad Iqbal met in a tank during World War II, they did not expect that they would meet again years later, become friends, and raise their families together. Archie marries Clara, the daughter of a Jehovah's Witness, and Iqbal marries Alsana. The story follows this unlikely pair of friends as they struggle with the trials of the underclass and try to understand their own children, who are caught between the old world of their parents' upbringing and the new world of modern Britain.

Smith's characters are the best part of this book. Her ability to create utterly unique but completely believable people is just one of her many talents as a writer. Then she puts them in situations that test their limits, and makes you wonder about your own as she tackles issues like multiculturalism, religion, and social class with humor and sensitivity. The heavy issues can make this book a bit difficult to wade through at times, but it is an amazing read that will make you laugh and is completely worth the effort.

Mary Kate Castellani, Editor

> ### Next?
>
> *Brick Lane* By Monica Ali tells a multicultural story of London, too.
>
> More Zadie Smith? Try *The Autograph Man* or *On Beauty*.
>
> *The Buddha of Suburbia* by Hanif Kureishi is a fabulous book about London, being Asian, and sex (of all sorts!).

WHO IS JESSE FLOOD? Malachy Doyle

12+

> ### Next?
>
> If you enjoyed *Jesse Flood* you might also like to try *Feather Boy* (UTBG 115) by Nicky Singer and *Snow Spider* by Jenny Nimmo, both of which feature boys who feel different and who struggle to find their identity. All three books look at how teenage boys are affected by family events such as divorce or bereavement.
>
> *Fat Boy Swim* (UTBG 113) by Catherine Forde is about a boy who finds a most original way of making a difficult life bearable.
>
> Or try Patrick Jones's much grittier look at a teenage boy's struggle to find his niche in *Nailed* (UTBG 239).

Jesse Flood is different from other kids—he's hopeless at school, sports, and talking to girls (though he's a whizz at ping-pong). Jesse lives in his head to shut out the world, and his diary reveals his thoughts on life and love, as well as his embarrassing failures with girls. He describes teenage life in a small town like being in a long tunnel, waiting for the light to shine through. Malachy Doyle shows great sympathy for the pain of being a teenager and the boredom of small-town life, and creates a distinctive character in Jesse Flood.

Anne Flaherty, Journalist

WICKED Gregory Maguire

12+

Next?

Gregory Maguire has written many retellings of classic fairy tales: *Confessions of an Ugly Stepsister* (*Cinderella*), *Mirror Mirror* (*Snow White*), and *Son of a Witch* (the sequel to *Wicked*).

Reading *The Wonderful Wizard of Oz* by L. Frank Baum isn't the same once you've seen it from the Wicked Witch's perspective.

There are always two sides to every story, especially in the *Wizard of Oz*. Not much is said about the Wicked Witch of the West in the book or movie—until now. Gregory Maguire depicts the witch's life from many perspectives. The Wicked Witch comes across so many issues that stretch so deep and are so exhilarating and unthinkable. She endures many failures but tries to keep moving on, never knowing if it means life or death.

Wicked was very interesting to read. It sparked my imagination and made me soar to greater heights than I knew possible. This novel made me think about the meaning of life itself and the concepts of good and evil. Each of the characters had a unique personality that had a big impact on the plot line. I would recommend *Wicked* for people who want reading that will make them think, and who enjoy a challenge!

Lisa La Beau, age 16

WIDE SARGASSO SEA Jean Rhys

14+

The Sargasso Sea, mysterious and sluggish, swirls between Europe and the West Indies, its waters choked with seaweed, its floor strewn with shipwrecks. Edward Rochester marries Antoinette Cosway, a Creole (white West Indian) for her money, only to find she has none. Once in England, Antoinette finds herself renamed Bertha and locked away in a secret annex. Mad with grief, Bertha burns the house to the ground. This is *Jane Eyre* from the point of view of the Creole woman, sidelined and despised in the original book: the "madwoman in the attic" has been given a voice at last.

Gill Vickery, Author

Next?

The Awakening by Kate Chopin is another account of a woman desperate to escape from a stifling life.

The Yellow Wallpaper (UTBG 403) by Charlotte Perkins Gilman is a brilliant, absolutely terrifying, "madwoman in the attic" story.

You may also enjoy Andrea Levy's *Small Island*, a modern novel about the Windrush generation arriving in Britain.

A WILD SHEEP CHASE Haruki Murakami

Murakami is one of those authors you just have to trust. In his books the strange runs parallel with the mundane. Sometimes the two blur until it's hard to tell the difference. His books read like dreams, and this one is no exception. The hero is quiet, ordinary, but his life, with its endless circular journeys, its despair, is changed when he's hired by Mr. Big to find the sheep that changed *his* life. Yes, the title is almost literal! On his quest, he meets a girl with the most beautiful ears in the world, talks with the dead, meets a Sheep Man, and reads *Sherlock Holmes*. Surreal, darkly comic, utterly engrossing, this is a wonderfully written book that just might change *your* life.

Leonie Flynn, Editor

Next?

Try the **Sherlock Holmes** stories (UTBG 319) by Sir Arthur Conan Doyle for more mysteries within mysteries.

Another Murakami? Read *Norwegian Wood*, a novel in two volumes, one red, one green, which became a national obsession in Japan; or the wonderfully surreal *The Wind-up Bird Chronicle*.

Or how about surrealism without the humor? Try Kafka's dark and disturbing *The Trial*.

WILD SWANS: THREE DAUGHTERS OF CHINA Jung Chang

A mind-opening and mind-blowing account of three generations of Chinese women living in Maoist China. From the painful practice of binding women's feet so that they could only take dainty steps to the struggles of the Long March, it is the fascinating and often shocking details that make this true story so gripping. It reads like a novel, and you have to keep reminding yourself that it's not.

The way the Communist authorities imposed control and turned friend against friend and relative against relative is vividly brought to life—but what shines through most of all is the sheer power of individual human will and determination. It's an inspirational book.

Nicola Morgan, Author

Next?

For another true and moving story about the Chinese way of life, try Adeline Yen Mah's *Falling Leaves*.

Jung Chang has followed this up with a biography of the larger-than-life Chinese leader, *Mao: The Unknown Story* (written with her husband, Jon Halliday).

Or if you want to read another story of surviving traumatic early years, try *A Child Called "It"* (UTBG 65) by Dave Pelzer.

THE WIND ON FIRE trilogy

12+

William Nicholson

This is a fantasy trilogy as full of human truth as it is of adventure, and you may well love it even if fantasy's not usually your thing.

In *The Wind Singer*, the Hath family live in the city of Aramanth, where the whole of life is controlled by exams. Even two-year-olds have to play their part, taking tests that will help decide on their family's future. When Kestrel Hath dares to rebel against the system, she starts off a chain of events that launches her on an epic journey with her twin brother, Bowman, and their friend Mumpo, their aim to bring love and kindness back into the city.

Slaves of the Mastery and *Firesong* are set five years later: the peace of Aramanth is shattered when the entire population is taken as slaves by warrior invaders. The Hath family emerge as true leaders as they struggle to set their people free and to lead them to their homeland.

Susan Reuben, Editor

Next?

William Nicholson wrote the screenplay for the film *Gladiator*, and you may notice some similarities to the Manaxas in *Slaves of the Mastery*. His new series begins with *Seeker* (UTBG 309).

Pullman's **His Dark Materials** trilogy (UTBG 153) is also loved by fantasy fans and fantasy haters alike.

The Ultimate Teen Readers' Poll

BOOK THAT CHANGED YOUR LIFE

1 **The Harry Potter series**

2 *A Child Called "It"*

3 **The Bible**

4 **The Lord of the Rings trilogy**

5 *Twilight*

6 *The Diary of a Young Girl*

7 **The His Dark Materials trilogy**

8 *Noughts & Crosses*

9 **A Series of Unfortunate Events**

10 *Holes*

THE WISH HOUSE Celia Rees

Next?

More Celia Rees? Try *Witch Child* (UTBG 393), a gripping historical novel.

For another recent coming-of-age novel involving some suspense, try *Desert Crossing* by Elise Broach.

Linda Newbery's *Set in Stone* (UTBG 314) also features a striking country house and an impressionable young man who falls under its spell, though with a late-Victorian setting.

Readers who know Celia Rees through her best-selling *Witch Child* or *Sorceress* are likely to be surprised by this more recent coming-of-age novel, set in the 1970s.

On vacation in South Wales with his completely dull parents, Richard is captivated by the Wish House and its unconventional inhabitants—in particular Clio, the beautiful, troubled girl who befriends him, and with whom he has his first sexual experience. Her father, the egotistical artist Jethro Dalton, exerts an autocratic rule over the household; as secrets emerge, Richard realizes how thoroughly he has been manipulated.

An enticing feature of this novel is the art-show catalogue preface to each chapter, which Celia Rees has written so skillfully that the reader almost sees the exhibits.

Linda Newbery, Author

WITCH CHILD Celia Rees

Forget boring historical novels about long-dead people; *Witch Child* is so "now" and so vivid that you sometimes forget that the heroine, Mary, lived in the 17th century. Celia Rees is one of those writers with the magical gift of drawing the reader into a relationship with her characters by the end of page one, with the result that homework goes undone, sleep is set aside, and a vast amount of chocolate is munched until the adventure comes to an end. Except that in *Witch Child*, it doesn't. So gripping is the writing and so believable the plot that when you reach the final page—and no, I'm not going to tell you just how cleverly executed it is— you simply have to rush out and buy the sequel, *Sorceress*.

This is a book for readers who want believable characters, loads of emotion, and a vivid insight into how prejudice and bullying have affected lives for centuries. Without a doubt, this is an unforgettable read.

Rosie Rushton, Author

Next?

Pirates! (UTBG 271) is another Celia Rees book set in the past, this time a swashbuckling romance.

Or for another book about outsiders, try *Chocolat* (UTBG 67) by Joanne Harris.

The Minister's Daughter (UTBG 227) by Julie Hearn is a story of superstition and witchcraft.

A WIZARD OF EARTHSEA
Ursula K. Le Guin

Long before Harry Potter went to Hogwarts, on a faraway island an unloved boy named Ged discovered he could do magic. This is a story about how frightening magic can be, the danger and the responsibility of it. Ged's talent leads him into wonderful adventures, on marvelous islands, and you won't be able to put the book down until you finish it. And when you do finish it, you will know something important about yourself. You may not be a Harry Potter, but you are certainly a Ged. The world you live in has a deep balance, and the best magicians learn to use magic only in the greatest emergency . . .
Jill Paton Walsh, Author

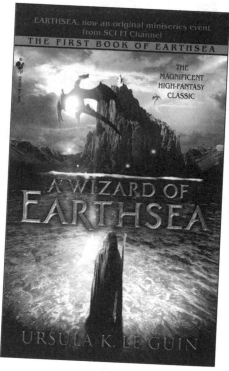

Next?

If you love *A Wizard of Earthsea*, there's good news for you—there are sequels: *The Tombs of Atuan*, *The Farthest Shore*, *Tehanu*, and *The Other Wind*.

There is also a collection of stories in Le Guin's *Tales from Earthsea*.

And when you've finished those you can read Le Guin's adult sci-fi. Start with *The Left Hand of Darkness* (UTBG 202). This is an author you never grow out of—you grow into her!

Frank Herbert's *Dune* (UTBG 100) and its sequels mix science fiction and fantasy in an epic that chronicles the adventures of a young man who fulfills an ancient prophecy about his birth.

Ursula K. Le Guin's books sink their claws into you and don't let go. Written in simple yet powerful prose, they deal with classic themes of Good and Evil, and what it means to grow up. Her world of Earthsea is one of the great creations in fantasy: a place of many peoples, with a wild surging ocean, dragons, ancient magic, and wizards both wise and foolish. This book, the first in her Earthsea Quartet, taught me the power of words. To me, *A Wizard of Earthsea* feels like a myth or legend, a half-remembered song. If you are looking for a grand saga, I cannot recommend it highly enough.
Christopher Paolini, Author

WOLF BROTHER Michelle Paver

Wolf Brother brilliantly recreates the world of 6,000 years ago and follows a young boy, Torak, as he learns to survive in a vast and dangerous forest following the violent death of his father. There are raging rivers, hostile tribes, fever, starvation, and most frightening of all, a demon that has taken the shape of a giant bear.

Michelle Paver certainly knows her stuff—and she doesn't pull any punches. Torak is totally convincing as a primitive hero. When he kills a roe buck and cuts it up to use every bit of it either as food, clothes, or weapons (he turns the stomach into a waterskin) you begin to see just how difficult it's going to be for him to survive. Paver is also a great storyteller. Just about every chapter ends on a cliffhanger, although personally I could have done without the slightly old-fashioned illustrations.

Anthony Horowitz, Author

Next?

More Michelle Paver? There will be five books in the **Chronicles of Ancient Darkness**. *Spirit Walker* is next

Jenny Nimmo's **Red King** quintet, starting with *Midnight for Charlie Bone*, is a magical thriller.

Looking for another action-packed series? Try *The Lightning Thief*, book one of Rick Riordan's adventure series with a mythological twist, **Percy Jackson and the Olympians**.

THE WOLVES IN THE WALLS Neil Gaiman

Next?

How about John Masefield's *The Box of Delights*, a surreal Christmas classic?

Or for slightly friendlier lupine fun, read *Wolf Brother* (UTBG 395) by Michelle Paver.

Or try Neil Gaiman and Dave McKean's other collaboration, the rather less scary but no less brilliant *The Day I Swapped My Dad for Two Goldfish*. Good title, too.

Lucy knows there are wolves in the walls of her house, but nobody believes her. She can hear them creeping around, scratching and whispering, hatching their wolfish schemes. And if the wolves come out of the walls, it's all over.

Although this is intended for young children (and only recommended if you never want them to sleep again), Gaiman and Dave McKean, the illustrator, prove that you're never too old for a picture book. McKean's combination of traditional painting and photography lends the book an eerie feel, and Gaiman's story is deeply unsettling. Beautifully illustrated, extremely sinister, and all-round good fun, it feels like reading a modern-age fairy tale. Buy this and relive every nighttime terror you've ever had.

Chris Wooding, Author

SHORT AND GRIPPING BOOKS
by Patrick Jones

"I want you to kiss me."

That's the first line of my novel *Things Change* and the intent is obvious: get the reader's attention like a slap in the face or a kiss on the lips. While a great beginning is important for any book, it is vital for authors who want to reach reluctant readers. These readers are often aliterate—that is, they can read, however, they choose not to—in part, because they've never found reading to be enjoyable. Reading equals boredom not pleasure.

But there is hope, and often it comes in small packages, or under 225 pages. Just because a book is thin, however, doesn't necessarily mean that it is great for the nonreader, and there are plenty of big books that nonreaders will devour. But for many reluctant readers, size does matter. There's a committee called "Quick Picks" from the Young Adult Library Services Association that identifies books for these readers. The annual list it compiles features books that read quickly and get readers' attention even quicker.

"Bret, what the hell is wrong with you?"

That's the first line from my second novel, *Nailed*. Almost every teenager has heard this question during their adolescent years. The question asked by a short and gripping book is normally simple and carried out by a few characters. A quick read is about plot, not theme or purpose. A quick read is about what happens. A quick read asks a question, like "what happened to Cass McBride?" and then can answer it in one sentence: she's buried alive. Like a great short story, the gripping reluctant-reader book can't waste a word, from the get-go.

"Simon Glass was easy to hate."

That's the first line of *Shattering Glass* by Gail Giles. Giles is the new queen of the quick read; the old king of the short and gripping novel was R. L. Stine. Stine was more productive; Giles is more polished. Giles writes a book a year, while Stine used to write one a month. But the similarities between them are as long as the books are short. Both pen novels that feature clear writing without long, convoluted sentences of sophisticated vocabulary. They start with a bang and a hook, have plots that turn the pages

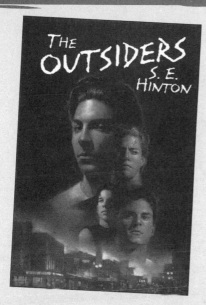

so fast readers get paper cuts, and have endings of the "Holy s&^t!" variety. The plots unfold through dialogue and action, not description or introspection. People do stuff; they don't think about it.

"When I stepped out into the bright sunlight from the darkness of the movie house, I had only two things on my mind: Paul Newman and a ride home."

That's the first line of *The Outsiders* (UTBG 264) by S. E. Hinton; that's the big bang of the YA lit universe, but it wasn't even 200 pages long. It announces the common thread on which most great thin teen books dangle: the search for identity. Yes, thin books are about plots, characters, and powerful scenes: the loud stuff. But beneath the surface is the silent search for identity. From *The Outsiders* in 1967 to Giles's *What Happened to Cass McBride?* (UTBG 385) in 2006, there's a long list of short and gripping teen novels to turn the nonreader around, especially when read the night before a report is due!

Patrick's quick picks: the top 20 teen tomes under 225 pages

Don't You Dare Read This, Mrs. Dunphrey by Margaret Peterson Haddix (128 pages)

Inside Out by Terry Trueman (128 pages)

The Long Night of Leo and Bree by Ellen Wittlinger (128 pages)

Miracle's Boys by Jacqueline Woodson (144 pages)

Forged by Fire by Sharon M. Draper (160 pages)

Crosses by Shelley Stochr (164 pages)

The Afterlife by Gary Soto (168 pages)

Slumber Party by Christopher Pike (170 pages)

The Skin I'm In by Sharon G. Flake (176 pages)

Playing in Traffic by Gail Giles (176 pages)

The Boy Who Couldn't Die by William Sleator (184 pages)

The Outsiders by S. E. Hinton (192 pages)

Driver's Ed by Caroline B. Cooney (208 pages)

Speak by Laurie Halse Anderson (208 pages)

Blind Date by R. L. Stine (208 pages)

Black and White by Paul Volponi (208 pages)

Acceleration by Graham McNamee (210 pages)

Shattering Glass by Gail Giles (224 pages)

What Happened to Cass McBride? by Gail Giles (224 pages)

Hidden Talents by David Lubar (224 pages)

THE WOMAN IN WHITE Wilkie Collins

You must read *The Woman in White* when you're a teenager—you'll love it, forever.

This is a Gothic story of love through richer and poorer, and there is nothing conditional about Walter Hartright's feelings for Laura Fairlie. It has an ethereal quality, a ghostliness, and a sense of place that is both eerie and satisfying, and gives a rich and fascinating insight into how different and difficult mid-Victorian life could be for girls. The strangeness, the madness, the ghostliness resonated for me long after I finished this book, and it sent me on a journey through many other Wilkie Collins novels.

Raffaella Barker, Author

Next?

More Wilkie Collins? My favorites to go on to are *The Moonstone* (UTBG 231) (another thriller) and *No Name*.

Another great Gothic romance: Ann Radcliffe's *The Mysteries of Udolpho* or the parody of such things, Jane Austen's *Northanger Abbey* (UTBG 247).

Or try *The Warden* by Anthony Trollope, the first of the **Chronicles of Barsetshire**, which tell the complex stories of a cathedral town.

THE WONDERFUL STORY OF HENRY SUGAR Roald Dahl

Next?

The Sandman series (UTBG 302) by Neil Gaiman has a similar mixture of myth and reality.

I Am the Cheese (UTBG 168) by Robert Cormier tells the strange story of Adam, who is being interrogated by a psychiatrist with an ulterior motive.

More Roald Dahl? Try *Tales of the Unexpected* (UTBG 349).

Roald Dahl isn't just the author of wickedly funny, wildly imagined children's books. He also wrote these surreal and disturbing stories, creating a host of different worlds, each one compelling, moving, and terrifying. There's a modern-day Peter Pan, who travels the seas on the back of a giant turtle; there's a bullied boy who has a swan's wings strapped to his arms. In a third tale, the discovery of buried treasure corrupts everyone who touches it. The title story is the best of the lot, as Henry Sugar learns to stare into a flame, see through a blindfold, and become a real magician. There's even the story of how Dahl himself became a writer. This is Roald Dahl as you've never read him before.

Ariel Kahn, Academic

THE WORLD ACCORDING TO GARP

John Irving

Next?

More John Irving—*The Hotel New Hampshire*, *A Prayer for Owen Meany* (UTBG 274), *The Cider House Rules*—you can't go wrong.

For an odd, all-encompassing novel with the most bizarre characters, read Tom Robbins's *Another Roadside Attraction* (UTBG 21).

Or how about a weird and sprawling mass of a novel set in a Scottish family—Iain Banks's *The Crow Road*?

This is a great, big, wonderful book, and while the movie has a good stab at getting John Irving's extraordinary story up on screen, this is one you *have* to read. It'll make you laugh, possibly out loud, it'll make you sad, and it will definitely stay with you long after you've put it down.

What's it about? It may sound like a big cop-out to say it's beyond description, but that's the truth, although I can tell you it has a lot to do with wrestling (with other people as well as with consciences), and that this man is one of the best writers ever. Really.

Graham Marks, Author

THE WORST JOURNEY IN THE WORLD

Apsley Cherry-Garrard

Killer whales, deadly blizzards, temperatures of minus 70 degrees—this is without a doubt the greatest adventure story ever written.

Author Cherry-Garrard was 24 when he was chosen by Scott to be part of the South Polar expedition. The book is a mixture of personal reminiscences together with extracts from diaries and letters, and it covers far more than just Scott's doomed walk to the Pole.

The account is written by the one man who could have saved Scott, if only he'd known it—and I for one will be forever grateful that Cherry-Garrard had the courage to publish this account. Without it, men such as Captain Oates and Birdie Bowers would have remained nothing but names in a history book.

Laura Hutchings, Teacher

Next?

For a futuristic take on polar exploration, try *Surviving Antarctica* by Andrea White.

Or try Geraldine McCaughrean's *The White Darkness*, about a girl obsessed with Captain Oates.

You may want to move on to the thrills of mountaineering literature. One of the best books has to be *Touching the Void* (UTBG 361) by Joe Simpson.

A WREATH FOR EMMETT TILL

Marilyn Nelson

Emmett Till, an African American teenage boy visiting family in Mississippi in 1955, made one innocent mistake in speaking to a white woman and was brutally beaten and murdered. This lynching and the acquittal of his murderers is one of the events that sparked the civil rights movement.

Nelson tells Emmett's story and delves into the subject of lynching through a heroic crown of sonnets, in which the last line of each sonnet becomes the first line of the next. This is an incredible accomplishment! Illustrator Philippe Lardy uses stark paintings to complement the sonnets and continues the mood of the words in his art.

The book is the size of a picture book, but it is truly amazing. It is a book that everyone should read, discuss, and contemplate.

Kimberly Paone, Librarian

> **Next?**
>
> Marilyn Nelson has written other wonderful nonfiction including *Carver*, a biography of George Washington Carver.
>
> John Grisham's *A Time to Kill* is a story about racism in the Deep South.
>
> For more about Emmett Till's story, try *Getting Away with Murder* by Chris Crowe, a book that includes photographs and interviews.

WRESTLING STURBRIDGE Rich Wallace

> **Next?**
>
> Another novel by Rich Wallace, *Playing Without the Ball*, has the same intensity as *Wrestling Sturbridge*, but it takes on basketball instead.
>
> If you like wrestling stories, try Alfred C. Martino's *Pinned* or E. M. J. Benjamin's *Takedown*.

Ben weighs 135 pounds. So does his best friend Al, which means that they're competing for the wrestling championship in their weight class. Everyone assumes that Al is going to win . . . but why should Ben settle for second place?

Winning the state championship would make his father proud. And it would help him get out of Sturbridge. Ben isn't sure what his future holds, but he is sure of one thing—he doesn't want to spend the rest of his life dying of boredom in Sturbridge.

Ben hasn't beaten Al in a match in three years. Does he have the ability to beat his friend, win the state championship, and possibly change both of their futures?

This is a sports book that can be enjoyed by everyone. Ben's internal voice rings clear and true, and readers will follow him through the story wondering if they would make the same choices that he does.

Andrea Lipinski, Librarian

A WRINKLE IN TIME
Madeleine L'Engle

12+

Written in 1963, this award-winning book still manages to hover in the top 500 of Amazon.com and has a fanatical following.

It's the story of Meg Murry and her genius baby brother—children of two brilliant scientists—and their quest to rescue their father from a faraway planet overtaken by the dark shadow of evil. It's not really science fiction (phew!), though there are enough challenging scientific ideas about time travel to keep you on your toes. Instead, it's about the triumph of Meg's difficult, unruly, passionate personality where intellect alone has failed. And it's the perfect book for those of us with messy, stubborn characters, who don't always feel appreciated by the rest of the world.

Meg Rosoff, Author

Next?

This is part of the **Time** quintet. The others are *A Swiftly Tilting Planet*, *A Wind in the Door*, *Many Waters*, and *An Acceptable Time*.

From the Mixed-up Files of Mrs. Basil E. Frankweiler by E. L. Konigsburg has another great brother and sister relationship. This time, the siblings run away from their boring suburban life to live in the Metropolitan Museum in New York.

MADELEINE L'ENGLE

A Wrinkle in Time

THE DECADENT FRENCH

Bonjour Tristesse by Françoise Sagan

Chocolat by Joanne Harris

Claudine at School by Colette

Le Grand Meaulnes by Alain-Fournier

Les Misérables by Victor Hugo

Thérèse Raquin by Émile Zola

WUTHERING HEIGHTS Emily Brontë

Next?

If you prefer better-mannered lovers and happier endings, then check out *Pride and Prejudice* (UTBG 276) by Jane Austen.

Or if you'd like a more suspenseful tale with a brooding yet irresistible love interest, try *Rebecca* (UTBG 287) by Daphne du Maurier.

Forget Mr. Darcy—Heathcliff is the sexiest man in English literature. I first read this book when I was 13 and reread it pretty much every year for the next decade. It's a monumental love story carved of passion and brutality. In a dilemma that has resonated with women down the centuries, Cathy Earnshaw must choose between the "good" and civilized man, Edgar Linton, and the "bad" wild foundling of nature, Heathcliff. Cathy's final decision, and the revenge that follows, exact a terrible penalty on two generations of Earnshaws and Lintons.

A beautiful and savage book that makes you grateful to be alive.

Nicky Singer, Author

THE YEAR OF SECRET ASSIGNMENTS
Jaclyn Moriarty

Three 10th-grade girls at an upscale prep school embark on a school letter-writing project, corresponding with boys at the tough school in the same town. Emily, Cassie, and Lydia find themselves drawn in by their pen pals and end up getting way more than they bargained for. Spying! Car-jacking! Identity theft! And romance. Emily embarks on a flirtation; Lydia gets her pen pal to execute hilarious pranks and mysterious tasks; and Cassie keeps writing, even when her pen pal threatens her.

Unbelievably witty. Bright-and-shiny clever. And it's Australian, so there's cool slang, plus Emily's constant and comical misuse of words. I really admire Moriarty's style—the entire novel consists of letters, e-mails, and journal entries, always snappy and hilarious. Her plot is completely unusual even as the emotions of the girls are universal.

E. Lockhart, Author

Next?

Emily, Cassie, and Lydia also show up in Moriarty's *Feeling Sorry for Celia* and *The Murder of Bindy Mackenzie*.

Other books with a similar feel to Jaclyn Moriarty's writing are Ann Brashares's *The Sisterhood of the Traveling Pants* (UTBG 324) or Megan McCafferty's *Sloppy Firsts* (UTBG 328).

If you enjoy the epistolary format, try Lauren Myracle's novel *ttyl* (UTBG 368), told completely in Instant Messages.

THE YELLOW WALLPAPER

Charlotte Perkins Gilman

Written in the first person, this short story reads like a diary. The protagonist, a married woman with a young child, has just been relocated to the country. Her husband thinks she is tired and in need of a good long rest. Essentially he wants her to do nothing at all, and is even opposed to her writing in her diary. But she continues to write, and thus we have a story. Desperate for something to do, but not allowed to do anything, she begins to obsess about the wallpaper in her bedroom.

The Yellow Wallpaper was written in a time when women who were artistic, creative, or just a little different were often shunned by society. Their desire to be actively engaged was considered strange and unnatural, and they were often deemed insane; and sometimes they did, quite literally, lose their minds. This book was written in homage to these women.

Candida Gray, Teacher

Next?

The Awakening by Kate Chopin was considered shocking when it was published.

Virginia Woolf's *A Room of One's Own* (UTBG 293) set out her ideas about the role of women compared to that of men.

Daisy Miller (UTBG 85) by Henry James is the story of a young woman and her potential.

YOU DON'T KNOW ME David Klass

Next?

For another shocking trip through a teen's mind, try *Trigger* (UTBG 365) by Susan Vaught, in which a teen must relearn his own life after his failed suicide attempt.

The lead character in *Martyn Pig* (UTBG 220) by Kevin Brooks accidentally commits an act of violence.

For the strangest journey any teenager could take, dip into *Lady: My Life as a Bitch* by Melvin Burgess, in which a girl is transformed into a mischievous dog.

Anther David Klass? Try *The Braves*, about gangs, football, and fitting in.

The voice of John, the narrator of this novel, is one of the best-ever achieved in fiction for teen readers. By turns incredibly funny and then uncomfortably violent, the book tells the story of 14-year-old John and the images in his head, his life inside a life, as he tries to escape the crushing reality of his mother's abusive new boyfriend. At school he feels isolated, despite being liked by his teachers and peers. And John is a likable character, ordinary in many ways, but his view on the absurdities of modern life make him very special indeed. In trying to make himself unknowable, he inadvertently reveals everything that he is. A powerful and moving novel.

John McLay, Literary Scout

THE ZIGZAG KID David Grossman

Nonny is about to turn 13. And what a birthday it's going to be . . . You see, he thinks he's getting on a train to visit his uncle Samuel, The Great Educator, who will give him an unbearable lecture on responsible behavior. But Nonny wasn't counting on meeting Felix Glick, and he wasn't expecting what happened next.

For Nonny's father and stepmother have cooked up a magical birthday surprise, a mystery adventure tour of discovery and self-discovery. And author David Grossman has done just the same for us. His little miracle of a book is funny, thought-provoking, and touching (the three most important things in a book, I think). It may seem like an odd thing to say, but I'm just glad this book exists; I hope you will be, too.

Daniel Hahn, Editor

> ### Next?
>
> There's another David Grossman you're bound to love: *Someone to Run With*, about life in modern Jerusalem.
>
> For a story about stories, mixing fantasy and reality, try Salman Rushdie's beautiful *Haroun and the Sea of Stories*.
>
> Or have a look at our Coming of Age feature on pp. 278–279.

ZOO Graham Marks

> ### Next?
>
> More Graham Marks? Try *Missing in Tokyo*, about a boy searching for his lost sister in the seedy backstreets of Tokyo.
>
> If you like fast-paced adventure stories, why not try *The Burning City* (UTBG 55) by Ariel and Joaquin Dorfman? Its plot lunges forward like the main character's hurtling courier bike.
>
> John Grisham has written many equally addictive and unputdownable legal suspense novels. Start with *The Runaway Jury* (UTBG 297) or *The Firm* (UTBG 118).
>
> A similar psychological thriller is *Kissing the Rain* (UTBG 195) by Kevin Brooks.

Cam Stewart's comfortable, laid-back lifestyle is shattered when he is kidnapped and held up for ransom with no explanation. Escaping and killing a man on the way, Cam relies on the kindness of strangers to pick him up physically and mentally as he desperately tries to run away from the past, and starts to discover the unexpected and shocking truth of who he really is.

Edgy, hard-hitting, and high-octane, Cam's disaster-ridden narrative unfolds like an episode of *24*. Cleverly timed chapters accelerate the action and maintain the momentum in this edge-of-the-seat action adventure.

Eileen Armstrong, Librarian

About the Contributors

DAVID ALMOND has been a teacher and is now a writer, best known for *Skellig*. He lives with his family in Northumberland, England.

ABIGAIL ANDERSON is a freelance theater director who has worked on a number of plays for teenagers, including an adaptation of Melvyn Burgess's *Smack*.

ALICIA ANDERSON is a teen services librarian for Hennepin County Library near Minneapolis, MN. She frequently and enthusiastically reads below her age level. Her reviews and general book-related ranting can be found at http://bookbarker.blogspot.com.

KRISTIN ANDERSON is a youth services librarian at the Columbus Metropolitan Library in Ohio. She lives with her husband, two stepdaughters, and two dogs in Dublin, OH.

NOGA APPLEBAUM is in the final stages of a PhD in Children's Literature. Her research on children's science fiction will be published in 2008. She also writes for children and has twice won the London Writers' Competition (2005 and 2006).

JON APPLETON has been a reviewer of children's books, and has spent the last ten years editing them. He is now having fun being Senior Editor at Orion Children's Books.

PHILIP ARDAGH recently collaborated with Paul McCartney and Geoff Dunbar on Sir Paul's first children's book, *High in the Clouds*, but is probably best known for his Eddie Dickens adventures.

MAX AREVUO is 13 years old. An enthusiastic reader, he prefers autobiographies but enjoys most books that are put in front of him.

NEIL ARKSEY writes for TV when he's not being an author. His books for teens include *Brooksie*, *MacB*, *Playing on the Edge,* and *As Good as Dead in Downtown*. He is now lead writer on a medical drama in Hungary (in Hungarian).

OLIVIA ARMES is 15 and lives in London. She enjoys relaxing with friends, photography, and most of all surfing.

EILEEN ARMSTRONG is a high school librarian in Northumberland, UK; a reviewer; feature writer for a variety of professional journals; and author of *Fully Booked! Reader Development and the Secondary School LRC*.

SHERRY ASHWORTH has written many novels for teenagers, including, most recently, *Close-Up*. She lives in Manchester, UK, and has a husband, two grown-up daughters, and two very lazy cats.

MAY AUNG is a senior who attends Eleanor Roosevelt High School in New York City. She enjoys reading, writing, and watching television in her spare time.

SHELBI BALL, 16, lives in Hudson, WI. Reading is her favorite pastime. When she really gets into a book, she blocks out everything around her and becomes part of the story.

LYNNE REID BANKS has written many books but is best known for *The L-Shaped Room* for adults and *The Indian in the Cupboard* for children. She also has the distinction of being the first-ever female TV news reporter!

ANDREW BARAKAT was born in New York, NY, and moved to London in 2002. He attends Arnold House School and enjoys visiting the library and reading.

DAVID BARD is talkative, inquisitive, sporty, and enthusiastic. Now 13, he attends Arnold House School in England.

RAFFAELLA BARKER lives in Norfolk, UK. She has written seven adult novels and one for teens called *Phosphorescence*.

SUSAN CAMPBELL BARTOLETTI has written many fiction and nonfiction books for young readers. *Hitler Youth: Growing Up in Hitler's Shadow* received a Newbery Honor and a Siebert Award. *Black Potatoes: The Story of the Great Irish Famine, 1845–1850* also received a Siebert Award. Susan lives in Pennsylvania with her husband and two children.

JOAN BAUER, a *New York Times* bestselling author, has won numerous book awards. She lives in Brooklyn, NY, with her husband.

NINA BAWDEN has written more than 40 novels. Her best known book is *Carrie's War*, and she has recently written *Dear Austen*, about the Potter's Bar railroad crash which injured her and killed her husband.

SUSILA BAYBARS has spent the last 13 years immersed in children's books. She's hopped around publishers, working with the good and the great, loving every minute of it.

K. K. BECK is the author of 21 crime thrillers. Her novels for young adult readers are *Fake* and *Snitch*.

DAVID BELBIN is the author of *Love Lessons*, The Beat series, *Denial*, and many other novels for young adults. He has also written numerous short stories for both adult and younger readers.

JULIA BELL is a novelist and lecturer at Birkbeck, UCL. Her publications include the novels *Massive* and *Dirty Work*, and the *Creative Writing Coursebook*.

JULIE BERTAGNA's first published work was a glowing review of her brother's appalling rock band, and she has been writing ever since. She is currently completing *Zenith*, the sequel to *Exodus*. She lives in Glasgow, Scotland, with her family.

THOMAS BLOOR has always lived in London. As well as writing, he also teaches adults part-time. He's married and has two children.

BAILEY BORON, 16, is a sophomore at Hudson High School in Hudson, WI. She loves to read because she gets to experience life from a whole new perspective.

TIM BOWLER has written seven novels for teenagers. *Midget* and *Dragon's Rock* established him as a powerful new voice, and his third novel, *River Boy*, won the Carnegie Medal. His most recent novel is *Frozen Fire*.

TONY BRADMAN published his first children's book in 1984, and since then he has written or edited nearly 200 more titles.

GERALDINE BRENNAN is a freelance journalist; she spent 10 years as books editor of the *Times Educational Supplement*. She has also judged the Nestlé Smarties Book Prize and the Booktrust Teenage Prize.

THERESA BRESLIN loves reading and writing books for young people. Her novel *Whispers in the Graveyard*, about a boy who struggles to read and write, won the Carnegie Medal.

KEVIN BROOKS lives in Essex, UK. He's had loads of horrible jobs and also spent many years involved in music and art. He's

been a full-time writer for the last seven years.

ANGELA BRYAN-BROWN is a sophomore at Eleanor Roosevelt High School in New York. She is a writer, a dreamer, a reader, an actress, a singer, a friend, a student, and a perfectionist intertwined with insecurity. But first and foremost, she's a rainbow.

MEG CABOT is the bestselling author of several series for young adults, including The Princess Diaries, The Mediator, and Missing, as well as *All-American Girl*, *Teen Idol*, *Nicola and the Viscount*, *Victoria and the Rogue*, and many books for older readers.

NICHOLAS CAMPBELL is 17 years old and lives in Dallas, TX. He wants to be a writer, and reading books inspires him a lot in his writing. He sees reading as both an art and an adventure, and as a large part of his everyday life.

NOAH CANTOR, 19, is a student at the University of Miami. His literary interests include graphic novels, Kurt Vonnegut, and John Irving. In the future, Noah hopes to pursue a career as an opera performer.

STACY CANTOR has been working in the publishing industry since 2004. She enjoys swimming, knitting, and of course reading. She lives in New York City on an island even smaller than Manhattan.

JAMIE CAPLAN is now 12 years old and attends an all-boys prep school. He reads to relax and prefers books about real-life issues.

BJORN CARLSON is a 16-year-old from Hudson, WI. He is currently a tenth grader at Hudson High School, and he loves music.

ALEXANDER CARN is 13 years old and lives in London with his mother, father, and sister. He

prefers academic work and enjoys clay-pigeon shooting.

ROSEMARY CASS-BEGGS, after a degree in psychology, specialized in focus groups for consumer research and tutored in the Open University. She rediscovered literature for children in the 1960s and has read it ever since. She is the author of *The Penguin Book of Rounds*.

ANNE CASSIDY has written 20 crime novels for teenagers. She lives in east London with her husband and son. When she's not writing she is shopping.

MARY KATE CASTELLANI has worked in the publishing industry since 2005. She lives in New York City, where she likes to take long walks through new neighborhoods, and can usually be found sitting in a coffee shop with a book.

CASEY CHARTIER, 11, is in the fifth grade at Clinton Valley Elementary in Clinton Township, MI. He has lots of pets, including a bearded dragon lizard, a cat, and a dog.

GARY CHOW is a 17-year-old Hong Konger living in Rugby, UK. He has many hobbies, such as reading, reading, and more reading.

EMILY CICIOTTE, 13, lives in Ellsworth, ME. She's not an author or anything like that. She can, however, jump off buildings without breaking bones, thanks to stunt camp. She's also into rock climbing, reading, and any other kind of adventures you can think of.

DORIAN CIRRONE is the author of *Dancing in Red Shoes Will Kill You*, *Prom Kings and Drama Queens*, and the Lindy Blues books.

JONATHAN COE is the author of seven novels, including *The Rotters' Club* and *The Closed Circle*, as well as a biography of the novelist B. S. Johnson.

ADAM COHEN is 13 years old and lives in London. He loves adventure books and is a loyal supporter of Cardiff City and Glamorgan Cricket Club.

RACHEL COHN is the author of the teen novels *Gingerbread, Shrimp, Cupcake*, and, along with David Levithan, *Nick & Norah's Infinite Playlist* and *Naomi and Ely's No Kiss List*. Her books have been selected as ALA Best Books for Young Adults, ALA Quick Picks for Reluctant Readers, and NYPL Books for the Teen Age. She mostly lives in California but sometimes in New York; she can't really make up her mind.

EOIN COLFER was born and still lives in Ireland. He is the author of many books including the best-selling Artemis Fowl, a series that grew from his love of Irish history and legend.

CLIO CONTOGENIS, 14, lives in uptown Manhattan in a little-known neighborhood called Hudson Heights. She occupies herself by ruthlessly devouring books, writing her own stories, and singing. She also enjoys acting and is usually involved in some sort of play.

WENDY COOLING is a children's books consultant and the creator of Bookstart, which gives free books to every baby in England. She has also edited many story and poetry collections. She was the winner of the prestigious Eleanor Farjeon Award for 2007.

YVONNE COPPARD was a teacher and then a child protection adviser before taking up writing full-time. She writes serious and humorous novels for children and teenagers.

MICHAEL COX has written more than 35 children's books and is published in more than a dozen countries, including Russia, Brazil, and Korea.

MICHAEL CRONIN is an actor and a writer. He has worked throughout the world on stage, in film, and on TV. *In the Morning . . .* , the final title of his World War II trilogy, was just published.

GILLIAN CROSS has been writing for young people for 30 years. Four of her Demon Headmaster books have been televised and she has won the Smarties Prize, the Whitbread Children's Book Award, and the Carnegie Medal.

BENJAMIN CUFFIN-MUNDAY is a pupil at the King's School Chester, UK. He plays clarinet and piano and in 2004 he was a judge for the Blue Peter Book Awards.

KAREN CUSHMAN's first book, *Catherine, Called Birdy*, was named a 1995 Newbery Honor Book. *The Midwife's Apprentice* won the Newbery Medal for 1996 and changed Cushman's life. She is also the author of *The Ballad of Lucy Whipple, Matilda Bone*, and *Rodzina*. Cushman lives on Vashon Island in Washington with her husband, and is at work on a new book.

ISSIE DARCY is 13 and likes singing, dancing, and drama. She loves reading everything from Harry Potter to *Lord of the Flies*.

JANE DARCY taught English for years before going back to school, where she is now studying English again and can read books all day.

DEBORAH DAVIS's books include *The Secret of the Seal*, an IRA Teacher's Choice, and *My Brother Has AIDS*. She is also the editor of *You Look Too Young to Be a Mom: Teen Mothers Speak Out on Love, Learning, and Success*. Her most recent novel is *Not Like You*. Deborah lives in Berkeley, CA, with her husband, son, and two cats.

CHRIS D'LACEY has written a wide variety of books for children aged four to 14. He is a regular visitor to schools, libraries, and book festivals.

BERLIE DOHERTY has written nearly 50 books and is translated into 21 languages. Her most recent titles are *The Starburster, Jinnie Ghost*, and *Abela*.

JENNIFER DONNELLY lives in Brooklyn, NY, with her husband, daughter, and two greyhounds. As a child, she loved to read, and the high point of her week was a Saturday trip to the library. It still is.

MALACHY DOYLE writes picture books, young fiction, and teenage novels. His work as a special needs teacher inspired his first novel, *Georgie*. Malachy is Irish, lives in Wales, and is married to an Englishwoman.

BRITTNY DUNLOP is 17 years old and lives in Hudson, WI. She discovered reading in fourth grade, where she first understood how reading takes you into another world.

JEANNE DUPRAU is the author of *The City of Ember, The People of Sparks*, and *The Prophet of Yonwood*. (A fourth and final volume of the series is forthcoming.) Her books are *New York Times* bestsellers, and they've also won many state readers' choice awards. She lives in California, where she keeps a big garden and a small dog.

FLORENCE EASTOE is 13 and lives in East Kent, UK, with her parents and younger brother. Her pastimes include reading, shopping, and caring for a menagerie of household pets.

CLAIRE EASTON is 16 and lives in New Jersey, which must be why she has an extreme fondness for diners and malls. She also enjoys books, good music, and eating Chinese food at Man Hing with her friends. She might become a writer someday.

PATRICIA ELLIOTT's first novel was *The Ice Boy*. Her most recent novel is *Ambergate*. Patricia lives in London with her husband, two sons, and a loopy Labrador.

SUSAN ETTENHEIM teaches Art and Computer Arts and is responsible for the library at Eleanor Roosevelt High School in New York City. She is the advisor to the Library Club and was thrilled to be involved, with her students, in this book project.

SHARI FESKO is the teen services librarian at the Southfield Public Library in Southfield, MI. She truly enjoys her work with teens and especially loves matching them up with the right book!

ANNE FINE has written 12 books for older readers. She was England's Children's Laureate from 2001–03 and has won the Whitbread and the Carnegie (both twice) and the Guardian Children's Fiction Prize.

DEBBIE REED FISCHER is the author of *Braless in Wonderland* and *Swimming with the Sharks*. She has worked as a modeling agent and as an English teacher, where she was the recipient of her school's Teacher of the Year award. Debbie lives in Florida with her husband and two sons. Visit her at Debbiereedfischer.com.

CATHERINE FISHER is a poet and novelist. Her best-known works include *Corbenic*, *Darkwater Hall*, and the acclaimed Book of the Crow series. Catherine's latest publications are *The Scarab* and *Darkhenge*. She lives in Wales with her two cats.

ANNE FLAHERTY worked as a news journalist in Ireland, South Africa, and Hong Kong before studying for an MA in children's literature. She now lives in London and is a freelance writer.

HALEY FLETCHER is 17 years old and a junior at the Hudson High School in Hudson, WI. She loves reading because it is the most relaxing thing to do. It allows her to create images and stories she couldn't do otherwise.

ALEX FLINN is the author of six novels. Her first novel, *Breathing Underwater*, was selected as an ALA Top 10 Best Book for Young Adults, while her novels *Breathing Underwater* and *Nothing to Lose* have been selected by teens for the IRA Young Adults Choices list. Her latest novel is *Beastly*, a modern, urban *Beauty and the Beast*.

MELINDA HOWARD FLORES graduated from New School University's MFA program in Writing for Children in 2005. Both Melinda's fiction and nonfiction works have appeared in print, and her young adult novel, *Ring Finger*, was a Merit Finalist for the 2004 Work-in-Progress Grant from the SCBWI. Melinda lives in New York City.

CATHERINE FORDE writes stories with young adults as her central characters. Her novels *Fat Boy Swim, Skarrs,* and *The Drowning Pond* have contemporary settings and dialogue.

LAURA FOX is 16 and lives in Salt Lake City, UT. She loves soccer and enjoys watching Manchester United play. She loves English and is thinking about pursuing a career in writing.

LINDSEY FRASER was a children's bookseller and is now a partner in Fraser Ross Associates, a literary agency in Edinburgh, Scotland.

MARIAH FREDERICKS is the author of many books for teens, including *The True Meaning of Cleavage*, *Head Games*, and her most recent book, *Crunch Time*. She lives with her husband in Queens, NY. You can visit her online at www.mariahfredericks.com.

KATHY FREDRICKSON is a librarian and Assistant Director of Youth Services at the Rolling Meadows Library in Illinois. She is also a storyteller, belly dancer, singer, and voracious reader. She lives with her fiancé and their two dogs.

EDWARD FRY is a small, scruffy-haired boy. He is 12 and is fanatical about rugby, jaffa cakes, and Scotland.

LAURA GAJDOSTIK lives and teaches English in Hudson, WI. She loves reading and loves sharing books with her high school students.

DAVID GARDNER is a student and National Literacy Trust accredited Reading Champion. Anyone who says teenagers don't read anymore has obviously never met David.

GRAHAM GARDNER wanted to be a writer from age eight. He is now 30, and went through at least 30 jobs before he saw his first novel published. Graham lives in West Wales.

SUSAN GATES lives in the north of England. She has taught in schools in Malawi, Africa, and County Durham, UK. Her latest teenage novels are *Dusk* and *Firebird*.

JAMILA GAVIN is known for her books reflecting her Anglo-Indian background, such as the Surya trilogy, though her Whitbread Children's Books prize winner was *Coram Boy*.

ADÈLE GERAS has written more than 90 books for children and two books for adults. Her latest young-adult novel is *Ithaka*.

ALAN GIBBONS went to Warwick University. He was a teacher and is now a full-time writer. He lives in

Liverpool, UK, with his wife and four children.

MADALYN GIBSON is 16 years old. She loves playing basketball, fishing, and hanging with her friends. She enjoys reading because it lets her step out of her world and walk into someone else's.

GAIL GILES is the author of *Breath of the Dragon*, *Shattering Glass*, *Dead Girls Don't Write Letters*, *Playing in Traffic*, and *What Happened to Cass McBride?* *Shattering Glass* was listed as one of the 100 best books of the last 10 years by the ALA. She has far too many pets and names all of them after authors, but none of them have written anything yet.

K. L. GOING is the award-winning author of books for children and teens. Her first novel, *Fat Kid Rules the World*, was named a Michael L. Printz Honor book by the ALA, as well as one of the Best Books for Young Adults from the past decade. Her newest novel is called *The Garden of Eve*. You can visit her online at www.klgoing.com.

ED GOLDBERG is the teen services librarian at the Syosset Public Library on Long Island, NY. Ed and his teen reviewers have been reviewing books for *VOYA* for the past three years.

JUDY GOLDSCHMIDT is the author of *Raisin Rodriguez & the Big-Time Smooch*, *Will the Real Raisin Rodriguez Please Stand Up?* and *The Secret Blog of Raisin Rodriguez*, which was a *VOYA* Top Shelf Fiction for Middle Grade Readers in 2005, as well as an ALA Popular Paperbacks/Humor in 2006.

SAHIL GOSWAMI is a 15-year-old boy residing in Queens, NY. He attends Stuyvesant High School and he loves to read, play chess, and participate in policy debate. He is a member of his school math team and neighborhood drum corps.

K. M. GRANT is the author of the de Granville trilogy and *How the Hangman Lost His Heart*. Her first novel, *Blood Red Horse*, was a Booksense Top Ten Pick and a *Booklist* Top Ten in Youth First Novels. She lives with her husband in Glasgow, Scotland.

ALAN GRATZ's first novel, *Samurai Shortstop*, was named one of YALSA's Top Ten Best Books of the Year and was also selected as one of the *Booklist* 2006 Top Ten Best Sports Books and 2006 Top Ten First Books for Youth. Alan is also the author of *Something Rotten*, *Something Wicked*, and *The Brooklyn Nine*. He lives in western North Carolina.

CANDIDA GRAY has degrees in theater, art history, and history, but she has always wanted to have one in literature, too! Candida works in education.

KEITH GRAY's first book, *Creepers*, was published when he was only 24. He has written several award-winning novels, including *The Runner* and *The Fearful*. He lives in Edinburgh, Scotland.

JOHN GREEN is the Michael L. Printz Award–winning author of *Looking for Alaska* and *An Abundance of Katherines*. When he was little, he made a list of things he was good at. The list included "telling lies" and "sitting." So he became a writer. You can visit him at www.sparksflyup.com.

JULIA GREEN writes mainly for young adults. She lives in Bath, UK, with her two teenage children, and lectures in creative writing at Bath Spa University.

ELENA GREGORIOU is a teacher in a London prep school. She believes the best thing about summer vacation is being able to read all day in the sun.

SARAH GRISTWOOD is the author of

three historical biographies—*Arabella: England's Lost Queen*, *Bird of Paradise: The Colorful Career of the First Mrs. Robinson*, and *Elizabeth and Leicester*—as well as a book on women's diaries.

HATTIE GRYLLS is now 13. She lives in Islington, UK. When not playing with her dog she reads, swims, and listens to her iPod.

LIAM HALLATT, 15, attends Myrtle Springs School in the UK. His review of *Stormbreaker* placed third in the Schools' Competition.

CRESS HANSON is 17 years old and lives in Hudson, WI. She loves riding horses and spends her time on schoolwork and track and field. She loves to read scary stories and about teens.

MARY ANN HARLAN has been a high school teacher and librarian in Northern California for seven years. She prefers teen books to adult books, has been a member of the ALA Quick Picks committee, and has coauthored *Young Adult Literature and Multimedia: A Quick Guide*.

JESSICA HARRINGTON, 17, lives in the ever-expanding river town of Hudson, WI. She absolutely loves to read, using it as a getaway from the everyday stressors in her life. She also loves to play softball, work, and spend time with her friends.

ALLISON HAWTHORNE is your average literature-loving 16-year-old from Hudson, WI. She has been reading since she was a toddler and has only gained speed and interest since.

KATIE HEATON, 18, has always used books as her getaway for exploring the world. Working in her town's local public library has made her love even more passionate, as well as inspiring her to write, and she has been rewarded with the NCTE Award for Most Promising Young Writer.

DIANA TIXIER HERALD, a former library director and Popular Materials librarian, has had a lifelong passion for reading. She has written articles and reviews for *Booklist, School Library Journal*, and *VOYA*. Diana has maintained a Web site focused on genre fiction since 1995—visit it at www.genrefluent.com.

BECCA HIEKEL is 16 years old and lives in Hudson, WI. She *loves* reading because it takes her mind off everything in her life and lets her focus on the book. Reading lets her mind imagine the unimaginable.

MARY HOFFMAN is the author of at least 85 books for children and teenagers. Her two most famous series are Amazing Grace and its sequels, and the Stravaganza series of teenage fantasy.

ZOE HOLDER is 16 and goes to Devonport High School for Girls in the UK. Her review of *Fat Kid Rules the World* won first place in the Schools' Competition.

ANTONIA HONEYWELL is taking a break from being a teacher of English to study for an MA. Her interest in children's literature was heightened by the birth of her first baby, Oliver.

MARY HOOPER has been writing for young adults for an awfully long time and enjoys the variety of being able to write historical fiction one day and funny stuff the next. She has two grown-up children and lives in Hampshire, UK.

CATHY HOPKINS lives in North London. She has had 34 books published. She is the author of the Mates Dates . . . teen-fiction series and the Truth or Dare . . . series. The books are now published in 22 different countries.

ANTHONY HOROWITZ is the author of the bestselling Alex Rider series— the first of which, *Stormbreaker*, has now been made into a film. He

lives in Crouch End, UK, with his wife, his children, and his dog.

LESLEY HOWARTH has written more than 20 books for children and teenagers. Her novel *MapHead* won the Guardian Children's Fiction Prize. Her latest novel is *Calling the Shots*.

LAURA HUTCHINGS is an English teacher at a boys' prep school in North London. She loves the fact that it gives her an excuse to read all the children's books that she'd be reading anyway!

BENEDICT JACKA is half-Australian, half-Armenian, and grew up in London. He's now 25 and divides his time between writing, reading, martial arts, and playing games.

JULIA JARMAN thinks that writing is another way of talking, and she has written more than 100 books. *Peace Weavers* is her latest for teens.

KATIE JENNINGS edits children's fiction and nonfiction for a London publishing house. Like most people who work in children's books, she owns two cats.

MERIDETH JENSON-BENJAMIN is a youth services librarian at Glendale Public Library in Glendale, AZ. A self-professed geek, she loves fantasy, sci-fi, and comic books— though not necessarily in that order.

CATHERINE JINKS was born in Brisbane, Australia, in 1963. She is the author of many children's books and also writes for adults.

ROBERT JOHNSTON, 18, graduated from high school in 2007 and is now attending Mesa State College in Colorado. He has been writing book reviews for about eight years and hopes to one day be an author of YA fiction.

PATRICK JONES is the author of four teen novels for older readers: *Things Change, Nailed, Chasing Tail Lights*, and *Cheated*.

In another life he was a teen librarian. He can be found on the Web at www.connectingya.com.

ANN JUNGMAN was born in London of refugee parents. Teaching led to writing, and Ann has published more than 100 books for children. Ann also runs Barn Owl Books, which reprints out-of-print quality children's books.

ARIEL KAHN's cultural world is occupied with The Sandman, *Buffy*, and other highbrow literary figures. A fiction and poetry writer, Ariel is currently working on his first novel as well as teaching both creative writing and graphic novels.

ELIZABETH KAY is half-Polish and half-English, and she went to art school. She wrote the Divide trilogy.

BRIAN KEANEY was born and lives in London. He made up his mind at an early age that he wanted to be a writer, and he considers it the best job in the world. He has written 14 novels for young people.

M. E. KERR is the author of 27 YA books. She has received the Margaret A. Edwards Award, a Christopher Award, the Knickerbocker Lifetime Achievement Award, and SCBWI Awards. Her latest book is called *Someone Like Summer*.

KELLI KONICEK is 15 years old and lives in Grand Junction, CO. She loves to snowboard, but her main passion is reading. She loves to be taken away from her bland, monotonous daily routine and placed into worlds she could never have dreamed up on her own.

KATHERINE KRAULAND, 18, lives in western Colorado. Somewhere between schoolwork, speech and debate, two musical instruments, and about a million other interests, she finds the time to read, even at the cost of running into a door between classes.

BOB KRECH lives in Lawrenceville, NJ, and teaches in Princeton Junction. Bob has written over 20 books and many articles on teaching and parenting. His debut novel, *Rebound*, was a 2007 ALA Best Book for Young Adults.

LISA LA BEAU is 16 years old. From a young age she has loved reading. She loves books that draw her in right away and make her keep reading. She hopes to read for the rest of her life because without it, she wouldn't be whole.

ELIZABETH LAIRD has always been a traveler. Born in New Zealand, she has lived in Malaysia, Ethiopia, Iraq, Lebanon, and Austria. Some of her books reflect her travels.

KELLY JO LASHER lives in Woodbine, NJ. She was a kid who loved to read, was a teenager who devoured Sweet Valley High books, and is now a high school librarian. She and her husband have a house, two dogs, and lots of tractors.

CAROLINE LAWRENCE is a Californian whose obsession with ancient history and languages brought her to England. She stayed to teach at a London primary school. In 1999 she began writing the Roman Mysteries.

MICHAEL LAWRENCE became a writer for young people with the publication of *When the Snow Falls* in 1995. Since then he has published many more books, including the bestselling Jiggy McCue series and the acclaimed *A Crack in the Line*.

LAURA LEHNER-ENNIS is a young adult librarian in Hudson, OH, although she herself is not a young adult. But she lives with some and reads a lot of their books.

KARA LEONARDI, age 17, lives in Grand Junction, CO. She regularly writes reviews of teen books, which can be found at www.genrefluent.com.

GAIL CARSON LEVINE grew up in New York City and has been writing all her life. Her first book for children, *Ella Enchanted*, was a 1998 Newbery Honor Book. She lives in a 200-year-old farmhouse in the Hudson River Valley in New York.

FRANCESCA LEWIS graduated in 1995 and has worked in publishing and public relations ever since.

SUE LIMB is a writer and broadcaster specializing in comedy. She lives in Gloucestershire, UK. Her favorite animal is the toad.

ANDREA LIPINSKI is a senior young adult librarian in the New York Public Library system. She has been reviewing young adult books for NYPL for over a decade, and she also reviews books for *School Library Journal*. She reads so many teen books that she hardly has room for grown-up books anymore, but she manages to fit in a couple each year.

E. LOCKHART is the author of *The Boyfriend List*, *The Boy Book*, *Dramarama*, and *Fly on the Wall*. Visit her on the Web at www.theboyfriendlist.com.

AMBER LYON, a tenth grader, lives in Hudson, WI. She loves to read whenever she has the time. When the weather is nice she can be found on her three-wheeler.

CATHERINE MACPHAIL lives in Scotland. She always wanted to be a writer, but it was only after her children were born that she had the courage to send off her first short story. Since then she has written short stories, romance novels, and comedy series for radio, but her major success has been with her teenage novels.

KERRY MADDEN is the author of *Gentle's Holler*, which received starred reviews from both *Kirkus Reviews* and *Publishers Weekly*, as

well as *Louisiana's Song*, *Jessie's Mountain*, *Writing Smarts*, and *Offsides*. She is currently at work on a biography of Harper Lee. You can visit her at www.kerrymadden.com.

JUSTIN MAHES, 12, lives in Manhattan. In school, reading is one of his favorite subjects. Justin likes to read horror and comedy books, as well as suspense and mystery. Justin is also very fond of writing book reviews.

MARGARET MAHY has written more than 180 books, including picture books, middle school books, senior and young-adult books, and collections of short stories.

LOUISE MANNING lives in London. She loves to read (obviously). In her free time she likes going out with her friends or going swimming.

JAN MARK lived in Oxford and wrote many novels for all ages. She gave up teaching to become a full-time writer, and she won the Carnegie Medal twice. Jan died suddenly at the beginning of 2006.

GRAHAM MARKS is an ex-graphic designer turned author. When he's not writing teen/young-adult novels and younger fiction, he is children's books editor for the trade paper *Publishing News*.

BRENDA MARSHALL is an English teacher and librarian at Port Regis, a prep school in Dorset, UK.

ROSA MATEO, 17, was born in the Dominican Republic and is looking forward to graduating from the In-tech Academy 368, class of 2008. She's been a volunteer for the New York Public Library for about five years and loves books.

SUE MAYFIELD was originally a teacher. Sue often leads workshops in schools and has been a youth worker and writing therapist. Born near Newcastle, she now lives in Cheltenham, UK.

MEGAN MCCAFFERTY is the *New York Times* bestselling author of *Sloppy Firsts*, *Second Helpings*, *Charmed Thirds*, and *Fourth Comings*, and the editor of the short story collection *Sixteen*. Her books have won awards from the ALA and the New York Public Library, and have been translated into ten languages. For more, go to www.meganmccafferty.com.

GERALDINE MCCAUGHREAN writes for all ages. She has won the Carnegie Medal, Guardian Children's Fiction Prize, Blue Peter Book Award, four Smarties Bronzes, and three Whitbread Children's Book Awards. In 2006 she published the official sequel to *Peter Pan*: *Peter Pan in Scarlet*.

PATRICIA MCCORMICK, a 2006 finalist for the National Book Award, is the author of three critically acclaimed novels for young adults—*Sold*, *My Brother's Keeper*, and *Cut*. She is currently working on a book that explores the grief of a 15-year-old girl whose brother was killed in the war in Iraq. McCormick lives in Manhattan with her husband and teenage son.

STEPHEN MCGRUER, age 14, attends the Boclair Academy in England. His review of *Montmorency* took third place in the Schools' Competition.

JOHN MCLAY is a children's books literary scout. He is also a lecturer, an anthologist, and a book reviewer. He has previously worked for Puffin Books, been a children's bookseller, and sold translation rights internationally. He is founding director of the Bath Festival of Children's Literature in the UK.

ANDY MCNAB's novel *Bravo Two Zero*, McNab's account of the Gulf War operation that he led in 1991, is the UK's bestselling war book of all time and launched his career as a writer.

CLIFF MCNISH is a fantasy writer whose first series, the Doomspell trilogy, won him an instant and avid readership. He has followed up the success of this series with his Silver sequence.

VALERIE MENDES knew she wanted to be a writer when she was six. Since then she has written two picture books and four novels for teenagers, including *Girl in the Attic*, *The Drowning,* and *Lost and Found*.

LIVI MICHAEL has written four award-winning books for adults, the Frank series for younger children, and *The Whispering Road* for older children.

HEATHER E. MILLER is the young adult librarian at Homewood Public Library in Alabama, where she has worked for more than 11 years. When not enjoying teens and teen books, she spends time doing glass art, which she displays in local galleries.

ELEANOR MILNES-SMITH has always been an avid reader of fantasy and now, aged 13, is a fan of Terry Pratchett and Christopher Paolini.

PHILIPPA MILNES-SMITH is a literary agent and children's specialist at the LAW agency (Lucas Alexander Whitley). She has worked for many years in children's publishing and was previously the managing director of Puffin Books.

SHAZIA MIRZA, age 15, attends Dixons City Technology College in the United Kingdom. Her review of *Eragon* placed second in the Schools' Competition.

CAITLIN MOHWINKEL is 16 years old and lives in Wisconsin. She likes to read because it can take her to places that she has never been before.

ROZ MONETTE is the author of an

edgy teen fiction series. She lives in Colorado and is learning to master the balancing act of being a wife, mother, and writer and having a day job. Visit her Web site at www.rozmonette.com.

NICOLA MORGAN has written around 70 books, mostly home-learning titles based on her specialty in literacy acquisition. In 2002 she achieved her overriding ambition to be a novelist with *Mondays Are Red*. She now writes nonfiction and fiction.

SAMUEL MORTIMER lives in Devon, UK. His hobbies include playing guitar, judo, and reading.

AN NA was born in Korea and grew up in San Diego, CA. A former middle school English and history teacher, she now divides her time writing in Oakland, CA, and Warren, VT. *A Step from Heaven*, a Printz award winner, was her first novel.

BEVERLEY NAIDOO grew up in Johannesburg, South Africa. As a student she joined the resistance to apartheid, ending up exiled in England. Her first book, *Journey to Jo'burg*, was banned in South Africa. That spurred her to keep writing! She won the Carnegie Medal for *The Other Side of Truth*.

LINDA NEWBERY writes fiction for all ages. Her young-adult novels, *The Shell House* and *Sisterland*, were both shortlisted for the Carnegie Medal. She also writes short stories and poems.

MACKENZEE NICELY is 15 and lives in Wisconsin. She loves to read, swim, and—the typical answer—hang out with her friends.

DEBORAH NICHOLL has worked in libraries for more than 20 years and is currently the young adult liaison for a branch of the San Antonio Public Library system. She lives with her own personal library, her husband, and a pet turtle named Plato.

SARA NICKERSON wrote for TV and film before publishing her first novel, *How to Disappear Completely and Never Be Found.*

JENNY NIMMO lives in Wales. She worked in the theater before becoming a writer/director in children's TV. She won the Smarties Gold Award for *The Snow Spider* in 1986 and for *The Owl Tree* in 1997. She is currently writing a quintet: Children of the Red King.

ANDREW NORRISS has, over 20 years, written and cowritten some 150 episodes of sitcoms and children's drama for television, and six books for children, including *Aquila*, which won the Whitbread Children's Book Award in 1997.

IAN OGILVY is best known as an actor—in particular for his title role in *The Saint*. He has written two novels and four children's books all about his hero, Measle Stubbs. He lives in Southern California.

KENNETH OPPEL is the author of *Airborn*, its sequel, *Skybreaker*, as well as the Silverwing trilogy, which has sold more than a million copies worldwide. He published his first novel at 17, after receiving encouragement from Roald Dahl.

CHARLI OSBORNE is the head of toon services at the Oxford Public Library in Oxford, MI. She reviews regularly for *School Library Journal* and *Library Journal.* A former Michael L. Printz Committee Member, she is now serving her second term on the Alex Awards Committee.

TERRI PADDOCK is the author of one teen novel, *Come Clean*, and one adult novel, *Beware the Dwarfs.* Formerly a freelance journalist, she's now the editor of www.whatsonstage.com, the UK's leading theater Web site.

MELANIE PALMER works as an editor in children's books and lives in North London with seven other vagabonds.

CHRISTOPHER PAOLINI was born in 1983 and was homeschooled by his parents in Montana. He began writing *Eragon* as a hobby, and the book is now on sale all over the world. On completing the trilogy, Christopher plans to take a long vacation.

KIMBERLY L. PAONE is the Supervisor of Adult and Teen Services at the Elizabeth Public Library in Elizabeth, NJ. She has served on a number of professional committees, including YALSA's Best Books for Young Adults, the Michael L. Printz Award, and the Margaret A. Edwards Award. Kimberly is also a regular reviewer for *VOYA.*

AMY PATTEE is an assistant professor of library science at the Graduate School of Library and Information Science at Simmons College in Boston, MA. When not teaching future librarians all about children's and young adult literature, Amy enjoys reading and writing about young adult novels and playing with her cat, Spooky.

PHILIPPA PEARCE was a highly acclaimed children's writer whose most famous title is *Tom's Midnight Garden,* for which she won the Carnegie Medal. Her last book is *The Little Gentleman.* She died in 2006.

DANIEL PEASE is a junior at Eleanor Roosevelt High School in New York. He is a talented musician and an avid reader.

MAL PEET grew up in Norfolk, UK, before settling down to write and illustrate books for children—his first novel was *Keeper.* His novel *Tamar* won him the 2005 Carnegie Medal.

YARDLEY SAGE PERESMAN, a

sophomore at Eleanor Roosevelt High School, is 15 years old and lives in New York City. She loves reading, writing, and the beach.

ZOEY PERESMAN, 15, is a sophomore at Eleanor Roosevelt High School who resides in New York City. She loves film, literature, and relaxation.

NORMA N. PEREZ-HERNANDEZ is a 17-year-old writer from the Bronx, NY, whose reviews have been featured in the New York Public Library's "Books for the Teen Age." Her plans include college and a successful career, along with reading as many books as she can get her hands on.

HELENA PIELICHATY won a bar of chocolate for writing a story when she was 10. She can't remember the story but she does remember the chocolate. She has been interested in chocolate and other people's problems ever since.

CAROLINE PITCHER writes stories for all ages. *Cloud Cat* and *Sky Shifter* are the first two books in the Year of Changes quartet.

ANNA PLOCIAK is 16 and a junior at Eleanor Roosevelt High School in New York City. Her favorite subjects are English and Science. She enjoys participating in basketball, gymnastics, and fencing.

ANNA POSNER is a high school senior in England.

SUSAN PRICE had her first novel published when she was 16. Since then she has written many more, including the award-winning *The Sterkarm Handshake.*

SALLY PRUE wasn't great at writing stories at school, but as she grew up she gradually realized she couldn't do anything else, much, either. After only 15 years of toil, she had her first novel, *Cold Tom*, published.

LOGAN RAGAR, 14, lives in Grand Junction, CO. Reading is her way of not only entertaining herself but also of keeping her imagination alive. When not being a complete bookworm/nerd, she also spends many an hour practicing her violin or playing with her fat blond Lab, Buddy.

BALI RAI is a fairly young and occasionally exciting author. He has written over 10 books that deal with the realities of life in modern Britain for young adults/teens.

JANETTE RALLISON is the author of many novels for young adults, including *All's Fair in Love, War, and High School*; *It's a Mall World After All*; and *How to Take the Ex Out of Ex-Boyfriend*. She lives in Chandler, AZ, with her husband and their children.

CELIA REES writes for teenagers. Her novels include *Witch Child, Sorceress,* and *Pirates!* She lives in Leamington Spa, UK, and divides her time between writing, talking to readers, acting as a tutor on creative writing courses, and reviewing.

DOUGLAS REES lives at the south end of San Francisco Bay, CA, where he works as a young adult librarian and writes books. He is the author of *Lightning Time*, which was an ALA Best Book and a NYPL Best Book for the Teen Age, as well as *Grandy Thaxter's Helper, Vampire High, Smoking Mirror,* and *The Janus Gate*. His most recent novel is called *Uncle Pirate*.

PHILIP REEVE worked in a bookshop before becoming known as an illustrator. His first book for children, *Mortal Engines*, created one of the most intriguing worlds in fantasy fiction.

ANTHONY REUBEN is a business journalist for BBC Online. He lives in England.

JAMES REYNOLDS is the China correspondent for the BBC.

ELIZABETH RICE is a senior at Hudson High School in Wisconsin. She has been an avid reader since she read her first book, *Silly Sally Went to Town*. With her overactive imagination, there is usually a book in hand or very close by.

JAMES RIORDAN is Emeritus Professor at the University of Surrey, UK. He also writes both picture books and novels for young people.

KATHERINE ROBERTS always wanted to be a fantasy writer. Her debut novel was *Song Quest*, and 10 years of working as a racehorse groom led to her Alexander epic, *I Am the Great Horse*.

CATHERINE ROBINSON has been writing books for children of all ages, from preschool to teens, for nearly 20 years. Her most recent work has been a series of one-off teenage novels.

MEG ROSOFF won great acclaim for her first novel, *How I Live Now*, which was published in 2004. Her second novel, *Just in Case*, won the 2006 Carnegie Medal. An American, she lives in London with her husband and daughter.

KATHRYN ROSS is a former English teacher and independent bookseller. She is now a partner in Fraser Ross Associates, an Edinburgh-based literary agency.

ROSIE RUSHTON has had more than 30 books published worldwide. She is a secondary-school principal, a lay minister in the Church of England, and has three young grandchildren.

KAREN SANTAMARIA is a teen librarian in charge of materials selection at Kalamazoo (MI) Public Library. She also serves as advisor to the Galley Review Group, hoping to inspire young library patrons to want to write and talk about the books they are reading.

HUGH SCOTT wrote *The Plant That Ate the World*, *Freddie and the Enormouse*, and *Why Weeps the Brogan?*

KIERAN SCOTT is a young adult author who lives in New Jersey with her husband, Matt. Her book *I Was a Non-Blonde Cheerleader* was an ALA Quick Pick and a NYPL Book for the Teen Age. She is also the author of *Brunettes Strike Back*, *A Non-Blonde Cheerleader in Love*, and *Jingle Boy*. Kieran is currently hard at work on her next novel, *Geek Magnet*.

MARCUS SEDGWICK is an award-winning author of children's books. He has worked in publishing for 15 years, as a bookseller, an editor, and a publisher, as well as in sales.

DARREN SHAN always wanted to be a writer and is now a publishing phenomenon! His Saga of Darren Shan has sold in huge numbers and each new volume is eagerly awaited across the globe.

NICK SHARRATT is the illustrator of Jacqueline Wilson's multimillion selling novels. He also illustrates picture books for writers like Julia Donaldson and Giles Andreae, as well as writing his own.

RACHEL SHAW enjoys spending time with her friends. These are her first book reviews—and she enjoyed doing them!

HELEN SIMMONS works in a small independent bookshop in Bath, UK, and has specialized in children's books for most of her career. She also has a job as a school librarian and is a reviewer.

NICKY SINGER's first novel for children, *Feather Boy*, was made into a TV drama. Her second, *Doll*, was short-listed for the Booktrust

Teenage Prize, and her latest, *The Innocent's Story*, is about terrorism and moral responsibility.

GARETH SMITH lives in South Wales. Like most contributors to this book, Gareth loves reading. He was a judge for the 2004 Blue Peter Book Awards.

SONYA SONES is the author of four young adult novels in verse: *Stop Pretending: What Happened When My Big Sister Went Crazy*, *What My Mother Doesn't Know*, *One of Those Hideous Books Where the Mother Dies*, and *What My Girlfriend Doesn't Know*. Her books have received many awards and have been chosen by the ALA as Best Books for Young Adults and Quick Picks for Reluctant Young Adult Readers. She hopes you'll visit her at www.sonyasones.com.

JERRY SPINELLI is the author of many books, which have been translated into many languages around the world. Jerry and his wife, fellow author Eileen, live in Willistown, PA.

STEPHANIE A. SQUICCIARINI is the Teen Services Librarian at Fairport (NY) Public Library. A recovering retail manager, she lives in Rochester, NY, with her husband and requisite three cats. She is active in YALSA as well as the Youth Services Section (YSS) of the New York Library Association.

TODD STRASSER is the author of more than 120 books for teens and middle schoolers, including the best-selling Help! I'm Trapped in . . . series, and numerous award-winning YA novels, including *The Wave*, *Give a Boy a Gun*, *The Accident*, *Can't Get There from Here*, and *Boot Camp*. His novel *How I Created My Perfect Prom Date* became the feature release *Drive Me Crazy*. He also writes for television, newspapers, and magazines.

WILLIAM SUTCLIFFE was born in 1971 in London. He is the author of four novels—*New Boy*, *Are You Experienced?*, *The Love Hexagon*, and *Bad Influence*—which have been translated into 17 languages.

CECILE SVENSGAARD is 18 years old and attends the University of Minnesota at Duluth. She has loved to read ever since she was a little girl. Her mom used to tell her she would "eat books." Reading is her way of escaping reality and "teleporting" into a different world.

REBECCA SWIFT is an editor, writer, and director of The Literary Consultancy. She has also published poems and has written the libretto for the opera *Spirit Child*.

MARIANNE TAYLOR lives in North London. She is the sub-editor for *Birdwatch* magazine, and she is also a freelance writer, an artist, and a cartoonist.

ALAN TEMPERLEY lives in Scotland and has written many books including *Harry and the Wrinklies*.

ALAN THIERFELDER is 18 and has never left the state of Wisconsin, a place where there isn't much else to do but read. He generally sticks to reading horror but does dabble every once in a while. He's about six feet tall and generally sarcastic.

KATE THOMPSON was born in Yorkshire but lives in Ireland. In 2005 she won the Guardian Children's Fiction Prize for *The New Policeman*.

MATT THORNE is the author of the 39 Castles series and six novels for adults, including *Eight Minutes Idle* and *Cherry*, which was long-listed for the Booker Prize.

JEREMY TRAMER, 17, lives in Santa Monica, CA. The son of two professional writers, Tramer is the author of the impressive literary works *What I Did Over Summer*

Break, *Why Soda Should Be Allowed in the Vending Machines*, and *What I Did Over Spring Break*. His writing has received an A and three Bs in Mr. Barazza's AP English class, which is kind of a big deal considering that Mr. Barazza grades really hard.

JORDYN TURNEY is 17 years old. She lives in California and has been reading and writing for as long as she can remember. Her favorite novel so far is *Gone with the Wind*.

ELEANOR UPDALE's historical novel *Montmorency* won the Blue Peter Book Award for "The Book I Couldn't Put Down." It has three sequels. Eleanor is working on a PhD in history at the University of London.

JEAN URE had her first book published while she was still at school, and she has been writing ever since. She lives in a 300-year-old house in South London with her family.

FELIX VAN DER VAART, 14, of Annandale, VA, plays all sports, although he likes tennis and, more than anything, he loves baseball. Felix enjoys reading and likes history. He also enjoys hanging out with his dog, Zack, and his friends.

ALLISON RAE VAN SICLEN is 16 years old and a junior at St. Anthony Village High School. She enjoys acting, singing, and writing, as well as reading whatever she has time for. Allison is an aspiring writer who hopes to go into the film industry.

SUSAN VAUGHT is the author of the young adult novels *Trigger* and *Stormwitch*. *Trigger* was a Book Sense Children's Pick and a 2006 ALA Best Book for Young Adults. Her newest novel is called *Big Fat Manifesto*. She lives in Tennessee.

GILL VICKERY studied fine art and

painting at college and since then has worked as a children's librarian and English teacher. She is the author of the novel *The Ivy Crown*.

LAUREN VILLARROEL is 17 years old and is a senior at Eleanor Roosevelt High School in New York City. She likes to read books that seem real and relate to her life. In her spare time she likes to listen to music and write lyrics and poems.

NED VIZZINI is the author of *It's Kind of a Funny Story*, *Be More Chill*, and *Teen Angst? Naaah* . . . He has written for *The New York Times Book Review*, *The New York Sun*, Bookslut, Huffington Post, Dogmatika, 3:AM, and Underground Voices. His work has been translated into six languages. He lives in Brooklyn, NY.

RACHEL WADHAM is the education librarian at Brigham Young University in Utah. Rachel holds an MLS from the University of North Texas and will soon graduate with an MEd from Pennsylvania State University. Her published works include hundreds of book reviews as well as works on fantasy and other young adult literature topics.

JILL PATON WALSH has been a professional writer most of her working life. She has written for children and for adults. She lives in Cambridge, UK.

MEGAN WEBB is a youth services librarian in High Point, NC. She has received a BA in English from Lees-McRae College and an MA in Information Science from the University of Tennessee.

ARABELLA WEIR is a comedy writer/performer. She wrote the bestseller *Does My Bum Look Big in This?* after developing and performing the character for the BBC.

NANCY WERLIN has been a devoted reader since the age of four. She is the author of six young adult novels,

including *The Killer's Cousin* (winner of the Edgar Award for Best Mystery), *Double Helix* (a *School Library Journal* and *Booklist* Best Book of the Year), and *The Rules of Survival* (a National Book Award finalist). Visit her Web site at www.nancywerlin.com.

SARA WHEELER writes nonfiction books, sometimes travel narratives and sometimes biographies.

GLORIA WHELAN has published over 30 award-winning books for young readers. Her novel *Homeless Bird* received the National Book Award. She also writes fiction and poetry for adults. After many years of living in the woods of Northern Michigan, she now lives in Detroit.

MAGGIE WHITACRE is 16 years old and lives in Wisconsin. She loves to read because it's interesting and lets you see life through another person's point of view.

SARAH ILEEN WHITSON, 17, is from a small town in Kansas— El Dorado. She loves reading because there is so much to discover in a book. It's so different from a movie and television because you, as the reader, get to create how the characters look.

MATT WHYMAN is the author of several acclaimed novels, including *Boy Kills Man* and *So Below*—an urban fantasy series.

JEANNE WILLIS lives in North London. Since 1980 she has had more than 100 books published. She's won several awards and was short-listed for the Whitbread Children's Book Award.

ELLEN WITTLINGER has published 12 young adult novels, many of which have been ALA Best Books of the Year. Her novel *Hard Love* won a Michael L. Printz Honor Award and the Lambda Literary Award. Her most recent novel,

Parrotfish, is about a transgendered teenager.

CHRIS WOODING writes screenplays, books for children and adults, cartoon series, graphic novels, TV shows, and just about anything else he can. He lives in London.

SARA ZARR is the author of *Story of a Girl* and the forthcoming *Sweethearts*. *Story of a Girl* has been named a NYPL Book for the Teen Age and won the Utah Arts Council Original Writing Competition before it was published. Sara lives in Salt Lake City, UT, with her husband.

JONNY ZUCKER writes for children and teenagers. His work includes the Venus Spring—Stunt Girl series. He has worked as a stand-up comedian and a primary school teacher.

STACEY ZUEHLK is 15 and lives in Lapeer, MI. One of her favorite things to do is read. She loves to write poetry and short stories, and she is obsessed with music and her guitar.

Acknowledgments

We thought that the second book would be easier, and that we wouldn't need to depend on quite as much help from other people this time around. We were really very wrong indeed. The list of people to whom we owe a debt for helping to bring this book out is enormous. And still we're bound to have forgotten people—if we have, our apologies.

To begin with, we must give thanks to all those who made the first book a success—in particular to Jill Coleman who commissioned it, and to Jon Appleton, who turned our chaotic manuscript into an exciting and special book; and then to Nicky Potter, Tabitha Pelly, and Rebecca Caine, who made sure everyone in the press knew just how exciting and special it was. We were lucky enough to receive awards for the first book from Blue Peter and the National Literacy Association, for which, too, we are grateful; they helped to enhance the success of the first book, but more importantly worked wonders for our morale as we trudged through the assembling of volume two.

And so to this, the *UTBG*. Our most important thanks must be to our contributors, whose words make up the bulk of the book. From those who wrote single exquisite entries to those who heroically took on a dozen or more (special round of applause for Eileen Armstrong here, please): your work is—of course—what makes this book what it is. We are especially pleased that our contributors to this volume include a number of teenagers; the quality of their work, their enthusiasm, their professionalism were admirable—the rest of us could learn a great deal from them. As last time, many of our contributors have generously waived their fees, and proceeds in the UK have been donated to our chosen charity, Hope and Homes for Children (www.hopeandhomes.org)—we are delighted to have been able to raise well over £2,000 from this book to help them to continue their vital and inspiring work.

Support from publishers' publicists and authors' agents has allowed us to get hold of new titles to review and contributors to review them, without which this really wouldn't have been much of a book; so thanks to them, too.

All three of us have friends and family who have helped in any number of ways with the *UTBG* process—some of them by writing entries or making useful suggestions, others by taking us out for drinks to take our minds off the uglier aspects of our proofreading obsessions. To Jenny Hicks for her encouragement; to Simon and Sarah and all at the Kilburn Bookshop; to Nicholas Allen and all at Arnold House School; to Noga Applebaum; to Miranda Duffy for another day spent sifting through hundreds and hundreds and hundreds of reviews sent to us by teenagers from around the country; to Sarah and David for keeping Leonie sane (not the easiest of tasks)—thanks to you all. In particular, Laura Hutchings and Anthony Reuben have shown extraordinary patience as the *UTBG* invaded every room of their homes and every moment of their lives—their work on the *UTBG* has been tireless, as has their work on other matters that have freed up the editors to get on with *UTBG* work when it was really their turn to do the dishes. Laura moved house almost single-handedly on Leonie's behalf. If Anthony could possibly have carried Susan's pregnancy on her behalf, to allow her to get on with drafting her editing suggestions, we have no doubt that he wouldn't have hesitated.

Which brings us to the latest member of the UBG team, Isaac, who very thoughtfully resisted the temptation to be born too early and throw our schedules out of kilter. His patience is more appreciated than he yet knows. In fact he turned up very efficiently a matter of hours before our deadline—before the deadline, mind, but at the last possible moment. His mother's dominant publishing gene is clearly in evidence here.

And thanks, too, to David Almond who kindly agreed to write an introduction to this book, though we did all have some doubts about whether we should invite him to write it, as on the whole we don't want him to do anything with the hours in his day but write more and more books for us to be enchanted by. Leonie and Susan disagree vigorously about the merits of almost every book they discuss—David is possibly unique in earning the highest praise from both.

Not forgetting the designers of the book, Helen Taylor and Terry Woodley, a massive thanks for making it all look so fantastic.

In the *UBG* we described our agent, Philippa Milnes-Smith, as the book's godmother, and we're delighted to say that as we graduated to book two she hasn't shirked that important role one bit. She and her assistants, Helen Mulligan (last book) and Helen Norris (this book), have been more than generous with their time and thoughts, more than efficient in their work and—of course—a delight always. We do know how lucky we are to have them.

Finally to Susila Baybars and Katie Jennings at A & C Black, who bravely took on this project. Thanks so much for the huge amount of work you've put in. We three have enjoyed working with you on the *UTBG* tremendously—and just hope you have enjoyed it, too.

About this edition

This volume is based on an edition we produced for the UK, which was published at the start of 2006. A fair amount of cutting away and replacing was needed to make that volume into this, to take into account which books are or aren't available in which country and how reading tastes and markets differ between the two. Indeed, the extent of these differences never ceases to surprise and baffle us.

None of us is particularly expert on publishing trends or reading habits in the United States, though, so we knew that if this book was to have any chance of working there we would have to depend on the expertise of others, in this case the team at Walker & Company in New York who have—we think—done a fantastic job. From the designers, Donna Mark and Yelena Safronova, through the production team, Jennifer Healey and Melissa Kavonic, copyeditor Nira Hyman and proofreader Lola Kavonic, everyone has worked to produce something the three of us are extremely proud of and for which we are very grateful. And most of all, of course, our gratitude goes to the people behind all the editorial work, the planning and commissioning and editing of all the new entries: Stacy Cantor, Mary Kate Castellani, and Emily Easton—who have quietly got on with it and seemingly effortlessly (but surely not so in hard reality!) produced a book that shows they understood absolutely 100% what we feel the Ultimate Book Guides are about. Thank you.

—D. H., L. F., and S. R.

419

Front cover from *The Hound of the Baskervilles* by Sir Arthur Conan Doyle, which appears on pages 96 and 319, used by permission of Penguin Books Ltd. 1996.

Jacket cover from *How I Live Now* by Meg Rosoff, which appears on page 279, used by permission of Random House Children's Books, a division of Random House, Inc.

Front cover from *How the García Girls Lost Their Accents* by Julia Alvarez, which appears on pages 166 and 374, used by permission of Penguin Group (USA) Inc.

"Book Cover," from *Interview with the Vampire* by Anne Rice, copyright © 1997. Used by permission of Ballantine Books, a division of Random House, Inc. Jacket appears on pages 250 and 346.

Front cover from *Looking for Alaska* by John Green, which appears on page 278, used by permission of Penguin Group (USA) Inc. Books for Young Readers.

Front cover from *Lord of the Flies* by William Golding, which appears on page 209, used by permission of Penguin Group (USA) Inc.

Cover from *The Lord of the Rings* by J. R. R. Tolkien. Copyright © 1954, 1965 by J. R. R. Tolkien. Copyright © renewed 1982 by Christopher R. Tolkien, Michael H. R. Tolkien, John F. R. Tolkien and Priscilla M. A. R. Tolkien. Reprinted by permission of Houghton Mifflin Company. All rights reserved. Jacket appears on pages 36 and 210.

Vintage front cover from *Love in the Time of Cholera* by Gabriel García Márquez, translated by Edith Grossman, copyright © 1988 by Gabriel García Márquez. Used by permission of Alfred A. Knopf, a division of Random

House, Inc. Jacket appears on page 212.

Front cover from *Mates, Dates, and Inflatable Bras* by Cathy Hopkins, which appears on page 222, used by permission of Simon & Schuster, Inc.

Front cover from *Monster* by Walter Dean Myers, which appears on pages 189 and 228. Cover art © 1999 by Christopher Myers. Cover © 2001 by HarperCollins Publishers, Inc. Used by permission of HarperCollins Publishers.

Front cover from *Nick & Norah's Infinite Playlist* by Rachel Cohn and David Levithan, which appears on pages 163 and 242, used by permission of Alfred A. Knopf Books for Young Readers, a division of Random House, Inc.

Jacket cover from *Night* by Elie Wiesel, which appears on page 243, used by permission of Bantam Books, a division of Random House, Inc.

Front cover from *No More Dead Dogs* by Gordon Korman, which appears on page 246, used by permission of Hyperion Books.

Front cover from *Noughts & Crosses* by Malorie Blackman, which appears on page 252, used by permission of The Random House Group Ltd.

Front cover from *On the Road* by Jack Kerouac, which appears on page 251, used by permission of Penguin Group (USA) Inc.

Front cover from *The Outsiders* by S. E. Hinton, which appears on pages 264 and 397, used by permission of Penguin Group (USA) Inc. Books for Young Readers.

Front cover from *Pirates!* by Celia Rees, which appears on page

271, used by permission of Bloomsbury Children's Books, a division of Bloomsbury U.S.A.

"Book Cover," copyright © 2005, from *Prep* by Curtis Sittenfeld. Used by permission of Random House, Inc. Cover appears on page 275.

Front cover from *The Princess Diaries* by Meg Cabot, which appears on page 70. Cover photographs © 2003 by Timothy Hampson. Cover © 2001 by HarperCollins Publishers, Inc. Used by permission of HarperCollins Publishers.

Front cover from *Refugee Boy* by Benjamin Zephaniah, which appears on page 375, used by permission of Bloomsbury Children's Books, a division of Bloomsbury U.S.A.

Front cover from *Rhymes with Witches* by Lauren Myracle, © 2005 Lauren Myracle. Published by Harry N. Abrams, Inc., New York. All Rights Reserved. Cover appears on pages 71 and 290.

Front cover from *The Rules of Survival* by Nancy Werlin, which appears on page 296, used by permission of Penguin Group (USA) Inc. Books for Young Readers.

Front cover from *The Secret Life of Bees* by Sue Monk Kidd, which appears on pages 278 and 308, used by permission of Penguin Group (USA) Inc.

Front cover from *The Shell House* by Linda Newbery, which appears on page 318, used by permission of The Random House Group Ltd.

Jacket cover from *Skellig* by David Almond, which appears on page 325, used by permission of Random House Children's Books, a division of Random House, Inc.

Jacket cover from *Slaughterhouse-Five* by Kurt Vonnegut, Jr., which appears on page 218, used by permission of Dell publishing, a division of Random House, Inc.

Front cover from *Smack* by Melvin Burgess, which appears on pages 188 and 329. Cover © 2003 by HarperCollins Publishers. Used by permission of HarperCollins Publishers.

Front cover from *Speak* by Laurie Halse Anderson, which appears on page 334, used by permission of Penguin Group (USA) Inc. Books for Young Readers.

Front cover from *Staying Fat for Sarah Byrnes* by Chris Crutcher, which appears on page 338. Jacket photograph © 2003 by Ali Smith. Jacket © 2003 by HarperCollins Publishers. Used by permission of HarperCollins Publishers.

Front cover from *A Step from Heaven* by An Na, which appears on page 374, used by permission of Penguin Group (USA) Inc. Books for Young Readers.

Front cover from *Stormbreaker: An Alex Rider Adventure* by Anthony Horowitz, which appears on page 11, used by permission of Penguin Group (USA) Inc. Books for Young Readers.

Front cover from *Surrender* by Sonya Hartnett. Copyright © 2005 Sonya Hartnett. Reproduced by permission of the publisher, Candlewick Press, Inc., Cambridge, MA. Cover appears on page 344.

Front cover from *Tales of Mystery and Imagination* by Edgar Allan Poe, which appears on page 347, used by permission of Wordsworth Classics.

Front cover from *Things Change* by Patrick Jones, which appears on page 396, used by permission of

Walker Books for Young Readers, a division of Bloomsbury U.S.A.

Front cover from *To Kill a Mockingbird* by Harper Lee, which appears on page 360, used by permission of Grand Central Publishing, a division of Hachette Book Group USA, Inc.

Front cover from *The True Meaning of Cleavage* by Mariah Fredericks, which appears on page 367, used by permission of Simon & Schuster, Inc.

Front cover from *ttyl* by Lauren Myracle, © 2004 Lauren Myracle. Published by Harry N. Abrams, Inc., New York. All Rights Reserved. Cover appears on page 162.

Front cover from *Twilight* by Stephenie Meyer, which appears on page 369, used by permission of Little, Brown and Company, a division of Hachette Book Group USA, Inc.

Front cover from *Uglies* by Scott Westerfeld, which appears on page 370, used by permission of Simon & Schuster, Inc.

Front cover from *V for Vendetta* by Alan Moore and David Lloyd, which appears on pages 123 and 373, used by permission of Titan Books. Copyright © 1990, 2006 DC Comics Inc. All rights reserved.

Front cover from *Watchmen* by Alan Moore and Dave Gibbons, which appears on pages 122 and 381, used by permission of Titan Books. Copyright © 1986, 1987, 2006 DC Comics Inc. All rights reserved.

Front cover from *What Happened to Cass McBride?* by Gail Giles, which appears on page 347, used by permission of Little, Brown and Company, a division of Hachette Book Group USA, Inc.

Front cover from *Witch Child* by

Celia Rees, which appears on page 313, used by permission of Bloomsbury Publishing Plc.

Jacket cover from *A Wizard of Earthsea* by Ursula K. Le Guin, which appears on page 394, used by permission of Bantam Books, a division of Random House, Inc.

Jacket from *A Wrinkle in Time* by Madeleine L'Engle. Copyright © 1962, renewed 1990 by Madeleine L'Engle Franklin. Reprinted by permission of Farrar, Straus and Giroux, LLC. Jacket appears on pages 36 and 401.

Front cover from *Zoo* by Graham Marks, which appears on page 218, used by permission of Bloomsbury Children's Books, a division of Bloomsbury U.S.A.

Herald, Diana Tixier. *Teen Genreflecting*. Second Edition. Libraries Unlimited, 2003. Reprinted reviews for *Burning Up* by Caroline B. Cooney, which appears on page 55, and *Define "Normal"* by Julie Anne Peters, which appears on page 90.

Herald, Diana Tixier. "Beige" *Reader's Advisor Online*. Libraries, Unlimited, 2007. Reprinted review for *Beige* by Cecil Castellucci, which appears on page 31.

All efforts have been made to seek permission for copyrighted material, but in the event of any omissions, the publisher would be pleased to hear from copyright holders and to amend these acknowledgments in subsequent editions of *The Ultimate Teen Book Guide*.

Index of authors featured in the *UTBG* (and the pages where you'll find their books recommended)